HISTORY'S
DAYBOOK

HISTORY'S DAYBOOK

*A History of the
World in
366 Quotations*

PETER FURTADO

Atlantic Books
London

First published in Great Britain in 2011 by Atlantic Books,
an imprint of Atlantic Books Ltd.

1 2 3 4 5 6 7 8 9 10

A CIP catalogue record for this book is available from the British Library.

ISBN: 978 1 84887 670 5

Designed by carrstudio.co.uk
Printed in Great Britain by the MPG Books Group

Atlantic Books
An Imprint of Atlantic Books Ltd
Ormond House
26–27 Boswell Street
London
WC1N 3JZ

www.atlantic-books.co.uk

CONTENTS

∞

INTRODUCTION

Some of the best historical quotations, like the best stories, improve in the telling. Martin Luther did not tell the Diet of Worms in 1521, 'Here I stand; I can do no other', but spoke much less pithily. Marie Antoinette did not say in 1789 'Let them eat cake' (these words in fact appear in an anecdote in the *Confessions* of Jean-Jacques Rousseau). It was a British tabloid headline writer, not the then prime minister James Callaghan, who came out with 'Crisis, What Crisis?' during Britain's 'winter of discontent' of 1978–9. And the Chinese premier Zhou Enlai never suggested to the US secretary of state Henry Kissinger in 1972 that it was 'too early to tell' what might be the impact of the French Revolution – he was actually referring to France's '*événements*' of May 1968.

Misquotations, as much as true quotations, can act as what the biologist Richard Dawkins called 'memes' – heritable units of cultural memory encapsulating a hinterland of knowledge, each one competing for our attention. The capacity of quotation to bear this weight of meaning is, perhaps, just one good reason among several for a collection of excerpts describing or reflecting on notable events in the past, and placed in their historical context.

History's Daybook offers a genuine quotation from or about history for every day of the calendar year. Each quotation consists of words actually spoken on that day, or relating to events that took place on it. Some of the quotations refer to famous or notorious anniversaries – 6 June, 1 July, 14 July, 11 September, to name but a few – others to less immediately familiar but still significant events, from the ancient world to the twenty-first century.

History's Daybook includes some the most celebrated of all 'historical quotations', from Caesar's cry of '*Alea iacta est!*' as he crossed the River Rubicon in 49 BC, to Marx's and Engels' 'Workers of the world, unite!' in *The Communist Manifesto* of 1848. But here I present these words in the larger context in which they were originally placed. The sound-bites of history may be memorable, but they become far more revealing when their preceding and succeeding paragraphs are also read, and when their historical context is fully understood.

As an anthology of original source materials – some of them key documents, others the reports of eyewitnesses, or written shortly after the event – *History's Daybook* offers a shortcut to the heart of history. Diary entries and memoirs, letters and interviews, *bons mots* and sound-bites, narratives and journalistic accounts, speeches and sermons, official reports and briefings; the entries selected are as wide-ranging in form as they are in geography and timescale. In some cases two disparate accounts throw contrasting light on the same happening. They are limited only by the need to pin the event – or the quote – to a specific date in the calendar.

It is important to add a health warning: not every entry in *History's Daybook* should be taken at face value. Some of the statements here are self-serving, others deluded. And some may be accurate as far as they go, but are still partial accounts that more recent historians have reassessed in the light of a fuller understanding of their historical context. Yet as the raw material of history they remain vital and fascinating. The great British scholar G.M. Young once advised young historians to 'Read until you can hear the people talking' – and it is my hope that the 366 extracts in *History's Daybook* provide a wealth of opportunities to do just that.

Peter Furtado
Oxford
August 2011

JANUARY

∞

1 JANUARY

THE DEBUT OF *THE TIMES*, 1785

To the Public

To bring out a new paper in the present day, when so many others are already established and confirmed in the public opinion, is certainly an arduous undertaking; and no-one can be more fully aware of its difficulties than I am; I, nevertheless, entertain very sanguine hopes that the nature of the plan on which this paper will be conducted will ensure it a moderate share at least of public favour; but my pretensions to encouragement, however strong they may appear in my own eyes, must be tried before a tribunal not liable to be blinded by self-opinion; to that tribunal I shall now, as I am bound to do, submit these pretensions with deference, and the public will judge whether they are well or ill founded.

...A paper that... by steering clear of extremes, hit the happy medium, has long been expected by the public. Such, it is intended, shall be the UNIVERSAL REGISTER, the great objects of which will be to facilitate the commercial intercourse between the different parts of the community through the channel of advertisements, to record the principal occurrences of the times, and to abridge the account of debates during the sitting of Parliament.

EDITORIAL, *DAILY UNIVERSAL REGISTER*, 1 JANUARY 1785.

The former underwriter John Walter launched his newspaper, under the title *Daily Universal Register*, on the first day of 1785. Exactly three years later he renamed it *The Times* and broadened its appeal to include society gossip, something that landed him in Newgate Prison for two years after libelling the Prince of Wales. By the 19th century its independent viewpoint and innovative technology had made it the leading newspaper in Britain, campaigning for Parliamentary Reform before 1832, and for army reform during the Crimean War of 1854–6, a conflict that showcased the journalism of *Times* reporter W.H. Russell (*see* 25 October). *The Times* was nicknamed the 'Thunderer', originally a self-description ('We thundered out the other day...') after an editorial challenged the verdict of an inquest into the death of the peer Lord Graves in 1830.

ALSO ON THIS DAY

1863 US President Lincoln's Emancipation Proclamation is issued.
1900 The Australian Commonwealth is established.
1993 Czechoslovakia splits into the Czech Republic and the Slovak Republic.

2 JANUARY

THE CAPITULATION OF MUSLIM SPAIN, 1492

The Emirate of Granada was Islam's last stronghold on the Iberian peninsula. It finally surrendered to the forces of Ferdinand of Aragon and Isabella of Castile on 2 January 1492. Having besieged Sultan Boabdil in Granada since the spring of 1491, the recently married monarchs received his surrender in person, and in recognition of their victory the pope awarded them the title of 'Most Catholic Kings'.

The Christian 'reconquest' of Muslim Spain – the *Reconquista* – had been spread over four centuries, though for much of that time a policy of *convivencia*, or peaceful co-existence, had been practised, and the words of the capitulation document in 1492 echo the tolerance of former centuries.

∞

That both great and small should be perfectly secure in their persons, families, and properties.

That their laws should be preserved as they were before.

That their mosques should remain as they were in the times of Islam.

That no Christian should enter the house of a Muslim, or insult him in any way.

That the Christians who had embraced Islam should not be compelled to relinquish it and adopt their former creed.

That no Christian should be allowed to peer over the wall, or into the house of a Muslim or enter a mosque.

That any Muslim choosing to travel or reside among the Christians should be perfectly secure in his person and property.

CAPITULATION AGREEMENT, GRANADA, SPAIN, 1492.

∞

The reality of what was to come was very different, for a resurgent, more aggressive form of Christianity was on the rise in Spain. The Alhambra Decree, also in 1492, ordered the expulsion of Jews from Spain; just four years later, the remaining Muslim population of the former emirate was forced to convert to Christianity, and in 1609 the 'Moriscos', as they were called, were expelled from Spain entirely.

ALSO ON THIS DAY

AD 366 Barbarian Alemanni invade the Roman Empire across the Rhine.
1905 Russo-Japanese War: Port Arthur falls to the Japanese.
1945 WWII: heavy Allied bombing of Nuremberg takes place.

4

3 JANUARY

THE SIEGE OF SIDNEY STREET, 1911

The street had been cleared of all onlookers, but a group of detectives slunk along the walls on the anarchists' side of the street at such an angle that they were kept safe from the slanting fire of the enemy. They had to keep very close to the wall because Peter and his pals were dead shots and maintained something like a barrage fire with their automatics. Any detective or policeman who showed himself would have been sniped in a second, and these men were out to kill.

...In the top floor room... we observed a gas jet burning, and presently some of us noticed the white ash of burnt paper fluttering out of a chimney pot.

...They were setting fire to the house... The window curtains were first to catch alight, then volumes of black smoke, through which little tongues of flame licked up, poured through the empty window frames. They must have used paraffin... for the whole house was burning with amazing rapidity.

...A moment later I had one quick glimpse of a man's arm with a pistol in his hand. He fired and there was a quick flash. At the same moment a volley of shots rang out from the guardsmen opposite. It is certain that they killed the man for afterwards they found his body with a bullet through the skull. It was not long afterwards that the roof fell in with an upward rush of flame and smoke. The inside of the house from top to bottom was a furnace.

The detectives, with revolvers ready, now advanced in Indian file. One of them ran forward and kicked at the front door. It fell in... Peter the Painter and his fellow bandits were charred cinders in the bonfire they had made.

PHILIP GIBBS, *WEEKLY GRAPHIC*, JANUARY 1911.

Journalist Philip Gibbs observed the violent siege of a flat at Sidney Street, Mile End, London, on 3 January 1911. It followed the shooting of two policemen in December by thieves, believed to be anarchist revolutionaries; led by a Latvian Jewish immigrant known as Peter the Painter, they were tracked to the East End terraced house. Controversially, Home Secretary Winston Churchill arrived on the scene. He called in Scots Guards, and a gun battle ensued. Eventually, the house caught fire, but Churchill refused to allow the fire brigade to put out the flames, and two charred bodies were found in the debris.

ALSO ON THIS DAY

1521 Pope Leo X excommunicates Martin Luther.
1946 William Joyce, the pro-Nazi broadcaster 'Lord Haw-Haw', is hanged for treason.
1959 Alaska becomes the 49th US state.

4 JANUARY

THE DEFENCE OF PARLIAMENTARY INDEPENDENCE, 1642

May it please Your Majesty, I have neither eyes to see nor tongue to speak in this place but as the House is pleased to direct me, whose servant I am here.

WILLIAM LENTHALL, 4 JANUARY 1642.

∞

This dignified statement of the independence of the House of Commons – directed at the monarch – was also an affirmation of the authority of the Speaker, a position then held by William Lenthall. It was occasioned when Charles I went in person, at the head of a band of soldiers, to arrest five MPs – John Pym, John Hampden, Denzil Holles, Sir Arthur Haselrig and William Strode – and one member of the House of Lords, Lord Mandeville, all of whom he believed to have been stirring popular opposition to his rule. The king marched into the Chamber, sat in the Speaker's chair and, on seeing none of his intended victims, commented: 'I see the birds have flown.' When he commanded Speaker Lenthall to locate them, he refused. Up to that point, Lenthall had sought a compromise between the parties, and six months earlier had argued 'no peace to the king, no prosperity to the people'. But this attempt to assert royal authority was a step too far. Shortly afterwards Charles I moved his court and government to Oxford and called his own parliament there, a move that led inexorably to civil war (see 14 June).

William Lenthall remained Speaker for much of the so-called Long Parliament, and survived Colonel Pride's purge (1648) of members opposed to putting King Charles on trial, which reduced its membership to a 'Rump'. Following the period of Cromwellian rule, and its intermittent, shortlived and fractious parliaments, Lenthall reluctantly resumed his Speakership when the Long Parliament was re-formed in 1659. Thus he took a role in the restoration of the monarchy in 1660. Instead of a tomb to glorify himself, he insisted on a plain plaque inscribed *vermis sum*, 'I am a worm'.

ALSO ON THIS DAY

1885 The first successful appendectomy is carried out, in the USA.
1959 The Soviet spacecraft *Luna 1* flies close to the Moon.
1965 The death of the US-born British poet T.S. Eliot.

5 JANUARY

THE DEATH OF 'SILENT CAL', 1933

How can you tell?

DOROTHY PARKER, 5 JANUARY 1933.

∞

The poet and wit Dorothy Parker was unimpressed on hearing that Calvin Coolidge (1873–1933), the most laconic of US presidents, sometimes called 'Silent Cal', had died at home after a heart attack. Vice-President Coolidge had been sworn into the top job on his family Bible by his father, a Vermont storekeeper, following the death in office of President Warren Harding in August 1923. The sense of homeliness and lack of ostentation stayed with him throughout his career – qualities out of kilter with the materialist flamboyance of American high society in the 1920s. Yet he won an easy victory in the 1924 presidential election, defeating his Democratic Party challenger John W. Davis.

According to his adviser Walter Lippmann, people liked Coolidge for doing nothing:

This active inactivity suits the mood and certain of the needs of the country admirably. It suits all the business interests which want to be let alone… And it suits all those who have become convinced that government in this country has become dangerously complicated and top-heavy.

He applied the same principle to his dealings with people, once explaining: 'Many times I say only "yes" or "no" to people. Even that is too much. It winds them up for twenty minutes more.' According to Dorothy Parker, on one occasion a woman sitting next to Coolidge at a dinner party told him she had bet that she could get him to say at least three words. He quietly replied: 'You lose.'

His innate conservatism made him reluctant to intervene at a federal level, whether it was to initiate projects of aid for farmers or to invest in public works. History has laid blame at his door for leaving America unprepared for the depth and duration of the Great Depression that followed the Wall Street Crash (*see* 29 October). He left office in 1929 and settled into a – naturally – quiet retirement.

ALSO ON THIS DAY

1066 The death of England's Anglo-Saxon king Edward the Confessor.
1477 Charles the Bold, duke of Burgundy, is killed at the Battle of Nancy.
1941 The British aviator Amy Johnson drowns in the Thames Estuary.

6 JANUARY

ROOSEVELT'S THIRD INAUGURAL ADDRESS, 1941

This is no time for any of us to stop thinking about the social and economic problems which are the root cause of the social revolution which is today a supreme factor in the world. For there is nothing mysterious about the foundations of a healthy and strong democracy.

The basic things expected by our people of their political and economic systems are simple. They are:

Equality of opportunity for youth and for others.

Jobs for those who can work.

Security for those who need it.

The ending of special privilege for the few.

The preservation of civil liberties for all.

The enjoyment – the enjoyment of the fruits of scientific progress in a wider and constantly rising standard of living.

These are the simple, the basic things that must never be lost sight of in the turmoil and unbelievable complexity of our modern world. The inner and abiding strength of our economic and political systems is dependent upon the degree to which they fulfill these expectations.

...I have called for personal sacrifice, and I am assured of the willingness of almost all Americans to respond to that call. A part of the sacrifice means the payment of more money in taxes. In my budget message I will recommend that a greater portion of this great defense program be paid for from taxation than we are paying for today. No person should try, or be allowed to get rich out of the program, and the principle of tax payments in accordance with ability to pay should be constantly before our eyes to guide our legislation.

If the Congress maintains these principles the voters, putting patriotism ahead of pocketbooks, will give you their applause.

In the future days, which we seek to make secure, we look forward to a world founded upon four essential human freedoms.

The first is freedom of speech and expression – everywhere in the world.

The second is freedom of every person to worship God in his own way – everywhere in the world.

The third is freedom from want, which, translated into world terms, means economic understandings which will secure to every nation a healthy peacetime life for its inhabitants – everywhere in the world.

The fourth is freedom from fear, which, translated into world terms, means a world-wide reduction of armaments to such a point and in such a thorough fashion that no nation will be in a position to commit an act of physical aggression against any neighbour – anywhere in the world.

That is no vision of a distant millennium. It is a definite basis for a kind of world attainable in our own time and generation. That kind of world is the very antithesis of the so-called 'new order' of tyranny which the dictators seek to create with the crash of a bomb.

To that new order we oppose the greater conception – the moral order. A good society is able to face schemes of world domination and foreign revolutions alike without fear.

...This nation has placed its destiny in the hands and heads and hearts of its millions of free men and women, and its faith in freedom under the guidance of God. Freedom means the supremacy of human rights everywhere. Our support goes to those who struggle to gain those rights and keep them. Our strength is our unity of purpose.

To that high concept there can be no end save victory.

US President Franklin D. Roosevelt, 6 January 1941.

∞

Franklin D. Roosevelt's visionary statement of freedom, delivered as part of his third Inaugural Address, was intended to encourage the US Congress to pass the Lend-Lease Bill, which would commit the United States to materially support the fight against Hitler – at a time when Britain was the last man standing against Nazi Germany, its cities and factories bearing the brunt of the night-time bombing of the Blitz. Up until his successful election for a third term, Roosevelt had had to tread carefully; although personally disposed to put the United States' considerable weight behind the struggle to defeat Nazi aggression, he was battling for the presidency in a context of widespread popular isolationism.

But victory liberated his voice, and unleashed the idealism and determination evident in his address. The universal terms in which he framed 'freedom' also inspired the foundation and charter of the United Nations a few years later.

ALSO ON THIS DAY

1066 Harold Godwinson is crowned king of England.
1540 Henry VIII of England marries Anne of Cleves, his fourth wife.
1919 The death of Theodore Roosevelt, 26th US president.

7 JANUARY

ENGLAND LOSES CALAIS, 1558

When I am dead and opened, you shall find 'Calais' lying within my heart.

QUEEN MARY I, DYING WORDS (ATTRIBUTED), NOVEMBER 1558.

∞

By the mid-16th century, the port town of Calais had been an English-governed outpost on the European mainland for hundreds of years. Henry VIII had found Calais a convenient launching pad both for military adventures and diplomatic initiatives, and Francis II of France had met him, and his future queen Anne Boleyn, there in 1532. Now, this last remaining enclave fell to the Duc de Guise in January 1558, never to be recovered. England's Catholic queen Mary I had allowed her country to become embroiled in the war between her husband Philip II of Spain and Henri II of France. There had been successes, including the Anglo-Spanish capture of the town of St Quentin in August 1557, after which the Earl of Pembroke's army had returned home to spend the winter. But the loss of Calais was a devastating blow to the national psyche, recorded by one ordinary Londoner, Henry Machyn, as 'the heaviest tidings… that ever was heard of'.

Writing about Mary's death in November 1558, Raphael Holinshed, the Elizabethan historian whose enthusiastic Protestantism inclined him to say little that was favourable about Mary, was careful to ascribe her famous words to eye-witnesses. He described how, on her deathbed, 'Bloody Mary' had admitted being troubled by twin losses, those of King Philip, whom she had not seen since his return to Spain in July 1557, and Calais.

After the loss of Calais, Mary's successor, her younger sister Elizabeth I (*see* 15 January), accepted that England could not reassert a permanent presence across the Channel, although later in her reign she supported military expeditions to aid the Protestant Dutch in their revolt against Catholic Spanish rule. She preferred to expand English influence on a global scale, encouraging many trading and exploratory ventures beyond Europe, sowing the seeds of empire.

ALSO ON THIS DAY

1536 The death of Catherine of Aragon, Henry VIII's first wife.
1610 Galileo discovers three of Jupiter's moons.
1927 A London–New York telephone service begins to operate.

8 JANUARY

THE BATTLE OF ASHDOWN, 871

Roused by this calamitous defeat at Reading, the Christians, in shame and indignation, within four days, assembled all their forces, and again encountered the pagan army at a place called Ashdune which means the 'Hill of the Ash'...

Now the Christians had determined that King Ethelred, with his men, should attack the two pagan kings, but that his brother Alfred, with his troops, should take the chance of war against the two earls. Things being so arranged, the king remained a long time in prayer, and the pagans came up rapidly to fight. Then Alfred, though possessing a subordinate authority, could no longer support the troops of the enemy, unless he retreated or charged upon them without waiting for his brother. At length he bravely led his troops against the hostile army...

...The pagans occupied the higher ground, and the Christians came up from below. There was also a single thorn-tree, of stunted growth, and we have with our own eyes seen it. Around this tree the opposing armies came together with loud shouts from all sides, the one party to pursue their wicked course, the other to fight for their lives, their dearest ties, and their country. And when both armies had fought long and bravely, at last the pagans, by the divine judgment, were no longer able to bear the attacks of the Christians, and having lost great part of their army, took to a disgraceful flight. One of their two kings, and five earls were there slain, together with many thousand pagans, who fell on all sides, covering with their bodies the whole plain of Ashdune... The Christians followed, slaying all they could reach, until it became dark.

ASSER, *LIFE OF ALFRED* (9TH CENTURY).

∽

The Battle of Ashdown, on the Berkshire Downs, represented the beginning of the Anglo-Saxon fightback – of Asser's 'Christians' – against the 'pagan' Danes, who had already conquered East Anglia. Prince Alfred demonstrated his military ardour, in contrast to his more cautious older brother, King Ethelred of Wessex. Within three months, Ethelred was dead and Alfred was king. During the long struggle with the Danes that lay ahead, Alfred's statesmanship and military prowess would justify his enduring epithet of 'The Great'.

ALSO ON THIS DAY

1815 US forces defeat the British in the Battle of New Orleans.
1886 The Severn Railway Tunnel opens in England.
1959 General de Gaulle becomes the first president of the French Fifth Republic.

9 JANUARY

THE PROBLEM OF THE SUDAN, 1884

No one who has been in a Turkish province... will need to be told why the people of the Sudan have risen in revolt against the Khedive [the Egyptian ruler]... Oppression begat discontent; discontent necessitated an increase of the armed force at the disposal of the authorities; this increase of the armed force involved an increase of expenditure, which again was attempted to be met by increasing taxation, and that still further increased the discontent... That the people were justified in rebelling nobody who knows the treatment to which they were subjected will attempt to deny. Their cries were absolutely unheeded at Cairo... and they rallied round the Mahdi [Muhammad Ahmad], who exhorted them to revolt against the Turkish yoke. I am convinced that it is an entire mistake to regard the Mahdi as in any sense a religious leader: he personifies popular discontent... The movement is not religious, but an outbreak of despair...

During the three years that I wielded full powers in the Sudan I taught the natives that they had a right to exist... I had taught them something of the meaning of liberty and justice, and accustomed them to a higher ideal of government than that with which they had previously been acquainted. As soon as I had gone... a population which had begun to appreciate something like decent government was flung back to suffer the worst excesses of Turkish rule.

GENERAL CHARLES GORDON, *PALL MALL GAZETTE*, 9 JANUARY 1884.

∞

General Charles George Gordon (1833–85) had been governor-general for the British-Egyptian-dominated Sudan during 1877–80. His interview with the journalist W.T. Stead for the *Pall Mall Gazette* gave him a platform to present his views on the Sudan, now under the inept rule of the Ottoman Khedive of Egypt. It resulted in a popular clamour for Gordon's return to the Sudan, and the British government acquiesced. By then, the Sudan was in tumult from the rebellion raised by the Islamist-nationalist forces of the 'Mahdi' (Muhammad Ahmad). On 26 January 1885, while attempting to organize the evacuation of Khartoum, Gordon was killed by Mahdist rebels, an event that shocked public opinion in Britain, and which would redefine 'Chinese Gordon' for posterity as 'Gordon of Khartoum'.

ALSO ON THIS DAY

1799 The British prime minister William Pitt the Younger introduces income tax.
1873 The death of the former French emperor Napoleon III.
1969 The Anglo-French supersonic airliner *Concorde* makes its first test flight.

10 JANUARY

THE CROSSING OF THE RUBICON, 49 BC

When the news came that the interposition of the tribunes in his [Julius Caesar's] favour had been utterly rejected, he sent forward some cohorts secretly, to prevent any suspicion; and to keep up appearances, he attended the public games and examined the model of a fencing school which he proposed building, then, as usual, sat down to table with a large company of friends.

After sunset some mules were put in his carriage and he set out privately, with a very small retinue. It grew dark and he lost his way until a guide led him on foot through some narrow paths, and he reached the road again. Coming with his troops on the banks of the Rubicon, which was the frontier of his province, he halted and, revolving in his mind the importance of the step he meditated, he turned to those about him, saying: 'Still we can retreat! But once we pass this little bridge, nothing is left but to fight.'

As he hesitated, a man of noble mien and graceful aspect appeared close by, and played a pipe. Some shepherds came to listen, as did soldiers, including some trumpeters. The man snatched a trumpet and ran to the river with it; then, sounding the Advance, crossed to the other side. Caesar cried out, 'Let us go where the omens of the Gods and the crimes of our enemies summon us! The die is now cast!'

He marched his army over the river; then he showed them the tribunes of the Plebs, who had come from Rome to meet him, and in their presence, called on the troops to pledge him their fidelity.

SUETONIUS, *THE TWELVE CAESARS*, AD 121.

∞

In 49 BC Julius Caesar, the triumphant conqueror-governor of Cisalpine Gaul (which included what is now northern Italy), found himself in conflict with his erstwhile political collaborator Pompey and the Roman Senate. They ordered Caesar to resign and return to Rome to stand trial. On hearing the news, on or around 10 January, his response was to lead his army across the Rubicon, a small river – flowing into the Adriatic – which marked the southern boundary of Cisalpine Gaul; this action was tantamount to a declaration of war. The ensuing civil war led to Pompey's death and to Caesar's triumph, and ultimately to the downfall of the Roman Republic.

ALSO ON THIS DAY

1840 The Penny Post is introduced in Britain.
1863 The first line of the London Underground (the Metropolitan Railway) opens.
1946 The UN General Assembly meets for the first time.

11 JANUARY

THE IDENTIFICATION OF A KILLER, 1964

Cigarette smoking is causally related to lung cancer in men; the magnitude of the effect of cigarette smoking far outweighs all other factors. The data for women, though less extensive, point in the same direction. The risk of developing lung cancer increases with duration of smoking and the number of cigarettes smoked per day, and is diminished by discontinuing smoking. In comparison with non-smokers, average male smokers of cigarettes have approximately a 9- to 10-fold risk of developing lung cancer and heavy smokers at least a 20-fold risk. The risk of developing cancer of the lung for the combined group of pipe smokers, cigar smokers, and pipe and cigar smokers is greater than for non-smokers, but much less than for cigarette smokers. Cigarette smoking is much more important than occupational exposures in the causation of lung cancer in the general population...

On the basis of prolonged study and evaluation of many lines of converging evidence, the Committee makes the following judgment:

Cigarette smoking is a health hazard of sufficient importance in the United States to warrant appropriate remedial action.

SMOKING AND HEALTH: REPORT OF THE ADVISORY COMMITTEE
TO THE SURGEON GENERAL OF THE UNITED STATES, 1964.

On 11 January 1964, after a committee of ten medical experts had sat for months, the US Surgeon General's office issued its most famous report, a conclusion to decades of burgeoning evidence that smoking was injurious to health. A particular impetus had been the alarming rise in cases of lung cancer during the century, which the report laid squarely on the tobacco habit; but the experts also pointed to a wider range of cancers associated with smoking, as well as to the development of chronic bronchitis, emphysema, and increasing rates of coronary heart disease.

It was not, in itself, an end to the argument. The jury was still out on whether smoking could be classified as an addiction, and decades later tobacco companies were still attempting to show that health claims were unproven. But, by the end of the 1960s it was commonly acknowledged that – for all its allure and nerve-calming capabilities – the cigarette was a killer.

ALSO ON THIS DAY

1569 England's first state lottery is held.
1923 Franco-Belgian troops occupy the Ruhr.
1928 The death of the English novelist and poet Thomas Hardy.

12 JANUARY

THE FOUNDING OF THE NATIONAL TRUST, 1895

The need of quiet, the need of air, the need of exercise, and the sight of sky and of things growing seem human needs, common to all men.

OCTAVIA HILL, 1895.

∞

Britain's National Trust was established in January 1895 by three visionaries: the housing reformers Octavia Hill (1838–1912) and Sir Robert Hunter (1844–1913), the latter being solicitor of the Commons Preservation Society, and the clergyman Hardwicke Rawnsley (1851–1920), who had once collected rents for Hill. They all believed in the healing power of Nature and its contribution to the welfare of all, including the poorest. Hill was a protégée of the art critic and philosopher John Ruskin, absorbing his concerns about the degrading effects of urban squalor; she had acquired slums in Marylebone (London) and renovated them to improve the living conditions of their residents. Eighteen years earlier, and also under the influence of Ruskin, the utopian socialist William Morris had set up the Society for the Preservation of Ancient Buildings (SPAB), arguing that such buildings 'belong, partly to those who built them, and partly to all generations of mankind who are to follow us'.

Over the following century the National Trust became custodian of large numbers of period houses and many tracts of land in areas of natural beauty, including coastline. It tended to acquire a reputation for preserving the houses of the wealthy for the vicarious delight of a well-heeled middle class, and – concomitant with that impression – a growing difficulty in interesting inner-city dwellers in the beauties of what it had to offer. Nevertheless, by 2010 the National Trust, now describing itself as 'For ever, for everyone', had become Britain's largest membership organization, with well over 3.5 million members; and its remit had broadened to include vernacular buildings such as Birmingham's 'back-to-back' houses and even the childhood homes of Beatles John Lennon and Paul McCartney.

ALSO ON THIS DAY

1915 The US House of Representatives rejects female suffrage.
1976 The death of the English detective novelist Agatha Christie.
2010 An earthquake in Haiti kills 230,000 people.

13 JANUARY

THE GUILTY MEN OF THE DREYFUS CASE, 1898

J'ACCUSE...!

...I accuse Major Du Paty de Clam as the diabolic workman of the miscarriage of justice, without knowing – I would like to believe – and of then defending his harmful work, for three years, by the most evil and absurd of machinations.

I accuse General Mercier of being an accomplice, if only by mental weakness, in one of the greatest iniquities of the century.

I accuse General Billot of having held in his hands the unquestionable evidence of Dreyfus's innocence and of suppressing it, and making himself guilty of this crime against humanity and justice, with a political aim and to protect the compromised Chief of High Command.

I accuse General de Boisdeffre and General Gonse as accomplices of the same crime, one undoubtedly by religious passion, the other perhaps by this *esprit de corps* that has made the War Office an unassailable icon.

I accuse General de Pellieux and Commander Ravary of performing a rogue investigation, by which I mean a monstrously partial one, as proved by the latter in a report that is an imperishable monument to naive audacity.

I accuse the three handwriting experts, Messieurs Belhomme, Varinard and Couard, of submitting untrue and fraudulent reports, unless a medical examination declares them to be suffering from a disease of sight and judgment.

I accuse the War Office of carrying out an abominable press campaign, particularly in *L'Eclair* and *L'Echo de Paris*, to mislead the public and cover up their malfeasance.

Finally, I accuse the first court martial of violating the law by convicting the defendant on the basis of secret evidence, and I accuse the second court martial of covering up this illegality, on orders, and thereby committing the crime of knowingly acquitting a guilty man.

While proclaiming these charges, I am aware of subjecting myself to Articles 30 and 31 of the press law of July 29, 1881, which makes libel a punishable offence. I voluntarily expose myself to that danger.

As for the people I accuse, I do not know them, I have never seen them, I have neither resentment nor hatred for them. They are for me only entities, spirits of evil in society. The action I am taking is only a radical means for hastening the explosion of truth and justice.

I have only one passion, that of enlightenment, in the name of humanity which has suffered so and is entitled to happiness. My heated protest is no more than a *cri de coeur*. Let them dare to bring me to court, and let the investigation take place in the light of day!

I am waiting.

Émile Zola, L'Aurore, 13 January 1898.

∞

The headline of what has been called the 'greatest newspaper article of all time' announced the French novelist Émile Zola's front-page open letter to President Félix Faure (*see also* 16 February). It appeared in the Paris newspaper *L'Aurore*. In it Zola analyzed in detail the scandal that had engulfed France since Captain Alfred Dreyfus (1859–1935) was accused of passing artillery secrets to Germany, convicted of treason and sentenced to life imprisonment on Devil's Island in 1894. Zola, convinced that the Jewish Dreyfus was the victim of a conservative and anti-Semitic conspiracy within the army and French high society, named the guilty men one by one, then added:

> *Truth is on the march and nothing shall stop it. Today is only the beginning for this case, since it is only today that the positions have been made clear: on one side, the guilty parties, who do not want the light to shine forth, on the other, those who seek justice and who will give their lives to see that light shine. When truth is buried underground, it builds up and acquires an explosive force that is destined to blast everything away with it.*

Eventually, and after a dispute that soured French political life for years, Dreyfus was exonerated in 1906. Four years earlier, though, Zola himself had died, asphyxiated in a domestic fire sometimes thought to have been the result of sabotage by his enemies. At his funeral the writer Anatole France proclaimed: 'He was a moment in the conscience of humanity.'

ALSO ON THIS DAY

1893 The Independent Labour Party is formed in Britain.
1941 The death of the Irish novelist James Joyce.
1964 The Beatles' first single is released in the United States.

14 JANUARY

A HUMAN BE-IN, 1967

A new concept of celebrations beneath the human underground must emerge, become conscious, and be shared, so a revolution can be formed with a renaissance of compassion, awareness, and love, and the revelation of unity for all mankind.

SAN FRANCISCO ORACLE, JANUARY 1967.

The words 'turn on, tune in, drop out' were first publicly uttered in New York during a September 1966 press conference by Timothy Leary (1920–96). They were to become the defining slogan of the 1960s' counter-culture, providing the theme of the first and arguably most radical 'happening' of that movement: the 'Gathering of the Tribes for a Human Be-In', which took place in San Francisco's Golden Gate Park on 14 January 1967 and was attended by 30,000 people. Promoted mainly through the 'underground' newspaper the *San Francisco Oracle*, it brought together the New Age hippies of the city's Haight-Ashbury district with the Berkeley campus radicals and the anti-Vietnam War agitators.

Many movers and shakers of the United States' counter-culture were present, including San Francisco bands such as The Grateful Dead and Jefferson Airplane, the poet Allen Ginsberg (1926–97), the activist Jerry Ruben (1938–94), and Timothy Leary himself, the apostle of personal liberation achieved through liberal use of the hallucinogen lysergic acid diethylamide ('acid' or LSD). The drug had been developed for therapeutic use in 1947 but made illegal in California in October 1966.

The Be-In was originally conceived by the *Oracle* art editor Michael Bowen as a piece of performance art, and as a model that could be infinitely replicated. His plan succeeded spectacularly. A vast amount of 'acid' was 'dropped', the media lapped up everything that happened and San Francisco's so-called Summer of Love, as 1967 became known, was off to an early start.

ALSO ON THIS DAY

1129 The Council of Troyes endorses the military-religious Templar Order.
1898 The death of the English writer Lewis Carroll (Charles Lutwidge Dodgson).
1943 WWII: the Casablanca Conference discusses Allied war strategy.

15 JANUARY

THE CORONATION OF ELIZABETH I, 1559

On the 15th day she was crowned with the usual ceremonies at Westminster Abbey. She first came to Westminster Hall. There went before her trumpets, knights, and lords, heralds of arms in their rich coats: then the nobles in their scarlet, and all the bishops in scarlet; then the queen and all the footmen waiting upon her to the hall. There Her Grace's apparel was changed. In the hall they met the bishop of Carlisle that was to perform the ceremony, and all the chapel, with three crosses borne before them, in their copes, the bishop mitred; and singing as they passed, *'Salve Festa Dies'* [A Gregorian chant]. All the streets new laid with gravel and blue cloth, and railed in on each side. And so to the abbey to mass; and there Her Grace was crowned. Thence, the ceremony ended, the queen and her retinue went to Westminster Hall to dinner; and every officer took his office at service upon their lands and so did the Lord Mayor of London, and the aldermen.

JOHN STRYPE, *ANNALS OF THE REFORMATION...*
DURING QUEEN ELIZABETH'S HAPPY REIGN, 1709–25.

∞

Thus was England's Virgin Queen invested with her symbols of majesty, the orb, sceptre and crown, on 15 January 1559, some three months after the death of her Catholic half-sister and predecessor Mary I (*see* 7 January).

The lead-up to the coronation had begun two days before, with a symbolic 'possession' of the Tower of London – to emphasize the monarch's actual hold on power – followed the next day by a procession through the City of Westminster, accompanied by pageants, popular acclamation and a variety of orations.

At the formal ceremony itself, there was no Archbishop of Canterbury – in an act of historical neatness, Mary's Catholic archbishop, Reginald Pole, had died within 24 hours of his queen, and his successor remained unappointed. With the Catholic bishops nervous and suspicious, it fell to the Bishop of Carlisle to perform the ceremony. The proceedings remained Catholic in nature, yet it appears that Elizabeth managed to have it both ways by absenting herself during the Latin Mass, thus exemplifying her distinction between the right to personal belief and the obligations of outward behaviour. The political astuteness that would account for much that was successful in her reign was already in evidence.

ALSO ON THIS DAY

1535 In England Henry VIII becomes 'Supreme Head of the Church'.
1759 The British Museum opens.
1929 The birth of the US civil rights leader Martin Luther King, Jr.

16 JANUARY

THE BEGINNING OF IMPERIAL ROME, 27 BC

Augustus, Princeps et Imperator Caesar divi filius

[The illustrious one, the first head, and commander Caesar, son of the deified one]

SENATORIAL DECREE ANNOUNCING OCTAVIAN'S NEW TITLES, 16 JANUARY 27 BC.

When the Roman Senate awarded him these titles, Octavian – adoptive son of Julius Caesar – became supreme ruler of Rome and supreme commander of the Roman legions. With the transmogrification of Octavian into Augustus, Rome's transition from Republic to Empire was complete. Nonetheless, Augustus preferred to work within old institutions and claim that he was merely 'first among equals'.

After Octavian (63 BC–AD 14) had triumphed in the wars that followed his uncle's murder in 44 BC (*see* 15 March) – defeating first the Republican conspirators Brutus and Cassius in 42 BC, and later Mark Antony and Cleopatra in 31 BC – he sought to accumulate power in his person while appearing to respect the rights of the Roman Senate and its patrician families.

He refused to accept the controversial title of 'dictator', which Julius Caesar had borne, but, already permanent consul, he was rewarded on 16 January 27 BC with this array of new titles. They asserted the scope of his power and the benevolence of his rule, and they established him as the leading senator, the head of the army and the descendant of the now-deified Julius Caesar. The last of these titles effectively made his family name Caesar a synonym with the holder of imperial power – a meaning it retained in Russia (Czar/Tsar) and Germany (Kaiser) into the 20th century.

Augustus's own, inevitably highly partial, first-person reflections in *Res Gestae Divi Augusti* reveal a man of some modesty as well as his absolute certainty as to his objectives. Despite his ruthlessness on occasion, he prided himself on the peace, prosperity and cultural glory of his Augustan reign, often called the Silver Age; as the historian Suetonius put it, 'He could boast that he inherited Rome a city of brick and left it one of marble.' (*See also* 19 August.)

ALSO ON THIS DAY

1547 Ivan the Terrible is crowned as Russia's first tsar.
1605 Cervantes' prose work *Don Quixote* is published in Madrid.
1970 Colonel Gaddafi assumes control of Libya after a military coup.

17 JANUARY

THE MOTHER OF ALL BATTLES, 1991

The great duel, the mother of all battles has begun. The dawn of victory nears as this great showdown begins!... The evil and satanic intentions of the White House will be crushed and so will all the blasphemous and oppressive forces.

IRAQI PRESIDENT SADDAM HUSSEIN, SPEECH, 17 JANUARY 1991.

Thus the Iraqi dictator and Ba'ath Party leader Saddam Hussein addressed his people on the day that a US-led coalition launched Operation Desert Storm, the aim of which was to expel Iraqi forces from Kuwait following Iraq's annexation of that country. Saddam had been supported by US and European money and *matériel* in the long and bloody Iran–Iraq War of the 1980s, but lost all support internationally when he invaded Kuwait in August 1990. Saddam had sought to exploit a historic claim that Kuwait was an integral part of Iraq, made independent only through the machinations of the British between the world wars. With Kuwait swiftly overwhelmed, tales of Iraqi atrocities committed there stoked the world's repugnance. The US president, George Bush, Snr, supported by United Nations resolutions, led a coalition to restore Kuwaiti independence and protect a vulnerable Saudi Arabia. The offensive, launched on 16 January 1991, was met by defiant words but little effective military response, other than setting fire to Kuwait's oil wells.

Having expelled Iraqi forces from Kuwait, coalition troops pursued Saddam's retreating forces to within 150 miles of Baghdad before withdrawing from Iraq. After a ceasefire was declared by President Bush on 28 February, the US commander of the Allied forces, Norman Schwarzkopf, was scathing about his beaten adversary: 'As far as Saddam Hussein being a great military strategist: he is neither a strategist, nor is he schooled in the operational art, nor is he a tactician, nor is he a general, nor is he a soldier. Other than that, he's a great military man.'

ALSO ON THIS DAY

1706 The birth of the US polymath Benjamin Franklin.
1912 Robert Falcon Scott reaches the South Pole.
1945 WWII: Soviet forces liberate the Polish capital Warsaw from the Germans.

18 JANUARY

CONFLICTING INTERESTS AT THE
PARIS PEACE CONFERENCE, 1919

The allotment of delegates was a delicate business. Brazil got three, since there are many German interests there and they hope, by implicating her fully in the Conference, to cajole her into repressive measures there. It sounds almost unworthy of American principles.

The Portuguese were greatly sorrowful. The French went to their minister, and said how they regretted the inadequate representation, but that the English were quite firm. The Portuguese came to us more in anger than in sorrow, and protested. Sir Eyre Crowe [head of the British Foreign Office] had to cut out an extract from the official proceedings and send it them secretly, that they might see the protest against the extra delegate came from the French.

Mr Balfour [British foreign secretary] completely forgot the Hejaz [western Arabia] representatives at the first sitting. I got Mallet, Tyrrell [William Tyrrell, minister-plenipotentiary], and Cecil [Lord Robert Cecil] to go and protest. Then I went to see Eric Drummond [future Secretary-General of the League of Nations], and explained myself vigorously. He tried first to persuade me that we had no standing, but later came round and promised to do his best. I dined with Mr Balfour, and got his promise to the same effect, and loaded him full of ammunition. Philip Kerr did the same for Lloyd George [British prime minister] on Lionel Curtis' [writer and public servant] advice. Meanwhile I told Feisal [leader of the Arab delegation] that his question was not prejudiced, only postponed a day for production of necessary papers. Next day Balfour proposed the Hejaz. Pichon [French foreign minister] protested. Clemenceau [French prime minister] accepted one delegate, and Pichon said they could have no more since they were an embryo nationality, not an independent state. Balfour and Lloyd George countered sharply with the statement that they and France had recognised its independence, and the point – two delegates – was carried.

Feisal had meanwhile been visited by Gout, who told him his omission was intentional, and the English were only playing with him. He said France was strong, and the sooner Feisal ceased to listen to the mischief-makers in Mesopotamia and Syria who were working against France, the better it would be for him. They recognised no Arab army in Syria, and Allenby [British commander in Syria] lied if he said they did. So Feisal saw that his representation was contested, and spent a very miserable night in consequence. I found him wandering about the hotel at 2 a.m. When we won he took it as a good augury of all the future battles and was very joyful.

At the first sitting he was amused when Clemenceau, as temporary president, put the question of his own confirmation in the office to the delegates. He voted with the rest for him. Lloyd George in seconding the proposal said that while he was a boy at school Clemenceau was holding office.

The campaign in favour of America co-operating in the East, to secure the practice of her ideals, goes well. Kipling's enthusiasm had turned over Doubleday that night in England. Ellis is now in his sixth article, all tending that way, in the 'Herald'. Mrs. Egan has adhered, and of course old McClure. I want to frighten America with the size of the responsibility, and then that she should run us for it instead. The Americans are rather fed up with France. 'Reminiscences of the second Empire' are too common for their taste. Weizmann [Zionist leader] was asked by Wilson [US president] how he got on with the British – he said so well that he wanted them as his trustee. Then how he got on with the French. He said he knew French perfectly, but he could not understand, or make himself understood by, the French politicians. 'Exactly what I find,' said Wilson.

T. E. LAWRENCE, DIARY OF THE PARIS PEACE CONFERENCE, 1919.

∞

The Paris Peace Conference, called by the Allies to redraw the world map in the aftermath of the First World War, opened on 18 January 1919. At the opening ceremony, French President Raymond Poincaré said: 'You are assembled in order to repair the evil that it has done and to prevent a recurrence of it. You hold in your hands the future of the world.' The result was rather less idealistic. Amid a welter of competing interests, there was a great deal of political infighting, with the major Allies – especially the French delegation led by Prime Minister Georges Clemenceau – determining the outcome. Germany was not invited to send a delegation but was nevertheless forced to sign the eventual Treaty of Versailles in June 1919.

One factor in the complexity of the conference was that as well as representatives of all the belligerent countries, there were many non-state delegations too. They were seeking new nation-states following the principle of national self-determination, one of the 'Fourteen Principles' enunciated by US President Woodrow Wilson early in 1918. Negotiating on behalf of the Arabs, who had fought to free themselves from the Ottoman Empire, was the man who had trained and led them and who was so much associated with their cause: T.E. Lawrence (1888–1935). He provided a vivid behind-the-scenes account as the conference opened.

ALSO ON THIS DAY

1778 Captain James Cook reaches the 'Sandwich Islands' – Hawaii.
1871 Wilhelm of Prussia is proclaimed Kaiser (emperor) of a united Germany.
1967 Alberto DeSalvo, the 'Boston Strangler', is sentenced to life imprisonment for thirteen murders.

19 JANUARY

THE DEATH OF THE FIRST ANARCHIST, 1865

Pierre-Joseph Proudhon was born in 1809 and died on 19 January 1865, in the Parisian suburb of Passy. He was one of the early utopian socialists – and the first person to call himself an anarchist. An autodidact from Besançon, in eastern France, Proudhon argued consistently for workers to hold goods in common and to work co-operatively, opposing both capitalism and state power. Having devised a memorable formula with the phrase 'property is theft' (1840), he mined the seam a little deeper with its companion, 'anarchy is order'.

∞

To be governed is to be watched, inspected, spied upon, directed, law-driven, numbered, regulated, enrolled, indoctrinated, preached at, controlled, checked, estimated, valued, censured, commanded, by creatures who have neither the right nor the wisdom nor the virtue to do so. To be governed is to be at every operation, at every transaction noted, registered, counted, taxed, stamped, measured, numbered, assessed, licensed, authorized, admonished, prevented, forbidden, reformed, corrected, punished. It is, under pretext of public utility, and in the name of the general interest, to be placed under contribution, drilled, fleeced, exploited, monopolized, extorted from, squeezed, hoaxed, robbed; then, at the slightest resistance, the first word of complaint, to be repressed, fined, vilified, harassed, hunted down, abused, clubbed, disarmed, bound, choked, imprisoned, judged, condemned, shot, deported, sacrificed, sold, betrayed; and to crown all, mocked, ridiculed, derided, outraged, dishonoured. That is government; that is its justice; that is its morality.

PIERRE-JOSEPH PROUDHON, *GENERAL IDEA OF THE REVOLUTION IN THE NINETEENTH CENTURY*, 1845.

∞

Unlike those anarchists of the later 19th century who adopted what they called 'propaganda by the deed' – encouraging others to see the benefits of revolution through bombs and attempted assassinations (some of them successful) – Proudhon eschewed violence, even during the Parisian revolution of 1848 that gave birth to the French Second Republic. The originator of 'anarchism' preferred the pen as a means of advancing his cause, and he used it to potent effect, as in this energetic summation of the evils of government.

ALSO ON THIS DAY

1419 Hundred Years' War: Rouen surrenders to Henry V of England.
1915 WWI: German Zeppelin airships bomb England for the first time.
1966 Indira Gandhi, daughter of Jawaharlal Nehru, becomes India's prime minister.

20 JANUARY

THE INAUGURATION OF BARACK OBAMA, 2009

In reaffirming the greatness of our nation, we understand that greatness is never a given. It must be earned. Our journey has never been one of short-cuts or settling for less. It has not been the path for the faint-hearted – for those who prefer leisure over work, or seek only the pleasures of riches and fame. Rather, it has been the risk-takers, the doers, the makers of things – some celebrated but more often men and women obscure in their labour – who have carried us up the long, rugged path towards prosperity and freedom...

We will not apologize for our way of life, nor will we waver in its defence, and for those who seek to advance their aims by inducing terror and slaughtering innocents, we say to you now that our spirit is stronger and cannot be broken; you cannot outlast us, and we will defeat you.

For we know that our patchwork heritage is a strength, not a weakness. We are a nation of Christians and Muslims, Jews and Hindus – and non-believers. We are shaped by every language and culture, drawn from every end of this Earth; and because we have tasted the bitter swill of civil war and segregation, and emerged from that dark chapter stronger and more united, we cannot help but believe that the old hatreds shall someday pass; that the lines of tribe shall soon dissolve; that as the world grows smaller, our common humanity shall reveal itself; and that America must play its role in ushering in a new era of peace...

US PRESIDENT BARACK OBAMA, INAUGURATION ADDRESS, 20 JANUARY 2009.

The 2008 US presidential election followed a Democratic Party primary with two candidates who promised to break the mould of American politics: a woman, in the shape of Hillary Clinton, and an African-American, in the shape of Barack Obama. Eventual victory went to Obama, and on 20 January 2009 the 44th president of the United States made his inaugural address. He arrived at the White House on a wave of optimism. For many, he symbolized the end of a long road from slavery, through segregation and the struggle for civil rights. The expectations were that he would now heal the wounds, within the United States and around the world, of the previous few years. The challenge of living up to his soaring rhetoric was immense.

ALSO ON THIS DAY

1265 The first English Parliament meets.
1841 China cedes Hong Kong to the British.
1942 WWII: Nazi leaders discuss 'the Final Solution of the Jewish Question'.

21 JANUARY

THE EXECUTION OF THE FORMER LOUIS XVI, 1793

The youngest of the guards, who seemed about eighteen, immediately seized the head, and showed it to the people as he walked round the scaffold; he accompanied this monstrous ceremony with the most atrocious and indecent gestures. At first an awful silence prevailed; at length some cries of 'Vive la République!' were heard. By degrees the voices multiplied and in less than ten minutes this cry, a thousand times repeated, became the universal shout of the multitude, and every hat was in the air.

HENRY ESSEX EDGEWORTH, *MEMOIRS*, 1815.

∞

On 21 January 1793 Louis Bourbon, the former Louis XVI – who had lost his throne when the French monarchy was abolished in September 1792 – mounted the scaffold and calmly placed his head beneath the guillotine. It was the culminating moment of more than three years of revolutionary ferment in France.

At his trial, Louis had presented a strong but futile defence. On 9 December 1792, two days before it opened, the leading light of the Jacobin faction, Maximilien Robespierre, had already made clear his view: 'It is with regret that I pronounce the fatal truth: Louis must die that the country may live.' The National Convention, the new legislative assembly established in September 1792, narrowly voted for execution, the verdict was delivered on 20 January, and the execution was set for the following morning.

On his final journey Louis was accompanied by Henry Essex Edgeworth, an Irish-born priest. When, on the scaffold, his guards tried to bind his arms, he insisted: 'To bind me? No! I shall never consent to that; do what you have been ordered, but you shall never bind me.'

The execution shocked monarchists across Europe, and France was soon at war with Spain, Britain, Holland, Austria and Prussia. The threat fuelled Robespierre's rise to power within the new 'Committee for Public Safety', where he instituted a policy of state terror to protect the Revolution (*see* 5 February).

ALSO ON THIS DAY

1919 Sinn Féin members of the UK Parliament proclaim the Irish Republic.
1924 The death of the founding leader of the Soviet Union, Vladimir Ilyich Lenin.
1950 The death of George Orwell, the British journalist, broadcaster and novelist.

22 JANUARY

BRITAIN'S FIRST LABOUR GOVERNMENT, 1924

Today 23 years ago dear Grandmama died. I wonder what she would have thought of a Labour government.

KING GEORGE V, DIARY, 22 JANUARY 1924.

∞

In his diary entry of 22 January 1924, King George V – grandson of Queen Victoria – reflected on Britain's first-ever Labour government. The general election of December 1923 had been inconclusive, but Stanley Baldwin, leader of the Conservative Party majority, proved unable to form a coalition government and lost a vote of no confidence as soon as Parliament returned in January 1924. His resignation ushered in Ramsay MacDonald – illegitimate son of a farm labourer from northeast Scotland – as the first Labour Party leader to reach the prime ministership, at the head of a minority government.

The party had been founded as the Independent Labour Party (ILP) only 30 years earlier. From 1906, when it was renamed the Labour Party and when MacDonald first entered Parliament, it had replaced most of its revolutionary Marxist ideology with a commitment to parliamentary politics. The political establishment, though, remained fearful and when Prime Minister MacDonald arrived at Buckingham Palace for the traditional kissing of hands, the king complained that the 'Red Flag' and the 'Marseillaise' had been sung in triumph at a Labour rally a few days earlier. MacDonald replied it had been hard to restrain his followers from singing the 'Red Flag' in the House of Commons after the vote of no confidence in Baldwin.

The king needn't have worried. MacDonald had little effective power, and his government lasted just nine months, without seriously alarming the wealthy.

23 JANUARY

ZULU DEFEAT AT RORKE'S DRIFT, 1879

It was about 3.30 o'clock in the afternoon that we heard of that fatal disaster of Isandhlwana... Bromhead asked me to get onto the top of the house... I could see that Zulus had got as near to us as they could without us seeing them... Mr Bromhead asked me how many I thought there were. I told him they numbered 4–6,000... A few minutes later one appeared on top of the mountain... He then moved steadily to the right and signalled with his arm. The main body at once began to advance... and in a few minutes was all round us...

...It was not until the bayonet was freely used that they flinched the least bit. Had the Zulus taken the bayonet as freely as they took the bullets we could not have stood more than fifteen minutes. They pushed on right up... and got in with us, but they seemed to have a great dread of the bayonet...

A fine big Zulu saw me shoot his mate down. He sprang forward... seizing hold of the muzzle of my rifle with his left hand and with his right hand getting hold of the bayonet... He pulled... but I had a firm hold of the small of the butt of my rifle with my left hand.

My cartridges were on the top of the mealie sweetcorn bags, which enabled me to load my rifle and shoot the poor wretch whilst holding on to his grasp. For some few moments they dropped back into the garden which served as a great protection for them... Their next object was to get possession of the hospital which they did by setting fire to it.

...Bromhead & myself & five others took up the position on the right of the second line of defence, in which we were exposed to three crossfires. Bromhead took the centre and was the only one that did not get wounded. There was four killed and two wounded... Bromhead & myself had it to our two selves about an hour & a half...

About this time we was pressed very much... We were so busy that one had got inside and was in the act of assegai-ing Bromhead, Bromhead not knowing he was there. I put my rifle on him knowing at the same time it was empty... He dodged down and hopped out of the laager again... They seemed to me as if they made up their minds to take Rorke's Drift with this rush. They rushed up madly notwithstanding the heavy loss they had already suffered.

It was in this struggle that I was shot... I knew this one had got his rifle presented at me, but... I had got my hands full in front and... he shot me through the right shoulder-blade and the bullet passed through my shoulder... I tried to keep my feet but could not; he could have assegaied me had not Bromhead shot him with his revolver... I was down not more than a few minutes, stripped in my shirt... I put my wounded arm under my waist belt. I was able to make another stand, getting Bromhead's revolver... Bromhead at this time was keeping a strict eye on the ammunition and telling the men not to waste one round as we were getting short. I was serving out ammunition myself when I became thirsty and faint... I got so thirsty that I could not do much...

Deacon said to me as I was leaning back against biscuit boxes: 'Fred, when it comes to the last shall I shoot you?' I declined. 'No, they have very near done for me and they can finish me right out when it come to the last.' I don't remember much after that. When I came to myself again, Lord Chelmsford had relieved us of our task. Bromhead brought His Lordship to me and His Lordship spoke very kindly to me and the doctor dressed my wound. Bromhead was my principal visitor and nurse while I was at the Drift.

PRIVATE FREDERICK HITCH, PRIVATE ACCOUNT.

On 23 January 1879 a small force of 152 British soldiers stationed at Rorke's Drift, a mission on the borders of the British colony of Natal and the kingdom of the Zulu nation, defied some 4,000 Zulus who had won a dramatic victory the previous day at nearby Isandhlwana. The battle for Rorke's Drift, which left at least 350 Zulus dead, was widely celebrated in Britain, and an unprecedented 11 Victoria Crosses were awarded to the defenders. The recipients included lieutenants John Chard and Gonville Bromhead, and 22-year-old Private Hitch, who later recorded his memories; Hitch died in 1913. With the end of the Anglo-Zulu War in 1879, the Zulu threat to British ambitions in southern Africa was effectively neutered.

ALSO ON THIS DAY

1556 An earthquake in China kills up to 830,000 people.
1806 The death of William Pitt the Younger, British prime minister.
1989 The death of the Surrealist painter and film-maker Salvador Dalí.

24 JANUARY

NO SURRENDER AT STALINGRAD, 1943

Surrender is forbidden. The Sixth Army will hold their positions to the last man and the last round and by their heroic endurance will make an unforgettable contribution towards the establishment of a defensive front and the salvation of the Western World.

ADOLF HITLER, ORDERS ISSUED ON 24 JANUARY 1943.

∞

When Friedrich Paulus, commander of the German Sixth Army, asked permission to withdraw from around the Soviet city of Stalingrad after months of desperate fighting, Adolf Hitler refused, seeing the fight as a decisive battle on the Eastern Front. The Axis advance into the Soviet Union had reached the Volga, at Stalingrad, in the summer of 1942, but Soviet leader Stalin was determined to defend the city: it was the communications hub of southern Russia and, as a city bearing his own name since 1925, a symbol of Soviet pride. His orders were: 'Not a step backwards' (*see* 28 July).

By the end of October 1942 the German forces had encircled Stalingrad, with the Soviet defenders pushed back to the river; but a massive counter-offensive, and the fierce winter, weakened the Sixth Army. The fighting degenerated into a relentless street-by-street battle. In November the Red Army, massively reinforced, was able to encircle the German army; by 24 January the last German airfield was overrun. When Paulus asked Hitler for permission to surrender, he received an uncompromising answer – and promotion to field marshal. The subtext was clear, as no German field marshal in history had ever surrendered, preferring suicide if all other options failed.

Paulus (1890–1957), however, was different, asserting that he had 'no intention of shooting myself for that Austrian corporal'. He surrendered on 31 January and was taken into Soviet captivity. The remnants of the German army – 90,000 men – were taken prisoner, and many of them would not survive their captivity. In all, up to 2 million people may have lost their lives during the battle for Stalingrad. When he heard the news of the surrender, Hitler stripped Paulus of his rank and commented: 'The god of war has gone over to the other side.' He was right: with Stalingrad, the once all-conquering *Wehrmacht* had experienced its most serious defeat to date.

In the post-Stalin era, Stalingrad was renamed Volgograd. But the epic battle that it had witnessed ensured the historical resonance of its former name.

ALSO ON THIS DAY

AD 41 The Roman emperor Caligula is assassinated.
1965 The death of the British statesman and wartime premier Winston Churchill.
1984 The first Apple Macintosh computer goes on sale.

25 JANUARY

THE BIRTH OF SCOTLAND'S NATIONAL POET, 1759

The birth in Alloway, Ayrshire, in 1759 of Robert Burns, Scotland's unofficial national poet, is celebrated on 25 January across the world – with a ceremonial supper involving a haggis, whisky, and a declaiming of Burns's eight-stanza 'Address to a Haggis'. The offal concoction is traditionally cut during the recitation of the third stanza:

> His knife see rustic Labour dicht,
> An' cut you up wi' ready slicht,
> Trenching your gushing entrails bricht,
> Like ony ditch;
> And then, O what a glorious sicht,
> Warm-reekin, rich!

The Burns Night ceremony begins, though, with the Selkirk Grace, which dates back to the 17th century and which Burns himself delivered at a dinner given by the Earl of Selkirk:

> Some hae meat and canna eat,
> And some wad eat that want it;
> But we hae meat, and we can eat,
> Sae let the Lord be thankit.

Robert Burns, brought up in poverty, achieved great acclaim with his lyric poetry, much of it written in the Scots language. His first volume appeared in 1786; with it, he hoped to raise money to emigrate to Jamaica, to escape retribution from the father of a girl he had impregnated. But the book's success encouraged him to move to Edinburgh instead, where he was lauded by the literary establishment. He also travelled throughout the country, collecting traditional songs.

The first Burns Night supper was held in Alloway by the poet's friends in 1802, four years after his death at the age of 37 – though on this occasion, and for the next decade, it was held on 29 January, owing to confusion over the poet's birth date.

26 JANUARY

THE COLONIZATION OF AUSTRALIA, 1788

We had the satisfaction of finding the finest harbour in the world, in which a thousand sail of the line may ride in the most perfect security.

CAPTAIN ARTHUR PHILLIP, FIRST DESPATCH TO HOME SECRETARY LORD SYDNEY, 1788.

∞

The 'First Fleet' of 11 convict ships, carrying 792 prisoners for transportation to Australia and 160 marines to guard them, left England in May 1787. It arrived in Botany Bay in January 1788. The site had been noted as ideal for settlement by Captain James Cook on his visit 18 years earlier. For Cook, initially 'the great quantity of these sort of fish found in this place occasioned my giving it the name of Stingrays Harbour'. He later revised his preference to 'Botany Bay' on account of 'the great quantity of plants' collected there, and Botany Bay was the name that stuck.

The First Fleet's commander, Captain Arthur Phillip, was also to be the governor of Britain's new convict colony. After realizing that Botany Bay itself was not the ideal place to land, he moved a little further north and selected Port Jackson – today's Sydney Harbour – and began disembarkation there on 26 January 1788. He named the disembarkation point Sydney Cove after Thomas Townshend, Lord Sydney, the British home secretary who had planned the expedition, and to whom he wrote regular despatches reporting progress. Already he was aware of the potential of one of the world's great harbours and its implications for Britain's imperial growth. His vision served him well, helping him create a colony in which the residents, although sent there by no choice of their own, were prepared to work together to create a society in which they could have a second chance.

ALSO ON THIS DAY

1885 General Gordon is killed by Mahdist rebels in Khartoum, Sudan.
1939 General Franco's Spanish Nationalists capture Barcelona.
1950 India becomes a republic within the British Commonwealth.

27 JANUARY

THE LIBERATION OF AUSCHWITZ-BIRKENAU, 1945

It was by the greatest miracle that I survived. Every barrack had a little cabin in the front, with a breadbox in which the bread was supplied. But the hinge of the box was torn off, and I hid in that box upside down. Someone came in to search, he even kicked it, but luckily I was so skinny, it gave. This is how I remained alive.

When they left, the Germans, I wanted to go back to the barracks, but the Poles and the Ukrainians, they wouldn't let me in. So I hid out in the heap of dead bodies because in the last week when the crematoria didn't function at all, the bodies were just building up higher and higher. And I sneaked among those dead bodies because I was afraid they'd come back. So there I was at night time; in the daytime I was roaming around in the camp. January 27, I was one of the very first, Birkenau was one of the very first camps liberated.

BART STERN, INTERVIEWED IN 1992, US HOLOCAUST MEMORIAL MUSEUM.

∞

Hungarian-born Bart Stern was one of the survivors found by the Soviet Red Army when it entered the Nazi extermination-camp complex at Auschwitz-Birkenau, in southern Poland, on 27 January 1945. By then, having seen the murder of well over a million people, the complex housed around 7,000 inmates, most too old or sick to join the 60,000 others who had been forced to undertake a murderous evacuation march ordered by the Nazis a fortnight earlier.

Among the other prisoners liberated that day were Otto Frank (1889–1980), father of the young Dutch diarist and Holocaust victim Anne Frank (*see* 12 June), and the Italian chemist Primo Levi (1919–87), who was too ill with scarlet fever to be evacuated. After his return to Italy, Levi spent much of his subsequent years writing about the experience of the camps, notably in *If This is a Man* (1947). Yet even he felt unqualified to bear complete testimony. In a later interview he said: 'We who survived the camps are not true witnesses. We are those who, through prevarication, skill or luck, never touched bottom. Those who have, and who have seen the face of the Gorgon, did not return, or returned wordless.'

ALSO ON THIS DAY

1756 The birth of the composer Wolfgang Amadeus Mozart in Salzburg, Austria.
1944 WWII: the German siege of Leningrad is lifted.
1973 The Paris Peace Accord ends the Vietnam War.

28 JANUARY

THE EXPLOSION OF THE SPACE SHUTTLE
CHALLENGER, 1986

The crew of the Space Shuttle *Challenger* honoured us by the manner in which they lived their lives. We will never forget them, nor the last time we saw them, this morning, as they prepared for the journey and waved goodbye and 'slipped the surly bonds of earth' to 'touch the face of God'.

US PRESIDENT RONALD REAGAN, OVAL OFFICE ADDRESS, 28 JANUARY 1986.

∞

President Ronald Reagan spoke for the nation after the catastrophic explosion of the Space Shuttle *Challenger*, broadcast live on television earlier that day. Following the American missions to the Moon, the Space Shuttle project – for a reusable craft that could enter the Earth's orbit – had been NASA's prime focus, and the first launch into orbit had occurred in 1981. But public interest was increasingly unexcited by the 'routine' nature of the Space Shuttle's functions: conducting experiments, and launching and maintaining satellites.

As a result of a novel attempt to engage the public, on 28 January 1986 the world was watching as the first civilian was sent into space aboard *Challenger*. Christa McAuliffe, a 37-year-old schoolteacher from New Hampshire, had been chosen from more than 11,000 applicants for this extraordinary opportunity. She described her looming adventure as 'the ultimate field trip'. Tragically, it was to last just 73 seconds, when a fuel leak caused the rocket carrying the Shuttle to disintegrate into a peel of white smoke, seen etched against the deep blue sky. McAuliffe and the six other crew members died instantly.

The disaster was felt widely and deeply in the United States, and that night President Reagan, the 'Great Communicator', consoled the nation from the Oval Office. He quoted from the poem 'High Flight' by John Gillespie Magee, an aviator who had died in a mid-air collision over England in 1941. He also pointed out a coincidence:

On this day 390 years ago, the great explorer Sir Francis Drake died aboard ship off the coast of Panama. In his lifetime the great frontiers were the oceans, and a historian later said: 'He lived by the sea, died on it, and was buried in it.' Well, today we can say of the Challenger crew: their dedication was, like Drake's, complete.

In 2011, NASA scheduled its last mission for the Space Shuttle programme.

ALSO ON THIS DAY

814 The death of the Frankish emperor Charlemagne.
1547 The death of King Henry VIII, England's second Tudor monarch.
1807 London becomes the first city to be illuminated by gas light.

29 JANUARY

AN AXIS OF EVIL, 2002

Our... goal is to prevent regimes that sponsor terror from threatening America or our friends and allies with weapons of mass destruction. Some of these regimes have been pretty quiet since September the 11th. But we know their true nature. North Korea is a regime arming with missiles and weapons of mass destruction, while starving its citizens.

Iran aggressively pursues these weapons and exports terror, while an unelected few repress the Iranian people's hope for freedom.

Iraq continues to flaunt its hostility toward America and to support terror. The Iraqi regime has plotted to develop anthrax, and nerve gas, and nuclear weapons for over a decade...

States like these, and their terrorist allies, constitute an axis of evil, arming to threaten the peace of the world. By seeking weapons of mass destruction, these regimes pose a grave and growing danger. They could provide these arms to terrorists, giving them the means to match their hatred. They could attack our allies or attempt to blackmail the United States. In any of these cases, the price of indifference would be catastrophic...

We can't stop short... If we stop now – ...leaving terror states unchecked – our sense of security would be false and temporary. History has called America and our allies to action, and it is both our responsibility and our privilege to fight freedom's fight.

US President George W. Bush, State of the Union Address, 29 January 2002.

∞

President George W. Bush's second State of the Union Address was dominated by his response to the attacks by al-Qaeda on 11 September the previous year (*see* 11 September), and by the subsequent war in Afghanistan that was meant to deprive that organization of its bases and destroy its leadership. The address expressed the fear that terrorists of the al-Qaeda type might form mutually advantageous relationships with three states in particular: thereby introducing the notion of Saddam Hussein's Iraq as a legitimate target of US and Western action, which was realized 14 months later in the invasion of that country.

ALSO ON THIS DAY

1820 The death of the periodically 'mad' King George III of Britain.
1886 Karl Benz's petrol-driven motor car is patented.
1916 Paris is bombed from the air, by German Zeppelins, for the first time.

30 JANUARY

THE EXECUTION OF CHARLES I, 1649

I stood amongst the crowd in the street before Whitehall Gate, where the scaffold was erected, and saw what was done but was not so near as to hear any thing. The blow I saw given, and I can truly say with a sad heart at the instant thereof I remember well, there was such a groan by the thousands then present, as I never heard before and desire I may never hear again.

PHILIP HENRY, DIARY, 1649.

∞

The 17-year-old Philip Henry, later a leading Nonconformist clergyman, stood among the crowds on 30 January 1649 that observed the execution of 'Charles Stuart' outside the Whitehall Banqueting House in London. The execution of King Charles I followed a trial in December 1648 that was manipulated by Oliver Cromwell and the army, and enabled by the compliant 'Rump' of MPs left in Parliament. Charles, refusing to recognize the court's jurisdiction, mounted no proper defence of his actions.

The beheading of Charles I represented an unprecedented regicide, observed with misgivings even by its few supporters, with horror by staunch royalists, and with simple shock by most others. The event was quickly turned into propaganda, with graphic accounts of the chilly morning written by both sides of the recent civil wars. By all accounts, though, Charles conducted himself with more dignity than at many other key moments of his life; and he was quickly turned into 'Charles the Martyr', whose purported spiritual autobiography, *Eikon Basilike* (Greek for 'Royal Portrait'), published in mid-February 1649, became an instant best-seller. Powerful words were put into his mouth by the still-unidentified author:

But, O, let the blood of me, though their king, yet a sinner, be washed with the blood of my innocent peacemaking Redeemer, for in that Thy justice will find not only a temporary expiation but an eternal plenary satisfaction, both for my sins and the sins of my people, whom I beseech Thee still own for Thine; and when thy wrath is appeased by my death, O remember thy mercies toward them and forgive them, O my Father, for they know not what they do.

ALSO ON THIS DAY

1933 Adolf Hitler is appointed German chancellor.
1965 The state funeral of Winston Churchill takes place.
1972 Thirteen marchers die during 'Bloody Sunday' in Derry, Northern Ireland.

31 JANUARY

THE TET OFFENSIVE, 1968

Crack the sky, shake the earth.

Vo Nguyen Giap, message to North Vietnamese troops, January 1968.

∞

To say that we are closer to victory today is to believe, in the face of the evidence, the optimists who have been wrong in the past. To suggest we are on the edge of defeat is to yield to unreasonable pessimism. To say that we are mired in stalemate seems the only realistic, yet unsatisfactory, conclusion. On the off chance that military and political analysts are right, in the next few months we must test the enemy's intentions, in case this is indeed his last big gasp before negotiations. But it is increasingly clear to this reporter that the only rational way out then will be to negotiate, not as victors, but as an honourable people who lived up to their pledge to defend democracy, and did the best they could.

Walter Cronkite, CBS Television News, 27 February 1968.

∞

31 January, known as the Feast of the First Morning or *Tet Nguyen Dan*, is the first day of the year in the Vietnamese calendar, and in 1968 it saw the start of a major offensive by Communist forces against South Vietnamese targets and the supporting US forces. It was organized by North Vietnam's defence minister, General Giap, as simultaneous surprise attacks by 80,000 troops on 100 towns, cities and airfields across the country – including Saigon and Hue. In most areas they were quickly defeated, but some major battles ensued, notably at Khe Sanh; US casualties mounted and Communist losses were enormous. In military terms, the 'Tet Offensive' was a failure, and the human cost high. But with the broadcasting of footage showing Communists attacking central Saigon, the impression created in the USA was of a beleaguered South Vietnam. When the respected journalist Walter Cronkite – no anti-war 'leftie' – delivered his verdict, that the United States was 'mired in a stalemate', he registered for the nation this new self-doubt. In February Robert McNamara, US secretary for defence, resigned; and in June, President Johnson replaced William Westmoreland, the US commander in Vietnam. To the surprise of the Viet Cong commanders, a military defeat had become an important propaganda victory.

ALSO ON THIS DAY

1747 London's first clinic for venereal diseases opens.
1876 Native Americans are ordered into reservations by Congressional order.
2000 The British serial killer Dr Harold Shipman is jailed for life.

FEBRUARY

1 FEBRUARY

THE AYATOLLAH'S REVOLUTION, 1979

These people [the interim government of Iran] are trying to bring the shah back. I'll knock their teeth out. From now on, it's me who'll be appointing the government. I am doing it with the support of this whole nation.

AYATOLLAH RUHOLLAH KHOMEINI,
TEHRAN AIRPORT PRESS CONFERENCE, 1 FEBRUARY 1979.

∞

In 1979 the Shi'ite cleric Ayatollah Khomeini had been in exile for 15 years from the Iranian regime of Mohammed Reza Shah Pahlavi. The shah's rule was corrupt and repressive, but (in the Cold War context) pro-Western and backed by the United States and its allies. Protests against the shah had begun in 1977, co-ordinated by the Shi'ite clergy, and they culminated in huge demonstrations in December 1978. An interim government was set up under Shapour Bakhtiar; on 16 January 1979 the shah left the country and Bakhtiar invited Khomeini to return from his Parisian exile – in spite of the fact that just the previous week Khomeini had opined: 'I will not become a president nor accept any other leadership role. Just like before, I limit my activities only to guiding and directing the people.'

On the plane to Tehran, he was asked what he felt about his return; his answer, 'nothing', was taken to mean that he cared little for patriotism, only for Islam. He later explained more fully: 'We do not worship Iran, we worship Allah. For patriotism is another name for paganism. I say let this land go up in smoke, provided Islam emerges triumphant in the rest of the world.' More than a million people were waiting to greet him at the airport on 1 February, where they heard his fierce rejection of Bakhtiar. The interim government collapsed ten days later, and Khomeini won a referendum to establish an Islamic republic under Sharia law, with a reported 98.2 per cent voting in favour.

In December 1979 Khomeini was officially appointed 'Supreme Leader of the Revolution', and there followed a brutal purge of the professional classes and intelligentsia as the rule of the mullahs was established.

2 FEBRUARY

THE REAL ROBINSON CRUSOE, 1709

Immediately our pinnace return'd from the shore, and brought abundance of craw-fish, with a man cloth'd in goat-skins, who look'd wilder than the first owners of them. He had been on the Island four Years and four Months, being left there by Capt. Stradling in the Cinque-Ports; his name was Alexander Selkirk a Scotch man, who had been Master of the Cinque-Ports, a ship that came here last with Capt. Dampier, who told me this was the best man in her; so I immediately agreed with him to be a Mate on board our ship... At his first coming on board us, he had so much forgot his language for want of use, that we could scarce understand him, for he seem'd to speak his words by halves... He had with him his clothes and bedding, with a firelock, some powder, bullets and tobacco, a hatchet, a knife, a kettle, a Bible, some practical pieces, and his mathematical instruments and books.

WOODES ROGERS, *A CRUISING VOYAGE ROUND THE WORLD*, 1712.

∞

On 2 February 1709 a young Scot named Alexander Selkirk, who had run away to sea at age 19 and disappeared, was picked up by the pirate Woodes Rogers while visiting the island of Juan Fernandez, 500 miles off the coast of Chile. According to Rogers's diary, Selkirk had been marooned there for more than four and a half years, having voluntarily abandoned the privateering vessel on which he had been serving, and which he had believed to be unseaworthy. He had then fended for himself alone for all that time. When Selkirk eventually returned to Britain in 1711, Rogers's account made him a celebrity.

During his island sojourn, Selkirk had had to confront 'the terror of being left alone in such a desolate place'. To survive he shot – and later chased down – goats, made clothes from their skins, and sang psalms. In 1719 Daniel Defoe published *The Life and Strange Surprising Adventures of Robinson Crusoe of York, Mariner*, based heavily on Selkirk's adventures. There was, however, no real-life Man Friday.

ALSO ON THIS DAY

1901 The funeral of Queen Victoria is held, and filmed.
1913 Grand Central Terminal opens in New York City.
1970 The death of the philosopher and pacifist Bertrand Russell.

3 FEBRUARY

THE WIND OF CHANGE ACROSS AFRICA, 1960

The most striking of all the impressions I have formed since I left London a month ago is of the strength of this African national consciousness. In different places it takes different forms, but it is happening everywhere. The wind of change is blowing through this continent and, whether we like it or not, this growth of national consciousness is a political fact.

HAROLD MACMILLAN, ADDRESS TO THE SOUTH AFRICAN PARLIAMENT, 3 FEBRUARY 1960.

∞

Towards the end of a 1960 tour of Africa, Britain's Conservative prime minister, Harold Macmillan, acknowledged the growing momentum of African nationalism. Ghana had won its independence in 1957, and most of Britain's other African colonies would become independent over the next six years. Macmillan's words, delivered to the South African Parliament in Cape Town, were also aimed at South Africa's policy of *apartheid*, which he criticized in terms forthright enough to lose him friends on the right of his party at home. He said he wanted 'a society which respects the rights of individuals – a society in which individual merit, and individual merit alone, is the criterion for a man's advancement'. His words were received in silence, and Henrik Verwoerd, South Africa's prime minister, retorted:

> ...to do justice to all, does not only mean being just to the black man of Africa, but also to be just to the white man of Africa. We set up a country bare, and the Bantu came in this country and settled certain portions for themselves... we believe in allowing exactly those same full opportunities to remain within the grasp of the white man who has made all this possible.

Six weeks later, 69 black protesters, objecting to the regime's notorious 'pass laws' (which restricted the movement of black South Africans), were shot dead by police at Sharpeville. It would be 30 years before Macmillan's 'wind of change' in South Africa became reality (*see* 11 February).

ALSO ON THIS DAY

AD 313 The Edict of Milan ends the persecution of Christians in the Roman Empire.
1488 The explorer Bartolomeu Dias lands in South Africa after rounding the Cape of Good Hope.
1959 The rock 'n' roll singer Buddy Holly dies in a plane crash.

4 FEBRUARY

THE CAPTURE OF VALDIVIA, 1820

As soon as it was dark, a picked party silently advanced to the attack, expecting to fall in with the enemy outside the fort, but our men were unopposed.

The main body moved forward, cheering and firing in the air, to intimate to the Spaniards that their chief reliance was on the bayonet. The enemy kept up an incessant fire in the direction of the shouts, but without effect, as no aim could be taken in the dark. Whilst the patriots were thus noisily advancing, a gallant young officer, Ensign Vidal, got under the inland flank of the fort...

A volley from Vidal's party convinced the Spaniards that they had been taken in flank. They instantly took to flight. The Chileans bayoneted them by dozens. A number of the enemy escaped in boats to Valdivia, others plunged into the forest, whilst upwards of a hundred, besides officers, fell into our hands, the like number being found bayoneted on the following morning. Our loss was seven men killed, and nineteen wounded.

The Spaniards had, no doubt, regarded their position as impregnable, which, considering its almost natural impenetrability, it ought to have been. An attack where least expected is almost invariably crowned with success.

THOMAS COCHRANE, *NARRATIVE*, 1859.

On 4 February 1820, after a decade of struggle against Spanish and pro-Royalist forces, Chilean patriots moved to complete their independence struggle by capturing the city of Valdivia. They overcame its impressive defences through an audacious land attack. It was a key moment in the liberation of that country from colonial rule.

The attack was led by a Scotsman, Admiral Thomas Cochrane, 10th Earl of Dundonald. He was an adventurous former Royal Navy commander, who had been disgraced following conviction for fraud on the Stock Exchange; he then pursued a dramatic new naval career in South America, offering his services to nationalist and independence movements. Cochrane had been recruited by the Spanish-Irish 'Liberator of Chile' Bernardo O'Higgins (and Chile's first president, 1817–23) who, with Argentine General José de San Martín – the 'Simón Bolívar of the south' – shaped the independence struggle.

ALSO ON THIS DAY

1789 George Washington is elected as the first US president.
1945 WWII: the Yalta Conference discusses Europe's postwar organization.
1948 Ceylon (later Sri Lanka) becomes independent from Britain.

5 FEBRUARY

THE TERROR OF REVOLUTIONARY FRANCE, 1794

France is the theatre of a mighty struggle. Without, all the tyrants encircle you; within, all the friends of tyranny conspire – they will conspire until crime has been robbed of hope. We must smother the internal and external enemies of the Republic or perish with them. In this situation, the first maxim of your policy ought to be to lead the people by reason and the people's enemies by terror.

If the mainspring of popular government in peacetime is virtue, amid revolution it is at once virtue and terror: virtue, without which terror is fatal; terror, without which virtue is impotent. Terror is nothing but prompt, severe, inflexible justice; it is therefore an emanation of virtue. It is less a special principle than a consequence of the general principle of democracy applied to the country's most pressing needs.

It has been said that terror was the mainspring of despotic government. Does your government, then, resemble a despotism? Yes, as the sword which glitters in the hands of liberty's heroes resembles the one with which tyranny's lackeys are armed. Let the despot govern his brutalized subjects by terror; he is right to do this, as a despot. Subdue liberty's enemies by terror, and you will be right, as founders of the Republic. The government of the revolution is the despotism of liberty against tyranny. Is not force made to protect crime? And is it not to strike the heads of the proud that lightning is destined?

MAXIMILIEN ROBESPIERRE, *REPORT OF THE PRINCIPLES OF PUBLIC MORALITY*,

FEBRUARY 1794.

Maximilien Robespierre was leader of the radical Jacobin faction in France, who achieved prominence with the so-called Committee of Public Safety in summer 1793, several months after the execution of Louis XVI (*see* 21 January). He saw the French Revolution as under mortal threat from the Prussian, Austrian and other pro-monarchical forces threatening to invade France – and he believed these forces had many supporters within France itself. In February 1794, he delivered his major *Report* to the National Convention in which he construed state 'terror' as the means to achieve the desired goals. Moderates on both sides were now threatened by the guillotine. After more than 1,200 people had died by this means, Robespierre himself was guillotined on 28 July 1794.

ALSO ON THIS DAY

1818 Jean-Baptiste Jules Bernadotte becomes king of Norway and Sweden.
1919 Charlie Chaplin, D.W. Griffith, Mary Pickford and Douglas Fairbanks launch United Artists.
1953 The rationing of sweets ends in Britain.

6 FEBRUARY

THE BRITISH GAIN NEW ZEALAND, 1840

1. The Chiefs of the Confederation of the United Tribes of New Zealand... cede to Her Majesty the Queen of England absolutely and without reservation all the rights and powers of Sovereignty which the said... Chiefs respectively exercise or possess, or may be supposed to exercise or to possess, over their respective Territories as the sole Sovereigns thereof.

2. Her Majesty the Queen of England confirms and guarantees to the Chiefs and Tribes of New Zealand and to the respective families and individuals thereof the full exclusive and undisturbed possession of their Lands and Estates Forests Fisheries and other properties which they may collectively or individually possess so long as it is their wish and desire to retain the same in their possession; but the Chiefs... yield to Her Majesty the exclusive right of Pre-emption over such lands as the proprietors thereof may be disposed to alienate at such prices as may be agreed upon between the respective Proprietors and persons appointed by Her Majesty to treat with them in that behalf.

3. In consideration thereof Her Majesty the Queen of England extends to the Natives of New Zealand Her royal protection and imparts to them all the Rights and Privileges of British Subjects.

TREATY OF WAITANGI, 6 FEBRUARY 1840.

These three brief Articles of the Treaty of Waitangi, signed by British representative Captain William Hobson and Maori chiefs in 1840, read somewhat differently in Maori; but there was no question that they gave the British sovereignty over New Zealand, which now became a separate colony. The treaty was signed after an all-night discussion among Maori chiefs. Afterwards, one said that he believed 'the shadow of the land is to the Queen, but the substance remains to us'. And land remained the subject of debate and – in the 1840s and 1860s – violent conflict between Maoris and settlers.

Although the treaty was never actually ratified, its signing is seen as the foundation day of the modern nation. In recent decades, parts of the treaty have been used as a basis to challenge perceived injustices suffered by Maoris in the years after settler occupation.

ALSO ON THIS DAY

1817 Sir Thomas Stamford Raffles founds Singapore.
1958 Twenty people, including 8 Manchester United footballers, die in the Munich air disaster.
1994 A Serbian mortar bomb kills many civilians in Sarajevo's market square.

7 FEBRUARY

BEATLEMANIA HITS NEW YORK, 1964

'They've got everything over there. What do they want us for?'

GEORGE HARRISON, 7 FEBRUARY 1964.

∞

The Beatles, having taken the British pop scene by storm in 1963 with their interpretation of American rock and roll and rhythm and blues music, were surprised and awed to make a similar impact in the United States the next year. In early February 1964, when the band members heard they were Number 1 in the US charts, they 'hit the roof', in Paul McCartney's words.

The idea of exporting rock 'n' roll to its American birthplace seemed, on the face of it, preposterous, and there was no precedent for it. John Lennon later said: 'The thing is, in America, it just seemed ridiculous – I mean, the idea of having a hit record over there. It was just something you could never do.' But a few days later they were on their way to New York. Even in mid-Atlantic, George Harrison was still expressing disbelief, and on arrival they were shocked by the scale of the reception.

Their press conference on arrival introduced Americans to their irreverent wit, quite different to the show-business norm:

Journalist: 'Why does it [the Beatles' music] excite them so much?' ...
John Lennon: 'If we knew, we'd form another group and be managers.'...
Journalist: 'What do you think of Beethoven?'
Ringo Starr: 'Great. Especially his poems.'

On 9 February, no fewer than 75 million US television viewers watched The Beatles' appearance on the prime-time *Ed Sullivan Show*. The magazine *Newsweek* didn't think much of them: 'Visually they are a nightmare: tight, dandified Edwardian beatnik suits and great pudding bowls of hair. Musically they are a near disaster, guitars and drums slamming out a merciless beat that does away with secondary rhythms, harmony and melody.' But the rest of the country clearly disagreed.

ALSO ON THIS DAY

1497 Inhabitants of Florence destroy precious articles in the 'Bonfire of the Vanities'.
1812 The birth of the English novelist Charles Dickens.
1992 The Maastricht Treaty is signed, creating the modern European Union.

8 FEBRUARY

THE EXECUTION OF MARY, QUEEN OF SCOTS, 1587

Her prayers being ended, the executioners, kneeling, desired her Grace to forgive them her death: who answered: 'I forgive you with all my heart, for now, I hope, you shall make an end of all my troubles.' Then they, with her two women, helping her up, began to disrobe her of her apparel: then she, laying her crucifix upon the stool, one of the executioners took from her neck the *Agnus Dei*, which she, laying hands off it, gave to one of her women, and told the executioner he should be answered money for it. Then she suffered them, with her two women, to disrobe her of her chain of pomander beads and all other her apparel most willingly, and with joy rather than sorrow, helped to make unready herself, putting on a pair of sleeves with her own hands which they had pulled off, and that with some haste, as if she had longed to be gone.

All this time they were pulling off her apparel, she never changed her countenance, but with smiling cheer she uttered these words: 'that she never had such grooms to make her unready, and that she never put off her clothes before such a company'.

…One of the women having a Corpus Christi cloth lapped up three-corner-ways, kissing it, put it over the Queen of Scots' face, and pinned it fast to the caule of her head… Kneeling down upon the cushion most resolutely, and without any token or fear of death, she spake aloud this Psalm in Latin: '*In Te Domine confido, non confundar in eternam*', etc. Then, groping for the block, she laid down her head, putting her chin over the block with both her hands, which, holding there still, had been cut off had they not been espied. Then lying upon the block most quietly, and stretching out her arms cried: '*In manus tuas, Domine*', etc., three or four times. Then she, lying very still upon the block, one of the executioners holding her slightly with one of his hands, she endured two strokes of the other executioner with an axe, she making very small noise or none at all, and not stirring any part of her from the place where she lay: and so the executioner cut off her head, saving one little gristle, which being cut asunder, he lift up her head to the view of all the assembly and bade God save the Queen. Then, her dress of lawn falling from off her head, it appeared as grey as one of threescore and ten years old, polled very short, her face in a moment being so much altered from the form she had when she was alive, as few could remember her by her dead face. Her lips stirred up and down a quarter of an hour after her head was cut off.

Then Mr Dean said with a loud voice: 'So perish all the Queen's enemies', and afterwards the Earl of Kent came to the dead body, and standing over it, with a loud voice said: 'Such end of all the Queen's and the Gospel's enemies.'

Then one of the executioners, pulling off her garters, espied her little dog which was crept under her clothes, which could not be gotten forth but by force, yet afterward would not depart from the dead corpse, but came and lay between her head and her shoulders, which being imbrued with her blood was carried away and washed...

ROBERT WYNKEFIELD, LETTER TO LORD WILLIAM CECIL, 1587.

∞

The tumultuous life of Mary, Queen of Scots, ended at Fotheringhay Castle in Northamptonshire on 7 February 1587. On that day she was executed for treason, the pretext being her involvement in the Babington Plot to assassinate Elizabeth I. Since 1568 Mary had been under house arrest, having fled her opponents in Scotland. But her presence remained a thorn in the side of Elizabeth: through descent – Mary's grandmother Margaret was sister of Henry VIII – Mary held a claim to the English throne; and her Catholicism attracted the support of those English who yearned for the Old Religion as well as those foreign Catholic powers who desired an end to Elizabeth's Protestant regime.

In 1587, after much indecision and a natural disinclination to execute a fellow monarch (and relative), Elizabeth allowed events to take their course. For Philip II of Spain, the execution of Mary compounded existing Anglo-Spanish hostilities and confirmed his determination to attempt to remove Elizabeth, expressed in 1588 through the launching of his vast – but futile – Armada (*see* 9 August).

ALSO ON THIS DAY

1265 The death of the Mongol leader Hulagu Khan.
1575 The University of Leiden is founded in the Netherlands.
1924 The first execution by means of the gas chamber takes place in the USA.

9 FEBRUARY

THE BEGINNINGS OF A
COMMUNIST WITCHUNT, 1950

The State Department is infested with Communists. I have here in my hand a list of 205 – a list of names that were made known to the Secretary of State as being members of the Communist Party and who nevertheless are still working and shaping policy in the State Department.

The reason why we find ourselves in a position of impotency is not because the enemy has sent men to invade our shores, but rather because of the traitorous actions of those who have had all the benefits that the wealthiest nation on earth has had to offer – the finest homes, the finest college educations, and the finest jobs in Government we can give... Today we are engaged in a final, all-out battle between communistic atheism and Christianity. The modern champions of communism have selected this as the time, and ladies and gentlemen, the chips are down – they are truly down.

SENATOR JOSEPH MCCARTHY, SPEECH, WHEELING, WEST VIRGINIA, 9 FEBRUARY 1950.

∞

The US Red Scare began when Joseph McCarthy, senator for Wisconsin, made a speech to the Republican Women's Club at Wheeling, West Virginia, on 9 February 1950. He argued that members of the State Department were working for the Soviet Union, and followed up his claims with a detailed speech in the Senate two weeks later – though now claiming the list held just 57 names, and not the 205 he had mentioned previously.

McCarthy was able to trade on unsubstantiated insult and accusation against a wide variety of targets, from the US president downwards. From 1953, he chaired the Senate Committee on Government Operations, which included the Permanent Subcommittee on Investigations, and this gave him a platform for pursuing his agenda of 'flushing out' suspected Communists from US institutions.

Eventually, McCarthy met his match when he took on on the US Army in 1954: these televised hearings revealed his crudely hectoring style – and often the paucity of his evidence. Shown up as a dishonest, drunk, bully, he was censured by the Senate, and his political influence rapidly declined – as did he himself, dying in 1957 from alcohol-related liver disease.

ALSO ON THIS DAY

1737 The birth of the radical libertarian Thomas Paine.
1967 The Boeing 747 airliner makes its first test flight.
1996 IRA bombs strike London's Canary Wharf financial district.

10 FEBRUARY

FRANCE CEDES CANADA TO BRITAIN, 1763

Article IV. His Most Christian Majesty renounces all pretensions which he has heretofore formed or might have formed to Nova Scotia or Acadia in all its parts, and guarantees the whole of it, and with all its dependencies, to the King of Great Britain: Moreover, his Most Christian Majesty cedes and guarantees to his said Britannic Majesty, in full right, Canada, with all its dependencies, as well as the island of Cape Breton, and all the other islands and coasts in the gulf and river of St Lawrence... His Britannic Majesty, on his side, agrees to grant the liberty of the Catholic religion to the inhabitants of Canada: he will, in consequence, give the most precise and most effectual orders, that his new Roman Catholic subjects may profess the worship of their religion according to the rites of the Romish church, as far as the laws of Great Britain permit. His Britannic Majesty farther agrees, that the French inhabitants, or others who had been subjects of the Most Christian King in Canada, may retire with all safety and freedom wherever they shall think proper, and may sell their estates, provided it be to the subjects of his Britannic Majesty, and bring away their effects as well as their persons, without being restrained in their emigration, under any pretence whatsoever, except that of debts or of criminal prosecutions.

TREATY OF PARIS, 1763.

∞

The Treaty of Paris between the 'Most Christian King' (Louis XV of France) and 'His Britannic Majesty' (George III) ended the Seven Years' War, a far-reaching conflict whose North American theatre is known as the French and Indian Wars. The outcome produced major territorial adjustments on that continent, spelling the end of 'New France'. British control over Quebec (conquered by General Wolfe in 1759; *see* 13 September) and Cape Breton was confirmed, while further south France renounced interests in land east of the Mississippi, other than New Orleans.

With the demise of 'New France', many French Canadians seized the chance to emigrate. But the province of Quebec that later formed an uneasy part of modern Canada is still mainly Francophone in its language, culture and politics.

ALSO ON THIS DAY
1258 Baghdad falls to the Mongols, ending the Abbasid Caliphate.
1355 The St Scholastica's Day riot in Oxford leaves 93 scholars and locals dead.
1840 Queen Victoria marries Prince Albert of Saxe-Coburg-Gotha.

11 FEBRUARY

NELSON MANDELA'S LONG MARCH TO FREEDOM, 1990

Friends, Comrades and fellow South Africans. I greet you all in the name of peace, democracy and freedom for all. I stand here before you not as a prophet but as a humble servant of you, the people. Your tireless and heroic sacrifices have made it possible for me to be here today. I therefore place the remaining years of my life in your hands...

Today, the majority of South Africans, black and white, recognize that apartheid has no future. It has to be ended by our own decisive mass action in order to build peace and security.

The mass campaigns of defiance and other actions of our organization and people can only culminate in the establishment of democracy.

The destruction caused by apartheid to our subcontinent is incalculable. The fabric of family life of millions of my people has been shattered. Millions are homeless and unemployed. Our economy lies in ruins and our people are embroiled in political strife.

Our resort to the armed struggle in 1960 with the formation of the military wing of the ANC (Umkho–to We Sizwe) was a purely defensive action against the violence of apartheid. The factors which necessitated the armed struggle still exist today. We have no option but to continue. We express the hope that a climate conducive to a negotiated settlement would be created soon, so that there may no longer be the need for the armed struggle...

There must be an end to white monopoly on political power, and a fundamental restructuring of our political and economic systems to ensure that the inequalities of apartheid are addressed and our society thoroughly democratized.

It must be added that Mr de Klerk himself is a man of integrity who is acutely aware of the dangers of a public figure not honouring his undertaking.

But as an organization, we base our policy and our strategy on the harsh reality we are faced with, and this reality is that we are still suffering under the policies of the nationalist government.

Our struggle has reached a decisive moment: We call on our people to seize this moment, so that the process toward democracy is rapid and uninterrupted.

We have waited too long for our freedom. We can no longer wait. Now is the time to intensify the struggle on all fronts. To relax our efforts now would be a mistake which generations to come will not be able to forgive.

The sight of freedom looming on the horizon should encourage us to redouble our efforts. It is only through disciplined mass action that our victory can be assured.

We call on our white compatriots to join us in the shaping of a new South Africa. The freedom movement is a political home for you, too.

We call on the international community to continue the campaign to isolate the apartheid regime. To lift sanctions now would run the risk of aborting the process toward the complete eradication of apartheid.

Our march to freedom is irreversible. We must not allow fear to stand in our way. Universal suffrage on a common voters' roll in a united, democratic and non-racial South Africa is the only way to peace and racial harmony.

NELSON MANDELA, SPEECH, 11 FEBRUARY 1990.

∞

On the morning of 11 February 1990, 71-year-old Nelson Mandela walked hand in hand with his wife Winnie down the long road from Viktor Verster Prison, in the Western Cape of South Africa. Although he had been locked up for 27 years – most of them on the offshore facility of Robben Island – his courage and dignity had maintained his status as the moral authority of the African National Congress (ANC) and the broader anti-*apartheid* movement. The previous September F.W. de Klerk, the new state president, had announced the dismantling of *apartheid* policies, unbanned the ANC and entered into negotiations for a transition from white-minority rule to a multi-racial state.

On the evening of his release, Mandela spoke in public for the first time. His address combined his characteristically measured rhetoric with an analysis of the choices facing the ANC in the coming months of tense negotiations. That transition, against the expectations of many inside the country and out, proved to be largely peaceable. Mandela and de Klerk were jointly awarded the Nobel Peace Prize in 1993; multi-party elections were held on 27 April 1994, and Mandela became the country's first black president – and the first South African leader elected by universal franchise.

ALSO ON THIS DAY

1826 University College London is founded.
1847 The birth of the American inventor Thomas Edison.
1929 Fascist Italy and the Vatican sign the Lateran Treaty.

12 FEBRUARY

DONALD RUMSFELD'S
KNOWNS AND UNKNOWNS, 2002

US Journalist: In regard to Iraq weapons of mass destruction and terrorists, is there any evidence to indicate that Iraq has attempted to or is willing to supply terrorists with weapons of mass destruction? Because there are reports that there is no evidence of a direct link between Baghdad and some of these terrorist organizations.

Donald Rumsfeld: The absence of evidence is not evidence of absence, or vice versa… There are known knowns. These are things we know that we know. There are known unknowns. That is to say, there are things that we now know we don't know. But there are also unknown unknowns. These are things we do not know we don't know.

US Secretary of Defence Donald Rumsfeld, press conference, 12 February 2002.

∞

The US Secretary of Defence Donald Rumsfeld resorted to these ostensibly runic observations in the course of an uncomfortable press conference mostly about the war in Afghanistan; this was a few days after Mohammed Karzai had been installed as the new Afghan president, following the toppling of the Taliban regime. But it was not the moment of rejoicing that Rumsfeld and President George W. Bush had hoped for, as the hunt for the al-Qaeda and Taliban leadership had stalled and civilian casualties were rising. There were also unsettling rumours that the US-declared Global War on Terror might be expanded into Iraq (*see* 29 January).

The journalist's question, and its answer, would come back to haunt Rumsfeld – as well as President Bush and his British ally Tony Blair – the following year, after the US-led invasion of Iraq produced no evidence of hidden weapons of mass destruction. Rumsfeld's on-the-hoof sophistry appeared to carry a whiff of arrogance and dissimulation, which – unfairly or otherwise – came to stick and left him politically vulnerable. Nevertheless, he had his catchphrase, and when he published his memoir in 2011 it was entitled *Known and Unknown*.

ALSO ON THIS DAY

1554 Lady Jane Grey, England's 'nine days' queen', is beheaded.
1804 The death of the German philosopher Immanuel Kant.
1809 The future US president Abraham Lincoln is born in rural Kentucky.

13 FEBRUARY

THE MASSACRE OF GLENCOE, 1692

You are to fall upon the rebels, the M'Donalds, of Glencoe and put all to the sword under seventy. You are to have special care that the old fox and his sons do upon no account escape your hands. You are to secure all the avenues, that no man may escape. This you are to put in execution at five o'clock in the morning precisely. This is by the king's special command, for the good of the country, that these miscreants be cut off root and branch.

JOHN DALRYMPLE, MASTER OF STAIR, ORDERS TO JOHN CAMPBELL, 1692.

The notorious 1692 massacre of members of the Clan MacDonald in Glencoe, in the Scottish Highlands, was a spasm that followed in the aftermath of Britain's Glorious Revolution of 1688. That coup had seen the Stuart King James II (who was James VII of Scotland), a Catholic, flee into exile to be replaced by his Protestant daughter Mary and her Dutch husband, William of Orange. The Scottish Parliament accepted William, but James retained support among Catholic and Church of Scotland Highlanders, and rebellion ensued. After initial success turned to defeat (and with James's cause severely damaged in Ireland, at the Battle of the Boyne; *see* 12 July), in late 1691 the clans were disposed to accept William's offer of a pardon to those who would take an oath of allegiance to him. Alasdair Maclain, chief of the Clan MacDonald, was prominent among those who took the oath, though he did so reluctantly and after the set deadline of 1 January.

However, for William's secretary of state in Edinburgh, Sir John Dalrymple – a Lowlander and Protestant – Maclain's failure to meet the deadline presented an opportunity to prove his own loyalty to the new regime and exact some exemplary punishment. In his words, 'Glencoe had not taken the oath, at which I rejoice! It will be a proper vindication of public justice to extirpate that sect of thieves. It must be quietly done. Let it be secret, and sudden.' Dalrymple sent a force to Glencoe, led by Robert Campbell, where they were billeted on the MacDonalds, accepting hospitality according to the traditions of the Highlands. Yet, early on 13 February, the guests turned on their hosts and Maclain and about 80 others were massacred in their homes or died from exposure after their houses were destroyed.

ALSO ON THIS DAY

1542 Catherine Howard, Henry VIII's fifth wife, is executed for her indiscretions.
1931 New Delhi becomes the capital of India.
1945 WWII: the historic German city of Dresden is incinerated by Allied air raids.

14 FEBRUARY

THE DEATH OF CAPTAIN COOK, 1779

Matters had apparently a different appearance at our return to our old station. We were very little visited and provisions did not flow upon us as before, and the people were shy and reserved from reasons no doubt variously assigned by us. The *Resolution* since our departure from this place found the head of her foremast so much damaged as to take it out and send it on shore to be repaired which was accordingly done and had our carpenters to assist them with a marker and a Guard of Marines from the *Resolution*. On the 14th our large cutter moored at our sml br. buoy was missing. Boats were manned and armed from both ships with orders from Capt. Cook to lay at the mouth of the bay and keep the passage, that nothing should enter or go out while he himself with three of his own boats manned and armed went to the town on the NW side of the harbour to secure the Chief of all the Islands at his residence there. Capt. Cook landed with the Marine officer and party of Marines and visited the chief's house, but was opposed in his demands upon Tireoboo the Chief and was returning to the shore where the boats lay surrounded both him [sic] and his guard with a vast crowd who were alarmed at his boldness and perhaps at a loss to account for his return to the boats – or from whatever motives it was soon perceived that many of them were armed – tho at the same time others were crowding presents upon him, which with much anger he threw from him – some insolence was afterwards shown him and he fired some small shot at the offender without doing any damage, this is perhaps partly nearly the situation of matters when a skirmish ensued and the fire became general from the boats and then from the Marines, but without any orders from any quarter as I can understand, for Capt. Cook turned to the boats enquired the reason of it and was ordering them to cease firing when a chief came behind and stabbed him between the shoulders with an iron instrument like a dirk (a type of knife) of which they had many made by Capt. Cook by their own directions. He fell immediately at the receipt of the blow with his face in the water but did not expire till he had received several other wounds in different parts of his body – everything was in confusion now, the Indians were elevated at their success and a corporal and three Marines shared the fate of their commander before the others got on board the boats, the Lieut. of Marines was stabbed in the shoulder and others badly wounded with stones which came like hail from such a multitude.

LIEUTENANT JOHN RICKMAN, *JOURNAL OF CAPTAIN COOK'S*
LAST VOYAGE TO THE PACIFIC OCEAN, 1781.

Captain James Cook (1728–79) revolutionized knowledge of the Pacific and Australasia in more than 30 years' worth of voyaging, charting and discovery. He visited Australia, New Zealand, the coast of Newfoundland, many Pacific islands and both the extreme south and north of that ocean. He also consistently preached tolerance and understanding of the peoples he encountered, and was notably concerned for the welfare of his crew.

In 1779, on his third major voyage, he was attempting to prove (or disprove) the existence of a Northwest Passage linking the Pacific and Atlantic oceans across the top of Canada; but the impenetrable ice forced his return to the Hawaiian islands, which he had first encountered the previous year. The great explorer met his end on a Hawaiian beach on 14 February 1779, as a disagreement with Native Hawaiians turned into a skirmish.

Seaman George Gilbert described the feeling among his crew on the *Resolution* immediately afterwards:

When on the return of the boats informing us of the captain's death, a general silence ensued throughout the ship, for the space of near half an hour – it appearing to us somewhat like a dream that we could not reconcile ourselves to for some time. Grief was visible in every countenance.

1797 The British defeat a Spanish fleet at the Battle of Cape St Vincent.
1929 Intra-gangster violence produces the Valentine's Day massacre in Chicago.
1989 Salman Rushdie, author of *The Satanic Verses*, is subjected to an Iranian *fatwa*.

15 FEBRUARY

THE OUTBREAK OF THE
SPANISH–AMERICAN WAR, 1898

'Remember the Maine, to hell with Spain!'

US PATRIOTIC SLOGAN.

∞

The *casus belli* in the 1898 war between the United States and Spain – a war that was heavily stirred up by the American press – was the sinking of the US Navy battleship *Maine*, which operated down the US East Coast and in the Caribbean. On the evening of 15 February 1898 she was in Havana Harbour, on a mission seen as provocative by the Spanish authorities that controlled Cuba. A massive explosion tore through the ship and sank her, with the loss of 268 men. Although the cause was never determined, suspicions were raised of Spanish or Cuban rebel responsibility. The Spanish minister for the colonies told the governor of Cuba 'to gather every fact you can to prove the *Maine* catastrophe cannot be attributed to us'. The official US inquiry stated: 'In the opinion of the court, the *Maine* was destroyed by the explosion of a submarine mine, which caused the partial explosion of two or more of her forward magazines. The court has been unable to obtain evidence fixing the responsibility for the destruction of the *Maine* upon any person or persons.'

US public opinion, however, had little doubt and pinned the blame firmly on Spain. Newspapers stoked war fever. In a possibly apocryphal, but telling, example, William Randolph Hearst reputedly told his *New York Morning Journal* illustrator in Cuba (who had been telegraphing to say 'there will be no war') to stay put, with the words: 'Please remain. You supply the pictures and I'll supply the war.' In May war was declared on Spain, and by December 1898 the Spanish colonies of Puerto Rico and the Philippines were being ceded to the United States, while Cuba gained its independence under US administrative control.

16 FEBRUARY

THE 'MYSTERIOUS' DEATH OF A FRENCH PRESIDENT, 1899

Towards midnight (I had been in bed for some time), I was awakened by the bell of the telephone in my room. It was M. Bordelongue, a director in the Ministry of *Postes et Telegraphes*, and an old friend.

'What's the matter?' I asked.

And then I heard the news, the dreadful news: 'The president is dead.'

I could not believe what I heard. 'It's impossible,' I exclaimed. 'I saw him today. He was tired, weak, upset, but there seemed to be nothing particularly wrong with his health.' I asked Bordelongue all kinds of questions, but he merely replied: 'Nothing is known. They say the president died of an apoplectic stroke.'

The next morning at six o'clock I was told that my faithful agent 'wished to see me on a matter of importance'. This 'agent'... was a private detective who had been specially selected and appointed by Félix Faure to keep guard over me wherever I went, and see that no harm befell me...

I guessed what the man came about, so I hastily dressed and met him.

'Ah ! Madame, I see you know the news... There's some mystery in the president's death. They say he died of congestion of the brain, but I hear his agony lasted several hours... I am myself being shadowed, and it will be better if I do not call again... But you know my address and if at any time I can be of some use to you I beseech you to apply to me.'

MARGUERITE STEINHEIL, *MY MEMOIRS*, 1912.

The death of Félix Faure, French president during *L'Affaire Dreyfus* (*see* 13 January), was widely judged to be much less of a mystery than Marguerite Steinheil's sanitized memoirs suggest. The fatal moments were credited to over-excitement, at a critical juncture, during his last sexual encounter with Mme Steinheil, his mistress. She went on to enjoy other high-profile liaisons, before becoming embroiled in a genuinely mysterious crime in 1908 in which she was bound and gagged while her husband and stepmother were suffocated.

ALSO ON THIS DAY

1923 The archaeologist Howard Carter unseals Tutankhamun's burial chamber.
1936 The Popular Front comes to power in Spain, instituting left-wing republican rule.
1959 Fidel Castro gains power in Cuba.

17 FEBRUARY

THE BURNING OF GIORDANO BRUNO, 1600

Perhaps you pronounce this sentence against me with greater fear than I receive it.

GIORDANO BRUNO, 17 FEBRUARY 1600.

∞

The execution of Neapolitan philosopher and astronomer Giordano Bruno (1548–1600) has been seen – probably wrongly – as an attempt by the Catholic Church to hold back the tide of modern science. Yet he was perhaps the first to envisage an infinite universe, in which the stars and sun are similar objects. Such a belief took him far beyond the heliocentric observations of Nicolaus Copernicus, and his conviction of the importance of a sceptical attitude towards accepted 'truths' led him to explore a multitude of avenues, including mathematics, alchemy and the pseudo-scientific 'hermetic' beliefs of his day. For Bruno, 'everything, however men may deem it assured and evident, proves, when it is brought under discussion, to be no less doubtful than are extravagant and absurd beliefs'. In *On Cause, Principle and Unity*, he espoused a radical relativism that led him to doubt the Church's message:

> This entire globe, this star, not being subject to death, and dissolution and annihilation being impossible anywhere in Nature, from time to time renews itself by changing and altering all its parts. There is no absolute up or down, as Aristotle taught; no absolute position in space; but the position of a body is relative to that of other bodies. Everywhere there is incessant relative change in position throughout the universe, and the observer is always at the centre of things.

Bruno was arrested in Venice and sent to Rome in 1593, where he was handed over to the Roman Inquisition and imprisoned for seven years while he was subjected to a long trial. He refused to recant several heretical beliefs (it is not known which), and eventually the pope condemned him and handed him over to the secular authorities, who burned him in Rome's Campo de' Fiori on 17 February 1600.

ALSO ON THIS DAY

1673 The French playwright Molière dies after acting in *The Hypochondriac*.
1871 Prussians parade in Paris after their victory in the Franco-Prussian War.
1904 The premiere of Puccini's opera *Madame Butterfly* takes place in Milan.

18 FEBRUARY

THE DEATH OF CLARENCE, 1478

Clarence: How darkly and how deadly dost thou speak!
Your eyes do menace me. Why look you pale?
Who sent you hither? Wherefore do you come?
Second Murderer: To, to, to –
Clarence: To murder me?
Both Murderers: Ay, ay…
Clarence: Are you drawn forth among a world of men
To slay the innocent? What is my offense?
Where is the evidence that doth accuse me?
What lawful quest have given their verdict up
Unto the frowning judge? Or who pronounced
The bitter sentence of poor Clarence' death
Before I be convict by course of law?
To threaten me with death is most unlawful:
I charge you, as you hope to have redemption
By Christ's dear blood shed for our grievous sins,
That you depart, and lay no hands on me.
The deed you undertake is damnable.
First Murderer: What we will do, we do upon command.
Second Murderer: And he that hath commanded is our king…
    WILLIAM SHAKESPEARE, *KING RICHARD III*, ACT I SCENE IV, 1597 AND IN FIRST FOLIO (1613).

∞

The real George Plantagenet, 1st Duke of Clarence, was killed behind closed doors on 18 February 1478, concluding his sojourn in the Tower of London on charges of treason against his elder brother, Edward IV. More memorably, though, Shakespeare projected the event into the reign of Clarence's other brother, Richard III – and played upon Clarence's bewildered innocence to emphasize Richard's villainy. But the Bard retained the unique method of dispatch: drowning in a butt of Malmsey wine.

ALSO ON THIS DAY

1294 The death of the Mongol emperor Kublai Khan.
1861 Victor Emmanuel II of Sardinia-Piedmont becomes king of most of Italy.
1965 The Gambia, in West Africa, achieves independence from Britain.

19 FEBRUARY

A PROBLEM WITH NO NAME, 1963

Gradually, without seeing it clearly for quite a while, I came to realize that something is very wrong with the way American women are trying to live their lives today. I sensed it first as a question mark in my own life, as a wife and mother of three small children, half-guiltily, and therefore half-heartedly, almost in spite of myself, using my abilities and education in work that took me away from home.

The problem lay buried, unspoken, for many years in the minds of American women. It was a strange stirring, a sense of dissatisfaction, a yearning that women suffered in the middle of the 20th century in the United States. Each suburban wife struggled with it alone. As she made the beds, shopped for groceries... she was afraid to ask even of herself the silent question — 'Is this all?'

BETTY FRIEDAN, *THE FEMININE MYSTIQUE*, 1963.

The American middle-class domestic dream, so pervasive in the 1950s, was blown apart by journalist Betty Friedan's discovery that most of her contemporaries at the elite Smith College in 1942 were leading lives of quiet desperation, with few of them in any kind of paid employment. Her book *The Feminine Mystique*, published on 19 February 1963, considered this 'problem with no name' and exposed the widespread nature of American women's dissatisfaction:

> *For over fifteen years women in America found it harder to talk about the problem than about sex. Even the psychoanalysts had no name for it. When a woman went to a psychiatrist for help, as many women did, she would say, 'I'm so ashamed,' or 'I must be hopelessly neurotic.' 'I don't know what's wrong with women today,' a suburban psychiatrist said uneasily. 'I only know something is wrong because most of my patients happen to be women. And their problem isn't sexual.' Most women with this problem did not go to see a psychoanalyst, however. 'There's nothing wrong really,' they kept telling themselves, 'There isn't any problem.'*

Friedan's book became a prime stimulus for the emerging women's movements of the 1960s, particularly in the United States. In 1966, Friedan founded the National Organization for Women and became its first president, retiring in 1970 before going on to found other organizations. She died in 2006.

ALSO ON THIS DAY

1473 The birth of the astronomer Nikolaus Copernicus.
1878 Thomas Edison patents the phonograph.
1915 WWI: an Anglo-French force attacks Ottoman positions on the Dardanelles.

20 FEBRUARY

THE FUTURIST MANIFESTO, 1909

1. We intend to sing the love of danger, the habit of energy and fearlessness...

9. We will glorify war – the world's only hygiene – militarism, patriotism, the destructive gesture of freedom-bringers, beautiful ideas worth dying for, and scorn for woman.

10. We will destroy the museums, libraries, academies of every kind, will fight moralism, feminism, every opportunistic or utilitarian cowardice.

11. We will sing of great crowds excited by work, by pleasure, and by riot; we will sing of the multicoloured, polyphonic tides of revolution in the modern capitals; we will sing of the vibrant nightly fervour of arsenals and shipyards blazing with violent electric moons; greedy railway stations that devour smoke-plumed serpents; factories hung on clouds by the crooked lines of their smoke; bridges that stride the rivers like giant gymnasts, flashing in the sun with a glitter of knives; adventurous steamers that sniff the horizon; deep-chested locomotives whose wheels paw the tracks like the hooves of enormous steel horses bridled by tubing; and the sleek flight of planes whose propellers chatter in the wind like banners and seem to cheer like an enthusiastic crow.

FILIPPO MARINETTI, *THE FUTURIST MANIFESTO*, 1909.

∽

The manifesto of the Italian avant-garde art movement, one that unrestrainedly celebrated speed, modernity and youth, was published on the front page of the French newspaper *Le Figaro* on 20 February 1909. On publication its provocations aroused controversy, and brought its author Filippo Marinetti (1876–1944) – the Italian poet and playwright – considerable notoriety. After the First World War, Marinetti published a four-volume edition of *Manifesti*, in 1920. He also actively supported the Fascist Party leader Benito Mussolini and tried to persuade him to adopt Futurism as Italy's state ideology of art – a concept that Mussolini, for all his other faults, managed to resist.

ALSO ON THIS DAY

1628 The death of the English composer John Dowland.
1872 The Metropolitan Museum of Art opens in New York City.
1877 Tchaikovsky's ballet *Swan Lake* premieres in Moscow.

21 FEBRUARY

THE COMMUNIST MANIFESTO, 1848

A spectre is haunting Europe – the spectre of communism. All the powers of old Europe have entered into a holy alliance to exorcise this spectre: Pope and Czar, Metternich and Guizot [the leading conservatives of Austria and France], French radicals and German police-spies.

The history of all hitherto existing society is the history of class struggles.

Freeman and slave, patrician and plebeian, lord and serf, guild-master and journeyman, in a word, oppressor and oppressed, stood in constant opposition to one another, carried on an uninterrupted, now hidden, now open fight, a fight that each time ended, either in a revolutionary re-constitution of society at large, or in the common ruin of the contending classes.

...The communists everywhere support every revolutionary movement against the existing social and political order of things.

The communists disdain to conceal their views and aims. They openly declare that their ends can be attained only by the forcible overthrow of all existing social conditions. Let the ruling classes tremble at a communistic revolution. The proletarians have nothing to lose but their chains. They have a world to win.

Workers of the world, unite!

KARL MARX AND FRIEDRICH ENGELS, *THE COMMUNIST MANIFESTO*, 1848.

In 1847 the Manchester-based industrialist Friedrich Engels (1820–95) introduced a group of idealistic German socialists in exile in Britain to the radical journalist Karl Marx (1818–83), who insisted they set up a Communist League and produce a stirring manifesto to rouse the workers to action. A few weeks later the 23-page *Communist Manifesto* was ready. It was the world's first great political manifesto, the blueprint for countless other attempts by intellectuals to change reality through forceful words.

The *Manifesto* was first published in German on 21 February 1848, in a year that, coincidentally, was witnessing a rash of nationalist and republican fervour across Continental Europe. The first English translation, by Helen MacFarlane, appeared in 1850, in which the first line unfortunately read: 'A frightful hobgoblin stalks through Europe.'

ALSO ON THIS DAY

1677 The death of the Dutch philosopher Baruch Spinoza.
1916 WWI: the Battle of Verdun commences on the Western Front.
1972 US President Nixon makes his historic visit to China.

22 FEBRUARY

THE EXECUTION OF SOPHIE SCHOLL, 1943

Such a fine, sunny day, and I have to go, but what does my death matter, if through us thousands of people are awakened and stirred to action?

SOPHIE SCHOLL, QUOTED BY CELL-MATE ELSE GEBEL, 22 FEBRUARY 1943.

∞

On 22 February 1943 Sophie Scholl (aged 21), a biology student in Munich, and her brother Hans (aged 24), studying medicine, were executed by the Gestapo, having been arrested a few days earlier for throwing leaflets from a window. They were guillotined the same day; the rest of their group of anti-Nazi dissidents were rounded up over the succeeding months and also executed.

In 1941 they had formed the White Rose society to encourage passive resistance to the Nazi regime and the Nazi war effort. From 1942 they produced several anonymous leaflets under the title *The White Rose*, which they distributed throughout southern Germany, in one of them arguing:

> *We want to try and show that everyone is in a position to contribute to the overthrow of the system. It can be done only by the co-operation of many convinced, energetic people – people who are agreed as to the means they must use. We have no great number of choices as to the means. The meaning and goal of passive resistance is to topple National Socialism, and in this struggle we must not recoil from our course, any action, whatever its nature. A victory of fascist Germany in this war would have immeasurable, frightful consequences.*

In another leaflet they asserted that 'The name of Germany is dishonoured for all time if German youth does not finally rise, take revenge, smash its tormentors. Students! The German people look to us.' Today, the group is memorialized in Munich and throughout Germany.

ALSO ON THIS DAY

1732 The birth of the future US general and president George Washington.
1987 The death of the American pop artist and socialite Andy Warhol.
1997 Scientists in Scotland announce the cloning of Dolly – a sheep.

23 FEBRUARY

THE PROPHET MUHAMMAD BIDS FAREWELL, 632

O People, lend me an attentive ear, for I know not whether after this year, I shall ever be amongst you again. Therefore listen to what I am saying to you very carefully and take these words to those who could not be present here today.

. O People, just as you regard this month, this day, this city [Mecca] as sacred, so regard the life and property of every Muslim as a sacred trust. Return the goods entrusted to you to their rightful owners. Hurt no one so that no one may hurt you. Remember that you will indeed meet your Lord, and that He will indeed reckon your deeds. God has forbidden you to take usury, therefore all interest obligation shall henceforth be waived. Your capital, however, is yours to keep. You will neither inflict nor suffer any inequity. God has judged that there shall be no interest and that all the interest due to Abbas ibn 'Abd'al Muttalib [Muhammad's uncle] shall henceforth be waived...

Beware of Satan, for the safety of your religion. He has lost all hope that he will ever be able to lead you astray in big things, so beware of following him in small things.

O People, it is true that you have certain rights with regard to your women, but they also have rights over you. Remember that you have taken them as your wives only under God's trust and with His permission. If they abide by your right then to them belongs the right to be fed and clothed in kindness. Do treat your women well and be kind to them for they are your partners and committed helpers. And it is your right that they do not make friends with any one of whom you do not approve, as well as never to be unchaste.

O People, listen to me in earnest, worship God, say your five daily prayers [Salah], fast during the month of Ramadan, and give your wealth in Zakat. Perform Hajj [pilgrimage to Mecca] if you can afford to.

All mankind is from Adam and Eve, an Arab has no superiority over a non-Arab nor a non-Arab has any superiority over an Arab; also a white has no superiority over black nor a black has any superiority over white except by piety and good action. Learn that every Muslim is a brother to every Muslim and that the Muslims constitute one brotherhood. Nothing shall be legitimate to a Muslim which belongs to a fellow Muslim unless it was given freely and willingly. Do not, therefore, do injustice to yourselves.

Remember, one day you will appear before God and answer your deeds. So beware, do not stray from the path of righteousness after I am gone.

O People, no prophet or apostle will come after me and no new faith will be born. Reason well, therefore, O People, and understand words which I convey to you. I leave behind me two things, the Qur'an and my example, the Sunnah, and if you follow these you will never go astray.

All those who listen to me shall pass on my words to others and those to others again; and may the last ones understand my words better than those who listen to me directly. Be my witness, O God, that I have conveyed your message to your people.

THE PROPHET MUHAMMAD, FAREWELL SERMON, AD 632.

The Prophet Muhammad completed his life with a pilgrimage to Mecca in 632, which was the tenth year after his migration to Medina (the event known as the *Hijra*) and hence dated 10 AH in the Islamic calendar. He thus initiated the practice of pilgrimage (*hajj*) to Mecca that Muslims, wherever they reside, are supposed to attempt at least once in their lifetimes.

During the pilgrimage, on which he was accompanied by tens of thousands of supporters, he gave his final sermon on 23 February and completed the Islamic holy book of revelations, the Qur'an (Koran). In the account of Shia Islam, Muhammad was also said to have chosen his cousin and son-in-law Ali as his successor – a claim that has divided Shi'ite and Sunni Muslims ever since, with the latter instead following a line of leadership stretching back to Muhammad's close associate and the first caliph, Abu Bakr. The text of the sermon itself is disputed, and several versions exist – the Shia version being twice as long as the Sunni, which is reproduced here in its entirety.

Muhammad died on 8 June 632, in his wife Aisha's house in Medina, aged 63.

24 FEBRUARY

THE GREAT PERSECUTION OF CHRISTIANS, AD 303

This was the nineteenth year of the reign of Emperor Diocletian, when the feast of the Saviour's passion was near at hand, and royal edicts were published everywhere, commanding that the churches should be razed to the ground, the Scriptures destroyed by fire, those who held positions of honour degraded, and the household servants, if they persisted in the Christian profession, be deprived of their liberty.

And such was the first decree against us. But issuing other decrees not long after, the Emperor commanded that all the rulers of the churches in every place should be first put in prison and afterwards compelled by every device to offer sacrifice.

Then as the first decrees were followed by others commanding that those in prison should be set free, if they would sacrifice, but that those who refused should be tormented with countless tortures; who could again at that time count the multitude of martyrs throughout each province, and especially throughout Africa and among the race of the Moors, in Thebais and throughout Egypt, from which having already gone into other cities and, provinces, they became illustrious in their martyrdoms.

EUSEBIUS, *HISTORIA ECCLESIAE*, C. AD 325.

The fourth-century Bishop of Caesarea and 'Father of Church History', Eusebius gave a first-hand account of the 'Great Persecution' of Christians that was begun by the Roman emperor Diocletian on 24 February AD 303, after he had sought advice from the Oracle of Apollo in Delphi. Diocletian abdicated in AD 305, but it has been estimated that some 3,000 people lost their lives as a result of the persecution, while many others were imprisoned over a period of ten years until Emperor Constantine finally introduced religious toleration across the Roman Empire, via the Edict of Milan, in AD 313.

ALSO ON THIS DAY

1500 The birth of the future Habsburg emperor Charles V.
1607 Claudio Monteverdi's *L'Orfeo*, perhaps the first true opera, receives its first performance.
1981 Prince Charles and Lady Diana Spencer announce they are to marry.

25 FEBRUARY

KHRUSHCHEV'S DENUNCIATION OF STALIN, 1956

Stalin originated the concept of the enemy of the people. This term automatically rendered it unnecessary that the ideological errors of a man or men engaged in a controversy be proven; this term made possible the usage of the most cruel repression, violating all norms of revolutionary legality, against anyone who in any way disagreed with Stalin, against those who were only suspected of hostile intent, against those who had bad reputations. This concept, enemy of the people, actually eliminated the possibility of any kind of ideological fight or the making of one's views known on this or that issue, even those of a practical character. In the main, and in actuality, the only proof of guilt used, against all norms of current legal science, was the 'confession' of the accused himself; and, as subsequent probing proved, confessions were acquired through physical pressures against the accused.

This led to the glaring violations of revolutionary legality, and to the fact that many entirely innocent persons, who in the past had defended the Party line, became victims.

NIKITA KHRUSHCHEV, SPEECH, 25 FEBRUARY 1956.

In 1956, three years after Stalin's death, he was still seen as the saviour of the nation; but at the 20th Congress of the Communist Party, the new General Secretary Nikita Khrushchev gave a four-hour-long speech behind closed doors on, denouncing the 'cult of personality' and detailing the abuses of the Stalin era, especially the purges of 1937–8. He ranged over many aspects of Stalin's rise and rule. A large number of specific abuses were laid at the door of Lavrenti Beria, the secret-police chief whom Khrushchev called 'the rabid enemy of our party'. Many of the audience left shocked, having learned for the first time about the comprehensive mendacity underlying the Soviet state and the true fates of former party members; it was said that some delegates had heart attacks and others subsequently killed themselves.

No word was released, officially, of the speech, but it was soon leaked to the West, where it was pored over with fascination. Ushering in the Soviet 'Thaw', the speech is seen as a decisive break from the abuses and megalomania of Stalinism while attempting to reclaim Leninism and the values of the Russian Revolution.

ALSO ON THIS DAY

1723 The death of the English architect Sir Christopher Wren.
1901 J.P. Morgan incorporates the US Steel Corporation.
1964 Cassius Clay defeats Sonny Liston to become the world heavyweight boxing champion.

26 FEBRUARY

THE RAPE OF THE CONGO, 1885

Our only programme, I am anxious to repeat, is the work of moral and material regeneration, and we must do this among a population whose degeneration in its inherited conditions it is difficult to measure. The many horrors and atrocities which disgrace humanity give way little by little before our intervention.

LEOPOLD II, KING OF THE BELGIANS, QUOTED BY ARTHUR CONAN DOYLE, 1909.

∞

The Berlin Conference of European powers, which met in November 1884, agreed the terms for a carve-up of the African continent – the so-called Scramble for Africa – by its conclusion on 26 February 1885. One result was that a vast swathe of Central Africa designated as the 'Congo Free State' (now the Democratic Republic of the Congo) was established as the personal property of Leopold II, King of the Belgians. It was 'Free' in that it was open to international traders, without tariffs, and politically neutral. It proved not to be 'free' for its native inhabitants; Leopold's pledge to them would be shamefully betrayed.

Over the next two decades the Congo's rubber and other raw materials provided a huge source of wealth for Leopold while his regime became a byword for forced labour, mutilations and other atrocities. According to one Belgian soldier, 'They ordered us to cut off the heads of the men and hang them on the village palisades, also their sexual members, and to hang the women and the children on the palisade in the form of a cross.' A Danish missionary, after seeing a native killed, reported the excuses of the soldier involved: 'They kill us if we don't bring the rubber. The Commissioner has promised us if we have plenty of hands he will shorten our service.'

In 1904 the Irish journalist Roger Casement wrote an influential report on the abuses, while American writer Mark Twain described Leopold as 'a greedy, grasping, avaricious, cynical, bloodthirsty old goat'. In 1905 the Belgian Parliament set up its own inquiry, and in 1908 it annexed the state as the Belgian Congo. Leopold was now condemned as a mass murderer responsible for the deaths of up to 10 million people. The British writer Arthur Conan Doyle commented that Leopold 'stands in 1909 with such a cloud of terrible direct personal responsibility resting upon him as no man in modern European history has had to bear'.

ALSO ON THIS DAY

1802 The birth of the French poet and novelist Victor Hugo.
1815 Napoleon escapes from his supposed exile on Elba.
1993 An Islamist bomb attack on New York's World Trade Center kills six.

27 FEBRUARY

THE BURNING OF THE REICHSTAG, 1933

'This is a God-given signal! If this fire, as I believe, turns out to be the handiwork of Communists, then there is nothing that shall stop us now crushing out this murder pest with an iron fist.'

Adolf Hitler, Fascist Chancellor of Germany, made this dramatic declaration in my presence tonight in the hall of the burning Reichstag building.

The fire broke out at 9:45 tonight in the Assembly Hall of the Reichstag.

It had been laid in five different corners and there is no doubt whatever that it was the handiwork of incendiaries.

One of the incendiaries, a man aged thirty, was arrested by the police as he came rushing out of the building, clad only in shoes and trousers, without shirt or coat, despite the icy cold in Berlin tonight...

Never have I seen Hitler with such a grim and determined expression. His eyes, always a little protuberant, were almost bulging out of his head.

Captain Goering, his right-hand man, who is the Prussian Minister of the Interior, and responsible for all police affairs, joined us in the lobby. He had a very flushed and excited face.

'This is undoubtedly the work of Communists, Herr Chancellor,' he said.

D. SEFTON DELMER, *DAILY EXPRESS*, 28 FEBRUARY 1933.

The Reichstag, Berlin's parliament building, suffered a devastating fire on the evening of 27 February 1933, a month after Hitler had been appointed German Chancellor. A Dutch Communist, Marinus van der Lubbe, was convicted of starting it. The event allowed the Nazi regime to pass an emergency decree against the Communist Party. Many Communist parliamentary delegates were arrested, thereby giving the Nazis a majority in the chamber for the first time. The following year all the powers of the Reichstag were transferred to Hitler.

Today it is thought that van der Lubbe did indeed begin the fire, but whether as part of a Communist Party plot is still disputed. What is undeniable is that the destruction of the Reichstag helped pave the way for the consolidation of the Nazi grip on power and the Nazification of all facets of the German state.

ALSO ON THIS DAY

AD 272 The birth of the future Roman emperor Constantine.
1594 Henry IV is crowned king of France.
1844 The Dominican Republic gains independence from Haiti.

28 FEBRUARY

THE COMING OF THE RAILWAY TO AMERICA, 1827

At a meeting in Baltimore, on the twelfth of February last, the report... was presented, embracing the reasonings of various writers on railroads, with some estimates of the cost of extending one from Baltimore to the Ohio, and of the amount of trade which might be presumed to take that course. A charter was afterwards obtained from the states of Maryland and Virginia... for a company called the Baltimore and Ohio Railroad Company, with a capital of three millions, and the power of extending it to five...

Little known as railroads are in America, and their more extended use not yet fully proved in England, the scheme is certainly a bold one, of constructing a road of this sort, not less than two hundred and fifty miles in length, and surmounting an elevation of three thousand feet...

The substitution of railroads for canals, which appears to be generally contemplated in England, is rendered by some circumstances of climate, still more advantageous in this country than in that. Our rigorous winters would obstruct canals with ice, during several weeks, and sometimes months... and our tropical summer presents a serious objection to canals, on the score of health. It may therefore be fortunate that Baltimore has reserved her means for the completion of a mode of conveyance which, besides being better adapted to the country, far excels the other in speed, in economy of construction, and in cheapness of carriage.

PROCEEDINGS OF SUNDRY CITIZENS OF BALTIMORE, CONCERNED FOR THE PURPOSE OF DEVISING THE MOST EFFICIENT MEANS OF IMPROVING INTERCOURSE BETWEEN THAT CITY AND THE WESTERN STATES, 1827.

∞

Thus, in the spirit of assertive western expansion, did the citizens of Baltimore embark on the United States' first 'railroad'. Incorporated on 28 February 1827, and opening in 1830, it was a project of comparable far-sightedness to England's Liverpool and Manchester Railway (*see* 15 September). Charles Carroll, last surviving signatory of the Declaration of Independence, turned the first shovelful of earth, remarking: 'I consider what I have just done to be among the most important acts of my life, second only to my signing the Declaration of Independence, if indeed it be even second to that.'

ALSO ON THIS DAY

1916 The death of the expatriate American novelist Henry James.
1975 Forty-three commuters die in the Moorgate Underground crash, London.
1986 Sweden is shocked by the assassination of its prime minister, Olof Palme.

29 FEBRUARY

THE SALEM WITCH TRIALS, 1692

'Sarah Good, what evil spirit have you familiarity with?'
  'None.'

'Have you made no contract with the Devil?'
  Good answered no.

'Why do you hurt these children?'
  'I do not hurt them; I scorn it.'

'Who do you employ then to do it?'
  'I employ nobody.'

'What creature do you employ then?'
  'No creature but I am falsely accused.'

INTERROGATION OF SARAH GOOD BY MAGISTRATE JOHN HATHORNE,
SALEM, MASSACHUSETTS, 1692.

∞

The Salem witch trials in colonial North America began with the arrest of the pregnant Sarah Good, a twice-married woman impoverished by her first husband's debt. She was known in the Puritan community of Salem, Massachusetts, as a dirty, aggressive woman and a virtual beggar. On 29 February 1692 she and two others were accused of 'afflicting' two children – biting, pinching and harassing them – and others came forward to testify against her, accusing her of consorting with the Devil, flying on broomsticks and other unnatural acts. She in her turn made accusations against another arrested woman, which gave rise to a wider witch-hunt in Salem.

Good was hanged, with four others, in July 1692, shortly after giving birth; her baby died immediately. In all, during the 15 months of the witch-hunt in Salem and surrounding towns, 150 people were accused, 29 convicted of witchcraft and 19 were executed. These events, as imaginatively transformed in Arthur Miller's classic play *The Crucible* (1953), achieved new life as a vehicle for anatomizing the anti-Communist paranoia whipped up during the McCarthyite era (*see* 9 February).

ALSO ON THIS DAY

1792 The birth of the Italian composer Gioachino Rossini.
1960 An earthquake in Morocco kills 3,000 people.
1996 Bosnian War: the siege of Sarajevo is lifted.

MARCH

∞

1 MARCH

THE WORLD'S FIRST NATIONAL PARK, 1872

An Act to set apart a certain tract of land lying near the headwaters of the Yellowstone River as a public park. Be it enacted by the Senate and House of Representatives of the United States of America in Congress assembled, that the tract of land in the Territories of Montana and Wyoming is hereby reserved and withdrawn from settlement, occupancy, or sale under the laws of the United States, and dedicated and set apart as a public park or pleasuring ground for the benefit and enjoyment of the people; and all persons who shall locate, or settle upon, or occupy the same or any part thereof, except as hereinafter provided, shall be considered trespassers and removed there from.

US PRESIDENT ULYSSES S. GRANT, ACT ESTABLISHING YELLOWSTONE NATIONAL PARK, 1872.

∞

The world's first national park, Yellowstone, an area of almost 3,500 square miles now in Wyoming and surrounding states of the northwestern USA, was created in 1872 following a campaign by explorers and geologists to protect and preserve the area's remarkable geothermal features and its unique flora and fauna. Thomas Moran revealed the region's beauty in his watercolours. His diary of his trip there in 1871 also expressed the wonder of the place:

> The route lay through a magnificent forest of pines & firs all growing straight as a ships mast, & growing but a few feet apart, passed over the debris of a great landslide, where the whole face of the mountain had fallen down at some time, laying bare a great cliff some 500 feet high. The view of the lake, as we approached it, was very beautiful. The Mountains surrounding it are about 11,000 feet high & about 3000 ft. above the level of the lake having snow still upon them. After descending to the shore of the lake, some of the party fished in it & caught a few of the finest trout that I have yet seen.

Protection of the area from hunters, poachers and settlers proved difficult until the army arrived in 1886. Native Americans were also removed from the park's borders.

ALSO ON THIS DAY

1867 Nebraska becomes the 37th US state.
1950 The British scientist Klaus Fuchs is jailed for passing nuclear secrets to the USSR.
1981 The imprisoned IRA member Bobby Sands begins a (fatal) hunger strike.

2 MARCH

ETHIOPIAN VENGEANCE AFTER VICTORY, 1896

So ended the day's fight, which was spread over a very large area of country, all favouring the tactics of the defenders of their country and ending so disastrously for Italy... The day after the battle King Menelek [of Ethiopia] could calculate the cost of his victory and what he had gained by it. He had utterly defeated his enemy and taken about 4,000 prisoners, Italian and native in about equal numbers... The whole of the Italian artillery, some 65 cannon, about 11,000 rifles...

The Italian native prisoners, soldiers in the Italian service who had fought against the Abyssinians [Ethiopians], were tried by a council of war consisting of all the chief Abyssinian leaders, and the horrible sentence of mutilation was passed; which Menelek sanctioned, after, it is said, great pressure had been brought to bear upon him, he being greatly against any harsh measures being used. The sentence of mutilation – that is, the cutting off the right hand and left foot – is the customary punishment for the offences of theft, sacrilege and treason... Nearly 800 of them were operated on at the same place... and the severed hands and feet put in a pile. I saw it when I visited Adowa, a rotting heap of ghastly remnants. The joints of wrist and ankle are articulated and the stumps plunged into boiling fat to stop the haemorrhage; the wound then heals over, and afterwards a piece of the stump of the bone that is destroyed by the contact with the boiling fat comes away.

AUGUSTUS WYLDE, *MODERN ABYSSINIA*, 1901.

Italy's belated attempt to enter the 'Scramble for Africa' by invading and annexing Ethiopia (Abyssinia) in 1896 resulted in ignominious defeat at the hands of the Ethiopian emperor Menelek II at Adowa on 1 March 1896. The gruesome aftermath was witnessed by British journalist Augustus Wylde, as the Ethiopian ruler took measures against those inhabitants of his kingdom who had sided with the Italians.

In October 1896 Italy recognized Abyssinian independence. Forty years later, in an atmosphere of resurgent imperial pretensions, Benito Mussolini took national revenge for Adowa when he unleashed tanks, aircraft and poison gas on Abyssinia.

ALSO ON THIS DAY

1797 The Bank of England prints the first £1 note.
1956 Morocco achieves independence from France.
1962 General Ne Win of Burma seizes power in a coup.

3 MARCH

THE EMANCIPATION OF RUSSIA'S SERFS, 1861

The serfs will receive in time the full rights of free rural inhabitants.

Aware of the unavoidable difficulties of this reform, we rely upon the zealous devotion of our nobility for the unselfish support it has given to the realization of our designs. Russia will not forget that the nobility, motivated by its respect for the dignity of man and its Christian love of its neighbour, has voluntarily renounced serfdom, and has laid the foundation of a new economic future for the peasants. We also expect that it will continue to express further concern for the realization of the new arrangement in a spirit of peace and benevolence, and that each nobleman will realize, on his estate, the great civic act of the entire group by organizing the lives of his peasants and his domestics on mutually advantageous terms.

And now we confidently expect that the freed serfs, on the eve of a new future which is opening to them, will appreciate and recognize the considerable sacrifices which the nobility has made on their behalf.

TSAR ALEXANDER II, EMANCIPATION PROCLAMATION, 3 MARCH 1861.

∞

Tsar Alexander II released the 23 million serfs on Russia's private estates – a third of the country's population – in 1861, giving them, among other things, the right to own and run businesses and to marry without consent. But the parcels of land that they received had to be paid for by way of 'redemption' fees. As well as becoming hopelessly indebted, the peasants found that the plots were frequently smaller than those they had previously worked, and they no longer enjoyed traditional rights of grazing or firewood.

Tensions over serfdom had existed for centuries, and by the mid-19th century the antiquated system could not even be justified on the grounds of serving Russia's real economic needs. Alexander saw abolition as a means to bring sweeping reform and was proud of his achievement – ahead of Abraham Lincoln's emancipation proclamations in the United States (see 22 September). But he did not reap the rewards he might have expected, and in 1881 he was assassinated by bombs thrown at his carriage by members of the left-wing People's Will – a group seeking, among other things, revolutionary land reform.

ALSO ON THIS DAY

1792 The death of the Scottish neoclassical architect Robert Adam.
1918 Russia exits the First World War via the Treaty of Brest-Litovsk.
1931 The 'Star-Spangled Banner' becomes the US national anthem.

4 MARCH

BLACK-MAJORITY RULE IN ZIMBABWE, 1980

There can never be any return to the state of armed conflict. Surely this is now time to beat our swords into ploughshares so we can attend to the problems of developing our economy and our society.

My party recognizes the fundamental principle that in constituting a government it is necessary to be guided by the national interest rather than by strictly party considerations. What I envisage is a coalition which, in the interests of reconciliation, can include, by co-option, members of other communities whom the Constitution has denied the right of featuring as our candidates by virtue of their being given parliamentary representation. We should certainly work to achieve a national front.

Whatever government I succeed in creating will certainly adhere to the letter and spirit of our Constitution. I urge you, whether you are black or white, to join me in a new pledge to forget our grim past, forgive others and forget, join hands in a new amity, and together, as Zimbabweans, trample upon racialism, tribalism and regionalism, and work hard to reconstruct and rehabilitate our society.

ZIMBABWEAN PRIME MINISTER ROBERT MUGABE, SPEECH, 4 MARCH 1980.

∞

Speaking in the aftermath of the election victory that made him the first prime minister of the newly independent Zimbabwe (formerly Rhodesia), Robert Mugabe offered peace and reconciliation. The leader of ZANU (Zimbabwe African National Union) had waged a long guerrilla struggle until the illegal white-minority regime of Ian Smith recognized the necessity of reaching a settlement. That was finally realized when the legitimate colonial power, Britain, brokered a deal in December 1979.

Despite the high ideals and constitutionalism of the early years, Mugabe's rule became steadily more partisan and arbitrary. The policy of allowing 'war veterans' to seize white-owned farms, in a belated attempt at land reform, drove hundreds of white Zimbabweans to emigrate, leaving the once agriculturally abundant country dependent on food aid. At the same time, hyper-inflation reached eye-watering levels. Extreme crisis was averted in 2008 by a fragile power-sharing agreement with the main opposition group, the Movement for Democratic Change.

ALSO ON THIS DAY

1152 Frederick I (Barbarossa) becomes king of the Germans.
1789 The American Constitution is enacted at the first Congress in New York.
1817 James Monroe becomes the fifth US president.

5 MARCH

CHURCHILL'S IRON CURTAIN, 1946

I have a strong admiration and regard for the valiant Russian people and for my wartime comrade, Marshal Stalin. There is deep sympathy and goodwill in Britain – and I doubt not here also – toward the peoples of all the Russias and a resolve to persevere through many differences and rebuffs in establishing lasting friendships.

It is my duty, however, to place before you certain facts about the present position in Europe.

From Stettin in the Baltic to Trieste in the Adriatic an iron curtain has descended across the Continent. Behind that line lie all the capitals of the ancient states of Central and Eastern Europe. Warsaw, Berlin, Prague, Vienna, Budapest, Belgrade, Bucharest and Sofia; all these famous cities and the populations around them lie in what I must call the Soviet sphere, and all are subject, in one form or another, not only to Soviet influence but to a very high and in some cases increasing measure of control from Moscow.

WINSTON CHURCHILL, SPEECH AT WESTMINSTER COLLEGE, FULTON, MISSOURI,

5 MARCH 1946.

∞

Winston Churchill, Britain's wartime prime minister but now leader of His Majesty's Loyal Opposition, travelled to Westminster College, Fulton, Missouri in 1946. On 5 March, with US President Harry S Truman in attendance, he was awarded an honorary degree and gave a long speech in reply, surveying the postwar condition of the world, drawing attention not only to the Communist threat but also to the dangers of the 'two marauders, nuclear war and tyranny'. He also addressed the responsibilities of the 'new temple of peace', the United Nations, and asserted the role of the British Empire and Commonwealth in the future preservation of liberty around the world. The speech also drew considerable criticism for its frankness about the Soviet threat, but it was that subject that gave the speech its most memorable phrase, in the enduring metaphor of the Soviet 'iron curtain' falling across Europe.

ALSO ON THIS DAY

1770 British soldiers kill five American colonists – the 'Boston Massacre'.
1933 The Nazi Party wins German federal elections.
1953 The death of the Soviet leader Joseph Stalin.

6 MARCH

THE DIVINELY INSPIRED JOAN OF ARC, 1429

I was at the castle of Chinon [in the Loire] when Joan arrived, and I saw her when she presented herself before the King's Majesty with great lowliness and simplicity; a poor little shepherdess! I heard her say these words: 'Most noble Lord Dauphin, I am come and am sent to you from God to give succour to the kingdom and to you.'

After having seen and heard her, the king put her under the protection of Guillaume Bellier, whose wife was most devout. Then he had her visited by the clergy, by doctors, and by prelates, to know if he could lawfully put faith in her. Her deeds and words were examined during three weeks. The examinations finished, the clergy decided that there was nothing evil in her deeds nor in her words. After numerous interrogations, they ended by asking her what sign she could furnish, that her words might be believed? 'The sign I have to show,' she replied, 'is to raise the siege of Orléans.'

LORD RAOUL DE GAUCOURT, TRIAL EVIDENCE, 1429.

The future Grand Master of France, Lord Raoul de Gaucourt, described how Joan, a teenage peasant girl from Domrémy in eastern France, arrived at the royal court in 1429, inspired to drive the English from France and crown the dauphin at Reims. Having impressed the dauphin at this meeting (he had disguised himself, but she correctly identified him anyway), her claims to be divinely inspired by 'voices' acquired increasing credibility in the eyes of the court and the Church, with the result that she was allowed to take up arms.

Joan was given armour (men's, of course) at Blois, and two months later led a successful assault on the English armies laying siege to Orléans, which she finally relieved on 7 May. By mid-July she had led the French army to Reims, and in the cathedral there Joan saw the dauphin crowned as King Charles VII. It was the high point of her extraordinary story, for her further ambitions to relieve Paris were confounded by her capture and sale to the English. Tried for heresy, she was burned at the stake in 1431. Almost 500 years later, the peasant girl from Domrémy was canonized.

ALSO ON THIS DAY

1475 The birth of the Italian artist and sculptor Michelangelo.
1888 The death of Louisa May Alcott, author of *Little Women*.
1957 Ghana becomes the first British colony in Africa to gain independence.

7 MARCH

THE BIRTH OF BANGLADESH, 1971

Yahya Khan, you are the president of this country. Come to Dhaka, come and see how our poor Bengali people have been mown down by your bullets, how the laps of our mothers and sisters have been robbed and left empty and bereft, how my helpless people have been slaughtered.

As we have given blood, we will give more blood. God-willing, the people of this country will be liberated... Turn every home into a fortress against their onslaught. Use whatever you can put your hands on to confront this enemy. Every last road must be blocked.

The struggle now is a struggle for our emancipation; the struggle now is a struggle for our independence. Joy Bangla! Victory to Bengal!

MUJIBUR RAHMAN, SPEECH, 7 MARCH 1971.

∞

At the Indian subcontinent's Partition in 1947, the new state of Pakistan comprised West Pakistan, the dominant part, and East Pakistan, consisting of much of eastern Bengal. An increasingly tense relationship developed in which the East Pakistanis felt oppressed and marginalized.

Bengali politician Mujibur Rahman's call of 'Victory to Bengal', to a vast crowd in Dhaka on 7 March 1971, was seen as a *de facto* declaration of independence. It followed protests against the domination of West Pakistan and against the overbearing rule of President Yahya Khan in particular. West Pakistan reacted with an attempt to suppress opposition by force, and on 26 March Sheikh Mujib (as he was also known) formally declared independence as Bangladesh ('Free Bengal'):

This may be my last message. From today Bangladesh is independent. I call upon the people of Bangladesh wherever you are and with whatever you have, to resist the occupation army. Our fight will go on till the last soldier of the Pakistan Occupation Army is expelled from the soil of independent Bangladesh. Final victory is ours. Joy Bangla!

A few minutes later he was arrested and imprisoned. Pakistani forces committed widespread atrocities, until intervention by India led to the international recognition of Bangladesh. Mujib became prime minister, then president, of the new republic before being assassinated by army officers in 1975.

ALSO ON THIS DAY

1274 The death of the Italian theologian and priest Thomas Aquinas.
1936 German troops begin the remilitarization of the Rhineland.
1945 WWII: Allied forces finally cross the Rhine at Remagen, to close in on Germany.

8 MARCH

RONALD REAGAN'S 'EVIL EMPIRE', 1983

It was C.S. Lewis who wrote: 'The greatest evil is not done now in those sordid "dens of crime" that Dickens loved to paint. It is not even done in concentration camps and labor camps. In those we see its final result. But it is conceived and ordered (moved, seconded, carried and minuted) in clean, carpeted, warmed, and well-lighted offices, by quiet men with white collars and cut fingernails and smooth-shaven cheeks who do no need to raise their voices.'

Well, because these 'quiet men' do not 'raise their voices', because they sometimes speak in soothing tones of brotherhood and peace, because they're always making 'their final territorial demand', some would have us accept them at their word. But if history teaches anything, it teaches that simple-minded appeasement or wishful thinking about our adversaries is folly. It means the betrayal of our past, the squandering of our freedom.

So, I urge you to speak out against those who would place the United States in a position of military and moral inferiority. In your discussions of the nuclear-freeze proposals, I urge you to beware the temptation of pride – the temptation of blithely declaring yourselves above it all and label both sides equally at fault, to ignore the facts of history and the aggressive impulses of an evil empire, to simply call the arms race a giant misunderstanding and thereby remove yourself from the struggle between right and wrong and good and evil.

US President Ronald Reagan, speech to the
National Association of Evangelicals, 8 March 1983.

∞

With this speech, Ronald Reagan was trying to argue the case for deployment of Pershing II nuclear missiles in Western Europe. But the speech is better remembered for its undiplomatic characterization of the Soviet Union as an 'evil empire'. Reagan's hard-line stance in his first presidential term has been credited with bankrupting the Soviet Union through an unwinnable arms race, and thereby incubating the revolutions of 1989 and the end of the Cold War. But senior Soviet politicians and military men were also genuinely alarmed that the West intended war, and the later Reagan notably softened his rhetoric.

ALSO ON THIS DAY

1702 Queen Anne succeeds to the British throne, its last Stuart monarch.
1817 The New York Stock Exchange is created.
1917 The 'February' Revolution (Old Style calendar) ends tsarist rule in Russia.

9 MARCH

LENIN'S VERDICT ON STALIN, 1923

Stalin is too rude and this defect, although quite tolerable in our midst and in dealing among us communists, becomes intolerable in a secretary-general. That is why I suggest that the comrades think about a way of removing Stalin from that post and appointing another man in his stead who differs from Comrade Stalin in only one respect, namely, that of being more tolerant, more loyal, more polite and more considerate to the comrades, less capricious, etc. This circumstance may appear to be a negligible detail. But I think that from the standpoint of safeguards against a split and from the standpoint of what I wrote above about the relationship between Stalin and Trotsky it is not a detail, but something that can assume decisive importance.

V. I. Lenin, 'Last Testament', 1923.

∞

Vladimir Ilyich Lenin, the Father of the Russian Revolution, dictated his so-called Last Testament to his wife Nadezhda Krupskaya over the winter of 1922–3. At the time his health was in severe decline, following two strokes; by the time of his third stroke, which occurred on 9 March 1923, he could do no more.

In the document he proposed changes to the political structure of the Soviet governing bodies and commented on his possible successor. His intention was that his wishes be read at the Communist Party Congress in April 1923. However, his third stroke left him immobilized and mute and he died the following January. After his death, Krupskaya sent the Testament to the Communist Party Central Committee, which permitted only limited circulation. Stalin remained in his key post of secretary-general, and had consolidated his hold over power before the document was published in English in 1926.

ALSO ON THIS DAY

1661 The death of Cardinal Jules Mazarin, France's powerful chief minister.
1796 Napoleon marries his fragrant mistress, Josephine.
1959 The Barbie doll is launched by the US Mattel company.

10 MARCH

THE WORLD'S FIRST TELEPHONE CALL, 1876

The improved instrument was constructed this morning and tried this evening...
Mr Watson was stationed in one room with the receiving instrument. He pressed
one ear closely against S [the armature] and closed the other ear with his hand.
The transmitting instrument was placed in another room and the doors of both
rooms were closed.

I shouted into M [the mouthpiece] the following words: 'Mr Watson, come here,
I want you.' To my delight he came and declared that he had understood what I
had said. I asked him to repeat the words. We then changed places and listened
at S while Mr Watson read a few passages from a book into the mouthpiece. It
was certainly the case that loud and articulate sounds proceeded from S. Finally
the sentence 'Mr Bell do you understand what I say? MR-BELL-DO-YOU-UNDER-
STAND-WHAT-I-SAY?' came quite clearly and intelligibly. No sound was audible
when the armature S was removed.

ALEXANDER GRAHAM BELL, JOURNAL ENTRY, 10 MARCH 1876.

The world's first telephone call was made on 10 March 1876 by the Scottish-born
Alexander Graham Bell to his assistant, the electrical designer Thomas A. Watson, who
was in the next room of their Boston office. The landmark call was made three days
after Bell had been granted a patent for his invention – and three weeks after he had
applied for it – and the very same day that rival inventor Elisha Gray had filed an
application for a similar device. Bell's first working phone, which he sketched in his
journal alongside a description of the call, used a transmitter that closely resembled
the drawing on Gray's patent application.

Bell, whose mother and other family members suffered profound deafness, had
been long interested in elocution and voice reproduction. Later that summer he
displayed the telephone at the Philadelphia Centennial Exhibition, and set up the Bell
Telephone Company the following year. In 1878, New Haven, Connecticut, acquired
the company's first telephone exchange and issued the first telephone directory – of
just 50 numbers.

ALSO ON THIS DAY

1762 The death under torture of the Huguenot Jean Calas inspires Voltaire
to campaign for religious tolerance.
1864 General Ulysses S. Grant assumes the leadership of Lincoln's Union armies.
1906 In the Courrières mining disaster, France, an explosion kills 1,099 people.

11 MARCH

THE EMERGENCE OF A SOVIET REFORMER, 1985

I am cautiously optimistic. I like Mr Gorbachev. We can do business together. We both believe in our own political systems. He firmly believes in his; I firmly believe in mine. We are never going to change one another. So that is not in doubt, but we have two great interests in common: that we should both do everything we can to see that war never starts again, and therefore we go into the disarmament talks determined to make them succeed. And secondly, I think we both believe that they are the more likely to succeed if we can build up confidence in one another and trust in one another about each other's approach, and therefore, we believe in cooperating on trade matters, on cultural matters, on quite a lot of contacts between politicians from the two sides of the divide.

BRITISH PRIME MINISTER MARGARET THATCHER, BBC INTERVIEW, DECEMBER 1984.

∞

Margaret Thatcher's comments about the up-and-coming Soviet politician Mikhail Gorbachev were made during his visit to Britain in December 1984, when Soviet General Secretary Konstantin Chernenko was terminally ill. Chernenko died on 10 March 1985, and Gorbachev (born 1931) was elected to the post by his fellow Politburo members just three hours later, the youngest-ever general secretary.

A believer in reform, rather than replacement, of the Soviet system, Gorbachev introduced the twin principles of *perestroika* (restructuring) and *glasnost* (openness). But the momentum was unstoppable, and these novelties – combined with an economy in freefall, the pressures of the Cold War arms race, military failure in Afghanistan, and a host of satellite nations that were now burdens rather than assets – led to the collapse and breakup of the Soviet Bloc and the Soviet Union itself within six years. For his pains, Gorbachev was lauded by the West for far-sighted vision, modernity and common sense; while in Russia he was widely vilified for throwing away an empire.

ALSO ON THIS DAY

1941 WWII: the US Lend-Lease Bill supports the British war effort.
1966 France becomes semi-detached from NATO.
2011 An earthquake and tsunami off the coast of Japan kills 15,000.

12 MARCH

THE ANNEXATION OF AUSTRIA, 1938

Last night groups of cheering Nazis tore up the borderline posts along the German and Austrian border to signify that it is now but one nation. Adolf Hitler after a tiring day spent in the Imperial Hotel within a block of the art academy which years ago refused to accept him as a student. Hitler spent last evening in his hotel conferring with Nazi leaders but he was frequently called out onto the balcony of his suite to face the cheering crowd. Several times he attempted to make an announcement but the crowd was so wild he was unable to make himself heard. Meantime former Chancellor Kurt Schuschnigg refused to leave Austria when he was told he was free to go where he liked but that his 11-year-old son Kurt must remain as a hostage as a pledge of his father's discretion. Schuschnigg said that his conscience is clear and that in any case he would not abandon his little boy but would remain and face whatever might be his fate. Meanwhile it is announced that Chancellor Hitler will leave Vienna for Berlin either tonight or Wednesday morning.

Hitler arose this morning at 2.30 am Eastern Time. His breakfast consisted of two glasses of milk, a cup of chocolate and two prunes and a roll. Far into the night Hitler had talked with Foreign Secretary von Ribbentrop and other high German officials. As he was talking with them, an unidentified man fired on Nazi Stormtroopers from a window and then shot himself dead. Later at a downtown café a man got up on a table, shouted Heil Hitler and then stabbed himself.

A hysterical roar of cheers greeted Chancellor Hitler today as he drove slowly across Hero Square in Vienna. The crowd was described as one of the greatest gatherings ever assembled in the Austrian capital. Hitler reviewed 20,000 Austro-German and Nazi troops today in Vienna's most famous street, the Ringstrasse. The review started after memorial services were held for the Austrian war dead in the Imperial Palace. The spectacle of the marching troops was the most impressive seen in Austria since the [First] World War. Dr Arthur Seyss-Inquart, the former Austrian chancellor, preceded Chancellor Hitler to the microphone in the Ringstrasse mass meeting in greeting to Hitler. Chancellor Hitler began addressing more than a million Austro-Germans today shortly after five o'clock Eastern Standard Time after Chancellor Seyss-Inquart concluded a brief address of introduction. Seyss-Inquart confined his remarks to thanks to Hitler for sending troops to Austria and reuniting Austria with Germany. Hitler's appearance before the microphone was the signal for a roar of 'Heils'. Chancellor Hitler termed Austria the latest and greatest addition to the German Reich. He said that he wanted to assure the other 80 million Germans in the world that Austria's allegiance to the Reich is second to none. He ended his brief address with the cry 'Germany! New Germany! Nazi Germany! Our army! Hail victory!'

US Mutual Broadcasting System, 13 March 1938.

The unidentified US reporter in Vienna caught the extraordinary drama of the *Anschluss*, the Nazi invasion and incorporation of Austria into Germany, the first major step in Hitler's expansion in Central and Eastern Europe. Hitler had given the Austrian chancellor, Kurt Schuschnigg (1897–1977), a virtual ultimatum to hand power to the Austrian Nazis in February 1938, but Schuschnigg attempted to hold a referendum on Austrian independence. Then, knowing that Hitler's troops were mobilizing to march across the border, he resigned on 11 March. He was replaced by the Nazi-supporting Arthur Seyss-Inquart (1892–1946), who immediately invited in the German troops. Hitler, moved by the enthusiastic reception he received in Vienna, decided to unite Austria with the German Reich.

Schuschnigg was arrested and held until 1945, and after the war he took up an academic post in the United States; Seyss-Inquart governed Nazi-occupied Poland and the Netherlands, and in recompense was sentenced to death at the Nuremberg trials and hanged in 1946.

ALSO ON THIS DAY

1925 The death of Sun Yat-sen, Chinese revolutionary.
1940 Finland finally submits in its Winter War with the Soviet Union.
1999 The Czech Republic, Hungary and Poland are admitted to NATO.

13 MARCH

THE INIQUITIES OF THE CORN LAWS, 1845

The cry of protection carried the counties at the last election, and politicians gained honours, emoluments, and place by it. But is that old tattered flag of protection, tarnished and torn as it is already, to be kept hoisted still in the counties for the benefit of politicians? I can not believe that the gentry of England will be made mere drumheads to be sounded upon by a prime minister to give forth unmeaning and empty sounds, and to have no articulate voice of their own. No! ...You are the aristocracy of England. Your fathers led our fathers; you may lead us if you will go the right way...

This is a new era. It is the age of improvement; it is the age of social advancement, not the age for war or for feudal sports. You live in a mercantile age, when the whole wealth of the world is poured into your lap... I, who am not one of you, have no hesitation in telling you that there is a deep-rooted, an hereditary prejudice, if I may so call it, in your favour in this country. But you never got it, and you will not keep it, by obstructing the spirit of the age. If you are indifferent to enlightened means of finding employment to your own peasantry; if you are found obstructing that advance which is calculated to knit nations more together in the bonds of peace by means of commercial intercourse; if you are found fighting against the discoveries which have almost given breath and life to material nature, and setting up yourselves as obstructives of that which destiny has decreed shall go on, – why, then, you will be the gentry of England no longer, and others will be found to take your place.

RICHARD COBDEN, HANSARD, 13 MARCH 1845.

Britain's advocate of Free Trade, Richard Cobden (1804–65), decisively won the argument against the Corn Laws in the House of Commons in March 1845. The existing rules – notably legislation passed in 1815 – imposed high tariffs on imported corn, keeping prices artificially high in the interests of the aristocratic landlords, impoverishing both the rural labourers and the urban working classes. Prime Minister Robert Peel refused to answer his Radical critic, saying: 'Those may answer him who can.' The following year Peel repealed the Corn Laws, splitting his Tory Party in the process.

ALSO ON THIS DAY

1781 Uranus is discovered by the English astronomer Sir William Herschel.
1881 Tsar Alexander II is assassinated by the revolutionary 'People's Will' group.
1933 Joseph Goebbels becomes the Nazi propaganda minister.

14 MARCH

THE EXECUTION OF ADMIRAL BYNG, 1757

The shore on each side of the harbour was lined with a multitude of people, whose eyes were steadfastly fixed on a lusty man who was kneeling down on the deck of one of the men-of-war, with something tied before his eyes. Opposite to this personage stood four soldiers, each of whom shot three bullets into his skull, with all the composure imaginable; and when it was done, the whole company went away perfectly well satisfied. 'What the devil is all this for?' said Candide, 'and what demon, or foe of mankind, lords it thus tyrannically over the world?' He then asked who was that lusty man who had been sent out of the world with so much ceremony. When he received for answer, that it was an admiral. 'And pray why do you put your admiral to death?' 'Because he did not put a sufficient number of his fellow-creatures to death. You must know, he had an engagement with a French admiral, and it has been proved against him that he was not near enough to his antagonist.' 'But,' replied Candide, 'the French admiral must have been as far from him.' 'There is no doubt of that; but in this country it is found requisite, now and then, to put an admiral to death, in order to encourage the others to fight.'

VOLTAIRE, *CANDIDE*, 1759.

∞

Admiral John Byng (1704–57) followed in the seafaring footsteps of his father by joining the Royal Navy at the age of 14. But in the year of his promotion to admiral he met his downfall. Britain and France were locked in the Seven Years' War, and in 1756 Byng was ordered to relieve the British base at Minorca, in the Balearics, from a French blockade. In choosing not to pursue the larger French fleet but to protect his own, the base was lost and Byng found himself charged with cowardice. He was found guilty on a lesser charge of neglect of duty, but the verdict remained the death penalty; the prime minister suggested that King George II should show mercy, but to no avail. Thus, on 14 March 1757, a firing squad dispatched Admiral Byng on board the *Monarque*, at Portsmouth.

The extreme penalty paid by this solid and courageous British sailor proved irresistible to the satirical instincts of the French writer Voltaire, who portrayed it in *Candide* as a peculiarly English method *pour encourager les autres*.

ALSO ON THIS DAY

1879 The birth of the German physicist Albert Einstein.
1883 The death of the German political philosopher Karl Marx.
1900 The United States joins the Gold Standard.

15 MARCH

THE ASSASSINATION OF JULIUS CAESAR, 44 BC

Caesar's approaching murder was foretold by unmistakable signs. When the settlers assigned to the colony at Capua were demolishing some tombs of great antiquity to build country houses, there was discovered in a tomb, which was said to be that of Capys, the founder of Capua, a bronze tablet, inscribed: 'Whenever the bones of Capys shall be moved, it will come to pass that a son of Ilium shall be slain at the hands of his kindred, and presently avenged at heavy cost to Italy.' Shortly before his death, as he was told, the herds of horses which he had dedicated to the river Rubicon when he crossed it, and had let loose without a keeper, stubbornly refused to graze and wept copiously. Again, when he was offering sacrifice, the soothsayer Spurinna warned him to beware of danger, which would come not later than the Ides of March; and on the day before the Ides of that month a little bird called the king-bird flew into the Hall of Pompey with a sprig of laurel, pursued by others of various kinds from the grove hard by, which tore it to pieces in the hall. The night before his murder he dreamt that he was flying above the clouds, and that he was clasping the hand of Jupiter; and his wife Calpurnia thought that the pediment of their house fell, and that her husband was stabbed in her arms; and on a sudden the door of the room flew open of its own accord.

Both for these reasons and because of poor health he hesitated whether to stay at home; but, urged by Decimus Brutus not to disappoint the meeting which had been waiting for him, he went forth; and when a note revealing the plot was handed him by someone on the way, he put it with others which he held in his left hand, intending to read them presently. Then, after several victims had been slain, and he could not get favourable omens, he entered the House in defiance of portents, laughing at Spurinna and calling him a false prophet, because the Ides of March were come without bringing him harm; though Spurinna replied that they had of a truth come, but they had not gone.

As he took his seat, the conspirators gathered about him as if to pay their respects, and straightway Tillius Cimber, who had assumed the lead, came nearer as though to ask something; and when Caesar with a gesture put him off to another time, Cimber caught his toga by both shoulders; then as Caesar cried, 'Why, this is violence!', one of the Cascas stabbed him from one side just below the throat. Caesar caught Casca's arm and ran it through with his stylus, but as he tried to leap to his feet, he was stopped by another wound. When he saw that he was beset on every side by drawn daggers, he muffled his head in his robe, and at the same time drew down its lap to his feet with his left hand, in order to fall more decently, with the lower part of his body also covered. And in this wise he was stabbed with three and twenty wounds, uttering not a word, but merely a groan at the first stroke, though some have written that when Marcus Brutus rushed at him, he said in Greek, 'You too, my child?' All the conspirators made off, and he lay there lifeless for some time, and finally three common slaves put him on a litter and carried him home, with one arm hanging down.

SUETONIUS, *THE TWELVE CAESARS*, AD 121.

After five years of struggling for the mastery of Rome with the forces and allies of his rival Pompey, by 44 BC Julius Caesar had established an astonishing pre-eminence as 'dictator for life', whose image was everywhere, from statues to coins. If that were not enough, he was declared to be sacred. In his case godhead did not, however, bring with it immortality, as the events foretold (according to Suetonius) for the 'Ides' (15th) of March came to pass. On that day a group of former friends led by Brutus and Cassius, who feared Caesar's dominance and the threat to aristocratic and republican traditions, assassinated him. The result was not, though, restoration of republican ideals but civil war, which only ended with the creation of the Roman Empire by Caesar's nephew Octavius in his new persona as Augustus (*see* 16 January).

The events of 15 March, as described by Suetonius (AD 69/75–after AD 130), formed the basis of Shakespeare's play *Julius Caesar*, which portrays the conspiracy against Caesar, his assassination and its aftermath, and which popularized the injunction to 'beware the Ides of March'.

ALSO ON THIS DAY

1493 Christopher Columbus arrives back in Spain after his first voyage to the Americas.
1917 The last Russian tsar, Nicholas II, abdicates.
1956 The musical *My Fair Lady* has its Broadway premiere.

93

16 MARCH

THE LAST WALK OF AN ENGLISH GENTLEMAN, 1912

He has borne intense suffering for weeks without complaint and to the very last was able and willing to discuss outside subjects. He did not – would not – give up hope till the very end. He was a brave soul. This was the end: he slept through the night before last hoping not to wake – but he woke in the morning – yesterday it was blowing a blizzard; he said I am just going outside and may be some time. He went out into the blizzard and we have not seen him since. I take this opportunity of saying that we have stuck to our sick companions to the last.

We knew that poor Oates was walking to his death but though we tried to dissuade him we knew it was the act of a brave man and an English gentleman. We all hope to meet the end with a similar spirit and assuredly the end is not far.

CAPTAIN ROBERT FALCON SCOTT, 16–17 MARCH 1912.

∞

After months of hardship and exceptionally low temperatures, the British 'Terra Nova' expedition to the South Pole, led by Robert Falcon Scott, eventually ended with the deaths of all members in March 1912. They had reached the Pole only to discover that the Norwegian Roald Amundsen's expedition had beaten them to it, and were attempting to make their way back in the face of an appalling deterioration in the weather. The last men alive were just over ten miles from one of their route's foodstores, which might have saved them.

In his diary Scott recorded the demise of his colleague, the 32-year-old Captain Lawrence Oates, who had been chosen as an expert pony-handler but who had suffered frostbite for several weeks. The contents of the diary transformed the expedition's failure into a triumph of British heroism and pluck, and Oates's selfless action as the ultimate in understated self-sacrifice. His body was never found, but in November 1912 a search party erected a memorial inscribed: 'Hereabouts died a very gallant gentleman, Captain L.E.G. Oates, of the Inniskilling Dragoons. In March 1912, returning from the Pole, he walked willingly to his death in a blizzard, to try and save his comrades, beset by hardships.'

ALSO ON THIS DAY

1660 Britain's Long Parliament is formally dissolved after 20 years.
1872 In the first Football Association Cup Final, Wanderers beat the Royal Engineers.
1968 US troops massacre Vietnamese civilians in the village of My Lai.

17 MARCH

A DREAM OF IRELAND, 1943

The ideal Ireland that we would have, the Ireland that we dreamed of, would be the home of a people who valued material wealth only as a basis for right living, of a people who, satisfied with frugal comfort, devoted their leisure to the things of the spirit – a land whose countryside would be bright with cosy homesteads, whose fields and villages would be joyous with the sounds of industry, with the romping of sturdy children, the contest of athletic youths and the laughter of happy maidens, whose firesides would be forums for the wisdom of serene old age. The home, in short, of a people living the life that God desires that men should live. With the tidings that make such an Ireland possible, St Patrick came to our ancestors fifteen hundred years ago promising happiness here no less than happiness hereafter. It was the pursuit of such an Ireland that later made our country worthy to be called the island of saints and scholars. It was the idea of such an Ireland – happy, vigorous, spiritual – that fired the imagination of our poets; that made successive generations of patriotic men give their lives to win religious and political liberty; and that will urge men in our own and future generations to die, if need be, so that these liberties may be preserved.

IRISH *TAOISEACH* EAMON DE VALERA, SPEECH, 17 MARCH 1943.

The founding father of the Irish Republic, Eamon de Valera (1882–1975), was a veteran of the 1916 Easter Rising against British rule (*see* 24 April). He had spent his entire adult life as a political campaigner, agitator and fundraiser, and although he opposed the partition of Ireland between north and south, he eventually compromised and in 1932 became head of the government of the Irish Free State as leader of his Fianna Fáil Party. He served as Ireland's prime minister for a total of 21 years, 1932–48 (*taoiseach* from 1937), 1951–4 and 1957–9.

Defining himself and his vision of a self-sufficient Ireland in opposition to Britain, he maintained Ireland's neutrality in the Second World War. Campaigning in 1943 he used the opportunity of a radio broadcast on the saint's day of Patrick, Ireland's national saint, to reassert the values of the traditionalist, Catholic and patriotic society that he hoped to build.

ALSO ON THIS DAY

AD 180 The death of the Roman emperor and author of *Meditations* Marcus Aurelius.
1938 The birth of the Russian ballet *premier danseur* Rudolf Nureyev.
1968 A major anti-Vietnam War demonstration takes place in London.

18 MARCH

THE PUNISHMENT OF
THE TOLPUDDLE MARTYRS, 1834

He [the judge, Baron Williams] told the jury that if such Societies were allowed to exist, it would ruin masters, cause a stagnation in trade, destroy property, – and if they should not find us guilty, he was certain they would forfeit the opinion of the Grand Jury. I thought to myself, there is no danger but we shall be found guilty, as we have a special jury for the purpose, selected from among those who are most unfriendly towards us – the Grand Jury, landowners, the Petty Jury, land-renters. Under such a charge, from such a quarter, self-interest alone would induce them to say, 'Guilty.'

GEORGE LOVELESS, *VICTIMS OF WHIGGERY*, 1837.

George Loveless, a Methodist lay preacher, and five agricultural workers from Tolpuddle, Dorset, were tried in March 1834 for secretly swearing an oath to the Friendly Society of Agricultural Labourers. This embryonic form of trade union was fighting the reduction of agricultural wages at a time of economic depression and rural discontent. The case was brought by landowner James Frampton on the recommendation of the home secretary Lord Melbourne, whose brother-in-law – one William Ponsonby, MP – served as foreman of the Grand Jury. The verdict was a foregone conclusion, certainly in the eyes of George Loveless.

The punishment meted out – transportation to Australia for seven years – was widely seen as oppressively harsh and, following widespread protest that included a petition signed by 200,000 people, the men were allowed to return to England in 1836. Loveless recorded the events – a landmark in 19th-century trade unionism – in his pamphlet *Victims of Whiggery*, which he sold to raise funds to support the families of the men. He and several of the other 'Tolpuddle Martyrs' eventually emigrated to Canada.

ALSO ON THIS DAY

1766 Britain repeals the Stamp Act, unpopular in the American colonies.
1871 Radicals of the Paris Commune exert control in the city.
1925 The most destructive US tornado ever recorded kills nearly 700.

19 MARCH

THE CONDEMNATION OF THE CATHARS, 1179

Canon 27: St Leo says, though the discipline of the church should be satisfied with the judgment of the priest and should not cause the shedding of blood, yet it is helped by the laws of catholic princes so that people often seek a salutary remedy when they fear that a corporal punishment will overtake them. For this reason, since in Gascony and the regions of Albi and Toulouse and in other places the loathsome heresy of those whom some call the Cathars... has grown so strong that they no longer practise their wickedness in secret, as others do, but proclaim their error publicly and draw the simple and weak to join them, we declare that they and their defenders and those who receive them are under anathema, and we forbid under pain of anathema that anyone should keep or support them in their houses or lands or should trade with them. If anyone dies in this sin, then neither... is mass to be offered for them nor are they to receive burial among Christians... On all the faithful we enjoin, for the remission of sins, that they oppose this scourge with all their might and by arms protect the Christian people against them. Their goods are to be confiscated and princes free to subject them to slavery.

CANONS OF THE THIRD LATERAN COUNCIL, FINAL SESSION, 19 MARCH 1179.

∞

The 11th ecumenical Council of the Church (or Third Lateran Council, so called because these councils met at Rome's Lateran Palace) was called by Pope Alexander III in 1179. In three sessions it dealt with various matters of Church discipline; it also tackled heresy, including Catharism, which was popular in southwest France and the Pyrenees (where it was sometimes known as Albigensianism after the town of Albi).

Inspired by the third-century Persian teacher Mani, Cathars saw the world in stark Manichean terms of spiritual good battling material evil. This led to an austere anti-worldly stance and fundamental disagreements with Christian belief and Church teaching. The Church's consequent injunction to the faithful to root out Catharism led to an increasingly vigorous campaign, which became a full-scale and violent crusade in 1209.

ALSO ON THIS DAY

1859 Gounod's opera *Faust* premieres in Paris.
1918 The United States establishes time zones across the country.
1982 Argentina's seizure of the island of South Georgia begins the Falklands War with Britain.

20 MARCH

A PROMISE TO THE PHILIPPINES, 1942

The President of the United States ordered me to break through the Japanese lines and proceed from Corregidor to Australia for the purpose, as I understand it, of organizing the American offensive against Japan, a primary object of which is the relief of the Philippines. I came through and I shall return.

US General Douglas MacArthur, press conference, 20 March 1942.

∞

In 1942 the US general Douglas MacArthur had come out of retirement to defend the Philippines against an overwhelming Japanese advance following the attack on Pearl Harbor (7 December 1941). He was ordered to retreat to Australia by President Roosevelt, and he did so on 11 March 1942 but only reluctantly. He had been given a new appointment, as commander of the Allied forces in the Southwest Pacific, but he was also misled into believing that substantial reinforcements would be waiting for him, which would permit an immediate return to the Philippines. On arrival in Australia he discovered this was not the case, but the phrase he used on 20 March 1942 to assert his intentions – 'I shall return' – became the motto of Filipino resistance to the Japanese invaders.

On 20 October 1944 MacArthur was finally able to make good his word. Leading the US invading force at Leyte Gulf, he announced: 'People of the Philippines, I have returned. By the grace of Almighty God, our forces stand again on Philippine soil, soil consecrated in the blood of our two peoples. We have come dedicated and committed to the task of destroying every vestige of enemy control over your daily lives, and of restoring upon a foundation of indestructible strength, the liberties of your people.' By December, his hold on Leyte Island was complete and the 'return' could begin in earnest.

In September 1945 MacArthur witnessed Japan's formal and unconditional surrender.

ALSO ON THIS DAY

1727 The death of the English mathematician and natural philosopher Isaac Newton.
1852 Harriet Beecher Stowe's anti-slavery novel *Uncle Tom's Cabin* is published.
2003 US, British and other forces begin their invasion of Iraq.

21 MARCH

THE MARTYRDOM OF THOMAS CRANMER, 1556

'And now I come to the great thing that troubleth my conscience more than any other thing that ever I said or did in my life: and that is, the setting abroad of writings contrary to the truth. Which here now I renounce and refuse, as things written with my hand, contrary to the truth which I thought in my heart, and written for fear of death, and to save my life, if it might be: and that is, all such bills, which I have written or signed with mine own hand since my degradation: wherein I have written many things untrue. And forasmuch as my hand offended in writing contrary to my heart, therefore my hand shall first be punished: for if I may come to the fire, it shall be first burned. And as for the pope, I refuse him, as Christ's enemy and antichrist, with all his false doctrine.'

Fire being now put to him, he stretched out his right hand, and thrust it into the flame, and held it there a good space, before the fire came to any other part of his body; where his hand was seen of every man sensibly burning, crying with a loud voice, 'This hand hath offended.' As soon as the fire got up, he was very soon dead, never stirring or crying all the while.

JOHN FOXE, *BOOK OF MARTYRS*, 1563.

∞

Thomas Cranmer (1489–1556), Archbishop of Canterbury to Henry VIII and Edward VI, was convicted of heresy during the Catholic restoration pursued by Mary I. Though condemned to death, he recanted and repudiated his Protestant beliefs. When he was forced to make a second recantation on 21 March 1556, this time in public in the University Church in Oxford, this further humiliation pushed him too far: as he spoke, he departed from his text and renounced the recantation itself. He was pulled from the pulpit and taken to Broad Street, where the pyre awaited him. His final act, to thrust the hand that had signed his recantation into the flames, became a key part of the Protestant mythology of resistance to Marian persecution.

The graphic account of Cranmer's and other martyrdoms was collected by John Foxe and published as *Actes and Monuments of These Latter and Perilous Days*. Massively popular, Foxe's *Book of Martyrs*, as it was better known, powerfully sustained anti-Catholic feeling in England.

ALSO ON THIS DAY

1413 The Plantagenet King Henry V accedes to the English throne.
1960 In the Sharpeville Massacre, 69 black South Africans are killed by police.
1963 The island prison of Alcatraz in San Francisco Bay closes.

22 MARCH

THE DEATH OF GOETHE, 1832

The morning after Goethe's death, a deep desire seized me to look once again upon his earthly garment. His faithful servant, Frederick, opened for me the chamber in which he was laid out. Stretched upon his back, he reposed as if asleep; profound peace and security reigned in the features of his sublimely noble countenance. The mighty brow seemed yet to harbour thoughts. I wished for a lock of his hair; but reverence prevented me from cutting it off. The body lay naked, only wrapped in a white sheet; large pieces of ice had been placed near it, to keep it fresh as long as possible. Frederick drew aside the sheet, and I was astonished at the divine magnificence of the limbs. The breast was powerful, broad, and arched; the arms and thighs were elegant, and of the most perfect shape; nowhere, on the whole body, was there a trace of either fat or of leanness and decay. A perfect man lay in great beauty before me; and the rapture the sight caused me made me forget for a moment that the immortal spirit had left such an abode. I laid my hand on his heart – there was a deep silence – and I turned away to give free vent to my suppressed tears.

JOHANN PETER ECKERMANN, *CONVERSATIONS WITH GOETHE*, 1832.

Peter Eckermann played a similar role in the life and memory of the great German literary polymath Goethe (1749–1832) as James Boswell had done for Samuel Johnson, and his awestruck, faintly erotic, description of the poet's fine bodily form evince a deep reverence for the man. He published his recollections in *Conversations with Goethe* in 1836, four years after the death of the writer on 22 March 1832, in Weimar.

Not that Goethe needed posthumous reclamation. By the end of his life, having published over 90 books – poetry, plays (including his dramatic masterpiece *Faust*, 1808, 1832), novels, children's stories, philosophical and scientific works – as well as many of his letters, he was an international celebrity. In the German theatre, via the lessons of Shakespeare, he liberated drama from neoclassical strictures. And in his epistolary best-seller *The Sorrows of Young Werther* (1774), he unleashed on the world a version of the Romantic persona in the novella's eponymous hero: a sensitive, unrequited and ultimately suicidal lover.

ALSO ON THIS DAY

1622 Several hundred of the Jamestown colonists are killed by Native Americans.
1888 The Football League is founded in England.
1963 British war secretary John Profumo lies to Parliament about links with Christine Keeler.

23 MARCH

A CALL TO AMERICAN ARMS, 1775

If we wish to be free – if we mean to preserve inviolate those inestimable privileges for which we have been so long contending – if we mean not basely to abandon the noble struggle in which we have been so long engaged, and which we have pledged ourselves never to abandon until the glorious object of our contest shall be obtained – we must fight! I repeat it, sir, we must fight! An appeal to arms and to the God of hosts is all that is left us!

It is in vain, sir, to extenuate the matter. Gentlemen may cry 'Peace, Peace' – but there is no peace. The war is actually begun! The next gale that sweeps from the north will bring to our ears the clash of resounding arms! Our brethren are already in the field! Why stand we here idle? What is it that gentlemen wish? What would they have? Is life so dear, or peace so sweet, as to be purchased at the price of chains and slavery? Forbid it, Almighty God! I know not what course others may take; but as for me, give me liberty or give me death!

PATRICK HENRY, SPEECH, RICHMOND, VIRGINIA, 23 MARCH 1775.

Patrick Henry's stirring address to the Virginian House of Burgesses assembled at Richmond in March 1775 was a rallying call to resist the British army, which had been sent to Boston following the Boston Tea Party in 1773 (*see* 16 December) and which led to preparations for war on both sides. Ten years earlier and in similarly uncompromising terms, the lawyer Henry had argued for opposition to the Stamp Act – the tax imposed on the American colonies that had provoked the cry 'No taxation without representation!'. Once again, Henry made a huge impression. Although no transcript was kept, his speech was later reconstructed, and it was recorded that in response the other delegates jumped up shouting: 'To arms! To arms!'

The first hostilities of what became the American Revolution broke out at Lexington, Massachusetts, less than a month later (*see* 19 April).

ALSO ON THIS DAY

1743 Handel's *Messiah* receives its first London performance.
1815 A British corn law limits the import of cheaper foreign corn.
1984 US President Reagan announces the Strategic Defense Initiative – 'Star Wars'.

24 MARCH

A CHANGE OF ROYAL DYNASTIES, 1603

Forasmuch as it has pleased Almighty God to call to his mercy out of this transitory life our sovereign lady the high and mighty prince Elizabeth late Queen of England, France and Ireland, by whose death and dissolution the imperial crown of these realms aforesaid is now absolutely, wholly and solely come to the high and mighty prince James the Sixth King of Scotland, who is lineally and lawfully descended from the body of Margaret, daughter to the high and renowned prince Henry the Seventh King of England, France and Ireland, his great-grandfather, the said Margaret being lawfully begotten of the body of Elizabeth, daughter to King Edward the Fourth, the same Lady Margaret being also the eldest sister of Henry the Eighth, of famous memory King of England as aforesaid.

PROCLAMATION, READ IN WHITEHALL, LONDON, 1603.

∞

The day of 24 March 1603 saw the first peaceful transition in English history from one dynasty to another, with the death of Elizabeth Tudor at the age of 69, and the accession of James VI, Stuart King of Scots, as James I of England. James was the grandson of Elizabeth's aunt Margaret Tudor, who was sister of Henry VIII; he had been on the Scottish throne since infancy, after his mother, Mary, Queen of Scots, had been forced to abdicate for her scandalous affairs.

The childless, unmarried Elizabeth had executed Mary, Queen of Scots, in 1587, for plotting (*see* 8 February). She had also declined to name a successor; but in the years before her death her chief minister Robert Cecil had negotiated in secret with James, and on her death he read out the proclamation of his rule at Whitehall. Copies were immediately circulated around the country, and James – standing by – was invited to London from Edinburgh. The union of the crowns of Scotland and England was followed, 104 years later, by a more thoroughgoing union of parliaments at Westminster in 1707.

ALSO ON THIS DAY

809 The death of the cultured fifth Abbasid caliph, Haroun al-Rashid.
1980 El Salvador's outspoken Archbishop Oscar Romero is assassinated.
1989 The *Exxon Valdez* tanker spills oil off Alaska – an environmental disaster.

25 MARCH

THE FIGHT FOR VOTING RIGHTS, 1965

Last Sunday, more than 8,000 of us started on a mighty walk from Selma, Alabama. We have walked through desolate valleys and across the trying hills. We have walked on meandering highways and rested our bodies on rocky byways. Some of our faces are burned from the outpourings of the sweltering sun. Some have literally slept in the mud. We have been drenched by the rains. Our bodies are tired and our feet are somewhat sore.

I know you are asking today, 'How long will it take?' Somebody's asking, 'How long will prejudice blind the visions of men, darken their understanding, and drive bright-eyed wisdom from her sacred throne?' Somebody's asking, 'When will wounded justice, lying prostrate on the streets of Selma and Birmingham and communities all over the South, be lifted from this dust of shame to reign supreme among the children of men?' Somebody's asking, 'When will the radiant star of hope be plunged against the nocturnal bosom of this lonely night, plucked from weary souls with chains of fear and the manacles of death? How long will justice be crucified, and truth bear it?' I come to say to you this afternoon, however difficult the moment, however frustrating the hour, it will not be long, because 'truth crushed to earth will rise again'. How long? Not long, because 'no lie can live forever'. How long? Not long, because 'you shall reap what you sow'. How long? Not long, because the arc of the moral universe is long, but it bends toward justice.

MARTIN LUTHER KING, JR, SPEECH AT MONTGOMERY, ALABAMA, 25 MARCH 1965.

∞

Martin Luther King, Jr's speech to civil rights protesters on 25 March 1965 was heard by thousands who had marched from Selma, Alabama, to the state capital, Montgomery, demanding that African-Americans be permitted to exercise their lawful right to vote. Protests had been attempted for three weeks, but had encountered obstruction from the Alabama authorities; the first march, on 7 March, saw marchers attacked by state police with billy clubs and tear gas. A second march, a few days later, was stopped by court order; but a week after that, the right to march was affirmed by a federal judge, and on 21–25 March the protesters were actually able to mount their march. In August 1965, President Lyndon B. Johnson signed into law the Voting Rights Act, to ensure national registration of electors, irrespective of colour.

ALSO ON THIS DAY

AD 421 By tradition, the city of Venice is founded – at noon.
1807 Parliament outlaws the trade in slaves in the British Empire.
1975 King Faisal of Saudi Arabia is assassinated by his nephew.

26 MARCH

PEACE BETWEEN EGYPT AND ISRAEL, 1979

During the past 30 years, Israel and Egypt have waged war. But for the past 16 months, these same two great nations have waged peace. Today we celebrate a victory – not of a bloody military campaign, but of an inspiring peace campaign. Two leaders who will loom large in the history of nations, President Anwar al-Sadat and Prime Minister Menachem Begin, have conducted this campaign with all the courage, tenacity, brilliance, and inspiration of any generals who have ever led men and machines onto the field of battle.

At the end of this campaign, the soil of the two lands is not drenched with young blood. The countrysides of both lands are free from the litter and the carnage of a wasteful war. Mothers in Egypt and Israel are not weeping today for their children fallen in senseless battle. The dedication and determination of these two world statesmen have borne fruit. Peace has come to Israel and to Egypt.

I honour these two leaders and their government officials who have hammered out this peace treaty which we have just signed. But most of all, I honour the people of these two lands whose yearning for peace kept alive the negotiations which today culminate in this glorious event.

...Let us now lay aside war. Let us now reward all the children of Abraham who hunger for a comprehensive peace in the Middle East. Let us now enjoy the adventure of becoming fully human, fully neighbours, even brothers and sisters. We pray God, we pray God together, that these dreams will come true. I believe they will.

US President Jimmy Carter, speech, 26 March 1979.

∞

Today, a new dawn is emerging out of the darkness of the past. Never before had men encountered such a complex dispute, which is highly charged with emotions. Never before did men need that much courage and imagination to confront a single challenge. Never before had any cause generated that much interest in all four corners of the globe.

...Let there be no more wars or bloodshed between Arabs and Israelis – let there be no more wars or bloodshed between Arabs and Israelis. Let there be no more suffering or denial of rights. Let there be no more despair or loss of faith. Let no mother lament the loss of her child. Let no young man waste his life on a conflict from which no one benefits. Let us work together until the day comes when they beat their swords into ploughshares and their spears into pruning hooks. And God does call to the abode of peace. He does guide whom He pleases to His way.

EGYPTIAN PRESIDENT ANWAR SADAT, RESPONSE, 26 MARCH 1979.

∞

It is the third greatest day in my life. The first was May 14, 1948, when our flag was hoisted. Our independence in our ancestors' land was proclaimed after 1,878 years of dispersion, persecution, humiliation and, ultimately, physical destruction.

The second day was when Jerusalem became one city and our brave, perhaps most hardened soldiers, the parachutists, embraced with tears and kissed the ancient stones of the remnants of the wall destined to protect the chosen place of God's glory. Our hearts wept with them in remembrance.

This is the third day in my life. I have signed a treaty of peace with our great neighbour, with Egypt. The heart is full and overflowing. God gave me the strength to persevere, to survive the horrors of Nazism and of the Stalinist concentration camps, to endure, not to waver in nor flinch from my duty, to accept abuse from foreigners and, what is more painful, from my own people, and even from my close friends.

ISRAELI PRIME MINISTER MENACHEM BEGIN, RESPONSE, 26 MARCH 1979.

∞

Substantive negotiations for an Egyptian–Israeli peace treaty took place at the US presidential retreat of Camp David in September 1978, following the Egyptian president Sadat's gesture of peace in November 1977 – when he flew to Jerusalem and addressed the Israeli Knesset. The negotiations resulted in Sadat and the Israeli prime minister Begin sharing the 1978 Nobel Peace Prize.

The 1979 bilateral agreement allowed for mutual recognition of the two countries and the withdrawal of Israeli forces from the Sinai peninsula, which Israel had occupied since the 1967 Six Day War. It did not solve the question of the Occupied Territories or the Palestinians, and Israel continued to be regarded with hostility in the region; however, there has been no full-scale war between Israel and her Arab neighbours since 1979. For his pains, Sadat was assassinated by discontented military officers during a parade in 1981.

The '1878 years of dispersion' referred to in Begin's speech began with the destruction of the Temple in Jerusalem by troops of the future Roman emperor Titus in AD 70 (*see* 10 August).

ALSO ON THIS DAY

1892 The death of the American poet Walt Whitman.
1971 Bangladesh achieves independence from Pakistan.
1973 Women begin working on the London Stock Exchange for the first time.

27 MARCH

THOREAU OBSERVES THE ARRIVAL OF SPRING, 1859

Of our seven indigenous flowers which begin to bloom in March, four, i.e. the two alders, the aspen, and the hazel, are not generally noticed so early, if at all, and most do not observe the flower of a fifth, the white maple. The first four are yellowish or reddish brown at a little distance, like the banks and sward moistened by the spring rain. The browns are the prevailing shades as yet, as in the withered grass and sedge and the surface of the earth, the withered leaves, and these brown flowers.

I see from a hilltop a few very bright green spots a rod in diameter in the upper part of Farrar's meadow, which the water has left within a day or two. Going there, I find that a very powerful spring is welling up there, which, with water warm from the bowels of the earth, has caused the grass and several weeds, as Cardamine rhomboidea, etc., to grow thus early and luxuriantly, and perhaps it has been helped by the flood standing over it for some days. These are bright liquid green in the midst of brown and withered grass and leaves. Such are the spots where the grass is greenest now.

HENRY DAVID THOREAU, JOURNAL, 27 MARCH 1859.

The American writer and environmentalist Henry David Thoreau (1817–62) explored the joys of a simple lifestyle living close to nature when he spent two years living in a cabin by Walden Pond, outside Concord in Massachusetts, in 1845–7. The journal was published as Walden (1854). He continued to live in the area for the rest of his life, working as a land surveyor, maintaining a nature diary and writing on a wide range of subjects and campaigning for the abolition of slavery. In his essay On Civil Disobedience (1849) – in which he wrote 'That government is best which governs least' – he argued that individuals should not allow government to override their individual conscience. Through this he influenced many later thinkers, including 19th-century anarchists and 20th-century campaigners for civil rights including Mahatma Gandhi and Martin Luther King.

ALSO ON THIS DAY

1306 Robert I, the Bruce, is crowned King of Scots at Scone.
1613 Charles I becomes king of England, Scotland and Ireland.
1989 Soviet parliamentary elections permit non-Communist candidates for the first time.

28 MARCH

BRITAIN JOINS THE CRIMEAN WAR, 1854

It is with deep regret that Her Majesty announces the failure of her anxious and protracted endeavours to preserve for her people and for Europe the blessings of peace.

The unprovoked aggression of the Emperor of Russia against the Sublime Porte [the Ottoman government] has been persisted in with such disregard of consequences, that after the rejection by the Emperor of Russia, of terms which the Emperor of Austria, the Emperor of the French, and the King of Prussia, as well as Her Majesty, considered just and equitable, Her Majesty is compelled to come forward in defence of an ally whose territory is invaded, and whose dignity and independence are assailed.

...The time has now arrived when it is but too obvious that the Emperor of Russia has entered upon a course of policy which, if unchecked, must lead to the destruction of the Ottoman Empire.

In this conjuncture, Her Majesty feels called upon, by regard for an ally, the integrity and independence of whose empire have been recognized as essential to the peace of Europe, by the sympathies of her people with right against wrong, by a desire to avert from her dominions most injurious consequences, and to save Europe from the preponderance of a Power which has violated the faith of treaties, and defies the opinion of the civilized world, to take up arms, in conjunction with the Emperor of the French, for the defence of the sultan.

BRITISH DECLARATION OF WAR ON RUSSIA, LONDON, 28 MARCH 1854.

In October 1853 the sultan of the Ottoman Empire declared war on Russia, following Russian aggression in the Balkans and Black Sea area. The British and French – worried about Russian expansionism and Ottoman inability to resist it – jointly set an ultimatum for withdrawal, which expired in March 1854, resulting in this British declaration of war.

The ensuing Crimean War, fought mainly in that Black Sea peninsula, proved more costly than anticipated, revealing many weaknesses in the preparedness and organization of the British Army. (*See also* 25 October.)

ALSO ON THIS DAY

1881 The death of the Russian composer Modest Mussorgsky.
1939 The fall of Madrid ends the Spanish Civil War, in the Nationalists' favour.
1979 A serious accident befalls the US nuclear plant at Three Mile Island.

29 MARCH

THE PUNISHMENT OF THE ROSENBERG SPIES, 1953

I consider your crime worse than murder... I believe your conduct in putting into the hands of the Russians the A-Bomb years before our best scientists predicted Russia would perfect the bomb has already caused, in my opinion, the Communist aggression in Korea, with the resultant casualties exceeding 50,000 and who knows but that millions more of innocent people may pay the price of your treason. Indeed, by your betrayal you undoubtedly have altered the course of history to the disadvantage of our country. No one can say that we do not live in a constant state of tension. We have evidence of your treachery all around us every day for the civilian defence activities throughout the nation are aimed at preparing us for an atom bomb attack.

US JUDGE IRVING KAUFMAN, SENTENCING THE ROSENBERG SPIES, 29 MARCH 1953.

∞

Julius and Edith Rosenberg, two New York Communists, were convicted in 1953 of passing nuclear secrets to the Soviet Union in 1944 and 1945, thus hastening the Soviet acquisition of the atomic bomb. Ethel's brother David Greenglass, who supplied them with documents from the US secret nuclear research centre at Los Alamos, was given a 15-year jail sentence; but the Rosenbergs were both executed in June 1953.

Many considered their penalty harsh insofar as the information obtained was relatively insignificant and they had not been charged with treason; some claimed that the Rosenbergs were victims of anti-Semitism. Among those to speak out against the sentence were Pope Pius XII, Albert Einstein, Jean-Paul Sartre and Pablo Picasso. But the voices of dissent could make little impact against the clamour that characterized the period of the Korean War and the 'Red Scare' in US political and cultural life (*see also* 9 February).

ALSO ON THIS DAY

1461 In England, Yorkist forces defeat the Lancastrians at the bloody Battle of Towton.
1867 The Dominion of Canada is created from four provinces.
1941 WWII: British and Australian ships emasculate the Italian navy at the Battle of Cape Matapan.

30 MARCH

THE SICILIAN VESPERS, 1282

Sicilians!... to pursue our course, glory and deliverance. Our forces are sufficient to raise the whole country as far as Messina, and Messina must not belong to the foe; we share the same origin, the same language, the same past glory and present shame, the same experience that slavery and misery are the result of division. All Sicily is stained with the blood of the strangers; she is strong in the courage of her sons, in the ruggedness of her mountains, in the protection of the seas which are her bulwarks. Who then shall set foot upon her soil, except to find in it a yawning grave? Christ, who preached liberty to mankind, who inspired you to effect this blessed deliverance, now extends to you his Almighty hand, if you will but act like men in your own defence. Citizens; captains of the people – it is my counsel that messengers be sent to all the other towns, inviting them to unite with us for the maintenance of the commonwealth, that by force of arms, by daring, and by rapidity of action, we should aid the weak, determine the doubtful, and combat the froward. For this purpose, let us divide into three bands, which may simultaneously traverse the whole island; then let a general parliament mature our counsels, unite our views, and regulate the form of government; for I call God to witness, that Palermo aspires not to dominion, but seeks only liberty for all, and for herself the glory of being foremost in peril.

ROGER MASTRANGELO, IN THE CHRONICLE BY SABA MALASPINA, *C.*1285.

∞

With such declarations of defiance – according to the contemporary chronicler Saba Malaspina – the people of late 13th-century Sicily rebelled against the French rule of Charles of Anjou, beginning a wider war for regional control between France and a papal–Aragonese alliance. It commenced on 30 March 1282, with the declaration of 'Death to the French' and an explosion of violence at a riot in Palermo. The timing and location, at evening prayers outside a church, gave the rebellion its name of the 'Sicilian Vespers', and it went on to become a rampage of extermination against thousands of French inhabitants. But true Sicilian liberation had to wait for some 600 years (*see* 26 October).

ALSO ON THIS DAY

1856 The Crimean War ends with the Treaty of Paris.
1867 For just over $7 million, the United States buys Alaska from Russia.
2002 Queen Elizabeth The Queen Mother dies aged 101.

31 MARCH

THE DEATH OF KING HEROD OF JUDAEA, 4 BC

But now Herod's distemper increased. A fire glowed in him, which did not so much appear to the touch, but augmented his pains inwardly, bringing him a vast appetite to eat. His entrails were also ulcerated, especially his colon; a watery liquid collected itself about his feet. His penis putrefied and produced worms; and when he sat upright, he had difficulty in breathing; his breath stank and he had convulsions in all parts of his body. Those pretended to be able to divine the future claimed that God inflicted this punishment on him on account of his great impiety.

When he had no more hope of recovering, he gave every soldier 50 drachmae; and also gave a great deal to their commanders, and to his friends, and moved to Jericho, where he grew so furious that he behaved like a madman. He commanded that all the principal men of the entire Jewish nation be called to him. The king was in a wild rage against them all, the innocent as well as those that had given him grounds; and when they had come, he had them all shut up in the hippodrome, then sent for his sister Salome and spake thus to them: 'I shall soon meet death, a death which a man should welcome and bear cheerfully. But I am troubled: I shall die unlamented, and without the kind of mourning a king should expect.'

So he requested that, as soon as they saw he had died, they should keep his death secret until they had posted soldiers around the hippodrome. Then they should order all those inside to be shot with their darts. This slaughter would be a double cause for rejoicing: first because they would enact the wishes of a dying man, and second because he would have the honour of a memorable mourning at his funeral.

As he was giving these commands, letters came from his ambassadors, who had been sent to Rome to Caesar [the emperor Augustus]. They announced that Acme [a Jewish servant in the household of Livia, Caesar's wife] had been killed by Caesar for his indignation at the part she had played in Antipater's [Herod's son's] wicked practices; but as for Antipater himself, Caesar left it to Herod himself either to banish him, or to take his life, whichever he pleased.

Now Antipater, thinking his father had died, was emboldened to hope he would be immediately released, and would take the kingdom; he asked the gaoler to let him go, and promised him great things. But the gaoler informed the king of his intentions; whereupon Herod – although he was at death's door – beat his head, sent for some of his guards, and commanded them to kill Antipater instantly.

Herod died, five days after having Antipater slain. He had reigned 34 years from the murder of Antigonus [of the Hasmonean dynasty], or 37 since being declared king by the Romans. He showed great barbarity towards all men, and was a slave to his passion; yet he was also favoured by fortune, insofar as he rose from a private man to become a king, and though threatened with a myriad dangers, he got clear of them all, and lived to a very old age.

JOSEPHUS, *THE ANTIQUITIES OF THE JEWS*, BOOK XVII, 1ST CENTURY AD.

Herod 'the Great', king of Judaea and client of the Romans who elected him 'King of the Jews' in 40 BC, was an ambitious and ruthless tyrant responsible for huge building projects around Jerusalem. In the Bible he looms large in the story of the birth of Jesus, perpetrating the 'massacre of the innocents'. In the description of the first-century AD Romano-Jewish historian Josephus, Herod died grotesquely at the end of March in (probably) 4 BC, shortly after ordering the death of his son Antipater, who had been implicated in an earlier plot to kill his father. Herod's kingdom was subsequently divided among his three remaining sons; but in AD 6 a Roman province was established in Judaea, as a sub-province of Syria, and ruled by a prefect.

ALSO ON THIS DAY

1631 The death of the English metaphysical poet John Donne.
1959 The Dalai Lama escapes to India from Chinese-ruled Tibet.
1990 In London, protesters riot against the government's poll tax (community charge).

APRIL

1 APRIL

AN ENGLISH LADY TAKES A TURKISH BATH, 1717

I went to the Bagnio about 10 o'clock. It was already full of women. I was in my travelling habit and certainly appeared very extraordinary to them, yet there was not one of them that showed the least surprise or impertinent curiosity, but received me with all the obliging curiosity possible. I know no European court where the ladies would have behaved in so polite a manner to a stranger.

The first sofas were covered with cushions and rich carpets, on which sat the ladies, and on the second their slaves behind them., but without any distinction of rank by their dress, all of them being in a state of nature, that is, in English, stark naked, without any beauty or defect concealed, yet there was not the least wanton smile or immodest gesture amongst them.

I was at last forced to open my skirt and show them my stays, which satisfied them very well, for I saw they believed I was so locked up in that machine that it was not in my own power to open it, which contrivance they attributed to my husband.

LADY MARY WORTLEY MONTAGU, LETTER, 1717.

Lady Mary Wortley Montagu (1689–1762), *née* Pierrepoint – belle-lettrist, hostess and orientalist – eloped with Edward Wortley Montagu in 1712. Four years later she travelled overland with her husband to the Ottoman Empire's capital in Constantinople (modern Istanbul), where he was to spend two years in an ambassadorial capacity.

En route, the couple were able to acquaint themselves with Islamic and Turkish culture during stays in Belgrade and Sofia, and it was in the latter city that Mary first visited a Turkish bath, on 1 April 1717. Although she stayed little over a year in the Near East, her visit provided rich material for her *Embassy Letters*, which became classics of epistolary travel writing. Her trip also proved important in introducing Turkish practices to the West, in particular inoculation against smallpox.

ALSO ON THIS DAY

1204 The death of Eleanor of Aquitaine, mother of Richard (I) 'the Lionheart'.
1918 The British Royal Air Force comes into being.
1945 WWII: US forces invade the Japanese island of Okinawa.

2 APRIL

ADMIRAL NELSON DISOBEYS ORDERS, 1801

Nelson was at this time... pacing the quarter-deck. A shot through the mainmast knocked the splinters about; and he observed to one of his officers with a smile, 'It is warm work, and this day may be the last to any of us at a moment' – and then stopping short at the gangway, added, with emotion – 'But mark you! I would not be elsewhere for thousands.' About this time the signal-lieutenant called out that number Thirty-Nine the signal for discontinuing the action was thrown out by the Commander-in-Chief. He continued to walk the deck, and appeared to take no notice of it. The signal officer met him at the next turn, and asked if he should repeat it. 'No,' he replied, 'acknowledge it'... He now paced the deck, moving the stump of his lost arm in a manner which always indicated great emotion. 'Do you know,' said he to Mr Ferguson, 'what is shown on board the Commander-in-Chief? Number Thirty-Nine!' Mr Ferguson asked what that meant. 'Why, to leave off action!' Then shrugging up his shoulders, he repeated the words – 'Leave off action? Now, damn me if I do! You know, Foley,' turning to the captain, 'I have only one eye, – I have a right to be blind sometimes': and then putting the glass to his blind eye, in that mood of mind which sports with bitterness, he exclaimed, 'I really do not see the signal!'

ROBERT SOUTHEY, *LIFE OF HORATIO LORD NELSON*, 1813.

∞

At the Battle of Copenhagen on 2 April 1801, a British fleet was attempting to disrupt the Russo-Swedish-Danish 'neutral' alliance, which was effectively bolstering Napoleon by blocking access to the Baltic for British shipping. With the right show of force, it appeared possible to prise Denmark away from the Russian-dominated pact.

Horatio Nelson, second-in-command to Admiral Sir Hyde Parker, famously disobeyed Parker's orders and, within the hour, defeated the Danes. Parker gave Nelson considerable freedom of action, and it was later claimed that he had said, when ordering Nelson to leave off action, 'If he is in a condition to continue the action successfully, he will disregard it [the order]; if he is not, it will be an excuse for his retreat and no blame can be imputed to him.' However, the episode ruined Parker's reputation and a month after the battle he lost his command – to Nelson.

ALSO ON THIS DAY

1792 The US Mint is established by Congress.
1982 Argentine forces invade the Falkland Islands.
2005 The death of the Polish pope John Paul II.

3 APRIL

THE KILLING OF JESSE JAMES, 1882

A great sensation was created this morning by the announcement that Jesse James, the notorious bandit and train-robber, had been shot and killed... In a small shanty in the south-east part of the city, Jesse James had lived with his wife since sometime in November last. Robert and Charles Ford, two of his gang, have made their headquarters at the same house... The three of them have been making preparations for a raiding expedition on which they were to start tonight.

James and the two Fords were in the front room together at 9 o'clock this morning. James took off his belt and laid his pistols on the bed, preparing to wash himself, when Robert Ford sprang up behind him and sent a bullet through his brain. The ball entered the back of his head at the base of the right brain, coming out over the eye. The Ford brothers at once made known what they had done and gave themselves up...

A look at the body... showed that he was a fine-looking man, apparently 40 years old, with broad forehead, and his physiognomy was that of an intelligent as well as a resolute and daring man. The house where James lived has the appearance of an armoury. James was in the habit of wearing two belts with a brace of very fine revolvers and 25 extra cartridges...

New York Times, 4 April 1882.

By 1882, the American outlaw Jesse James had become infamous, leading a gang of bank- and train-robbers (with his brother Frank) in the decade following the American Civil War, during which conflict he had fought as a Confederate guerrilla. A foiled raid on a bank in Northfield, Minnesota, in 1876 depleted his gang, and James returned to St Joseph, in his home state of Missouri. His new colleagues, the Ford brothers, now plotted with the state governor to kill James; after the shooting, they were tried for murder and sentenced to death, only to be immediately pardoned and given part of the proffered reward. James's prolific lawbreaking and ruthlessness continued to fascinate long after his death, inspiring many filmic interpretations.

ALSO ON THIS DAY

1860 The Pony Express makes its first run.
1865 US Civil War: the fall of the Confederate capital of Richmond, Virginia.
1948 US President Truman signs the Marshall Aid Plan.

4 APRIL

HEALING THE WOUNDS OF CIVIL WAR, 1660

If the general distraction and confusion which is spread over the whole kingdom doth not awaken all men to a desire and longing that those wounds which have so many years together been kept bleeding, may be bound up, all we can say will be to no purpose; however, after this long silence, we have thought it our duty to declare how much we desire to contribute thereunto; and that as we can never give over the hope, in good time, to obtain the possession of that right which God and nature hath made our due, so we do make it our daily suit to the Divine Providence, that He will, in compassion to us and our subjects, after so long misery and sufferings, remit and put us into a quiet and peaceable possession of that our right, with as little blood and damage to our people as is possible; nor do we desire more to enjoy what is ours, than that all our subjects may enjoy what by law is theirs...

And to the end that the fear of punishment may not engage any, conscious to themselves of what is past, to a perseverance in guilt for the future, by opposing the quiet and happiness of their country, in the restoration of king, peers and people to their just, ancient and fundamental rights, we do, by these presents, declare, that we do grant a free and general pardon, which we are ready, upon demand, to pass under our Great Seal of England, to all our subjects, of what degree or quality so ever, who, within forty days after the publishing hereof, shall lay hold upon this our grace and favour, and shall, by any public act, declare their doing so, and that they return to the loyalty and obedience of good subjects; excepting only such persons as shall hereafter be excepted by Parliament, those only to be excepted. Let all our subjects, how faulty so ever, rely upon the word of a king, solemnly given by this present declaration, that no crime whatsoever, committed against us or our royal father before the publication of this, shall ever rise in judgment, or be brought in question, against any of them, to the least endamagement of them, either in their lives, liberties or estates or (as far forth as lies in our power) so much as to the prejudice of their reputations, by any reproach or term of distinction from the rest of our best subjects...

And because the passion and uncharitableness of the times have produced several opinions in religion... we do declare a liberty to tender consciences, and that no man shall be disquieted or called in question for differences of opinion in matter of religion, which do not disturb the peace of the kingdom; and that we shall be ready to consent to such an Act of Parliament, as, upon mature deliberation, shall be offered to us, for the full granting of that indulgence.

And because, in the continued distractions of so many years, and so many and great revolutions, many grants and purchases of estates have been made to and by many officers, soldiers and others, who are now possessed of the same, and who may be liable to actions at law upon several titles, we are likewise willing that all such differences, and all things relating to such grants, sales and purchases, shall be determined in Parliament, which can best provide for the just satisfaction of all men who are concerned.

And we do further declare, that we will be ready to consent to any Act or Acts of Parliament to the purposes aforesaid, and for the full satisfaction of all arrears due to the officers and soldiers of the army under the command of General Monck; and that they shall be received into our service upon as good pay and conditions as they now enjoy.

Charles II, Declaration of Breda, 4 April 1660.

In the months before his restoration to the English throne in 1660, Charles II paved the way by reassuring his prospective subjects as to his intentions. In the so-called Declaration of Breda – issued from exile in the Netherlands – he offered a general pardon, to those who would offer him their loyalty, for acts committed during the Civil War and Interregnum; confirmed he would give 'liberty to tender consciences' in religion; he promised that Parliament would decide about titles to estates that had been lost; and he assured the army that it would be paid.

The promise about a general pardon was kept, but the aggressively Anglican religious settlement that emerged proved less generous than that suggested here. Nor were the regicides who had signed the death warrant of Charles I (*see* 30 January) forgiven: several were arrested and executed or imprisoned, while others were driven into exile. Three who had previously died, including Oliver Cromwell, were exhumed and their bodies desecrated.

ALSO ON THIS DAY

1581 The English explorer Francis Drake receives a knighthood.
1721 Robert Walpole becomes the first British prime minister.
1968 Martin Luther King, Jr is assassinated in Memphis, Tennessee.

5 APRIL

'POWER TENDS TO CORRUPT', 1887

If the thing is criminal, if, for instance, it is a licence to commit adultery, the person who authorizes the act shares the guilt of the person who commits it...

I cannot accept your canon that we are to judge pope and king unlike other men, with a favourable presumption that they did no wrong. If there is any presumption it is the other way, against the holders of power, increasing as the power increases. Historic responsibility has to make up for the want of legal responsibility. Power tends to corrupt, and absolute power corrupts absolutely. Great men are almost always bad men, even when they exercise influence and not authority, still more when you superadd the tendency or the certainty of corruption by authority. There is no worse heresy than that the office sanctifies the holder of it.

Here are the greatest names coupled with the greatest crimes; you would spare those criminals, for some mysterious reason. I would hang them higher than Haman, for reasons of quite obvious justice, still more, still higher for the sake of historical science.

Quite frankly, I think there is no greater error. The inflexible integrity of the moral code is, to me, the secret of the authority, the dignity, the utility of History.

LORD ACTON, LETTER TO BISHOP MANDELL CREIGHTON, 5 APRIL 1887.

The aristocratic historian Lord Acton (1834–1902) wrote little but, in this letter, produced one of the most famous aphorisms in, and about, history: 'Power tends to corrupt, and absolute power corrupts absolutely.' He was writing to the Cambridge University professor of ecclesiastical history (and later Anglican Bishop of London) Mandell Creighton, who had recently published his *History of the Papacy*. Acton, a liberal Catholic known for his volumes of essays *A History of Freedom in Antiquity* and *A History of Freedom in Christianity*, criticized Creighton's book for having been too soft on the medieval popes, the Renaissance pope Sixtus IV and the Spanish Inquisition.

The 'Haman' Acton refers to was a Persian noble of the fifth century BC, who instigated a plot to kill the Jews of ancient Persia but was foiled by the Persian king's Jewish wife, Esther, and subsequently hanged.

ALSO ON THIS DAY

1792 The first US presidential veto is exercised by George Washington.
1955 Sir Winston Churchill resigns as British prime minister.
1964 The death of the US general Douglas MacArthur.

6 APRIL

GANDHI COMPLETES THE SALT MARCH, 1930

With this, I am shaking the foundations of the British Empire.

MOHANDAS K. GANDHI, 1930.

In 1930 Mohandas K. Gandhi (1869–1947), or 'Mahatma' as he was fondly known, continued his broad challenge to the British government of India by means of a high-profile campaign against its tax on salt production and sale – a potent symbol of Indians' dispossession from the resources of their land. Seeking a cause that would unite India's Hindus and Muslims, on 12 March he and a few dozen supporters began a long journey by foot from his ashram in Gujarat to the sea. By the time he arrived on the coast at Dandi, after a trip of 240 miles, on 5 April, he had some 60,000 followers. That evening he gave an interview:

> I cannot withhold my compliments from the government for the policy of complete non-interference adopted by them throughout the march. I wish I could believe this non-interference was due to any real change of heart or policy. The only interpretation I can put upon this non-interference is that the British Government, powerful though it is, is sensitive to world opinion which will not tolerate repression of extreme political agitation which civil disobedience undoubtedly is, so long as disobedience remains civil and therefore necessarily non-violent.

Early the next morning he went to the sea, collected a handful of salty mud which he boiled with seawater to make salt, and urged everyone to do the same. Gandhi's arrest came in May, but thousands followed his example and within the month nearly 600,000 people had been arrested, and 60,000 imprisoned, for breaking the salt laws. A boycott of British goods followed, and a peaceful march on the Dharasana Salt Works in Surat led to worldwide publicizing of the cold-blooded assault by soldiers on thousands of peaceful protesters, which injured hundreds and killed at least two.

ALSO ON THIS DAY

1199 The death of the English king Richard I 'the Lionheart'.
1917 The USA declares war on the German Empire.
1971 The death of the Russian composer Igor Stravinsky.

7 APRIL

THE UNVEILING OF THE DOMINO THEORY, 1954

First of all, you have the specific value of a locality in its production of materials that the world needs. Then you have the possibility that many human beings pass under a dictatorship that is inimical to the free world. Finally, you have broader considerations that might follow what you would call the 'falling domino' principle. You have a row of dominoes set up, you knock over the first one, and what will happen to the last one is the certainty that it will go over very quickly. So you could have a beginning of a disintegration that would have the most profound influences.

US President Dwight D. Eisenhower, press conference, 7 April 1954.

At the height of the Cold War, US President Eisenhower used the metaphor of falling dominoes to argue that the fall of one country to Communism could weaken its neighbours, causing them too to collapse. The so-called 'domino theory' was voiced during a press conference on Indochina, at a time when the nationalist and Communist-backed Viet Minh were besieging the French stronghold of Dien Bien Phu and in the process of driving the French out of their colony. Eisenhower was asked to explain the strategic importance of Indochina to the Free World – an importance which, the questioner pointed out, was not fully appreciated across the United States. During this period, several other countries in the region, including Indonesia, Malaya and Burma, were experiencing Communist-backed insurgencies, and stopping them was seen as a crucial aspect of the Cold War.

With the retreat of the French from Indochina, the United States ratcheted up its own regional involvement, and the 'domino theory' came back into prominence in the 1960s and early 1970s as a justification for US intervention in Vietnam, Laos and Cambodia.

ALSO ON THIS DAY

1862 US Civil War: a Union army defeats the Confederates at the Battle of Shiloh.
1947 The death of the automotive industrialist Henry Ford.
1948 The World Health Organization is founded.

8 APRIL

THE SENTENCING OF JOMO KENYATTA, 1953

You have successfully plunged many Africans back to a state which shows little humanity. You have persuaded them in secret to murder, burn and commit atrocities which will take many years to forget. Make no mistake about it, Mau Mau will be defeated.

JUDGE RANSLEY THACKER, COMMENTS DURING SENTENCING, 8 APRIL 1953.

∞

The Mau Mau insurgency in Kenya arose from the loss of native rights over the land during the years between the world wars. Tensions heightened from 1950, and by 1956 tens of thousands of Kenyans had died – many of them members of the Kikuyu people, who were the dominant element within the Mau Mau as well as being their main victims – along with a small number of Europeans. The insurgency drew a strong and sometimes brutal response from the British colonial authorities, whose methods included the calling in of troops, bomber aircraft and mass incarceration.

Six nationalist leaders – the so-called Kapenguria Six – were also imprisoned, on charges of managing a proscribed society and conspiring to murder all the white inhabitants of Kenya. They included Jomo Kenyatta (c.1894–1978), even though he had spoken out against Mau Mau violence. The judge, a close associate of Kenya's Governor Evelyn Baring, was hostile to the defendants throughout the trial. Evidence later came to light that key witnesses in the case had been bribed and intimidated. The Indian prime minister, Jawaharlal Nehru, sent a lawyer to assist the defendants, but they were convicted nonetheless and sentenced to between three and seven years' hard labour.

In contrast, when a few months later a young British officer was found guilty of ordering his African troops to tie up Mau Mau suspects with thongs round their necks, whip the soles of their feet and burn their ears with lighted cigarettes, the same judge commented: 'It is easy to work oneself up into a state of pious horror over these offences, but they must be considered against their background. All the accused were engaged in seeking out inhuman monsters and savages of the lowest order.'

In 1962 Kenyatta became prime minister, taking Kenya to independence, and he later became president of the country.

ALSO ON THIS DAY

1587 The death of the Protestant martyrologist John Foxe.
1904 Britain and France agree the *Entente Cordiale*.
1973 The death of the artist Pablo Picasso.

9 APRIL

THE SURRENDER OF GENERAL ROBERT E. LEE, 1865

At a little before 4 o'clock General Lee shook hands with General Grant, bowed to the other officers, and with Colonel Marshall left the room. One after another we followed, and passed out to the porch. Lee signalled to his orderly to bring up his horse, and while the animal was being bridled the general stood on the lowest step and gazed sadly in the direction of the valley beyond where his army lay – now an army of prisoners. He smote his hands together a number of times in an absent sort of way; seemed not to see the group of Union officers in the yard who rose respectfully at his approach, and appeared unconscious of everything about him. All appreciated the sadness that overwhelmed him, and he had the personal sympathy of every one who beheld him at this supreme moment of trial. The approach of his horse seemed to recall him from his reverie, and he at once mounted. General Grant now stepped down from the porch, and, moving toward him, saluted him by raising his hat. He was followed in this act of courtesy by all our officers present; Lee raised his hat respectfully, and rode off to break the sad news to the brave fellows whom he had so long commanded.

GENERAL HORACE PORTER, *BATTLES AND LEADERS OF THE CIVIL WAR*, 1887.

∞

The Battle of Appomattox Courthouse in Virginia ended the American Civil War, when the Confederate General Robert E. Lee, at the head of the Army of Northern Virginia, found himself surrounded by superior forces and cut off from the Army of Tennessee. Realizing in mid-morning that his position was impossible, Lee concluded: 'There is nothing left for me to do but to go and see General Grant and I would rather die a thousand deaths.' The two men met in a farmhouse belonging to a Wilmer Maclean, and by 4pm on 9 April the surrender terms were agreed, with Ulysses S. Grant taking care to preserve the dignity of the defeated army and its general. The following day Lee gave his farewell address to his troops before ordering them to surrender their arms:

> *After four years of arduous service, marked by unsurpassed courage and fortitude, the Army of Northern Virginia has been compelled to yield to overwhelming numbers and resources.*
>
> *I need not tell the survivors of so many hard-fought battles who have remained steadfast to the last that I have consented to this result from no distrust of them; but feeling that valour and devotion could accomplish nothing that could compensate for the loss that would have attended the continuance of the contest, I determined to avoid the useless sacrifice of those whose past services have endeared them to*

their countrymen. By the terms of the agreement, officers and men can return to their homes and remain until exchanged.

You may take with you the satisfaction that proceeds from the consciousness of duty faithfully performed, and I earnestly pray that a merciful God will extend to you his blessing and protection.

With an unceasing admiration of your constancy and devotion to your country, and a grateful remembrance of your kind and generous consideration of myself, I bid you all an affectionate farewell.

A formal ceremony on 12 April 1865 disbanded the army and finally ended the war.

After the war Robert E. Lee served as a much-respected president of Washington College, Lexington, Virginia (now Washington and Lee University), until his death in 1870. He remains a revered figure in both the southern and northern states of the USA. Ulysses S. Grant served – as a Republican – two scandal-riven terms as 18th US president (1869–77). He died in 1885.

ALSO ON THIS DAY

1917 WWI: the Battle of Arras begins.
1940 WWII: Germany invades Norway and Denmark.
2003 Iraq War: the statue of Saddam Hussein is toppled in Baghdad.

125

10 APRIL

THE GOOD FRIDAY AGREEMENT, 1998

1. We, the participants in the multi-party negotiations, believe that the agreement we have negotiated offers a truly historic opportunity for a new beginning.

2. The tragedies of the past have left a deep and profoundly regrettable legacy of suffering. We must never forget those who have died or been injured, and their families. But we can best honour them through a fresh start, in which we firmly dedicate ourselves to the achievement of reconciliation, tolerance, and mutual trust, and to the protection and vindication of the human rights of all.

3. We are committed to partnership, equality and mutual respect as the basis of relationships within Northern Ireland, between North and South, and between these islands.

4. We reaffirm our total and absolute commitment to exclusively democratic and peaceful means of resolving differences on political issues...

5. We acknowledge the substantial differences between our continuing, and equally legitimate, political aspirations. However, we will endeavour to strive... towards reconciliation and rapprochement... It is accepted that all of the institutional and constitutional arrangements... are interlocking and interdependent and that in particular the functioning of the Assembly and the North/South Council are so closely inter-related that the success of each depends on that of the other.

PREAMBLE, GOOD FRIDAY AGREEMENT, 10 APRIL 1998.

The Northern Ireland Troubles, which had blighted the province for almost 30 years, finally ended with an agreement between Sinn Féin, the Ulster Unionists and the British government. Thanks in part to the interventions of the British premier Tony Blair ('This is no time for sound-bites. But I feel the hand of history on our shoulder in respect to this') and US President Bill Clinton, an agreement was hammered out on 10 April 1998. A referendum brought power-sharing among the former enemies and ushered in a transformation of the province, despite lingering threats from republican fringe groups.

ALSO ON THIS DAY

1606 The Virginia Company acquires its charter for American colonization.
1912 RMS *Titanic* leaves Southampton.
1966 The death of the English novelist and journalist Evelyn Waugh.

11 APRIL

IMPOTENCE IN THE FACE OF GENOCIDE, 1994

April 11, the fifth day of slaughter. The Security Council and office of the secretary-general were obviously at a loss as to what to do. I continued to receive demands to supply them with more information... What more could I possibly tell them that I hadn't already described in horrific detail? The odour of death in the hot sun; the flies, maggots, rats and dogs that swarmed to feast on the dead. At times it seemed the smell had entered the pores of my skin. My Christian beliefs had been the moral framework that had guided me through my adult life. Where was God in all this horror? Where was God in the world's response?

Two thousand Rwandans had lost their lives that day as a direct result of the Belgian withdrawal. They had taken refuge after April 7 at the Belgian camp set up at the Dom Bosco School, joined by a few expatriates. That morning, French troops had come to the school to evacuate the foreigners, and after they left, the company commander, Captain Lemaire, called Lieutenant Colonel Dewez, his CO, to request permission for his company to consolidate at the airport. He didn't mention the 2,000 Rwandans his troops were protecting at the school. When Dewez approved the move and the troops pulled out, the Interahamwe moved in, killing almost all the Rwandans.

...I mark April 12 as the day the world moved from disinterest in Rwanda to the abandonment of Rwandans to their fate. The swift evacuation of the foreign nationals was the signal for the génocidaires to move toward the apocalypse. That night I didn't sleep at all for guilt.

LIEUTENANT-GENERAL ROMÉO DALLAIRE, *SHAKE HANDS WITH THE DEVIL*, 2003.

Dallaire commanded the UN peacekeeping force for Rwanda in 1993–4 but was powerless to prevent the genocide waged by Hutu extremists against the minority Tutsis. In the early summer of 1994, machete-wielding government-sponsored forces murdered at least 800,000 people, massacres that were given a pretext on 6 April by the shooting down of the Hutu president of Rwanda's plane. The insurgent Tutsi-led Rwandan Patriotic Front eventually toppled the regime, ending the genocide – but sparking off reprisals and a flood of refugees across Rwanda's borders.

ALSO ON THIS DAY

1689 William III and Mary II are crowned as Britain's monarchs.
1713 The Treaty of Utrecht is signed, ending the War of the Spanish Succession.
1945 WWII: Buchenwald concentration camp is liberated by the US army.

12 APRIL

BYZANTINE CONSTANTINOPLE
FALLS TO CRUSADERS, 1204

Thus it was that Constantine's fair city, the common delight and boast of all nations, was laid waste by fire and blackened with soot, taken and emptied of all wealth, public and private, as well as that which was consecrated to God, by the scattered nations of the West. Feeble and unspeakable, these assembled to undertake a voyage of piracy, and their pretext to backwater [sic] against us, like a painted mask concealing their true motives, was to avenge the Byzantine Emperor Isaakios Angelos... The supine and stay-at-home ministers of the Roman empire ushered in the pirates as judges to condemn and punish us.

On the day on which the city fell, the despoilers took up quarters in the houses spread out in all directions, seized everything inside as plunder and interrogated their owners as to the whereabouts of their hidden treasures, beating some, holding gentle discourse with many, and using threats to all. They spared nothing and shared none of the belongings with their owners, nor were they willing to share food and house with them; and because they showed them utter contempt, taking them captives while heaping abuse on them, the chiefs decided to allow those who desired to depart from the city.

NIKETAS CHONIATES, *ANNALS OF BYZANTIUM*, 1204.

The participants in the Fourth Crusade, led by the blind 80-year-old Doge of Venice, Enrico Dandolo, allowed themselves to become embroiled in the political infighting of the wealthy Byzantine Empire by committing themselves to restore the deposed emperor, Isaakios II Angelos. The Crusade was thus diverted from its main object – the retaking of Jerusalem, which had fallen to the Muslim Kurdish leader Saladin in 1187 – to besiege the Byzantine capital Constantinople (modern Istanbul) instead. After the city fell on 12 April 1204, its treasures were looted and sent back to the West *en masse*, and a new 'Latin Empire' of Constantinople, a Crusader state, was established, which survived to 1261. Few of the crusaders travelled on to the Holy Land.

Constantinople fell, irrevocably, to the Ottoman Turks in 1453 (*see* 29 May).

ALSO ON THIS DAY

1861 A Confederate attack on Fort Sumter, South Carolina, begins the US Civil War.
1945 The death of US President Franklin D. Roosevelt.
1961 Soviet cosmonaut Yuri Gagarin becomes the first man in space.

13 APRIL

THE AMRITSAR MASSACRE, 1919

The firing was directed towards the exit gates through which the people were running out. There were small three or four outlets in all and bullets were actually rained over the people at all these gates... and many got trampled under the feet of the rushing crowds and thus lost their lives... even those who lay flat on the ground were fired upon.

GIRDHARI LAL, EYEWITNESS TO THE MASSACRE, 13 APRIL 1919.

∞

The massacre of between 379 (official estimate) and 1,000 (Indian estimate) unarmed Indians in the Punjabi city of Amritsar, on 13 April 1919, was ordered by the local British commander Brigadier-General Dyer. It occurred after a crowd of 20,000 had assembled at the Jallianwala Bagh garden to protest against conscription and heavy taxation. Dyer ordered the firing of live ammunition into the crowd without warning; many died by jumping into a well to escape the bullets. The following day Dyer issued a chilling challenge to the people of Amritsar:

Do you want war or peace? If you wish for a war, the government is prepared for it, and if you want peace, then obey my orders and open all your shops; else I will shoot. For me the battle-field of France or Amritsar is the same... You people talk against the government, and persons educated in Germany and Bengal talk sedition. I shall report all these. Obey my orders. I do not wish to have anything else. I have served in the military for over 30 years. I understand the Indian sepoy and Sikh people very well. You will have to obey my orders and observe peace. Otherwise the shops will be opened by force and rifles... Obey my orders.

Dyer received the support of India's viceroy, and although Winston Churchill denounced his actions in the House of Commons in July, Dyer was unrepentant when summoned to an inquiry in Westminster, saying that had he been able to bring his machine guns to bear on the crowd, he would have used them.

ALSO ON THIS DAY

1598 Henry IV's Edict of Nantes gives toleration to French Protestants.
1970 Technical problems imperil the *Apollo 13* astronauts.
1975 A Palestinian–Christian street battle in Beirut sparks the Lebanese Civil War.

14 APRIL

THE ASSASSINATION OF ABRAHAM LINCOLN, 1865

On the fourth anniversary of the fall of Fort Sumter, the beloved president, his great heart filled with peaceful thoughts and charity for all, entered Ford's Theater amid the acclamations of the loyal multitude assembled to greet him. Mr Lincoln sat in a high-backed upholstered chair in the corner of his box nearest the audience, and only his left profile was visible to most of the audience; but from where I sat, almost under the box, in the front row of orchestra chairs, I could see him plainly. Mrs Lincoln rested her hand on his knee much of the time, and often called his attention to some humorous situation on the stage. She seemed to take great pleasure in witnessing his enjoyment.

All went on pleasantly until half-past ten o'clock, when, during the second scene of the third act, the sharp report of a pistol rang through the house. The report seemed to proceed from behind the scenes on the right of the stage, and behind the president's box. While it startled every one in the audience, it was evidently accepted by all as an introductory effect preceding some new situation in the play... A moment afterward a hatless and white-faced man leaped from the front of the president's box down, twelve feet, to the stage. As he jumped, one of the spurs on his riding-boots caught in the folds of the flag draped over the front, and caused him to fall partly on his hands and knees as he struck the stage. Springing quickly to his feet with the suppleness of an athlete, he faced the audience for a moment as he brandished in his right hand a long knife, and shouted, *'Sic semper tyrannus.'* Then, with a rapid stage stride, he crossed the stage, and disappeared from view. A piercing shriek from the president's box, a repeated call for 'Water! Water!' and ' A surgeon!' in quick succession, conveyed the truth to the almost paralysed audience. A most terrible scene of excitement followed. With loud shoots of 'Kill him!' 'Lynch him!' part of the audience stampeded toward the entrance and onto the stage.

I leaped from the top of the orchestra railing in front of me upon the stage, and, announcing myself as an army surgeon, was immediately lifted up to the president's box by several gentlemen who had collected beneath...

When I entered the box, the president was lying upon the floor surrounded by his wailing wife and several gentlemen who had entered from the private stairway and dress-circle. Assistant Surgeon Charles A. Leale, USV [United States Volunteer], was in the box, and had caused the coat and waistcoat to be cut off in searching for the wound. Dr A.F.A. King of Washington was also present, and assisted in the examination... He was removed to a bed in a house opposite the theater... When the dying president was laid upon the bed in a small but neatly furnished room opposite the theater, it was found necessary to arrange his great length diagonally upon it...

There was scarcely a dry eye in the room, and it was the saddest and most pathetic death-bed scene I ever witnessed. Captain Robert Lincoln, of General Grant's staff, entered the room and stood at the headboard, leaning over his dying father. At first his terrible grief overpowered him, but, soon recovering himself, he leaned his head on the shoulder of Senator Charles Sumner, and remained in silent grief during the long, terrible night.

...When it was announced that the great heart had ceased to beat, Mr. Stanton said in solemn tones, 'He now belongs to the Ages.' Shortly after death, finding that the eyes were not entirely closed, one of the young surgeons reverently placed silver half-dollars upon them. The lower jaw fell slightly, and one of the medical men bound it up with his handkerchief. Secretary Stanton pulled down the window-shades, a guard was stationed outside the door, and the martyred President was left alone.

DR CHARLES SABIN TAFT, RECOLLECTIONS IN *CENTURY MAGAZINE*, FEBRUARY 1893.

The assassination by John Wilkes Booth of President Abraham Lincoln (1809–65) took place on 14 April 1865, just a few days after Lincoln had secured victory in the American Civil War (*see* 9 April). The president's killer was an actor; more importantly, he was a diehard Confederate supporter and opponent of the emancipation of slaves. Booth shot Lincoln in the back of the head at close quarters, and the president died the following day. Vice-President Andrew Johnson and Secretary of State William Seward were also intended victims of Booth's co-conspirators, but both survived. Booth's own final moments came later that month, also from a gunshot wound, after he was tracked down to a Virginian farm.

ALSO ON THIS DAY

1471 Wars of the Roses: the Earl of Warwick, 'the Kingmaker', is killed at the Battle of Barnet.
1759 The death of the composer George Frideric Handel.
1931 The Spanish Republic is declared.

15 APRIL

THE SINKING OF THE *TITANIC*, 1912

I went to the place I had seen the collapsible boat on the boat deck, and to my surprise I saw the boat and the men still trying to push it off. They couldn't do it. I went up to them and was just lending a hand when a large wave came awash of the deck. The big wave carried the boat off. I had hold of an oarlock and I went off with it. The next I knew I was in the boat. But that was not all, I was in the boat and the boat was upside down, and I was under it… How I got out from under the boat I do not know, but I felt a breath of air at last…

There were men all around me – hundreds of them. The sea was dotted with them, all depending on their life belts. I felt I simply had to get away from the ship. She was a beautiful sight then.

Smoke and sparks were rushing out of her funnel. There must have been an explosion, but we had heard none. We only saw the big stream of sparks. The ship was gradually turning on her nose – just like a duck that goes down for a dive. I had only one thing on my mind – to get away from the suction. The band was still playing. I guess all of the band went down. They were playing 'Autumn' then. I swam with all my might. I suppose I was 150 feet away when the *Titanic*, on her nose, with her after-quarter sticking straight up in the air, began to settle – slowly.

When at last the waves washed over her rudder there wasn't the least bit of suction I could feel. She must have kept going just so slowly as she had been.

HAROLD BRIDE, *NEW YORK TIMES*, 19 APRIL 1912.

After the luxury White Star liner RMS *Titanic* hit an iceberg in the North Atlantic shortly before midnight on 14 April 1912, the radio operator Harold Bride went on sending distress messages until his last moment to escape. The supposedly unsinkable liner was on its maiden voyage, from Southampton to New York, but she sank less than three hours after the collision. Following his rescue by RMS *Carpathia*, Bride helped with that ship's radio communications too, sending a stream of messages to the families of survivors. He told his story to the *New York Times* immediately on arrival on dry land. More than 1,500 died in the *Titanic* disaster, and 713 were rescued.

ALSO ON THIS DAY

1450 Hundred Years' War: the English are defeated at the Battle of Formigny.
1755 Samuel Johnson's *Dictionary* is published.
1980 The death of the French philosopher Jean-Paul Sartre.

16 APRIL

JACOBITE DEFEAT AT CULLODEN MOOR, 1746

The morning was cold and stormy – snow and rain blowing against us. Before long we saw the red soldiers in front of us and we could see the red coats of the soldiers and the blue tartan of the Campbells. The battle began and the pellets came at us like hail-stones. The big guns were thundering and causing frightful break up among us, but we ran forward and – oh dear! oh dear! – what cutting and slicing there was and many the brave deeds performed by the Gaels. I saw Iain Mor MacGilliosa cutting down the English as if he was cutting corn and Iain Breac Shiosallach killing them as though they were flies. But the English were numerous and we were few and a large number of our friends fell. The dead lay on all sides and the cries of pain of the wounded rang in our ears. You could see a riderless horse running and jumping as if mad.

DONALD MACKAY OF ACHMONIE, EYE-WITNESS RECOLLECTIONS, 1746.

∞

On 16 April 1746 the Battle of Culloden Moor, near Inverness, saw the rout of the Scottish Highlanders supporting the Jacobite claimant to the British crown, 'Bonnie Prince Charlie' – Charles Edward Stuart. It was the end of the Jacobite Rising, which had broken out in 1745, and the end of Stuart ambitions to dislodge the House of Hanover from the throne. The Jacobites' nemesis, commanding the government troops, was the Duke of Cumberland; his nickname, 'Butcher Cumberland', had been awarded by political opponents, but the description was apt for the ferocity with which he subsequently pursued the Highlanders.

Culloden Moor was the last pitched battle to be fought in Britain. The fighting lasted for an hour, during which the outgunned and exhausted Highlanders – despite the fear-instilling screeches of their Highland charge – failed to break the government formations. Up to 2,000 Jacobites died. Donald Mackay, an eyewitness, escaped to Inverness but was transported to the West Indies for his part in the uprising, though he later returned to the Highlands. Bonnie Prince Charlie famously fled back to the Continent, aided by Flora Macdonald, to nurse his sorrows.

ALSO ON THIS DAY

1850 The death of Mme Tussaud, founder of London's waxwork museum.
1917 Vladimir Ilyich Lenin returns to Russia from exile.
1964 The UK's Great Train Robbers are sentenced.

17 APRIL

THE SAN FRANCISCO EARTHQUAKE, 1906

I wake about 5 o'clock, feeling my bed rocking, and for a moment I think I am dreaming that I am crossing the water. I go to the window and look out. And what I see makes me tremble with fear. I see the buildings toppling over, big pieces of masonry falling, and from the street below I hear the screams of men and women and children.

I remain speechless, thinking I am in some dreadful nightmare, and for forty seconds I stand there, while the buildings fall and my room rocks like a boat.

My valet advises me to dress quickly and go into the open. By this time the plaster on the ceiling has fallen in a great shower, covering the bed and the carpet and the furniture. We run down the stairs and into the street, and my valet, brave fellow that he is, goes back and bundles all my things into trunks and drags them down six flights of stairs and out into the open one by one.

I make my way to Union Square, where I see some friends. And they tell me to come to a house that is still standing; but I prefer to remain where there is no fear of being buried. So I lie down in the square, while my valet goes and looks after the luggage, and soon all the city seems to be on fire.

ENRICO CARUSO, THE THEATRE MAGAZINE, JULY 1906.

The San Francisco earthquake on the night of 17–18 April 1906 devastated the young American city, destroying gas mains and causing fires that raged for four days. Perhaps as many as 20,000 people died, and hundreds of thousands were made homeless. One survivor was the 33-year-old Italian tenor Enrico Caruso, who had triumphantly sung in Bizet's *Carmen* the previous evening. Eventually, the singer's resourceful valet found a man with a cart to expedite his escape, and Caruso was able to narrate his 'dreadful nightmare' to *Theatre* magazine.

ALSO ON THIS DAY

1790 The death of the US polymath Benjamin Franklin.
1961 The 'Bay of Pigs': Cuban exiles invade Castro's Cuba.
1984 London police officer Yvonne Fletcher is killed by a Libyan Embassy sniper.

18 APRIL

MARTIN LUTHER STANDS FIRM, 1521

Unless I am convinced by the testimonies of the Holy Scriptures or evident reason (for I believe neither in the pope nor councils alone, since it has been established that they have often erred and contradicted themselves), I am bound by the Scriptures adduced by me, and my conscience has been taken captive by the Word of God, and I am neither able nor willing to recant, since it is neither safe nor right to act against conscience. God help me. Amen.

MARTIN LUTHER, STATEMENT AT THE DIET OF WORMS, 18 APRIL 1521.

∞

Martin Luther's affirmation of the authority of scripture above the directions of the Catholic Church was spoken at the Diet (general assembly) of the Holy Roman Empire, presided over by Emperor Charles V. The last phrases are traditionally – but perhaps apocryphally – rendered as 'Here I stand, I can do no other, so help me God. Amen.'

Following his summons to appear at the diet, the Augustinian friar had arrived in Worms, a town on the River Rhine, two days earlier and had been challenged to renounce his writings. Luther declined to do so, except insofar as he had been unfair to individuals within the Church. Through his robust defence of his views he turned his protests against abuses in the Church into a thoroughgoing challenge to its spiritual and political authority.

Luther left Worms before being formally declared a heretic, and – for his own protection – was captured in a faked ambush by Frederick of Saxony, who kept him in Wartburg Castle for nine months. Luther did not waste the time he spent in captivity, translating the New Testament into German; on publication this quickly became a bestseller and the challenge to papal, and imperial, authority became unstoppable.

ALSO ON THIS DAY

1506 Building starts on the present St Peter's Basilica, Rome.
1949 Ireland becomes a republic.
1954 In Egypt, Colonel Nasser seizes power in a military coup.

19 APRIL

THE FIRST SHOTS OF
THE AMERICAN REVOLUTION, 1775

The Company under the command of Captain John Parker being drawn up (sometime before sunrise) on the green or common, and I being in the front rank, there suddenly appeared a number of the King's Troops, about a thousand, as I thought, at the distance of about sixty or seventy yards from us, huzzaing and on a quick pace toward us, with three officers in their front on horseback, and on full gallop towards us; the foremost of which cried, 'Throw down your arms, ye villains, ye rebels'; upon which said Company dispersing, the foremost of the three officers ordered their men, saying 'Fire, by God, fire,' at which moment we received a very heavy and close fire from them; at which instant, being wounded, I fell, and several of our men were shot dead by one volley. Captain Parker's men, I believe, had not then fired a gun.

JOHN ROBBINS, LEXINGTON MILITIAMAN, 1775.

The first encounter of the American Revolutionary War (or American War of Independence) occurred when a 700-strong force of regular British Army troops moved inland from Boston to Concord to destroy the rebel colonists' reported military supplies. The colonists, alerted by silversmith Paul Revere's 'midnight ride' – though possibly not with the oft-quoted phrase 'The British are coming!' – prepared to face them, and the 77-strong Lexington Militia met the British regulars at dawn.

The course of events, including the question of who fired the first shot, remains confused; but Militia Captain John Parker was later supposed to have said: 'Stand your ground; don't fire unless fired upon, but if they mean to have a war, let it begin here.' Eight Massachusetts men were killed and ten were wounded before they fell back. Later in the day a second battle, at Concord, resulted in a retreat by the army regulars. The poet Ralph Waldo Emerson later described the Battle of Concord as 'the shot that rang around the world'.

ALSO ON THIS DAY

1587 Francis Drake 'singes the king of Spain's beard' by raiding the Spanish port of Cadiz.
1943 The uprising of the Warsaw Jewish Ghetto begins.
2005 The German Cardinal Ratzinger is elected Pope Benedict XVI.

20 APRIL

NELSON MANDELA DEFENDS HIS ACTIONS, 1964

Above all, we want equal political rights, because without them our disabilities will be permanent. I know this sounds revolutionary to the whites in this country, because the majority of voters will be Africans. This makes the white man fear democracy.

But this fear cannot be allowed to stand in the way of the only solution which will guarantee racial harmony and freedom for all. It is not true that the enfranchisement of all will result in racial domination. The ANC has spent half a century fighting against racialism. When it triumphs it will not change that policy.

This then is what the ANC is fighting. Their struggle is a truly national one. It is a struggle of the African people, inspired by their own suffering and their own experience. It is a struggle for the right to live.

During my lifetime I have dedicated myself to this struggle of the African people. I have fought against white domination and I have fought against black domination. I have cherished the ideal of a democratic and free society in which all persons live together in harmony and with equal opportunities. It is an ideal which I hope to live for and to see realized. But if needs be, my lord, it is an ideal for which I am ready to die.

NELSON MANDELA, DEFENCE SPEECH, 20 APRIL 1964.

∞

In 1963 leaders of the African National Congress were arrested, most of them in the Johannesburg suburb of Rivonia. Eight were put on trial, facing the death penalty for 221 acts of sabotage designed to 'foment violent revolution'. Prominent at the so-called Rivonia Trial was Nelson Mandela, leader of *Umkhonto we Sizwe* (Spear of the Nation), the ANC's armed wing. The legal-trained Mandela spoke in his own defence for four and a half hours, admitting he had organized sabotage, but explaining his rationale; he ranged far and wide, recounting the ANC's struggle, the iniquities of *apartheid* and his aspirations for a representative democracy in South Africa.

In June 1964 the defendants were sentenced to life imprisonment, and Mandela remained incarcerated until 1990 when his release paved the way for the transformation of his, and his country's, life (*see* 11 February).

ALSO ON THIS DAY

1792 French Revolutionary Wars: France declares war on Austria.
1885 The birth of Adolf Hitler in Austria.
1902 The French chemists Marie and Pierre Curie isolate radium chloride.

21 APRIL

THE FOUNDING OF ROME, 753 BC

The Fates had already decreed the origin of this great city and the foundation of the mightiest empire under heaven. The Vestal was raped and gave birth to twins. She named Mars as their father, either because she believed it, or because the fault might appear less heinous if a deity were the cause of it. But she was thrown into prison, the boys were ordered to be thrown into the river. It happened that the Tiber was then overflowing its banks, and stretches of standing water prevented any approach to the main channel. The boys were exposed at the nearest point of the overflow, in a wild, empty place. A thirsty she-wolf from the surrounding hills, attracted by the crying of the children, came to them, gave them her teats to suck and was so gentle towards them that the king's shepherd found her licking the boys. As the boys grew older they took joy in roaming the woods, hunting. As their strength and courage developed, they used to lie in wait for fierce beasts of prey, and even attacked brigands loaded with plunder.

Romulus and Remus decided to build a city near where they had been exposed. But the ancestral curse – ambition – led to a quarrel over a trivial matter. As twins, neither could claim seniority over the other, so they decided to consult the deities of the place as to who should give his name to the new city, and who should rule it. Romulus selected the Palatine as his station for observation, Remus the Aventine.

Remus was the first to receive an omen: six vultures appeared to him. The augury had just been announced to Romulus when twice the number appeared to him. Each was saluted as king by his supporters. An argument began; passions led to bloodshed; in the tumult Remus contemptuously jumped over the newly raised walls and was killed by the furious Romulus, who exclaimed: 'So shall it be henceforth with every one who leaps over my walls.'

LIVY, *HISTORY OF ROME*, BOOK I, 27–25 BC.

∞

The traditional founding of Rome was celebrated annually on 21 April for more than a thousand years, and the founding legend was recorded by the historian Livy in the first century BC, some 700 years after the purported events.

Several Etruscan city-states flourished in central Italy, while the Italic tribes known as the Latins lived in the region of the Tiber around modern Rome, with its main centre at Alba Longa. The daughter of King Numitor of Alba Longa, called Rea Silvia, was a Vestal Virgin, dedicated to the goddess Vesta and therefore sworn to chastity. Her twin sons were exposed at a site traditionally identified with Velabro, near the Palatine Hill. The boys were raised by the shepherd who found them, made aware of their origins and helped Numitor to regain his throne before deciding to found a city of their own.

Archaeology has shown that the site of Rome had been inhabited from Neolithic times, but that the eighth century BC did indeed see the creation of a new settlement.

Livy's (59 BC–AD 17) *Ab Urbe Condita Libri* ('Chapters from the Foundation of the City') described the history of Rome from its earliest, legendary beginnings to the age of the emperor Augustus. The traditional epithet for Rome, the 'Eternal City', occurs in the work of Ovid, Tibullus and other classical writers.

ALSO ON THIS DAY

1910 The death of the US author Mark Twain.
1918 The German fighter ace 'Red Baron' Manfred von Richthofen is killed in action.
1967 A Greek military coup topples the government.

22 APRIL

THE SETTLEMENT OF OKLAHOMA, 1889

Unlike Rome, the city of Guthrie was built in a day. To be strictly accurate in the matter, it might be said that it was built in an afternoon. At twelve o'clock on Monday, April 22nd, the resident population of Guthrie was nothing; before sundown it was at least ten thousand. In that time streets had been laid out, town lots staked off, and steps taken toward the formation of a municipal government.

Harper's Weekly, 18 May 1889.

∞

The opening to white settlement of the Unassigned Lands, a portion of Indian Territory in what is now Oklahoma, set off a bizarre episode that instantly created two cities twenty miles apart. The federal government decided that, at noon on 22 April 1889, people would be allowed to cross the Arkansas or Texas borders, seek a parcel of unclaimed land from the 2 million acres available, and file a claim of ownership. There was a mad rush of some 50,000 people, and by the end of the day Oklahoma City and Guthrie, which previously had been nothing more than water-points on the railroad, were both home to thousands of so-called 'boomers', in tents.

By August 1889, the Guthrie city directory included six banks, 16 barbers, 16 blacksmiths, 17 carpenters, two cigar manufacturers, five newspapers, seven hardware stores, 15 hotels, 19 pharmacists, 22 lumber companies, 39 doctors, 40 restaurants, and no fewer than 81 lawyers – to service the many legal disputes concerning 'sooners', who were said to have entered the territory and staked their claims before the permitted date. Six similar land grabs were organized in the succeeding decade.

ALSO ON THIS DAY

1509 Henry VIII accedes to the English throne.
1529 The Spanish–Portuguese Treaty of Zaragoza divides the eastern hemisphere between these two powers.
1994 The death of the former US president Richard Nixon.

23 APRIL

A POST-CORONATION CELEBRATION, 1661

I took my wife and Mrs Frankleyn (who I proffered the civility of lying with my wife at Mrs Hunt's to-night) to Axe-yard, in which at the further end there were three great bonfires, and a great many great gallants, men and women; and they laid hold of us, and would have us drink the King's health upon our knees, kneeling upon a faggot, which we all did, they drinking to us one after another. Which we thought a strange frolique; but these gallants continued thus a great while, and I wondered to see how the ladies did tipple. At last I sent my wife and her bedfellow to bed, and Mr Hunt and I went in with Mr Thornbury (who did give the company all their wine, he being yeoman of the wine-cellar to the king) to his house; and there, with his wife and two of his sisters, and some gallant sparks that were there, we drank the king's health, and nothing else, till one of the gentlemen fell down stark drunk, and there lay spewing; and I went to my lord's pretty well. But no sooner a-bed with Mr Shepley but my head began to hum, and I to vomit, and if ever I was foxed it was now, which I cannot say yet, because I fell asleep and slept till morning. Only when I waked I found myself wet with my spewing.

SAMUEL PEPYS, DIARY, 23 APRIL 1661.

∞

Diarist and future naval administrator Samuel Pepys (1633–1703) had spent the day of Charles II's coronation first in Westminster Abbey, where he had watched the ceremonies, and later in Westminster Hall, where the coronation feast was held. Finally he went off to these more informal celebrations with family and friends, which evidently proved too much for his normally robust constitution.

Pepys's diary, written in a code devised by the author between 1660 and 1669, had to wait until the 19th century to be deciphered – and even later for an unbowdlerized edition. But his vivid recounting of his life and times has embedded itself in modern perceptions of the Restoration era. (*See also* 2 September.)

ALSO ON THIS DAY

1014 The Irish king Brian Boru defeats a Viking army at Clontarf.
1616 The death of the Spanish writer Cervantes.
1616 The death of the English dramatist William Shakespeare.

24 APRIL

THE EASTER RISING, 1916

IRISHMEN AND IRISHWOMEN: In the name of God and the dead generations from which she receives her old tradition of nationhood, Ireland, through us, summons her children to her flag and strikes for her freedom... We declare the right of the people of Ireland to the ownership of Ireland, and to the unfettered control of Irish destinies, to be sovereign and indefeasible. The long usurpation of that right by a foreign people and government has not extinguished the right, nor can it ever be extinguished except by the destruction of the Irish people... Standing on that fundamental right and again asserting it in arms in the face of the world, we hereby proclaim the Irish Republic as a sovereign independent state, and we pledge our lives and the lives of our comrades-in-arms to the cause of its freedom, of its welfare, and its exaltation among the nations.

The Irish Republic is entitled to, and hereby claims, the allegiance of every Irishman and Irishwoman. The Republic guarantees religious and civil liberty, equal rights and equal opportunities to all its citizens, and declares its resolve to pursue the happiness and prosperity of the whole nation and of all its parts, cherishing all the children of the nation equally, and oblivious of the differences carefully fostered by an alien government, which have divided a minority from the majority in the past.

PADRAIG PEARSE *ET AL.*, PROCLAMATION, 24 APRIL 1916.

When members of the insurrectionist Irish Volunteers and Irish Citizens' Army took over Dublin's main post office on 24 April 1916, the oratorically gifted Padraig (Patrick) Pearse read this assertion of Ireland's independence on the building's steps. With these words he announced what became known as the Easter Rising against British rule in Ireland. The other signatories were Thomas J. Clarke, Seán Mac Diarmada, Thomas MacDonagh, Éamonn Ceannt, James Connolly and Joseph Plunkett. After a bloody week, British Army units retook the building, and later the seven signatories and eight others were executed for their rebellion.

Independence for all but the six counties of Northern Ireland was finally agreed in 1921, but only at a cost of splitting the republican movement (*see* 6 December).

ALSO ON THIS DAY

1731 The death of the English novelist Daniel Defoe.
1877 The Russo-Turkish War begins.
1915 The Ottoman authorities begin the roundup and killing of Armenians.

25 APRIL

HEROIC FAILURE AT GALLIPOLI, 1915

The boats had almost reached the beach when a party of Turks entrenched ashore opened a terrible fusillade with rifles and a Maxim... The Australians... sprang into the sea... and rushed the enemy's trenches. Their magazines were uncharged, so they just went in with cold steel. It was over in a minute...

Then the Australians found themselves facing an almost perpendicular cliff of loose sandstones, covered with thick shrubbery. Somewhere about half way up the enemy had a second trench, strongly held, from which poured a terrible fire on the troops below and the boats pulling back to the destroyers for a second landing party. Here was a tough proposition to tackle in the darkness, but those colonials ... went about it in a practical way. They... proceeded to scale the cliff without responding to the enemy's fire... In less than a quarter of an hour the Turks were out of their second position, and either bayoneted or fleeing.

As daylight came it was seen that the landing had been effected... at a point where the cliffs rise very sheer... To the sea it presents a steep front, broken into innumerable ridges, bluffs, valleys, and sandpits. Rising to a height of several hundred feet the surface is bare, crumbly sandstone, with thick shrubbery about six feet in height, which is ideal for snipers, as the Australasians soon found to their cost.

There has been no finer feat in this war than this sudden landing in the dark and the storming of the heights, and above all, the holding on whilst reinforcements were landing. These raw colonial troops in these desperate hours proved worthy to fight side by side with the heroes of Mons, the Aisne, Ypres, and Neuve Chapelle.

ELLIS ASHMEAD-BARTLETT, *SYDNEY MORNING HERALD*, 8 MAY 1915.

On 25 April 1915 the Australian and New Zealand (ANZAC) forces attempting to take the Gallipoli peninsula from the Turks in the First World War encountered a more challenging environment than expected. The troops found themselves pinned to the beach and cliff for months before being evacuated in December after suffering high losses to fighting and disease. The landing at 'Anzac Cove', as it is still known, is commemorated in both countries.

ALSO ON THIS DAY

1792 A French highwayman becomes the guillotine's first victim.
1898 The USA declares war on Spain.
1945 WWII: US and Soviet soldiers finally link up in Germany.

26 APRIL

THE DESTRUCTION OF GUERNICA, 1938

Guernica, the most ancient town of the Basques and the centre of their cultural tradition, was completely destroyed yesterday afternoon by insurgent air raiders. The bombardment of this open town far behind the lines occupied precisely three hours and a quarter, during which a powerful fleet of aeroplanes consisting of three German types, Junkers and Heinkel bombers, did not cease unloading on the town bombs weighing from 1,000 lbs. downwards and, it is calculated, more than 3,000 two-pounder aluminium incendiary projectiles. The fighters, meanwhile, plunged low from above the centre of the town to machine-gun those of the civilian population who had taken refuge in the fields.

The whole of Guernica was soon in flames except the historic Casa de Jontas with its rich archives of the Basque race, where the ancient Basque Parliament used to sit. The famous oak of Guernica, the dried old stump of 600 years and the young new shoots of this century, was also untouched...

At 2 am today when I visited the town the whole of it was a horrible sight, flaming from end to end. The reflection of the flames could be seen in the clouds of smoke above the mountains from 10 miles away. Throughout the night houses were falling until the streets became long heaps of red impenetrable debris...

In the form of its execution and the scale of the destruction it wrought, no less than in the selection of its objective, the raid on Guernica is unparalleled in military history. Guernica was not a military objective. A factory producing war material lay outside the town and was untouched. So were two barracks some distance from the town. The town lay far behind the lines. The object of the bombardment was seemingly the demoralization of the civil population and the destruction of the cradle of the Basque race. Every fact bears out this appreciation, beginning with the day when the deed was done.

Monday was the customary market day in Guernica for the country round. At 4.30 pm, when the market was full and peasants were still coming in, the church bell rang the alarm for approaching aeroplanes, and the population sought refuge in cellars and in the dugouts prepared following the bombing of the civilian population of Durango on March 31, which opened General Mola's offensive in the north. The people are said to have shown a good spirit. A Catholic priest took charge and perfect order was maintained.

Five minutes later a single German bomber appeared, circled over the town at a low altitude, and then dropped six heavy bombs, apparently aiming for the station. The bombs with a shower of grenades fell on a former institute and on houses and streets surrounding it. The aeroplane then went away. In another five minutes came a second bomber, which threw the same number of bombs into the middle of the town. About a quarter of an hour later three Junkers arrived to continue the work of demolition, and thenceforward the bombing grew in intensity and was continuous, ceasing only with the approach of dusk at 7.45. The whole town of 7,000 inhabitants, plus 3,000 refugees, was slowly and systematically pounded to pieces. Over a radius of five miles round a detail of the raiders' technique was to bomb separate caserios, or farmhouses. In the night these burned like little candles in the hills. All the villages around were bombed with the same intensity as the town itself, and at Mugica, a little group of houses at the head of the Guernica inlet, the population was machine-gunned for 15 minutes.

GEORGE STEER, *THE TIMES*, 28 APRIL 1938.

∞

During the Spanish Civil War (1936–9), British journalist and Republican sympathizer George Steer arrived in Guernica a few hours after the town had been destroyed on 26 April 1938 by bombs of the German Condor Legion, supporting General Franco's Nationalist insurgency. This was the first manifestation in Europe of the much-feared horrors of mass aerial bombardment – although similar incidents had taken place in Abyssinia (Ethiopia), where Steer had also worked, and in Japanese assaults on Chinese cities since 1937. Steer was able to demonstrate German involvement in the attack, which killed a reported 1,600 people. The figure remains disputed, but worldwide outrage followed the bombing, memorably expressed in Pablo Picasso's epic painting of the horrors.

The military lessons of the Spanish Civil War were not solely of the bombers' efficacy, however. Successful interception of bombers by Soviet fighter-planes, supporting the Republicans, suggested that the fatalistic 'bomber would always get through' mindset of the time was questionable.

ALSO ON THIS DAY

1865 John Wilkes Booth, the assassin of Abraham Lincoln, is shot dead.
1964 Tanzania is created, combining Tanganyika and Zanzibar.
1986 A serious nuclear accident takes place at Chernobyl, in Ukraine.

27 APRIL

THE EXPLORER MAGELLAN MEETS HIS DEATH, 1521

The captain-general [Magellan] sent some men to burn their houses in order to terrify them. When they saw this, they were roused to fury. Two of our men were killed while we burned twenty or thirty houses. So many of them charged down upon us that they shot the captain through the right leg with a poisoned arrow. On that account, he ordered us to retire slowly.

The natives continued to pursue us, and picking up the same spear, hurled it at us again and again. Recognizing the captain, they knocked his helmet off his head twice, but he stood firm like a good knight. An Indian hurled a bamboo spear into his face, but the latter immediately killed him with his lance, which he left in the Indian's body. Then, trying to lay hand on sword, he could draw it out but halfway, because he had been wounded in the arm. When the natives saw that, they hurled themselves upon him. One wounded him on the left leg with a cutlass like a large scimitar. That caused the captain to fall face downward, when they rushed upon him with iron and bamboo spears and cutlasses, until they killed our mirror, our light, our comfort, and our true guide. Thereupon, beholding him dead, we, wounded, retreated, as best we could, to the boats, which were already pulling off.

ANTONIO PIGAFETTA (CREW-MEMBER), *REPORT ON THE FIRST VOYAGE AROUND THE WORLD*, 1521.

Having become the first European to sail around South America and cross the Pacific – which ocean he named – the Portuguese navigator Ferdinand Magellan (*c.*1480–1521) was killed when trying to convert a chieftain on the small island of Mactan, in the modern Philippines, to Christianity. Just one ship from his fleet of five eventually arrived home in September 1522, three years after setting sail; the rest had been wrecked, captured or become unusable because of depleted crews. Nevertheless, the skeleton crew of Magellan's ship *Victoria*, captained by the Spaniard Juan Sebastian del Cano, became the first Europeans to complete the circumnavigation of the world. Fewer than ten per cent of the original expedition's sailors returned, but they were able to confirm Magellan's route, exploits and discoveries.

ALSO ON THIS DAY

1296 The Scots are defeated by Edward I at the Battle of Dunbar.
1882 The death of the US poet Ralph Waldo Emerson.
1994 The first post-*apartheid* elections take place in South Africa.

28 APRIL

A JOHNSONIAN CONVERSATION, 1779

At General Paoli's were Sir Joshua Reynolds, Mr Langton, Marchese Gherardi of Lombardy, and Mr John Spottiswoode the younger, of Spottiswoode, the solicitor. At this time fears of an invasion were circulated; to obviate which, Mr Spottiswoode observed, that Mr Fraser the engineer, who had lately come from Dunkirk, said, that the French had the same fears of us.

Johnson: 'It is thus that mutual cowardice keeps us in peace. Were one half of mankind brave, and one half cowards, the brave would be always beating the cowards. Were all brave, they would lead a very uneasy life; all would be continually fighting: but being all cowards, we go on very well.'

We talked of drinking wine.

Johnson: 'I require wine, only when I am alone. I have then often wished for it, and often taken it.'

Spottiswoode: 'What, by way of a companion, Sir?'

Johnson: 'To get rid of myself, to send myself away. Wine gives great pleasure; and every pleasure is of itself a good. It is a good, unless counterbalanced by evil. A man may have a strong reason not to drink wine; and that may be greater than the pleasure. Wine makes a man better pleased with himself. I do not say that it makes him more pleasing to others. Sometimes it does. But the danger is, that while a man grows better pleased with himself, he may be growing less pleasing to others. Wine gives a man nothing. It neither gives him knowledge nor wit; it only animates a man, and enables him to bring out what a dread of the company has repressed. It only puts in motion what has been locked up in frost. But this may be good, or it may be bad.'

JAMES BOSWELL, *LIFE OF JOHNSON*, VOLUME III, 1791.

Scottish lawyer James Boswell's wonderfully detailed *Life of Johnson* revealed the wide-ranging opinions and ready wit of his friend the lexicographer Samuel Johnson (1709–84); it also offered an intimate portrait of mid-Georgian society. At the time of this conversation, 28 April 1779, France had recently declared war on Britain in support of the American revolutionaries – but the invasion rumour was to come to nothing.

ALSO ON THIS DAY

1192 Conrad I of Jerusalem is killed by the 'Assassins' sect.
1789 The crew of the *Bounty* mutiny against Captain Bligh.
1945 Partisans execute the Italian Fascist leader Benito Mussolini.

THE LAST TESTAMENT OF ADOLF HITLER, 1945

More than thirty years have now passed since I in 1914 made my modest contribution as a volunteer in the First World War that was forced upon the Reich.

In these three decades I have been actuated solely by love and loyalty to my people in all my thoughts, acts, and life. They gave me the strength to make the most difficult decisions which have ever confronted mortal man. I have spent my time, my working strength, and my health in these three decades.

It is untrue that I or anyone else in Germany wanted the war in 1939. It was desired and instigated exclusively by those international statesmen who were either of Jewish descent or worked for Jewish interests. I have made too many offers for the control and limitation of armaments, which posterity will not for all time be able to disregard, for the responsibility for the outbreak of this war to be laid on me. I have further never wished that after the first fatal world war a second against England, or even against America, should break out. Centuries will pass away, but out of the ruins of our towns and monuments the hatred against those finally responsible whom we have to thank for everything, International Jewry and its helpers, will grow.

Three days before the outbreak of the German–Polish war I again proposed to the British ambassador in Berlin a solution to the German–Polish problem – similar to that in the case of the Saar district, under international control. This offer also cannot be denied. It was only rejected because the leading circles in English politics wanted the war, partly on account of the business hoped for and partly under influence of propaganda organized by International Jewry.

I have also made it quite plain that, if the nations of Europe are again to be regarded as mere shares to be bought and sold by these international conspirators in money and finance, then that race, Jewry, which is the real criminal of this murderous struggle, will be saddled with the responsibility. I further left no one in doubt that this time not only would millions of children of Europe's Aryan people die of hunger, not only would millions of grown men suffer death, and not only hundreds of thousands of women and children be burnt and bombed to death in the towns, without the real criminal having to atone for this guilt, even if by more humane means.

After six years of war, which in spite of all setbacks, will go down one day in history as the most glorious and valiant demonstration of a nation's life purpose, I cannot forsake the city which is the capital of this Reich. As our forces are too small to make any further stand against the enemy attack at this place and since our resistance is gradually being weakened by men who are as deluded as they are lacking in initiative, I should like, by remaining in this town, to share my fate with those, the millions of others, who have also taken upon themselves to do so. Moreover I do not wish to fall into the hands of an enemy who requires a new spectacle organized by the Jews for the amusement of their hysterical masses.

I have decided therefore to remain in Berlin and there of my own free will to choose death at the moment when I believe the position of the Führer and Chancellor itself can no longer be held.

I die with a joyful heart, aware of the immeasurable deeds and achievements of our soldiers at the front, our women at home, the achievements of our farmers and workers and the work, unique in history, of our youth who bear my name.

ADOLF HITLER, 1945

In 1945, holed up in his bunker in Berlin and with the Soviet Red Army less than a mile away, Adolf Hitler dictated his last testament to his secretary, Traudl Junge, during the night of 28–29 April. In it, he heaped responsibility for the Second World War at the door of the Jewish people, justifying the genocidal Nazi policy towards them as 'humane' recompense. That same night he married his mistress, Eva Braun. On 30 April he said goodbye to his staff, killed his dog and, as Braun took cyanide, shot himself through the temples. Their bodies were burned and buried in a crater outside the bunker.

ALSO ON THIS DAY

1429 Joan of Arc relieves the English siege of Orléans.
1945 WWII: German forces in Italy surrender.
2006 The death of the US economist John Kenneth Galbraith.

30 APRIL

HENRY VIII, RENAISSANCE PRINCE, 1515

His Majesty is the handsomest potentate I ever set eyes on; above the usual height, with an extremely fine calf to his leg, his complexion very fair and bright, with auburn hair combed straight and short in the French fashion and a round face so very beautiful that it would become a pretty woman, his throat rather long and thick. He speaks French, English, Latin and a little Italian, plays well on the lute and harpsichord, sings from book at sight, draws the bow with greater strength than any man in England, and jousts marvellously. Believe me, he is in every respect a most accomplished Prince.

PIERO PASQUALIGO, LETTER, 30 APRIL 1515.

∞

In 16th-century Europe ambassadors frequently sent home detailed descriptions of the countries and the princes at whose courts they served, and these provide some of the most vivid reporting of royal life. The Venetian Ambassador Piero Pasqualigo had arrived at Henry VIII's court on 23 April 1515 – St George's Day – charged with gaining the Tudor monarch's support for Venice's war in Lombardy.

In his twenties, Henry was seen as a model Renaissance prince, educated and *sportif*, cutting an impressive figure on the European stage – a far cry from the bloated, overweight tyrant of his later years. He was often compared with the powerful Francis I of France, who had come to the throne on New Year's Day 1515 and who was to dominate northern Italy after a dramatic victory against the Venetians and Swiss at Marignano in September. Over the succeeding decade, European politics involved shifting alliances around these two young monarchs and (from 1516) Charles I of Spain, who was elected Holy Roman Emperor as Charles V in 1519 and who was the nephew of Henry's first wife, Catherine of Aragon. (*See also* 7 June.)

ALSO ON THIS DAY
1812 Louisiana becomes the 18th US state.
1945 Adolf Hitler and Eva Braun commit suicide in their Berlin bunker.
1975 Saigon falls to North Vietnamese Communist troops.

MAY

1 MAY

THE OPENING OF THE GREAT EXHIBITION, 1851

Yesterday I went for the second time to the Crystal Palace. We remained in it about three hours, and I must say I was more struck with it on this occasion than at my first visit. It is a wonderful place – vast, strange, new and impossible to describe. Its grandeur does not consist in *one* thing, but in the unique assemblage of *all* things. Whatever human industry has created you find there, from the great compartments filled with railway engines and boilers, with mill machinery in full work, with splendid carriages of all kinds, with harness of every description, to the glass-covered and velvet-spread stands loaded with the most gorgeous work of the goldsmith and silversmith, and the carefully guarded caskets full of real diamonds and pearls worth hundreds of thousands of pounds. It may be called a bazaar or a fair, but it is such a bazaar or fair as Eastern genii might have created. It seems as if only magic could have gathered this mass of wealth from all the ends of the earth – as if none but supernatural hands could have arranged it this, with such a blaze and contrast of colours and marvellous power of effect. The multitude filling the great aisles seems ruled and subdued by some invisible influence. Amongst the thirty thousand souls that peopled it the day I was there not one loud noise was to be heard, not one irregular movement seen; the living tide rolls on quietly, with a deep hum like the sea heard from the distance.

CHARLOTTE BRONTË, LETTER TO HER FATHER, 7 JUNE 1851.

∾

London's Great Exhibition of 1851 was the first 'world's fair', designed at the height of Britain's imperial sway to showcase developments in design, industry and commerce. It would be the first of several world's fairs over the next century.

The Great Exhibition was conceived by Queen Victoria's consort Prince Albert, with Henry Cole, to focus on the display of British industry and ingenuity. It was housed in the huge iron-and-glass Crystal Palace in Hyde Park, its innovative design conceived by Joseph Paxton. Queen Victoria opened the event on 1 May 1851, and around 2,500 tickets were sold for that day alone. One of the early attendees was the author of *Jane Eyre*, Charlotte Brontë. Over the next six months at least 3 million people swarmed to the spectacle.

ALSO ON THIS DAY

1707 The Union Treaty creates the Kingdom of Great Britain.
1873 The death of the Scottish missionary David Livingstone.
1960 Gary Powers's US spyplane is shot down over the Soviet Union.

2 MAY

THE PUBLICATION OF THE KING JAMES BIBLE, 1611

But it is high time to show in brief what we proposed to ourselves, and what course we held in this our perusal and survey of the Bible. Truly (good Christian reader) we never thought from the beginning, that we should need to make a new translation, nor yet to make of a bad one a good one, but to make a good one better, or out of many good ones, one principal good one, not justly to be excepted against; that hath been our endeavour, that our mark. To that purpose there were many chosen, that were greater in other men's eyes than in their own, and that sought the truth rather than their own praise. Again, they came or were thought to come to the work learned, not to learn: For the chief overseer under His Majesty [James I] knew by his wisdom, that it is a preposterous order to teach first and to learn after, yea that to learn and practice together, is neither commendable for the workman, nor safe for the work.

PREFACE, KING JAMES BIBLE, 1611.

The Authorized Version of the Bible – which would become the most familiar and best-loved English-language translation into the 20th century and beyond – was commissioned by King James I (James VI of Scotland) in 1604. It was completed seven years later and included a long preface justifying the procedures used to create it and emphasizing the learned credentials of those who undertook the translation. Almost 50 translators were involved, including Richard Bancroft who, as Archbishop of Canterbury, oversaw the process, and the scholarly cleric Lancelot Andrewes. They built on earlier translations, and their brief was in part political – to resolve the objections to the previous translation, the Bishops' Bible of 1568, that had been voiced by Puritans. In the centuries that followed, its phraseology profoundly suffused not only the religious life of the English-speaking world but the English language itself.

Once in print, the King James Bible underwent revisions and corrections over the years, though as some errors departed others arrived, perhaps most famously an injunction in the 1631 printing: 'Thou shalt commit adultery.'

ALSO ON THIS DAY

1519 The death of Leonardo da Vinci.
1945 WWII: the Soviet Red Flag is raised over Berlin.
2011 The al-Qaeda leader Osama bin Laden is killed in Pakistan.

3 MAY

IN FLANDERS FIELDS, 1915

In Flanders fields the poppies blow
Between the crosses, row on row,
That mark our place; and in the sky
The larks, still bravely singing, fly
Scarce heard amid the guns below.

We are the Dead. Short days ago
We lived, felt dawn, saw sunset glow,
Loved and were loved, and now we lie
In Flanders fields.

Take up our quarrel with the foe:
To you from failing hands we throw
The torch; be yours to hold it high.
If ye break faith with us who die
We shall not sleep, though poppies grow
In Flanders fields.

JOHN MCCRAE, 3 MAY 1915.

'In Flanders Fields', one of the most poignant – and earliest – poems of the First World War was begun by Canadian doctor Major John McCrae, of the 1st Brigade Canadian Field Artillery, on the evening of 2 May 1915 and completed on 3 May. McCrae's lyrical reflection on transient life followed the death and funeral of his friend Alexis Helmer earlier that day, during the Second Battle of Ypres. The poem was sent to *Punch* magazine and published in December 1915, and it has been regularly used in Remembrance Day services ever since the end of the war. McCrae himself died in France (of pneumonia) in January 1918.

ALSO ON THIS DAY

1916 Patrick Pearse, a leader of the Easter Rising, is executed in Dublin.
1937 *Gone With the Wind* wins the Pulitzer Prize for Fiction.
1951 George VI opens the Festival of Britain.

4 MAY

MASS-MARKET NEWSPAPERS HIT BRITAIN, 1896

The 'note' of the Daily Mail is not so much economy of price as conciseness and compactness. It is essentially the busy man's paper. The mere halfpenny saved each day is of no consequence to most of us.

...Our type is set by machinery, and we can produce many thousands of papers per hour cut, folded and if necessary with the pages pasted together. It is the use of these new inventions on a scale unprecedented in any English newspaper office that enables the *Daily Mail* to effect a saving of from 30 to 50 per cent and be sold for half the price of its contemporaries. That is the whole explanation of what otherwise appears a mystery.

INAUGURAL ISSUE OF THE DAILY MAIL, 4 MAY 1896.

The 30-year-old Alfred Harmsworth revolutionized the staid late-Victorian British newspaper industry by launching the American-style *Daily Mail* on 4 May 1896. It sold at half the price of its rivals, thanks to new technology and a new concept of short, snappy writing – plus the innovation of serials, which had readers coming back for more. Its first issue had gone through 65 dummy-runs before publication, including an experiment with a large front-page cartoon, though in the event the first issue's front page carried nothing but advertisements: in that respect at least, it was in line with other newspapers. Expected to sell 100,000 copies, the first day's issue of 'the Busy Man's Daily Newspaper' sold almost four times that number, and a message of goodwill was received from the Grand Old Man, the octogenarian former Prime Minister W.E. Gladstone.

The *Daily Mail* became the most popular paper in the world a few years later when circulation rose to over a million during the Second Anglo-Boer War, as Harmsworth's uncomplicated patriotism struck a chord with readers.

ALSO ON THIS DAY

1471 Wars of the Roses: Edward IV defeats a Lancastrian army at the Battle of Tewkesbury.
1927 The US Academy of Motion Picture Arts and Sciences is founded.
1970 US National Guardsmen shoot dead four Kent State University anti-war protesters.

5 MAY

THE CENTENARY OF NAPOLEON'S DEATH, 1921

Sire, sleep in peace; from the tomb itself you labour continually for France. At every danger to the country, our flags quiver at the passage of the Eagle. If our legions have returned victorious through the triumphal arch which you built, it is because the sword of Austerlitz marked out their direction, showing how to unite and lead the army that won the victory. Your masterly lessons, your determined labours, remain indefeasible examples. In studying them and meditating on them the art of war grows daily greater. It is only in the reverently and thoughtfully gathered rays of your immortal glory that generations of the distant future shall succeed in grasping the science of combat and the management of armies for the sacred cause of the defence of the country.

MARSHAL FERDINAND FOCH, ORATION, 5 MAY 1921.

∞

In a ceremony in Les Invalides in Paris, Ferdinand Foch – Marshal of France and the supreme Allied commander at the end of the First World War – eulogized Napoleon on the anniversary of the latter's death in 1821. He made special reference to the 1805 Battle of Austerlitz, the emperor's greatest military success, over a combined Russo-Austrian enemy. Keen to present the more recent defence of France against German attack as a triumph, despite the loss of a million men, Foch invoked the spirit of his remarkable predecessor, whose career he had studied in depth.

Although Napoleon had died – possibly of stomach cancer, but possibly poisoned by one of his entourage – and been buried in exile on the remote island of St Helena, the British authorities had agreed to the return of his body to France in 1840. There it was installed in Les Invalides, in great splendour, a symbol of the military glories of the past.

6 MAY

THE INCINERATION OF THE *HINDENBURG*, 1937

It's practically standing still now. They've dropped ropes out of the nose of the ship, and it's been taken a hold of down on the field by a number of men. It's starting to rain again; the rain had slacked up a little bit. The back motors of the ship are just holding it, just enough to keep it from... It's burst into flames! Get out of the way! Get out of the way! Get this, Charlie! Get this, Charlie! It's fire and it's crashing! It's crashing terrible! Oh, my! Get out of the way, please! It's burning, bursting into flames and is falling on the mooring mast, and all the folks agree that this is terrible. This is the worst of the worst catastrophes in the world! Oh, it's crashing... oh, four or five hundred feet into the sky, and it's a terrific crash, ladies and gentlemen. There's smoke, and there's flames, now, and the frame is crashing to the ground, not quite to the mooring mast... Oh, the humanity, and all the passengers screaming around here!

HERB MORRISON, WLS RADIO REPORT, 1937.

∞

In May 1937 the *Hindenburg* was the world's largest and newest airship, manufactured by the German company Zeppelin. On 6 May it was about to complete its maiden transatlantic journey with 97 people on board when the hydrogen-filled dirigible exploded, 500 feet up, while attempting to dock at Lakehurst, New Jersey. The event was watched, aghast, by film crews, reporters and celebrities, and most memorably described by Chicago WLS reporter Herb Morrison, whose account – bursting with the immediacy of the event – was broadcast the next morning.

Of those on board the *Hindenburg*, 35 died. The cause of the disaster has never been fully determined, but it put paid to this form of passenger transport. Airship development continued, however, for military, scientific and sightseeing purposes – though generally using the rather safer helium gas and hot-air methods for their lift.

ALSO ON THIS DAY

1881 Militant nationalists carry out the Phoenix Park murders in Dublin.
1915 The baseball legend Babe Ruth hits his first Major League home run.
1954 The British athlete Roger Bannister runs a mile in under four minutes.

7 MAY

A BLOOMSBURY VIEW OF THE GENERAL STRIKE, 1926

No change... The only news that the archbishops are conferring, & ask our prayers that they may be guided right. Whether this means action, we know not. We know nothing. Mrs Cartwright walked from Hampstead. She & L. [Leonard Woolf] got heated arguing, she being anti-labour; because she does not see why they should be supported, & observes men in the street loafing instead of working... Leonard went to the office, I to the Brit[ish] Mus[eum]... I came home & found L. & Hubert [Henderson] arriving from the office – Hubert did what is now called 'taking a cup of tea', which means an hour & a halfs talk about the strike. Here is his prediction: if it is not settled, or in process, on Monday, it will last 5 weeks. Today no wages are paid. Leonard said he minded this more than the war & Hubert told us how he had travelled in Germany, & what brutes they were in 1912. He thinks gas & electricity will go next; had been at a journalists meeting where all were against labour (against the general strike that is) & assumed government victory. L. says if the state wins & smashes T[rades] U[nion]s he will devote his life to labour: if the archbishop succeeds, he will be baptised. Now to dine at the Commercio to meet Clive [Bell].

VIRGINIA WOOLF, DIARY, 7 MAY 1926.

Despite her own upper-middle-class background, the novelist Virginia Woolf (1882–1941) and her husband Leonard supported the strikers during Britain's General Strike of 1926, called by the Trades Union Congress (TUC) in response to the mine-owners' plan to reduce wages. The strike began on 3 May 1926 and, despite fears of revolution, it proved generally peaceable. The action ended after ten days, with the TUC backing down, though the miners' union remained out for several months.

The Woolfs were at the heart of the literary and artistic Bloomsbury Group, which included Virginia's brother-in-law, the art critic Clive Bell.

ALSO ON THIS DAY

1915 The SS *Lusitania* is sunk by German torpedoes.
1945 WWII: Germany signs its unconditional surrender.
1954 The French are defeated at Dien Bien Phu in Indochina.

8 MAY

'VICTORY IN EUROPE' DAY, 1945

It was like no other day that anyone can remember. It had a flavor of its own, an extemporaneousness which gave it something of the quality of a vast, happy village fete as people wandered about, sat, sang, and slept against a summer background of trees, grass, flowers, and water... The bells had begun to peal and, after the night's storm, London was having that perfect, hot, English summer's day which, one sometimes feels, is to be found only in the imaginations of the lyric poets.

By lunchtime, in the [Piccadilly] Circus, the buses had to slow to a crawl in order to get through the tightly packed, laughing people. A lad in the black beret of the Tank Corps was the first to climb the little pyramidal Angkor Wat of scaffolding and sandbags which was erected early in the war to protect the pedestal of the Eros statue after the figure had been removed to safekeeping. The boy shinnied up to the top and took a tiptoe Eros pose, aiming an imaginary bow, while the crowd roared. He was followed by a paratrooper in a maroon beret, who, after getting up to the top, reached down and hauled up a blond young woman in a very tight pair of green slacks. When she got to the top, the Tank Corps soldier promptly grabbed her in his arms and, encouraged by ecstatic cheers from the whole Circus, seemed about to enact the classic role of Eros right on the top of the monument. Nothing came of it, because a moment later a couple of G.I.s joined them and before long the pyramid was covered with boys and girls. They sat jammed together in an affectionate mass, swinging their legs over the sides, wearing each other's uniform caps, and calling down wisecracks to the crowd. 'My God,' someone said, 'think of a flying bomb coming down on this!' When a firecracker went off, a hawker with a tray of tin brooches of Monty's head happily yelled that comforting, sometimes fallacious phrase of the Blitz nights, 'All right, mates, it's one of ours!'

It was without any doubt Churchill's day. Thousands of King George's subjects wedged themselves in front of the Palace throughout the day, chanting ceaselessly 'We want the king' and cheering themselves hoarse when he and the queen and their daughters appeared, but when the crowd saw Churchill there was a deep, full-throated, almost reverent roar. He was at the head of a procession of Members of Parliament, walking back to the House of Commons from the traditional St Margaret's Thanksgiving Service. Instantly, he was surrounded by people – people running, standing on tiptoe, holding up babies so that they could be told later they had seen him, and shouting affectionately the absurd little nurserymaid name, 'Winnie, Winnie!' One of two happily sozzled, very old, and incredibly

160

dirty cockneys who had been engaged in a slow, shuffling dance, like a couple of Shakespearean clowns, bellowed, 'That's 'im, that's 'is little old lovely bald 'ead!'

...American sailors and laughing girls formed a conga line down the middle of Piccadilly and cockneys linked arms in the Lambeth Walk. It was a day and night of no fixed plan and no organized merriment. Each group danced its own dance, sang its own song, and went its own way as the spirit moved it. The most tolerant, self-effacing people in London on V-E Day were the police, who simply stood by, smiling benignly, while soldiers swung by one arm from lamp standards and laughing groups tore down hoardings to build the evening's bonfires... The young service men and women who swung arm in arm down the middle of every street, singing and swarming over the few cars rash enough to come out, were simply happy with an immense holiday happiness. They were the liberated people who, like their counterparts in every celebrating capital that night, were young enough to outlive the past and to look forward to an unspoilt future. Their gaiety was very moving.

Mollie Panter-Downes, The New Yorker, 19 May 1945.

The vast, spontaneous party in London on 8 May 1945 that greeted the end of the war in Europe was described by Mollie Panter-Downes in her fortnightly 'Letter from London' column, which was published in the *New Yorker* magazine from 1939 to the 1980s. Her descriptions of the war years had done much to alert Americans to the grim realities of life under the Blitz and rationing.

On that day, Prime Minister Winston Churchill reminded the House of Commons that Japan remained 'unsubdued', but later he was brought onto the balcony of Buckingham Palace – a rare honour for a civilian – to absorb the cheers of the jubilant crowds.

ALSO ON THIS DAY

1450 Cade's rebellion breaks out in Kent, England.
1794 The French chemist Antoine Lavoisier is executed.
1970 The Beatles' last-released album *Let It Be* appears.

9 MAY

AN ATTEMPT ON THE CROWN JEWELS, 1671

The doctor [Thomas Blood] told [Mr Edwards, keeper of the regalia] that he had some friends at his house who wanted to see the regalia. Accordingly two of them came, accompanied by the doctor, about eight in the morning. They had no other apparatus but a wallet and a wooden mallet.

The old man had no sooner opened the door than the doctor silenced him, by knocking him down with the mallet. They made flat the bows of the crown to make it more portable, seized the sceptre and dove, put them into the wallet, and were preparing to make their escape when the old man's son returned from sea at the very instant and met Blood and his companions as they were coming out, who hurried away with the crown and globe. The warder at the drawbridge put himself in a posture to stop their progress. Blood discharged a pistol at the warder, who fell to the ground through fear. They got safe to the little ward-house gate, where one Still, who had been a soldier under Oliver Cromwell, stood sentinel. He made no resistance against Blood and his associates, who got through the outer gate upon the wharf.

At this place they were overtaken by Captain Beckman. Blood discharged a pistol at Beckman's head; but the shot missed him, and he seized Blood. Blood struggled to preserve his prize; and when it was wrested from him he said: 'It was a gallant attempt, how unsuccessful so-ever; for it was for a crown!'

NEWGATE CALENDAR, 1770.

∞

The Irish-born con-man, adventurer and spy Thomas Blood (c.1617–80) almost succeeded in his attempt to seize the English Crown Jewels from the Tower of London in 1671. Instead of being harshly punished, he was summoned to the presence of King Charles II, who pardoned him and gave him estates in Ireland. The reasons for this were never explained, but Blood had some powerful supporters; and, although he was a strong Protestant Nonconformist and suspicious of Charles's regime, he may well also have acted as a government informant.

The *Newgate Calendar* – its title deriving from London's notorious Newgate Prison – was a popular collection of 'true' crime stories, published between 1770 and the 1820s.

ALSO ON THIS DAY

1874 The birth of the English archaeologist Howard Carter.
1887 Buffalo Bill Cody's Wild West Show opens in London.
1974 Impeachment hearings begin against US President Richard Nixon.

10 MAY

THE OUTBREAK OF THE INDIAN MUTINY, 1857

The Sirkar [British authorities] sent parties of men from each regiment to different garrisons for instruction in the use of the new rifle. These men performed the new drill for some time until a report got about, by some means or other, that the cartridges used for these new rifles were greased with the fat of cows and pigs. The men from our regiment wrote to others in the regiment telling them of this, and there was soon excitement in every regiment. Some men pointed out that in forty years' service nothing had ever been done by the Sirkar to insult their religion, but the sepoys' minds had been inflamed by the seizure of [the Principality of Oudh]. Interested parties were quick to point out that the great aim of the English was to turn us all into Christians and they had therefore introduced the cartridge in order to bring this about, since both Mahommedans [Muslims] and Hindus would be defiled by using it.

SITA RAM, INDIAN ARMY SEPOY, OFFICIAL MEMOIR, 1857.

∞

Sita Ram, who remained loyal to the British throughout the events of the so-called Indian Mutiny (also referred to as the Rebellion, or Uprising, or War of Independence) in 1857–8, was one of the few Indian soldiers to write his account of the events. Prompted by insensitivity to native culture, and following the rapacious annexation of the wealthy principality of Oudh by the British East India Company, 'sepoys' – rank-and-file soldiers – stationed at Meerut rebelled on 10 May 1857; they believed that the bullets they were required to use insulted the religion of both Hindus and Muslims.

The revolt spread quickly across the north, and the British found themselves besieged in Kanpoor and Lucknow; nevertheless, by the following summer the conflict had been put down, often harshly. The British government now resolved to take direct responsibility for the running of the subcontinent from the East India Company, a transfer of authority that prompted Prime Minister Disraeli to push through legislation conferring on Queen Victoria the title of Empress of India in 1877.

ALSO ON THIS DAY

1869 In the USA, the First Transcontinental Railroad is completed.
1924 J. Edgar Hoover begins his tenure at the FBI.
1941 WWII: the leading Nazi Rudolf Hess lands in Scotland by parachute.

11 MAY

THE ASSASSINATION OF A PRIME MINISTER, 1812

The prisoner [John Bellingham] repeated 'I admit the fact; but wish, with permission, to state something in my justification. I have been denied redress of my grievances by the government; I have been ill-treated. They all know who I am and what I am through the Secretary of State and Mr Becker with whom I have had frequent communication. I was accused most wrongfully by a Governor-General in Russia, in a letter from Archangel to Riga, and have sought redress in vain. I am a most unfortunate man, and feel here' (placing his hand on his breast) 'sufficient justification for what I have done.' He did not talk at all incoherently, except on the subject of the assassination: respecting that deed, he said that he expected to be brought before a tribunal where ample justice would be done to him; and that he expected to be liberated and ultimately to have his claims satisfied.

THE TIMES, 13 MAY 1812.

∞

Spencer Perceval (1762–1812) possesses the dubious honour of being the only British prime minister to have been assassinated. The religious-minded and conservative lawyer was shot at close range on 11 May 1812, at the entrance of the House of Commons. His assailant was John Bellingham, a merchant who had been imprisoned in Russia for debt and who had unsuccessfully sought compensation from the government for his suffering. Perceval died moments after the shooting.

After a brief stay at Newgate Prison, Bellingham's trial commenced on 15 May. The accused claimed that Perceval, who had been prime minister since 1809, mainly at the head of a weak Tory government, had trampled on his liberties and that he (Bellingham) had acted as a warning for future politicians. In the febrile political atmosphere that existed at the time, dominated by the struggle to contain post-revolutionary Napoleonic France, Bellingham's actions appeared to symbolize a threat to public order rather than what they really were – an extreme response to a private grievance. He was condemned and hanged on 18 May.

ALSO ON THIS DAY

1502 Christopher Columbus's final voyage to the Caribbean departs.
1971 Britain's first tabloid newspaper, the *Daily Sketch*, closes.
1998 The first euro coins are minted, in France.

164

12 MAY

MacARTHUR ADDRESSES WEST POINT CADETS, 1962

'Duty', 'Honour', 'Country' – those three hallowed words reverently dictate what you ought to be, what you can be, what you will be. They are your rallying points to build courage when courage seems to fail, to regain faith when there seems to be little cause for faith, to create hope when hope becomes forlorn...

These are some of the things they do. They build your basic character. They mould you for your future roles as the custodians of the nation's defence. They make you strong enough to know when you are weak, and brave enough to face yourself when you are afraid.

They teach you to be proud and unbending in honest failure, but humble and gentle in success; not to substitute words for action; not to seek the path of comfort, but to face the stress and spur of difficulty and challenge; to learn to stand up in the storm, but to have compassion on those who fall; to master yourself before you seek to master others; to have a heart that is clean, a goal that is high; to learn to laugh, yet never forget how to weep; to reach into the future, yet never neglect the past; to be serious, yet never take yourself too seriously; to be modest so that you will remember the simplicity of true greatness; the open mind of true wisdom, the meekness of true strength.

They give you a temperate will, a quality of imagination, a vigour of the emotions, a freshness of the deep springs of life, a temperamental predominance of courage over timidity, an appetite for adventure over love of ease. They create in your heart the sense of wonder, the unfailing hope of what next, and the joy and inspiration of life. They teach you in this way to be an officer and a gentleman.

DOUGLAS MACARTHUR, ADDRESS, US MILITARY ACADEMY
AT WEST POINT, NEW YORK, 12 MAY 1962.

∞

In 1962 the 82-year-old soldier Douglas MacArthur could look back on an extraordinary career: supreme commander of Allied forces in the Pacific in the Second World War, postwar governor of Japan, and head of the United Nations forces in the Korean War – until disagreements with the president prompted his dismissal. On 12 May he exhorted US Army cadets for the last time. (*See also* 20 March.)

ALSO ON THIS DAY

1700 The death of the English poet and dramatist John Dryden.
1932 The aviator Charles Lindbergh's kidnapped son is found dead.
1949 The Soviet blockade of (West) Berlin ends.

13 MAY

WINSTON CHURCHILL TAKES CHARGE, 1940

On Friday evening last I received His Majesty's commission to form a new administration. It was the evident wish and will of Parliament and the nation that this should be conceived on the broadest possible basis and that it should include all parties, both those who supported the late government and also the parties of the Opposition. I have completed the most important part of this task. A War Cabinet has been formed of five Members, representing, with the Opposition Liberals, the unity of the nation. The three party leaders have agreed to serve, either in the War Cabinet or in high executive office. The three fighting services have been filled. It was necessary that this should be done in one single day, on account of the extreme urgency and rigour of events. A number of other positions, key positions, were filled yesterday, and I am submitting a further list to His Majesty to-night. I hope to complete the appointment of the principal ministers during to-morrow…

I considered it in the public interest to suggest that the House should be summoned to meet today. Mr Speaker agreed, and took the necessary steps, in accordance with the powers conferred upon him by the Resolution of the House …I now invite the House, by the motion which stands in my name, to record its approval of the steps taken and to declare its confidence in the new government.

To form an administration of this scale and complexity is a serious undertaking in itself, but it must be remembered that we are in the preliminary stage of one of the greatest battles in history, that we are in action at many other points in Norway and in Holland, that we have to be prepared in the Mediterranean, that the air battle is continuous and that many preparations, such as have been indicated by my Hon. Friend below the gangway, have to be made here at home. In this crisis I hope I may be pardoned if I do not address the House at any length today. I hope that any of my friends and colleagues, or former colleagues, who are affected by the political reconstruction, will make allowance, all allowance, for any lack of ceremony with which it has been necessary to act. I would say to the House, as I said to those who have joined this government: 'I have nothing to offer but blood, toil, tears and sweat.'

We have before us an ordeal of the most grievous kind. We have before us many, many long months of struggle and of suffering. You ask, what is our policy? I can say: It is to wage war, by sea, land and air, with all our might and with all the strength that God can give us; to wage war against a monstrous tyranny, never surpassed in the dark, lamentable catalogue of human crime. That is our policy.

You ask, what is our aim? I can answer in one word: It is victory, victory at all costs, victory in spite of all terror, victory, however long and hard the road may be; for without victory, there is no survival. Let that be realized; no survival for the British Empire, no survival for all that the British Empire has stood for, no survival for the urge and impulse of the ages, that mankind will move forward towards its goal. But I take up my task with buoyancy and hope. I feel sure that our cause will not be suffered to fail among men. At this time I feel entitled to claim the aid of all, and I say: 'Come then, let us go forward together with our united strength.'

WINSTON CHURCHILL, SPEECH, HOUSE OF COMMONS, 1940.

∞

Winston Churchill, First Lord of the Admiralty, was appointed Britain's prime minister in tumultuous circumstances on 10 May 1940, in the wake of Neville Chamberlain's resignation. British forces were reeling in the face of an (ultimately successful) German invasion of Norway, and Hitler's *Blitzkrieg* onslaught on Belgium and the Netherlands was now under way. The so-called 'Phoney War' of unnatural calm, in which neither side provoked the other too much, had ended.

The new prime minister immediately formed an all-party government. At the first meeting of his new Cabinet on 13 May, he said he offered nothing more than 'blood, toil, sweat and tears', a phrase he may have borrowed from Theodore Roosevelt. He used it again in the Commons the same day. His defiance to the threat posed by Hitler cheered the nation, which was further challenged within weeks by the fall of France and the humiliation of the evacuation of the British Expeditionary Force from Dunkirk (*see* 1 June).

ALSO ON THIS DAY

1373 The mystic Julian of Norwich experiences her religious visions.
1787 The First Fleet leaves England to establish the Australian penal colony.
1981 Mehmet Ali Ağca attempts to assassinate Pope John Paul II in Rome.

14 MAY

THE BIRTH OF THE JAMESTOWN COLONY, 1607

Now falleth every man to work, the council contrive the fort, the rest cut down trees to make place to pitch their tents; some provide clapboard to relade the ships, some make gardens, some nets, &c. The savages often visited us kindly... Captain Kendall, Newport, Smith, and twenty others, were sent to discover the head of the river: by divers small habitations they passed, in six days they arrived at a town called Powhatan, consisting of some twelve houses, pleasantly seated on a hill; before it three fertile isles, about it many of their cornfields, the place is very pleasant, and strong by nature, of this place the prince is called Powhatan, and his people Powhatans, to this place the river is navigable: but higher within a mile, by reason of the rocks and isles, there is not passage for a small boat, this they call the falls, the people in all parts kindly entreated them, till being returned within twenty miles of Jamestown, they gave just cause of jealousy, but had God not blessed the discoverers otherwise than those at the fort, there had then been an end of that plantation; for at the fort, where they arrived the next day, they found 17 men hurt, and a boy slain by the savages, and had it not chanced a cross bar shot from the ships struck down a bough from a tree amongst them, that caused them to retire, our men had all been slain, being securely all at work, and their arms in dry fats.

CAPTAIN JOHN SMITH, *THE GENERAL HISTORIE OF VIRGINIA*, 1624.

∞

In the 1580s English attempts to found a North American colony at Roanoke in Virginia (though now in North Carolina) failed, leaving a mystery that has lasted to this day: by 1590 the settlement was deserted, the colonists having vanished without trace. But the English colony at Jamestown, Virginia, founded on 14 May 1607, endured. That it did so was due in no small part to the energy and resolution of John Smith, who was responsible for creating good relations with the local Native Americans and whose (somewhat self-serving) account of the colony became a best-seller in Jacobean England.

ALSO ON THIS DAY

1610 Henry IV of France is assassinated by a Catholic fanatic.
1940 WWII: the Netherlands surrenders to Nazi Germany.
1955 The Warsaw Pact alliance of Soviet bloc states is signed into being.

15 MAY

THE GREEK OCCUPATION OF SMYRNA, 1919

The Greek occupation with all its attendant horrors and crimes has fallen also on the vilayet [district] of Smyrna... One of the rare Ottoman provinces on whose soil no fighting had been witnessed for five hundred years, has just been the theatre of a hideous invasion... they have transformed this marvellous country into a vast desert. Nearly 50,000 Turks have perished there in the most frightful torments, whilst 300,000 other fugitives wander about without medicaments, without shelter and without resource all round the zone of Greek occupation...

At Smyrna itself in the great port of the Aegean Sea, under the very eyes of indignant foreigners, no infamy has been spared the Turkish population... Almost the whole Turkish population of Menemen were massacred without any provocation, without any motive which even the existence of disturbances could justify. As to the tragedy of Aidin, it exceeds in horror all that can be imagined.

Nero, in setting fire to Rome, had not condemned the population to be burnt alive in their dwellings. That is however what the Greeks did at Aidin. From Smyrna as far as Nazilli all the towns, villages, hamlets are nothing but a heap of ruins and ashes. Most of them scarcely hide amongst their still smoking wreckage, the carbonised corpses, the bleeding remains of thousands of poor innocent Turks, of women, of children, of old men sacrificed to the ferocity of the Hellenic hordes. From all this devastated region, formerly one of the most prosperous, a cry of frightful distress arises to-day.

TURKISH CONGRESS AT LAUSANNE, *GREEK ATROCITIES IN THE VILAYET OF SMYRNA*, 1919.

∞

Following the end of the First World War, during which the Allies had promised Greece territory in exchange for Greek support against the Ottoman Turks, the Greeks occupied the Turkish town of Smyrna (Izmir), a city with a large Greek population, on 15 May 1919. The atrocities that resulted brought a furious reaction, especially from the nationalist Young Turks led by Mustafa Kemal, who were seeking to oust the Ottoman regime. In September 1922 the Turks retook the city, which was destroyed by fire, leading to an exodus of hundreds of thousands of Greeks from Asia Minor. It was a brutal chapter in the long history of Graeco-Turkish animosity.

ALSO ON THIS DAY

1885 The death of the US poet Emily Dickinson.
1948 Israel's War of Independence – the first Arab–Israeli War – breaks out.
1957 The first British hydrogen bomb test is carried out, over Christmas Island.

16 MAY

THE ANNIHILATION OF THE WARSAW GHETTO, 1943

What a wonderful sight! I called out 'Heil Hitler!' and pressed the button. A terrific explosion brought flames right up to the clouds. The colours were unbelievable. An unforgettable allegory of the triumph over Jewry.

WAFFEN-SS COMMANDER JÜRGEN STROOP, OFFICIAL REPORT, 1943.

∞

We knew perfectly well that we had no chance of winning. We fought simply not to allow the Germans alone to pick the time and place of our deaths. We knew we were going to die. Just like all the others who were sent to Treblinka... Their death was far more heroic. We didn't know when we would take a bullet. They had to deal with certain death, stripped naked in a gas chamber or standing at the edge of a mass grave waiting for a bullet in the back of the head... It was easier to die fighting than in a gas chamber.

JEWISH RESISTANCE LEADER MAREK EDELMAN, *RESISTING THE HOLOCAUST*, 2004.

∞

The Warsaw Ghetto uprising of Jews against the Nazis, which had begun in January 1943 following a new wave of Jewish deportations, was finally brought to an end on 16 May, having cost over 10,000 Jewish lives. The resistance fighters were few in number, poorly armed and received little support from outside; but they were able to resist the Germans for several months despite the German tactics of burning the area block by block. A few Jews, such as Marek Edelman, were able to escape to the forests; most died in the Ghetto.

Jürgen Stroop, who was sent to Warsaw in April to complete the destruction of the ghetto, wrote a detailed report of the action, illustrated with many photographs, several of which have become iconic images of Nazi persecution. He had the remaining 50,000 inhabitants of the Ghetto sent to concentration or extermination camps, and had the Ghetto itself – once Europe's largest – razed to the ground.

Edelmann survived the war, and continued to live in postwar Communist Poland, combining his status as a public figure with his career as a cardiologist. Stroop also survived the war, but was captured by American forces in 1945 and later extradited to Poland, where he was tried and executed in 1951.

ALSO ON THIS DAY

1568 Mary, Queen of Scots, flees Scotland for England.
1975 The first female climber conquers Everest.
1997 President Mobutu of Zaire (Congo) falls from power.

17 MAY

THE RELIEF OF MAFEKING, 1900

Some letters came to us from the Boers on one or two occasions in an unorthodox way, being fired into the town in shells. They were to convey news of their friends to Boer families we had in the place. In one instance the gunner who fired the shell said that he only wished he had something to drink our health in. This was so nice of him that I sent him out a bottle of whisky under the white flag. When I was in South Africa again recently a man came to me in De Aar and said that for many years he had wanted to meet me and thank me for an excellent bottle of whisky I had sent him, and this was my friend the gunner.

I received a letter from the Boer Commandant, Sarel Eloff, one day, in which he said that he and his friends proposed coming into Mafeking shortly to play cricket with us. To which I replied: 'My side is in at present and yours is in the field. You must bowl us out before your side can come in.' Not long afterwards he made his effort to do so, but the attempt failed and Commandant Eloff and over a hundred of his officers and men were captured by us. A week after our repulse of Eloff's attack Mafeking was finally relieved, on the 17th May, by Mahon and Plumer's columns in co-operation.

We received then the inspiring telegram sent to me by the Queen: 'I and my whole Empire greatly rejoice at the Relief of Mafeking, after the splendid defence made by you through all these months. I heartily congratulate you and all under you, military and civil, British and Native, for the heroism and devotion you have shown. V.R. and I [Victoria, Queen and Empress].'

ROBERT BADEN-POWELL, *LESSONS FROM THE VARSITY OF LIFE*, 1933.

∞

The British garrison at Mafeking, commanded by Baden-Powell and numbering around 2,000 Europeans and 500 Africans, was besieged and shelled by some 8,000 Boers for seven months in the early stages of the Second Boer War (1899–1902). A final assault on 12 May was driven back, and on 17 May a relief column arrived and the Boers withdrew. The Boer irregulars had provided British imperial might with its most serious challenge in decades, and the relief of Mafeking in May, following the lifting of the siege of Ladysmith in February, led to scenes of wild celebration in London.

ALSO ON THIS DAY

1510 The death of the artist Sandro Botticelli.
1943 The RAF carries out its 'Dambusters' raids on the Ruhr Valley.
1954 The US Supreme Court declares against racially segregated schools.

18 MAY

MASSACRE AT ANTIOCH, 1268

Death came from all sides: we killed all that you had ordered to guard the city or defend its approaches. Had you seen your knights trampled under the feet of the horses, your provinces pillaged, your riches looted, the wives of your subjects sold publicly; if you had seen the pulpits and crosses overturned, the pages of the Gospel torn and cast to the winds, and the tombs of your patriarchs profaned; if you had seen your enemies, the Muslims, trampling on the tabernacle, and murdering monks, priests and deacons in the churches; if you had seen your palaces burned, the dead consumed by fire, the church of St Paul and that of St Peter utterly destroyed, then surely you would have wished you had never been born.

MAMLUK SULTAN BAYBARS, LETTER TO PRINCE BOHEMUND VI OF ANTIOCH, 1268.

∞

Baybars, leader of the Mamluks, an Egyptian-based military caste, dominated the Middle East after defeating the previously invincible Mongols at Ain Jalut in 1260. Having made himself sultan of Egypt, he attacked the Crusader states in Syria. Although he failed to take Acre (now in Israel), he destroyed the garrison in Antioch (now in southern Turkey), whose Prince Bohemund had allied with the Mongols.

Antioch surrendered in return for a promise of safety; but as soon as Baybars was in the city his forces began a massacre: some 15,000 died and many more were taken into slavery. Discovering that Bohemund himself was not present in the city, Baybars wrote him an exultant letter that graphically outlined his victory.

Bohemund, reduced to his stronghold at Tripoli, remained an obsession with Baybars, who attacked in 1271, having written to him: 'Our yellow flags have repelled your red flags, and the sound of the bells has been replaced by the call: "Allah Akbar!" ...Warn your walls and your churches that soon our siege machinery will deal with them, your knights that soon our swords will invite themselves in their homes.' Bohemund was saved by the arrival in Acre of the Ninth Crusade.

ALSO ON THIS DAY

1756 The Seven Years' War breaks out.
1804 Napoleon is proclaimed emperor of France.
1911 The death of the Austrian composer Gustav Mahler.

19 MAY

THE EXECUTION OF ANNE BOLEYN, 1536

At eight of the clock in the morning, Anne Boleyn, Queen, was brought to execution on the green in the Tower of London by the great White Tower, the Lord Chancellor of England, the Duke of Richmond, Duke of Suffolk, with more of the king's council, as earls, lords and nobles of this realm being present at the same; also the Mayor of London, with the aldermen and sheriffs and certain of the best crafts of London being there present also. On a scaffold made there for the said execution, Queen Anne said thus: 'Masters, I here humbly submit me to the law as the law has judged me, and as for mine offences, I here accuse no man, God knoweth them; I remit them to God beseeching him to have mercy on my soul and I beseech Jesu, save my sovereign and master the king, the most godly, noble and gentle prince that is, and long to reign over you'; which words were spoken with a goodly smiling countenance; and this done she kneeled down to her knees and said: 'To Jesus Christ I commend my soul'; and suddenly the hangman smote off her head at a stroke with a sword.

WRIOTHESLEY'S CHRONICLE, MID-16TH CENTURY.

∞

In 1536 Anne Boleyn – Queen Consort of Henry VIII and mother of the future Queen Elizabeth I – had been tried and convicted of committing adultery with a musician, Mark Smeaton, and a groom, Henry Norris, and of committing incest with her brother George, Viscount Rochford; in due course other names were added to the list of supposed adulterous liaisons. Anne was tried and found guilty on 15 May, at a trial presided over by her uncle Thomas Howard, Earl of Norfolk; her alleged lovers were executed two days later. Her marriage was annulled and on 19 May she was executed – with a special sword and executioner that Henry had brought over from Calais. This was a merciful intervention by the king, as the queen's adultery was considered traitorous, and burning was the usual penalty for female traitors.

Thus ended the marriage that had been a catalyst for the king's break with the Church of Rome. Henry became betrothed to Jane Seymour (*see* 24 October) the following morning, who had been introduced into Anne's household as a lady-in-waiting. Anne Boleyn's body was put in an unmarked grave.

Charles Wriothesley's contemporary chronicle covered events from 1485 to 1559.

ALSO ON THIS DAY

1898 The death of the British statesman W.E. Gladstone.
1935 T.E. Lawrence 'of Arabia' is killed in a motorcycle crash.
1980 The volcano Mount St Helens erupts in Washington state.

20 MAY

THE SHOOTING OF GEORGE ORWELL, 1937

I had been about ten days at the front when it happened. The whole experience of being hit by a bullet is very interesting and I think it is worth describing in detail.

It was at the corner of the parapet, at five o'clock in the morning. This is always a dangerous time because we had the dawn at our back, and if you stuck your head above the parapet it was clearly outlined against the sky. I was talking to the sentries preparatory to changing the guards. Suddenly, in the very middle of saying something, I felt – it is very hard to describe what I felt, though I remember it with the utmost vividness.

Roughly speaking it was the sensation of being at the centre of an explosion. There seemed to be a loud bang and a blinding flash of light all round me, and I felt a tremendous shock – no pain, only a violent shock, such as you get from an electric terminal; with it a sense of utter weakness, a feeling of being stricken and shrivelled up to nothing. The sandbags in front of me receded into immense distance. I fancy you would feel much the same if you were struck by lightning. I knew immediately that I was hit, but because of the seeming bang and flash I thought it was a rifle nearby that had gone off accidentally and shot me. All this happened in a space of time much less than a second. The next moment my knees crumpled up and I was falling, my head hitting the ground with a violent bang which, to my relief, did not hurt. I had a numb, dazed feeling, a consciousness of being very badly hurt, but no pain in the ordinary sense.

The American sentry I had been talking to had started forward. 'Gosh! Are you hit?' People gathered around. There was the usual fuss – 'Lift him up! Where's he hit? Get his shirt open!' etc. The American called for a knife to cut my shirt open. I knew there was one in my pocket and tried to get it out, but discovered that my right arm was paralysed. Not being in pain, I felt a vague satisfaction. This ought to please my wife, I thought; she had always wanted me to be wounded, which would save me from being killed when the great battle came. It was only now that it occurred to me to wonder where I was hit, and how badly; I could feel nothing but I was conscious that the bullet had struck me somewhere in the front of my body. When I tried to speak I found that I had no voice, only a faint squeak, but at the second attempt I managed to ask where I was hit. In the throat, they said…

As soon as I knew that the bullet had gone clean through my neck I took it for granted I was done for… I had never heard of a man or an animal getting a bullet through the middle of the neck and surviving it. The blood was dribbling out of the corner of my mouth. 'The artery's gone,' I thought. I wondered how long you last when your carotid artery is cut; not many minutes, presumably. Everything was very blurry. There must have been about two minutes when I assumed that I was killed. And that too was interesting – I mean it is interesting to know what your thoughts would be at such a time. My first thought, conventionally enough, was for my wife. My second was a violent resentment at having to leave this world which, when all is said and done, suits me so well.

GEORGE ORWELL, *HOMAGE TO CATALONIA*, 1938.

The British journalist George Orwell (1903–50) had gone to Spain in 1936 to fight on behalf of the Republican cause against the Nationalist insurgency launched by General Franco; but he became embroiled in internecine disputes among Republican factions and joined the Trotskyist Partido Obrero de Unificación Marxista (POUM) rather than the International Brigades as he had planned. Fighting the Nationalists at Huesca, in Aragon, he received a bullet wound in the throat. As he was recuperating, the POUM were denounced as Fascist by the Communist Party, and many members were arrested; Orwell and his wife Eileen narrowly escaped and returned to England in June 1937.

In the next decade Orwell's politics became increasingly hostile to the authoritarianism he observed in rigid ideologies, as expressed in the Stalinist satire *Animal Farm* (1945) and the dystopian novel *Nineteen Eighty-Four* (1949).

ALSO ON THIS DAY

1609 Shakespeare's sonnets are published for the first time.
1861 Richmond, Virginia, becomes the capital of the Confederacy.
1932 Amelia Earhart begins her solo transatlantic flight from Newfoundland.

21 MAY

A FLIGHT ACROSS THE ATLANTIC, 1927

The sun went down shortly after passing Cherbourg and soon the beacons along the Paris–London airway became visible. I first saw the lights of Paris a little before 10pm, or 5pm New York time, and a few minutes later I was circling the Eiffel Tower at an altitude of about four thousand feet.

The lights of Le Bourget were plainly visible, but appeared to be very close to Paris. I had understood that the field was farther from the city, so continued out to the northeast into the country for four or five miles to make sure that there was not another field farther out which might be Le Bourget. Then I returned and spiralled down closer to the lights. Presently I could make out long lines of hangars, and the roads appeared to be jammed with cars.

I flew low over the field once, then circled around into the wind and landed. I saw there was danger of killing people with my propeller and I quickly came to a stop.

CHARLES LINDBERGH, WE, 1927.

∞

The aviator Charles Lindbergh (1902–74) took off from Long Island, New York, early in the morning of 20 May 1927 in his monoplane *The Spirit of St Louis* to fly to Europe. He arrived in Le Bourget, Paris, 33½ hours later, to a hero's welcome. A literally overnight celebrity, Lindbergh was the first man to fly solo and non-stop across the Atlantic, and his flight proved a huge boost to the young aviation industry.

Charles Lindbergh's starry status continued for the rest of his life, but the later headlines that attached to him were for darker and more controversial matters. His toddler son was kidnapped, leading to a massive and public investigation; the boy was found tragically murdered in 1932. In the later 1930s Lindbergh gave his support to Hitler, becoming a chief advocate of American isolationism. After the war he became an early proponent of environmentalism, spending much of his time in the Philippines.

ALSO ON THIS DAY

1881 The US Red Cross is founded.
1917 The Commonwealth War Graves Commission is established.
1991 The Indian politician Rajiv Gandhi is assassinated.

22 MAY

THE 'PACT OF STEEL', 1939

The German Reich Chancellor and His Majesty the King of Italy and Albania, Emperor of Ethiopia, consider that the time has come to confirm through a solemn pact the close relation of friendship and affinity which exists between National Socialist Germany and Fascist Italy.

Since a secure bridge for mutual help and assistance has been established through the common boundary between Germany and Italy, fixed for all time, the two governments acknowledge anew the principles and aims of the policy previously agreed upon by them, and which has shown itself successful in furthering the interests of the two countries as well as in ensuring the peace of Europe.

Firmly bound together through the inner unity of their ideologies and the comprehensive solidarity of their interests, the German and the Italian people are determined also in future to stand side by side and to strive with united effort for the securing of their Lebensraum [living space] and the maintenance of peace. In this way, prescribed for them by history, Germany and Italy wish, in a world of unrest and disintegration, to carry out the assignment of making safe the foundations of European culture.

PREAMBLE TO THE ITALO-GERMAN ALLIANCE, 22 MAY 1939.

∞

The 1939 treaty between Nazi Germany and Fascist Italy to 'make safe the foundations of European culture' was signed on 22 May 1939 in Berlin by Joachim von Ribbentrop and Count Ciano, foreign ministers of the two states. Even at the time Ciano thought it might prove disastrous for Italy. The Italian leader Mussolini, *Il Duce*, gave the agreement – which dealt with economic, military and propaganda co-operation between the two countries for ten years – its popular name 'Pact of Steel'.

In September the following year the Tripartite Pact, sometimes called the Axis Pact, was signed by Germany, Italy and Japan; they would become referred to as the Axis Powers during the Second World War.

ALSO ON THIS DAY

1377 Papal bulls are issued against the ideas of the English reformer John Wyclif.
1868 The US 'Great Train Robbery' takes place near Marshfield, Indiana.
1942 WWII: Mexico declares war on Germany and Japan.

23 MAY

THE BURNING OF SAVONAROLA, 1498

On 23 May, 1498, a Wednesday morning, the execution of the three friars [Girolamo Savonarola, Fra Silvestro Maruffi and Fra Domenico da Pescia] took place. They led them from the Palazzo della Signoria and had them walk on a platform that had been placed near the ringhiera [balcony]. The Otto di guardia [Florentine magistrates] and the collegi were there, as well as the papal legate, the general, canons, priests, monks and Bishop Paganotti, who had been entrusted with the task of demoting the friars. The friars were divested of all their paraments while the formulae proper to the ceremony were pronounced. Throughout the procedure, while their heads and hands were being shaved, as is typical of the demotion ceremony, it was claimed by people that Fra Girolamo was being condemned to the stake because he was a heretic and a schismatic.

When the demotion was done, they handed the friars over to the Otto, who ordered that they be hanged and burned. They were taken to the cross at the end of the platform. The first to be hanged from one of the arms of the cross was Fra Silvestro. Since the rope did not choke him, it took a while before he passed away; one could hear him repeating 'O Jesus' while hanging from the cross. The second to be hanged was Fra Domenico, who also continually repeated 'O Jesus'. The third was the friar Girolamo [Savonarola] who had been called a heretic, who did not speak in a loud voice, but softly. None of them addressed the crowd, and this was regarded as surprising, since everyone expected to see signs from God and thought that on such an occasion the friar would somehow reveal the truth. This is what was expected, especially by the righteous people, who were eagerly awaiting God's glory, the beginning of a virtuous life, the renovation of the Church, and the conversion of the infidels. They were disappointed, therefore, that neither Savonarola nor the other two made any sort of speech. As a consequence, many lost their faith.

Once all three had been hanged with their faces turned to the Palazzo della Signoria with Fra Girolamo in the centre, the platform was moved away from the ringhiera, and a fire was prepared under the circular end of the platform. They placed gunpowder under it and then set it aflame. The heap burned amid a great noise of crackling and explosions. Within a few hours their bodies were completely burned, and their arms and legs fell off bit by bit. Since part of their torsos had remained attached to the chains, people threw stones to make them fall down. Being afraid that some might try to take pieces of the corpses, the executioner and those in charge of the ceremony pulled the cross down to the ground and burned it with a great quantity of wood. They set fire to the corpses and saw to it that none of their remains were left. They then sent for some carts to have each speck of dust brought to the Arno. The guards escorted them to Ponte Vecchio, and from there they dumped the ashes into the river, causing every last trace to disappear. Nonetheless, a number of the faithful attempted to gather the coals floating on the water. Those who did so, however, acted in secret and with fear. No one, in fact, could either mention what had happened or speak about it without risking his life, as Savonarola's enemies wanted to extinguish all memory of the friar.

Luca Landucci, diary, 1498.

Luca Landucci was an apothecary who had supported the firebrand preacher Friar Girolamo Savonarola in his mission to institute a 'Christian and religious republic' in Florence after the fall of the Medici regime in 1494. Wielding large influence in the city, Savonarola made homosexuality punishable by death and forbade gambling, and in 1497 carried out a 'bonfire of the vanities' in which artworks, fine clothes, musical instruments and other items decreed to be immoral were publicly burned. He excoriated Church luxury and the corruption of the Borgia Pope Alexander VI, earning first a ban on preaching (which he ignored) and then his excommunication in May 1497.

Eventually, political realignments in Florence empowered the government – the *Signoria* – to take action. Savonarola and his associates were arrested and tortured, before being condemned as heretics and burned before a large audience on 23 May 1498. Before his death, Savonarola recanted his trenchant views, shattering the faith of those who had come to be true believers in him.

ALSO ON THIS DAY

1701 The pirate captain William Kidd is hanged in London.
1707 War of the Spanish Succession: the Duke of Marlborough defeats a French army at Ramillies.
1934 The US outlaws Bonnie Parker and Clyde Barrow are ambushed and killed.

24 MAY

THE CONVERSION OF JOHN WESLEY, 1738

I went very unwillingly to a society in Aldersgate Street, where one was reading Luther's preface to the Epistle to the Romans. About a quarter before nine, while he was describing the change which God works in the heart through faith in Christ, I felt my heart strangely warmed. I felt I did trust in Christ, Christ alone, for salvation; and an assurance was given me that He had taken away my sins, even mine, and saved me from the law of sin and death.

I began to pray with all my might for those who had in a more especial manner despitefully used me and persecuted me. I then testified openly to all there what I now first felt in my heart. But it was not long before the enemy suggested: 'This cannot be faith; for where is thy joy? Then was I taught that peace and victory over sin are essential to faith in the Captain of our salvation; but that, as to the transports of joy that usually attend the beginning of it, especially in those who have mourned deeply, God sometimes giveth, sometimes withholdeth, them according to the counsels of His own will.

After my return home, I was much buffeted with temptations, but I cried out, and they fled away. They returned again and again. I as often lifted up my eyes, and He 'sent me help from his holy place'. And herein I found the difference between this and my former state chiefly consisted. I was striving, yea, fighting with all my might under the law, as well as under grace. But then I was sometimes, if not often, conquered; now, I was always conqueror.

JOHN WESLEY, JOURNAL, 1738.

∞

The English cleric John Wesley (1703–91) discovered a powerful, emotional and charismatic version of Christianity on 24 May 1738 – what became known as Aldersgate Day. He spent the remainder of his life travelling throughout England preaching and promoting his evangelical faith, Methodism, within the Church of England. After Wesley's death in 1795 Methodism became a separate denomination. The social doctrines of Methodism exerted an influence on progressive politics in Britain and became a key ingredient in the identity of working people in some English regions, notably the Southwest.

ALSO ON THIS DAY

1487 Lambert Simnel, a pretender to the English throne, is 'crowned' in Dublin.
1798 The insurrection of the United Irishmen breaks out.
1976 The supersonic airliner *Concorde* begins commercial service.

25 MAY

THE USELESSNESS OF HISTORY, 1916

I don't know whether Napoleon did or did not try to get across there to Britain and I don't care. I don't know much about history, and I wouldn't give a nickel for all the history in the world. It means nothing to me. History is more or less bunk. It's tradition. We don't want tradition. We want to live in the present and the only history that is worth a tinker's damn is the history we make today.

HENRY FORD, *CHICAGO TRIBUNE*, 1916.

∞

The motor manufacturer Henry Ford (1863–1947), who had transformed industrial production with his assembly lines for the 'Model T' in Detroit in 1908, had political views that often set him in conflict with the orthodoxies of his day. As a leading advocate of pacifism during the First World War, he travelled to Norway and Sweden in 1915–16 in an attempt to convene a peace conference, but was not taken seriously and proved unable to attract delegates from the belligerent countries.

He later explained his much-quoted comment on the limitations of conventional history as follows:

History as it is taught in the schools deals largely with wars, major political controversies, territorial extensions and the like. When I went to our American history books to learn how our forefathers harrowed the land, I discovered that the historians knew nothing about harrows [agricultural implements]. Yet our country depended more on harrows than on guns or great speeches. I thought a history which excluded harrows and all the rest of daily life is bunk and I think so yet.

Despite his validation of 'daily life', Ford's populism did not always have a sure touch politically. His anti-Semitism prompted him to publish and disseminate the notorious *Protocols of the Elders of Zion*, a fabricated Jewish plan for world domination: he was forced to apologize for it in 1927. And in 1929 he tried to expand his commercial empire into Stalin's Soviet Union.

ALSO ON THIS DAY

1895 The writer Oscar Wilde is jailed for 'gross indecency'.
1935 The baseball star Babe Ruth makes his last (714th) home run.
1961 US President Kennedy announces his goal of putting a man on the Moon.

26 MAY

THE SECRET PROMISE OF CHARLES II, 1670

The King of England will make a public profession of the Catholic faith, and will receive the sum of two millions of crowns, to aid him in this project, from the Most Christian King [Louis XIV], in the course of the next six months. The date of this declaration is left absolutely to his own pleasure. The King of France will faithfully observe the Treaty of Aix-la-Chapelle, as regards Spain, and the King of England will maintain the Treaty of the Triple Alliance in a similar manner. If new rights to the Spanish monarchy revert to the King of France, the King of England will aid him in maintaining these rights. The two kings will declare war against the [Dutch] United Provinces. The King of France will attack them by land, and will receive the help of 6,000 men from England. The King of England will send 50 men-of-war to sea, and the King of France 30; the combined fleets will be under the Duke of York's command. His Britannic Majesty will be content to receive Walcheren, the mouth of the Scheldt, and the isle of Cadzand, as his share of the conquered provinces. Separate articles will provide for the interests of the Prince of Orange. The Treaty of Commerce, which has already begun, shall be concluded as promptly as possible.

THE ANGLO-FRENCH TREATY OF DOVER, 26 MAY 1670.

∞

The so-called Secret Treaty of Dover (26 May 1670) bound the impecunious King Charles II to the French king Louis XIV, who gave Charles 2 million crowns in exchange for a promise to convert publicly to Catholicism – an act that they both knew would outrage most of Charles's subjects – and for support for Louis's foreign-policy objectives. For Charles, tramelled by obstreperous parliamentarians and Protestant zealots, the treaty was a practical arrangement with the country in which he had lived as an exile, whose culture he admired, and whose king he envied.

In the event, the wily Charles delayed his religious conversion until his deathbed, 15 years later. His less subtle brother, the Duke of York, who succeeded him as James II in 1685, had never hidden his own Catholicism and now actively attempted to foist it on the country. Within three years he was driven from his throne.

ALSO ON THIS DAY

1897 Bram Stoker's *Dracula* is published in hardback.
1908 Major oil reserves are discovered in the Middle East, in Iran.
1940 WWII: British and French forces begin their evacuation from Dunkirk.

27 MAY

'LES ÉVÉNEMENTS' IN PARIS, 1968

Liberté! Egalité! Sexualité!	Liberty! Equality! Sexuality!
L'ennui est contre-révolutionnaire.	Boredom is counter-revolutionary.
Le masochisme aujourd'hui prend la forme du réformisme.	Today masochism takes the form of reformism.
Je suis marxiste tendance Groucho.	I'm a Marxist – Groucho tendency.
Ne changeons pas d'employeurs, changeons l'emploi de la vie.	Don't change bosses, change life.
Travailleurs de tous les pays, amusez-vous.	Workers of the world, enjoy yourselves!
Plus je fais l'amour, plus j'ai envie de faire la révolution. Plus je fais la révolution, plus j'ai envie de faire l'amour.	The more I make love, the more I want to make revolution. The more I make revolution, the more I want to make love.
Soyez réalistes, demandez l'impossible.	Be realistic – demand the impossible.

REVOLUTIONARY SLOGANS POSTED IN PARIS, 1968.

The student-led uprising of May 1968 against the French state and all the norms of bourgeois society involved an uneasy alliance of Maoists, anarchists, surrealists, avant-gardists and others with the trade unions and the Communist Party. Together they almost succeeded in toppling the government of President Charles de Gaulle.

After weeks of frenetic agitation based on the Sorbonne, on 27 May a huge and highly militant demonstration resulted in the flight of de Gaulle two days later. He reappeared after several days, having visited Germany and confirmed he had the backing of the French military and key authorities; he then dissolved the National Assembly. The impetus to revolution died away over the rest of the summer; de Gaulle easily won an election held in June but resigned in 1969 and died in 1970.

ALSO ON THIS DAY

1647 The first known execution for witchcraft takes place in the American colonies.
1703 St Petersburg is founded by Peter the Great of Russia.
1964 The death of India's founding prime minister, Jawaharlal Nehru.

28 MAY

THE DEFEAT OF THE COMMUNARDS, 1871

As I was driving along the Champs-Élysees in a cab, I saw, in the distance, people's legs running towards the great avenue. The whole avenue was filled by a vast crowd between two lines of soldiers. I descended and joined the people running to see what it was. It was the prisoners who had just been captured at the Buttes-Chaumont, walking in groups of five with a few women among them. 'There are six thousand of them,' a soldier in the escort said. 'Five hundred were shot on the spot.' At the head of this haggard multitude an old man in his nineties was walking along on shaky legs.

For all the horror one felt for these men, one felt pity at the sight of this melancholy procession, in the midst of which one could see some soldiers – they were army deserters – who had their tunics on inside out, with their pockets of grey cloth hanging by their sides, and who seemed to be already half-stripped in readiness for the firing-squad.

I ...went to see how much of Paris had been burned by the Federates. The Palais-Royal has been burnt down. The Tuileries need to be rebuilt.

I eventually come to the Hôtel de Ville. It is a magnificent ruin. All pink and ash-green and the colour of white-hot steel... With its... jagged silhouette outlined against the blue sky, it is a picturesque marvel. Amid the complete devastation of the building, on a marble plaque intact in its new gilt frame, there shines the mendacious inscription: 'Liberty, Equality, Fraternity'.

EDMOND DE GONCOURT, *JOURNAL*, 28 MAY 1871.

The renowned journal of Parisian life by Edmond de Goncourt (co-written with his brother Jules until the latter's death in 1870) described the aftermath of the defeat of the Commune, the revolutionary government set up after the shock French defeat in the Franco-Prussian War, which had seen the city besieged. After a week of bloody fighting, during which government troops shot as many as 30,000 'Communards', on 28 May the government commander, Marshal Mac-Mahon, issued a proclamation: 'To the inhabitants of Paris. The French army has come to save you. Paris is freed! At 4 o'clock our soldiers took the last insurgent position. Today the fight is over. Order, work and security will be reborn.'

ALSO ON THIS DAY

1905 The Russian fleet is defeated by the Japanese at the Battle of Tsushima.
1937 President F.D. Roosevelt opens the Golden Gate Bridge, San Francisco.
1982 Falklands War: British victory at the Battle of Goose Green.

29 MAY

THE FINAL FALL OF CONSTANTINOPLE, 1453

When the people heard that the Turks had got into the city, they all abandoned their posts and went rushing towards the harbour in the hope of escaping in the ships and the galleys. At this moment of confusion our omnipotent God came to His most bitter decision and decided to fulfil all the prophecies, and at sunrise the Turks entered the city near San Romano, where the walls had been razed to the ground by their cannon... Anyone they found was put to the scimitar, women and men, old and young, of any conditions. This butchery lasted until midday... The Turks made eagerly for the piazza five miles from the point where they made their entrance at San Romano, and as soon as they reached it some of them climbed a tower where the flags of Saint Mark and the Most Serene Emperor were flying, and they cut down the flag of Saint Mark and took away the flag of the Most Serene Emperor and then they raised the flag of the Sultan... When their flag was raised and ours cut down, we saw that the whole city was taken, and that there was no further hope of recovering.

NICCOLO BARBERO, *DIARY OF THE SIEGE OF CONSTANTINOPLE*, 1453.

The seizure of Constantinople by the Ottoman sultan Mehmet II on 29 May 1453, and the killing there of Emperor Constantine XI, marked the effective end of the Byzantine Empire, the offspring of the Eastern Roman Empire. It was not unexpected, as the Ottoman Turks had been encroaching on Byzantine territory ever since the 13th century and by the 1450s had left Constantinople with almost no hinterland; nor did it change the balance of power in the Mediterranean or Balkans; but it was a symbolic event of huge importance. It saw a new migration of Greek scholars to the West, while it confirmed the Turks as a Mediterranean power of the first importance.

Pope Nicholas V announced a crusade to reclaim Constantinople for Christendom, but to no avail. His own legate to the city had narrowly escaped with his life, after discarding his ecclesiastical robes; on his arrival in Venice he reported that the sultan was 'more powerful than Caesar or Alexander'.

The very last vestige of the once mighty Byzantine Empire, the Black Sea city of Trebizond, fell in 1461.

ALSO ON THIS DAY

1848 Wisconsin becomes the 30th US state.
1953 Mount Everest is climbed for the first time, by Edmund Hillary and Sherpa Tenzing.
1984 The 'Battle of Orgreave' takes place during the UK miners' strike.

30 MAY

A THOUSAND BOMBERS STRIKE COLOGNE, 1942

The Nazis entered this war under the rather childish delusion that they were going to bomb everyone else, and nobody was going to bomb them. At Rotterdam, London, Warsaw, and half a hundred other places, they put their rather naive theory into operation. They sowed the wind, and now they are going to reap the whirlwind.

AIR MARSHAL ARTHUR 'BOMBER' HARRIS, 1942.

∞

The Royal Air Force Bomber Command's Operation Millennium, also known as the first 'thousand bomber raid', on Cologne on the night of 30–31 May 1942, was the first major implementation of the new British policy of area-bombing German cities. It had been determined by the prime minister, Winston Churchill, in April on the recommendation of his scientific adviser Frederick Lindemann, and the intention was to disrupt German industrial capacity by destroying the areas where factory workers lived.

Air Chief Marshal Harris (1892–1984) adopted the policy, which would restore the reputation of Bomber Command after the relative failure of night-bombing campaigns the previous year. The raid comprised 1,047 aircraft, which dropped almost 1,500 tons of bombs, most of them incendiaries rather than high-explosive since the former – as Harris had learned from the London Blitz – produced a more devastating impact. The raid killed fewer than 500 people, as much of the population of the city had been evacuated, but 12,000 buildings were damaged.

Operation Millennium was, though, exceeded in scope and destructiveness by events to come, perhaps most prominently the obliteration of Dresden (and the deaths of around 25,000 of its population) by Anglo-American bombers in February 1945. Harris's unrepentant attitude towards enemy civilian deaths made him a controversial figure for many years after the war. But at the time, the conscience of even the thoughtful George Orwell was clear, broadcasting in 1942 that: 'The people of this country are not revengeful, but they remember what happened to themselves two years ago, and they remember how the Germans talked when they thought themselves safe from retaliation.'

ALSO ON THIS DAY

1431 Joan of Arc is burned at the stake in Rouen, Normandy.
1922 The Lincoln Memorial in Washington, DC is dedicated.
1967 The secession of southeastern Nigeria sparks the Biafran War.

31 MAY

THE SPIRIT OF REFORM, 1823

Good government is known from bad government by this infallible test: that under the former the labouring people are well fed and well clothed, and under the latter, they are badly fed and badly clothed.

WILLIAM COBBETT, *POLITICAL REGISTER*, 31 MAY 1823.

The English reformer William Cobbett (1763–1835) wrote a regular commentary on the state of the country after the end of the Napoleonic Wars, which was published in his own journal the *Political Register*; it quickly proved popular with working people. In the 1820s he began travelling around the English countryside in order to hear 'what gentlemen, farmers, tradesmen, journeymen, labourers, women, girls, boys, and all have to say; reasoning with some, laughing with others, and observing all that passes'; the record of these journeys would be collected in *Rural Rides* (1830).

In these he laid bare the injustices of many people's living and working conditions, especially those of the rural poor, during this early period of the Industrial Revolution. During his career he moved from a strong Toryism, fearful of revolutionary sentiments, to an increasing sympathy for electoral reform and for the right of Roman Catholics to sit as members of parliament – the latter eventually achieved in 1829 – and he warned the government of the dangers of the rural poverty that he observed. These warnings proved justified on the outbreak of the 'Captain Swing' riots across the South of England in the early 1830s.

Cobbett was tried in 1831 on suspicion of fomenting the discontent but acquitted; and after his agitation for electoral reform finally achieved legislative results in the Great Reform Act of 1832, he entered Parliament as member for Oldham.

ALSO ON THIS DAY

1594 The death of the Italian artist Tintoretto.
1902 The Treaty of Vereeniging ends the Second Anglo-Boer War.
1916 WW1: the Anglo-German naval Battle of Jutland is fought in the North Sea.

JUNE

∞

1 JUNE

THE MIRACLE OF DUNKIRK, 1940

The homeward route was a wonderful sight. Hundreds of small craft of every description, making towards Dunquerque. The German bombers were busy dropping their loads all over the place. There were more than seventy enemy planes overhead dropping their bombs all round on us, like hail-stones, but our luck held good. We escaped undamaged. The gunner put in some great work with his gun and hit three enemy planes, two of which came down. I was just coming along Folkestone pier at 8.30 when a violent explosion occurred. Another lucky escape. A mine had gone off behind us. We had brought home 504 troops, 70 of them French.

A SHIPMASTER, QUOTED IN JOHN MASEFIELD, *THE NINE DAYS WONDER*, 1941.

In May 1940 the British Expeditionary Force, supporting France and Belgium against German attack, found itself overwhelmed by the German *Blitzkrieg*. Retreating fast, the BEF was, from 20 May, cut off and surrounded at Dunkirk, pinned against the Channel. In response, an urgent and audaciously improvised evacuation commenced on 26 May.

The German advance had been so rapid that Panzer divisions, having stretched their supply lines, paused, allowing the Allies a vital breathing space. A hasty Allied rearguard action now attempted to protect the Dunkirk enclave, while *matériel* that had to be abandoned was destroyed.

Bombed and strafed by *Luftwaffe* aircraft, many Allied troops were eventually taken off the open beach after waiting in line for hours, up to their shoulders in water. Following a public appeal, a flotilla of privately owned 'little ships', sailing vessels and even pleasure steamers crossed the Channel to assist, despite the constant threat of attack from the air. John Masefield's shipmaster summed up the pride in, and relief at, the rescue efforts on 1 June.

The 'miracle' of the extraction of almost 200,000 British and 140,000 French troops by 3 June turned defeat into a morale-boosting demonstration of British resolve, and on 4 June Prime Minister Winston Churchill announced the completion of the operation, adding: 'We shall defend our island whatever the cost may be. We shall fight on the beaches, we shall fight on the landing grounds, we shall fight in the fields and in the streets, we shall fight in the hills. We shall never surrender.'

ALSO ON THIS DAY

1215 Beijing falls to Genghis Khan.
1533 Anne Boleyn is crowned as Henry VIII's queen.
1792 Kentucky becomes the 15th US state.

2 JUNE

THE POLISH POPE RETURNS HOME, 1979

It is right to understand the history of the nation through man, each human being of this nation. At the same time man cannot be understood apart from this community that is constituted by the nation... It is impossible without Christ to understand the history of the Polish nation – this great thousand-year-old community... It is impossible without Christ to understand this nation with its past so full of splendour and also of terrible difficulties. It is impossible to understand this city, Warsaw, that undertook in 1944 an unequal battle against the aggressor, a battle in which it was abandoned by the Allied powers, a battle in which it was buried under its own ruins – if it is not remembered that under those same ruins there was also the statue of Christ the Saviour with his cross that is in front of the church at Krakowskie Przedmiescie. It is impossible to understand the history of Poland from Stanislaus in Skalka to Maximilian Kolbe at Oswiecim unless we apply to them that same single fundamental criterion that is called Jesus Christ.

...We are before the tomb of the Unknown Soldier. In the ancient and contemporary history of Poland this tomb has a special basis, a special reason for its existence. In how many places in our native land has that soldier fallen! In how many places in Europe and the world has he cried with his death that there can be no just Europe without the independence of Poland marked on its map! On how many battlefields has that soldier given witness to the rights of man, indelibly inscribed in the inviolable rights of the people, by falling for 'our freedom and yours'.

POPE JOHN PAUL II, ADDRESS, 2 JUNE 1979.

∞

At the 1979 mass held in Victory Square, Warsaw, attended by a quarter of a million people, the newly elected Polish pope, John Paul II, spoke of the centrality of Catholicism to Poland's history. Born Karel Wojtyla, he had begun his religious studies in secret during the Nazi occupation. For many Poles, the Church represented the only substantial institutional counterweight to Communist ideology, and so Wojtyla's election as pope in 1978 was loaded with symbolism. Appropriately, John Paul's 1979 visit proved a key moment in the rise of opposition to the regime, inspiring the Solidarity trade union movement that emerged in 1980.

ALSO ON THIS DAY

AD 455 The Vandals sack Rome.
1946 The Italian monarchy is abolished.
1953 Elizabeth II is crowned queen of Great Britain and Northern Ireland.

3 JUNE

THE FIRST CRUSADE CAPTURES ANTIOCH, 1098

A certain Frank, Fulger by name, was the first boldly to ascend the wall; the Count of Flanders, following, sent word to Bohemund and the duke to ascend; and since all hurried, each to go ahead of the other, the ladder was broken. But those who had climbed up went down into the city and opened a certain little postern. Thus our men went in, and they did not take captive any of those whom they found. When the dawn of day appeared, they shouted out. The whole city was disturbed at this shout, and the women and small children began to weep. Those who were in the castle of the count, aroused at this outcry since they were nearer it, began to say to one another: 'Their aid has come!' Others replied: 'That does not sound like the voice of joyful people.' And when the day whitened, our standards appeared on the southern hill of the city. When the disturbed citizens saw our men on the mountain above them, some fled through the gate, others hurled themselves headlong. No one resisted; in truth, the Lord had confounded them. Then after a long time, a joyful spectacle was made for us, in that those who had so long defended Antioch against us were now unable to flee from Antioch. Even if some of them had dared to take flight, yet they could not escape death...

How great were the spoils captured in Antioch it is impossible for us to say, except that you may believe as much as you wish, and then add to it. Moreover, we cannot say how many Turks and Saracens then perished; it is, furthermore, cruel to explain by what diverse and various deaths they died.

RAYMOND D'AGUILERS, *HISTORIA FRANCORUM*.

The First Crusade, which had been called by Pope Urban II in 1095 (*see* 27 November), succeeded in its first objective when Bohemund of Taranto led a successful assault on the Seljuk stronghold of Antioch (in southern Turkey) after a six-month siege. The following year Bohemund took the title of Prince of Antioch. The style of the Christian victory set the tone for future crusader triumphs, with a massacre of the defending garrison, as was the case with Jerusalem the following year. Raymond d'Aguilers travelled to the Holy Land with the army of Raymond IV of Toulouse, and was an eye-witness observer of many of the events of the First Crusade.

ALSO ON THIS DAY

1924 The death of the Czech novelist Franz Kafka.
1937 The Duke of Windsor (the former Edward VIII) marries Wallis Simpson.
1989 The death of the Iranian leader Ayatollah Khomeini.

4 JUNE

DEATH OF DISSENT IN TIANANMEN SQUARE, 1989

The student said that around 2am he was positioned in the Changanjie Avenue of Everlasting Peace, just north of the east end of the Great Hall of the People. The students believed that when troops came in to take the square they would fire rubber bullets. Consequently, many of the students in the first line of barricades held up padded coats to protect themselves from the projectiles. However, the first lines of students fell after the troops opened fire. The student said that he had also been convinced that rubber bullets would be used. He had a sickening feeling when he noticed the bullets striking sparks off the pavement near his feet. He said that he saw many students fall during the ensuing hour. He became enraged at the deaths of his colleagues, he said, and threw bricks at the oncoming troops out of a desire for revenge and a hatred of what the troops were doing, even though he knew there was no match. 'In battle you stop thinking and just fight,' he said.

When resistance was clearly futile, perhaps around 4am, the student said that the leaders announced over the broadcasting system that they would put to a voice vote whether everyone should stay or vacate the square. The student said that the voices shouting 'stay' were actually just as numerous as those who voted 'leave', but the leaders announced the majority decision as 'leave'. The student said that most of those who voted to stay were out-of-towners who had come in for the demonstrations and who really had nowhere else to go. After talking with the troop commanders sent in to clear the square, the student leaders agreed to vacate the square along a southeast corridor from the central monument. Five thousand actually exited via the corridor.

The large group of students that exited the square turned west on Qianmendajie, passing the Kentucky Fried Chicken and the Beijing Duck restaurants. The students were organized, for the most part, by their institutions of study, with Beijing University at the head followed by Qinghua University. As the students rounded the corner gate of Changanjie they shouted at the four to six stationary tanks that the troops were beasts and fascists.

The student said that without warning the tanks started towards them. On the north side of the street, tank number 154 suddenly did a U-turn near the telegraph building entrance where the students and many others had run for refuge.

The student said that only the telegraph building offered a break in the metal fence on both sides of the street so he was fortunate to get into the fully crowded entrance way. Tank number 154 then raced back ('quicker than a public bus normally does') into other oncoming students marching west. The student said that one of his colleagues attempted to leap the south fence but only succeeded in hanging onto the fence. His legs were cut off.

After some sort of gas was thrown from a tank and all the tanks had passed, the student said he walked over from the telegraph building entrance to count the bodies so there would be at least one reliable witness later to the killings. He said that the bodies were squashed flat, 11 in all – just as in a Donald Duck cartoon – except that he noticed the brains squished out beside the flattened heads. A few bicycles in the group were smashed to caricatures of vehicles. The sight would never leave him, he said, and he hoped that by reporting it, someday justice would ultimately be done in avenging those deaths.

TELEGRAM FROM THE AMERICAN EMBASSY, BEIJING,

TO THE STATE DEPARTMENT, 22 JUNE 1989.

∞

In 1989 the eventual hardline response by the Communist authorities and the People's Army to students demonstrating in Beijing for democratic reform was reported worldwide but suppressed in China itself. The protest had begun after the death of an anti-corruption and pro-democracy official Hu Yaobang, on 15 April, when 100,000 people collected in Beijing's Tiananmen Square, demanding free media and dialogue between the authorities and representatives elected by the students themselves. The demonstrations turned into a camp, with a statue of the 'goddess of democracy' erected on 30 May; they were generally orderly and apparently commanded support within Beijing and elsewhere. Perhaps between 2,000 and 3,000 were killed when the demonstrations were broken up – most, as here, in the streets around the Square.

The demonstrations exposed splits and initial indecision among the ruling elite as to how to respond. But with the ruthless resolution that was finally displayed, the Chinese Communist Party demonstrated to the world that it was not about to go the way of Communist regimes in Eastern and Central Europe or follow the political liberalization of the Soviet Union.

ALSO ON THIS DAY

1913 The Suffragette Emily Davison runs in front of the royal horse during the Epsom Derby.
1944 WWII: the liberation of Rome by the US Army begins.
1971 The death of the Hungarian Marxist philosopher György Lukács.

5 JUNE

THE ASSASSINATION OF ROBERT KENNEDY, 1968

Kennedy moved slowly into the area, shaking hands, smiling, heading a platoon of reporters, photographers, staffers, the curious, TV men. I was in front of him, walking backward. I saw him turn to his left and shake the hand of a small Mexican cook. We could still hear the chants of 'We want Bobby!' from the Embassy Room. The cook was smiling and pleased.

Then a pimply messenger arrived from the secret filthy heart of America. He was curly haired, wearing a pale blue sweatshirt and blue jeans, and he was planted with his right foot forward and his right arm straight out and he was firing a gun.

The scene assumed a kind of insane fury, all jump cuts, screams, noise, hurtling bodies, blood. The shots went pap-pap-pap-pap-pap-pap, small sharp noises like a distant firefight or the sound of firecrackers in a backyard. Rosey Grier of the Los Angeles Rams came from nowhere and slammed his great bulk into the gunman, crunching him against a serving table. George Plimpton grabbed the guy's arm, and Rafer Johnson moved to him, right behind Bill Barry, Kennedy's friend and security chief, and they were all making deep animal sounds and still the bullets came.

PETE HAMILL, *THE VILLAGE VOICE*, VOL. XIII, No. 35.

Robert (Bobby) Kennedy (1925–68), the US senator and attorney general, and younger brother of the assassinated President John F. Kennedy, himself succumbed to sudden violence on 5 June 1968. As he walked through the kitchens of the Los Angeles Ambassadors Hotel, late that night, he was shot at close range. Kennedy had just won the Californian primary for the Democratic presidential nomination; he died the next day.

The gunman was a Palestinian called Sirhan Sirhan, whose motives remain uncertain, but conspiracy theories abounded, many drawing on the antipathy Kennedy had earned from vested interests over the years, including the Mafia. Kennedy's death prompted a rethink on protocol, and in future candidates in US presidential elections were to receive Secret Service protection.

Hubert Humphrey went on to win the Democratic nomination, but lost the subsequent presidential election to his Republican opponent Richard Nixon.

ALSO ON THIS DAY

1851 The serial publication of Harriet Beecher Stowe's *Uncle Tom's Cabin* begins.
1862 The Treaty of Saigon cedes the city to France.
1967 The Six-Day War begins in the Middle East.

6 JUNE

THE D-DAY LANDINGS, 1944

People of Western Europe: A landing was made this morning on the coast of France by troops of the Allied Expeditionary Force. This landing is part of the concerted United Nations' plan for the liberation of Europe, made in conjunction with our great Russian allies.

I have this message for all of you. Although the initial assault may not have been made in your own country, the hour of your liberation is approaching.

All patriots, men and women, young and old, have a part to play in the achievement of final victory. To members of resistance movements, I say: 'Follow the instructions you have received.' To patriots who are not members of organized resistance groups, I say: 'Continue your passive resistance, but do not needlessly endanger your lives until I give you the signal to rise and strike the enemy. The day will come when I shall need your united strength.' Until that day, I call on you for the hard task of discipline and restraint.

...This landing is but the opening phase of the campaign in Western Europe. Great battles lie ahead. I call upon all who love freedom to stand with us. Keep your faith staunch – our arms are resolute – together we shall achieve victory.

SUPREME ALLIED COMMANDER DWIGHT D. EISENHOWER, BROADCAST, 6 JUNE 1944.

∞

The Allied landings in Normandy in June 1944 represented the largest amphibious invasion in history; but the operation's supreme commander Eisenhower came close to calling them off because of adverse weather conditions on the days before the planned landing date – 6 June, 'D-Day'. However, the need to maintain the morale of occupied Europe (and the support of Stalin in the Soviet Union, who had been calling for a second front in the West for a year) made further delay unacceptable.

Although some landings experienced terrible carnage, notably the American assault on Omaha Beach, overall the Allies had luck on their side. They achieved the element of surprise – extraordinary given the size of the undertaking – and the initial casualties were far fewer than Churchill, for one, had feared. And they had achieved a vital toehold in France.

ALSO ON THIS DAY

1889 The city of Seattle is destroyed by fire.
1961 The death of the Swiss psychologist Carl Jung.
1982 The Israeli arrmy invades southern Lebanon.

7 JUNE

THE FIELD OF CLOTH OF GOLD, 1520

It having been arranged that the conference between the kings of France and England should take place on the 7th of June, the King of England at the 21st hour quitted Guisnes, accompanied by Cardinal Wolsey, who rode beside him; then came the Papal Nuncio with the Archbishop of Canterbury, the Spanish ambassador with the Duke of Buckingham, and the Venetian ambassador with the Duke of Suffolk. The rest of the lords and gentlemen followed, about 500 in number, all splendidly attired in cloth of gold and silk. The king wore a simar [cope with a shoulder-cape] of silver brocade, joined with silver cords, from the extremities of which hung beautiful pendent jewels, and round his neck he wore a jewelled collar of great price. This band of 500 in part preceded, and in part followed the king in pairs. On the left-hand side of the king was his guard, 500 in number, dressed in doublets of white and green velvet in chequers, with the royal badge of the rose embroidered on their breasts, and with halberts in their hands. They headed a squadron of 4,000 footmen, a force so imposing that it caused some suspicion on the part of the French, who sent officials to inspect the number of the band, and ascertain whether it was armed, who found the men were without arms, according to the articles. The English in their turn made a similar inspection of the French.

At length, both parties, English and French, being assured, marched forward to a hill, at the bottom of which is a pleasant valley, called 'Vallis Aurea'. On this hill the King of England halted, and the whole retinue formed a ring; the like being done by the Most Christian King [of France] on his reaching the opposite hill, which also looked on the valley, in whose hollow a tent had been pitched, covered with cloth of gold, and an awning. The ambassadors having halted on the hill, the King of England caused the sword borne by the Marquis of Dorset to be unsheathed, and His Majesty, with Cardinal Wolsey alone, on horseback descended into the valley, with the Master of the Horse on foot, in a doublet of cloth of gold, and Sir Richard Wingfield, English ambassador to the King of France, from whom he had then arrived, dressed in a simar of brocatel [heavy, raised embroidery], which His Most Christian Majesty had given him. These descended into the valley, and the Most Christian King did the like from the opposite direction, he by himself on horseback, and the Lord High Constable on foot with the drawn sword, the Lord Admiral with the badge and the whistle, and the Master of the Horse on foot.

The kings on arriving in the valley below, and drawing nigh, saluted each other cap in hand, and then embraced very lovingly on horseback; after which, having dismounted, they embraced again, and entered the tent accompanied by Cardinal Wolsey. They remained there in private for half an hour, after which, on coming out, they again embraced each other repeatedly, and having mounted their horses, took loving leave, and with music and great rejoicing each went in his own direction; the Most Christian King to Ardres, and the English King to Guisnes: it being sunset when they got home.

MANTUAN AMBASSADOR SOARDINO, LETTER, 1520.

∞

The diplomatic summit of the 'Most Christian King' Francis I of France and King Henry VIII of England in northern France, in June 1520, produced an epic display of finery on the 'Field of Cloth of Gold'. For Cardinal Wolsey, Henry's principal adviser, it swelled his monarch's status and was something of a diplomatic coup.

The grandeur of the occasion bolstered the self-images that both the young and powerful men liked to propagate, as ambitious and ostentatious Renaissance princes. The events included a royal bout of wrestling (which Francis won), archery, feasting and jousting, and they went on until 24 June. The occasion inspired appropriately lavish descriptions and art to memorialize it.

The meeting took place in the wake of 1518's Treaty of London, promising a tripartite amity between Henry and Francis and the Holy Roman Emperor Charles V. But by the end of 1520, Henry, in alliance with Charles, was at war with France. The everlasting peace habitually declared by Renaissance princes was rarely anything other than temporary.

ALSO ON THIS DAY

1329 The death of Robert the Bruce, King of Scots.
1942 WWII: the Japanese navy is routed in the Battle of Midway.
1975 The Sony Betamax video cassette recorder is launched.

8 JUNE

THE VIKING RAID ON LINDISFARNE, 793

In this year fierce, foreboding omens came over the land of Northumbria. There were excessive whirlwinds, lightning storms, and fiery dragons were seen flying in the sky. These signs were followed by great famine, and on January 8th the ravaging of heathen men destroyed God's church at Lindisfarne.

ANGLO-SAXON CHRONICLE, 793.

∞

It is nearly 350 years that we and our fathers have inhabited this most lovely land, and never before has such terror appeared in Britain as we have now suffered from a pagan race, nor was it thought that such an inroad from the sea could be made. Behold, the church of St Cuthbert spattered with the blood of the priests of God, despoiled of all its ornaments; a place more venerable than all in Britain is given as a prey to pagan peoples.

ALCUIN, LETTER TO ETHELRED, KING OF NORTHUMBRIA, 793.

∞

The calamity of your tribulation saddens me greatly every day, though I am absent; when the pagans desecrated the sanctuaries of God, and poured out the blood of saints around the altar, laid waste the house of our hope, trampled on the bodies of saints in the temple of God, like dung in the street... What assurance is there for the churches of Britain, if St Cuthbert, with so great a number of saints, defends not its own?

ALCUIN, LETTER TO THE BISHOP OF LINDISFARNE, 793.

∞

Alcuin, a Northumbrian scholar working on the Continent at the court of Charlemagne, recorded the shock of the raid in 793 – the first by Viking marauders – on one of the wealthiest monasteries of Anglo-Saxon England and home of the important relics of St Cuthbert, at Lindisfarne. The *Anglo-Saxon Chronicle* used similarly heightened language to portray the raid, describing it as the most notable event of the year – though presumably mistaking January, an unlikely month for crossing the North Sea, for June.

ALSO ON THIS DAY

632 The death of Prophet Muhammad.
1949 George Orwell's *Nineteen Eighty-Four* is published.
1972 Nick Ut takes his celebrated photograph of a napalm-burned child, South Vietnam.

9 JUNE

THE SUICIDE OF NERO, AD 68

His companions urged him to save himself from the indignities that threatened him, but he bade them dig a grave in his presence, proportioned to the size of his own person, and bring water and wood for disposing of his body. As these things were done, he wept and repeated: 'What an artist the world is losing!'

While he hesitated, a letter arrived. Nero snatched it and read that he had been pronounced a public enemy by the senate, and that they were seeking him to punish in the ancient fashion; and he asked what manner of punishment that was. When he learned that the criminal was stripped, fastened by the neck in a fork and then beaten to death with rods, in mortal terror he seized two daggers, and then, after trying the point of each, put them up again, pleading that the fatal hour had not yet come. Eventually horsemen arrived with orders to take him off alive. When he heard them, he drove a dagger into his throat, aided by his private secretary. He was all but dead when a centurion rushed in, and as he placed a cloak to the wound, pretending that he had come to assist him, Nero merely gasped: 'Too late!' and 'This is fidelity!'

SUETONIUS, *THE TWELVE CAESARS*, C.AD 120.

Nero (AD 37–68) became Rome's emperor in AD 54 with the backing of the Praetorian Guard. By the time of his demise, fourteen years later, he was deeply unpopular both with the people of Rome, and with the aristocracy for his heavy taxation. Over those years he was credited with poisoning his half-brother Britannicus, executing his mother Agrippina, and despatching two wives, the second allegedly by kicking her while she was pregnant. He was also viewed by some as responsible for the fire that destroyed over half of Rome in AD 64, despite Nero's campaign to blame Christians.

It may be difficult to disentangle the real Nero from the debauched megalomaniac of early accounts; but certainly mounting challenges to his rule came to a head in AD 68, when the commander of the Praetorian Guard turned against him in favour of Nero's rival Galba. Nero considered moving to the East where his military success against the Parthians meant he remained popular, but instead, faced with possible execution, he chose to face his downfall and death in the traditional Roman manner.

ALSO ON THIS DAY

1672 The birth of the Russian tsar Peter the Great.
1815 The Congress of Vienna ends.
1870 The death of the English novelist Charles Dickens.

10 JUNE

THE DEATH OF ALEXANDER THE GREAT, 323 BC

Alexander was sitting at dinner with his friends and drinking far into the night. He had previously celebrated the customary sacrificial rites in thanks for his success, adding others in obedience to his seers' advice, and had also distributed wine and sacrificial victims among the various units and sections of the army. According to some accounts, when he wished to leave his friends at their drinking and retire to his bedroom, he happened to meet Medius, who at that time was the companion most closely in his confidence, and who asked him to come and continue drinking at his own table, adding that the party would be a merry one.

The royal diaries confirm that he drank with Medius after his first carouse. Then he left the table, bathed, and went to sleep, after which he supped with Medius and again set to drinking, continuing till late at night. Then, once more, he took a bath, ate a little, and went straight to sleep, with the fever already on him.

Next day he was carried out on his bed to perform his daily religious duties, and after the ceremony lay in the men's quarters till dark. He continued to issue orders to his officers, instructing those who were to march by land to be ready to start in three days and those who were going with himself by sea to sail one day later. He was carried on his bed to the river Euphrates, and crossed to the park on the further side, where he took another bath and rested.

Next day he lay in his room, where he chatted to Medius. He lay all night in a fever.

The following morning he issued to Nearchus and the other officers detailed instructions about the voyage, which was due to start in two days' time.

Next day he bathed again, went through regular religious duties, and was afterwards in constant fever: Nonetheless he sent for his staff and gave them further instructions. In the evening, after another bath, his condition was grave, and the following morning he was moved to the building near the swimming-pool.

The day after that he just managed to have himself carried to his place of prayer, and after the ceremony continued, in spite of his weakness, to issue instructions to his staff.

Another day passed. Now very seriously ill, he still refused to neglect his religious duties; he gave orders, however, that his senior officers should wait in the court, and the battalion and company commanders outside his door. Then, his condition already desperate, he was moved back to the palace. He recognized his officers when they entered his room but could no longer speak to them. From that moment until the end he uttered no word. That night and the following day, and for the next twenty-four hours, he remained in a high fever.

The soldiers were eager to see him; some hoped for a sight of him while he was still alive; others wished to see his body, for a report had gone round that he was already dead, and they suspected, I fancy, that his death was being concealed by his guards. But nothing could keep them from a sight of him, and the motive in almost every heart was grief and a sort of helpless bewilderment at the thought of losing their king. Lying speechless as the men filed by, he yet struggled to raise his head, and in his eyes there was a look of recognition for each man as he passed.

ARRIAN OF NICOMEDIA, ANABASIS, C.AD 140.

∞

The extraordinary Macedonian Alexander III, 'the Great', died in Babylon on 10 June 323 BC, while organizing the return journey of his army from India by land and sea. The nature of his final illness remains uncertain: some suspected that his wine was poisoned, and while it is possible he died of natural causes, the most likely scenario may be that he was inadvertently poisoned by herbs he was taking.

On his death, his body was taken to Alexandria, in Egypt, for burial, while his generals began a long war to divide his vast empire, which stretched from Greece and the Balkans in the West to what is now India in the East. Alexander's energetic achievements – conquests, empire-building, the founding of cities – all before the age of 33 gave him a quality of heroic pre-eminence that still endures.

ALSO ON THIS DAY

1692 Bridget Bishop is hanged for witchcraft in Salem, Massachusetts.
1793 French Revolution: the Jacobins install a revolutionary dictatorship.
1977 Apple launches the Apple II computer.

11 JUNE

THE LAST HOURS OF AN ARCTIC EXPLORER, 1847

April 25, 1848 – H.M. ships 'Terror' and 'Erebus' were deserted on the 22d April, 5 leagues N.N.W. of this, having been beset since 12th September 1846. The officers and crews, consisting of 105 souls, under the command of Captain F.R.M. Crozier, landed here in lat. 69 37' 42' N., long 98 41' W. Sir John Franklin died on the 11th June, 1847; and the total loss by deaths in the expedition has been to this date 9 officers and 15 men.

CAPTAINS FRANCIS CROZIER AND JAMES FITZJAMES, NOTE, 1848.

∞

The British explorer John Franklin (1786–1847) had fought at the Battle of Trafalgar in 1805 and later spent a decade governing Van Diemen's Land (modern Tasmania); he had also devoted much energy to the exploration of Canada and its northern seas.

In 1845 Franklin led an expedition in search of the Northwest Passage to the Pacific through Arctic Canada. The entire expedition – consisting of the two ships *Terror* and *Erebus* and 128 men – perished. Under strong pressure from Franklin's wife and public opinion in Britain, several expeditions were sent in search of the men, or at least to find the truth of their fate, and in 1850 some relics were found on Beechy Island. There were also tales from the local Inuits of survivors resorting to cannibalism. These suggestions have been supported by archaeological evidence in recent decades.

Finally, in 1859 Francis McLintock discovered the above note on King William Island, written around the edge of a naval certificate, indicating Franklin's death on 11 June 1847. It also suggested that in the spring of 1848 the remaining men had attempted to walk to safety; but nothing further was known of their fate.

ALSO ON THIS DAY

1509 Henry VIII marries Catherine of Aragon.
1955 Eighty-four die in the Le Mans race-track disaster.
2001 Timothy McVeigh is executed for the Oklahoma City bombing.

12 JUNE

THE BEGINNING OF ANNE FRANK'S DIARY, 1942

I hope I will be able to confide everything to you, as I have never been able to confide in anyone, and I hope you will be a great source of comfort and support.

ANNE FRANK, DIARY, 12 JUNE 1942.

∞

With these words, written in the diary she received on her thirteenth birthday, Anne Frank began to record her life, both the everyday details of school, and the wider impact of the German occupation of the Netherlands on a Jewish family like her own. A few days later she added: 'For someone like me, it is a very strange habit to write in a diary. Not only that I have never written before, but it strikes me that later neither I, nor anyone else, will care for the outpouring of a thirteen-year-old schoolgirl.'

On 6 July 1942, just three weeks after Anne began her diary, her sister Margot had received a call-up from the SS, and the family immediately hid in a secret annex of offices belonging to her father's company. They remained there for the next 25 months and Anne continued to record her experiences, hopes and fears of this cramped, secretive existence. But in August 1944 they were betrayed, and the family was sent to Auschwitz, where Anne's mother died. Anne was not selected for the gas chambers, but was instead sent to Bergen-Belsen; there, in March 1945, she died along with her sister Margot of typhus a few weeks before the camp's liberation.

Her diary, however, was to achieve a new life of its own in the years after the war, and countless readers across the world have come to care very much for the outpouring of a thirteen-year-old schoolgirl. (*See also* 1 August.)

ALSO ON THIS DAY

1776 The Virginia Declaration of Rights is adopted.
1798 British forces defeat a United Irish army at Ballynahinch.
1964 Nelson Mandela is sentenced to life imprisonment in South Africa.

13 JUNE

THE GREAT FALLS OF THE MISSOURI OBSERVED, 1805

I hurried down the hill to gaze on this sublimely grand spectacle... At the cascade the river is about 300 yds wide; about ninety or a hundred yards of this is a smooth even sheet of water falling over a precipice of at least eighty feet, the remaining part of about 200 yards on my right forms the grandest sight I ever beheld... the irregular and somewhat projecting rocks below receive the water in its passage down and break it into a perfect white foam which assumes a thousand forms in a moment sometimes flying up in jets of sparkling foam to the height of fifteen or twenty feet and are scarcely formed before large rolling bodies of the same beaten and foaming water is thrown over and conceals them. In short the rocks seem to be most happily fixed to present a sheet of the whitest beaten froth for 200 yards in length and about 80 feet perpendicular... There is a beautiful rainbow produced which adds not a little to the beauty of this majestically grand scenery. After writing this imperfect description I again viewed the falls and was so much disgusted with the imperfect idea which it conveyed of the scene that I determined to draw my pen across it and begin again... I wished for the pencil of Salvator Rosa or the pen of Thompson, that I might be enabled to give to the enlightened world some just idea of this truly magnificent and sublimely grand object, which has from the commencement of time been concealed from the view of civilized man.

MERIWETHER LEWIS, JOURNAL, 1805.

Meriwether Lewis (1774–1809) and William Clark (1770–1838) undertook an epic transcontinental journey of exploration on the command of President Thomas Jefferson.

The expedition left St Louis and followed the Missouri River northwestwards, continuing until they reached the mouth of the Columbia River on the Pacific coast in November 1805, and returning to St Louis in September 1806. The journals of the expedition recorded a mass of detail on geography, geology, flora and fauna, and on 13 June they encountered what became known as the Great Falls of the Missouri, in present-day Montana.

ALSO ON THIS DAY

1917 WWI: 162 die in a German air raid on London.
1971 Publication of the leaked Pentagon Papers begins in *The New York Times*.
1983 The *Pioneer 10* probe leaves the Solar System.

14 JUNE

A ROYALIST DEFEAT AT NASEBY, 1645

The field was about a mile broad where the battle was fought, and from the outmost flank of the right, to the left wing, took up the whole ground; The bodies lay slain about four miles in length, the most thick on the hill the king's men stood on; I cannot think there was few less than four hundred men slain, and truly I think not many more, and near 300 Horses; We took at least four thousand prisoners on the ground between Naseby and Harborough, near three hundred carriages, whereof twelve of them were ordnance. There was [sic] many of the wagons laden with rich plunder, and others with arms and ammunition.

A 'Gentleman of Northampton', 1645.

The Battle of Naseby, in Northamptonshire, fought on 14 June 1645, delivered a blow to the Royalist cause during the English Civil War from which it was never to recover.

The battle occurred as a result of manoeuvring by King Charles I, who hoped to relieve the Parliamentary siege of his capital Oxford, and who sought to disrupt Parliament's control in the East Midlands by taking Leicester. A few days earlier an optimistic Charles had written 'that since this rebellion my affairs were never in so hopeful a way', and this confidence led him to offer battle despite being heavily outnumbered. After a bad mistake by Prince Rupert, the king's cavalry commander, who allowed his troops to charge off the battlefield in an undisciplined manner at a critical moment, the Royalist army was trapped; more than 1,000 died and 5,000 were taken prisoner.

Charles lost much of his baggage train and artillery, and was unable to raise an army of similar size and quality again. By contrast, the reforms to conditions and tactics embraced by Parliament's New Model Army, under the leadership of Sir Thomas Fairfax and Oliver Cromwell, appeared to have paid off.

ALSO ON THIS DAY

1940 WWII: the first prisoners arrive at Auschwitz concentration camp.
1940 WWII: Paris is occupied by German troops.
1982 The surrender of Argentinian forces ends the Falklands War.

15 JUNE

RICHARD II SUPPRESSES THE PEASANTS' REVOLT, 1381

The king caused a proclamation to be made that all the commons of the country who were still in London should come to Smithfield, to meet him there...

The king bade the Mayor of London to make their chieftain come to him. Wat Tyler of Maidstone came to the king with great confidence, mounted on a little horse. And he dismounted, holding in his hand a dagger. And when he had dismounted he half bent his knee, and then took the king by the hand, and shook his arm forcibly and roughly, saying to him: 'Brother, be of good comfort and joyful, for you shall have, in the fortnight that is to come, praise from the commons even more than you have yet had, and we shall be good companions.' And the king said to Walter, 'Why will you not go back to your own country?' But the other answered, with a great oath, that neither he nor his fellows would depart until they had got their charter such as they wished to have it. And he demanded that there should be no more villeins [unfree tenants] in England, and no serfdom or villeinage, but that all men should be free and of one condition. To this the king gave an easy answer, and said that he should have all that he could fairly grant, reserving only for himself the regality of his crown. And he bade him go back to his home, without making further delay.

Presently Wat Tyler, in the presence of the king, sent for a flagon of water to rinse his mouth, and when it was brought he rinsed his mouth in a very rude and disgusting fashion before the king's face. And then he made them bring him a jug of beer, and drank a great draught, and then, in the presence of the king, climbed on his horse again. At this time a certain valet who was among the king's retinue, when he saw him, said aloud that he knew the said Walter for the greatest thief and robber in all Kent. And for these words Wat tried to strike him with his dagger, and would have slain him in the king's presence.

But for his violent behaviour, the Mayor of London, William Walworth, arrested him. Wat stabbed the mayor with his dagger in the stomach in great wrath. But the mayor was wearing armour and took no harm, but drew his cutlass, and gave him a deep cut on the neck, and then a great cut on the head. And during this scuffle one of the king's household drew his sword, and ran Wat two or three times through the body. And when the commons saw him fall, they began to bend their bows and to shoot, wherefore the king himself spurred his horse, and rode out to them, commanding them that they should all come to him to Clerkenwell Fields.

The Mayor had Wat's head set on a pole and borne before him to the king. And when the king saw the head he had it brought near him to abash the commons, and thanked the mayor greatly for what he had done. And when the commons saw that their chieftain, Wat Tyler, was dead in such a manner, they fell to the ground there among the wheat, like beaten men, imploring the king for mercy for their misdeeds. And the king benevolently granted them mercy, and most of them took to flight. But the king ordained two knights to conduct the Kentishmen, through London and over London Bridge, without doing them harm, so that each of them could go to his own home.

Afterwards the king sent out his messengers into divers parts, to capture the malefactors and put them to death. And many were taken and hanged at London, and they set up many gallows around the City of London, and in other cities and boroughs of the south country.

ANONIMALLE CHRONICLE, 1381.

∞

The Peasants' Revolt was a violent uprising in southeastern England precipitated by the recent government attempts to enforce a poll tax, which, in taxing at a flat rate per head, discriminated against the poor. The rebellion began in Essex, but soon mushroomed, as did the nature and number of the rebels' demands as they converged on London.

Led by the Kentishman Wat Tyler and the radical preacher John Ball, the rising convulsed the capital for several days; rebels occupied the Tower of London and destroyed tax records. The fourteen-year-old King Richard II, however, met them at Mile End on 14 June and agreed to their demands, but they proceeded to kill the Archbishop of Canterbury and royal treasurer. After a second meeting the next day, during which Tyler was killed in a confrontation, the peasants dispersed, and none of their demands was ever met. John Ball was hanged, drawn and quartered.

The narrative provided by the 14th-century Anonimalle Chronicle, written in Anglo-Norman French, has a level of detail that suggests an eye-witness account.

ALSO ON THIS DAY

1215 Magna Carta limits the power of the English monarchy.
1919 John Alcock and Arthur Brown complete the first non-stop transatlantic flight.
1996 An IRA bombing destroys part of central Manchester.

16 JUNE

ABRAHAM LINCOLN'S SENATORIAL BID, 1858

'A house divided against itself cannot stand.'* I believe this government cannot endure, permanently, half slave and half free. I do not expect the Union to be dissolved – I do not expect the house to fall – but I do expect it will cease to be divided. It will become all one thing or all the other.

Either the opponents of slavery will arrest the further spread of it, and place it where the public mind shall rest in the belief that it is in the course of ultimate extinction; or its advocates will push it forward, till it shall become alike lawful in all the States, old as well as new – North as well as South.

ABRAHAM LINCOLN, SPEECH, 16 JUNE 1858.

*Gospel of Matthew, 12:25

Although Abraham Lincoln's nomination speech to be a US senator for Illinois became one of the most famous of his career, he failed on this occasion to win the seat. In the speech, he made slavery, and its implications for the future of the Union – as new states were admitted to it – the central issue of his campaign. Slavery also lay at the heart of seven debates he undertook with his Democratic Party rival Stephen A. Douglas.

The intense interest taken in these debates made Lincoln a national figure, and he went on to win easily the Republican Party nomination for the presidency in 1860. It proved to be an election in which the issues of slavery and states' rights would again dominate discussion, such that Lincoln's eventual victory alarmed his opponents enough to accelerate the secession of the slave-owning South and the paroxysm of civil war.

ALSO ON THIS DAY

1904 The single day celebrated in the events of James Joyce's *Ulysses*.
1963 Valentina Tereshkova becomes the first woman space traveller.
1976 In South Africa, the Soweto uprising begins.

17 JUNE

FRANCIS DRAKE CLAIMS NOVA ALBION, 1579

Our general travelled up into the country, where we found herds of deer by a thousand. We found the whole country to be a warren of a strange kind of coneys; their bodies in bigness as be the Barbary coneys, their heads as the heads of ours, the feet of a want [mole], and the tail of a rat, being of great length. Under her chin is on either side a bag, into the which she gathereth her meat, when she hath filled her belly abroad. The people eat their bodies, and make great account of their skins, for their king's coat was made of them. Our general called this country Nova Albion, and that for two causes; the one in respect of the white banks and cliffs, which lie towards the sea, and the other, because it might have some affinity with our country. There is no part of earth here, wherein there is not some probable show of gold or silver.

Our general set up a monument of our being there, as also of Her Majesty's right and title to the same; namely a plate, nailed upon a fair great post, whereupon was engraved Her Majesty's name, the day and year of our arrival there, with the free giving up of the province and people into Her Majesty's hands, together with Her Highness' picture and arms, in a piece of six pence of current English money, under the plate, whereunder was also written the name of our General.

FRANCIS PRETTY, *SIR FRANCIS DRAKE'S FAMOUS VOYAGE ROUND THE WORLD*, 1580.

The English explorer Francis Drake's voyage around the world (1577–80) was recorded by crew-member Francis Pretty, who described the visit to Nova Albion in June 1579 in detail. The precise location of Nova Albion has long been disputed – either northern California or perhaps as far north as Oregon. A plaque purporting to be that described by Petty, and inscribed with the date 17 June 1579, was found north of San Francisco in 1936, but in 2003 it was shown to be a fake. Nevertheless, present-day California boasts a 'Drake's Bay', several miles northwest of San Francisco, which is part of a National Park and popularly held to be the site of the landing.

ALSO ON THIS DAY

1775 American Revolutionary War: the British gain a costly victory at Bunker Hill.
1885 The Statue of Liberty arrives in New York harbour from France.
1940 WWII: RMS *Lancastria* is sunk off St Nazaire, France, with 4,000 lives lost.

18 JUNE

THE BATTLE OF WATERLOO, 1815

About 4 p.m. the enemy's artillery in front of us ceased firing all of a sudden, and we saw large masses of cavalry advance: not a man present who survived could have forgotten in afterlife the awful grandeur of that charge. You discovered at a distance what appeared to be an overwhelming, long moving line, which, ever advancing, glittered like a stormy wave of the sea when it catches the sunlight. On they came until they got near enough, whilst the very earth seemed to vibrate beneath the thundering tramp of the mounted host. One might suppose that nothing could have resisted the shock of this terrible moving mass. They were the famous cuirassiers, almost all old soldiers, who had distinguished themselves on most of the battlefields of Europe. In an almost incredibly short period they were within twenty yards of us, shouting 'Vive l'Empereur!' The word of command, 'Prepare to receive cavalry', had been given, every man in the front ranks knelt, and a wall bristling with steel, held together by steady hands, presented itself to the infuriated cuirassiers.

CAPTAIN J.H. GRONOW, *REMINISCENCES AND RECOLLECTIONS*, 1862–6.

∞

21-year-old Captain J.H. Gronow of the Foot Guards described one moment in the day-long Battle of Waterloo, near Brussels. The eventual British and Prussian victory on 18 June 1815 finally ended Napoleon's resurgence – the so-called 'Hundred Days' since he escaped from his island exile in Elba in March 1815 and reimposed himself on France, to threaten Europe once more. However, as the famously unflappable Duke of Wellington, commanding the Allied forces, pointed out to his friend Thomas Creevey, 'It has been a damned serious business... Blücher and I have lost 30,000 men. It has been a damned nice thing – the nearest run thing you ever saw in your life... By God! I don't think it would have been done if I had not been there.' His victory resulted from the arrival of the Prussian Field Marshal von Blücher's forces; though exhausted from defeat by Napoleon just two days earlier at Ligny, and by a difficult march thereafter, the Prussians' assistance late in the day proved decisive.

With Waterloo, Napoleon was definitively thwarted (*see* 15 July).

ALSO ON THIS DAY

1812 The USA declares war against Britain.
1940 WWII: Winston Churchill delivers his 'Finest Hour' speech.
1940 WWII: broadcasting from London, General de Gaulle exhorts
the French people to resist German occupation.

19 JUNE

THE CREATION OF THE
METROPOLITAN POLICE, 1829

1. To prevent crime and disorder, as an alternative to their repression by military force and severity of legal punishment.

2. To recognise always that the power of the police to fulfil their functions and duties is dependent on public approval of their existence, actions and behaviour and on their ability to secure and maintain public respect.

3. To recognise always that to secure and maintain the respect and approval of the public means also the securing of the willing co-operation of the public in the task of securing observance of laws.

4. To recognise always that the extent to which the co-operation of the public can be secured diminishes proportionately the necessity of the use of physical force and compulsion for achieving police objectives.

5. To seek and preserve public favour, not by pandering to public opinion; but by constantly demonstrating absolutely impartial service to law...

6. To maintain at all times a relationship with the public that gives reality to the historic tradition that the police are the public and that the public are the police...
SIR RICHARD MAYNE, JOINT COMMISSIONER OF THE METROPOLITAN POLICE, JULY 1829.

The Act of Parliament creating the Metropolitan Police, the first modern police force in England, became law on 19 June 1829. The new force of 3,000 men replaced the multiplicity of local and amateur constabularies that had previously been responsible for law and order. It was the brainchild of Home Secretary Sir Robert Peel; he proposed – and the first commissioners enunciated in their 'General Instructions to Police' – a number of principles for 'vigorous preventive policing', that now form a canon of 'Peelian principles' influencing police forces worldwide.

ALSO ON THIS DAY

1953 The spies Julius and Ethel Rosenberg are executed in New York state.
1964 The Civil Rights Act is approved by the US Senate.
1970 The Conservatives under Edward Heath win the UK general election.

20 JUNE

QUEEN VICTORIA'S ACCESSION, 1837

I was awoke at 6 o'clock by Mamma, who told me that the Archbishop of Canterbury and Lord Conyngham were here, and wished to see me. I got out of bed and went into my sitting-room (only in my dressing-gown) and alone, and saw them. Lord Conyngham (the Lord Chamberlain) then acquainted me that my poor uncle, the king, was no more, and had expired at 12 minutes past 2 this morning, and consequently that I am queen. Lord Conyngham knelt down and kissed my hand, at the same time delivering to me the official announcement of the poor king's demise... I then went to my room and dressed.

Since it has pleased Providence to place me in this station, I shall do my utmost to fulfil my duty towards my country; I am very young and perhaps in many, though not in all things, inexperienced, but I am sure that very few have more real good-will and more real desire to do what is fit and right than I have.

...At 9 came Lord Melbourne [the prime minister], whom I saw in my room, and of course quite alone, as I shall always do all my ministers. He kissed my hand, and I then acquainted him that it had long been my intention to retain him and the rest of the present ministry at the head of affairs, and that it could not be in better hands than his... He was in full dress. I like him very much and feel confidence in him. He is a very straightforward, honest, clever and good man... At about half-past 11 I went downstairs and held a Council in the red saloon.

QUEEN VICTORIA, DIARY, 1837.

The 18-year-old Princess Victoria came to the throne on the death of her uncle William IV (1765–1837), who died without any legitimate children.

Victoria had been brought up in a sheltered manner by her overbearing widowed mother Princess Victoria of Saxe-Coburg-Saalfeld, whose second marriage was to King William's brother Prince Edward, the Duke of Kent and Strathearn (1767–1820). The young queen's references to being 'alone' hint at the way in which she used her new status to free herself from maternal influence. Indeed, her close association with Lord Melbourne in the early years of her reign drew adverse comment from political rivals.

ALSO ON THIS DAY

1863 West Virginia becomes the 35th US state.
1944 WWII: the US Fifth Fleet defeats the Japanese in the Battle of the Philippine Sea.
1975 Steven Spielberg's film *Jaws* is released in the USA.

21 JUNE

THE BLACK HOLE OF CALCUTTA, 1756

Figure to yourself, my friend, if possible, the situation of a hundred and forty-six wretches, exhausted by constant fatigue and action, crammed together in a cube of eighteen feet, in a close sultry night, in Bengal, shut up to the eastward and southward (the only quarters from whence air could reach us) by dead walls, and by a wall and door to the north, open only to the westward by two windows, strongly barred with iron, from which we could receive scarce the least circulation of fresh air.

What must ensue, appeared to me in lively and dreadful colours, the instant I cast my eyes round and saw the size and situation of the room.

...About a quarter after six in the morning, the poor remains of 146 souls, being no more than three and twenty, came out of the black hole alive, but in a condition which made it very doubtful whether they would see the morning of the next day. The bodies were dragged out of the hole by the soldiers and thrown promiscuously into the ditch of an unfinished ravelin [an earthwork] which was afterwards filled with earth.

JOHN ZEPHANIAH HOLWELL, *A GENUINE NARRATIVE*, 1758.

∞

This sole eyewitness account, written by an East India Company officer, described the fate of British and Anglo-Indian prisoners held overnight without water and air in cramped conditions in Fort William gaol, Calcutta. Conflict had come about when the East India Company began fortifying the city to protect its interests (chiefly against the French), incurring the hostility of Bengal's ruler, the Nawab Siraj ud-Daula, who seized Calcutta. The reported brutality of the 'Black Hole of Calcutta' quickly entered British imperial myth. However, the accuracy of the account has been questioned, particularly with regard to the number of victims.

Retribution came in 1757 when Robert Clive's victory at the Battle of Plassey put an end to Siraj ud-Daula's rule, and, through means of a puppet ruler, 190 years of British rule on the subcontinent commenced.

ALSO ON THIS DAY

1798 The United Irish rebels are defeated at the Battle of Vinegar Hill.
1945 WWII: Okinawa falls to US forces.
1964 Three civil rights workers are murdered by the Ku Klux Klan in Mississippi.

22 JUNE

THE FRENCH SURRENDER AT COMPIÈGNE, 1940

In the centre is a great granite block. Hitler walks slowly over to it, steps up, and reads the inscription engraved in great high letters on that block. It says:

HERE ON THE ELEVENTH OF NOVEMBER 1918 SUCCUMBED THE CRIMINAL PRIDE OF THE GERMAN EMPIRE... VANQUISHED BY THE FREE PEOPLES WHICH IT TRIED TO ENSLAVE.

Hitler reads it and Göring reads it. They all read it, standing there in the June sun and the silence. I look for the expression on Hitler's face... I have seen that face many times at the great moments of his life. But today! It is afire with scorn, anger, hate, revenge, triumph. He steps off the monument and contrives to make even this gesture a masterpiece of contempt. He glances back at it, contemptuous, angry – angry, you almost feel, because he cannot wipe out the awful, provoking lettering with one sweep of his high Prussian boot... He swiftly snaps his hands on his hips, arches his shoulders, plants his feet wide apart. It is a magnificent gesture of defiance, of burning contempt for this place now and all that it has stood for in the twenty-two years since it witnessed the humbling of the German Empire.

...The French have not yet appeared... Exactly at 3.30 p.m. they alight from a car... Their faces are solemn, drawn. They are the picture of tragic dignity...

At 3.42 p.m., twelve minutes after the French arrive, we see Hitler stand up, salute stiffly, and then stride out of the drawing-room... The German band strikes up the two national anthems, 'Deutschland, Deutschland über Alles' and the Horst Wessel song. The whole ceremony in which Hitler has reached a new pinnacle in his meteoric career and Germany avenged the 1918 defeat is over in a quarter of an hour.

WILLIAM SHIRER, *BERLIN DIARY*, 1941.

∞

The formalities of the French surrender to Germany in June 1940 took place in a replica of the railway carriage at Compiègne where the 1918 armistice had been signed. Under the terms of the 1940 surrender, much of France was occupied, while the rest was subject to the collaborationist Vichy regime headed by Marshal Pétain, the former French military hero.

ALSO ON THIS DAY

1633 The Vatican forces Galileo to retract his heliocentric assertions.
1941 WWII: the German invasion of the Soviet Union begins.
1948 The *Empire Windrush* brings the first West Indian immigrants to Britain.

23 JUNE

THE REINVENTION OF THE OLYMPIC GAMES, 1894

In this year 1894 and this city of Paris, we were able to bring together the representatives of international athletics, who voted unanimously for the restoration of a two-thousand-year-old idea which still quickens the human heart. And in the evening electricity transmitted the news that Hellenic Olympism had re-entered the world.

The Greek heritage is so vast that all those who have conceived physical exercise under one of its multiple aspects have been able to refer to Greece. Some have seen it as training for the defence of one's country, others as the search for physical beauty and health through a happy balance of mind and body, and yet others as that healthy drunkenness of the blood which is nowhere so intense and so exquisite as in bodily exercise.

At Olympia, there was all that, and something more which no-one has dared to put into words, because since the middle ages a sort of discredit has hovered over bodily qualities and they have been isolated from qualities of the mind. Recently the first have been admitted to serve the second but they are still treated as slaves and made every day to feel their dependence and inferiority. This was an error whose consequences are almost impossible to calculate. There are not two parts to a man – body and soul – but three, body, mind and character; character is formed not by the mind, but primarily by the body. The men of antiquity knew this, and we are painfully relearning it. The adherents of the old school groaned when they saw us: they realized we were rebels and that we would finish by casting down the edifice of their worm-eaten philosophy.

Pierre de Coubertin, speaking at the Sorbonne, 1894.

∞

The French aristocratic Baron de Coubertin (1863–1937) was interested in the renewal of the classical traditions of education, and his fascination with Ancient Greece led him to revive the Olympic Games, which had flourished among the Greek states between the 8th century BC and the 4th century AD. Founding the International Olympic Committee in 1893, de Coubertin organized the first manifestation of the modern Olympic Games – appropriately in Athens – in 1896.

ALSO ON THIS DAY

1757 The British East India Company defeats Bengali and French forces at Plassey.
1812 Napoleon embarks on his invasion of Russia.
1985 A bomb on an Air India plane kills 329 people over the Atlantic.

24 JUNE

THE BATTLE OF BANNOCKBURN, 1314

The Scots resolved to fight, and at sunrise marched out of the wood in three divisions of infantry. They directed their course boldly upon the English army, which had been under arms all night, with their horses bitted. The English mounted in great alarm, for they were not accustomed to fight on foot; whereas the Scots had taken a lesson from the Flemings, who had at Courtrai defeated on foot the power of France. The aforesaid Scots came in line of schiltrons [pike formations] and attacked the English columns, which were jammed together so their horses impaled on the pikes. The troops in the English rear fell back upon the ditch of Bannockburn, tumbling one over the other.

The English squadrons being thrown into confusion by the thrust of pikes upon the horses began to flee. Those attending upon the king [Edward II] led him by the rein off the field towards the castle. As the Scottish knights, who were on foot, laid hold of the housing of the king's charger to stop him, he struck out so vigorously with a mace that there was none whom he touched that he did not fell to the ground.

As those who had the king's rein were drawing him forward, one, Giles de Argentin, said: 'Sire, your rein was committed to me; you are now in safety; there is your castle where your person may be safe. I am not accustomed to fly, nor am I going to begin now. I commend you to God!' Setting spurs to his horse, he returned to the fray, where he was slain.

SIR THOMAS GRAY, *SCALACRONICA*, 1362.

Thomas Gray's account of the disastrous defeat of the English army led by Edward II at the hands of the much smaller force of the Scots king Robert (the) Bruce came from his book about the achievements of his father, also called Thomas Gray.

The armies met south of the English stronghold of Stirling, which the Scots were besieging – having already taken Edinburgh – and the battle lasted two days. The English dominance over Scottish affairs gained under Edward I was now reversed. In 1320 the pope accepted the Scottish Declaration of Arbroath, which not only reconciled Robert Bruce (ruled 1306–29) to Rome but also asserted Scottish independence.

ALSO ON THIS DAY

1497 John Cabot lands in Newfoundland.
1509 Henry VIII is crowned king of England.
1901 Pablo Picasso exhibits his work in Paris for the first time.

25 JUNE

CUSTER'S LAST STAND, 1876

Sioux thought the soldiers on the hill would charge them in rear, but when they did not the Sioux thought the soldiers on the hill were out of cartridges... All the Sioux watched around the hill on which were the soldiers until a Sioux man came and said many walking soldiers [infantry] were coming near. The coming of the walking soldiers was the saving of the soldiers on the hill. Sioux cannot fight the walking soldiers, being afraid of them, so the Sioux hurriedly left.

The soldiers charged the Sioux camp about noon. The soldiers were divided, one party charging right into the camp. After driving these soldiers across the river, the Sioux charged the different soldiers [Custer's battalion] below, and drive them in confusion; these soldiers became foolish, many throwing away their guns and raising their hands, saying, 'Sioux, pity us; take us prisoners.' The Sioux did not take a single soldier prisoner, but killed all of them; none were left alive for even a few minutes. These different soldiers discharged their guns but little. I took a gun and two belts off two dead soldiers; out of one belt two cartridges were gone, out of the other five.

The Sioux took the guns and cartridges off the dead soldiers and went to the hill on which the soldiers were, surrounded and fought them with the guns and cartridges of the dead soldiers. Had the soldiers not divided I think they would have killed many Sioux. The different soldiers [Custer's battalion] that the Sioux killed made five brave stands. Once the Sioux charged right in the midst of the different soldiers and scattered them all, fighting among the soldiers hand to hand.

LAKOTA CHIEF RED HORSE, RECORDED IN PICTOGRAPHS AND TEXT, 1881.

∞

The Battle of the Little Bighorn took place on 25–6 June 1876 in eastern Montana, during that portion of the Indian Wars known as the (Great) Sioux War. Confederated Native Americans of the Lakota, the northern Cheyenne and the Arapaho fought the US Seventh Cavalry, led by Lieutenant-Colonel George Custer. The result was a major defeat for the US Cavalry: more than half the entire force was killed, and all of those fighting in Custer's sector were annihilated, including the commander. But in 1877 the war ended with the Native American tribes, inevitably, surrendering to the government.

ALSO ON THIS DAY

1788 Virginia becomes the 10th US state.
1950 The Korean War begins.
2009 The death of the singer Michael Jackson.

26 JUNE

KENNEDY'S DEFIANCE IN BERLIN, 1963

Two thousand years ago the proudest boast was 'civis Romanus sum'. Today, in the world of freedom, the proudest boast is 'Ich bin ein Berliner'.

There are many people in the world who really don't understand, or say they don't, what is the great issue between the free world and the Communist world. Let them come to Berlin. There are some who say that Communism is the wave of the future. Let them come to Berlin. And there are some who say in Europe and elsewhere we can work with the Communists. Let them come to Berlin. And there are even a few who say that it is true that Communism is an evil system, but it permits us to make economic progress. Lass' sie nach Berlin kommen. Let them come to Berlin.

Freedom is indivisible, and when one man is enslaved, all are not free. When all are free, then we can look forward to that day when this city will be joined as one and this country and this great continent of Europe in a peaceful and hopeful globe. When that day finally comes, as it will, the people of West Berlin can take sober satisfaction in the fact that they were in the front lines for almost two decades.

All free men, wherever they may live, are citizens of Berlin, and, therefore, as a free man, I take pride in the words 'Ich bin ein Berliner'.

US PRESIDENT JOHN F. KENNEDY, SPEECH, 26 JUNE 1963.

US President Kennedy's defiant speech of solidarity, to a large crowd outside the Berlin Rathaus on 26 June 1963, came eight months after the Cuban Missile Crisis had nearly tipped the world into outright US–Soviet war. Kennedy sought to challenge the partition of the city brought about by the Soviet/East German construction of the Berlin Wall in 1961. That physical manifestation of Churchill's 'iron curtain' (*see* 5 March) reinforced the idea of Berlin as the frontline of the global Cold War.

Kennedy's phrase was later mocked by those who claimed that 'ein Berliner' more commonly meant a doughnut than an inhabitant of the city, and that he should have dropped the indefinite article 'ein' to be technically correct. Any ambiguity did not notably detract from the speech's rhetorical force at the time.

ALSO ON THIS DAY

AD 363 The death of the Roman emperor Julian the Apostate.
1917 WWI: the first US troops arrive in France.
1945 Fifty countries sign the United Nations Charter.

27 JUNE

THE SOLO CIRCUMNAVIGATION OF THE WORLD, 1898

Sailing on, she had one more danger to pass – Newport harbour was mined. The *Spray* hugged the rocks along where neither friend nor foe could come if drawing much water, and where she would not disturb the guard-ship in the channel... At last she reached port in safety, and there at 1 a.m. on June 27, 1898, cast anchor, after the cruise of more than forty-six thousand miles round the world, during an absence of three years and two months, with two days over for coming up.

Was the crew well? Was I not? I had profited in many ways by the voyage. I had even gained flesh, and actually weighed a pound more than when I sailed from Boston. As for aging, why, the dial of my life was turned back till my friends all said, 'Slocum is young again.' And so I was, at least ten years younger than the day I felled the first tree for the construction of the *Spray*.

...The *Spray* was not quite satisfied till I sailed her around to her birthplace, Fairhaven, Massachusetts, farther along... So on July 3, with a fair wind, she waltzed beautifully round the coast and up the Acushnet River to Fairhaven, where I secured her to the cedar spile [post] driven in the bank to hold her when she was launched. I could bring her no nearer home.

JOSHUA SLOCUM, *SAILING ALONE AROUND THE WORLD*, 1900.

On 27 June 1898 Massachusetts sailor Joshua Slocum (1844–1909) arrived in Newport, Rhode Island, after three years at sea in his 37-foot sloop *Spray*. His final hazard was underwater mines, laid to protect Newport harbour as a consequence of the current war between the United States and Spain (*see* 15 February). Slocum's original plan to sail eastwards through the Mediterranean changed after an encounter with Moroccan pirates, and thus he completed his solo circumnavigation of the globe by sailing westwards, around South America into the Pacific. His journey aroused great interest in the press, and two years later his book was a worldwide best-seller. Slocum, and the *Spray*, disappeared at sea in November 1909.

ALSO ON THIS DAY

1941 WWII: the beginning of the Iași pogrom, Romania, in which 13,000 Jews are murdered.
1977 Djibouti gains its independence from France.
2007 Gordon Brown succeeds Tony Blair as British prime minister.

28 JUNE

ASSASSINATION IN SARAJEVO, 1914

A tiny clipping from a newspaper, mailed without comment from a secret band of terrorists in Zagreb, capital of Croatia, to their comrades in Belgrade, was the torch which set the world afire with war in 1914. That bit of paper wrecked old, proud empires. It gave birth to new, free nations.

I was one of the members of the terrorist band in Belgrade which received it.

The clipping declared that Austrian Archduke Franz Ferdinand would visit Sarajevo, the capital of Bosnia, 28 June, to direct army manoeuvres in the neighbouring mountains.

...To understand how great a sensation that little piece of paper caused among us, and how greatly it inflamed our hearts, it is necessary to explain just why the Narodna Odbrana [Black Hand] existed, the kind of men that were in it, and the significance of that date, 28 June.

...How dared Franz Ferdinand, not only the representative of the oppressor but in his own person an arrogant tyrant, enter Sarajevo on that day? Such an entry was a studied insult. 28 June is a date engraved deeply in the heart of every Serb... It is the day on which the old Serbian kingdom was conquered by the Turks at the battle of Amselfelde [the Battle of Kosovo] in 1389. That was no day for Franz Ferdinand, the new oppressor, to venture to the very doors of Serbia for a display of the force of arms which kept us beneath his heel. Our decision was taken almost immediately. Death to the tyrant!

When Franz Ferdinand and his retinue drove from the station they were allowed to pass the first two conspirators. The motor cars were driving too fast to make an attempt feasible and in the crowd were many Serbians; throwing a grenade would have killed many innocent people.

When the car passed Gabrinovic, the compositor, he threw his grenade. It hit the side of the car, but Franz Ferdinand with presence of mind threw himself back and was uninjured. Several officers riding in his attendance were injured.

The cars sped to the Town Hall and the rest of the conspirators did not interfere with them. After the reception in the Town Hall General Potiorek, the Austrian Commander, pleaded with Franz Ferdinand to leave the city, as it was seething with rebellion. The archduke was persuaded to drive the shortest way out of the city and to go quickly.

The road to the manoeuvres was shaped like the letter V, making a sharp turn at the bridge over the River Milgacka. Franz Ferdinand's car could go fast enough until it reached this spot but here it was forced to slow down for the turn. Here Princip had taken his stand.

As the car came abreast he stepped forward from the kerb, drew his automatic pistol from his coat and fired two shots. The first struck the wife of the Archduke, the Archduchess Sofia, in the abdomen. She was an expectant mother. She died instantly.

The second bullet struck the Archduke close to the heart. He uttered only one word, 'Sofia' – a call to his stricken wife. Then his head fell back and he collapsed. He died almost instantly.

The officers seized Princip. They beat him over the head with the flat of their swords. They knocked him down, they kicked him, scraped the skin from his neck with the edges of their swords, tortured him, all but killed him. The next day they put chains on Princip's feet, which he wore till his death...

I was placed in the cell next to Princip's, and when Princip was taken out to walk in the prison yard I was taken along as his companion...

BORIJOVE JEVTIC, RECOLLECTIONS, 1914.

The assassination of Franz Ferdinand (1863–1914), Archduke of Austria and heir apparent to the Austro-Hungarian imperial crown, sparked off the events that brought general war across Europe within six weeks. The archduke and his wife were attending manoeuvres in Sarajevo, the capital of Bosnia-Herzegovina, which had been annexed by Austria in 1908. There they were ambushed by members of the Black Hand, an extreme nationalist Serbian group seeking to join Bosnia-Herzegovina with independent Serbia.

Six conspirators were ready to attack; the first attempt failed and the archduke continued to the town hall where he read his speech. After the reception he was to be driven to the station, but the car took a wrong turning. The 19-year-old Gavrilo Princip took the unexpected opportunity presented him and fired the fatal shots. Princip was arrested and, too young to receive the death penalty, was sentenced to twenty years in prison; he died in 1918.

The fragile stability of Europe soon unravelled, as Austria (supported by Germany) issued an ultimatum to Serbia (supported by Russia); when Austria-Hungary invaded Serbia on 28 July 1914, it ensured a rapid descent into war (*see* 4 August).

ALSO ON THIS DAY

1919 The Treaty of Versailles is signed, formally ending the First World War.
1922 The Irish Civil War begins.
1969 The Stonewall Riots in New York give birth to the modern gay rights movement.

29 JUNE

SHAKESPEARE'S THEATRE BURNS DOWN, 1613

I will entertain you at the present with what happened this week at the Banks side. The King's players had a new play called 'All is True', representing some principal pieces of the reign of Henry the Eighth, which set forth with many extraordinary circumstances of pomp and majesty even to the matting of the stage; the knights of the order with their Georges and Garter, the guards with their embroidered coats, and the like: sufficient in truth within awhile to make greatness very familiar, if not ridiculous. Now King Henry making a masque at the Cardinal Wolsey's house, and certain cannons being shot off at his entry, some of the paper or other stuff, wherewith one of them was stopped, did light on the thatch, where being thought at first but idle smoke, and their eyes more attentive to the show, it kindled inwardly, and ran round like a train, consuming within less than an hour the whole house to the very ground. This was the fatal period of that virtuous fabric, wherein yet nothing did perish but wood and straw, and a few forsaken cloaks; only one man had his breeches set on fire, that would perhaps have broiled him, if he had not by the benefit of a provident wit, put it out with a bottle of ale.

HENRY WOTTON, LETTER, 2 JULY 1613.

∞

The open-air Globe Theatre had been built in 1599 on Bankside, the southern side of the Thames in Southwark, which was host to all kinds of entertainments, from theatricals to bear-baiting and bordellos. The theatre was home to the Lord Chamberlain's Men, who were renamed the King's Men in 1603 when James I came to the throne. This was the company in which William Shakespeare was one of eight shareholders and for which he wrote the majority of his plays, many of them premiered at the Globe.

It was a performance of his *Famous History of the Life of King Henry the Eighth* that brought about the building's downfall on 29 June 1613, when ceremonial cannon-fire set the thatch ablaze. Despite the fact the theatre could accommodate 3,000 spectators and had just two doors, there were no serious casualties. The Globe was soon rebuilt; and in 1997 the efforts to revive it by way of a modern reconstruction on a nearby site bore fruit.

ALSO ON THIS DAY

1444 The Albanian leader Skanderbeg wins his first victory against the Ottomans.
1644 English Civil War: Charles I wins the Battle of Cropredy Bridge.
1995 The space shuttle *Atlantis* docks with the space station *Mir*.

30 JUNE

HONG KONG RETURNS TO CHINESE RULE, 1997

For Hong Kong as a whole, today is cause for celebration not sorrow. But here and there, perhaps there will be a touch of personal sadness...

...Of course, Hong Kong's story is not solely that of the century and a half of British responsibility, though it is the conclusion of that chapter that we mark tonight.

This chapter began with events that, from today's vantage point... none of us here would wish or seek to condone. But we might note that most of those who live in Hong Kong now do so because of events in our own century which would today have few defenders. All that is a reminder that sometimes we should remember the past the better to forget it.

What we celebrate this evening is the restless energy, the hard work, the audacity of the men and women who have written Hong Kong's success story. Mostly Chinese men and Chinese women. They were only ordinary in the sense that most of them came here with nothing. They are extraordinary in what they have achieved against the odds.

...I said that tonight's celebration will be tinged for some with sadness. So it will be for my family and myself and for others who like us will soon depart from this shore. I am the 28th governor. The last governor... Now, Hong Kong people are to run Hong Kong. That is the promise. And that is the unshakeable destiny.

GOVERNOR CHRIS PATTEN, SPEECH, 30 JUNE 1997.

Hong Kong – encompassing the Chinese island ceded as a crown colony to Britain for 150 years after the First Opium War in 1842, along with territory on the mainland ceded later – was returned to Chinese rule in 1997. The last governor, Chris Patten, attempted to ensure that a level of political pluralism would survive subsequently within China's one-party state, before tearfully taking his leave in the royal yacht Britannia.

Post-transition, the temptations of Hong Kong's economic might proved the best guarantor of its identity, as the Chinese Communist Party adopted a policy of 'one country, two systems' to account for the paradoxical embrace of Hong Kong's eager free enterprise.

ALSO ON THIS DAY

1859 Blondin, a French acrobat, crosses Niagara Falls on a tightrope.
1905 Albert Einstein's 'Special Theory of Relativity' is published.
1908 The 'Tunguska event': a meteorite causes devastation in Siberia.

JULY

∞

1 JULY

THE FIRST DAY OF THE SOMME OFFENSIVE, 1916

Went over the top at 7.30 a.m. after what seemed an interminable period of terrible apprehension. Our artillery seemed to increase in intensity and the German guns opened up on No Man's Land. The din was deafening, the fumes choking and visibility limited owing to the dust and clouds caused by exploding shells. It was a veritable inferno. I was momentarily expecting to be blown to pieces. My platoon continued to advance in good order without many casualties and until we had reached nearly half-way to the Boche front line. I saw no sign of life there. Suddenly, however, an appalling rifle and machine-gun fire opened against us and my men commenced to fall. I shouted 'down' but those that were still not hit had already taken what cover they could find. I dropped in a shell hole and occasionally attempted to move to my right and left but bullets were forming an impenetrable barrier and exposure of the head meant certain death. None of our men was visible but in all directions came pitiful groans and cries of pain... after what seemed hours of waiting I was almost tempted to take a chance and crawl back in daylight. I finally decided to wait until dusk and about 9.30 I started to crawl flat on my stomach. At times I made short dashes and finally came to our wire... At last the firing ceased and after tearing my clothes and flesh on the wire I reached the parapet and fell over into our trench now full of dead and wounded. I found a few of my men but the majority were still out and most were dead.

LIEUTENANT ALFRED BUNDY, 2ND MIDDLESEX REGIMENT, 1996.

∞

The first day of the Battle of the Somme, 1 July 1916, was the most disastrous in British military history, with almost 60,000 casualties – some 19,500 of them fatalities – sustained in an assault on German lines intended to break the deadlock of trench warfare. A week's worth of bombardment was supposed to have softened up the German lines enough to allow a decisive breakthrough. Instead, months of attritional warfare continued. The experience of Lieutenant Alfred Bundy, north of La Boisselle, was typical of those who survived the day.

The offensive continued until mid-November, when the Allies had advanced a maximum of ten miles. It was a gain, of sorts, but at a cost of over 1 million Allied and German casualties.

ALSO ON THIS DAY

1863 US Civil War: the Battle of Gettysburg begins.
1963 The British government confirms Kim Philby had been a Soviet agent.
2007 Smoking is banned in indoor public spaces in England and Wales.

2 JULY

THE INSPIRATION FOR THE SALVATION ARMY, 1865

When I saw those masses of poor people, so many of them evidently without God or hope in the world, and found that they so readily and eagerly listened to me, following from open-air meeting to tent, and accepting, in many instances, my invitation to kneel at the Saviour's feet there and then, my whole heart went out to them. I walked back to our West-End home and said to my wife:

'O Kate, I have found my destiny! These are the people for whose Salvation I have been longing all these years. As I passed by the doors of the flaming gin-palaces to-night I seemed to hear a voice sounding in my ears, "Where can you go and find such heathen as these, and where is there so great a need for your labours?" And there and then in my soul I offered myself and you and the children up to this great work. Those people shall be our people, and they shall have our God for their God.'

WILLIAM BOOTH, *IN DARKEST ENGLAND, AND THE WAY OUT*, 1890.

∞

Thus the Methodist evangelist William Booth (1829–1912) recorded his inspiration to rescue the poor of the East End of London from depravity, especially those brought low by alcohol. He and his wife set up a Christian mission in London's down-at-heel Whitechapel area in 1865, beginning in a tent set up in a Quaker burial ground. This developed into what he called the 'volunteer army' to save the poor, the criminal and those that were homeless – both spiritually and physically. The organization was renamed the Salvation Army in 1878, with Booth as its first 'General' – it took its nomenclature from more conventional armies.

At first, Booth's activists were perceived as troublesome radicals. But by the end of the century the Salvation Army had become a worldwide movement, and Booth a respected Establishment figure.

ALSO ON THIS DAY

1644 English Civil War: the Royalists are defeated at Marston Moor.
1900 The first Zeppelin flight takes place in Germany.
1961 The US writer Ernest Hemingway commits suicide.

3 JULY

THE CASUALTIES OF GETTYSBURG, 1863

Toward the close of the afternoon... the roar of the battle was subsiding, and... we started back... I fairly shrank back aghast at the awful sight presented. The approaches were crowded with wounded, dying and dead. The air was filled with moanings, and groanings. As we passed on toward the house, we were compelled to pick our steps in order that we might not tread on the prostrate bodies.

...Mrs Weikert went through the house, and... brought all the muslin and linen she could spare. This we tore into bandages and gave them to the surgeons, to bind up the poor soldiers' wounds.

Amputating benches had been placed about the house. Near the basement door... stood one of these benches. I saw them lifting the poor men upon it, then the surgeons sawing and cutting off arms and legs, then again probing and picking bullets from the flesh.

...I saw the surgeons hastily put a cattle horn over the mouths of the wounded ones, after they were placed upon the bench. At first I did not understand the meaning of this but upon inquiry, soon learned that that was their mode of administrating chloroform. But the effects in some instances were not produced; for I saw the wounded throwing themselves wildly about, and shrieking with pain while the operation was going on.

...Just outside of the yard, I noticed a pile of limbs higher than the fence. It was a ghastly sight! Gazing upon these, too often the trophies of the amputating bench, I could have no other feeling, than that the whole scene was one of cruel butchery.

TILLIE ALLEMAN (*NÉE* PIERCE), *AT GETTYSBURG*, 1888.

Tillie Pierce was a 15-year-old girl in July 1863 at the time of the Battle of Gettysburg, in Pennsylvania. Daughter of a local butcher, she witnessed the effects of the bloodiest confrontation of the American Civil War, which produced a combined figure of almost 50,000 casualties. Pierce wrote up her memories 25 years later.

The battle saw the South's invasion of the North arrested, and is considered the turning point in the war. It also memorably occasioned President Lincoln's Gettysburg Address (*see* 19 November).

ALSO ON THIS DAY

1608 Quebec City is founded.
1866 Prussia defeats Austria at the Battle of Königgrätz.
1886 The first motor-car is unveiled by Karl Benz in Mannheim, Germany.

4 JULY

THE AMERICAN
DECLARATION OF INDEPENDENCE, 1776

We hold these truths to be self-evident, that all men are created equal, that they are endowed by their Creator with certain unalienable rights, that among these are life, liberty and the pursuit of happiness. – That to secure these rights, governments are instituted among men, deriving their just powers from the consent of the governed, – That whenever any form of government becomes destructive of these ends, it is the right of the people to alter or to abolish it, and to institute new government, laying its foundation on such principles and organizing its powers in such form, as to them shall seem most likely to effect their safety and happiness... when a long train of abuses and usurpations, pursuing invariably the same object evinces a design to reduce them under absolute despotism, it is their right, it is their duty, to throw off such government, and to provide new guards for their future security. – Such has been the patient sufferance of these colonies; and such is now the necessity which constrains them to alter their former systems of government. The history of the present King of Great Britain is a history of repeated injuries and usurpations, all having in direct object the establishment of an absolute tyranny over these States. To prove this, let facts be submitted to a candid world.

He has refused his assent to laws, the most wholesome and necessary for the public good.

...He has kept among us, in times of peace, standing armies without the consent of our legislatures.

He has affected to render the military independent of and superior to the civil power.

He has combined with others to subject us to a jurisdiction foreign to our constitution, and unacknowledged by our laws; giving his assent to their Acts of pretended legislation:

For quartering large bodies of armed troops among us:

For protecting them, by a mock trial from punishment for any murders which they should commit on the inhabitants of these States:

For cutting off our trade with all parts of the world:

For imposing taxes on us without our consent:

For depriving us in many cases, of the benefit of trial by jury:

For transporting us beyond seas to be tried for pretended offences:

For abolishing the free system of English laws in a neighbouring province, establishing therein an arbitrary government, and

enlarging its boundaries so as to render it at once an example and fit
instrument for introducing the same absolute rule into these colonies:

For taking away our charters, abolishing our most valuable laws and
altering fundamentally the forms of our governments:

For suspending our own legislatures, and declaring themselves invested
with power to legislate for us in all cases whatsoever.

He has abdicated government here, by declaring us out of his protection and waging war against us.

He has plundered our seas, ravaged our coasts, burnt our towns, and destroyed the lives of our people.

He is at this time transporting large armies of foreign mercenaries to compleat the works of death, desolation, and tyranny, already begun with circumstances of cruelty & perfidy scarcely paralleled in the most barbarous ages, and totally unworthy of the head of a civilized nation.

...We, therefore, the Representatives of the United States of America, in General Congress, Assembled, appealing to the Supreme Judge of the world for the rectitude of our intentions, do, in the name, and by authority of the good people of these colonies, solemnly publish and declare, that these United Colonies are, and of right ought to be free and independent states; that they are absolved from all allegiance to the British Crown and that all political connection between them and the State of Great Britain, is and ought to be totally dissolved; and that as free and independent states, they have full power to levy war, conclude peace, contract alliances, establish commerce, and to do all other acts and things which independent states may of right do. And for the support of this declaration, with a firm reliance on the protection of Divine Providence, we mutually pledge to each other our lives, our fortunes and our sacred honour.

AMERICAN DECLARATION OF INDEPENDENCE,
SIGNED BY JOHN HANCOCK AND 55 OTHERS, 1776.

The declaration, drafted primarily by Thomas Jefferson from mid-June 1776, offered justification for opposition to the British crown in terms of the tyranny of King George III. War had broken out a year earlier, and the Continental Congress had voted for independence on 2 July. The declaration was adopted by the Congress two days later, and signed by representatives of the 13 former British colonies in August. The surrender of General Cornwallis in 1781 paved the way for the formal acknowledgement of the United States' independence in the Treaty of Paris of 1783.

ALSO ON THIS DAY

1946 The Philippines become fully independent of the USA.
1976 Passengers are rescued from a hijacked plane at Entebbe Airport, Uganda.
1987 The former Lyon Gestapo chief Klaus Barbie is sentenced to life imprisonment.

5 JULY

THE PUBLICATION OF NEWTON'S *PRINCIPIA*, 1687

Our design, not respecting arts, but philosophy, and our subject, not manual, but natural powers, we consider chiefly those things which relate to gravity, levity, elastic force, the resistance of fluids, and the like forces, whether attractive or impulsive; and therefore we offer this work as mathematical principles of philosophy.

For all the difficulty of philosophy seems to consist in this, from the phenomena of motions to investigate the forces of nature, and then from these forces to demonstrate the other phenomena. And to this end the general propositions in the first and second book are directed.

In the third book we give an example of this in the explication of the system of the world. For by the propositions mathematically demonstrated in the first book, we there derive from the celestial phenomena the forces of gravity with which bodies tend to the sun and the several planets. Then, from these forces, by other propositions which are also mathematical, we deduce the motions of the planets, the comets, the moon, and the sea.

I wish we could derive the rest of the phenomena of Nature by the same kind of reasoning from mechanical principles. For I am induced by many reasons to suspect that they may all depend upon certain forces by which the particles of bodies, by some causes hitherto unknown, are either mutually impelled towards each other, and cohere in regular figures, or are repelled and recede from each other; which forces being unknown, Philosophers have hitherto attempted the search of Nature in vain.

ISAAC NEWTON, *PHILOSOPHIAE NATURALIS PRINCIPIA MATHEMATICA*, PREFACE, 1687.

∞

Isaac Newton's three-volume *Principia*, as it is known, set out the principles of 'classical' mechanics and offered a mathematical explanation of the movement of the planets and other heavenly bodies in terms of his three laws of motion (Book 1), movement in fluids and gases (Book 2) and universal gravitation (Book 3), the last of which generated his celebrated equation for calculating gravitational force, the 'inverse square law'.

Principia, published on 5 July 1687, became the most famous work of science of its day, leading to a new concept of God as the creator of a remarkably ordered universe.

ALSO ON THIS DAY

1295 The 'Auld Alliance' between Scotland and France comes into being.
1809 Napoleon defeats an Austrian army at Wagram, near Vienna.
1948 The National Health Service is founded in the UK.

6 JULY

THE EXECUTION OF SIR THOMAS MORE, 1535

Sir Thomas More having remained a prisoner in the Tower [of London] about a week after his sentence, on the 6th of July early in the morning, his old friend Sir Thomas Pope came to acquaint him that his execution was appointed to be before nine that morning. Whereupon Sir Thomas thanked him heartily for his good news. 'I have been much obliged to His Majesty for the benefits and honours he has most bountifully conferred upon me; yet I am more bound to His Grace for confining me in this place, where I have had convenient place and opportunity to put me in mind of my last end. I am most of all bound to him, that His Majesty is pleased to rid me out of the miseries of this wretched world.'

...When he came to the scaffold, it seemed ready to fall, whereupon he said merrily to the lieutenant, 'Pray, Sir, see me safe up; and as to my coming down, let me shift for myself.' The executioner asked him forgiveness. He kissed him, and said: 'Pick up thy spirits, Man, and be not afraid to do thine office; my neck is very short, take heed therefore thou strike not awry for having thine honesty.' Laying his head upon the block, he bid the executioner stay till he had put his beard aside, for that had committed no treason. Thus he suffered with much cheerfulness; his head was taken off at one blow, and was placed upon London Bridge, where, having continued for some months, and being about to be thrown into the Thames, his daughter Margaret bought it, enclosed it in a leaden box, and kept it for a relic.

EDWARD HALL, *CHRONICLE*, 1542.

The lawyer, diplomat and lord chancellor Thomas More (1478–1535), who wrote the humanist political essay *Utopia*, was executed on 6 July 1535 for his adherence to the authority of the Church of Rome. By refusing to take an oath of succession, by which he would have accepted Henry VIII's divorce from Catherine of Aragon and the king's supreme governorship of the Church, he was charged with treason. Two weeks earlier, the bishop of Rochester, John Fisher, had met the same fate for the same reason. Their fates marked the start of a period of tyranny that brooked no opposition to royal wishes.

ALSO ON THIS DAY

1801 A French fleet is beaten by the Royal Navy at the Battle of Algeciras.
1942 WWII: Anne Frank and her family go into hiding.
1988 The Piper Alpha oil disaster in the North Sea claims 167 lives.

7 JULY

SUICIDE BOMBS IN LONDON, 2005

When the train slammed to a halt and the carriage flooded with thick black smoke, I thought: 'That's it, this is how I'm going to die.' The train's on fire and we're all going to asphyxiate slowly... I'm claustrophobic, and if anyone had asked me to describe hell, this would have been it...

The first five minutes were the worst. After that, it became clear that the smoke wasn't getting any thicker and some air was still circulating. Somewhere, a woman was still screaming hysterically, much to the annoyance of everyone around me. There was a feeling that if anyone lost their nerve, the situation would become impossible. I didn't let myself imagine the screamer was in a carriage full of corpses, as I now realize she probably was.

It was 30 interminable minutes until we were evacuated. As we straggled towards the bright lights of King's Cross I saw the injured for the first time: one young man staggering and soaked in blood, whose staring eyes are still imprinted on my brain; a middle-aged woman with her eye a sticky mess. I realized that I had been one of the lucky ones. I was crazed with shock when I got out of the station. I got through to my mum on the phone. She told me that there had been several incidents across London... I decided to try and get to her office in Old Street...

My mum didn't recognize me, as I was blackened and my eyes were still goggling with shock when I arrived at her office. I then watched events unfold on television. Now it all seems like a bad dream.

ALICE O'KEEFFE, *OBSERVER*, 10 JULY 2005.

∞

The British counterpart to America's 9/11 moment (*see* 11 September) came on 7 July 2005. Fifty-two people died when four British-born Islamist suicide bombers exploded their devices on three London Underground trains and a bus; 700 other people were injured. The justification given, in a pre-recorded video, was British involvement in Iraq and Afghanistan as part of the US-led 'War on Terror'. The subsequent investigations questioned whether better intelligence sharing could have prevented the events; but they also revealed the bravery of the injured and the humanity of those who had come to their assistance.

ALSO ON THIS DAY

1307 The death of England's King Edward I.
1954 Elvis Presley makes his radio debut.
1961 The death of the US novelist William Faulkner.

8 JULY

THE OPENING-UP OF JAPAN, 1853

At about 6:00am we went through a scatter of small islands southwest of Edo Bay. At 9:00 we watched the peaks of Nippon's mountains rise above the fog... We saw beautifully picturesque mountains and rocky slopes plunging to the water's edge.

...When we entered the bay, junks and a conflux of small fishing boats covered the water. At first they avoided us. Then a little fisher craft could not dodge fast enough and passed hard by us. The rest observed that we... ignored it. Emboldened, they paraded by, gaping in curious wonder at the fabulous sea monsters that moved without sails and against the wind besides.

...Presently many boats of appreciable size put out from land toward us. Two rowers worked each of a boat's six or eight oars... The boats carried officials who wanted to board us. After a parley the ranking one gained permission and boarded with his Dutch interpreter... Meanwhile the number of boats had multiplied. They threatened to surround and confine us with boats upon myriad boats. The commodore soon had it made clear to the officials that the boats must leave us alone; he would not suffer such a violation of maritime law. They looked nonplussed. His statement was repeated – in a threatening tone. They sent the boats home, then requested plainly and frankly that none of us go ashore for the time being, as they would have to answer for it. We gave our word. They returned to land in a calmer frame of mind.

WILLIAM HEINE, *WITH PERRY TO JAPAN: A MEMOIR*, 1876.

William Heine was the German-born illustrator who accompanied the American Commodore Matthew Perry's fleet of four steamships, led by USS *Powhatan*, which arrived in Edo (Tokyo) Bay on 8 July 1853. It was the first foreign penetration of mainland Japan – a country closed to outsiders except for one small island at Nagasaki, where Dutch traders were permitted. Perry's so-called 'Black Ships' were on a US government mission to negotiate a trade and maritime agreement, and a treaty followed in 1854 that opened up Japan to commerce with the West; in 1868 these developments led to a new Westernizing regime that rejected Japan's old feudal, isolationist ethos. (*See also* 29 November.)

ALSO ON THIS DAY

1709 Russia defeats Sweden at the Battle of Poltava.
1889 The *Wall Street Journal* is first published.
1932 The Dow Jones index reaches its lowest level of the Great Depression.

9 JULY

NASHVILLE'S 'GREAT TRAIN WRECK', 1918

Because somebody blundered, at least 121 persons were killed and fifty-seven injured... when Nashville, Chattanooga & St. Louis Railway passenger trains No. 1 from Memphis and No. 1 from Nashville crashed head-on together just around the sharp, steep-graded curve at Dutchman's Bend, about five miles from the city near the Harding road.

Both engines reared and fell on either side of the track, unrecognizable masses of twisted iron and steel, while the fearful impact of the blow drove the express car of the north-bound train through the flimsy wooden coaches loaded with human freight, telescoped the smoking car in front and piling high in the air the two cars behind it, both packed to the aisles with negroes en route to the powder plant and some 150 other regular passengers.

Just where lies the blame, it is impossible now to say. Officials of the road are silent. But one of three things is reasonably sure – that the engineer of No. 4 was given wrong instructions, ran by his signal, or overlooked, the schedule on which he was supposed to run... The speed of the two trains when they met is estimated by old and experienced railroad men as being not less than sixty miles an hour.

The scene immediately following the collision is indescribable. Those escaping unhurt or with lesser injuries fled from the spot in a veritable panic. The cornfield on both sides of the track was trampled by many feet, and littered with fragments, of iron and wood hurled from the demolished cars. The dead lay here and there, grotesquely sprawling where they fell. The dying moaned appeals for aid or, speechless, rolled their heads from side to side and writhed in agony. Everywhere there was blood and suffering and chaos.

NASHVILLE TENNESSEAN NEWSPAPER, 10 JULY 1918.

The 'Great Train Wreck' in Nashville, Tennessee, on 9 July 1918 killed a confirmed total of 101 people along with 171 injured, and it remains the worst train crash in US history; most of the victims were African-Americans hoping to work at a Nashville gunpowder factory. The two trains collided on a single stretch of line. The disaster led to the widespread replacement of wooden cars with metal ones.

ALSO ON THIS DAY

1816 Argentina declares its independence from Spain.
1877 The first Wimbledon tennis championships begins.
2011 The Republic of South Sudan secedes from Sudan.

10 JULY

THE ASSASSINATION OF WILLIAM THE SILENT, 1584

On Tuesday, the 10th of July, 1584, at about half-past twelve, the prince, with his wife on his arm... was going to the dining-room. William the Silent was dressed upon that day, according to his usual custom, in very plain fashion... Gerard presented himself at the doorway, and demanded a passport. The princess, struck with the pale and agitated countenance of the man, anxiously questioned her husband concerning the stranger... The princess... observed in an under-tone that 'she had never seen so villainous a countenance'... At two o'clock the company rose from table... The dining-room, which was on the ground floor, opened into a little square vestibule, which communicated, through an arched passageway, with the main entrance into the courtyard. This vestibule was also directly at the foot of the wooden staircase leading to the next floor, and was scarcely six feet in width. Upon its left side, as one approached the stairway, was an obscure arch, sunk deep in the wall, and completely in the shadow of the door... The prince came from the dining-room, and began leisurely to ascend. He had only reached the second stair, when a man emerged from the sunken arch, and, standing within a foot or two of him, discharged a pistol full at his heart. Three balls entered his body, one of which, passing quite through him, struck with violence against the wall beyond. The Prince exclaimed in French, as he felt the wound, 'O my God; have mercy upon my soul! O my God, have mercy upon this poor people.'

J.L. MOTLEY, *THE RISE OF THE DUTCH REPUBLIC*, 1856.

∞

Prince William of Orange (1533–84), also known as William the Silent, had participated in the Dutch rebellion against Spanish rule in the Netherlands since the early 1560s, and became ruler of the Protestant United Provinces when they declared their independence in 1579 and split from the predominantly Catholic provinces to the south. In 1582 William had narrowly escaped death from the bullet of a Spanish would-be assassin. On 10 July 1584, however, he fell victim to Balthasar Gérard, a French assassin attracted by a bounty placed on William's head by the Spanish king, Philip II.

Gérard was captured and, for killing the man perceived as father of the emerging nation, met a grisly judicial end. Dutch independence was confirmed in 1648.

ALSO ON THIS DAY

1940 WWII: Luftwaffe raids begin the Battle of Britain.
1943 WWII: the Allied invasion of Sicily begins.
1962 The *Telstar* communications satellite is launched.

11 JULY

ALEXANDER HAMILTON'S DEATH BY DUEL, 1804

Colonel Burr arrived first on the ground, as had been previously agreed. When General Hamilton arrived, the parties exchanged salutations, and the seconds proceeded to make their arrangements. They measured the distance, ten full paces, and cast lots for the choice of position. They then proceeded to load the pistols in each other's presence. The gentleman who was to give the word then explained to the parties the rules which were to govern them in firing.

He then asked if they were prepared; gave the word present, and both parties presented and fired in succession. The fire of Colonel Burr took effect, and General Hamilton almost instantly fell. Colonel Burr advanced toward General Hamilton with a manner and gesture that appeared to General Hamilton's friend to be expressive of regret; but, without speaking, turned about and withdrew, being urged from the field by his friend with a view to prevent his being recognized by the surgeon and bargemen who were then approaching. No further communication took place between the principals, and the barge that carried Colonel Burr immediately returned to the city. We conceive it proper to add, that the conduct of the parties in this interview was perfectly proper, as suited the occasion.

JUDGE NATHANIEL PENDLETON, STATEMENT TO THE PRESS, 1804.

Thus, by way of a duel, Thomas Jefferson's vice-president Aaron Burr killed his Federalist Party rival Alexander Hamilton (1757–1804), after a dispute over alleged insults by Hamilton brought to a head the men's simmering hostility. In 1800, after a deadlocked presidential election, Hamilton had supported Jefferson over Burr for the presidency, and their relations had soured thereafter.

Duelling was illegal in New York, so the encounter took place at Weehawken, across the Hudson River from Manhattan, and discretion was agreed by both parties. Judge Nathaniel Pendleton acted as Hamilton's second. Hamilton fired into the air (though whether intentionally is disputed); Burr hit him in the pelvis. After Burr's departure, Pendleton and the doctor took Hamilton home, where he died the next day. Burr was charged with murder but never reached trial, and he completed his term as vice-president in 1804. A charge of treason damaged his reputation further in 1807.

ALSO ON THIS DAY

1848 Waterloo Station opens in London.
1940 WWII: the collaborationist French Vichy regime is established.
1995 Bosnian Serb forces begin the Srebrenica massacre of Bosnian Muslims.

12 JULY

THE BATTLE OF THE BOYNE, 1690

His Majesty being mighty impatient of lying still... we marched down to Dundalk ...The next day... we came within four or five miles of Drogheda and then we marched to the right, to a ford over the Boyne called Old Ford about two miles to the west of Drogheda where we found the enemy, consisting of near 60,000 men and King James at the head of them, encamped on the south side of the river. They had raised two batteries which played very warmly upon us and we drew down our cannon and answered them in their own language...

The dispute was very sharp while it lasted, and I guess that the enemy lost 1,500 or 2,000 men but our loss far exceeds theirs for our general the Duke of Schomberg who charged at the head of a squadron naked without any sort of armour was killed in the first charge; his body was grievously hacked and bruised...

I had almost forgot to tell you that His Majesty do expose himself strangely, on Sunday night a cannon ball took away part of the sleeve of his coat and on Tuesday he led on the forlorn and is personally in every action.

ROBERT ALEWAY, JULY 1690.

∞

Robert Aleway, an artillery officer serving with William III, took part in the decisive Battle of the Boyne on 12 July 1690, which pitted the 'Williamite' Protestant forces (including contingents of Dutch, Danes and some French Protestants) against James II's inferior numbers of Catholic Irish and French troops supplied by Louis XIV. James and William faced one another across the banks of the River Boyne near Oldbridge, in County Louth, and William's tactics succeeding in splitting the Jacobite forces and winning the day, with the combined casualties numbering around 1,500.

After the battle, William was able to take Dublin. His victory in the so-called Williamite Wars confirmed the Protestant ascendancy in Ireland, checked French ambitions, and assured the victory of the 'Glorious Revolution' that, in 1688, had ejected James from the English and Scottish thrones. The Battle of the Boyne has been celebrated ever since by Protestants in Northern Ireland.

ALSO ON THIS DAY

972 King Athelstan unifies England.
1536 The death of the Dutch philosopher Erasmus.
1962 The Rolling Stones give their first-ever concert in London.

13 JULY

THE 'SCOPES MONKEY TRIAL', 1925

If today you can take a thing like evolution and make it a crime to teach in the public schools, tomorrow you can make it a crime to teach it in the private schools and next year you can make it a crime to teach it to the hustings or in the church. At the next session you may ban books and the newspapers... Ignorance and fanaticism are ever busy and need feeding. Always feeding and gloating for more. Today it is the public school teachers; tomorrow the private. The next day the preachers and the lecturers, the magazines, the books, the newspapers. After a while, Your Honour, it is the setting of man against man and creed against creed until with flying banners and beating drums we are marching backward to the glorious ages of the sixteenth century when bigots lighted faggots to burn the men who dared to bring any intelligence and enlightenment and culture to the human mind.

CLARENCE DARROW, TRIAL COMMENTS, 13 JULY 1925.

∞

Clarence Darrow (1857–1938) was one of interwar America's most controversial and charismatic lawyers, whose defence cases had included the infamous child murderers Leopold and Loeb (1924). In 1925 the liberal-leaning Darrow defended the young school-teacher John Scopes who was accused of breaking the laws of Tennessee by teaching the theory of evolution. The trial, which began on 12 July, aroused huge publicity and was broadcast on national radio as Darrow, a professed agnostic, clashed with prosecuting attorney (and Democratic presidential candidate) William Jennings Bryan, a fundamentalist Christian. It was nicknamed the 'Scopes Monkey Trial' by H. L. Mencken, who reported it in colourful terms for the *Baltimore Sun* newspaper.

The verdict on 21 July found Scopes guilty. But Bryan's victory was shortlived: he died on 26 July, and the conviction was overturned on appeal.

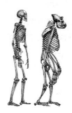

ALSO ON THIS DAY

100 BC The birth of Julius Caesar.
1793 French Revolution: Jean-Paul Marat is assassinated by Charlotte Corday.
1985 Live Aid charity concerts are held in London and Philadelphia.

14 JULY

THE STORMING OF THE BASTILLE, 1789

They send one of their members (Monsieur de Corny) to the Hotel des Invalides to ask arms for their Garde Bourgeoise. He was followed by, or he found there, a great mob. The governor came out and represented the impossibility of his delivering arms without orders...

De Corny advised the people to retire, and the people took possession of the arms. It was remarkable that not only the Invalids themselves made no opposition, but that a body of 5,000 foreign troops, encamped within 400 yards, never stirred.

Monsieur de Corny and five others were then sent to ask arms of Monsieur de Launai, Governor of the Bastille. They found a great collection of people already before the place... The deputation... advanced themselves to make their demand of the governor, and in that instant a discharge from the Bastille killed four people of those nearest to the deputies. The deputies retired, the people rushed against the place, and almost in an instant were in possession of a fortification, defended by 100 men, which in other times had stood several regular sieges and had never been taken. How they got in, has as yet been impossible to discover...

They took all the arms, discharged the prisoners and such of the garrison as were not killed in the first moment of fury, carried the governor and lieutenant governor to the Greve (the place of public execution), cut off their heads, and set them through the city in triumph to the Palais Royal.

...The alarm at Versailles increases instead of abating. They believed that the aristocrats of Paris were under pillage and carnage, that 150,000 men were in arms coming to Versailles to massacre the Royal family, the court, the ministers and all connected with them, their practices and principles.

THOMAS JEFFERSON, LETTER TO SECRETARY OF STATE JOHN JAY, 16 JULY 1789.

Thus Thomas Jefferson, US minister to France, described the events of 14 July 1789 in an official letter. The 'alarm at Versailles' that he reported was premature but not, in the end, an inaccurate summary of the fate that would befall King Louis XVI and his family and the institutions of the royalist state. Jefferson personally found the revolutionaries inspiring, but nevertheless returned to the United States in October 1789.

ALSO ON THIS DAY

1865 Edward Whymper makes the first ascent of the Matterhorn.
1881 The US outlaw Billy the Kid is shot dead by Lincoln County sheriff Pat Garrett.
1933 The Nazis outlaw all other German political parties.

15 JULY

NAPOLEON IN CAPTIVITY, 1815

My dear mother, you will be surprised at not hearing from me, and knowing the *Bellerophon's* arrival in England, but when I tell you no private letters were allowed to leave the ship before to-day, that will cease. It's unnecessary to say that we have got Buonaparte and suite on board, as it was known in England previous to our arrival... The circumstances which led to his surrender were his defeats in all points, and was it not for the strict blockade we kept up he would have escaped to America. We heard of his being on board the French frigate *Saale* off Rochfort, from which moment we watched his movements if possible more closely than before. On the morning of the 14th instant, observing a schooner bearing a flag of truce on board standing towards us, we hove to for her, when Count Lascazas and General Lallemande came on board with proposals from Buonaparte, in consequence of which we came to anchor in the evening in the roads off Rochelle. Next morning, 15th instant, at 4 a.m. observed a man-of-war brig standing out and beating towards us, we immediately dispatched all our boats. Lieut. Mott in the barge brought Buonaparte on board at 7, the boats were busily employed in bringing his retinue and baggage, and I never saw men exert themselves so much as ours did that day, lest Admiral Hotham should take him, as he was off the harbour in the *Superb*, and saw him coming on board here, and did all in his power to get in, but did not come to anchor before 11 in the forenoon.

Buonaparte is a fine-looking man, inclined to corpulency, is five feet six inches in height, his hair turning grey, and a little bald on the crown of the head, no whiskers, complexion French yellow, eyes grey, Roman nose, good mouth and chin, neck short, big belly, arms stout, small white hands, and shews a good leg. He wears a cocked hat somewhat like our old-fashioned three-cornered ones, with the tri-coloured cockade in it, plain green coat, cape red, and cuffs the same, plain gold epaulets, and a large star on the left breast, white waistcoat and breeches and white silk stockings, thin shoes and buckles. Eats but two meals in the day, breakfast and dinner, and these are sumptuous, fish, flesh, and fowl, wines, fruit, various French dishes &c. He breakfasts about eleven and dines at six, is about half an hour at each, when he generally comes on deck or goes into the after-cabin to study. We do not know what's to be done with him yet, he remains on board until we hear from the allies.

In his suite are Marshal Bertrand, Duc de Rovigo [Savary] once the French minister of police, Counts Lascazas and Montholon, Generals Lallemande and Gourgou, several Lieut.-Colonels and Captains. We have 33 on board, 17 were sent on board the *Myrmidon*, Captn. Gambier. There are two countesses on board, but not to be compared even to our English ladies. Their children are handsome… We performed the comedy of the 'Poor Gentleman' before Buonaparte and suite. I acted the part of Corporal Foss. It went off very well, our scenery was excellent. The female dresses were badly suited for Midshipmen… There are Admiralty orders not to allow any person whatever on board, but they crowd in boats round the ship, and he very condescendingly stands looking at them through a spyglass. There are two frigates, one on each side of us, the *Eurotas* and *Liffey*, and their boats are constantly rowing about the ship to keep off the boats. We prisoners have no other amusement than to look at them contending for places. I hope we will soon be allowed to go ashore, as I want to see Captain Sandys. You must be tired reading this long epistle… Give my affectionate love to Ally, Anne, Wilhelmina, Sophia and Jane… I remain, my dear mother, your affectionate son,

EPHRAIM GRAEBKE. 30 JULY 1815.

∞

After his defeat at Waterloo (*see* 18 June), Napoleon Bonaparte travelled first to Paris, where he abdicated, and then to Brittany in search of a passage across the Atlantic. When a Royal Navy blockade made this impossible, he surrendered to the commander of HMS *Bellerophon*, seeking asylum. He was taken to Torbay, in Devon, where Ephraim Graebke, an assistant surgeon, was able to observe the scourge of Europe in captivity and report on him to his own family.

Napoleon was not permitted ashore, and a few weeks later was exiled to the remote South Atlantic island of St Helena, where isolation from Europe allowed him to reflect on his triumphs and failures undisturbed. He died there in May 1821 (*see* 5 May).

ALSO ON THIS DAY

1685 The 1st Duke of Monmouth is executed after an unsuccessful rebellion.
1799 The Rosetta Stone is discovered in Egypt.
1918 WWI: the Second Battle of the Marne begins.

16 JULY

THE FIRST ATOMIC EXPLOSION, 1945

The tension increased by leaps and bounds. Everyone knew the awful potentialities of the thing that they thought was about to happen. The scientists felt that their figuring must be right and that the bomb had to go off but there was in everyone's mind a strong measure of doubt...

In that brief instant in the remote New Mexico desert the tremendous effort of the brains and brawn of all these people came suddenly and startlingly to the fullest fruition. Dr Oppenheimer... grew tenser as the last seconds ticked off. He scarce breathed. He held on to a post to steady himself. For the last few seconds, he stared directly ahead and then when the announcer shouted 'Now!' and there came this tremendous burst of light followed shortly thereafter by the deep growling roar of the explosion, his face relaxed into an expression of tremendous relief...

The tension in the room let up and all started congratulating each other. Everyone sensed 'This is it!' No matter what might happen now all knew that the impossible scientific job had been done. Atomic fission would no longer be hidden in the cloisters of the theoretical physicists' dreams. It was almost full grown at birth. It was a great new force to be used for good or for evil. There was a feeling in that shelter that those concerned with its nativity should dedicate their lives to the mission that it would always be used for good and never for evil.

As to the present war, there was a feeling that no matter what else might happen, we now had the means to ensure its speedy conclusion and save thousands of American lives.

GENERAL THOMAS FARRELL, US WAR DEPARTMENT RELEASE, 16 JULY 1945.

The so-called Trinity Test of the first atomic bomb, on 16 July 1945 in the Alamogordo Desert of New Mexico, was the fruit of three years' intensive and secret work at the Manhattan Project by its scientific director Robert Oppenheimer, its supremo General Leslie Groves and a large team of scientists. A few weeks later the bomb was dropped over the Japanese cities of Hiroshima and Nagasaki, to devastating effect (*see* 6 August). The thoughtful Oppenheimer later opposed the development of the more powerful hydrogen bomb and fell into political disfavour.

ALSO ON THIS DAY

1054 Differences between the Roman and Eastern Orthodox churches become a formal schism.
1951 J.D. Salinger's *The Catcher in the Rye* is published.
1965 The Mont Blanc Tunnel linking France and Italy opens.

17 JULY

THE EXECUTION OF THE ROMANOVS, 1918

About midnight Commandant Yurovsky woke the tsar's family. The family, the doctor, the maid and the waiters all got up, washed and dressed. Shortly after 1 a.m., they left their rooms, the tsar carrying the heir in his arms. The empress, her daughters and the others followed him.

None of the family asked any questions. When the room was reached, Yurovsky ordered chairs to be brought. The empress sat by the window, near the black pillar of the arch. Behind her stood three of her daughters (I knew their faces, because I had seen them every day in the garden, but I didn't know their names). The heir and the emperor sat side by side in the middle of the room. Doctor Botkin stood behind the heir. The maid stood at the left of the door leading to the store room; by her side stood one of the tsar's daughters. Two servants stood against the wall on the left.

It seemed as if they all guessed their fate, but no-one uttered a sound. Eleven men entered: Yurovsky, his assistant, two members of the Extraordinary Commission, and seven secret policemen.

Yurovsky ordered me to the street, to see if there was anybody there, and wait to see whether the shots had been heard. I went out, but before I got to the street I heard firing. I returned and saw all the tsar's family lying on the floor with many wounds. The blood was running in streams. The doctor, the maid and two waiters had also been shot. The heir was still alive and moaned a little. Yurovsky fired two or three more times at him. Then he was still.

PAVEL MEDVEDEV, GUARD, UNDER INTERROGATION.

Amid the turmoil of the Russian Revolution, the former tsar Nicholas II (he had abdicated in 1917) and his family had been placed under close arrest by the Bolsheviks in a merchant's house in Ekaterinburg, in the Urals, in April 1918. In July, following an order from Moscow, they were brutally murdered and their bodies dumped in the forest. For years details of what had happened were unclear. But in the post-Soviet years the remains of all the family were rediscovered and reburied – becoming the focus of a new cult.

ALSO ON THIS DAY

1936 A coup attempt begins the Spanish Civil War.
1945 WWII: Stalin, Churchill and Truman meet at the Potsdam Conference.
1975 The US *Apollo* and Soviet *Soyuz* craft link up in space.

18 JULY

THE MASSACRE AT SREBRENICA, 1995

The tragedy that occurred after the fall of Srebrenica is shocking for two reasons. It is shocking, first and foremost, for the magnitude of the crimes committed. Not since the horrors of the Second World War had Europe witnessed massacres on this scale. The mortal remains of close to 2,500 men and boys have been found on the surface in mass graves and in secondary burial sites. Several thousand more men are still missing, and there is every reason to believe that additional burial sites, many of which have been probed but not exhumed, will reveal the bodies of thousands more men and boys. The great majority of those who were killed were not killed in combat: the exhumed bodies of the victims show that large numbers had their hands bound, or were blindfolded, or were shot in the back or the back of the head. Numerous eyewitness accounts, now well corroborated by forensic evidence, attest to scenes of mass slaughter of unarmed victims.

The fall of Srebrenica is also shocking because the enclave's inhabitants believed that the authority of the United Nations Security Council, the presence of UNPROFOR [United Nations Protection Force] peacekeepers, and the might of NATO air power, would ensure their safety. Instead, the Bosnian Serb forces ignored the Security Council, pushed aside the UNPROFOR troops, and assessed correctly that air power would not be used against them. They overran the safe area of Srebrenica with ease, and then proceeded to depopulate the territory within 48 hours. Their leaders then engaged in high-level negotiations with representatives of the international community while their forces on the ground executed and buried thousands of men and boys within a matter of days.

In an effort to assign responsibility for the appalling events that took place in Srebrenica, many observers have been quick to point to the soldiers of the UNPROFOR Netherlands battalion as the most immediate culprits. They blame them for not attempting to stop the Serb attack, and they blame them for not protecting the thousands of people who sought refuge in their compound... However, after he [the battalion's commander] had been told that the risk of confrontation with the Serbs was to be avoided, and that the execution of his mandate was secondary to the security of his personnel, the battalion withdrew from observation posts under attack.

It is true that the UNPROFOR troops in Srebrenica never fired at the attacking Serbs. They fired warning shots over the Serbs' heads and their mortars fired flares, but they never fired directly on any Serb units. Had they engaged the Serbs directly it is possible that events would have unfolded differently...

The cardinal lesson of Srebrenica is that a deliberate and systematic attempt to terrorize, expel or murder an entire people must be met decisively with all necessary means, and with the political will to carry the policy through to its logical conclusion. In the Balkans, in this decade, this lesson has had to be learned not once, but twice...

The United Nations experience in Bosnia was one of the most difficult and painful in our history... Through error, misjudgement and an inability to recognize the scope of the evil confronting us, we failed to do our part to help save the people of Srebrenica from the Serb campaign of mass murder... The tragedy of Srebrenica will haunt our history forever.

Report of the Secretary-General Persuant to General Assembly Resolution 53/35:
The Fall of Srebrenica, 15 November 1999.

∞

On 18 July 1995, after a week of concerted killing, the greatest atrocity on European soil since the Second World War wound down. By then, thousands of Bosnian Muslim men, youths and boys – over 7,500 in most estimates – had been executed by Bosnian Serb forces, and their bodies dumped in mass graves.

As the UN Secretary-General's report made clear, the shock was not simply the death toll and the sheer human tragedy, it was the failure of the international bodies, in particular the United Nations, which had designated Srebrenica a 'safe haven' from the ravages of Bosnia's civil war. Ill-prepared, ill-briefed and hopelessly outnumbered, the mainly Dutch UN troops guarding the safe haven had simply allowed the Serb forces to help themselves to their victims.

In May 2011 Ratko Mladic, the Bosnian Serb general accused of organizing the massacre, was finally apprehended in Serbia and sent to the UN's International Criminal Tribunal for the Former Yugoslavia, where he was charged with 'genocide' and 'crimes against humanity'.

ALSO ON THIS DAY

AD 64 The Great Fire of Rome breaks out.
1290 The Jews are expelled from England by Edward I.
1976 Nadia Comăneci achieves the first perfect score in gymnastics at the Montreal Olympics.

19 JULY

THE LAUNCH OF SS *GREAT BRITAIN*, 1843

His Royal Highness... passed along a gallery erected alongside of the vessel to a pavilion at its farther end... the Prince being loudly cheered. The caisson having been opened during the banquet, the water had been let into the dock and the noble vessel was now fairly afloat, displaying her harmonious proportions of parts to the eye of the spectator. From her bows, a rope was made fast to the *Avon* steamer... on board of which vessel the 'steam had been up' for some time.

All was now ready. The cannon thundered away in every direction – the band struck up 'Rule Britannia' – and the *Avon* slowly drew from the dock the gigantic *Great Britain*. The first onward motion of the immense mass was the signal for a tremendous burst of cheering ... As the immense mass of iron floated majestically forward, Mrs Miles (to whom the prince had courteously deputed the christening ceremonial) broke a bottle of wine against the bows of the ship and pronounced the words – '*the Great Britain*'.

In about five minutes the vessel was clear of the dock and the Avon received the largest and most stupendous piece of naval mechanism which, since the Flood, has ever floated upon the waters.

The scene... was magnificent, and the effect not diminished by the reflection that (God willing) the noble bay of New York... would soon, in all probability, present an almost equally animated appearance in order to give a welcome to the second unrivalled Bristolian achievement in the art of steam navigation.

BRISTOL MERCURY, 22 JULY 1843.

Isambard Kingdom Brunel's iron-hulled steamship the *Great Britain* – the first to be equipped with a screw propeller – was launched by Prince Albert in Bristol on 19 July 1843. This was where Brunel's earlier transatlantic steamship, the *Great Western*, had also been built, in 1838. However, as the largest ship ever constructed, the *Great Britain* proved too large to leave the docks, and her maiden voyage was delayed for two years. After two years' service on the transatlantic route she ran aground off Ireland and was reallocated the role of conveying emigrants to Australia.

ALSO ON THIS DAY

1553 The accession of Mary I restores Catholicism to England.
1870 The Franco-Prussian War begins.
1979 The left-wing Sandinistas come to power in Nicaragua.

20 JULY

A LANDMARK DECLARATION
FOR WOMEN'S RIGHTS, 1848

The history of mankind is a history of repeated injuries and usurpations on the part of man toward woman...

He has never permitted her to exercise her inalienable right to the elective franchise.

...He has made her, morally, an irresponsible being, as she can commit many crimes with impunity, provided they be done in the presence of her husband. In the covenant of marriage, she is compelled to promise obedience to her husband, he becoming, to all intents and purposes, her master – the law giving him power to deprive her of her liberty, and to administer chastisement.

He has so framed the laws of divorce, as to what shall be the proper causes, and in case of separation, to whom the guardianship of the children shall be given, as to be wholly regardless of the happiness of women – the law... going upon a false supposition of the supremacy of man, and giving all power into his hands.

...He has endeavoured, in every way that he could, to destroy her confidence in her own powers, to lessen her self-respect, and to make her willing to lead a dependent and abject life.

Now, in view of this entire disfranchisement of one-half the people of this country, their social and religious degradation – in view of the unjust laws above mentioned, and because women do feel themselves aggrieved, oppressed, and fraudulently deprived of their most sacred rights, we insist that they have immediate admission to all the rights and privileges which belong to them as citizens of the United States.

DECLARATION, SENECA FALLS CONVENTION, 20 JULY 1848.

The convention for social reform held in Seneca Falls, New York, in July 1848 was organized by the franchise campaigner Elizabeth Cady Stanton (1815–1902) and the abolitionist Lucretia Mott (1793–1880). The adoption of its declaration by the convention is often considered to be the birth of the US movement for women's rights.

ALSO ON THIS DAY

1944 Hitler survives an assassination attempt led by Claus von Stauffenberg.
1974 Turkish forces invade Cyprus.
1976 *Viking 1* lands on Mars.

21 JULY

THE FIRST MOON LANDING, 1969

That's one small step for a man, a giant leap for mankind.

NEIL ARMSTRONG, SPEECH, 21 JULY 1969.

∞

US Navy pilot Commander Neil Armstrong (born 1930) became, as commander of the three-man crew of the *Apollo 11* space mission, the first man to set foot on the Moon in July 1969, watched live by a worldwide television audience estimated at almost 500 million. As he descended the ladder he spoke his famous words. They were slightly fluffed: he was heard to say 'small step for man' but NASA later confirmed he had meant to say 'for *a* man'.

His crew member 'Buzz' Aldrin joined him 20 minutes later; his comment was: 'beautiful, beautiful, magnificent desolation'. Shortly after stepping out, Armstrong and Aldrin spoke with President Nixon, in what the president described as 'the most historic phone call ever made from the White House'. They left on the Moon's surface an American flag, a silicon disk containing goodwill messages from scores of world leaders, and a plaque inscribed: 'Here men from planet Earth first set foot upon the Moon July 1969 A.D. We came in peace for all mankind.'

The risky mission fulfilled an optimistic vow made by President Kennedy on 25 May 1961, to put an American on the Moon by the end of the decade; it was a pledge made in the spirit of Cold War competitiveness, after the Soviet cosmonaut Yuri Gagarin had become the first man in space the previous month. (*See also* 4 October.)

Apollo 11 was launched on 16 July, and after three days reached lunar orbit; while the third member of the crew, Michael Collins, remained in orbit in the command module *Columbia*, Armstrong and Aldrin descended to the planned landing area of the Sea of Tranquillity in the 'lunar module' named *Eagle*. Armstrong reported the successful landing with the words 'Houston, Tranquillity Base here. The *Eagle* has landed.' After 21 hours on the Moon, the *Eagle* blasted off, blowing over the US flag in the process, and linked up with *Columbia*. And the astronauts returned to Earth on 24 July, their unprecedented achievement complete.

ALSO ON THIS DAY

AD 365 Alexandria is destroyed by a *tsunami*, after an earthquake in Crete.
1861 US Civil War: the Confederates prevail in the First Battle of Bull Run, Virginia.
1954 Vietnam is partitioned by the Geneva Conference.

22 JULY

THE BOMBING OF THE KING DAVID HOTEL, 1946

The dense column of acrid smoke spiralled several hundred feet into the air, completely hiding the southern wing of the hotel. When the billowing smoke started to drift off into the sunny, cloudless sky, there was a huge, gaping chasm where the six-storey corner had been. Wounded troops and civilians, their clothes spattered with blood, their faces covered with white dust and streaked with blood, staggered out of the wreckage dazed by the shock.

Inside the hotel all electric clocks had stopped at 12.37. The entire southern wall at the end of the corridor was blown out and the wall behind the bar was demolished. The bar itself was a shambles of broken bottles, windows and furniture. The lobby was caked with dust and a good deal of sand blown up through the loosened marble floor, which was covered with glass splinters. A whole row of tiles from the entrance hall to the south wing was raised a few inches. Broken woodwork was scattered about pell-mell in the lobby.

...As the *Daily Telegraph* correspondent was standing with Sir John Shaw, the figure of a civilian covered in dirt and with torn clothes emerged from the wreckage, walked up to the O.A.G. [Shaw], and said: 'I have got the ciphers and locked the safe, sir.'

PALESTINE POST, 23 JULY 1946.

∞

On 22 July 1946, British-administered Palestine was dealt a blow by the militant Jewish Irgun Zvai Leumi (or Stern Gang), which blew up part of Jerusalem's King David Hotel, housing British military headquarters and the Secretariat of the Palestine Government. The Officer Administering the Government (OAG), Sir John Shaw, escaped injury; but the death toll numbered upwards of 90 Britons, Jews and Arabs.

Menachem Begin, leader of Irgun and a future prime minister of Israel, justified the target for its military value and claimed the British had ignored three warnings to evacuate the building, including one to the English-language *Palestine Post*. While the action – condemned by mainstream Jewish organizations – hardened immediate British attitudes, it made palpable the determination of armed Zionists. Within two years, the British mandate in Palestine was over, and an embryonic Israel was fighting its Arab neighbours for survival.

ALSO ON THIS DAY

1456 The Ottomans are defeated by Hungary at the Siege of Belgrade.
1706 The Treaty of Union, leading to the formation of the Kingdom of Great Britain, is agreed.
2011 In Norway, Anders Behring Breivik kills 77 people in two terror attacks.

23 JULY

EGYPT'S MILITARY COUP, 1952

Egypt has endured a period characterized by bribery, mischief, and the absence of stability. All of these factors had a large influence on the army. Those who accepted bribes caused our defeat in the war [with Israel] of 1948. Following the war, the mischief-makers have been assisting one another, and traitors have been commanding the army. They appointed a commander who is either ignorant or corrupt. Egypt has reached the point of having no army to defend it.

Accordingly, we have undertaken to clean ourselves up and have appointed to command us men from within the army whom we trust in their ability, their character, and their patriotism. It is certain that Egypt will meet this news with enthusiasm and will welcome it...

I assure the Egyptian people that the entire army has become capable of operating in the national interest and under the rule of the constitution apart from any interests of its own. I request that the people never permit traitors to take refuge in deeds of destruction or violence. Should anyone behave in such ways, he will be dealt with forcefully in a manner such as has not been seen before and his deeds will meet immediately the reward for treason... I assure our foreign brothers that their interests, their personal safety and their property are safe, and that the army considers itself responsible for them. May God grant us success.

MUHAMMAD NAGUIB, RADIO BROADCAST READ BY ANWAR SADAT, 1952.

∞

The 'Free Officers Movement' of young soldiers, notably Major-General Muhammad Naguib and Colonel Gamal Nasser, seized power in Egypt in July 1952 and established a republic in 1953. Naguib, its first president, was forced out of office in 1954 by Nasser, whose Pan-Arabist aspirations and overtures to the Soviet Union contributed to suspicion of him by the West. In 1956 Nasser's nationalization of the Suez Canal had dramatic ramifications, notably when the Franco-British-Israeli conspiracy to seize the canal backfired with dire diplomatic consequences, especially for Britain.

Anwar Sadat succeeded Nasser as president in 1970, but was assassinated in 1981 after making peace with Israel (*see* 26 March). His successor, Hosni Mubarak, remained in office until 2011, when he was ousted by popular agitation.

ALSO ON THIS DAY

1903 The first Ford automobile is sold.
1914 Austria-Hungary issues an ultimatum to Serbia.
1983 Civil war begins in Sri Lanka: secessionist Tamil Tigers kill 13 army officers.

24 JULY

THE 'LOST CITY OF THE INCA' IS DISCOVERED, 1911

Without the slightest expectation of finding anything more interesting... I climbed farther up the ridge and around a slight promontory... They sent a small boy with me as a guide.

Hardly had we rounded the promontory when the character of the stonework began to improve. A flight of beautifully constructed terraces... had been recently rescued from the jungle by the Indians... I entered the untouched forest beyond, and suddenly found myself in a maze of beautiful granite houses! They were covered with trees and moss and the growth of centuries.

...Under a carved rock the little boy showed me a cave beautifully lined with the finest cut stone. It was evidently intended to be a Royal Mausoleum. On top of this particular boulder a semicircular building had been constructed. The wall followed the natural curvature of the rock and was keyed to it by one of the finest examples of masonry I have ever seen... The flowing lines, the symmetrical arrangement of the ashlars [sculpted blocks], and the gradual gradation of the courses, combined to produce a wonderful effect, softer and more pleasing than that of the marble temples of the Old World. Owing to the absence of mortar, there are no ugly spaces between the rocks. They might have grown together.

...Surprise followed surprise in bewildering succession. I climbed a marvellous great stairway of large granite blocks... and came into a little clearing. Here were the ruins of two of the finest structures I have ever seen in Peru. Not only were they made of selected blocks of beautifully grained white granite; their walls contained ashlars of Cyclopean size, ten feet in length, and higher than a man. The sight held me spellbound.

HIRAM BINGHAM, INCA LAND, 1922.

The wealthy young American academic Hiram Bingham (1875–1956) stumbled upon the 'lost city of the Inca', Machu Picchu, in July 1911. Dated to the 15th century and lying some 70 miles from the Inca capital Cuzco, its historical role is disputed. But there is no doubt as to the majesty of its dramatic setting, high in the Andes, or its popularity as a tourist destination, attracting almost half a million visitors a year.

ALSO ON THIS DAY

1567 Mary, Queen of Scots, is forced to abdicate.
1866 The first Southern state, Tennessee, is readmitted to the Union after the Civil War.
1943 WWII: Allied air raids begin the destruction of Hamburg.

25 JULY

BLÉRIOT FLIES THE ENGLISH CHANNEL, 1909

I rose at 2.30 this (Sunday) morning and, finding that the conditions were favourable, ordered the torpedo boat *Escopette*, which had been placed at my disposal, to start. Then I went to the garage at Sangatte and found that the motor worked well. At 4 a.m. I took my seat in the aeroplane and made a trial flight around Calais... descending to the spot chosen for the start across the Channel.

...At 4.35 'all's ready'. My friend Le Blance gives the signal and in an instant I am in the air, my engine making 1,200 revolutions, almost its highest speed, in order that I may get quickly over the telegraph wires at the edge of the cliff.

As soon as I am over the cliff I reduce my speed... I begin my flight, steady and sure, toward the coast of England.

The *Escopette* has seen me; she is driving ahead at full speed. She makes perhaps 42 kilometres an hour. What matters it? I am making at least 68 kilometres. Rapidly I overtake her at a height of 80 metres. Below me is the surface of the sea, disturbed by the wind which is freshening. The motion of the waves beneath me is pleasant. I drive on.

Ten minutes are gone. I have passed the destroyer, and I turn my head to see whether I am proceeding in the right direction. I am amazed. There is nothing to be seen – neither the torpedo boat destroyer nor France nor England. I am alone; I can see nothing at all.

For ten minutes I am lost. It is a strange position to be in, alone, guided without a compass in the air over the middle of the Channel... My hands and feet rest lightly on the levers. I let the aeroplane take its own course. I care not whither it goes.

...Twenty minutes after leaving the French coast, I see green cliffs and Dover Castle and away to the west the spot where I had intended to land...

I press a lever with my feet and turn easily toward the west. Now I am in difficulties for the wind here by the cliffs is much stronger and my speed is reduced as I fight against it, but my beautiful aeroplane responds still steadily.

I fly westward, chopping across the harbour, and reach Shakespeare Cliff. Although I am confident I can continue for an hour and a half, that I might indeed return to Calais, I cannot resist the opportunity to make a landing upon this green spot.

Once more I turn my aeroplane. I enter the opening and find myself again over dry land. Avoiding the red buildings on my right I attempt a landing, but the wind catches me and whirls me around two or three times. At once I stop my motor, and instantly my machine falls straight upon the ground from a height of twenty metres. In two or three seconds I am safe upon your shore.

Soldiers in khaki run up and policemen. Two of my compatriots are on the spot. They kiss my cheeks. The conclusion of my flight overwhelms me.

Thus ended my flight across the Channel – a flight which could easily be done again. Shall I do it? I think not. I have promised my wife that after a race for which I have already entered, I will fly no more.

LOUIS BLÉRIOT, *NEW YORK TIMES*, 26 JULY 1909.

Louis Blériot's flight across the English Channel – the first long flight across water – was undertaken after the *Daily Mail* offered £1,000 to the first man to fly the Channel. The newspaper had begun offering prizes for aviation in 1906, and it continued to do so up to 1930 when its £10,000 prize for the first solo flight from Britain to Australia was won by Amy Johnson.

Blériot (1872–1936) and two other rivals for the prize all arrived in Calais in July 1909; all three men suffered accidents in preparing for the flight, and the other two withdrew, whereas Blériot decided to continue despite a badly burned foot. His journey on 25 July, in a 24-horse-power monoplane he had designed himself, took 37 minutes.

Blériot's flight proved a staging post in the rapid development of flight; two years later André Beaumont won £10,000 in the *Mail's* challenge for the first flight around Britain.

ALSO ON THIS DAY

AD 306 Constantine becomes Roman emperor.
1603 James VI of Scotland is crowned as James I of England.
1978 The birth of Louise Brown in Oldham, the first IVF baby.

26 JULY

WINSTON CHURCHILL'S ELECTORAL DEFEAT, 1945

Just before dawn I woke suddenly with a sharp stab of almost physical pain. A hitherto subconscious conviction that we were beaten broke forth and dominated my mind. All the pressure of great events, on and against which I had mentally so long maintained my 'flying speed' would cease and I should fall. The power to shape the future would be denied me. The knowledge and experience I had gathered, the authority and goodwill I had gained in so many countries, would vanish. I was discontented at the prospect, and turned over at once to sleep again. I did not wake till nine o'clock. The first results had begun to come in. They were, as I now expected, unfavourable. By noon it was clear that the Socialists would have a majority. At luncheon my wife said to me: 'It may well be a blessing in disguise.' I replied: 'At the moment it seems quite effectively disguised.'

WINSTON CHURCHILL, *WAR MEMOIRS: TRIUMPH AND TRAGEDY*, 1953.

∞

The British general election of 1945 took place with the nation victorious over Nazi Germany (*see* 8 May) but still at war against Japan. During the campaign Churchill, the incomparably popular war leader, made the mistake of comparing the Labour Party with the Gestapo, a slip that exposed his unsuitability in the eyes of many to lead the country towards a new era of postwar reform.

With the votes – including those of servicemen in the Far East – taking several weeks to count, Churchill took part in the Potsdam Conference from 17 July with Soviet leader Stalin and US President Truman, to consider, among other things, the handling of defeated Germany. He returned to Britain on 25 July in anticipation of the election result; after his defeat, his place at the end of the conference was taken by his erstwhile coalition deputy and now Labour prime minister, Clement Attlee.

Although now in Opposition, Churchill nevertheless still bestrode the world stage (*see* 5 March), and in 1951 – in his late seventies – he resumed his prime-ministerial career until finally resigning in 1955.

ALSO ON THIS DAY

1847 Freed American slaves declare the independence of Liberia.
1947 The US Central Intelligence Agency is created.
1974 Civilian rule resumes in Greece after seven years of military rule.

27 JULY

PHILIP II WINS THE BATTLE OF BOUVINES, 1214

Oh the admirable clemency of the prince! Oh his incredible mercy, unheard of in this century! After the king and the barons had returned to the tents, on this very same evening he had brought to him all the noblemen who had been taken in battle. There were thirty of them, amongst whom were five counts and twenty-five men of such high nobility that each carried his own banner in battle, as well as other prisoners of lesser rank.

When they were all in front of him, he gave them all their lives through the great kindness and compassion of his heart; even though all those who were from his kingdom, were his liege-men and had conspired against him and sworn to kill him, deserved to be beheaded according to the customs of the land. Although an inflexible severity against rebels was burning in him, clemency for those who submitted flowered in him even more. His intent always was to spare the meek and defeat the haughty. In chains and in ropes they were loaded on carts to be taken to prisons in various locations.

WILLIAM THE BRETON, CHAPLAIN TO PHILIP II OF FRANCE.

The victory at the Battle of Bouvines, near Lille, of the Capetian French king Philip II (ruled 1180–1223) was a key moment in the emergence of a powerful French monarchy and French state. On that day the king's forces defeated an alliance of the Holy Roman Emperor Otto IV (who was subsequently deposed) and his ally the Duke of Flanders, assisted by Reginald of Boulogne and other former vassals of Philip.

The alliance against Philip had been assembled, though, by King John of England, in an attempt to regain Normandy and Anjou which had been lost ten years earlier. They were portions of the Plantagenet kings' Angevin Empire, which, at its height, included much of what is now western and southwestern France. Philip's victory enabled him to force John to accept a humiliating and expensive truce – and, on his return to England, to submit to the terms of the Magna Carta later imposed on him by his disgruntled barons.

ALSO ON THIS DAY

1794 French Revolution: Robespierre is arrested.
1866 The completion of the first transatlantic cable enables intercontinental telegraphy.
1921 Insulin is discovered, at the University of Toronto.

28 JULY

STALIN DEMANDS 'NOT ONE STEP BACK', 1942

The people of our country, for all the love and respect that they have for the Red Army, are losing faith in it, and many curse it for giving our people over to the yoke of the German oppressors while the army runs away to the east. Some foolish people comfort themselves by saying we can always retreat further east, since we have much territory, land and manpower, and that we will always have more than enough grain. They say this to excuse their shameful conduct at the front. Such talk is lies and falsehood, and only helps our enemies.

After the loss of the Ukraine, Byelorussia, the Baltic lands, the Donbass and other regions, we have much less territory, far fewer people, much less grain and metal, fewer factories and industrial plants. To retreat further would ruin ourselves and our motherland. Every scrap of land that we give up strengthens our enemy and weakens our defence, our motherland.

The time for retreating is over. Not one step back! That must now be our watchword.

Can we take the blows of the enemy and push them back to the west? Yes, we can, because our factories are doing excellent work and the front is receiving ever more aircraft, tanks, artillery and mortars.

We lack order and discipline. This is our main shortcoming. We must establish the strictest order and iron discipline if we want to rescue the situation and defend our motherland. Panickers and cowards will be eliminated on the spot. Commanders of companies, battalions, regiments and divisions, along with their commissars and political workers, will be considered traitors to the motherland if they retreat without orders.

JOSEPH STALIN, PEOPLE'S COMMISSAR OF DEFENCE, ORDER NO. 227, 28 JULY 1942.

Following the speedy Nazi advance through the Soviet Union after Hitler had unleashed his Operation Barbarossa invasion in June 1941, Stalin determined in the summer of 1942 to draw a line in the sand. The ensuing nightmarish battle and siege at Stalingrad (*see* 24 January) did indeed see 'panickers and cowards… eliminated on the spot'. However, at a huge human cost, it proved a turning point in the war.

ALSO ON THIS DAY

1868 The 14th Amendment to the US Constitution guarantees black citizenship.
1914 Austria-Hungary declares war on Serbia.
1976 An earthquake in Tangshan, China, kills hundreds of thousands.

29 JULY

THE DEATH OF VINCENT VAN GOGH, 1890

Our dear friend Vincent died four days ago.

...On Sunday evening he went out into the countryside near Auvers, placed his easel against a haystack and went behind the chateau and fired a revolver shot at himself. Under the violence of the impact (the bullet entered his body below the heart) he fell, but he got up again, and fell three times more, before he got back to the inn where he was staying (Ravoux, place de la Mairie) without telling anyone about his injury. He finally died on Monday evening, still smoking his pipe which he refused to let go of, explaining that his suicide had been absolutely deliberate and that he had done it in complete lucidity.

...On the walls of the room where his body was laid out all his last canvases were hung, making a sort of halo for him, and the brilliance of the genius that radiated from them made this death even more painful for us artists who were there. The coffin was covered with a simple white cloth and surrounded with masses of flowers, the sunflowers that he loved so much, yellow dahlias, yellow flowers everywhere. It was, you will remember, his favourite colour, the symbol of the light that he dreamed of as being in people's hearts as well as in works of art.

ARTIST ÉMILE BERNARD, LETTER TO ART COLLECTOR ALBERT AURIER,

4 AUGUST 1890.

∞

The Post-Impressionist artist Vincent Van Gogh shot himself in the stomach in a field near Auvers-sur-Oise, outside Paris, on 27 July 1890. It was the location of one of his last paintings, *Wheatfield with Flight of Crows*. His brother, the art dealer Théo (who had encouraged him to take up art), had been the troubled painter's vital emotional support and he now went to attend him, reporting Vincent's last words as: 'The sadness will last forever.' The 37-year-old Vincent died on 29 July.

Writing a few days later to their sister Elizabeth, Théo asserted: 'People should realize that he was a great artist, something which often coincides with being a great human being. In the course of time this will surely be acknowledged, and many will regret his early death.' Théo died a mere six months later, too soon to witness the global adulation that would indeed attach itself to Vincent and his work.

ALSO ON THIS DAY

1948 The Olympic Games open in London.
1981 Prince Charles and Lady Diana Spencer marry at St Paul's Cathedral, London.
2005 The discovery of the dwarf planet Eris is announced by the Palomar Observatory.

THE MARSEILLAISE IS SUNG IN PARIS, 1792

Allons enfants de la Patrie,	Arise, children of the Fatherland,
Le jour de gloire est arrivé!	The day of glory has arrived!
Contre nous de la tyrannie,	Against us is tyranny
L'étendard sanglant est levé,	The bloody banner is raised,
L'étendard sanglant est levé,	The bloody banner is raised,
Entendez-vous dans nos campagnes	Do you hear the sounds in the fields?
Mugir ces féroces soldats?	The howling of those ferocious soldiers?
Ils viennent jusque dans nos bras	They're coming right into our arms
Égorger nos fils et nos compagnes!	To slit the throats of our sons and our companions!
[chorus]	
Aux armes, citoyens,	To arms, citizens,
Formez vos bataillons,	Form your battalions,
Marchons, marchons!	Let's march, let's march!
Qu'un sang impur	So that impure blood
Abreuve nos sillons!	Waters our furrows!

The patriotic song 'La Marseillaise' (seven verses in all) was composed by Claude Joseph Rouget de Lisle in Strasbourg in April 1792, intended to be the 'Song of the Army of the Rhine' as the French attempted to defend their revolution against the invasion by Prussia and Austria. On 30 July 1972 it was heard for the first time in Paris when it was sung by an arriving troop of volunteers from Marseilles, in the south, who had adopted it as their marching song. In 1793 Rouget de Lisle, a royalist sympathizer, was threatened with the guillotine for refusing to take an oath to the new republic; he was reprieved for having written 'La Marseillaise'. By 1796 it was adopted as the first French national anthem, though later suppressed by Napoleon as dangerous until readopted in 1879. Since then it has been diffused far and wide, in the 20th century making notable cameo appearances in the film *Casablanca* and The Beatles' 'All You Need is Love'.

ALSO ON THIS DAY

762 The traditional date of the founding of Baghdad.
1945 WWII: the USS *Indianapolis sinks* with 883 lives lost.
2006 The final edition of BBC's *Top of the Pops* is broadcast, after a run of 42 years.

31 JULY

THE ARREST OF DR CRIPPEN, 1910

The *Montrose* was in port at Antwerp when I read that a warrant had been issued for Crippen and le Neve... Soon we sailed for Quebec... On the third day out I gave my wireless operator a message for Liverpool: 'One hundred and thirty miles west of Lizard... have strong suspicions that Crippen London cellar murderer and accomplice are among saloon passengers... Accomplice dressed as boy; voice, manner and build undoubtedly a girl.'

...Imagine my excitement when my operator brought me a message he had intercepted from a London newspaper to its representative aboard the White Star liner *Laurentic*... 'What is Inspector Dew doing? Is he sending and receiving wireless messages? Are passengers excited over chase? Reply.'

This was the first I knew that my message to Liverpool had caused Inspector Dew to catch the first boat out. She would reach the Newfoundland coast before me. I hoped that if she had any news she would leave it at the Belle Isle station.

She had news indeed: 'Will board you at Father Point... strictly confidential... from Inspector Dew, Scotland Yard, aboard *Laurentic*.'

The last night was dreary and anxious... I could see 'Mr Robinson' [Crippen] strolling about the deck. I had invited him up early to see the 'pilots' come aboard. When they did so they came straight to my cabin. I sent for Mr Robinson...

As he came in the detective said: 'Good morning, Dr Crippen. Do you know me? I'm Inspector Dew, from Scotland Yard.' Crippen quivered. Surprise struck him dumb. Then he said, 'Thank God it's over. The suspense has been too great. I couldn't stand it any longer.'

CAPTAIN H.G. KENDALL, CAPTAIN OF THE SS *MONTROSE*, RECOLLECTIONS.

∞

Hawley Crippen, the American homeopathic doctor suspected of poisoning his second wife and burying her body in the basement of their London house, was the first fugitive to be apprehended with the aid of wireless telegraphy. He was arrested as the *Montrose* – on which he and his lover, Ethel le Neve, were fleeing Europe in disguise – arrived in Canada, having been overtaken by Inspector Dew on the faster SS *Laurentic*.

ALSO ON THIS DAY

1784 The death of the French encyclopaedist and philosopher Denis Diderot.
1956 The cricketer Jim Laker takes 10 Australian wickets in a Test match innings.
1964 *Ranger 7* transmits the first detailed photographs of the Moon to Earth.

AUGUST

∽

1 AUGUST

ANNE FRANK'S LAST DIARY ENTRY, 1944

What I say is not what I feel, which is why I have a reputation for being a boy-chaser, a flirt, a smart aleck and a reader of romances. The happy-go-lucky Anne laughs, gives a flippant reply, shrugs her shoulders and pretends she couldn't care less. The quiet Anne reacts in just the opposite way.

If I'm being completely honest, I'll have to admit that it does matter to me, that I'm trying very hard to change myself, but that I'm always up against a more powerful enemy. A voice within me is sobbing, 'You see, that's what's become of you. You're surrounded by negative opinions, dismayed looks and mocking faces, people who dislike you, and all because you don't listen to the advice of your own better half.'

I'd like to listen, but it doesn't work, because if I'm quiet and serious, everyone thinks I'm putting on a new act and I have to save myself with a joke, and then I'm not even talking about my own family, who assume I must be ill, stuff me with aspirins and sedatives, feel my neck and forehead to see if I have a temperature, ask about my bowel movements and berate me for being in a bad mood, until I just can't keep it up any more, because when everybody starts hovering over me, I get cross, then sad, and finally end up turning my heart inside out, the bad part on the outside and the good part on the inside, and keep trying to find a way to become what I'd like to be and what I could be if... if only there were no other people in the world.

ANNE FRANK, DIARY, 1 AUGUST 1944.

∞

Thus went the final diary entry of the 15-year-old Jewish girl Anne Frank. It was written on 1 August 1944, after more than two years in hiding in the Nazi-occupied Netherlands (see 12 June). After Anne's death at Bergen-Belsen in March 1945, the diaries were found by Miep Gies, who had helped shelter the family in Amsterdam, and given to Anne's father Otto, who had survived his incarceration in Auschwitz. He published versions in 1947, and other editions followed, transforming the teenager Anne's private thoughts and fears into perhaps the most widely disseminated voice of the tragedy of the Holocaust, familiar to children and adults worldwide.

ALSO ON THIS DAY

30 BC Octavian enters Alexandria, annexing Egypt for Rome.
1834 The Slavery Abolition Act becomes operative in most of the British Empire.
1944 WWII: the Warsaw Uprising begins.

2 AUGUST

EINSTEIN ADVOCATES THE BOMB

In the course of the last four months it has been made probable – through the work of [Frédéric] Joliot in France as well as [Enrico] Fermi and [Leo] Szilard in America – that it may become possible to set up a nuclear chain reaction in a large mass of uranium, by which vast amounts of power and large quantities of new radium-like elements would be generated. Now it appears almost certain that this could be achieved in the immediate future.

…This new phenomenon would also lead to the construction of bombs, and it is conceivable – though much less certain – that extremely powerful bombs of a new type may thus be constructed. A single bomb of this type, carried by boat and exploded in a port, might very well destroy the whole port together with some of the surrounding territory. However, such bombs might very well prove to be too heavy for transportation by air.

ALBERT EINSTEIN, LETTER, 2 AUGUST 1939.

Albert Einstein's letter of 2 August 1939 warned the US president, Franklin D. Roosevelt, about the implications of recent advances in nuclear physics, and in effect encouraged Roosevelt to commence work on an atomic bomb before the Nazis could develop one. Although Einstein – himself a Jewish refugee from Germany – did not say so, physicists in Germany had achieved nuclear fission in 1938, and Einstein now feared that the work of Nobel prize-winner Frédéric Joliot-Curie might also fall into German hands. Leo Szilard, a Hungarian émigré, encouraged Einstein to write this letter; it inspired Roosevelt to accelerate research, eventually setting up the Manhattan Project to build the American bomb (*see also* 16 July and 6 August). Later, however, Einstein regretted his decision, saying: 'The release of atom power has changed everything except our way of thinking… the solution to this problem lies in the heart of mankind. If only I had known, I should have become a watchmaker.'

ALSO ON THIS DAY

216 BC Hannibal defeats the Romans at Cannae, southeast Italy.
1964 Vietnam War: North Vietnamese gunboats fire on US destroyers in the Gulf of Tonkin.
1980 The Bologna railway station bombing kills 85 people.

3 AUGUST

OLIVER CROMWELL DEMANDS A CHANGE OF POLICY IN SCOTLAND, 1650

Your own guilt is too much for you to bear: bring not therefore upon yourselves the blood of innocent men, deceived with pretences of King and Covenant; from whose eyes you hide a better knowledge! I am persuaded that divers of you, who lead the People, have laboured to build yourselves in these things; wherein you have censured others, and established yourselves 'upon the Word of God'. Is it therefore infallibly agreeable to the Word of God, all that you say? I beseech you, in the bowels of Christ, think it possible you may be mistaken.

...There may be a spiritual fulness, which the World may call drunkenness; as in the second Chapter of the Acts. There may be, as well, a carnal confidence upon misunderstood and misapplied precepts, which may be called spiritual drunkenness. There may be a Covenant made with Death and Hell. I will not say yours was so. But judge if such things have a politic aim: To avoid the overflowing scourge; or, To accomplish worldly interests? And if therein we have confederated with wicked and carnal men, and have respect for them, or otherwise 'have' drawn them in to associate with us, Whether this be a Covenant of God, and spiritual? Bethink yourselves; we hope we do.

OLIVER CROMWELL, LETTER TO THE SCOTTISH KIRK, 1650.

In July 1650, Oliver Cromwell, the dominant figure in the establishment of the Commonwealth set up after the execution of Charles I in January 1649, invaded Scotland. He was infuriated both by the proclamation of the young Charles II as King of Scots in February 1649 (he was crowned at Scone on 1 January 1651), and by their intention of restoring him to the English throne and imposing Presbyterianism across Britain. On 3 August, Cromwell wrote furiously to the General Assembly of the Kirk, accusing them of having failed to present his policies to the Scottish people and urging a change of heart. Their reply was equally blunt: 'Would you have us to be sceptics in our religion?' A month later, however, Cromwell defeated the Scots at Dunbar. After the battle, so historian John Morrill recounts, he 'laughed uncontrollably', calling it 'a high act of the Lord's Providence to us [and] one of the most signal mercies God hath done for England and His people'.

ALSO ON THIS DAY

1492 Christopher Columbus sets out from Spain on the first transatlantic voyage.
1914 WWI: Germany declares war on France.
1936 The African-American Jesse Owens wins the 100m sprint at the Berlin Olympics.

4 AUGUST

EUROPE DISSOLVES INTO THE GREAT WAR, 1914

The cascade of events that began with the assassination of the Austrian Archduke Franz Ferdinand in Sarejevo (*see* 28 June) led Austria to declare war on Serbia on 28 July 1914. Russian mobilization against Austria, German mobilization, French mobilization, a German declaration of war on Russia, and German invasion of Belgium *en route* to invasion of France all followed within the next seven days. Although Germany hoped to keep Britain out of the conflict, Prime Minister Herbert Asquith and Foreign Secretary Sir Edward Grey could not allow Germany to become a dominant power in Europe.

At 9.30 a.m. on 3 August, Asquith telegraphed to Sir Edward Goschen, the British ambassador in Berlin:

The King of the Belgians has made an appeal to His Majesty the King for diplomatic intervention on behalf of Belgium.

His Majesty's government are also informed that the German government has delivered to the Belgium government a note proposing friendly neutrality entailing free passage through Belgian territory and promising to maintain the independence and integrity of the kingdom and its possessions at the conclusion of peace, threatening in case of refusal to treat Belgium as an enemy. An answer was requested within twelve hours.

We also understand that Belgium has categorically refused this as a flagrant violation of the law of nations.

His Majesty's government are bound to protest against this violation of a treaty to which Germany is a party in common with themselves, and must request an assurance that the demand made upon Belgium will not be proceeded with, and that her neutrality will be respected by Germany. You should ask for an immediate reply.

Goschen described his subsequent meeting:

Herr von Jagow [the German foreign minister] replied ... that the safety of the [German] Empire rendered it absolutely necessary that the Imperial troops should advance through Belgium.

I gave His Excellency a written summary of your telegram and, pointing out that you had mentioned 12 o'clock as the time when His Majesty's government would expect an answer, asked him whether, in view of the terrible consequences which would necessarily ensue, it were not possible even at the last moment that their answer should be reconsidered.

He replied that if the time given were even 24 hours or more, his answer must be the same...

I then said that I should like to go and see the [German] chancellor, as it might be, perhaps, the last time I should have an opportunity of seeing him. He begged me to do so. I found the chancellor very agitated.

His Excellency Chancellor Theobald von Bethman-Hollweg at once began a harangue, which lasted for about twenty minutes. He said that the step taken by His Majesty's government was terrible to a degree; just for a word – 'neutrality', a word which in war time had so often been disregarded – just for a scrap of paper Great Britain was going to make war on a kindred nation who desired nothing better than to be friends with her.

Goschen now asked for his passport, a request that was taken by the Germans as a *de facto* declaration of war. In London that evening, Sir Edward Grey watched the street-lights being lit and commented:

The lamps are going out all over Europe; we shall not see them lit again during our lifetime.

On the next day, 4 August, Grey wrote to the German ambassador:

The result of the communication made at Berlin having been that His Majesty's ambassador has had to ask for his passports, I have the honour to inform Your Excellency that in accordance with the terms of the notification made to the German government today His Majesty's government consider that a state of war exists between the two countries as from today at 11 o'clock p.m.

Two days later Asquith told the House of Commons that:

I do not believe any nation ever entered into a great controversy – and this is one of the greatest history will ever know – with a clearer conscience and a stronger conviction that it is fighting, not for aggression, not for the maintenance even of its own selfish interest, but that it is fighting in defence of principles the maintenance of which is vital to the civilization of the world.

ALSO ON THIS DAY

1265 A royal army defeats and kills the rebellious Simon de Montfort at the Battle of Evesham.
1704 War of the Spanish Succession: the British capture Gibraltar.
1892 Lizzie Borden's parents are found murdered in their home in Massachusetts.

5 AUGUST

OSWALD OF NORTHUMBRIA DIES IN BATTLE, 642

Oswald, the most Christian king of Northumbria... fell in battle at Maserfield against the heathen king and people of Mercia, who had also slain his predecessor Edwin... Oswald's great devotion and faith in God was made evident by the miracles that took place after his death. For at the place where he was killed fighting for his country, sick men and beasts are healed to this day. Many people took away earth from the place where his body fell and put it in water, from which sick folk who drank it received great benefit. This practice became so popular that as the earth was gradually removed, a pit was left in which a man could stand

BEDE, *HISTORY OF THE ENGLISH CHURCH AND PEOPLE*, 731.

Oswald, king of Northumbria, had been the most powerful ruler in Britain in the 630s, and was responsible for the spreading and deepening of Christianity, which had been introduced to Northumbria by the Roman bishop Paulinus in 627. In 635 Oswald invited the Irish monk Aidan to his kingdom from the Scottish monastery of Iona, which he had visited in his youth. He gave Aidan the island of Lindisfarne for his see. Although Oswald was recognized as the high king across much of England, the Mercian king Penda refused to acknowledge him or his new religion, and Oswald died on his campaign against Mercia – probably at Oswestry in the Welsh borders.

The Celtic form of Christianity introduced by Aidan differed from the Roman form in a number of ways, notably in the degree of independence it permitted to monks. It also calculated the date of Easter – the most important day in the Christian calendar – differently. The tensions between the two forms were only resolved at the Synod of Whitby, called by Oswald's successor, his brother Oswiu, in 664. The Venerable Bede, a monk working at Jarrow, in Northumbria, completed his account of the establishment of the English church in 731.

ALSO ON THIS DAY

1861 The US government introduces income tax.
1962 The death of the actress and sex symbol Marilyn Monroe.
1963 The Anglo-US-Soviet nuclear test ban treaty is signed.

6 AUGUST

THE HIROSHIMA BOMB, 1945

Medical relief agencies from neighbouring districts cannot distinguish – much less identify – the dead from the injured. The impact of the bomb was so terrific that practically all living things – human and animal – were literally seared to death by the tremendous heat and pressure set up by the blast. All the dead and injured were burned beyond recognition.

TOKYO RADIO BROADCAST, 1945.

∞

If they do not now accept our terms, they may expect a rain of ruin from the air the likes of which has never been seen on this earth.

US PRESIDENT HARRY S TRUMAN, PRESIDENTIAL ADDRESS, 1945.

∞

The single bomb that dropped onto Hiroshima from a cloudless sky at 8.15 a.m. on 6 August 1945 shocked and awed the world. Releasing the energy locked up in the nuclei of its uranium atoms, it immediately killed up to 70,000 people and damaged or destroyed over 90 per cent of the Japanese city.

Although Japan's resources were now so depleted that defeat seemed inevitable, the country's regime was preparing its citizens to fight to the last. Not only did Allied forces face the prospect of further attritional fighting, but the United States was keen to act decisively to forestall Soviet involvement in Japan's future.

As the horror of Hiroshima sank in, leaflets were dropped throughout Japan:

We are in possession of the most destructive explosive ever devised by man... We have just begun to use this weapon against your homeland. If you still have any doubt, make inquiry as to what happened to Hiroshima... We urge that you accept these consequences and begin the work of building a new, better, and peace-loving Japan.

Three days later, the threat was made good with a second bomb on Nagasaki. On 15 August, Emperor Hirohito made his first-ever broadcast to his people and prepared them for imminent surrender, saying it was time to 'endure the unendurable'.

ALSO ON THIS DAY

1806 The abdication of Francis II signals the end of the Holy Roman Empire.
1890 The first execution of a US convict by means of the electric chair takes place.
1962 US President Lyndon Johnson signs the Voting Rights Act.

7 AUGUST

A LYNCHING IN INDIANA, 1930

Thousands of Indianans carrying picks, bats, axe handles, crowbars, torches, and firearms attacked the Grant County Courthouse, determined to 'get those goddamn Niggers.' A barrage of rocks shattered the jailhouse windows, sending dozens of frantic inmates in search of cover. A sixteen-year-old boy, James Cameron, one of the three intended victims, paralyzed by fear and incomprehension, recognized familiar faces in the crowd – schoolmates, and customers whose lawns he had mowed and whose shoes he had polished – as they tried to break down the jailhouse door with sledgehammers. Many police officers milled outside with the crowd, joking. Inside, fifty guards with guns waited downstairs.

The door was ripped from the wall, and a mob of fifty men beat Thomas Shipp senseless and dragged him into the street. The waiting crowd 'came to life.' It seemed to Cameron that 'all of those ten to fifteen thousand people were trying to hit him all at once.' The dead Shipp was dragged with a rope up to the window bars of the second victim, Abram Smith. For twenty minutes, citizens pushed and shoved for a closer look at the 'dead nigger.' By the time Abe Smith was hauled out he was equally mutilated. Those who were not close enough to hit him threw rocks and bricks. Somebody rammed a crowbar through his chest several times in great satisfaction. Smith was dead by the time the mob dragged him 'like a horse' to the courthouse square and hung him from a tree. The lynchers posed for photos under the limb that held the bodies of the two dead men.

Then the mob headed back for James Cameron and 'mauled him all the way to the courthouse square,' shoving and kicking him to the tree, where the lynchers put a hanging rope around his neck. Cameron credited an unidentified woman's voice with silencing the mob (Cameron, a devout Roman Catholic, believes that it was the voice of the Virgin Mary) and opening a path for his retreat to the county jail and, ultimately, for saving his life...

After souvenir hunters divvied up the bloodied pants of Abram Smith, his naked lower body was clothed in a Klansman's robe – not unlike the loincloth in traditional depictions of Christ on the cross. Lawrence Beitler, a studio photographer, took this [photograph of the bodies of Shipp and Smith]. For ten days and nights he printed thousands of copies, which sold for fifty cents apiece.

JAMES CAMERON, *A TIME OF TERROR*, 1982.

∞

James Cameron was the sole survivor of the last lynching to take place in the Northern United States, in Marion, Indiana, on 7 August 1930. He and the other two victims, all in their teens, were accused of a robbery, murder and sexual assault.

The woman who appealed for Cameron's life was never identified, and he continued to attribute his rescue to divine intervention. In later life he became a civil rights activist.

The photograph mentioned in the final paragraph inspired the poem 'Strange Fruit' by songwriter Abel Meeropol, which would later be sung by blues singer Billie Holiday as the closing number of every set she performed:

Southern trees bear a strange fruit,
Blood on the leaves and blood at the root,
Black body swinging in the Southern breeze,
Strange fruit hanging from the poplar trees.

Pastoral scene of the gallant South,
The bulging eyes and the twisted mouth,
Scent of magnolias sweet and fresh,
And the sudden smell of burning flesh.

Here is a fruit for the crows to pluck,
For the rain to gather, for the wind to suck,
For the sun to rot, for a tree to drop,
Here is a strange and bitter crop.

Lynchings in the South continued into the late 1960s.

ALSO ON THIS DAY

1942 WWII: US forces begin the campaign to recapture Guadalcanal in the Solomon Islands.
1960 Côte d'Ivoire achieves independence from France.
1998 Al-Qaeda bomb the US embassies in Kenya and Tanzania.

8 AUGUST

THE RESIGNATION OF RICHARD NIXON, 1974

I have never been a quitter. To leave office before my term is completed is abhorrent to every instinct in my body. But as president, I must put the interest of America first. America needs a full-time president and a full-time Congress, particularly at this time with problems we face at home and abroad.

To continue to fight through the months ahead for my personal vindication would almost totally absorb the time and attention of both the president and the Congress in a period when our entire focus should be on the great issues of peace abroad and prosperity without inflation at home.

Therefore, I shall resign the presidency effective at noon tomorrow.

...I regret deeply any injuries that may have been done in the course of the events that led to this decision. I would say only that if some of my judgments were wrong, and some were wrong, they were made in what I believed at the time to be the best interest of the nation.

RICHARD M. NIXON, TELEVISED PRESIDENTIAL ADDRESS, 8 AUGUST 1974.

After two years of increasingly embattled defence, the 37th president of the United States went on television to become the first one to resign the office. The initial crime, a break-in on 17 June 1972 at the Watergate Hotel in Washington, DC, the headquarters of the Democratic Party, appeared to be part of a dirty-tricks campaign by his election team; but it was quickly linked to the White House itself, and the cover-up that ensued involved destroying evidence and a clear implication of Nixon's knowledge and, to some extent at least, authorization. The president now faced the imminent prospect of impeachment. Meanwhile transcripts and taped recordings of the president's meetings revealed he was suffering a degree of paranoia that was widely felt to be stifling his ability to perform his official duties.

ALSO ON THIS DAY

1876 Thomas Edison patents the 'mimeograph' for printing.
1918 WWI: the Battle of Amiens begins the Allied push for victory.
1991 The Beirut hostage John McCarthy is freed after five years' captivity.

9 AUGUST

QUEEN ELIZABETH DEFIES THE SPANISH ARMADA, 1588

My loving people, We have been persuaded by some that are careful of our safety, to take heed how we commit our selves to armed multitudes, for fear of treachery; but I assure you I do not desire to live to distrust my faithful and loving people. Let tyrants fear. I have always so behaved myself that, under God, I have placed my chiefest strength and safeguard in the loyal hearts and good-will of my subjects; and therefore I am come amongst you, as you see, at this time, not for my recreation and disport, but being resolved, in the midst and heat of the battle, to live and die amongst you all; to lay down for my God, and for my kingdom, and my people, my honour and my blood even, in the dust.

I know I have the body but of a weak and feeble woman; but I have the heart and stomach of a king, and of a King of England too, and think foul scorn that [the Duke of] Parma or Spain, or any prince of Europe, should dare to invade the borders of my realm; to which rather than any dishonour shall grow by me, I myself will take up arms, I myself will be your general, judge, and rewarder of every one of your virtues in the field.

I know already, for your forwardness you have deserved rewards and crowns; and We do assure you in the word of a prince, they shall be duly paid you. In the mean time, my lieutenant general shall be in my stead, than whom never prince commanded a more noble or worthy subject; not doubting but… we shall shortly have a famous victory over those enemies of my God, of my kingdom, and of my people.

QUEEN ELIZABETH I, SPEECH, TILBURY, 9 AUGUST 1588.

∞

Elizabeth I's address at Tilbury to troops preparing to defend England against possible invasion was made shortly after the principal naval battle with the Spanish Armada, at Gravelines. The day before the battle English fireships had caused havoc among the Spanish foe, and during the next day's fighting several Spanish ships were sunk. It was the beginning of the end for the Spanish invasion plans, but England remained alert for a possible Spanish landing nevertheless. The speech was not written down until the later 1620s, almost 40 years later.

ALSO ON THIS DAY

1902 King Edward VII of Britain is crowned.
1945 WWII: the atomic bomb is dropped over Nagasaki, Japan.
1969 The actress Sharon Tate and four others are murdered by Charles Manson's 'Family'.

10 AUGUST

THE DESTRUCTION OF THE TEMPLE OF JERUSALEM, AD 70

Titus resolved to storm the temple the next day... But as for that house, God had, for certain, long ago doomed it to the fire; and now that fatal day was come, according to the revolution of ages...

These flames took their rise from the Jews themselves; for when Titus retired, the rebels lay still for a while, and then attacked the Romans again, while those that guarded the temple fought with those that quenched the fire that was burning the inner temple; but these Romans put the Jews to flight, and proceeded as far as the holy house itself. Now one of the soldiers, without staying for any orders, and without any concern or dread upon him at so great an undertaking, and inspired by a divine fury, snatched some of the burning materials and, lifted up by another soldier, set fire to a golden window through which was a passage to the rooms around the holy house, on the north side of it. As the flames went up, the Jews made a great clamour, and ran to prevent it; and let nothing get in their way as their holy house was perishing.

Now someone ran to Titus, and told him of this fire, as he was resting in his tent; he rose in great haste, and ran to the holy house, to have the fire put out ...Calling to the soldiers that were fighting, and giving a signal to them with his right hand, he ordered them to quench the fire. But they did not hear... as some were distracted with fighting, others with passion. As for the legions that came running, neither persuasions nor threats could restrain them from violence, but each man was ruled by his own passion. As they crowded into the temple, many were trampled, while others fell among the hot and smoking ruins of the cloisters, and were destroyed in the same miserable way as those whom they had conquered. When they came near the holy house, they pretended not to hear Caesar's orders; but they encouraged those that were ahead of them to set it on fire. As for the rebels, they could not help, as most were weak and without arms, and had their throats cut if they were caught. Around the altar lay a heap of dead bodies; a great quantity of their blood ran down its steps, while the bodies of those killed by the altar also fell down them.

Since Caesar could not restrain his soldiers, or stop the fire, he went into the holy place of the temple, and looked at it, with what was in it. He realized it was far superior to the reports he had received from foreigners, and not inferior to what the Jews themselves believed about it. As the flames had not as yet reached to its innermost parts, he again tried to persuade the soldiers to put out the fire, and gave order to the centurion to beat any soldier who refused; yet their passions were stronger than their regards for Caesar. The hope of plunder also drove many on, as they believed that the places within were full of money, and all round about it was made of gold. Then one of them obstructed Caesar, when he ran out to restrain the soldiers, and threw the fire upon the hinges of the gate, in the dark; whereby the flame immediately burst out from within the holy house itself. Thus the holy house was burnt down, against Caesar's wishes.

JOSEPHUS, *THE JEWISH WAR*, BOOK VI, *c.*AD 75.

The Romano-Jewish historian Josephus wrote a vivid account of the defeat by Titus, son of the emperor Vespasian, of the Jewish revolt against the Romans that had broken out in AD 66. The revolt ended with the Temple of Jerusalem burned and its treasures taken to Rome, and the further scattering (diaspora) of Jews outside Palestine. Josephus claimed to be writing a balanced account; however, he was working in Rome under the patronage of the ruling Flavian dynasty, and he blamed much of the disaster on the Jewish people themselves:

> *...No other city has ever endured such horrors, and no generation in history has fathered such wickedness. In the end they brought the whole Hebrew race into contempt in order to make their own impiety seem less outrageous in foreign eyes, and confessed the painful truth that they were slaves, the dregs of humanity, bastards, and outcasts of their nation.*

ALSO ON THIS DAY

991 Vikings defeat the Saxons at the Battle of Maldon, Essex.
1792 French Revolution: the royal palace is stormed and Louis XVI arrested.
1821 Missouri becomes the 24th US state.

11 AUGUST

HERBERT HOOVER ANNOUNCES
THE END OF POVERTY, 1928

One of the oldest and perhaps the noblest of human aspirations has been the abolition of poverty. By poverty I mean the grinding by undernourishment, cold and ignorance and fear of old age of those who have the will to work. We in America today are nearer to the final triumph over poverty than ever before in the history of any land. The poorhouse is vanishing from among us. We have not yet reached the goal, but given a chance to go forward with the policies of the last eight years, and we shall soon with the help of God be in sight of the day when poverty will be banished from this Nation. There is no guarantee against poverty equal to a job for every man. That is the primary purpose of the economic policies we advocate.

HERBERT HOOVER, SPEECH, 11 AUGUST 1928.

Herbert Hoover (1874–1964) gave an alarming hostage to fortune in his acceptance speech at the US Republican Party convention in 1928. Under the presidencies of Warren Harding and Calvin Coolidge, during the 1920s, Hoover had served as secretary of commerce: he appeared to know what he was talking about.

Hoover won the subsequent presidential election easily, partly by attacking the unpopular policy of Prohibition, partly by riding the wave of national prosperity. In his inauguration speech he repeated his promise to banish poverty, but eight months after taking office the Wall Street Crash initiated his country's descent into the Great Depression (*see* 29 October), and poverty, far from being banished, made a comeback across the United States. Hoover was reluctant to run up a budget deficit in order to combat unemployment through government action.

Shortly before his devastating electoral defeat by Democratic Party contender Franklin D. Roosevelt in 1932, Hoover belatedly introduced policies which, much expanded by the incoming president, proved to be the foundation of the New Deal. He remained, though, a critic of the large scope of the New Deal.

ALSO ON THIS DAY

1456 The death of John Hunyadi, ruler of Hungary.
1855 Charles Barrington becomes the first man to climb the Eiger, in the Bernese Oberland.
1965 The Watts Riots break out in Los Angeles.

12 AUGUST

THE DEATH OF CLEOPATRA, 30 BC

Cleopatra begged Caesar to be permitted to pour libations for Antony. When the request was granted, she embraced his urn, saying: 'Antony, I buried you with hands still free; now I pour libations for you as a captive, and so carefully guarded that I cannot with blows or tears disfigure this body of mine, which is a slave's body...'

She wreathed the urn, then... made a sumptuous meal. And there came a man from the country carrying a basket with a dish full of figs... After eating, Cleopatra took a sealed tablet and sent it to Caesar, and then, dismissing all the company except two women, she closed the doors.

When Caesar opened the tablet, he knew what had happened... He sent messengers to investigate... But though they ran, they found Cleopatra dead upon a golden couch, arrayed in royal state...

It is said that the asp was brought hidden beneath the figs, for so Cleopatra had given orders that the reptile might fasten itself upon her body without her being aware of it. But when she took some figs and saw it, she bared her arm and held it out for the bite. But others say that the asp was shut in a water jar, and that as Cleopatra stirred it with a golden distaff it fastened itself upon her arm. But the truth no one knows. It was also said that she carried poison in a hollow comb hidden in her hair... Some say that Cleopatra's arm had two slight punctures; and Caesar seems to have believed this, for in his triumph an image of Cleopatra with the asp clinging to her was carried.

PLUTARCH, *LIFE OF ANTONY*, C. AD 98.

The Roman historian Plutarch, writing over a century after the events he described, produced a rich and memorable account of the story of Antony, Octavian Caesar – later Augustus (*see* 16 January and 19 August) – and Cleopatra, the last queen of Ancient Egypt before her country became a Roman province. His account, well-known in 16th-century Europe, became the basis of Shakespeare's tragedy *Antony and Cleopatra*.

ALSO ON THIS DAY

1480 Ottoman forces capture Otranto, southern Italy.
1914 WWI: Britain declares war on Austria-Hungary.
1966 John Lennon apologizes for comparing The Beatles to Jesus Christ.

13 AUGUST

THE BERLIN WALL GOES UP, 1961

8 am. My colleague phoned and said 'Get out of bed and come to the office quickly because they've sealed off West Berlin, but before you do that tell your relatives.' My grandparents lived close and I went there then caught the tram. It stopped at Eberswalder Strasse, not very far from the office, because barbed wire had been rolled across the tramlines. I got out and thought I was dreaming. People jumped over the one roll of wire and made fun of it like a game even though they were told not to. They thought it was a joke but as another roll uncoiled the seriousness dawned on them. Many hung around jeering as one lot of wire unrolled after another. People watched from windows...

I walked to the office... I couldn't believe it, I couldn't believe that was it. All the people I spoke to said: 'Wait for the Americans to come, they will help us. The Allies will help us.'

ERDMUTE GRIES-BEHRENDT, INTERVIEW.

On 12 August 1961 Erdmute Gries-Behrendt, secretary at the Reuters press office in East Berlin, was visiting her family in West Berlin. She returned to her home in the East in the early hours of the Sunday morning – on what proved to be the last U-Bahn (underground) train to cross the border for 30 years. Her next, brief, visit to her family in the West was not until 1976.

Barbed-wire barricades were erected during the night of 12–13 August 1961 by the East German army, in many cases running down the centre of streets and sometimes even through buildings. In Western eyes, East Berlin remained the Soviet sector of the divided city, but in practice it was the capital of the Communist East German state, which was losing large numbers of its people to West Germany via Berlin's porous border. A more permanent barrier soon followed the barbed wire, becoming – literally – the most concrete manifestation of the Cold War divide. US presidents visited Berlin to protest at the wall's existence, most famously John F. Kennedy (*see* 26 June), but it endured until 1989 – during which time more than 200 people had died trying to cross from East to West.

At the time of the wall's demise (*see* 9 November), Gries-Behrendt was still working for Reuters.

ALSO ON THIS DAY

1704 War of the Spanish Succession: an Allied army defeats the French at Blenheim.
1863 The death of the French artist Eugène Delacroix.
1966 The Chinese Communist Party announces the 'New Leap Forward': the Cultural Revolution.

14 AUGUST

THE END OF THE BOXER REBELLION, 1900

At last our ears have heard the sweet music for which we have been listening for two months – the cannonading of the relief army – so plainly that we know that intense desire and imagination are not deceiving us, as so many times before. Our deliverance is at hand. Last night was a fearful one. There were at least six distinct attacks, the first beginning about eight in the evening, and there was almost incessant firing between these attacks. Our implacable foes seemed determined to use to the utmost this last chance to wipe us out. Our garrison returned fire more than at any other time, for now they are not afraid of exhausting their ammunition...

It was a little after two in the afternoon, as I was sitting writing under the trees in the tennis-court, where I have spent so many hours during these past weeks, when an American Marine from the city wall ran into the yard shouting, 'The troops are inside the city – almost here!' There was a wild rush for the south end of the compound, and there, sheltered by the barricades, we stood and saw the first of the relief army straggling up the streets. And who do you think they were? Black-faced, high-turbaned troops, Rajputs from India – great, fierce-looking fellows, but their faces were beaming with joy, and they hurrahed louder than we did. There were British officers with them, and one of them stooped in passing and kissed a pale-faced girlie who looked as if she needed to be rescued by a relief army. All that afternoon the troops came streaming in, Sihks, Bengal Lancers; English soldiers, and, most welcome of all, our American boys.

MINER LUELLA, *OUTLOOK*, 10 NOVEMBER 1900.

In 1900 Miner Luella was a teacher at an American school in Beijing, who, with hundreds of other Westerners, was attacked and besieged in the legation buildings for several weeks by the so-called 'Boxers' – Chinese nationalists of the Yihetuan ('Righteous Fists' or 'Harmonious Fists') opposed to foreign influence in the country, and latterly supported by the Chinese government. A multinational China Relief Expedition landed at Tianjin and arrived in Beijing in August. The following month China was forced to pay an indemnity and gave the Western powers further concessions.

ALSO ON THIS DAY

1917 WWI: China declares war on Austria-Hungary and Germany.
1941 WWII: Roosevelt and Churchill reveal their Atlantic Charter for the postwar world order.
1969 British troops arrive in Northern Ireland at the start of the 'Troubles'.

15 AUGUST

INDIA WINS ITS INDEPENDENCE, 1947

Long years ago we made a tryst with destiny, and now the time comes when we shall redeem our pledge, not wholly or in full measure, but very substantially. At the stroke of the midnight hour, when the world sleeps, India will awake to life and freedom. A moment comes, which comes but rarely in history, when we step out from the old to the new, when an age ends, and when the soul of a nation, long suppressed, finds utterance.

It is fitting that at this solemn moment we take the pledge of dedication to the service of India and her people and to the still larger cause of humanity.

At the dawn of history India started on her unending quest, and trackless centuries are filled with her striving and the grandeur of her success and her failures. Through good and ill fortune alike she has never lost sight of that quest or forgotten the ideals which gave her strength. We end today a period of ill fortune and India discovers herself again.

...And so we have to labour and to work, and work hard, to give reality to our dreams. Those dreams are for India, but they are also for the world, for all the nations and peoples are too closely knit together today for anyone of them to imagine that it can live apart.

Peace has been said to be indivisible; so is freedom, so is prosperity now, and so also is disaster in this one world that can no longer be split into isolated fragments.

...The appointed day has come – the day appointed by destiny – and India stands forth again, after long slumber and struggle, awake, vital, free and independent. The past clings on to us still in some measure and we have to do much before we redeem the pledges we have so often taken. Yet the turning point is past, and history begins anew for us, the history which we shall live and act and others will write about.

...On this day our first thoughts go to the architect of this freedom, the father of our nation, who, embodying the old spirit of India, held aloft the torch of freedom and lighted up the darkness that surrounded us.

We have often been unworthy followers of his and have strayed from his message, but not only we but succeeding generations will remember this message and bear the imprint in their hearts of this great son of India, magnificent in his faith and strength and courage and humility. We shall never allow that torch of freedom to be blown out, however high the wind or stormy the tempest.

Our next thoughts must be of the unknown volunteers and soldiers of freedom who, without praise or reward, have served India even unto death.

We think also of our brothers and sisters who have been cut off from us by political boundaries and who unhappily cannot share at present in the freedom that has come. They are of us and will remain of us whatever may happen, and we shall be sharers in their good and ill fortune alike.

The future beckons to us. Whither do we go and what shall be our endeavour? To bring freedom and opportunity to the common man, to the peasants and workers of India; to fight and end poverty and ignorance and disease; to build up a prosperous, democratic and progressive nation, and to create social, economic and political institutions which will ensure justice and fullness of life to every man and woman.

...To the nations and peoples of the world we send greetings and pledge ourselves to co-operate with them in furthering peace, freedom and democracy.

And to India, our much-loved motherland, the ancient, the eternal and the ever-new, we pay our reverent homage and we bind ourselves afresh to her service. Jai Hind [Victory to India].

JAWAHARLAL NEHRU, SPEECH, 14 AUGUST 1947.

∞

The speech made on 14 August 1947 by Jawaharlal Nehru, hours before becoming India's first prime minister, marked the climax of a long campaign led by the Indian National Congress to secure independence. But there had been an unbridgeable gap between the Hindu-dominated Congress and the Muslim League under Muhammad Ali Jinnah (c.1876–1948), and independence was achieved at the cost of partitioning the subcontinent largely along sectarian grounds, to create a smaller, Hindu-majority India and the new Muslim-majority state of Pakistan (also encompassing what is now Bangladesh). The transition was marred by enormous human suffering, as mass emigrations of Hindus and Muslims took place across the new borders, accompanied by mass ethnic violence. 'Mahatma' Gandhi, whom Nehru described as 'the architect of our freedom', consistently opposed Partition; he was assassinated six months after independence by a Hindu extremist.

ALSO ON THIS DAY

1461 The Ottomans capture Trebizond, the last remnant of the Byzantine Empire.
1914 The Panama Canal opens to commercial shipping.
1945 WWII: The Allies' V-J Day celebrates the end of the war in Asia.

16 AUGUST

THE PETERLOO MASSACRE, 1819

The sounds of music proclaimed the near approach of Mr Hunt and his party... their approach was hailed by one universal shout from probably 80,000 persons. The meeting was indeed a tremendous one. [Hunt] mounted the hustings; the music ceased... and Mr Hunt, stepping forward towards the front of the stage, took off his white hat and addressed the people.

...I saw a party of cavalry in blue and white uniform come trotting, sword in hand, round the corner of a garden wall and to the front of a row of new houses, where they reined up in a line.

On the cavalry drawing up they were received with a shout of goodwill as I understood it. They shouted again, waving their sabres over their heads; and then, slackening rein, and striking spur into their steeds, they dashed forward and began cutting the people.

The cavalry were in confusion; they evidently could not, with all the weight of man and horses, penetrate that compact mass of human beings; and their sabres were plied to hew a way through naked held-up hands and defenceless heads; and then chopped limbs and wound-gaping skulls were seen; and groans and cries were mingled with the din of that horrid confusion. For a moment the crowd held back as in a pause; then was a rush, heavy and resistless as a headlong sea, and a sound like low thunder, with screams, prayers and imprecations from the crowd-moiled and sabre-doomed who could not escape.

SAMUEL BAMFORD, *PASSAGES IN THE LIFE OF A RADICAL*, 1864.

∞

Samuel Bamford witnessed the demonstration in Manchester's St Peter's Fields, which had been summoned by Henry 'Orator' Hunt to call for parliamentary reform. But magistrates sent in troops, who killed 11 people and wounded a further 500. (Bamford himself was charged with treason for inciting a riot and sentenced to a year in Lincoln gaol.) The event fuelled radical discontent at the perceived repressiveness of Lord Liverpool's Tory government and, coming just a few years after Wellington's victory at Waterloo, acquired the ironic title of the 'Peterloo Massacre'. Electoral reform did not, in the end, begin until 1832.

ALSO ON THIS DAY

1513 An English and Imperial army defeats the French at the 'Battle of the Spurs'.
1977 The death of the rock 'n' roll icon Elvis Presley.
2003 The death of the former Ugandan dictator Idi Amin.

17 AUGUST

THE FIRST COMMERCIAL STEAMSHIP SERVICE, 1807

The surprise and dismay excited among the crews of these vessels by the appearance of the steamer was extreme. These simple people, the majority of whom had heard nothing of Fulton's experiments, beheld what they supposed to be a huge monster, vomiting fire and smoke from its throat, lashing the water with its fins, and shaking the river with its roar, approaching rapidly in the very face of both wind and tide. Some threw themselves flat on the deck of their vessels, where they remained in an agony of terror until the monster had passed, while others took to their boats and made for the shore in dismay, leaving their vessels to drift helplessly down the stream. Nor was this terror confined to the sailors. The people dwelling along the shore crowded the banks to gaze upon the steamer as she passed by.

JAMES DABNEY MCCABE, *GREAT FORTUNES, AND HOW THEY WERE MADE*, 1871.

∞

The world's first commercial steamship, the *North River Steamboat* (later called the *Clermont*), came into service in the United States on 17 August 1807, plying its way up the Hudson River from New York to Albany. Built by the Pennsylvania-born inventor Robert Fulton (1765–1815), she was a paddle steamer but fitted with masts and sails. Many were doubtful of her safety; as one of the first passengers, a Frenchman called Michaux, explained in a letter:

> So great was the fear of the explosion of the boiler that no one, except my companion and myself, dared to take passage in it for New York. We quitted Albany on the 20th of August in the presence of a great number of spectators… From every point on the river whence the boat, announced by the smoke of its chimney, could be seen, we saw the inhabitants collect; they waved their handkerchiefs and hurrahed for Fulton, whose passage they had probably noticed as he ascended the river.

18 AUGUST

THE DEATH OF GENGHIS KHAN, 1227

With Heaven's aid I have conquered for you a huge empire. But my life was too short to achieve the conquest of the world. That is left for you.

GENGHIS KHAN, 1227.

∞

The Mongol conqueror named Genghis Khan ('Universal Ruler'), creator of the largest land empire the world has ever seen, had been born in c.1162 under the name Temujin, and became leader of one of the disparate tribes of the East Asian steppes. By 1206 he had unified the tribes under his rule, and by the time of his death on 18 August 1227 he controlled the Central and East Asian steppes as far west as modern Iran and the Caspian Sea, east into northern China, and he had forced Kiev to sue for peace. His ruthlessness and violence were notorious across Eurasia, but his empire was marked by religious toleration.

He died after falling from a horse on his way back to his palace in Mongolia from a successful campaign against another nomadic tribe. Although he was venerated as a god, his tomb at his own request was hidden; all those involved in its construction were killed, and it has never been located.

He had appointed his third son Ogedei (ruled 1229–41) to be his successor as Great Khan, and with Ogedei's death the vast empire – now threatening Hungary – began to be divided into several increasingly independent khanates, including the Khanate of the Golden Horde: at its height, this stretched from Central Asia to the Danube, and forced the Russian principalities to its north to pay tributes as vassal states until as late as the 1480s.

Ogedei's successors continued to expand the empire, reaching as far west as modern Romania and Syria, conquering the whole of China (1268–79) and Korea (by 1260), and making two massive, though abortive, attempts, to invade Japan in 1274 and 1281. With the conquest of China, Genghis Khan's grandson Kublai Khan overturned the Song Dynasty to become its new emperor; and later descendants of Genghis Khan founded India's Mughal Dynasty in the early 16th century.

ALSO ON THIS DAY

1503 The death of Rodrigo Borgia, Pope Alexander VI.
1587 The birth of Virginia Dare at Roanoke, the first child born to English colonists in the Americas.
1969 The three-day Woodstock music festival in New York state closes.

19 AUGUST

THE DEATH OF EMPEROR AUGUSTUS, AD 14

On the last day of his life he asked every now and then whether there was any disturbance without on his account; then calling for a mirror, he had his hair combed and his falling jaw set straight. After that, calling in his friends and asking whether it seemed to them that he had played the comedy of life fitly, he added the tag: 'Since well I've played my part, all clap your hands / And from the stage dismiss me with applause.'

Then he sent them all off, and while he was asking some newcomers from the city about the daughter of Drusus, who was ill, he suddenly passed away as he was kissing Livia, uttering these last words: 'Live mindful of our wedlock, Livia, and farewell,' thus blessed with an easy death and such a one as he had always longed for. For almost always on hearing that anyone had died swiftly and painlessly, he prayed that he and his might have a like euthanasia, for that was the term he was wont to use. He gave but one single sign of wandering before he breathed his last, calling out in sudden terror that forty men were carrying him off. And even this was rather a premonition than a delusion, since it was that very number of soldiers of the Praetorian Guard that carried him forth to lie in state.

SUETONIUS, *LIFE OF AUGUSTUS*, AD 121.

Augustus Caesar, born Octavian, had ruled as emperor of Rome in all but name for more than 40 years (*see* 16 January), and he was said to have boasted that he inherited 'a city of brick and left it one of marble'. His reign witnessed a golden age of Latin writing, during which the historian Livy and the poets Horace, Virgil and Ovid flourished; it was the conscious emulation of these models by some 18th-century English writers that revived the term 'Augustan Age', to describe their endeavours.

Always concerned with his public image – even in his supposedly unguarded memoirs – the emperor Augustus maintained appearances to the very last, at least in the account of his death on 19 August AD 14, as related by the historian Suetonius a century later. He was proclaimed a god at his funeral.

ALSO ON THIS DAY

1692 In Salem, Massachusetts, five people are executed for witchcraft.
1772 Gustavus III assumes control of Sweden in a royal coup.
1936 The Spanish poet Federico García Lorca is murdered by Nationalists.

20 AUGUST

CHURCHILL HAILS THE ROYAL AIR FORCE, 1940

The gratitude of every home in our island, in our Empire, and indeed throughout the world except in the abodes of the guilty goes out to the British airmen who, undaunted by odds, unweakened by their constant challenge and mortal danger, are turning the tide of world war by their prowess and their devotion.

Never in the field of human conflict was so much owed by so many to so few. All hearts go out to the fighter pilots, whose brilliant actions we see with our own eyes day after day but we must never forget that all the time, night after night, month after month, our bomber squadrons travel far into Germany, find their targets in the darkness by the highest navigational skill, aim their attacks, often under the heaviest fire, often at serious loss, with deliberate, careful precision, and inflict shattering blows upon the whole of the technical and war-making structure of the Nazi power. On no part of the Royal Air Force does the weight of the war fall more heavily than on the daylight bombers, who will play an invaluable part in the case of invasion and whose unflinching zeal it has been necessary in the meanwhile on numerous occasions to restrain.

…Even if the Nazi legions stood triumphant on the Black Sea or indeed upon the Caspian, even if Hitler was at the gates of India, it would profit him nothing if at the same time the entire economic and scientific apparatus of German war power lay shattered and pulverized at home.

PRIME MINISTER WINSTON CHURCHILL, SPEECH, HOUSE OF COMMONS, 1940.

∞

Churchill gave his famous tribute to the Battle of Britain pilots – the 'few' – at the height of the great air battle that had begun on 10 July 1940. The 18th of August had seen the greatest numbers of casualties on both sides, while on 19 August Luftwaffe chief Hermann Goering had ordered the targeting of aircraft factories. But Churchill was equally keen to remind his listeners of the less visible efforts of RAF Bomber Command, which was carrying the fight into Germany on a regular basis.

The Battle of Britain continued to 30 October, when the Luftwaffe abandoned its attempt to defeat RAF Fighter Command, seeking instead to undermine morale by bombing Britain's cities by night.

ALSO ON THIS DAY

1914 WWI: Brussels is occupied by German troops.
1968 Warsaw Pact forces intervene in Czechoslovakia's 'Prague Spring'.
1989 51 drown when the *Marchioness* pleasure boat capsizes in the River Thames, London.

21 AUGUST

THE VIOLATION OF BELGIAN NEUTRALITY, 1914

The entrance of the German army into Brussels has lost the human quality. It was lost as soon as the three soldiers who led the army bicycled into the Boulevard du Regent and asked the way to the Gare du Nord. When they passed, the human note passed with them.

What came after them, and twenty-four hours later is still coming, is not men marching but a force of nature like a tidal wave, an avalanche or a river flooding its banks.

...At the sight of the first few regiments of the enemy we were thrilled with interest. After for three hours they had passed in one unbroken steel-grey column we were bored. But when hour after hour passed and there was no halt, no breathing time, no open spaces in the ranks, the thing became uncanny, inhuman. You returned to watch it, fascinated. It held the mystery and menace of fog rolling toward you across the sea.

...Then, as dusk came and as thousands of horses' hoofs and thousands of iron boots continued to tramp forward, they struck tiny sparks from the stones, but the horses and the men who beat out the sparks were invisible.

At midnight pack wagons and siege guns were still passing. At seven this morning I was awakened by the tramp of men and bands playing jauntily. Whether they marched all night or not I do not know; but now for twenty-six hours the grey army has rumbled by with the mystery of fog and the pertinacity of a steam roller.

RICHARD HARDING DAVIS, *NEWS CHRONICLE*, 23 AUGUST 1914.

In the opening month of the First World War, the American journalist Richard Harding Davis recorded the arrival of Kaiser Wilhelm's army in the capital of Belgium on 21 August 1914, a little over two weeks after they had entered the country. This violation of Belgium's neutrality, and the stories (many of them concocted) of atrocities committed by German troops against the civilian population, did much to fuel indignation and war fever in Britain. Davis himself was arrested by the Germans and narrowly avoided execution as a spy.

ALSO ON THIS DAY

1831 Nat Turner's slave revolt breaks out in Virginia.
1983 The Filipino opposition leader Benigno Aquino is assassinated.
1991 An attempted hardline Soviet coup against Mikhail Gorbachev collapses.

22 AUGUST

THE BATTLE OF BOSWORTH FIELD, 1485

King Richard did in his army stand,
He was numbered to forty thousand
  and three
Of hardy men of heart and hand,
That under his banner there did be.

Sir William Stanley wise and worthy
Remembered the breakfast he
  promised to him;
Down at a bank then cometh he,
And shortly set upon the King.

Then they countered together sad and
  sore;
Archers they let sharp arrows fly,
They shot guns both fell and far,
Bows of yews bended did be,

Springals [stone throwing machines]
  sped them speedily,
Harquebusiers' pellets throughly did
  thring [crowd];
So many banners began to sway
That was on Richard's party, their king.

Then our archers let their shooting be,
With joined weapons were grounded
  full right,
Brands rang on basinets [visored
  helmets] high,
Battle-axes fast on helms did light.

There died many a doughty knight,
There under foot can they thring;
Thus they fought with main and might
That was Henry's party, our king.

Then to King Richard there came a
  knight,
And said, 'I hold it time for to flee;
For yonder Stanleys' dints [blows] they
  be so wight,
Against them no man may dree.
  [endure]

'Here is thy horse at thy hand ready;
Another day thou may worship win,
And for to reign with royalty,
To wear the crown, and be our king.'

He said, 'Give me my battle-axe in my
  hand,
Set the crown of England on my head
  so high!
For by Him that shope [shaped] both
  sea and land,
King of England this day will I die!

One foot will I never flee
Whist the breath is my breast within!'
As he said it, so did it be;
If he lost his life, if he were king.

About his standard can they light,
The crown of gold they hewed him fro,
With doleful dints his death they
  dight,
The duke of Norfolk that day they
  slew.

...Then they moved to a mountain on
  height,
With a loud voice they cried 'King
  Henry!';

The crown of gold that was bright,
To the Lord Stanley delivered it be.

Anon to King Henry delivered it he,

The crown that was so delivered to
    him.
And said, 'Methink ye are best worthy
To wear the crown and be our King.'

ANONYMOUS BALLAD, LATE 16TH CENTURY OR EARLIER.

The Battle of Bosworth Field proved to be a major turning point in English history. The defeat and death of the Yorkist Richard III, the last Plantagenet king of England, and the coronation of the Lancastrian-descended Henry Tudor as Henry VII ushered in a new dynasty. Yet this ballad, probably written by a member of the entourage of Thomas Stanley but not recorded for 100 years, is the only likely eyewitness account.

Stanley, who waited on the sidelines, only intervened on Henry's side when the tide of battle was turning against Richard; he was created Earl of Derby for placing the crown on Henry's head.

ALSO ON THIS DAY

1846 The USA annexes New Mexico.
1911 The *Mona Lisa* is stolen from the Louvre (it will be returned in 1913).
1978 The death of Kenya's President Jomo Kenyatta.

23 AUGUST

THE MASSACRE OF ST BARTHOLOMEW'S EVE, 1572

King Charles IX, paying particular deference to his mother [Catherine de' Medici], and much attached to the Catholic religion, was now convinced of the intentions of the Huguenots. He suddenly resolved to follow his mother's counsel, and put himself under the safeguard of the Catholics...

Sending for M. de Guise and all the princes and Catholic officers, the 'Massacre of St Bartholomew' was that night resolved upon.

Immediately chains were drawn across the streets, alarm-bells were sounded, and every man repaired to his post, according to the orders he had received, whether it was to attack the Admiral's [Coligny's] quarters, or those of other Huguenots. M. de Guise hastened to the Admiral's, and Besme, a gentleman in the service of the former, a German by birth, forced into his chamber, killed him with a dagger, and threw his body out of a window to his master.

I was ignorant of what was happening... The Huguenots were suspicious of me because I was a Catholic, and the Catholics because I was married to the King of Navarre, who was a Huguenot. No one spoke a syllable of the matter to me.

MARGUERITE DE VALOIS, *MEMOIRS*, 1628.

The Massacre of St Bartholomew's Eve, 23 August 1572, was a key event in the long-running French Wars of Religion. Instigated by Henry, 3rd Duke of Guise (spurred on by the king's mother Catherine de' Medici), the massacres saw the murder of the Protestant Huguenot leader Admiral Gaspard de Coligny and thousands of other Huguenots in Paris and beyond. A botched attempt had been made on Coligny's life just two days earlier; its failure led to fears of Huguenot retribution, emboldening the Catholic faction to commence the bloodbath.

The massacre took place just six days after the marriage of King Charles IX's sister Marguerite de Valois to the Huguenot Prince of Navarre (the future Henry IV). In 1589 the over-mighty Duke of Guise was himself assassinated, along with his brother, Cardinal Louis, by order of King Henry III, who had inherited the throne after the death of his elder brother Charles.

ALSO ON THIS DAY

1305 The Scots leader William Wallace is hanged, drawn and quartered.
1939 The Nazi–Soviet Non-Aggression Pact is signed.
1985 West Germany's counter-intelligence supremo is revealed as an East German spy.

24 AUGUST

THE ERUPTION OF VESUVIUS, AD 79

About one in the afternoon, my mother desired him [Pliny the Elder] to observe a cloud of unusual size and shape. It was shooting up to a great height, resembling a pine tree with a very tall trunk and spreading out at the top into branches. This was occasioned, I imagine, either by the sudden gust of air that impelled it, the force of which decreased as it went higher, or as the cloud itself expanded and fell under its own weight. It was spotted bright and dark, depending of the amount of earth and cinders.

This phenomenon seemed so extraordinary to a man of such learning that he ordered a light vessel to be got ready. But he received a note from Rectina, the wife of Bassus; for her villa at the foot of Mount Vesuvius, there was no way of escape but by sea.

He changed his plan, ordered the galleys to be put to sea to assist not only Rectina, but other towns along that beautiful coast. As others fled, he steered straight towards the danger, with such presence of mind as to be able to dictate his observations upon all the phenomena of that dreadful scene. He was so close to the mountain that the cinders, which grew thicker and hotter the nearer he approached, fell into the ships, together with pumice-stones and black pieces of burning rock. They were in danger of being grounded by the sudden retreat of the sea, and also from vast lumps rolling down from the mountain, and obstructing the shore. The helmsman advised him to turn back but replied, 'Fortune favours the brave; steer to Stabiae, where Pomponianus is.'

PLINY THE YOUNGER, LETTER TO TACITUS, AD 106.

The devastating eruption of the volcano of Vesuvius, which destroyed Pompeii, Herculaneum and other nearby cities, was observed from close quarters by the naturalist and naval commander Pliny the Elder, who, while helping his friends escape, became the most memorable victim of the natural disaster. Pliny's nephew and secretary, Pliny the Younger, wrote this account in a letter to the historian Tacitus some years later.

ALSO ON THIS DAY

1349 A pogrom takes place in Mainz, when Jews are blamed for a plague outbreak.
1821 The Treaty of Córdoba wins Mexico its independence from Spain.
1949 The NATO Treaty becomes effective.

25 AUGUST

THE BRITISH TAKE THE WHITE HOUSE, 1814

Well, on the 24th of August, sure enough, the British reached Bladensburg, and the fight began between 11 and 12. Even that very morning General Armstrong assured Mrs Madison there was no danger. The president... rode out on horseback to Bladensburg to see how things looked. Mrs. Madison ordered dinner to be ready at 3, as usual; I set the table myself, and brought up the ale, cider, and wine, and placed them in the coolers, as all the Cabinet and several military gentlemen and strangers were expected. While waiting, at just about 3... James Smith, a free coloured man who had accompanied Mr Madison to Bladensburg, galloped up to the house, waving his hat, and cried out, 'Clear out, clear out! General Armstrong has ordered a retreat!' All then was confusion. Mrs Madison ordered her carriage, and passing through the dining-room, caught up what silver she could crowd into her old-fashioned reticule, and then jumped into the chariot with her servant girl Sukey, and Daniel Carroll; Jo Bolin drove them over to Georgetown Heights; the British were expected in a few minutes. Mr Cutts, her brother-in-law, sent me to a stable on 14th Street, for his carriage. People were running in every direction...

I will here mention that although the British were expected every minute, they did not arrive for some hours; in the mean time, a rabble, taking advantage of the confusion, ran all over the White House, and stole lots of silver and whatever they could lay their hands on.

About sundown I walked over to the Georgetown ferry, and found the president and all hands waiting for the boat. It soon returned, and we all crossed over, and passed up the road about a mile; they then left us servants to wander about. In a short time several wagons from Bladensburg passed up the road, having crossed the Long Bridge before it was set on fire. As we were cutting up some planks a white wagoner ordered us away, and told his boy Tommy to reach out his gun, and he would shoot us. I told him, 'he had better have used it at Bladensburg.' Just then we came up with Mr Madison and his friends... consulting what to do. I walked on to a Methodist minister's, and in the evening while he was at prayer, I heard a tremendous explosion, and, rushing out, saw that the public buildings, navy yard, ropewalks, &c., were on fire.

Mrs Madison slept that night at Mrs Love's, two or three miles over the river...

It has often been stated in print, that when Mrs Madison escaped from the White House, she cut out from the frame the large portrait of Washington (now in one of the parlours there), and carried it off. This is totally false. She had no time for doing it. It would have required a ladder to get it down. All she carried off was the silver in her reticule, as the British were thought to be but a few squares off, and were expected every moment. John Susé (a Frenchman, then door-keeper, and still living) and Magraw, the president's gardener, took it down and sent it off on a wagon, with some large silver urns and such other valuables as could be hastily got hold of. When the British did arrive, they ate up the very dinner, and drank the wines, &c., that I had prepared for the president's party.

PAUL JENNINGS, *A COLOURED MAN'S REMINISCENCES OF JAMES MADISON*, 1865.

∞

The British occupation of the city of Washington – including the burning of the White House itself – was the most dramatic moment of the so-called War of 1812, an Anglo-American conflict that in fact lasted until 1815. The United States had declared war on Britain for reasons that included the restrictions imposed on US trade with France (with which Britain was then at war). This account of the evacuation of the White House by Dolley Madison, wife of President James Madison, was written by one of her slaves, Paul Jennings.

While addressing both houses of Congress nearly 200 years later, in July 2003, British prime minister Tony Blair alluded to the events: 'On our way down here, Senator Frist was kind enough to show me the fireplace where, in 1814, the British had burnt the Congress Library. I know this is kind of late, but, "sorry".'

ALSO ON THIS DAY

AD 357 The Roman general Julian defeats the Alemanni at Argentoratum (Strasbourg).
1875 Matthew Webb completes the first unassisted cross-Channel swim.
1944 WWII: the Allies liberate Paris.

26 AUGUST

THE BATTLE OF CRÉCY, 1346

As soon as the French king came in sight of the English his blood began to boil, and he cried out: 'Order the Genoese forward and begin the battle.' There were about 15,000 Genoese crossbowmen, but they were quite fatigued, having marched on foot that day six leagues, completely armed and carrying their crossbows; they told the constable they were not in a condition to do any great thing in battle. The Earl of Alençon, hearing this, said: 'This is what one gets for employing such scoundrels, who fall off when there is any need for them.'

During this time a heavy rain fell, accompanied by thunder and a very terrible eclipse of the sun; and before the rain a great flight of crows hovered in the air over all the battalions, making a loud noise. Shortly afterwards it cleared up and the sun shone very bright, but the French had it in their faces and the English on their backs. When the Genoese were somewhat in order they approached the English and set up a loud shout; but the English remained quite quiet. Then they set up a second shout and advanced a little; the English never moved. They hooted a third time, advancing, and began to shoot. The English archers then took one step forward, and shot their arrows with such force and quickness that it seemed as if it snowed. When the Genoese felt these arrows which pierced their armour, some of them cut the strings of the crossbows, others flung them to the ground, and all turned about and retreated.

The French king, seeing them fall back, cried out; 'Kill me those scoundrels.'

JEAN FROISSART, *CHRONICLES*, 1373–1400.

∞

Thus the French chronicler Jean Froissart described the beginning of the French defeat at the hands of their English and Welsh opponents at the Battle of Crécy, near Calais, on 26 August 1346. The victory of King Edward III – who was attempting to press his claim to the French throne – over the far larger forces of Philip VI (including the kings of Bohemia and Navarre, as well as the Genoese mercenaries) saw the triumph of the longbow over the more powerful, but clumsy, crossbow, and demonstrated its effectiveness against even heavily armoured knights. Swiftly followed by the capture of Calais itself, the battle assured English control in northeastern France in the early years of the Hundred Years' War.

ALSO ON THIS DAY

1071 The Seljuk Turks defeat the Byzantines at Manzikert.
1974 The death of the US aviator Charles Lindbergh.
1991 Yugoslav and Serb forces begin the siege of Vukovar, Croatia.

27 AUGUST

THE ERUPTION OF KRAKATOA, 1883

Thousands of tongues of fire lit up the surroundings... As they disappeared they left a greenish light. Others quickly filled their place. On tops of the trees I saw flames. I heard a crack and noticed a sheet of fire right by me... Everything was smothered in ash. I could not see my hand before me. I went into the house again...

Suddenly it was pitch dark. The last thing I saw was the ash being pushed up through the cracks in the floorboards, like a fountain... It seemed as if the air was being sucked away and I could not breathe. Large lumps cluttered down on my head, my back and my arm... I could not stand.

After much effort I did finally manage to get to my feet, but I could not straighten my back or neck. I felt as if a heavy iron chain was fastened around my neck and was pulling me downward.

I tottered, doubled up, to the door... I tripped and fell. I realized the ash was hot and I tried to protect my face with my hands. The hot bite of the pumice pricked like needles.

Had I been in my right mind I would have understood what a dangerous thing it was to... plunge into the hellish darkness... Then something got hooked into my finger and hurt. I noticed for the first time that my skin was hanging off everywhere, thick and moist from the ash stuck to it. Thinking it must be dirty, I wanted to pull bits of skin off, but that was still more painful. My brain could not make out what it was. I did not know I had been burned. Worn out, I leaned against a tree.

JOHANNA BEIJERINCK, JAVANESE NEWSPAPER ACCOUNT, 1883.

On 27 August 1883 the climactic volcanic eruption that largely erased the island of Krakatoa, in the Dutch East Indies (modern Indonesia), produced the loudest explosion ever recorded; it also created a *tsunami* that killed more than 30,000 and generated pyroclastic flows of burning ash that survivors nearby, including 26-year-old Mrs Beijerinck and her family, were fortunate to escape. Ash from the volcano produced unusually cold conditions across the Northern hemisphere for five years afterwards.

ALSO ON THIS DAY

1776 American Revolutionary War: British victory at Long Island (Brooklyn Heights).
1896 Zanzibar surrenders to Britain in the world's shortest war: 45 minutes.
1979 Lord Louis Mountbatten is assassinated by the IRA.

28 AUGUST

MARTIN LUTHER KING HAS A DREAM, 1963

Even though we face the difficulties of today and tomorrow, I still have a dream. It is a dream deeply rooted in the American dream.

I have a dream that one day this nation will rise up and live out the true meaning of its creed: 'We hold these truths to be self-evident, that all men are created equal.'

I have a dream that one day on the red hills of Georgia, the sons of former slaves and the sons of former slave owners will be able to sit down together at the table of brotherhood.

I have a dream that one day even the state of Mississippi, a state sweltering with the heat of injustice, sweltering with the heat of oppression, will be transformed into an oasis of freedom and justice.

I have a dream that my four little children will one day live in a nation where they will not be judged by the colour of their skin but by the content of their character.

I have a *dream* today!

I have a dream that one day, down in Alabama, with its vicious racists, with its governor having his lips dripping with the words of 'interposition' and 'nullification' – one day right there in Alabama little black boys and black girls will be able to join hands with little white boys and white girls as sisters and brothers.

I have a *dream* today!

I have a dream that one day every valley shall be exalted, and every hill and mountain shall be made low, the rough places will be made plain, and the crooked places will be made straight; 'and the glory of the Lord shall be revealed and all flesh shall see it together'.

This is our hope, and this is the faith that I go back to the South with.

With this faith, we will be able to hew out of the mountain of despair a stone of hope. With this faith, we will be able to transform the jangling discords of our nation into a beautiful symphony of brotherhood. With this faith, we will be able to work together, to pray together, to struggle together, to go to jail together, to stand up for freedom together, knowing that we will be free one day.

And this will be the day – this will be the day when all of God's children will be able to sing with new meaning:

'My country 'tis of thee, sweet land of liberty, of thee I sing. / Land where my fathers died, land of the Pilgrim's pride, From every mountainside, let freedom ring!'

And if America is to be a great nation, this must become true. And so let freedom ring from the prodigious hilltops of New Hampshire. Let freedom ring from the mighty mountains of New York. Let freedom ring from the heightening Alleghenies of Pennsylvania. Let freedom ring from the snow-capped Rockies of Colorado. Let freedom ring from the curvaceous slopes of California.

But not only that: Let freedom ring from Stone Mountain of Georgia. Let freedom ring from Lookout Mountain of Tennessee. Let freedom ring from every hill and molehill of Mississippi. 'From every mountainside, let freedom ring!'

And when this happens, when we allow freedom to ring, when we let it ring from every village and every hamlet, from every state and every city, we will be able to speed up that day when *all* of God's children, black men and white men, Jews and Gentiles, Protestants and Catholics, will be able to join hands and sing in the words of the old Negro spiritual:

'Free at last! Free at last! / Thank *God* Almighty, we are free at last!'

MARTIN LUTHER KING, SPEECH, 28 AUGUST 1963.

∞

Martin Luther King, Jr's most famous speech was delivered on the steps of the Lincoln Memorial, Washington, DC, to a crowd of 200,000 at the climax of the March on Washington for Jobs and Freedom. Its language dug deep into strains of American identity – the legacy of the Founding Fathers and Abraham Lincoln, the Bible, the Pilgrims' idealism, the New World's promise as the land of freedom and enlightenment, the poignant yearnings of negro spirituals – all united in the cadences of King's delivery honed over his years as a Baptist minister. It defined the civil rights movement in the United States and increased pressure on the administration to introduce civil rights legislation. The peroration, repeating his 'dream', was unscripted, perhaps prompted by a cry from the Gospel singer Mahalia Jackson, 'Tell them about the dream, Martin.'

ALSO ON THIS DAY

1547 The death of King Henry VIII of England.
1996 Prince Charles and Diana, Princess of Wales, are divorced.
2005 New Orleans residents are ordered to evacuate in advance of Hurricane Katrina.

29 AUGUST

THE BIRTH OF CRICKET'S ASHES, 1882

In Affectionate Remembrance
of
ENGLISH CRICKET,
which died at the Oval
on
29th AUGUST, 1882,
Deeply lamented by a large circle of sorrowing friends
and acquaintances
R.I.P.
N.B. – The body will be cremated and the ashes taken to Australia.

'BLOOBS' (REGINALD BROOKS), *THE SPORTING TIMES*, 2 SEPTEMBER 1882.

One of the world's great sporting rivalries began with the narrow and tense defeat of the English cricket team by the Australians in a Test match at the Kennington Oval, London, on 29 August 1882. It was England's first defeat to what was then a British colony, and four days afterwards the mock obituary of English cricket was published.

A few months later an English team toured Australia, led by the Honourable Ivo Bligh. Following England's victories in the second and third Test matches, Bligh was presented with a terracotta urn, said to contain 'the ashes' of a ball, a bail or a stump, by a group of Melbourne women (one of whom, Florence Morphy, later became Bligh's wife). On the urn was pasted a label carrying six lines of doggerel celebrating Bligh's achievement and naming several members of the England team. These lines were published in *Melbourne Punch* in February 1883:

When Ivo goes back with the urn, the urn;
Studds, Steel, Read and Tylecote return, return;
The welkin will ring loud,
The great crowd will feel proud,
Seeing Barlow and Bates with the urn, the urn;
And the rest coming home with the urn.

The tradition of England and Australia doing battle for 'the Ashes' (the urn itself never leaves Lord's cricket ground, the home of MCC) emerged in the 1900s and has been hotly contested ever since.

ALSO ON THIS DAY

1526 Ottoman forces under Suleiman the Magnificent defeat the Hungarians at Mohács.
1966 The Beatles perform their last scheduled concert, in San Francisco.
1991 The Soviet Communist Party is suspended.

30 AUGUST

THE SECOND BATTLE OF MANASSAS, 1862

Bee, Bartow and others who fell on this field last year, have been amply revenged ...The Henry house, which was riddled by the artillery shots of the enemy last year, and where its aged owner, Mrs Henry, was killed, has also been removed piecemeal by the enemy, and probably sold as relics; but before its very doors, and within its demolished walls, sleep to-day the miserable myrmidons of the North.

Batteries were planted and captured yesterday where they were planted and captured last year. The pine thicket where the 4th Alabama and the 8th Georgia suffered so terribly in the first battle, is now strewn with the slain invader. We charged through the same woods yesterday, though from a different point, where Kirby Smith, the Blücher of the day, entered the fight before. These are remarkable coincidences; and they extend even to my own experience. In the road way where I relieved a wounded Irishman from Wisconsin late at night last year, I to-day found another Irishman crying for succour. As I rendered it to the first so I gave it to the second.

Is not the hand of God in all this? Who but He brought us again face to face with our enemies upon these crimsoned plains, and gave us the victory? When before did the same people ever fight two separate battles, upon the same ground, within so short a period? For the second time the God of Battles has spoken by the mouth of our cannon, and told the North to let us go unto ourselves.

'P.W.A', EYEWITNESS ACCOUNT, *SAVANNAH REPUBLICAN*, AUGUST 1862.

The Second Battle of Manassas (or Second Battle of Bull Run) in northern Virginia, which concluded on 30 August 1862, was the greatest Confederate victory of the American Civil War, and it resulted in some 10,000 Union casualties, vastly outnumbering the Confederate losses. The field had seen an earlier, far smaller, battle just 13 months previously, also won by the Confederates, whose cause had been helped by the late arrival of Brigadier-General Kirby Smith's reinforcements – hence the eyewitness's analogy with Prussian Field Marshal Blücher of Waterloo fame. The second battle's outcome ruined the reputation and career of the Union commander Major-General John Pope, who subsequently lost command of his Army of Virginia.

ALSO ON THIS DAY

1914 WWI: the Germans defeat the Russians at the Battle of Tannenberg.
1918 The Bolshevik leader V.I. Lenin survives an assassination attempt.
1963 A telephone 'hotline' is established between US and Soviet leaders.

31 AUGUST

THE DEATH OF THE 'PEOPLE'S PRINCESS', 1997

I feel like everyone else in this country today. I am utterly devastated.

Our thoughts and prayers are with Princess Diana's family, particularly her two sons. Our heart goes out to them.

We are today a nation in a state of shock, in mourning, in grief that is so deeply painful for us. She was a wonderful and a warm human being, although her own life was often sadly touched by tragedy. She touched the lives of so many others in Britain and throughout the world with joy and with comfort.

How many times shall we remember her in how many different ways – with the sick, the dying, with children, with the needy? With just a look or a gesture that spoke so much more than words, she would reveal to all of us the depth of her compassion and her humanity.

I am sure we can only guess how difficult things were for her from time to time. But people everywhere, not just here in Britain, kept faith with Princess Diana. They liked her, they loved her, they regarded her as one of the people. She was the People's Princess and that is how she will stay, how she will remain in our hearts and our memories for ever.

PRIME MINISTER TONY BLAIR, SPEECH, 31 AUGUST 1997.

When Diana, the recently divorced Princess of Wales, died in a Parisian car crash in the early hours of 31 August 1997, Prime Minister Tony Blair was the first to sum up the nation's feelings. They were to be vented over the coming days in an unprecedented public outpouring of grief for Diana – and, conversely, hostility towards the monarch and the Prince of Wales, whose supposed mistreatment of Diana during her marriage was now compounded by an ostensible lack of feeling on her death. For some, the public reaction was evidence of a welcome shift of the national character away from its traditional reticence; for others it was an undignified and entirely un-British display of mass hysteria. In death, as so often in life, Diana seemed to embody the unresolved relationship of a traditional royalty, a modern cult of celebrity, and the public's sometimes contradictory attitudes to both.

ALSO ON THIS DAY

1888 The body of Jack the Ripper's first victim is found in Whitechapel, London.
1949 The Greek Civil War comes to an end.
1962 Trinidad and Tobago achieve independence from Britain.

SEPTEMBER

∞

1 SEPTEMBER

THE BATTLE OF SEDAN, 1870

Now we have them in the mousetrap.

PRUSSIAN FIELD MARSHAL HELMUTH VON MOLTKE.

∞

We are in the chamber pot and about to be shat upon.

FRENCH GENERAL AUGUSTE-ALEXANDRE DUCROT.

∞

The crushing Prussian victory over the French at Sedan, in the Ardennes, was the culmination of the Franco-Prussian War of 1870–1, the result of years of tension between the European continent's two major military powers. Confused tactics from the French command – with the original commander Patrice de Mac-Mahon wounded early in the battle and then General Ducrot, followed by General Wimpffen, taking over command – produced a series of bungled manoeuvres and resulted in the army being surrounded and shelled from all sides. Attempts to break out failed and produced over 17,000 casualties; the remains of the French army were taken prisoner along with Emperor Napoleon III, who surrendered to German Chancellor Otto von Bismarck in person. This disaster was quickly followed by Napoleon's deposition and exile to England.

Meanwhile the Prussians marched on to besiege Paris, which fought on for several months under the newly proclaimed Third Republic. The city fell in January 1871 and the Second German Empire was proclaimed at Versailles, with the Prussian King Wilhelm I elevated as the new Kaiser Wilhelm, completing the unification of Germany. Soon afterwards Paris was engulfed in the civil violence that crushed the temporary revolutionary government of the Commune (*see* 28 May).

Napoleon III died in London in 1873. His last words to his friend Henri Conneau, who had also fought at Sedan, were: 'We were not cowards at Sedan, were we?'

ALSO ON THIS DAY

1715 The death of King Louis XIV of France.
1939 WWII: the German invasion of Poland signals the start of the war.
1967 The death of the English war poet Siegfried Sassoon.

2 SEPTEMBER

THE GREAT FIRE OF LONDON, 1666

I... walked to the Tower... and there I did see the houses at that end of the bridge all on fire, and an infinite great fire on this and the other side the end of the bridge ... So down, with my heart full of trouble, to the Lieutenant of the Tower, who tells me that it begun this morning in the king's baker's house in Pudding Lane, and that it hath burned St Magnus's Church and most part of Fish Street already. So I [go] down to the water-side, and... there saw a lamentable fire... Everybody endeavouring to remove their goods... poor people staying in their houses as long as till the very fire touched them, and then running into boats, or clambering from one pair of stairs by the water-side to another. And among other things, the poor pigeons, I perceive, were loath to leave their houses, but hovered about the windows and balconies till they were, some of them burned, their wings, and fell down...

I to Whitehall... where... the king commanded me to go to my Lord Mayor from him, and command him to spare no houses, but to pull down before the fire every way...

At last met my Lord Mayor in Canning Street, like a man spent, with a handkercher about his neck. To the king's message he cried, like a fainting woman, 'Lord! what can I do? I am spent: people will not obey me. I have been pulling down houses; but the fire overtakes us faster than we can do it.' That he needed no more soldiers; and that, for himself, he must go and refresh himself, having been up all night. So he left me, and I him, and walked home, seeing people all almost distracted, and no manner of means used to quench the fire. The houses, too, so very thick thereabouts, and full of matter for burning, as pitch and tar, in Thames street; and warehouses of oil, and wines, and brandy, and other things.

...I... walked, through the City, the streets full of nothing but people and horses and carts laden with goods... I observed that hardly one lighter or boat in three that had the goods of a house in, but there was a pair of virginals in it. Having seen as much as I could now, I away to Whitehall by appointment, and... then upon the water again, and to the fire up and down, it still increasing, and the wind great. So near the fire as we could for smoke; and all over the Thames, with one's face in the wind, you were almost burned with a shower of fire-drops... When we could endure no more upon the water; we to a little ale-house on the Bankside ... and there stayed till it was dark almost, and saw the fire grow; and, as it grew darker, appeared more and more, and in corners and upon steeples, and between churches and houses, as far as we could see up the hill of the City, in a most horrid malicious bloody flame, not like the fine flame of an ordinary fire... We stayed till, it being darkish, we saw the fire as only one entire arch of fire from this to the other side the bridge, and in a bow up the hill for an arch of above a mile long: it made me weep to see it. The churches, houses, and all on fire and flaming at once; and a horrid noise the flames made, and the cracking of houses at their ruins.

SAMUEL PEPYS, DIARY, 2 SEPTEMBER 1666.

∞

The Great Fire of London, which broke out in the early hours of 2 September 1666 and raged for three days in the old City of London, and rendered the majority of its 80,000 inhabitants homeless (although only a handful were killed). Along with over 13,000 houses, almost 90 churches were consumed by the fire along with over 40 livery halls. The conflagration was memorably described by Samuel Pepys, Secretary to the Admiralty, in his private diary (*see also* 23 April).

It was the second disaster to hit the city in succession, following the Great Plague of 1664–5. But in destroying so much of London's medieval heritage, it cleared the way for a new city to emerge. The grandiose plans for an Italianate city were ultimately deemed unsuited to London's commercial and practical requirements, but the shining glory of Christopher Wren's new St Paul's Cathedral (completed over a period of 35 years) was a direct consequence of the Great Fire – as was the Wren-designed column of 'The Monument', created 'to preserve the memory of this dreadful visitation'.

ALSO ON THIS DAY

31 BC Antony and Cleopatra are defeated by Octavian at the Battle of Actium.
1752 The Gregorian Calendar is adopted by Britain and its empire.
1969 The death of Ho Chi Minh, Vietnamese revolutionary leader.

3 SEPTEMBER

A DECLARATION OF WAR, 1939

This morning the British ambassador in Berlin handed the German government a final note stating that unless we heard from them by 11 o'clock that they were prepared at once to withdraw their troops from Poland, a state of war would exist between us. I have to tell you now that no such undertaking has been received, and that consequently this country is at war with Germany.

You can imagine what a bitter blow it is to me that all my long struggle to win peace has failed. Yet I cannot believe that there is anything more, or anything different, that I could have done and that would have been more successful. Up to the very last it would have been quite possible to have arranged a peaceful and honourable settlement between Germany and Poland. But Hitler would not have it. He had evidently made up his mind to attack Poland whatever happened, and although he now says he put forward reasonable proposals which were rejected by the Poles, that is not a true statement. The proposals were never shown to the Poles, nor to us, and though they were announced in the German broadcast on Thursday night, Hitler did not wait to hear comments on them, but ordered his troops to cross the Polish frontier the next morning.

His action shows convincingly that there is no chance of expecting that this man will ever give up his practice of using force to gain his will. He can only be stopped by force.

We have a clear conscience. We have done all that any country could do to establish peace. But the situation in which no word given by Germany's ruler could be trusted, and no people or country could feel itself safe, had become intolerable. And now that we have resolved to finish it, I know that you will all play your part with calmness and courage.

PRIME MINISTER NEVILLE CHAMBERLAIN, BBC RADIO ADDRESS, 3 SEPTEMBER 1939.

∞

The British declaration of war with Nazi Germany in 1939 represented the final failure of Neville Chamberlain's policy of appeasing Hitler's demands in Central and Eastern Europe (*see* 30 September). Poland quickly succumbed to Germany, but little action materialized in Western Europe until May 1940.

ALSO ON THIS DAY

1189 Richard I 'the Lionheart' is crowned king of England.
1783 The Treaty of Paris formally ends the American Revolutionary War.
2004 Over 380 die in the Beslan school hostage crisis, in the Russian Republic of North Ossetia.

4 SEPTEMBER

THE SURRENDER OF GERONIMO, 1886

General Miles said: 'I will take you under government protection; I will build you a house... I will give you cattle, horses, mules, and farming implements. You will be furnished with men to work the farm... In the fall I will send you blankets and clothing so that you will not suffer from cold in the winter time...' I said to General Miles: 'All the officers that have been in charge of the Indians have talked that way... I hardly believe you.' He said: 'This time it is the truth.' I said: 'General Miles, I do not know the laws of the white man, nor of this new country where you are to send me, and I might break the laws.' He said: 'While I live you will not be arrested.' Then I agreed to make the treaty...

We placed a large stone on the blanket before us. Our treaty was made by this stone, as it was to last until the stone should crumble to dust; so we made the treaty, and bound each other with an oath... When we had made the treaty General Miles said to me: 'My brother, you have in your mind how you are going to kill me, and other thoughts of war; I want you to put that out of your mind, and change your thoughts to peace'... I said: 'I will quit the war path and live at peace here after.' Then General Miles swept a spot of ground clear with his hand, and said: 'Your past deeds shall be wiped out like this and you will start a new life.'

GERONIMO'S *STORY OF HIS LIFE*, 1906.

The surrender of the Apache chief Geronimo on 4 September 1886 to General Nelson A. Miles represented the effective end of the Indian Wars in the United States. Geronimo (1829–1909) described it in his memoirs, dictated in 1905. In his adventure-filled life he had fought for some 30 years, in the Apache tribal lands of modern New Mexico, against Mexican and US settlers and troops. After his surrender, he spent most of the rest of his life in captivity, in Florida, Alabama and Oklahoma. In his old age he became something of a celebrity, appearing, for instance, at the 1904 World's Fair in St Louis.

ALSO ON THIS DAY

AD 476 Romulus Augustus is deposed, ending the Western Roman Empire.
1870 Napoleon III is deposed in France and the Third Republic declared.
1972 Mark Spitz becomes the first winner of seven Olympic gold medals.

5 SEPTEMBER

COUNTEROFFENSIVE ON THE MARNE, 1914

The Field Marshal [French commander Joseph Joffre] was standing at a table waiting for him [British commander-in-chief Sir John French], flanked by Murray, Wilson, Huguet, 'looking, as usual, as if he had lost his last friend', and several other members of his staff. Joffre walked over and for once took the floor at the outset. Instead of his usual laconic sentences, a passionate flood of speech poured forth punctuated by a gesture of his forearms which 'seemed to throw his heart on the table'. He said the 'supreme moment' had arrived, his own orders were given and whatever happened the last company of the French Army would be thrown into the battle to save France. The 'lives of all French people, the soil of France, the future of Europe' depended upon the offensive. 'I cannot believe the British Army will refuse to do its share in this supreme crisis... history would severely judge your absence.'

Joffre's fist crashed down on the table. 'Monsieur le Maréchal, the honour of England is at stake!'

At these words Sir John French, who had been listening with 'passionate attention', suddenly reddened. Silence fell on the company. Slowly tears came into the eyes of the British commander-in-chief and rolled down his cheeks. He struggled to say something in French and gave up. 'Damn it, I can't explain. Tell him we will do all we possibly can.'

Joffre looked enquiringly at Wilson who translated. 'The Field Marshal says "Yes".' It was hardly needed, for the tears and the tone already carried conviction.

BARBARA TUCHMAN, *THE GUNS OF AUGUST*, 1962.

'Gentlemen, we will fight on the Marne,' was Field Marshal Joffre's rallying-cry to his officers following his exchange with Sir John French, commander of the British Expeditionary Force in 1914. The 'Miracle of the Marne', which began on 5 September 1914 and in which more than 2 million men fought, followed a period characterized by a lack of co-ordination and bitter recriminations between the high commands of the two Allies; but it forced the German army to abandon its push on Paris and retreat northeastwards, ushering in four years of trench warfare.

ALSO ON THIS DAY

1793 French Revolution: the National Convention begins the Reign of Terror.
1905 The Treaty of Portsmouth ends the Russo-Japanese War.
1978 Israel and Egypt begin peace talks at Camp David, USA.

6 SEPTEMBER

THE SHOOTING OF PRESIDENT McKINLEY, 1901

On Wednesday I stood near the president, right under the stand from which he spoke. I thought... of shooting while he was speaking, but could not get close enough... The great crowd was always jostling, and I was afraid lest my aim fail ...My spirits were getting pretty low. I was almost hopeless that night as I went home.

Yesterday I went again to the Exposition grounds. Emma Goldman's speech was still burning me up. I waited... for the president, who was to board his special train... but the police allowed nobody but the president's party to pass out while the train waited.

Yesterday I thought of hiding my pistol under my handkerchief. I was afraid if I had to draw it from my pocket I would be seized by the guards. I got to the Temple of Music, and waited at the spot where the reception was to be held.

Then he came, the president – the ruler – and I got in line and trembled and trembled until I got right up to him, and then I shot him twice through my white handkerchief. I would have fired more, but I was stunned by a blow in the face – a frightful blow that knocked me down – and then everybody jumped on me. I thought I would be killed, and was surprised the way they treated me.

I am an Anarchist. I am a disciple of Emma Goldman. Her words set me on fire. I don't regret my act, because I was doing what I could for the great cause... I had no confidants, no one to help me. I was alone absolutely.

LEON FRANK CZOLGOSZ, CONFESSION TO POLICE, 1901.

William McKinley (1843–1901), 25th president of the United States, was shot at the Pan-American exhibition at Buffalo, New York, and died a little over a week later. His killer, unemployed factory worker Leon Czolgosz, had been inspired by the anarchist Emma Goldman and by the assassination, the previous year, of Italy's King Umberto I, and he had resolved on violent action of his own. Thus Czolgosz ended the life of a president associated strongly with US power projection, most palpably expressed in the 1898 war with Spain (*see* 15 February).

Czolgosz was executed by electric chair on 29 October 1901.

ALSO ON THIS DAY

1966 The architect of *apartheid*, South African prime minister Hendrik Verwoerd, is assassinated.
1972 Nine Israeli hostages are killed by Palestinian terrorists at the Munich Olympics.
1997 The funeral of Diana, Princess of Wales, takes place in London.

7 SEPTEMBER

THE FIRST DAY OF THE BLITZ, 1940

The brilliant sky was crisscrossed from horizon to horizon by innumerable vapour trails. The sight was a completely novel one. We watched, fascinated, and all work stopped. The little silver stars sparkling at the heads of the vapour trails turned east. This display looked so insubstantial and harmless, even beautiful. Then, with a dull roar which made the ground across London shake as one stood upon it, the first sticks of bombs hit the docks. Leisurely, enormous mushrooms of black and brown smoke shot with crimson climbed into the sunlit sky. There they hung and slowly expanded, for there was no wind and the great fires below fed more smoke into them as the hours passed.

DESMOND FLOWER, *THE WAR 1939–1945*, 1960.

The concerted aerial bombing of London by the Luftwaffe in 1940 began in the late afternoon of 7 September 1940, with a raid comprising 364 bombers accompanied by 515 fighters, aimed at the docks. More than 400 people were killed.

The 'Blitz' (after *Blitzkrieg*) began as a new tactic in the Battle of Britain, as Hitler and Goering moved away from attempting to achieve air superiority to pummelling the British people into demanding their government's surrender. It did no such thing, rather generating a 'Blitz spirit' of defiance. Nevertheless, the attacks on London continued for 72 consecutive nights. From November, the raids spread out to include many other industrial cities and ports, the worst raid being on Coventry (*see* 14 November).

ALSO ON THIS DAY

1812 Napoleon defeats the Russians in the bloody Battle of Borodino.
1893 The Genoa Cricket & Athletic club, later Italy's first football club, is founded.
1990 The death of the English historian A.J.P. Taylor.

8 SEPTEMBER

THE UNVEILING OF MICHELANGELO'S *DAVID*, 1504

Many disputes took place as to how to transport the statue to the Piazza della Signoria. Giuliano da San Gallo and his brother Antonio made a framework of wood and suspended the figure from it with ropes... and they drew it with windlasses over flat beams laid upon the ground, then set it in place...

Piero Soderini [Florence's *gonfaloniere*, 'leader'] was pleased, but said that it seemed to him that the nose was too thick. Michelangelo noticed that the *gonfaloniere* was beneath the Giant, and that his point of view prevented him from seeing it properly; he climbed upon the stagin ... took up a chisel, with a little of the marble-dust that lay upon the planks of the staging, and then, striking lightly with the chisel, let fall the dust little by little, but changed the nose not a whit from what it was before. 'I like it better,' said the *gonfaloniere*, 'you have given it life.' Michelangelo came down, laughing to himself...

In it may be seen most beautiful contours of legs, with attachments of limbs and slender outlines of flanks that are divine; nor has there ever been seen a pose so easy, or any grace to equal that in this work, or feet, hands and head so well in accord, one member with another, in harmony, design, and excellence of artistry. Whoever has seen this work need not trouble to see any other work executed in sculpture, either in our own or in other times, by no matter what craftsman.

GIORGIO VASARI, *LIVES OF THE ARTISTS*, 1550.

Michelangelo's marble sculpture of the biblical hero David was commissioned for Florence Cathedral but was erected in the city's Piazza della Signoria on 5 September 1504. It was celebrated as a symbolic assertion of the Florentine Republic's defiance in the face of the challenge from the resurgent 'Goliath' of Rome, where the aggrandizing pontificate of Pope Alexander VI had nurtured the territorial ambitions of his son Cesare Borgia, threatening Florence (*see also* 30 October).

One of the most celebrated and widely recognized masterpieces of Renaissance sculpture, Michelangelo's *David* now resides in Florence's Galleria dell'Accademia.

1900 A hurricane hits Galveston, Texas, killing 8,000 people.
1941 WWII: German forces begin their 872-day siege of Leningrad – a million deaths will result.
1944 WWII: the first German V2 rocket hits London.

9 SEPTEMBER

THE DEATH OF WILLIAM THE CONQUEROR, 1087

I treated the native inhabitants of the kingdom with unreasonable severity, cruelly oppressed high and low, unjustly disinherited many, and caused the death of thousands by starvation and war, especially in Yorkshire… In mad fury I descended on the English of the north like a raging lion, and ordered that their homes and crops with all their equipment and furnishings should be burnt at once and their great flocks and herds of sheep and cattle slaughtered everywhere. So I chastized a great multitude of men and women with the lash of starvation and, alas! was the cruel murderer of many thousands, both young and old, of this fair people.

WILLIAM I's FINAL CONFESSION, ORDERIC VITALIS, *GESTA REGUM ANGLORUM*, c.1140.

The ageing and overweight William the Conqueror died in Rouen in September 1087, following a fall from his horse in Mantes, Normandy. The main account of his life, written by the monk Orderic Vitalis, was probably based on interviews with eyewitnesses; but as an Englishman himself, Orderic may have used this episode as an opportunity to express the resentment still felt by the English towards their Norman conqueror, not least because of William's harsh treatment of northern rebels in the so-called 'Harrying of the North' (1069–70). He described how, on William's death, all his clothes and furniture were taken by his attendants, leaving his body almost naked. The bloated body was taken to Caen for burial, but, during the ceremony, it could not be fitted into its stone sarcophagus; the internal organs burst, to the distress of all those present. In the concise eloquence of the *Anglo-Saxon Chronicle* (1087):

> *He who was earlier a powerful king, and lord of many a land, he had nothing of any land but a seven-foot measure; and he who was at times clothed with gold and with jewels, lay then covered over with earth.*

A fine tomb was later erected, but it was destroyed in the 16th century.

ALSO ON THIS DAY

1543 Mary Stuart is crowned 'Queen of Scots' at nine months old.
1976 The death of Chinese Communist Party Chairman Mao Zedong.
1993 The Palestinian Liberation Organization recognizes the state of Israel.

10 SEPTEMBER

A WESTERNER IN MECCA, 1853

Scarcely had the first smile of morning beamed upon the rugged head of the eastern hill, Abu Kubays, when we arose, bathed, and proceeded in our pilgrim-garb to the Sanctuary. We entered by the Bab al-Ziyadah, or principal northern door, descended two long flights of steps, traversed the cloister, and stood in sight of the Bayt Allah.

There at last it lay, the bourn of my long and weary pilgrimage, realizing the plans and hopes of many and many a year... There were no giant fragments of hoar antiquity as in Egypt, no remains of graceful and harmonious beauty as in Greece and Italy, no barbarous gorgeousness as in the buildings of India; yet the view was strange, unique – and how few have looked upon the celebrated shrine! I may truly say that, of all the worshippers who clung weeping to the curtain, or who pressed their beating hearts to the stone, none felt for the moment a deeper emotion than did the Haji from the far north [i.e. himself]. It was as if the poetical legends of the Arab spoke truth, and that the waving wings of angels, not the sweet breeze of morning, were agitating and swelling the black covering of the shrine. But, to confess humbling truth, theirs was the high feeling of religious enthusiasm, mine was the ecstasy of gratified pride.

Few Moslems contemplate for the first time the Ka'abah, without fear and awe: there is a popular jest against new comers, that they generally inquire the direction of prayer. This being the Kiblah, or fronting place, Moslems pray all around it; a circumstance which of course cannot take place in any spot of Al-Islam but the Harim.

RICHARD BURTON, *A PERSONAL NARRATIVE OF A PILGRIMAGE*, 1855.

The British explorer and orientalist Richard Burton (1821–90) visited Mecca in disguise in 1853, on an expedition sponsored by the Royal Geographical Society. (By the conventions of Islam's holiest city, the presence of a non-Muslim would have resulted in his death, had his disguise been penetrated.) There he was able to observe what Muslim pilgrims on the annual *Hajj* would have been able to see: the cuboid shrine of the Ka'aba that lay at the centre of the Masjid al-Harem, the large mosque complex.

ALSO ON THIS DAY

1797 The death of Mary Wollstonecraft, author of *A Vindication of the Rights of Woman*.
1823 Simón Bolivar becomes the president of Peru.
2008 Proton beams are circulated in the Large Hadron Collider at CERN, Geneva, for the first time.

11 SEPTEMBER

AL-QAEDA ATTACKS THE UNITED STATES, 2001

Today, our fellow citizens, our way of life, our very freedom came under attack in a series of deliberate and deadly terrorist acts. The victims were in airplanes or in their offices: secretaries, business men and women, military and federal workers, moms and dads, friends and neighbors. Thousands of lives were suddenly ended by evil, despicable acts of terror. The pictures of airplanes flying into buildings, fires burning, huge – huge structures collapsing have filled us with disbelief, terrible sadness, and a quiet, unyielding anger. These acts of mass murder were intended to frighten our nation into chaos and retreat. But they have failed. Our country is strong.

A great people has been moved to defend a great nation. Terrorist attacks can shake the foundations of our biggest buildings, but they cannot touch the foundation of America. These acts shatter steel, but they cannot dent the steel of American resolve. America was targeted for attack because we're the brightest beacon for freedom and opportunity in the world. And no one will keep that light from shining. Today, our nation saw evil – the very worst of human nature – and we responded with the best of America. With the daring of our rescue workers, with the caring for strangers and neighbors who came to give blood and help in any way they could.

…This is a day when all Americans from every walk of life unite in our resolve for justice and peace. America has stood down enemies before, and we will do so this time. None of us will ever forget this day, yet we go forward to defend freedom and all that is good and just in our world.

PRESIDENT GEORGE W. BUSH, 2001

The attacks by members of the Islamic militant al-Qaeda group on the World Trade Center in New York and the Pentagon in Washington resulted in the deaths of some 3,000 people, including 343 firefighters and 60 police officers from New York City and the Port Authorities. US President George W. Bush addressed the nation that evening. The following week he declared war on the Afghan Taliban regime and its al-Qaeda allies.

Ten years later, US and other forces were still battling a Taliban insurgency in Afghanistan; but on 2 May 2011 American Special Forces located and killed al-Qaeda's founder Osama bin Laden at a compound in Abbottabad, northern Pakistan.

ALSO ON THIS DAY

1297 The Scots under William Wallace defeat the English at Stirling Bridge.
1973 A CIA-backed coup in Chile deposes left-wing President Salvador Allende.
1989 The Iron Curtain opens between Communist Hungary and Austria.

12 SEPTEMBER

THE BATTLE OF MARATHON, 490 BC

And when it came round to Miltiades' turn to command, then the Athenians were drawn up for battle... And when they had been arranged in their places and the sacrifices proved favourable, then the Athenians were let go, and they set forth at a run to attack the Barbarians. Now the space between the armies was not less than eight furlongs: and the Persians seeing them advancing to the attack at a run, made preparations to receive them; and in their minds they charged the Athenians with madness which must be fatal, seeing that they were few and yet were pressing forwards at a run, having neither cavalry nor archers. Such was the thought of the Barbarians; but the Athenians... fought in a memorable fashion: for they were the first of all the Hellenes about whom we know who went to attack the enemy at a run, and they were the first also who endured to face the Median garments and the men who wore them, whereas up to this time the very name of the Medes was to the Hellenes a terror to hear.

Now while they fought in Marathon, much time passed by; and in the centre of the army, where the Persians themselves and the Sacans were drawn up, the Barbarians were winning... but on both wings the Athenians and the Plataians severally were winning the victory... they left that part of the Barbarians which had been routed to fly without molestation, and bringing together the two wings they fought with those who had broken their centre, and the Athenians were victorious. So they followed after the Persians as they fled, slaughtering them, until they came to the sea; and then they called for fire and began to take hold of the ships.

HERODOTUS, *HISTORIES*, BOOK 6, TRANSLATED BY G.C. MACAULAY, 1890.

∞

The 'Father of History', Herodotus (c.484–425 BC) left a vivid account of the celebrated Greek victory on the plain of Marathon, whereby, in a pincer movement, the outnumbered Athenians and Plataeans defeated the invading 'Barbarians' – the Persians and their allies, including the fearsome Medes and the Sacans (Scythians). While the invaders suffered 7,000 casualties, the Athenian dead numbered a mere 192. In Plutarch's later account, the Athenian Pheidippides ran the 26 miles back to the city to announce the victory – the inspiration for the modern marathon race.

ALSO ON THIS DAY

1940 Palaeolithic cave paintings are discovered at Lascaux, southwest France.
1974 Emperor Haile Selassie is deposed in Ethiopia.
1977 The anti-*apartheid* activist Steve Biko is killed in South African police custody.

13 SEPTEMBER

THE FALL OF QUEBEC, 1759

Let not my brave fellows see me fall. The day is ours – keep it.

GENERAL JAMES WOLFE, 13 SEPTEMBER 1759.

∞

The Battle of the Plains of Abraham in 1759 was the decisive encounter in the North American theatre of the Seven Years' War – the so-called French and Indian Wars, fought between the French and British (with their respective Native American allies). It led to the deaths of the charismatic commanders of both armies and resulted in the British capture of nearby Quebec City, the capital of 'New France'. It was one of the high points of a year in which the British won decisive victories across the globe.

Following a three-month siege of the city, the 32-year-old General James Wolfe initiated a daring assault by his far smaller force. He sent an advance party to cross the St Lawrence River at night and scaled a near-vertical cliff, clearing the way for the bulk of the British army to reach the plateau in darkness and surprise the French defenders from behind. Louis-Joseph, Marquis de Montcalm, ordered an immediate attack; Wolfe was shot during the subsequent hour-long encounter and died as his victory was becoming clear. This death, mythologized in the heroic painting *The Death of General Wolfe* (1771) by Benjamin West, made him one of the first cult figures of British military history.

Montcalm, who had led the French defence against the British in North America since 1756, had dismissed the possibility of an attack up the cliff; but he was wounded during the French retreat and died the next day within the walls of Quebec City. On being told he had only a few hours to live he observed: 'So much the better. I shall not see the surrender of Quebec.' That surrender came a few days later. (*See also* 10 February.)

ALSO ON THIS DAY

AD 122 The building of Hadrian's Wall begins in northern England.
1584 The building of El Escorial, residence of the kings of Spain, is completed.
1953 Nikita Khrushchev becomes general secretary of the Soviet Communist Party.

14 SEPTEMBER

THE BURNING OF MOSCOW, 1812

A curious and impressive sight was this sudden appearance of this great city, Asiatic rather than European, spreading out at the end of a desert and naked plain, topped with its 1,200 spires and sky-blue cupolas, strewn with golden stars and linked one to another with golden chains. This conquest had been dearly paid for but Napoleon at the time lulled himself in the hope that he would be able to dictate peace there.

The Russian army had taken away the majority of the inhabitants in its train. There remained in the city only a few thousand people belonging to the lowest classes of society who had nothing to lose by awaiting the course of events.

...Hardly had the emperor entered the Kremlin than fire broke out in the Kitaigorod or Chinese city, an immense bazaar surrounded by porticoes in which were heaped up, in large shops or cellars, precious goods of every kind such as shawls, furs, Indian and Chinese textiles. The burning of the bazaar became the signal for a general conflagration of the city. This conflagration, spreading rapidly, devoured three-quarters of Moscow in three days... The town was one mighty furnace from which sheaves of fire burst heavenward, lighting up the horizon with glaring flames and spreading a searing heat... Motionless and in the silence of stupor we looked on at this horrible and magnificent spectacle, with our feeling of our absolute helplessness.

BARON CLAUDE FRANÇOIS DE MÉNEVAL, *MEMOIRS*, 1827.

∞

Baron de Méneval, Napoleon's private secretary, accompanied the French emperor as he led his 600,000-strong Grande Armée into Moscow in September 1812. Meanwhile the Russians, led by Prince Kutuzov, staged a tactical retreat following the indecisive Battle of Borodino in August. But the burning of the city forced the French themselves to retreat in October, harried by the Russians and tormented by the onset of the bitter winter. The campaign took a terrible toll of Napoleon's army – fewer than 100,000 men made it back to France – and it proved the turning point in the Napoleonic Wars, with the emperor thereafter on the defensive. Three years later, after the temporary resurgence of his 'Hundred Days', Napoleon met his Waterloo (*see* 18 June).

ALSO ON THIS DAY

1741 George Frideric Handel completes his oratorio *Messiah*.
1901 US President William McKinley dies eight days after being shot by Leon Czolgosz.
1959 Soviet *Luna 2*, the first spacecraft to reach Earth's satellite, crash-lands on the Moon.

15 SEPTEMBER

THE DEADLY LIVERPOOL–MANCHESTER
RAILWAY, 1830

We started to the number of about eight hundred people, in carriages. The most intense curiosity and excitement prevailed, and though the weather was uncertain, enormous masses of densely packed people lined the road, shouting and waving hats and handkerchiefs as we flew by them. What with the sight and sound of their cheering multitudes and the tremendous velocity with which we were borne past them, my spirits rose to the true champagne height, and I never enjoyed anything so much as the first hour of our progress. I had been unluckily separated from my mother in the first distribution of places, but by an exchange of seats which she enabled to make she rejoined me when I was at the height of my ecstasy, which was considerably damped by finding that she was frightened to death, and intent upon nothing but devising means of escaping from a situation which appeared to her to threaten with instant annihilation herself and all her travelling companions.

While I was chewing the cud of this disappointment... a man flew by us called out through a speaking trumpet to stop the engine, for that somebody in the directors' carriage had sustained an injury. We were all stopped accordingly and presently a hundred voices were heard exclaiming that Mr Huskisson was killed ...At last we distinctly ascertained that the unfortunate man's thigh was broken ...The engine had stopped to take in a supply of water and several gentlemen in the directors' carriage had jumped out to look about them. Lord Wilton, Count Batthyany, Count Matuscenitz and Mr Huskisson among the rest were standing talking in the middle of the road when an engine on the other line, which was parading up and down merely to show its speed, was seen coming down upon them like lightning. The most active of those in peril sprang back into their seats ...while poor Mr Huskisson, less active from the effects of age and ill-health, bewildered too by the frantic cries of 'Stop the engine! Clear the track!' that resounded on all sides, completely lost his head, look helplessly to the right and left, and was instantaneously prostrated by the fatal machine which dashed down like a thunderbolt upon him and passed over his leg, smashing and mangling it in the most horrible way.

Mr Huskisson was placed in a carriage with his wife and Lord Wilton and the engine, having been detached from the directors' carriage, conveyed them to Manchester. So great was the shock produced upon the whole party by this event that the Duke of Wellington declared his intention not to proceed, but to return immediately to Liverpool. However, upon its being represented to him that the whole population of Manchester had turned out to witness the procession and that a disappointment might give rise to riots and disturbances, he consented to go on, and gloomily enough the rest of the journey was accomplished.

...As we neared Manchester the sky grew cloudy and dark and it began to rain. The vast concourse of people who had assembled to witness the triumphant arrival of the successful travellers was of the lower order of mechanics and artisans, among whom great distress and a dangerous spirit of discontent with the government at that time prevailed. Groans and hisses greeted the carriage, full of influential personages, in which the Duke of Wellington sat. High above the grim and grimy crowd of scowling faces a loom had been erected, at which sat a tattered starved-looking weaver, evidently set there as a representative man, to protest against the triumph of machinery and the gain and glory which the wealthy Liverpool and Manchester men were likely to derive from it.

FRANCES KEMBLE, *RECORD OF A GIRLHOOD*, 1878.

The world's first inter-city passenger railway, planned by the railway pioneers George Stephenson (1781–1848) and his son Robert, was opened with great ceremony on 15 September 1830, with the prime minister, the Duke of Wellington, in attendance. However, the injuries sustained by the MP for Liverpool, William Huskisson, who stepped onto the track at an inopportune time, marred the occasion: he was run over by George Stephenson's *Rocket*. The unfortunate politician was then conveyed by the same engine, driven by Stephenson, to Manchester where he died shortly afterwards, thus achieving enduring fame as the first reported victim of a railway accident.

Frances ('Fanny') Kemble, aged 21 at the time of the railway's opening, became a leading actress in Britain and America. She evoked the incident in her *Recollections*, written in her retirement.

ALSO ON THIS DAY

1859 The death of the English civil engineer Isambard Kingdom Brunel.
1916 WWI: tanks are used in warfare for the first time, at the Battle of the Somme.
1935 The Nuremberg Laws deprive all German Jews of citizenship.

16 SEPTEMBER

THE STIRRINGS OF MEXICAN REVOLUTION, 1810

My friends and countrymen: neither the king nor tributes exist for us any longer. We have borne this shameful tax, which only suits slaves, for three centuries as a sign of tyranny and servitude; a terrible stain which we shall know how to wash away with our efforts. The moment of our freedom has arrived, the hour of our liberty has struck; and if you recognized its great value, you will help me defend it from the ambitious grasp of the tyrants. Only a few hours remain before you see me at the head of the men who take pride in being free. I invite you to fulfil this obligation. Without a *patria* nor liberty we shall always be at a great distance from true happiness. It has been imperative to take this step as now you know, and to begin this has been necessary. The cause is holy and God will protect it. The arrangements are hastily being made and for that reason I will not have the satisfaction of talking to you any longer. Long live the Virgin of Guadalupe! Long live America for which we are going to fight!

MIGUEL HIDALGO, *GRITO DE DOLORES*, 16 SEPTEMBER 1810.

The Mexican *Grito de Dolores*, also known as the Cry of Independence, was issued by the priest-turned-military-leader Father Miguel Hidalgo y Costilla (1753–1811), the figurehead of the Mexican fight for independence. In 1810 he led a revolt of Native Americans and Creoles (locally born people of Spanish ancestry) demanding land reform, the abolition of slavery, and an end to the rule of the Spanish vice-regent. He adopted the banner of the Virgin of Guadalupe, symbol of a miraculous appearance of the Virgin Mary to the suffering native population in 1531.

Hidalgo was captured and executed in 1811, but he inspired others and Mexican independence was eventually achieved in 1821. The date of 16 September, on which Hidalgo first raised the *Grito de Dolores*, became a national holiday in Mexico.

ALSO ON THIS DAY

1620 The *Mayflower* sails from Plymouth for North America.
1920 An anarchist bombing of Wall Street, New York, claims 38 lives.
1975 Papua New Guinea becomes independent from Australia.

17 SEPTEMBER

DARWIN ENCOUNTERS
THE GALÁPAGOS ISLANDS, 1835

The Bay swarmed with animals: Fish, Shark & Turtles were popping their heads up in all parts. Fishing lines were soon put overboard & great numbers of fine fish 2 & even 3 ft long were caught. This sport makes all hands very merry; loud laughter & the heavy flapping of the fish are heard on every side. – After dinner a party went on shore to try to catch tortoises, but were unsuccessful. – These islands appear paradises for the whole family of reptiles. Besides three kinds of turtles, the tortoise is so abundant; that single ship's company here caught from 500–800 in a short time. – The black lava rocks on the beach are frequented by large (2–3 ft) most disgusting, clumsy lizards. They are as black as the porous rocks over which they crawl & seek their prey from the sea. – Somebody calls them 'imps of darkness'. – They assuredly well become the land they inhabit. – When on shore I proceeded to botanize & obtained 10 different flowers; but such insignificant, ugly little flowers, as would better become an Arctic, than a tropical country. – The birds are strangers to Man & think... him as innocent as their countrymen the huge tortoises. Little birds within 3 & four feet, quietly hopped about the bushes & were not frightened by stones being thrown at them. Mr King killed one with his hat & I pushed off a branch with the end of my gun a large Hawk.

CHARLES DARWIN, *DIARY*, 17 SEPTEMBER 1835.

The journey undertaken by the naturalist Charles Darwin aboard HMS *Beagle*, which had begun in December 1831 and took him around South America, reached a climax on 17 September 1835 when the ship anchored off the Galápagos Islands. His observations over the next few weeks of the unique flora and fauna of those islands, notably the giant tortoises and the many species of finch, contributed importantly to his theory of evolution by natural selection, as advanced in his transformative best-seller *On the Origin of Species*, published in 1859.

ALSO ON THIS DAY

1630 The city of Boston, Massachusetts, is founded.
1948 The UN mediator Folke Bernadotte is murdered in Jerusalem by militant Zionists.
1980 In Poland, Solidarity becomes a nationwide trade union.

18 SEPTEMBER

THE JEWISH STAR IN NAZI GERMANY, 1941

The 'Jewish star', black on yellow cloth, at the centre in Hebrew-like lettering 'Jew', to be worn on the left breast, large as the palm of a hand, issued to us yesterday for 10 pfennigs, to be worn from tomorrow. The omnibus may no longer be used, only the front platform of the train. For the time being at least Eva will take over all the shopping. I shall breathe in a little fresh air only under shelter of darkness.

Today we were outside together in daylight for the last time. First cigarette hunt, then on the tram (seat!) to Loschwitz over the suspension bridge, from there along the right bank down by the river toward town as far as the Waldschlossen. In 21 years we have never taken this route. The Elbe, very high, broad, flowing strongly and quietly, a lot of mist, the park gardens behind the high walls autumnal with flowers and falling leaves. A first chestnut fell and burst at our feet. It was like a last day out, a last little bit of freedom before a long (how long?) imprisonment. The same feeling, as we ate in the Löwenbrau in Moritzstrasse.

When one occupant of this house visits another, he rings three times. That has been agreed, so that no-one catches fright. A simple ring could be the police.

VICTOR KLEMPERER, *I WILL BEAR WITNESS: A DIARY OF THE NAZI YEARS*, 1998.

∞

The German literary academic and writer Victor Klemperer (1881–1960) was born the son of a rabbi. From the age of 16 he kept a diary, and during the Nazi years he recorded, in detail, the daily humiliations of life for a Jewish family, including the direction to wear the Jewish star for racial identification. He was probably saved from the extreme fate that befell many of Europe's Jews by the fact that he could boast distinguished service in the First World War, that he had been baptized in his early twenties, and that (most importantly) his wife, Eva, was not Jewish.

In 1945 he and Eva survived the devastating Allied bombing of his home city of Dresden, which fortuitously also destroyed the Gestapo's files on him. After the war, Klemperer was able to resume his professorship of Romance Studies in what was now East Germany – and continued to keep his diary.

ALSO ON THIS DAY

1838 Richard Cobden establishes the Anti-Corn Law League in Britain.
1911 The Russian prime minister Pyotr Stolypin is assassinated.
1961 UN Secretary General Dag Hammarskjöld dies in an unexplained plane crash.

19 SEPTEMBER

THE FINAL SPEECH OF AN IRISH NATIONALIST, 1803

My lords, you are impatient for the sacrifice – the blood which you seek is not congealed by the artificial terrors which surround your victim; it circulates warmly and unruffled, through the channels which God created for noble purposes, but which you are bent to destroy, for purposes so grievous that they cry to heaven. Be yet patient! I have but a few words more to say.

I am going to my cold and silent grave: my lamp of life is nearly extinguished: my race is run: the grave opens to receive me, and I sink into its bosom! I have but one request to ask at my departure from this world – it is the charity of its silence!

Let no man write my epitaph: for as no man who knows my motives dare now vindicate them. Let not prejudice or ignorance asperse them. Let them and me repose in obscurity and peace, and my tomb remain uninscribed, until other times, and other men, can do justice to my character; when my country takes her place among the nations of the earth, then, and not till then, let my epitaph be written. I have done.

ROBERT EMMET, DUBLIN CASTLE, TRIAL SPEECH, 19 SEPTEMBER 1803.

∞

In 1803 the 25-year-old Robert Emmet, an idealistic member of the nationalist Society of United Irishmen, staged an abortive revolt against British rule in Dublin, following the loss of the separate Irish Parliament by the Act of Union (1800). He had spent some time on the Continent, hoping for French military aid; the rising was timed to coincide with the resumption of hostilities between France and Britain, but it went ahead without any foreign help. Emmet wore a green general's uniform, but his insurgents – mostly drunken workers – proved hopelessly ill-disciplined and were easily dispersed by regular troops. Perhaps 50 people died in the rebellion, and Emmet was captured after fleeing Dublin.

At his brief trial, Emmet made this famous speech from the dock on 19 September, asserting the nobility of his cause, which made him an enduringly romantic hero to future generations of Irish nationalists. He was executed the following day, adding martyrdom to heroism.

ALSO ON THIS DAY

1870 Franco-Prussian War: Prussian forces begin the siege of Paris.
1881 US President James Garfield dies of wounds from an assassination attempt on 2 July.
1991 A 5,300-year-old mummy, Ötzi the Iceman, is discovered on the Austro-Italian border.

20 SEPTEMBER

THE END OF THE MUGHAL EMPIRE, 1857

Captain Hodson then went out into the middle of the road in front of the gateway, and said that he was ready to receive his captives and renew his promise.

You may picture yourself the scene before the magnificent gateway, with the milk-white domes of the tomb towering up from within, one white man among a host of natives, yet determined to secure his prisoner or perish in the attempt.

Soon a procession began to come slowly out, first [the empress] Zeenat Mahal, on one of the close native conveyances used for women... Then came the king in a palkee [palanquin], on which Capt. Hodson rode forward and demanded his arms. Before giving them up, the king asked whether he was 'Hodson Bahadoor,' and if he would repeat the promise made by the herald? Captain Hodson answered that he would, and repeated that the government had been graciously pleased to promise him his life, and that of Zeenat Mahal's son, on condition of his yielding himself prisoner quietly, adding very emphatically, that if any attempt was made at a rescue he would shoot the king on the spot like a dog.

The old man then gave up his arms, which Capt. Hodson handed to his orderly, still keeping his own sword drawn in his hand. The same ceremony was then gone through with the boy (Jumma Bukh), and the march towards the city began, the longest five miles, as Captain Hodson said, that he ever rode, for, of course, the palkees only went at foot pace, with his handful of men around them, followed by thousands, any one of whom could have shot him down in a moment.

His orderly told me that it was wonderful to see the influence which his calm and undaunted look had on the crowd. They seemed perfectly paralyzed at the fact of one white man (for they thought nothing of his 50 black sowars [mounted soldiers]) carrying off their king alone. Gradually as they approached the city the crowd slunk away, and very few followed up to the Lahore Gate. Then Captain H. rode on a few paces and ordered the gate to be opened. The officer on duty asked simply as he passed what he had got in his palkees. 'Only the King of Delhi' was the answer; on which the officer's enthusiastic exclamation was more emphatic than becomes ears polite. The guard were for turning out to greet him with a cheer, and could only be repressed on being told that the king would take the honour to himself. They passed up that magnificent deserted street to the palace gate, where Captain Hodson met the civil officer (Mr Sanders), and formally delivered over his royal prisoners to him. His remark was amusing: 'By Jove, Hodson, they ought to make you commander-in-chief for this.'

Illustrated London News, March 1858.

The hostilities of the Indian Mutiny (*see* 10 May), which began in 1857, ended with the recapture of Delhi by the British, and the surrender of the elderly Bahadur Shah Zafar (1775–1862), king of Delhi and the last of the Mughal dynasty, who had become a figurehead for the rebels.

The elderly but cultured shah – a poet and calligrapher – had presided over a reduced and impoverished 'kingdom' – mostly consisting of the Red Fort at Delhi – but he had nevertheless made his court a vibrant centre of Urdu learning and literature. It came to an end with his abject surrender to Captain William Hodson; by that time, his sons had already been shot. The shah was put on trial and exiled to Burma, where he ended his days in a Rangoon prison. It was an ignominious end, and a bloody beginning to the era of the British Raj. But the last Mughal proved an inspirational symbol for later Indian nationalists.

21 SEPTEMBER

THE GRISLY DEMISE OF EDWARD II, 1327

Roger Mortimer sent orders as to how and in what manner the king should be killed. When they had seen the letter and the order, they were friendly towards King Edward at supper-time, so that the king knew nothing of their treachery. And when he had gone to bed and was asleep, the traitors... went quietly into his chamber and laid a large table on his stomach and with other men's help pressed him down... [They inserted] a long horn into his fundament as deep as they might, and took a spit of burning copper and put it through the horn into his body and oft-times rolled therewith his bowels, and so they killed their lord, and nothing was perceived.

BRUT CHRONICLE, 1330s.

King Edward II of England, much disliked by his nobility for his supposedly homosexual relationship with his favourite Piers Gaveston and for his military failures in Scotland, was deposed in January 1327 by Roger Mortimer, Earl of March – with the help of Mortimer's lover, Edward's French wife Isabella. With his 14-year-old son Edward III now placed on the throne, under the regency of Mortimer, Edward II was reported to have died on 21 September 1327 in custody at Berkeley Castle, Gloucestershire.

Several chronicles elaborate on the gruesome method of that death, but none is exactly contemporary or wholly reliable. Not only has doubt been cast on whether this was indeed the method of despatch (similar stories unrelated to Edward crop up elsewhere, for example in Chaucer), but historians have also queried whether he was in fact killed at this time, or whether he might have escaped and lived for a further decade in an Italian monastery.

22 SEPTEMBER

LINCOLN'S FIRST EMANCIPATION
PROCLAMATION, 1862

I... do hereby proclaim and declare that hereafter, as heretofore, the war will be prosecuted for the object of practically restoring the constitutional relation between the United States, and each of the States, and the people thereof, in which States that relation is, or may be, suspended or disturbed.

That it is my purpose... to again recommend the adoption of a practical measure tendering pecuniary aid to the free acceptance or rejection of all slave States, so called, the people whereof may not then be in rebellion against the United States and which States may then have voluntarily adopted, or thereafter may voluntarily adopt, immediate or gradual abolishment of slavery within their respective limits; and that the effort to colonize persons of African descent, with their consent, upon this continent, or elsewhere, with the previously obtained consent of the governments existing there, will be continued.

That on [1 January 1863], all persons held as slaves within any State, or designated part of a State, the people whereof shall then be in rebellion against the United States shall be then, thenceforward, and forever free; and the executive government of the United States, including the military and naval authority thereof, will recognize and maintain the freedom of such persons, and will do no act or acts to repress such persons, or any of them, in any efforts they may make for their actual freedom.

...And the executive will in due time recommend that all citizens of the United States who shall have remained loyal thereto throughout the rebellion, shall be compensated for all losses by acts of the United States, including the loss of slaves.

PRESIDENT ABRAHAM LINCOLN, PROCLAMATION, 22 SEPTEMBER 1862.

President Abraham Lincoln's first Emancipation Proclamation was followed in January 1863 by a second Order naming the ten states still in rebellion, in which the slaves were declared free. Slavery itself was not made illegal in the United States until 18 December 1865, when the Thirteenth Amendment to the Constitution was passed.

ALSO ON THIS DAY

1499 By the Treaty of Basel Switzerland becomes independent within the Holy Roman Empire.
1598 The English playwright Ben Jonson kills an actor in a duel, and is tried for manslaughter.
1896 Queen Victoria overtakes George III as Britain's longest-reigning monarch.

23 SEPTEMBER

THE BATTLE OF FLAMBOROUGH HEAD, 1779

A general chase commenced... The *Serapis* passed ahead of the *Bonhomme Richard*, and... put his helm a-lee, which brought the two ships on a line, and the *Bonhomme Richard* ran her bows into the stern of the *Serapis*.

We were hailed: 'Has your ship struck?' To which Captain Jones answered: 'I have not yet begun to fight!'

There was not a man on board the *Bonhomme Richard* ignorant of the superiority of the *Serapis*. The crew of that ship was picked seamen, and the ship itself had been only a few months off the stocks, whereas the crew of the *Bonhomme Richard* consisted of part Americans, English and French, and a part of Maltese, Portuguese and Malays, these latter contributing by their want of naval skill and knowledge of the English language to depress rather than to elevate a just hope of success in a combat.

The fire from the tops of the *Bonhomme Richard* was conducted with so much skill and effect as to destroy ultimately every man who appeared upon the quarter deck of the *Serapis*... Some of the hand-grenades thrown from the main-yard of the *Bonhomme Richard*... fell upon powder and produced a most awful explosion. The effect was tremendous; more than twenty of the enemy were blown to pieces, and many stood with only the collars of their shirts upon their bodies. In less than an hour afterward, the flag of Englan ... nailed to the mast of the *Serapis*, was struck by Captain Pearson's own hand, as none of his people would venture aloft on this duty; and this too when more than 1,500 persons were witnessing the conflict, and the humiliating termination of it, from Scarborough and Flamborough Head.

LIEUTENANT RICHARD DALE, *THE LIFE AND CHARACTER OF JOHN PAUL JONES*, 1825.

Although the Battle of Flamborough Head took place, on 23 September 1779, off England's Yorkshire coast, it was a minor incident in the American Revolutionary War (War of Independence), in which a small Franco-American fleet attempted to raid a British convoy. The defiance of the American commander John Paul Jones, captain of the *Bonhomme Richard*, and his demonstration that the Royal Navy was not invincible, ensured his entry into the annals of American national folklore.

ALSO ON THIS DAY

1846 The German astronomer Johann Galle becomes the first man to view the planet Neptune.
1939 The death of the Austrian founder of psychoanalysis, Sigmund Freud.
1943 WWII: Mussolini regains power in the 'Salò Republic' of northern Italy.

24 SEPTEMBER

THE PROPHET MUHAMMAD ARRIVES
IN MEDINA, 622

When news reached Medina that the apostle had left Mecca, Abdul-Rahman told how the followers of the apostle 'used to go morning prayers, expecting his arrival. We went out to a stony plain to look for him, and did not move until the sun drove us into the shade. The first man who caught sight of him on the day he arrived was a Jew, who knew that we were waiting for the apostle of Allah; and he at the top of his voice, 'See! Your good fortune has arrived'.'

The apostle of Allah took up his abode at Quba, two miles outside Medina. On Thursday he laid the foundation of a mosque; on Friday he left for Medina, and, during the short journey he prayed at the foot of the valley called Ranuna. These were the first Friday prayers he held in Medina.

Many tribes and families welcomed him and invited him to their houses, but he replied: 'Allow my camel to go where she will because she is guided by Allah.'

At last the camel stopped in a courtyard which was part burial ground, part date-grove, part camel enclosure, and knelt down; then it rose and went on a short distance. But it looked backwards and returned to the place where it had first intended to stop; there it knelt down, murmured and placed its chest on the ground. So the apostle of Allah alighted and took up his lodgings at the house of Abu Ayyub, near the courtyard. He inquired to whom the courtyard belonged and was told to two orphans, named Sahl and Suhayl; so he bought it to build a mosque.

IBN ISHAQ, EDITED BY IBN HISHAM, LIFE OF GOD'S MESSENGER, C.830.

The *hijra*, the Prophet Muhammad's flight from his native city of Mecca, where he was subjected to persecution, ended in September 622 when he arrived in Medina, north of Mecca. There he set up his new home, and it was in Medina that he was eventually buried, in 632. This journey is traditionally held to mark the beginning of the Islamic era, and the account by the eighth-century Ibn Ishaq is the earliest written record of these events.

ALSO ON THIS DAY

1664 England acquires New Amsterdam from the Dutch, later renaming it New York.
1957 Federal troops are sent to Little Rock, Arkansas, to enforce desegregation.
1988 Ben Johnson wins the Seoul Olympics 100m sprint, but is disqualified for doping.

25 SEPTEMBER

THE BATTLE OF STAMFORD BRIDGE, 1066

Now the battle began... And the fight at first was but loose and light, as long as the Northmen kept their order of battle; for although the English rode hard against the Northmen, they could do nothing against them. When the Northmen thought they perceived that the enemy were making but weak assaults, they set after them, and would drive them into flight; but when they had broken their shield-rampart the Englishmen rode up from all sides, and threw arrows and spears on them. Now when King Harald Sigurdson saw this, he went into the fray where the greatest crash of weapons was, and there was a sharp conflict, in which many people fell on both sides. King Harald then was in a rage, and ran out in front of the array, and hewed down with both hands; so that neither helmet nor armour could withstand him, and all who were nearest gave way before him. It was then very near with the English that they had taken to flight.

King Harald Sigurdson was hit by an arrow in the windpipe, and that was his death-wound. He fell, and all who had advanced with him, except those who retired with the banner. There was afterwards the warmest conflict, and Earl Tostig had taken charge of the king's banner. They began on both sides to form their array again, and for a long time there was a pause in fighting. But before the battle began again Harold Godwinson offered his brother, Earl Tostig, peace, and also quarter to the Northmen who were still alive; but the Northmen called out, all of them together, that they would rather fall, one across the other, than accept of quarter from the Englishmen. Then each side set up a war-shout, and the battle began again.

SNORRI STURELSON, *CHRONICLE OF THE KINGS OF NORWAY, C.*1230.

The Battle of Stamford Bridge, near York, pitted the forces of the Anglo-Saxon King Harold II (Godwinson) against the invading Norsemen, led by Harold's brother Tostig and Harald Sigurdson (later called Hardrada). It resulted in the deaths of both Harald and Tostig. But the fight left the Anglo-Saxons exhausted and unable, after a shattering march south, to meet the separate invasion of Duke William of Normandy – the Conqueror (*see* 14 October).

ALSO ON THIS DAY

1555 The Peace of Augsburg allows German princes to choose Lutheranism or Catholicism in their domains.
1789 The US Congress passes amendments to the Constitution: the Bill of Rights.
1942 WWII: Jewish refugees are henceforth refused entry into Switzerland.

26 SEPTEMBER

FAILURE AT ARNHEM, 1944

I underestimated the difficulties of opening up the approaches to Antwerp... I reckoned the Canadian Army could do it while we were going for the Ruhr. I was wrong. In my – prejudiced – view, if the operation had been properly backed from its inception, and given the aircraft, ground forces, and administrative resources necessary for the job, it would have succeeded in spite of my mistakes, or the adverse weather, or the presence of the 2nd SS Panzer Corps in the Arnhem area. I remain Market Garden's unrepentant advocate.

GENERAL SIR BERNARD MONTGOMERY, *MEMOIRS*, 1958.

∞

In 1944 Operation Market Garden, the Allied plan to parachute troops into the lower Rhine area of the Netherlands to seize bridges spanning the Dutch–German border, was the brainchild of General Bernard Montgomery, the senior British commander serving under General Eisenhower, supreme Allied commander in Europe. The intention was that these troops would hold the bridges until relieved by an Allied column from the Front, and thus the Allies would have their gateway into Germany.

But the operation, which began on 17 September 1944, ended in disaster, owing to unexpectedly strong German resistance at Arnhem, poor weather and a plan that required everything to go like clockwork. Lightly armed Allied paratroopers were no match for German armour and well-entrenched infantry. By 26 September, all Allied troops had been withdrawn or had surrendered, with casualties numbering over 17,000, and the Rhine remained a barrier until the following March.

Later Montgomery claimed the operation had been '90 per cent successful', but Prince Bernhardt of the Netherlands commented: 'My country can never again afford the luxury of another Montgomery success.' Beforehand, one of Montgomery's commanders had ventured that they might be going 'a bridge too far'. Eisenhower, who became increasingly exasperated with Montgomery during the final months of the war, said in his *Crusade in Europe* (1948) that:

I am certain that Field Marshal Montgomery, in the light of later events, would agree this [operation] was a mistaken one. But he vehemently declared that all he needed was adequate supply in order to go directly into Berlin.

ALSO ON THIS DAY

1687 The Parthenon, in Athens, is damaged by Venetian forces attacking the Ottoman Turks.
1960 Nixon and Kennedy take part in the first televised US presidential election debate.
1973 The supersonic airliner *Concorde* makes its first transatlantic flight.

27 SEPTEMBER

LAWRENCE OF ARABIA AND THE ARAB REVOLT, 1918

The village lay stilly under its slow wreaths of white smoke, as we rode near, on our guard. Some grey heaps seemed to hide in the long grass, embracing the ground in the close way of corpses. We looked away from these, knowing they were dead; but from one a little figure tottered off, as if to escape us. It was a child, three or four years old, whose dirty smock was stained red over one shoulder and side, with blood from a large half-fibrous wound, perhaps a lance thrust, just where neck and body joined...

We rode past the other bodies of men and women and four more dead babies, looking very soiled in the daylight, towards the village; whose loneliness we now knew meant death and horror. By the outskirts were low mud walls, sheepfolds, and on one something red and white. I looked close and saw the body of a woman folded across it, bottom upwards, nailed there by a saw bayonet whose haft stuck hideously into the air from between her naked legs. About her lay others, perhaps twenty in all, variously killed.

The Zaagi [one of the Arab leaders] burst into wild peals of laughter, the more desolate for the warm sunshine and clear air of this upland afternoon. I said: 'the best of you bring me the most Turkish dead,' and we turned after the fading enemy, on our way shooting down those who had fallen out by the roadside and came imploring our pity. One wounded Turk, half naked, not able to stand, sat and wept to us. Abdulla turned away his camel's head, but the Zaagi, with curses, crossed his track and whipped three bullets from his automatic through the man's bare chest. The blood came out with his heart beats, throb, throb, throb, slower and slower.

Tallal had seen what we had seen. He gave one moan like a hurt animal; then rode to the upper ground and sat there a while on his mare, shivering and looking fixedly after the Turks. I moved near to speak to him, but Auda caught my rein and stayed me. Very slowly Tallal drew his headcloth about his face; and then he seemed suddenly to take hold of himself, for he dashed his stirrups into the mare's flanks and galloped headlong, bending low and swaying in the saddle, right at the main body of the enemy.

It was a long ride down a gentle slope and across a hollow. We sat there like stone while he rushed forward, the drumming of his hoofs unnaturally loud in our ears, for we had stopped shooting, and the Turks had stopped. Both armies waited for him; and he rocked on in the hushed evening till only a few lengths from the enemy. Then he sat up in the saddle and cried his war cry, 'Tallal, Tallal,' twice in a tremendous shout. Instantly their rifles and machine-guns crashed out, and he and his mare riddled through and through with bullets, fell dead among the lance points.

Auda looked very cold and grim. 'God give him mercy; we will take his price.' He shook his rein and moved slowly after the enemy. We called up the peasants, now drunk with fear and blood, and sent them from this side and that against the retreating column. The old lion of battle waked in Auda's heart, and made him again our natural, inevitable leader. By a skilful turn he drove the Turks into bad ground and split their formation into three parts.

The third part, the smallest, was mostly made up of German and Austrian machine-gunners grouped round three motor cars and a handful of mounted officers or troopers. They fought magnificently and repulsed us time and again despite our hardiness. The Arabs were fighting like devils, the sweat blurring their eyes, dust parching their throats; while the flame of cruelty and revenge which was burning in their bodies so twisted them that their hands could hardly shoot. By my order we took no prisoners, for the only time in our war.

T.E. LAWRENCE, *SEVEN PILLARS OF WISDOM*, CHAPTER 117, 1926.

The British army officer T.E. Lawrence (1888–1935) achieved a renown he later tried to play down for his part in leading the people of Arabia in a guerrilla war against the Ottoman Turks during the First World War. In 1918 he attacked the vital Hejaz railway, and advanced towards the key Syrian city of Damascus. Turkish atrocities resulted in Arab reprisals, which Lawrence generally attempted to control. After the war he represented the Arabs at the Paris Peace Conference (*see* 18 January).

ALSO ON THIS DAY

1529 The Ottoman sultan Suleiman the Magnificent lays siege to Vienna.
1822 Jean-François Champollion announces the deciphering of the Rosetta Stone.
1996 The Taliban seize Kabul and take power in Afghanistan.

28 SEPTEMBER

THE DISCOVERY OF PENICILLIN, 1928

It was astonishing that for some considerable distance around the mould growth the staphylococcal colonies were undergoing lysis. What had formerly been a well-grown colony was now a faint shadow of its former self... I was sufficiently interested to pursue the subject.

ALEXANDER FLEMING (1929), QUOTED IN *BRITISH MEDICAL BULLETIN*, 23, 1944.

∞

The discovery of penicillin, the first antibiotic, has saved countless lives and was the result of a chance observation by the Scottish bacteriologist Alexander Fleming (1881–1955). While working on the *staphylococci* bacteria, he left some culture dishes exposed, and on 28 September 1928 he noticed that one had become contaminated by a fungus that appeared to have destroyed the surrounding bacterial colonies. He identified the mould and named the bacteriocidal substance it produced 'penicillin'.

Although Fleming published his findings in 1929, he was unable to isolate penicillin sufficiently to make it medically useful. This was done in the early 1940s by the Australian Howard Florey (1898–1968) and the Anglo-German Ernst Chain (1906–79), and penicillin contributed to the Allied victory in the Second World War by saving numerous injured troops from life-threatening infection. All three men won the Nobel Prize for Physiology in Medicine in 1945. At the ceremony, Fleming commented:

In my first publication I might have claimed that I had come to the conclusion, as a result of serious study of the literature and deep thought, that valuable antibacterial substances were made by moulds and that I set out to investigate the problem. That would have been untrue and I preferred to tell the truth that penicillin started as a chance observation. My only merit is that I did not neglect the observation and that I pursued the subject as a bacteriologist. My publication in 1929 was the starting-point of the work of others who developed penicillin especially in the chemical field.

ALSO ON THIS DAY

48 BC Pompey, Julius Caesar's military rival, is assassinated.
1066 The invasion of England by Duke William 'the Bastard' begins the Norman Conquest.
1994 The Swedish ferry *Estonia* sinks in the Baltic with the loss of 852 lives.

29 SEPTEMBER

SCOURGING THE BLACK DEATH, 1349

In 1349, about Michaelmas, over six hundred men came to London from Flanders, mostly of Zeeland and Holland origin. Sometimes at St Paul's and sometimes at other points in the city they made two daily public appearances wearing cloths from the thighs to the ankles, but otherwise stripped bare. Each wore a cap marked with a red cross in front and behind.

Each had in his right hand a scourge with three tails. Each tail had a knot and through the middle of it there were sometimes sharp nails fixed. They marched naked in a file one behind the other and whipped themselves with these scourges on their naked and bleeding bodies.

Four of them would cant in their native tongue and, another four would chant in response like a litany. Thrice they would all cast themselves on the ground in this sort of procession, stretching out their hands like the arms of a cross. The singing would go on and, the one who was in the rear of those thus prostrate acting first, each of them in turn would step over the others and give one stroke with his scourge to the man lying under him.

This went on from the first to the last until each of them had observed the ritual to the full tale of those on the ground. Then each put on his customary garments and always wearing their caps and carrying their whips in their hands they retired to their lodgings. It is said that every night they performed the same penance.

ROBERT OF AVESBURY, *DE GESTIS MIRABILIBUS REGIS EDWARDI TERTII*, C.1350.

Flagellation was one expedient attempted in order to avert the Black Death, the form of bubonic plague that cut a deadly swathe across Europe from the Mediterranean, beginning in 1348. Spread by fleas that were normally carried on black rats, but transported during an epidemic in wool and on clothes, the pestilence quickly spread along Europe's trade routes and was particularly destructive in the crowded towns and cities. The epidemic eventually declined in the early 1350s, having killed more than half the entire population of Europe.

30 SEPTEMBER

APPEASEMENT'S LAST GASP, 1938

The settlement of the Czechoslovakian problem which has now been achieved is, in my view, only the prelude to a larger settlement in which all Europe may find peace. This morning I had another talk with the German Chancellor, Herr Hitler, and here is the paper which bears his name upon it as well as mine. Some of you, perhaps, have already heard what it contains but I would just like to read it to you [Chamberlain reads out the agreement at this point]... We regard the agreement signed last night and the Anglo-German Naval Agreement, as symbolic of the desire of our two peoples never to go to war with one another again.

NEVILLE CHAMBERLAIN, PRESS CONFERENCE AT HESTON AERODROME,
30 SEPTEMBER 1938.

My good friends, this is the second time in our history that there has come back from Germany to Downing Street peace with honour. I believe it is peace for our time. We thank you from the bottom of our hearts. And now I recommend you to go home and sleep quietly in your beds.

NEVILLE CHAMBERLAIN, SPEECH AT DOWNING STREET, 30 SEPTEMBER 1938.

The Munich Agreement, thrashed out by Prime Minister Chamberlain after three visits to Germany (and signed in the early hours of 30 September, though dated the previous day), gave Hitler *carte blanche* to absorb the Sudeten German-majority region of Czechoslovakia, despite the existence of a previous alliance between Czechoslovakia, Britain and France. Chamberlain, whose policy sought to avoid war if at all possible, had won a promise from Hitler that this would be the end of his territorial ambitions – a promise that proved empty when he swallowed up more of Czechoslovakia in March the following year and invaded Poland in September 1939.

Although the agreement, and Chamberlain's words ('the second time' refers to Disraeli's return after the Congress of Berlin in 1878), are vilified today as the nadir of appeasement, at the time they were greeted with great acclaim and he was fêted for his achievement, including the rare honour of being invited onto the balcony of Buckingham Palace to receive the public's acclaim.

ALSO ON THIS DAY

1791 Mozart's last opera *The Magic Flute* receives its first performance, in Vienna.
1955 The death of the US actor James Dean in a car accident.
1965 An attempted communist coup in Indonesia triggers a brutal purge by the military.

OCTOBER

1 OCTOBER

THE SENTENCING OF THE NUREMBERG DEFENDANTS, 1946

Goering came down first and strode into his cell, his face pale and frozen, his eyes popping. 'Death!' he said as he dropped on the cot and reached for a book. His hands were trembling in spite of his attempt to be nonchalant. His eyes were moist and he was panting, fighting back an emotional breakdown. He asked me in an unsteady voice to leave him alone for a while.

When Goering collected himself enough to talk, he said that he had naturally expected the death penalty, and was glad that he had not gotten a life sentence, because those who are sentenced to life imprisonment never become martyrs. But there wasn't any of the old confident bravado in his voice. Goering seems to realize, at last, that there is nothing funny about death, when you're the one who is going to die.

Hess strutted in, laughing nervously, and said that he had not even been listening, so he did not know what the sentence was and what was more, he didn't care.

Ribbentrop wandered in, aghast, and started to walk around the cell in a daze, whispering, 'Death!-Death! Now I won't be able to write my beautiful memoirs. Tsk! Tsk! So much hatred! Tsk! tsk!' Then he sat down, a completely broken man, and stared into space...

Speer laughed nervously. 'Twenty years. Well; that's fair enough. They couldn't have given me a lighter sentence, considering the facts, and I can't complain. I said the sentences must be severe, and I admitted my share of the guilt, so it would be ridiculous if I complained about the punishment.'

G.M. GILBERT, *NUREMBERG DIARY*, 1947.

G.M. Gilbert was an American psychologist who observed the defendants throughout the Nuremberg war trials of 1945–6. On 1 October 1946, 18 leading Nazis were convicted of war crimes and crimes against humanity and Gilbert recorded their reactions. They included the Luftwaffe chief Hermann Goering; Joachim von Ribbentrop, Hitler's foreign minister; the architect-administrator Albert Speer; and Hitler's one-time deputy, Rudolf Hess.

ALSO ON THIS DAY

1908 The Ford Model-T automobile enters the marketplace.
1962 The admission of a black student to the University of Mississippi causes riots.
1975 The boxer Muhammad Ali defeats Joe Frazier in the 'Thriller in Manila'.

2 OCTOBER

JERUSALEM SURRENDERS TO SALADIN, 1187

The Christians were failing so that scarcely twenty or thirty men appeared to defend the city walls. No man could be found in the whole city brave enough to keep watch at the defences for a night, even for a hundred besants [gold coins].

Saladin laid down ransom terms for the inhabitants: each male, ten years old and over, was to pay ten besants for his ransom; females, five besants; boys, one. Those who wished would be freed on these terms and could leave securely with their possessions. Those who would not accept, or did not have ten besants, were to become booty, to be slain by the army's swords. This agreement pleased the Lord Patriarch and others who had money...

On Friday, 2 October, this agreement was read out through the streets of Jerusalem, so that everyone might within forty days provide for himself and pay Saladin the tribute for his freedom. When they heard it, the crowds wailed: 'Woe, woe! We have no gold! What are we to do?...' Who would have thought that such wickedness would be perpetrated by Christians?

Alas, by the hands of Christians Jerusalem was turned over to the wicked. The gates were closed and guards were posted. The *fakihs* and *kadis*, who are considered bishops and priests by the Saracens, came first to the temple of the Lord, which they call *Beithhalla* and in which they have great faith for salvation. They believed they were cleansing it and with unclean and horrible bellows they defiled the temple by shouting with polluted lips the Muslim precept: 'Allahu Akbar! Allahu Akbar!...'

DE EXPUGATIONE TERRAE SANCTAE PER SALADINUM, A CONTEMPORARY CHRONICLE.

∞

The city of Jerusalem, held by crusaders since 1099, fell in 1187 after a two-week siege by the Islamic Kurdish leader Saladin (1137–93), who was permitted to enter the city after surrender terms were agreed. He released many of those who were taken into captivity under those terms and allowed the freed inhabitants to leave unmolested. The recapture of Jerusalem would be the ultimate – but unrealized – aim of the Third Crusade in 1189–92.

ALSO ON THIS DAY

1919 US President Woodrow Wilson is paralyzed by a stroke.
1941 WWII: German forces begin their assault on Moscow.
1950 Charles M. Schultz's *Peanuts* comic strip appears for the first time.

3 OCTOBER

JULIUS CAESAR VANQUISHES THE GAULS, 52 BC

When the Gauls in the *oppidum* [hill fort] could see the slaughter and the rout of their countrymen; they gave up all hope of being saved and took their men back inside from the fortifications.

When news of our victory reached them, the Gallic relief force immediately fled from their camp. But for the fact that our men were exhausted by their exertions throughout the entire day and their constant efforts to relieve the threatened points, the Gauls' entire army could have been wiped out. Cavalry caught up with the enemy rearguard about midnight and killed or captured great numbers of them. The survivors fled.

The next day Vercingetorix called a council. He pointed out that he had undertaken the war not for any personal reasons but for the freedom of Gaul. Since he must now yield to fortune, he was putting his fate in their hands. They must decide whether to kill him and so make amends to the Romans, or hand him over alive.

Envoys were sent to me to discuss this. I ordered that their weapons should be surrendered and their tribal chiefs brought before me. I took my place on the fortifications in front of the camp and the chiefs were brought to me there. Vercingetorix was surrendered, and the weapons were laid down before me. I kept the Aeduan and Arvernian prisoners back, hoping to use them to regain the loyalty of their tribes. The rest I distributed as booty among the army, giving one prisoner to each of my men.

JULIUS CAESAR, *ON THE GALLIC WAR*, c.50 BC.

The decisive moment in the Roman conquest of Gaul came in October 52 BC. It took the form of Julius Caesar's siege of the hill fort (*oppidum*) of Alesia, in present-day Burgundy, which was occupied by an 80,000-strong army of confederated tribes, including the Aedui, former Roman allies; their leader was Vercingetorix, king of the Arverni. After a month, Vercingetorix launched an attack on the Roman positions but was heavily defeated. He gave himself up, to be displayed during Caesar's triumph in Rome later that year, and six years afterwards he was executed.

ALSO ON THIS DAY

1944 WWII: the Warsaw Uprising is crushed after 63 days of fighting.
1952 The UK becomes the third country to test a nuclear weapon.
1990 The reunification of Germany is declared.

4 OCTOBER

THE LAUNCH OF *SPUTNIK*, 1957

The USA has lost a battle more important and greater than Pearl Harbor.

DR EDWARD TELLER, CBS INTERVIEW, 4 OCTOBER 1957.

∞

4 October 1957 saw the launch of the world's first artificial satellite, the tiny *Sputnik 1*, by the Soviet Union. Soviet leader Nikita Khrushchev saw the achievement as a major public-relations victory over the United States at a key moment in the Cold War, and opinion in the United States was predictably horrified, prompting Dr Edward Teller's calamitous claim.

A Hungarian-born physicist, Teller was a veteran of the Manhattan Project that had developed the first atomic bomb; he had also been the intellect behind the far more powerful hydrogen bomb, which the United States had successfully tested in November 1952. But by then the Soviet Union was catching up in nuclear weaponry; nine months later a Soviet weapon was tested, and the result was an intensification of the Cold War, and a race to develop long-range delivery systems – and in particular to build a rocket capable of putting satellites into Earth's orbit or transporting a bomb halfway round the world. In this light Teller, renowned as a hardline Cold Warrior, saw *Sputnik* as a clear challenge to the technological superiority of the United States, and therefore as a direct threat; he also described it as a 'very serious defeat in a field where …the most important engagements are carried out: the classroom'. In the same vein, Senator Henry Jackson called the satellite 'a devastating blow to the prestige of the United States as the leader in the scientific and technical world'.

A month afterwards, *Sputnik II* was sent into orbit, this time carrying a dog called Laika. The result of these Soviet propaganda triumphs was firstly an American satellite, *Explorer I*, in January 1958, then an increase in funding for science education in America, and finally the 1960s' space race, with President Kennedy, in 1960, vowing to put a man on the Moon within the decade (*see* 21 July).

ALSO ON THIS DAY

1669 The death of the Dutch artist Rembrandt van Rijn.
1830 Belgium becomes independent of the Netherlands.
1958 The French Fifth Republic is signed into law.

5 OCTOBER

THE JARROW MARCH, 1936

I have suffered hardships for years. Rain and cold and wind on the way will mean nothing to me after that. I have suffered all that a man may suffer. Nothing that can happen on the road between here and London can be worse.

ANONYMOUS APPLICATION TO JOIN THE JARROW MARCH, OCTOBER 1936.

Thus reads an application from a 60-year-old man to join the Jarrow marchers. The 200 unemployed men who set off from Jarrow, in northeast England, on 5 October 1936 to march 300 miles to London were on a 'crusade' – to petition for assistance for the unemployed; they became a symbol of a divided Britain in the interwar years. Unemployment had reached 70 per cent in Jarrow following the closure of Palmers shipyard, and the local MP 'Red Ellen' Wilkinson described the town as:

> ...utterly stagnant. There was no work. No one had a job except a few railwaymen, officials, the workers in the co-operative stores, and a few workmen who went out of the town... the plain fact is that if people have to live and bear and bring up their children in bad houses on too little food, their resistance to disease is lowered and they die before they should.

The men sought to draw attention to their plight, holding public meetings in each town they passed through, despite fears (of some in the Labour Party and trade unions, among others) that they would be agitating for revolutionary change. In London a mass rally was held in Hyde Park, and Wilkinson handed in a petition to Downing Street; but the Conservative prime minister Stanley Baldwin refused to meet the marchers, claiming he was too busy.

The 60-year-old applicant died while preparing to make the return journey.

ALSO ON THIS DAY

1910 The Portuguese revolution abolishes the monarchy in favour of a republic.
1962 The premiere, in London, of the first James Bond film, *Dr No*.
1969 The first episode of *Monty Python's Flying Circus* is broadcast by the BBC.

6 OCTOBER

THE WORLD'S FIRST TALKIE, 1927

Wait a minute, wait a minute, you ain't heard nothin' yet! Wait a minute, I tell you. You ain't heard nothin' yet, folks. Listen to this! 'Lou, listen. You play 'Toot Toot Tootsie'. Three choruses, you understand, and in the third chorus I whistle. Now give it to 'em hard and heavy. Go right ahead!

AL JOLSON, THE JAZZ SINGER, 1927.

∞

Warner Theater, on Broadway, New York, witnessed tumultuous scenes in October 1927 when the premiere of *The Jazz Singer* broke into speech, with Lithuanian-born actor Al Jolson – who had just sung 'Dirty Hands, Dirty Face' – calling out to his orchestra before moving into the next musical number.

The Jazz Singer – a Broadway stage-hit for the last decade – became famous as the first full-length film to carry synchronized dialogue, though it was not the first with sound (or even the first film in which Jolson himself had been heard to sing). Previous experimental shorts had been made with the spoken voice, in which an actor talked to camera. *The Jazz Singer* carried only a few minutes of dialogue (most of which, in fact, was Jolson adlibbing), but it contained one moving sequence in which he addressed his character's mother as she sat on his knee:

> Did you like that, mama? I'm glad of it. I'd rather please you than anybody I know … Mama, listen, I'm gonna sing this like I will if I go on the stage. You know, with this show. I'm gonna sing it jazzy. Now get this.

He then launched into another song. It was enough to excite the audience, and reviewers immediately announced they had witnessed the death of the silent movie. The film proved a box-office success around the world, and 18 months later almost all films being produced in Hollywood were talkies.

7 OCTOBER

THE BATTLE OF LEPANTO, 1571

If I win the battle, I promise you your liberty. If the day is yours, then God has given it to you.

OTTOMAN ADMIRAL ALI PASHA, TO HIS CHRISTIAN GALLEY-SLAVES, 7 OCTOBER 1571.

∞

Let us no longer occupy ourselves with business, but let us go to thank the Lord. The Christian fleet has obtained victory.

POPE PIUS V, 7 OCTOBER 1571.

∞

In the naval Battle of Lepanto, fought off the Adriatic coast, the Ottoman Turkish fleet was defeated by a Christian coalition including Spanish, Venetian, Genoese and Savoyard elements, and commanded by Don John of Austria (half-brother to Philip II of Spain). After a clash of more than 200 galleys on each side, some 20,000 Christian galley-slaves with the Turkish fleet were granted their freedom.

On the very afternoon of the battle (before any messenger could possibly have reached Rome), Pope Pius V interrupted a meeting in the Vatican to stare out of the window and announce the victory. He later dedicated the victory to Mary of the Rosary. The Turkish grand vizier Mehmed Sokullu, however, shrugged off the defeat to the Venetian ambassador:

> You come to see how we bear our misfortune. But I would have you know the difference between your loss and ours. In wresting Cyprus from you [in 1570], we deprived you of an arm; in defeating our fleet, you have only shaved our beard. An arm when cut off cannot grow again; but a shorn beard will grow all the better for the razor.

The grand vizier was wrong, Lepanto proving to be one of the decisive battles of history. The Ottoman Empire was never again able to challenge the West at sea, though it continued to threaten Hungary and Austria by land for another century.

ALSO ON THIS DAY

1849 The death of the US writer Edgar Allan Poe.
1985 The *Achille Lauro* cruise liner is hijacked by Palestinian terrorists.
2001 US airstrikes begin the post-9/11 assault on Afghanistan.

8 OCTOBER

THE EXTRAORDINARY BRAVERY
OF CORPORAL YORK, 1918

This was our first offensive battle. We had to charge across a valley and rush the machine gun emplacements on the ridge on the far side. And there were machine guns on the ridges on our flanks too. The first and second waves got halfway and then were held up. Our losses were very heavy.

We couldn't go on until those machine guns were mopped up. So 17 boys went around on the left flank to see if we couldn't put those guns out of action. The brush hid us from the Germans.

We crossed over the hill and down into the gully behind. Then we swung around behind them, behind the German trench and the machine guns. When we jumped across a little stream, 15 or 20 Germans jumped up and threw up their hands and said, 'Kamerad!' The one in charge of us boys told us not to shoot.

It was headquarters. There were orderlies, stretcher bearers and runners, and a major and two other officers, They were just having breakfast and there was a mess of beef-steaks, jellies, jams, and loaf bread around.

By this time the Germans had got their machine guns turned around and fired on us. They killed six and wounded three of us. So that just left eight. We had a hard battle for a while.

I knowed that in order to shoot me the Germans would have to get their heads up to see where I was lying. My only chance was to keep their heads down. I covered their positions and let fly every time I seed anything to shoot at. Every time a head come up I done knocked it down.

The machine guns were spitting fire and cutting up all around me something awful. But they didn't seem to be able to hit me. As soon as I was able I stood up and begun to shoot off-hand. I used up several clips. The barrel was getting hot and my rifle ammunition was running low. But I had to keep on shooting.

A German officer and five men jumped out of a trench and charged me with fixed bayonets. I only had half a clip left in my rifle; but I had my pistol ready. I teched [sic] off the sixth man first; then the fifth; then the fourth; then the third; and so on. That's the way we shoot wild turkeys at home. We don't want the front ones to know that we're getting the back ones, and then they keep on coming until we get them all.

After he seen me stop the six with fixed bayonets, the German major got up and yelled 'English?' I said, 'No, not English.' He said, 'What?' I said, 'American.'

He said, 'Good ——! If you won't shoot any more I will make them give up.' He blew a whistle and they began to throw down their guns. All but one of them came off the hill with their hands up, and just before that one got to me he threw a hand grenade which burst in the air. I had to tech him off. The rest surrendered without any more trouble.

We had about 80 or 90 Germans disarmed.

It was their second line that I had captured. I marched straight at the German front line trench. More machine guns swung around and began to spit at us. I told the major to blow his whistle or I would take off his head and theirs too. So he blew his whistle and they all surrendered.

When I got back to my major's post of command, Lieutenant Woods counted 132 prisoners. He said, 'York, have you captured the whole German army?' I told him I had a tolerable few.

Next morning Captain Danforth sent me back to see if there were any American boys we had missed. But they were all dead. And there were a lot of German dead. We counted twenty-eight. And thirty-five machine guns and a whole mess of equipment and small arms.

ALVIN C. YORK, SERGEANT YORK: HIS OWN LIFE STORY AND WAR DIARY, 1928.

∞

On 8 October 1918 Corporal Alvin York (1887–1964), from Tennessee, performed his extraordinary feat of heroics during the Meuse-Argonne Offensive in the closing weeks of the First World War, as the German resistance was weakening. The battle was arguably the bloodiest in US military history in that there were more American casualties – 117,000, of whom 46,000 died – than in any other single encounter to date.

York was awarded the Medal of Honor, the highest US military award, as well as the French Croix de Guerre and other honours. His ghost-written memoirs appeared in 1928.

ALSO ON THIS DAY

AD 451 The first session of the Church's Council of Chalcedon opens.
1912 The First Balkan War: Bulgaria, Greece, Montenegro and Serbia attack the Ottoman Empire.
2003 The action-film star Arnold Schwarzenegger is elected governor of California.

9 OCTOBER

AN ASSASSINATION CAUGHT ON CAMERA, 1934

You are about to see the most amazing pictures ever made, the assassination of King Alexander of Yugoslavia. The ill-fated ruler arriving in Marseille aboard the Yugoslavian cruiser *Dubrovnik* is visiting friends on a mission of extreme importance. The final move in critical negotiations, he hopes, will cement the goodwill relationships of Yugoslavia, Italy and France, and banish the spectre of war from the Adriatic and Middle Europe. As he hastens ashore, where thousands wait to greet him and welcome him to France, the Balkan ruler is in a happy mood. He is on the eve of his greatest triumph: international amity for his country in the family of nations. And what a welcome he gets! As he sets foot on French soil, on the Quai des Belges in the ancient French port. He is to be escorted in regal fashion though the city to the railroad station accompanied by the aged French foreign minister Louis Barthou, mastermind of Europe's tangled diplomacy. For Barthou, too, tomorrow in Paris promises the fruition of his greatest work for France, the building of a Latin–Slavic bulwark across southern Europe against Germany and Hitlerism. And so the monarch and the revered French statesman begin their fateful ride, the ride of death, little dreaming of the terrible catastrophe that awaits them a block or so away.

Police line the streets and a mounted escort rides ahead, but no trouble is expected. It's a gala day in Marseille! *Vive Alexander! Vive L'Europe!* [the sound of gunfire erupts] Oh! They've been shot! [the film shows scenes of panic around the king's car] Oh, the king is dying and Barthou is fatally wounded. The crowd is infuriated and the police can't hold them. It's an eye for an eye and tooth for a tooth. Pandemonium has broken loose. The mob is out to beat the man [the assassin] to death. They'll do it, too. He's a Croatian conspirator, one of the king's own subjects, chosen by lot to do this foul deed. He tried to kill himself, after firing a fusillade into the king's car, but the police and the crowd were too quick for him. The fury of the crowd is not to be denied. Meanwhile, the king has breathed his last, victim of a tragedy that's rocking the very foundations of Europe.

GRAHAM MCNAMEE, *ALEXANDER MURDERED*, NEWSREEL, OCTOBER 1934.

∞

Alexander, son of Peter I of Serbia, had been regent of Serbia from 1914 and commander of the successful Serbian army in 1918, before acceding as king of the Serbs, Croats and Slovenes in 1921, and king of Yugoslavia in 1929. He abolished the parliamentary constitution and adopted the role of dictator, in his attempt to control his fractious country, a Balkan entity created in the aftermath of the First World War and beset by often violently divergent interests and nationalities – and with hostile neighbours.

In 1934, on a state visit to France, the Yugoslav king – and the French foreign minister – was shot and killed while in an open-top car, in circumstances that have not been definitively resolved. The assassin was killed by police; once his true identity was unearthed, he turned out to be member of a Macedonian secessionist organization, probably working in collaboration with the Ustaše (a Croatian fascist separatist movement) and sponsored by Italy's dictator Benito Mussolini (who was keen to extend Italian influence in the Balkans). But other conspiracy theories emerged too.

The event was captured by the commentary of the pioneering US broadcaster Graham McNamee (1888–1942), which accompanied United Newsreel's film of the event. McNamee, who was best known as a radio broadcaster, would open each of his broadcasts with the words, 'Good afternoon/evening, ladies and gentlemen of the radio audience.' He was also the narrator on Joe Rock's academy award-winning short documentary film *Krakatoa* (1933).

ALSO ON THIS DAY

1604 Supernova 1604 ('Kepler's Supernova') is observed in the night sky.
1962 Uganda achieves independence from Britain.
1967 The Marxist revolutionary 'Che' Guevara is executed in Bolivia.

10 OCTOBER

ARAB DEFEAT AT THE BATTLE OF TOURS, 732

While Abd ar-Rahman was pursuing Odo [of Aquitaine], he decided to despoil Tours by destroying its palaces and burning its churches. There he confronted Charles, the Consul of Austrasia, a man who, having proved himself as a warrior from his youth and an expert in things military, had been summoned by Odo.

After each side had tormented the other with raids for almost seven days, they finally prepared their battle lines and fought fiercely. The northern peoples remained as immobile as a wall, holding together like a glacier in the cold regions. In the blink of an eye, they annihilated the Arabs with the sword. The people of Austrasia, greater in number of soldiers and formidably armed, killed the king, Abd ar-Rahman, when they found him, striking him on the chest. But suddenly, within sight of the countless tents of the Arabs, the Franks despicably sheathed their swords, postponing the fight until the next day since night had fallen.

Rising at dawn, the Europeans saw the tents and canopies of the Arabs just as they had appeared the day before. Thinking that inside them there were Saracen forces ready for battle, they sent officers to reconnoitre and discovered that all the Ishmaelite troops had left. They had indeed fled silently by night in tight formation, returning to their own country.

MOZARABIC CHRONICLE, AD 754.

The seemingly unstoppable sweep of the Arabs across North Africa, into the Iberian Peninsula and north across the Pyrenees was eventually ended at Tours, in modern central France, in October 732. A previous victory won by Duke Odo of Aquitaine, at Toulouse in 721, had temporarily stalled ambitions to extend the reach of Al-Andalus – as Arab Spain was known. But at Tours, the Frankish 'Mayor of the Palace', Charles Martel, successfully led a Frankish and Burgundian army against the forces of the Umayyad Caliphate, under Abd ar-Rahaman. Martel's victory led to the emergence of a Frankish empire, which was brought to its height by his grandson Charlemagne.

The author of this chronicle was a Christian of Moorish descent, living in Toledo or Córdoba. 'Austrasia' refers to the northeastern part of the kingdom of the Merovingian Franks, in what is now eastern France, western Germany and the Low Countries.

ALSO ON THIS DAY

1780 The 'Great Hurricane' kills tens of thousands in the Caribbean.
1957 The world's first nuclear accident takes place at Windscale, northwest England.
1970 Quebec separatists kidnap and later murder a local politician.

11 OCTOBER

A ROYAL HUNTING PARTY, 1852

After luncheon, Albert decided to walk through the wood for the last time...
At half-past three o'clock we started, got out at Grant's and walked up part of
Carrop... when a stag was heard to roar... Albert soon left us to go lower, and we
sat down to wait for him; presently we heard a shot – then complete silence – and,
after another pause of some little time, three more shots. This was again succeeded
by complete silence. We sent someone to look, who shortly after returned, saying
the stag had been twice hit and they were after him... In about five minutes we
heard 'Solomon' give tongue, and knew he had the stag at bay. We listened a little
while, and then began moving down hoping to arrive in time; but the barking had
ceased, and Albert had already killed the stag; and on the road he lay...

He was a magnificent animal, and I sat down and scratched a little sketch of
him... while Albert and Vicky, with the others, built a little cairn to mark the spot.
We heard, after I had finished my little scrawl and the carriage had joined us,
that another stag had been seen near the road; and we had not gone as far as the
'Irons' before we saw one below the road, looking so handsome. Albert jumped
out and fired – the animal fell, but rose again, and went on a little way, and Albert
followed... I sat down to sketch, and poor Vicky unfortunately seated herself on a
wasps' nest and was much stung... Albert joined us in twenty minutes, unaware of
having killed the stag. What a delightful day!

QUEEN VICTORIA, *LEAVES FROM THE JOURNAL OF OUR LIFE IN THE HIGHLANDS*, 1868.

In 1848 Queen Victoria and Albert, Prince Consort, visited Balmoral, on Deeside, for
the first time and discovered the delights of the Scottish Highlands, where they could
indulge in aristocratic country pursuits, including the hunting of stags. The queen and
Albert returned there every year with their family, including their eldest child Vicky
(born 1840), the Princess Royal, who would later become empress of Germany as
the wife of Emperor Frederick III (he reigned for just three months in 1888). Victoria's
journal of this time proved an instant bestseller when published in 1868.

ALSO ON THIS DAY

1899 The Second Anglo-Boer War breaks out.
1963 The death of the French singer Édith Piaf.
1982 The remnants of Henry VIII's flagship *Mary Rose* are salvaged.

12 OCTOBER

COLUMBUS REACHES THE AMERICAS, 1492

At two o'clock in the morning the land was discovered, at two leagues' distance; they took in sail and remained under the square-sail lying to till day, which was Friday, when they found themselves near a small island, one of the Lucayos, called in the Indian language Guanahani. Presently they descried people, naked, and the admiral landed in the boat, which was armed, along with Martin Alonzo Pinzon, and Vincent Yanez his brother, captain of the *Niña*. The admiral bore the royal standard, and the two captains each a banner of the Green Cross, which all the ships had carried; this contained the initials of the names of the king and queen each side of the cross, and a crown over each letter. Arrived on shore, they saw trees very green many streams of water, and diverse sorts of fruits.

Bartolomé de las Casas (ed.), Journal of Christopher Columbus, 1492.

∞

The small fleet of Christopher Columbus's first transatlantic voyage left Spain on 3 August 1492, attempting to find what, he had theorized, would be a relatively short westward sea passage to the Indies. His three ships, the *Niña* (or, more formally, the *Santa Clara*), *Pinta* and *Santa Maria*, sighted land in the Bahamas early in the morning of 12 October, and a party led by Columbus went ashore later that day. He noted:

> As I saw that they were very friendly to us, and perceived that they could be more easily converted to our holy faith by gentle means than by force, I presented them with some red caps, and strings of beads, and other trifles with which they were delighted... Afterwards they came swimming to the boats, bringing parrots, balls of cotton thread, javelins, and many other things which they exchanged for articles we gave them, such as glass beads, and hawk's bells; which trade was carried on with the utmost good will. But they seemed on the whole to me, to be a very poor people. They all go completely naked, even the women, though I saw just one girl.

On this first voyage Columbus also visited Cuba and 'Hispaniola' (modern-day Haiti and Dominican Republic) before returning to Spain. His third expedition (1498) landed on the South American mainland for the first time.

13 OCTOBER

THE POISONING OF EMPEROR CLAUDIUS, AD 54

Nothing seemed to satisfy Agrippina... Although she exercised the same power as Claudius, she wanted his title outright; and once, when a great fire was consuming the city, she accompanied him as he lent his assistance.

Claudius was angered by her actions, of which he was now becoming aware, and sought for his son Britannicus, whom she had purposely kept out of his sight (for she was trying to secure the throne for Nero, her son by her former husband Domitius); and he displayed his affection whenever he met the boy. Claudius would not endure her behaviour, but was preparing to put an end to her power, to cause his son to assume the *toga virilis* [the symbol of adulthood], and to declare him heir to the throne.

Agrippina, learning this, became alarmed and decided to forestall anything of the sort by poisoning Claudius. He could not easily be harmed, owing to the great quantity of wine he was forever drinking and his general habits of life, such as all emperors as a rule adopt for their protection; but she sent for a famous dealer in poisons, a woman named Lucusta, who had recently been convicted on this very charge. They prepared a deadly poison, which Agrippina put into a mushroom.

She herself ate one of the mushrooms on the plate, but made her husband eat the largest and finest of them all, the one containing the poison. He was carried from the banquet apparently quite overcome by strong drink, as had happened many times before; but during the night the poison took effect and he passed away, without having been able to say or hear a word.

CASSIUS DIO, *ROMAN HISTORY*, BOOK 61, 3RD CENTURY AD.

∞

Cassius Dio's *Roman History* consisted of 80 books from the mythic past to AD 229. In Book 61 he described how Emperor Claudius, whose reign (AD 41–54) saw the conquest of Britain, fell victim to the plotting of his wife Agrippina, to be succeeded by his grand-nephew and adopted son Nero. The new emperor deified his predecessor, commenting that mushrooms must be the food of the gods, since a mushroom had made Claudius a god. Agrippina did not, perhaps, reap the rewards she expected: Nero had her killed five years later.

ALSO ON THIS DAY

1884 Greenwich, London, is established as the Prime Meridian by an international conference.
1905 The death of the English actor Sir Henry Irving.
1943 WWII: Post-fascist Italy declares war on Germany.

14 OCTOBER

THE BATTLE OF HASTINGS, 1066

The Norman infantry, with bows and arrows, formed the vanguard, while their cavalry, divided into wings, was placed in the rear. The duke, with serene countenance, declaring aloud that God would favour his as being the righteous side, called for his arms; and when, through the haste of his attendants, he put on his hauberk [shirt of chain mail] the hind part before, he corrected the mistake with a laugh, saying 'The power of my dukedom shall be turned into a kingdom.' Then starting the 'Song of Roland', in order that the warlike example of that hero might stimulate the soldiers, and calling on God for assistance, the battle commenced, and was fought with great ardour, neither side giving ground during the greater part of the day.

Observing this, William gave a signal to his troops, that, feigning flight, they should withdraw from the field. The solid phalanx of the English opened for the purpose of cutting down the fleeing enemy and thus brought upon itself swift destruction; for the Normans, facing about, attacked them, thus disordered, and compelled them to fly. In this manner, deceived by a stratagem, they met an honourable death in avenging their enemy; nor were they without their own revenge for, by frequently making a stand, they slaughtered their pursuers in heaps. Getting possession of an eminence, they drove back the Normans... into the valley beneath, where, by hurling javelins and rolling down stones, the English destroyed them to a man... This alternating victory, first of one side and then of the other, continued so long as Harold lived to check the retreat; but when he fell, his brain pierced by an arrow, the flight of the English ceased not until night.

WILLIAM OF MALMESBURY, *GESTA REGUM ANGLORUM*, C.1125.

∞

The Battle of Hastings in 1066, arguably the most significant ever fought on English soil, was recorded by several near-contemporary chroniclers, including William of Malmesbury, as well as pictorially in the Bayeux Tapestry. The defeat of Harold II marked the end of Anglo-Saxon rule in England and its replacement with the foreign, Norman dynasty founded by William the Conqueror. Now, the kingdom of England would be just one part of a wider, expansionist Norman empire.

ALSO ON THIS DAY

1944 WWII: the German field marshal Erwin Rommel commits suicide.
1969 The UK introduces the heptagonal 50-pence piece.
1999 The death of the former Tanzanian leader Julius Nyerere.

15 OCTOBER

EDWARD GIBBON'S ROMAN INSPIRATION, 1764

The use of foreign travel has been often debated as a general question; but the conclusion must be finally applied to the character and circumstances of each individual. With the education of boys, where or how they may pass over some juvenile years with the least mischief to themselves or others, I have no concern. But after supposing the previous and indispensable requisites of age, judgment, a competent knowledge of men and books, and a freedom from domestic prejudices, I will briefly describe the qualifications which I deem most essential to a traveller. He should be endowed with an active, indefatigable vigour of mind and body, which can seize every mode of conveyance, and support, with a careless smile, every hardship of the road, the weather, or the inn.

The benefits of foreign travel will correspond with the degrees of these qualifications; but, in this sketch, those to whom I am known will not accuse me of framing my own panegyric. It was at Rome, on the 15th of October 1764, as I sat musing amidst the ruins of the Capitol, while the bare-footed friars were singing vespers in the Temple of Jupiter, that the idea of writing the decline and fall of the city first started to my mind. But my original plan was circumscribed to the decay of the city rather than of the empire: and though my reading and reflections began to point towards that object, some years elapsed, and several avocations intervened, before I was seriously engaged in the execution of that laborious work.

EDWARD GIBBON, *MEMOIRS*, 1796.

Edward Gibbon did not begin work on his magisterial *The Decline and Fall of the Roman Empire* until 1772, and its six volumes were published between 1776 and 1788–9. In it, he presented a vision of a civilization brought down by a decadence induced, at least in part, by the triumph of the 'soft' religion of Christianity, with its promise of an afterlife, which overtook the civic virtues of Republican Rome and weakened its traditional martial spirit. Gibbon's vision was crystallized by his communing with the remains of Ancient Rome's once grand Temple of Jupiter, on the Capitoline Hill.

ALSO ON THIS DAY

1894 The French officer Alfred Dreyfus is arrested and accused of spying for Germany.
1946 The leading Nazi Hermann Goering commits suicide rather than face execution.
1964 Nikita Khrushchev falls from power in the Soviet Union.

16 OCTOBER

THE BURNING OF THE
PALACE OF WESTMINSTER, 1834

The mere announcement to our readers that the House of Lords, the House of Commons, and all their various offices, have become a prey to the unsparing element will awaken feelings in which sorrow, astonishment, and doubt will be singularly mingled.

At half-past five in the evening, a friend of ours passed between the Houses of Parliament and the Westminster Abbey, when all was still. Yet within a short hour, the interior of the House of Lords was filled with one vast flame, casting its lurid glare far over the horizon, spreading over the silent Thames a vast sheet of crimson that seemed to smother the more feeble rays of the rising moon – bringing out the stately and majestic towers of the abbey in strong relief against the deep blue western sky, playing with seemingly wayward and fantastic scintillations on the inimitable fretwork of the Seventh Harry's chapel [the King Henry VII Chapel].

The flames first shewed themselves about half-past six o'clock. They burst forth in the centre of the Lords, and burnt with such fury that in less than half an hour, the whole interior presented one entire mass of fire.

By half-past seven o'clock the engines were brought to play upon the building both from the river and the land side, but the flames had by this time acquired such a predominance that the quantity of water thrown upon them produced no visible effect.

In less than an hour the entire roof of the House of Lords had fallen in. The firemen now abandoned all hopes of saving any part of this portion of the building, and their efforts were wholly directed towards the House of Commons, and the preservation of Westminster Hall, which for the beauty of its architecture, and its close connection with some of the most important events of our country's history is equally admired and estimated by the antiquarian, the man of science, and the citizen.

For some time their efforts were successful, but not so ultimately. The wind veered somewhat towards the west, thus throwing the flames immediately upon the House of Commons, the angle of which abutting upon the House of Lords, caught fire, and the roof ignited, the woodwork of which being old and dry, the flames spread with the rapidity of wild fire.

In a very short time indeed, the whole of the roof fell in with a tremendous crash, emitting millions of sparks and flakes of fire. This appearance, combined with the sound resembling a piece of heavy ordnance, induced the assembled multitude to believe that an explosion of gunfire had taken place. The scene of confusion which followed baffled the power of description.

Manchester Guardian, 17 October 1834.

∞

The Palace of Westminster, seat of the British Parliament, was destroyed by a dramatic conflagration on 16 October 1834. While part of the lost building was old, much of it was of recent construction, built by James Wyatt in the 1790s and Sir John Soane in the 1820s. The 12th-century Westminster Hall was, thankfully, saved from the flames. The cause was later traced to medieval tally-sticks, used for centuries to record taxes and other financial transactions, being used as fuel in the boilers.

The fire attracted the attention of Londoners, including many artists, among them Joseph William Mallord Turner. It was not seen universally as a disaster: the architect Augustus Pugin, a proponent of the Gothic Revival and the man charged, in association with Charles Barry, with rebuilding the Palace, shed few tears at the destruction of buildings whose style he deplored; in a letter to Bishop Robert Willson, he wrote:

I was fortunate enough to witness the fire from almost the beginning. There is nothing much to regret and a great deal to rejoice in. A vast amount of Soane's mixtures and Wyatt's heresies have been effectively consigned to oblivion. Oh it was a glorious sight to see his composition mullions and cement pinnacles and battlements flying and cracking while his turrets were smoking like so many chimneys till the heat showered them into a thousand pieces. The old walls stood triumphantly amid this scene of ruin while brick walls and framed sashes, slate roofs etc fell faster than a pack of cards.

Pugin's scheme was copied, albeit in a somewhat toned-down way, in 1945–50, when the House of Commons had to be rebuilt yet again following its destruction by German bombs in 1941.

ALSO ON THIS DAY

1923 Walt and Roy Disney found a 'Cartoon Studio'.
1946 Ten leading Nazis convicted of war crimes, including Keitel and von Ribbentrop, are executed.
1987 An unforecast hurricane hits southern England.

17 OCTOBER

STANLEY LOCATES DR LIVINGSTONE, 1871

At this grand moment we do not think of the hundreds of miles we have marched, of the hundreds of hills that we have ascended and descended, of the many forests we have traversed, of the jungles and thickets that annoyed us, of the fervid salt plains that blistered our feet, of the hot suns that scorched us, nor the dangers and difficulties now happily surmounted... Selim said to me: 'I see the Doctor, Sir...' My heart beats fast, but I must not let my face betray my emotions, lest it shall detract from the dignity of a white man appearing under such extraordinary circumstances. So I did that which I thought was most dignified. I pushed back the crowds, and... walked down a living avenue of people until I came in front of the semicircle of Arabs, in the front of which stood the white man with the gray beard... He was pale, looked wearied, ...wore a bluish cap with a faded gold band round it, had on a red-sleeved waistcoat and a pair of gray tweed trousers. I would have run to him, only I was a coward in the presence of such a mob – would have embraced him, only, he being an Englishman, I did not know how he would receive me; so I did what cowardice and false pride suggested was the best thing: walked deliberately to him, took off my hat, and said, 'Dr Livingstone, I presume?'

'Yes,' said he, with a kind smile, lifting his cap slightly... I then say aloud, 'I thank God, Doctor, I have been permitted to see you.'

He answered, 'I feel thankful that I am here to welcome you.'

HENRY STANLEY, *HOW I FOUND LIVINGSTONE*, 1872.

The Scottish explorer and Congregationalist missionary David Livingstone (1813–73) had spent much of the 1840s and 1850s in Africa, during which time he had traced the course of the Zambezi River (and named its dramatic Victoria Falls). In 1866 he went in search of the source of the Nile, and little was heard of his movements for many months. This spurred the *New York Herald* to commission the American journalist Henry Morton Stanley to locate him. After a journey of eight months and 7,000 miles, he found the Scotsman at Ujiji, near Lake Tanganyika, in modern Tanzania. The ailing Livingstone remained in Africa, where he died eighteen months later.

ALSO ON THIS DAY

1448 Ottoman forces overwhelm a Hungarian-Wallachian force at the Second Battle of Kosovo.
1849 The death of the Polish composer Frédéric Chopin.
1968 African-American medal-winners give the Black Power salute at the Mexico Olympics.

18 OCTOBER

LOUIS XIV ENDS TOLERATION OF HUGUENOTS, 1685

I. We have, by this present perpetual and irrevocable edict, suppressed and revoked the edict of our grandfather, given at Nantes in April, 1598; we declare them null and void... and in consequence we desire... that all the temples of those of the said allegedly Reformed religion shall be demolished without delay.

II. We forbid our subjects of the allegedly Reformed religion to meet any more for the exercise of the said religion in any place or private house...

III. We forbid all noblemen to hold such religious exercises in their houses or fiefs.

IV. We enjoin all ministers of the allegedly Reformed religion, who do not choose to become converts and to embrace the Catholic, apostolic, and Roman religion, to leave our kingdom within a fortnight of the publication of our present edict.

VII. We forbid private schools for the instruction of children of the allegedly Reformed religion.

VIII. As for children who may be born of persons of the allegedly Reformed religion, we desire that from henceforth they be baptized by the parish priests, and thereafter the children shall be brought up in the Catholic, apostolic, and Roman religion...

X. We repeat our most express prohibition to all our subjects of the allegedly Reformed religion, together with their wives and children, against leaving our kingdom, or transporting their goods and effects therefrom.

Louis XIV, Edict of Fontainebleau, 18 October 1685.

Louis XIV's Edict of Fontainebleau reversed the policy of toleration articulated by his grandfather Henry IV's Edict of Nantes (1598). That document had finally ended France's crippling Wars of Religion. But Louis incrementally withdrew the liberties of Huguenots – the followers of the 'Reformed religion' – from 1661, and the new edict represented an effective re-Catholicizing of the country. The consequence was the mass emigration of Huguenots.

ALSO ON THIS DAY

1871 The death of Charles Babbage, the English 'father of the computer'.
1922 The precursor of the BBC is founded as the 'British Broadcasting Company'.
1989 East Germany's Erich Honecker falls from power.

19 OCTOBER

HANNIBAL MEETS HIS MATCH, 202 BC

Hannibal gave the word to the men on the elephants to charge the enemy. But as they heard the horns and trumpets braying all round them, some of the elephants became unmanageable and rushed back upon the Numidian contingents of the Carthaginian army; and this enabled Massinissa with great speed to deprive the Carthaginian left wing of its cavalry support. The rest of the elephants charged the Roman velites [light infantry] in the spaces between the maniples [legionary units] of the line, and while inflicting much damage on the enemy suffered severely themselves; until, becoming frightened, some of them ran away down the vacant spaces, the Romans letting them pass harmlessly along, according to Scipio's orders, while others ran away to the right under a shower of darts from the cavalry, until they were finally driven clear off the field.

It was just at the moment of this stampede of the elephants, that Laelius forced the Carthaginian cavalry into headlong flight, and along with Massinissa pressed them with a vigorous pursuit. While this was going on, the opposing lines of heavy infantry were advancing to meet others with deliberate step and proud confidence, except Hannibal's 'army of Italy', which remained in its original position. When they came within distance the Roman soldiers charged the enemy, shouting as usual their war-cry, and clashing their swords against their shields: while the Carthaginian mercenaries uttered a strange confusion of cries, the effect of which was indescribable, for, in the words of the poet [Homer] the 'voice of all was not one nor one their cry: But manifold their speech as was their race.'

...Hannibal provided himself with those numerous elephants, and put them in the van, for the express purpose of throwing the enemy's ranks into confusion and breaking their order. Again he stationed the mercenaries in front and the Carthaginians behind them, in order to wear out the bodies of the enemy with fatigue beforehand, and to blunt the edge of their swords by the numbers that would be killed by them; and moreover to compel the Carthaginians, by being in the middle of the army, to stay where they were and fight.

But the most warlike and steady part of his army he held in reserve at some distance, in order that they might not see what was happening too closely, but, with strength and spirit unimpaired, might use their courage to the best advantage when the moment arrived. And, if in spite of having done everything that could be done, he who had never been beaten before failed to secure the victory now, we must excuse him. For there are times when chance thwarts the plans of the brave; and there are others again, when a man 'Though great and brave has met a greater still'.

POLYBIUS, HISTORIES, BOOK XV, 2ND CENTURY BC.

∞

The great Carthaginian general Hannibal (247–183 BC), who had been undefeated through 15 years of campaigning in Italy in the Second Punic War (achieving remarkable victories at Trebbia [218 BC], Lake Trasimene [217 BC] and, most famously, at Cannae [216 BC]), was eventually worn down by the 'Fabian' tactics of Quintus Fabius Maximus. In 203 BC he was forced to return to his native North Africa by a Roman invasion led by Publius Cornelius Scipio (later called Africanus). In the decisive Battle of Zama, the Romans, assisted by the Carthaginians' former ally the Numidian King Massinissa, were able to frighten Hannibal's 85 elephants and neutralize their danger. Hannibal's surrender ended the Carthaginian Empire, though he shortly afterwards assumed a position of political power in Carthage itself. The Greek historian Polybius suggested that Hannibal, whom he admired, had done little wrong in the battle.

ALSO ON THIS DAY

1216 The death of King John I of England.
1469 Ferdinand II of Aragon marries Isabella I of Castile.
1813 Napoleon is defeated by a coalition army at the Battle of Leipzig.

20 OCTOBER

THE LOUISIANA PURCHASE, 1803

This accession of territory affirms forever the power of the United States, and I have given England a maritime rival who sooner or later will humble her pride.

NAPOLEON, LETTER TO THE MARQUIS DE LAFAYETTE, MARCH 1807.

∞

US President Thomas Jefferson's purchase of the French claim to Louisiana territory for $15 million – not just the modern state of Louisiana, but over 800,000 square miles of territory – doubled the size of the United States and changed the politics of North America at a stroke. The land encompassed all or part of 14 present-day states in what is now the central United States, including the city of New Orleans. US access to New Orleans and the Mississippi, previously a matter of concern, was now assured, and the danger of a new French or Spanish Empire on the continent was ended. France, which was losing its influence in the Caribbean, had little real interest in North America and Napoleon was happy to sell, and able to congratulate himself for creating a power with the potential to rival Britain.

Nevertheless, the scale and ease of the purchase took all by surprise. France had ceded its claim to this vast swathe of land to Spain in the aftermath of its defeat by Britain in the Seven Years' War (1763; *see* 10 February); but in the reshaped political landscape of Europe at the start of the 19th century, the claim had transferred back to France. The sale was agreed in Paris on 30 April 1803, when the US negotiator Robert Livingstone proclaimed: 'We have lived long, but this is the noblest work of our whole lives. From this day the United States take their place among the powers of the first rank.' Jefferson told the French ambassador: 'Your emperor has done more splendid things, but he has never done one which will give happiness to so great a number of human beings as the ceding of Louisiana to the United States.' He announced the purchase on 4 July, but faced opposition from those who saw his action as unconstitutional. It was not until 20 October that the US Senate ratified the treaty, and the purchase was completed on 1 January 1804.

ALSO ON THIS DAY

1818 The US–Canadian border is settled by an Anglo-US treaty.
1827 The Ottoman fleet is defeated by an Anglo-French-Russian fleet at the Battle of Navarino.
1984 The death of the English quantum physicist Paul Dirac.

366

21 OCTOBER

THE BATTLE OF TRAFALGAR, 1805

His Lordship came to me on the poop, and after ordering certain signals to be made, about a quarter to noon, he said: 'Mr. Pasco, I wish to say to the fleet, ENGLAND CONFIDES THAT EVERY MAN WILL DO HIS DUTY' and he added 'You must be quick, for I have one more to make which is for close action.' I replied: 'If your Lordship will permit me to substitute expects for confides, the signal will soon be completed, because the word "expects" is in the vocabulary, and "confides" must be spelled.' His Lordship replied, in haste, and with seeming satisfaction: 'That will do, Pasco, make it directly.'

JOHN PASCO, SIGNAL OFFICER, HMS *VICTORY*, 1805.

∞

Vice-Admiral Lord Nelson's celebrated encouragement to his fleet, transmitted in the recently introduced system of telegraph-flags, was followed by his equally well-known 'Engage the enemy more closely', as he led the first of two British lines in a right-angled assault on the centre of the Franco-Spanish line. His tactic, designed to split the enemy fleet and take advantage of his superior firepower, upset traditional assumptions about naval warfare and turned the Napoleonic Battle of Trafalgar, near Gibraltar, into a series of individual engagements. Nelson's flagship HMS *Victory* engaged in close combat with the second ship of the French line, the *Redoubtable*. As the ships tangled, Nelson was shot through the spine by a sniper in the French rigging. Carried down below, his death became the stuff of legend.

Among the admiral's last utterances, as reported by the ship's surgeon William Beattie, were an appeal on behalf of his mistress Emma Hamilton ('Take care of poor Lady Hamilton') and a farewell to Captain Thomas Hardy ('Kiss me, Hardy'). His final words encapsulated his life as a professional Royal Navy man: 'Thank God I have done my duty.' Nelson's body was returned to England for funeral, and his reputation as a hero who had ensured British naval dominance for a century or more was secure. (*See also* 2 April.)

ALSO ON THIS DAY

1854 The English nurse Florence Nightingale departs for the Crimea.
1861 US Civil War: the Confederates defeat Union forces at Ball's Bluff.
1966 A landslip of coal slag buries a school in Aberfan, South Wales, killing 144.

22 OCTOBER

THE CUBAN MISSILE CRISIS, 1962

For many years both the Soviet Union and the United States have deployed strategic nuclear weapons with great care, never upsetting the precarious status quo which ensured that these weapons would not be used in the absence of some vital challenge. Our own strategic missiles have never been transferred to the territory of any other nation under a cloak of secrecy and deception; and our history... demonstrates that we have no desire to dominate or conquer any other nation or impose our system upon its people. Nevertheless, American citizens have become adjusted to living daily on the bull's-eye of Soviet missiles located inside the USSR or in submarines.

In that sense, missiles in Cuba add to an already clear and present danger – although it should be noted the nations of Latin America have never previously been subjected to a potential nuclear threat.

But this secret, swift, and extraordinary buildup of Communist missiles – in an area well known to have a special and historical relationship to the United States and the nations of the Western Hemisphere... is a deliberately provocative and unjustified change in the status quo...

Acting, therefore, in the defence of our own security and of the entire Western Hemisphere... I have directed that the following initial steps be taken immediately:

First: To halt this offensive buildup, a strict quarantine on all offensive military equipment under shipment to Cuba is being initiated. All ships of any kind bound for Cuba from whatever nation or port will, if found to contain cargoes of offensive weapons, be turned back. This quarantine will be extended, if needed, to other types of cargo and carriers. We are not at this time, however, denying the necessities of life as the Soviets attempted to do in their Berlin blockade of 1948.

Second: I have directed the continued and increased close surveillance of Cuba and its military buildup... Should these offensive military preparations continue... further action will be justified. I have directed the Armed Forces to prepare for any eventualities; and I trust that in the interest of both the Cuban people and the Soviet technicians at the sites, the hazards to all concerned in continuing this threat will be recognized.

Third: It shall be the policy of this nation to regard any nuclear missile launched from Cuba against any nation in the Western Hemisphere as an attack by the Soviet Union on the United States, requiring a full retaliatory response upon the Soviet Union.

Fourth:... I have reinforced our base at Guantanamo, evacuated today the dependents of our personnel there, and ordered additional military units to be on a standby alert basis.

Fifth: We are calling for an immediate meeting of... the Organization of American States, to consider this threat to hemispheric security and to invoke articles 6 and 8 of the Rio Treaty in support of all necessary action...

Sixth: Under the Charter of the United Nations, we are asking tonight that an emergency meeting of the Security Council be convoked without delay... Our resolution will call for the prompt dismantling and withdrawal of all offensive weapons in Cuba, under the supervision of UN observers, before the quarantine can be lifted.

Seventh and finally: I call upon Chairman Khrushchev to halt and eliminate this clandestine, reckless and provocative threat to world peace and to stable relations between our two nations. I call upon him further to abandon this course of world domination, and to join in an historic effort to end the perilous arms race and to transform the history of man.

US PRESIDENT JOHN F. KENNEDY, TELEVISION ADDRESS, 22 OCTOBER 1962.

∞

The Cuban Missile Crisis – a stand-off that brought the world to the brink of nuclear war – began in September 1962 when US analysts suspected, from spy-plane photography, that the Soviet Union was transporting medium-range missiles to its new ideological bedfellow Cuba. This development, if allowed to proceed, would place the US mainland within the range of Soviet medium-range nuclear weaponry.

The central phase of the crisis lasted 13 days, beginning on 14 October, when US reconnaissance confirmed the existence of missile silos in Cuba. Options for US military strikes were urged upon President Kennedy by his military chiefs, but instead he resolved to enforce the 'quarantine' of Cuba, and the world waited to see whether the Soviet ships would breach it, with potentially catastrophic consequences. After Kennedy stated his position on television on 22 October, the crisis continued for another week until Khrushchev announced his intention to remove the missiles on 29 October. In fact, a deal was agreed behind closed doors, whereby in return the United States would remove its intermediate-range missiles from its ally Turkey.

ALSO ON THIS DAY

1906 The death of the French artist Paul Cézanne.
1944 WWII: Aachen becomes the first German city to fall to the Allies.
1966 The Soviet spy George Blake escapes from Wormwood Scrubs prison.

23 OCTOBER

THE BEGINNING OF THE WORLD, 4004 BC

We find that the year of our fore-fathers, and the years of the ancient Egyptians and Hebrews were of the same quantity with the Julian, consisting of twelve equal months, every of them containing 30 days... adjoining to the end of the twelfth month, the addition of five days, and every four year six. And I have observed by the continued succession of these years, as they are delivered in holy writ, that the end of the great Nebuchadnezzar's and the beginning of Evilmerodach's (his son's) reign, fell out in the 3442 year of the world, but by collation of Chaldean history and the astronomical canon, it fell out in the 186 year of Nabonasar, and, as by certain connexion, it must follow in the 562 year before the Christian account, and of the Julian Period, the 4152.

And from thence I gathered the creation of the world did fall out upon the 710 year of the Julian Period, by placing its beginning in autumn: but for as much as the first day of the world began with the evening of the first day of the week, I have observed that the Sunday, which in the year 710 aforesaid came nearest the autumnal equinox, by astronomical tables... happened upon the 23 day of the Julian October; from thence concluded that from the evening preceding that first day of the Julian year, both the first day of the creation and the first motion of time are to be deduced.

JAMES USSHER, *THE ANNALS OF THE WORLD*, 1658.

∞

James Ussher, Primate of All Ireland in 1625–56, estimated the date of the biblical Genesis story by combining calendrical calculation with a literal reading of the Bible. Starting with calculations of earlier scholars that time began in 4713 BC (Ussher in fact recalculated this 'Julian Period' to 4714 BC), he then used a biblical reference to the end of the reign of the Babylonian King Nebuchadnezzar as being in the 3,442nd year of the world's existence. Knowing this to have occurred in 562 BC, he calculated the world began in the Julian year 710, on the day we call 23 October 4004 BC. His conclusion, included in many an English Bible, became the most notorious of many such calculations. It was not until the early 19th century that the young science of geology, along with fossil evidence, added millions of years to estimates of the world's age.

ALSO ON THIS DAY

1642 English Civil War: the Parliamentarians defeat the Royalists at Edgehill.
1915 The death of the legendary English cricketer W.G. Grace.
1956 The Hungarian Uprising against Soviet-imposed policies begins.

24 OCTOBER

THE DEATH OF JANE SEYMOUR, 1537

QUEEN JEANY has travel'd for three days and more,
Till the ladies were weary, and quite gave her oer:
'O ladies, O ladies, do this thing for me,
To send for King Henry, to come and see me.'
King Henry was sent for, and sat by her bedside:
'Why weep you, Queen Jeany? your eyes are so red.'
'O Henry, O Henry, do this one thing for me,
Let my side straight be open'd, and save my babie!'
'O Jeany, O Jeany, this never will do,
It will leese thy sweet life, and thy young babie too.'
She wept and she wailed, till she fell in a swoon:
Her side it was opened, the babie was found.
Prince Edward was christened with joy and with mirth,
But the flower of fair England lies cold in the earth.
O black was King Henry, and black were his men,
And black was the steed that King Henry rode on.
And black were the ladies, and black were their fans,
And black were the gloves that they wore on their hands,
And black were the ribbands they wore on their heads,
And black were the pages, and black were the maids.

POPULAR BALLAD, COLLECTED BY FRANCIS JAMES CHILD IN 1882–98.

Jane Seymour became the third wife of Henry VIII on 30 May 1536, less than two weeks after the decapitation of her predecessor Anne Boleyn (*see* 19 May); she died on 24 October 1537, 12 days after giving birth to her son, the future Edward VI. She was the only one of Henry's six wives to receive a royal funeral.

The story of Jane's death was told in many popular ballads. Most of them told of a long labour, a Caesarean section (which would have been unlikely), and of the king's genuine grief at her loss. Henry wrote to the French king: 'Divine Providence has mingled my joy with the bitterness of the death of her who brought me this happiness'. The English king was eventually buried beside his lamented wife, in Windsor.

ALSO ON THIS DAY

1648 The Peace of Westphalia concludes the Thirty Years' War.
1857 Sheffield FC, the world's first football club, is founded.
1945 The United Nations organization comes into being.

25 OCTOBER

THE CHARGE OF THE LIGHT BRIGADE, 1854

At 11:00 our Light Cavalry Brigade rushed to the front... The Russians opened on them with guns from the redoubts on the right, with volleys of musketry and rifles.

They swept proudly past, glittering in the morning sun in all the pride and splendour of war. We could hardly believe the evidence of our senses. Surely that handful of men were not going to charge an army in position? Alas! It was but too true – their desperate valour knew no bounds, and far indeed was it removed from its so-called better part – discretion. They advanced in two lines, quickening the pace as they closed towards the enemy. A more fearful spectacle was never witnessed than by those who, without the power to aid, beheld their heroic countrymen rushing to the arms of sudden death. At the distance of 1,200 yards the whole line of the enemy belched forth, from thirty iron mouths, a flood of smoke and flame through which hissed the deadly balls. Their flight was marked by instant gaps in our ranks, the dead men and horses, by steeds flying wounded or riderless across the plain. The first line was broken – it was joined by the second, they never halted or checked their speed an instant. With diminished ranks, thinned by those thirty guns, which the Russians had laid with the most deadly accuracy, with a halo of flashing steel above their heads, and with a cheer which was many a noble fellow's death cry, they flew into the smoke of the batteries; but ere they were lost from view, the plain was strewed with their bodies and with the carcasses of horses. They were exposed to an oblique fire from the batteries on the hills on both sides, as well as to a direct fire of musketry.

Through the clouds of smoke we could see their sabres flashing as they rode up to the guns and dashed between them, cutting down the gunners as they stood. The blaze of their steel, like an officer standing near me said, 'was like the turn of a shoal of mackerel'. We saw them riding through the guns, as I have said; to our delight, we saw them returning, after breaking through a column of Russian infantry and scattering them like chaff, when the flank fire of the battery on the hill swept them down, scattered and broken as they were. Wounded men and dismounted troopers flying towards us told the sad tale – demigods could not have done what they had failed to do. At the very moment when they were about to retreat, a regiment of lancers was hurled upon their flank. Colonel Shewell, of the 8th Hussars, saw the danger and rode his men straight at them, cutting his way through with fearful loss. The other regiments turned and engaged in a desperate encounter. With courage too great almost for credence, they were breaking their way through the columns which enveloped them, where there took place an act of atrocity without parallel in modern warfare of civilized nations. The Russian gunners, when the storm of cavalry passed, returned to their guns. They saw their own cavalry mingled with the troopers who had just ridden over them, and to the eternal disgrace of the Russian name, the miscreants poured a murderous volley of grape and canister on the mass of struggling men and horses, mingling friend and foe in one common ruin. It was as much as our Heavy Cavalry Brigade could do to cover the retreat of the miserable remnants of that band of heroes as they returned to the place they had so lately quitted in all the pride of life.

At 11:35 not a British soldier, except the dead and dying, was left in front of those bloody Muscovite guns.

WILLIAM HOWARD RUSSELL, *THE TIMES*, 14 NOVEMBER 1854.

∞

Thus took place the most heroically foolhardy cavalry charge in British military history, during the Crimean War siege of Balaklava, when over 600 horsemen of the Light Brigade, led by Lord Cardigan, charged a battery of Russian cannon while being pounded by more cannon on their flanks. The incident quickly caught the public's imagination and was poetically memorialized as 'The Charge of the Light Brigade' by the Poet Laureate Alfred Lord Tennyson, after being inspired on reading Russell's despatch.

Observing the event unfold, Marshal Pierre Bosquet, fighting with the French allies, was compelled to declare: *C'est magnifique, mais ce n'est pa la guerre. C'est de la folie.* ('It's magnificent, but it's not war. It's madness'). Notoriously, the order to charge through the 'Valley of Death', as Tennyson called it, was the result of confused communications among the British commanders.

ALSO ON THIS DAY

1400 The death of the English poet Geoffrey Chaucer.
1415 Hundred Years' War: the English defeat the French at Agincourt.
1983 US forces invade the Caribbean island-state of Grenada.

26 OCTOBER

THE LIBERATION OF SOUTHERN ITALY, 1860

The king's discourteous proclamation to the people of Southern Italy, dated from Ancona, in which he informed them that he was 'coming to restore order, to close the era of revolutions in Italy,' preceded but a few days his entry into Naples. Coming from Venafro, the northern army defiled towards Teano. Garibaldi, at the head of his volunteers, crossed the Volturno to meet the king, crying, as he approached him: 'Hail to the King of Italy ! *Viva il re!*'...

The interview between the king and the dictator lasted but a few minutes; no invitation was given to Garibaldi to accompany His Majesty, who said to him: 'Your troops must be weary; mine are fresh.' Arrived at the bridge which crosses the little stream near Teano, they parted; Garibaldi halted at Calvi, fixing his head-quarters at a little church near the town, dining on bread and cheese, sleeping on straw... On November 2 Capua capitulated; such barren honours the king reserved to himself. Overlooking the discourtesy shown in every possible manner, Garibaldi ordered his troops to be drawn up for review by Their Majesty, who, after twice keeping them with ordered arms for more than six hours, failed to appear, sending General Della Rocca in his stead.

GIUSEPPE GARIBALDI, *AUTOBIOGRAPHY*, 1889 EDITION.

∞

The Italian revolutionary and republican Giuseppe Garibaldi (1807–82), having won a long military campaign to conquer the Bourbon Kingdom of The Two Sicilies (i.e. Naples and Sicily) in 1860, was stopped from advancing north to Rome – where he hoped to end the centuries-old papal rule – by the intervention of the Sardinian-Piedmontese king, Victor Emmanuel, at the head of an army. The king, with his chief minister Count Cavour, had been the prime shapers of Italian unification, but they had had an uneasy relationship with the unorthodox Garibaldi, whose advance now threatened possible conflict with the French troops protecting Rome.

The two men met at Teano, where Garibaldi effectively submitted, handing over his conquest to the king, shaking his hand and recognizing him as ruler of an independent, unified Italy.

ALSO ON THIS DAY

1881 The Gunfight at the O.K. Corral takes place in Tombstone, Arizona.
1944 WWII: the US Navy defeats the Japanese in the Battle of Leyte Gulf.
1951 Winston Churchill returns to power as British prime minister.

27 OCTOBER

CONSTANTINE RECEIVES A SIGN OF GOD, AD 312

Being convinced, however, that he needed some more powerful aid than his military forces could afford him, on account of the wicked and magical enchantments which were so diligently practised by the tyrant, he sought divine assistance, deeming the possession of arms and a numerous soldiery of secondary importance... Therefore felt it incumbent on him to honour his father's God alone. He called on him with earnest prayer and supplications to reveal to him who he was, and stretch forth his right hand to help him in his present difficulties. And while he was praying, a most marvellous sign appeared to him from heaven, the account of which it might have been hard to believe had it been related by any other person. But since the victorious emperor himself long afterwards declared it to the writer of this history, when he was honoured with his acquaintance and society, and confirmed his statement by an oath, who could hesitate to credit the relation, especially since the testimony of after-time has established its truth? He said that about noon, when the day was already beginning to decline, he saw with his own eyes the trophy of a cross of light in the heavens, above the sun, and bearing the inscription 'Conquer by this.' At this sight he himself was struck with amazement, and his whole army also, which followed him on this expedition, and witnessed the miracle.

EUSEBIUS, *CHURCH HISTORY*, C. AD 330.

The young Roman emperor Constantine, facing a challenge to his rule from his imperial rival Maxentius, committed himself to battle on 25 October AD 312 at Milvian Bridge over the Tiber, near Rome. Immediately before the battle, the pagan Constantine saw a vision of the cross in the sky. Having carried the day, he went on to issue the Edict of Milan in AD 313, proclaiming religious toleration in the Roman Empire. He himself was baptised on his deathbed 25 years later.

The 'Donation of Constantine', a forged document purporting to confer a range of rights and privileges on Pope Sylvester I (314–15) and his successors, became a central plank upon which the papacy justified its secular authority, including its rule over the Papal States in Italy.

ALSO ON THIS DAY

1787 The first Federalist Papers are published.
1870 Franco-Prussian War: Metz surrenders to Prussian forces.
1907 The first line of the New York Subway opens.

28 OCTOBER

TRUTH AND RECONCILIATION
IN SOUTH AFRICA, 1998

We have been given a great privilege. It has been a costly privilege but one that we would not want to exchange for anything in the world. Some of us have already experienced something of a post-traumatic stress and have become more and more aware of just how deeply wounded we have all been; how wounded and broken we all are. Apartheid has affected us at a very deep level more than we ever suspected. We in the Commission have been a microcosm of our society, reflecting its alienation, suspicions and lack of trust in one another. Our earlier Commission meetings were very difficult and filled with tension. God has been good in helping us to grow closer together. Perhaps we are a sign of hope that, if people from often hostile backgrounds could grow closer together as we have done, then there is hope for South Africa, that we can become united. We have been called to be wounded healers.

DESMOND TUTU, FOREWORD, *TRUTH AND RECONCILIATION COMMISSION REPORT*, 1998.

∞

In the process of turning *apartheid* South Africa into Nelson Mandela's vision of the Rainbow Nation, Desmond Tutu, Anglican archbishop of Cape Town, established the Truth and Reconciliation Commission (TRC) in 1995 to investigate many of the country's darkest moments between 1960 and 1994. Run in a spirit of Christian understanding, it offered restorative justice in which the victims and their families would come face to face with those who had hurt them; in return for fully disclosing involvement in politically motivated violence and human-rights violations, witnesses could be offered amnesty from criminal prosecution.

The TRC uncovered details of many atrocities, committed not only by the white-minority regime's security apparatus and pro-*apartheid* extremists but also by members of the African National Congress. In his Foreword to the much-awaited *Report*, published on 28 October 1998, Tutu faced up to his critics and justified the exercise as a necessary part of the healing of the nation. As such, and despite its flaws, it has remained a model for national conflict resolution.

ALSO ON THIS DAY

1704 The death of the English philosopher John Locke.
1922 King Victor Emmanuel III of Italy hands power to Benito Mussolini.
1958 Pope John XXIII is elected.

29 OCTOBER

THE WALL STREET CRASH, 1929

It was probably Wall Street's worst night. Not only had the day been bad, but everybody down to the youngest office boy had a pretty good idea of what was going to happen tomorrow.

The morning papers were black with the story of the Monday smash. Except for rather feeble hopes that the great banks would step into the gap they had no heart for cheerful headlines. In the inside pages, however, the sunshine chorus continued as merry as ever. Bankers said that heavy buying had been sighted on the horizon...

...The next day, Tuesday, was the worst of all. In the first half hour 3,259,800 shares were traded, almost a full day's work for the labouring machinery of the Exchange. The selling pressure was wholly without precedent. It was coming from everywhere. The wires to other cities were jammed with frantic orders to sell. So were the cables, radio and telephones to Europe and the rest of the world. Buyers were few, sometimes wholly absent. Often the specialists stood baffled at their posts, sellers pressing around them and not a single buyer at any price.

This was real panic. It was what the banks had prevented on Thursday, had slowed on Monday. Now they were helpless. Reportedly they were trying to force their associated corporations to toss their buying power into the whirlpool, but they were getting no results.

JONATHAN LEONARD, *THREE YEARS DOWN*, 1944.

Black Tuesday, 29 October 1929, was the culmination of panic-selling on the New York Stock Exchange. The beginnings of a decline in stock values had begun the preceding Thursday, but the banks had intervened over the weekend. Trading was very bad on Monday, but on Tuesday, 16 million shares were traded, with $40 billion wiped from the value of US companies. The events proved to be the beginning of a 'bear market', a long period of falling stock prices. And Black Tuesday represented the beginning of the decade-long economic slump of the 'Great Depression', which would affect every economy in the Western world.

ALSO ON THIS DAY

1618 The English adventurer Sir Walter Raleigh is executed.
1967 The off-Broadway opening of the counter-cultural musical *Hair*.
1975 The ailing General Franco steps down as Spanish head of state.

30 OCTOBER

A PAPAL ORGY IN RENAISSANCE ROME, 1501

On Sunday evening, October 30th, Don Cesare Borgia gave a supper in his apartment in the apostolic palace, with fifty decent prostitutes or courtesans in attendance, who after the meal danced with the servants and others there, first fully dressed and then naked. Following the supper too, lampstands holding lighted candles were placed on the floor and chestnuts strewn about, which the prostitutes, naked on the floor and on their hands and knees, had to pick up as they crawled in and out amongst the lampstands. The pope, Don Cesare and Donna Lucrezia were all present to watch. Finally, prizes were offered – silken doublets, pairs of shoes, hats and other garments – for those men who were most successful with the prostitutes. This performance was carried out in the Sala Reale [of the Vatican] and those who attended said in fact the prizes were presented by the servants to those who won the contest.

JOHANNES BURCHARD, *LIBER NOTARUM*, 1503.

The astute Spanish churchman Rodrigo Borgia gained election as Pope Alexander VI in 1492, and set about furthering his own enrichment and the worldly prospects of his illegitimate children, in particular the quick-tempered Cesare (who may have murdered his younger brother) and his beautiful daughter Lucrezia. On Alexander's election, Giovanni de' Medici – the future Pope Leo X – said: 'Now we are in the power of a wolf, the most rapacious perhaps that this world has ever seen. If we do not flee, he will inevitably devour us all.'

During Alexander's reign, the pope's court became a notorious focus for intrigue, extortion – and sexual immorality. He plundered the papal coffers to finance the ambitions of his son Cesare, who, after abandoning his cardinal's hat, attempted to carve a duchy for himself from large portions of the Emilia-Romagna region. Unsurprisingly, Cesare was one of Machiavelli's subjects for his 1513 study in cynical statecraft, *The Prince*.

Cesare's idea of a lavish banquet, on 30 October 1501, amply serviced by 50 courtesans, was recorded by the papal master-of-ceremonies Johannes Burchard. It has been called the 'Ballet of the Chestnuts'.

ALSO ON THIS DAY

1961 The Soviet Union explodes the largest (58 megaton) thermonuclear bomb ever tested.
1966 Barbados achieves independence from Britain.
2009 The death of the French anthropologist Claude-Lévi-Strauss.

31 OCTOBER

LUTHER SPARKS THE PROTESTANT REFORMATION, 1517

Out of love for the truth and the desire to bring it to light, the following propositions will be discussed at Wittenberg, under the presidency of the Reverend Father Martin Luther.

1. Our Lord and Master Jesus Christ, when He said *Poenitentiam agite*, willed that the whole life of believers should be repentance...

28. It is certain that when the penny jingles into the money-box, gain and avarice can be increased, but the result of the intercession of the Church is in the power of God alone.

37. Every true Christian, whether living or dead, has part in all the blessings of Christ and the Church; and this is granted him by God, even without letters of pardon...

73. The pope justly thunders against those who, by any art, contrive the injury of the traffic in pardons...

74. But much more does he intend to thunder against those who use the pretext of pardons to contrive the injury of holy love and truth...

94. Christians are to be exhorted that they be diligent in following Christ, their Head, through penalties, deaths, and hell;

95. And thus be confident of entering into heaven rather through many tribulations, than through the assurance of peace.

MARTIN LUTHER, 95 THESES, OCTOBER 1517.

When Martin Luther nailed his 95 Theses to the door of Wittenberg Cathedral in Saxony on 31 October 1517, he was protesting against the practice of raising money for the papacy by selling 'indulgences', or remission for time a soul would spend in purgatory for sins committed in his or her lifetime. Luther argued that true repentance was the only salvation. (*See also* 18 April.)

ALSO ON THIS DAY

1917 WWI: Australian cavalry overrun Ottoman trenches at the Battle of Beersheba.
1956 Suez Crisis: British and French air forces begin bombing Egypt.
1984 The Indian prime minister Indira Gandhi is assassinated by her Sikh bodyguards.

NOVEMBER

1 NOVEMBER

THE LISBON EARTHQUAKE, 1755

One moment has reduced one of the largest trading cities to ashes... There is hardly one merchant in a hundred that has saved anything, except some little part of their cash which they have been raking for among the ruins. As to their goods, their houses being burned to ashes, not one of them has been able to save a rag, nor can the Portuguese pay one single shilling of what they owe them... The shocks and tremulations having hardly discontinued since the first day of our disaster, three parts in four of the inhabitants remain encamped in the fields and gardens in and about this place. The houses which are yet standing in this city, as well as in the country for several miles around it, are for the most part in so shattered a condition that there is hardly one in fifty, tho' supported by props, that will be able to hold out the winter, if it should happen to blow and rain as heavily as we have sometimes experienced it at this season of the year.

WILLIAM STEPHENS, DIARY, 1755.

The Great Lisbon Earthquake killed up to 100,000 and devastated the Portuguese capital in 1755, causing a *tsunami* that was felt as far away as England. It was later estimated to have reached nine on the Richter Scale. William Stephens, an English merchant who was living and working in the city, was well placed to describe the event.

The earthquake also created philosophical shockwaves, as theologians struggled to reconcile the destruction of Lisbon with the notion of a benevolent deity. In his novel *Candide* (1759; *see also* 14 February), which contains numerous references to the earthquake, the writer Voltaire (who also wrote a *Poème sur le désastre de Lisbonne* ['A poem on the disaster of Lisbon']) satirized the philosophical optimism of the German thinker Gottfried Leibniz, who held that ours must be the 'best of all possible worlds' because it was created by an all-powerful and all-knowing God.

ALSO ON THIS DAY

1512 Michelangelo's Sistine Chapel ceiling in the Vatican is shown to the public for the first time.
1520 Ferdinand Magellan navigates the Strait of Magellan.
1894 Nicholas II accedes as tsar of Russia.

2 NOVEMBER

THE BALFOUR DECLARATION, 1917

Dear Lord Rothschild,

I have much pleasure in conveying to you, on behalf of His Majesty's government, the following declaration of sympathy with Jewish Zionist aspirations which has been submitted to, and approved by, the Cabinet:

'His Majesty's Government view with favour the establishment in Palestine of a national home for the Jewish people, and will use their best endeavours to facilitate the achievement of this object, it being clearly understood that nothing shall be done which may prejudice the civil and religious rights of existing non-Jewish communities in Palestine, or the rights and political status enjoyed by Jews in any other country.'

I should be grateful if you would bring this declaration to the knowledge of the Zionist Federation.

Yours sincerely

Arthur James Balfour

The so-called 'Declaration' of Arthur Balfour, British foreign secretary, to one of the leaders of the British Jewish community, constituted the statement of official British policy in the Middle East. The Zionists, led by Chaim Weizmann, had been pressing to have Palestine designated as the national home for the Jews, increasing numbers of whom had been immigrating to Palestine since the 1880s.

On 16 May 1916, some 18 months before the declaration, Sir Mark Sykes and Georges Picot, on behalf of Britain and France respectively, had signed a secret agreement to determine control and spheres of influence in the lands of the disintegrating Ottoman Empire, allocating Syria and Lebanon to France, and Iraq and Jordan to Britain, with the area of Palestine under an international condominium. This agreement only became public a few weeks after the Balfour Declaration.

Although the Sykes-Picot agreement set out 'to recognize and protect an independent Arab state or a confederation of Arab states', it ran counter to commitments given by the British to Emir Feisal, Sheriff of Mecca and leader of the Arabs in revolt against the Ottomans. The Balfour Declaration, 'viewing with favour' a Jewish state while promising to protect the interests of the existing non-Jewish peoples, proved a further disappointment of Arab aspirations.

On 7 November 1918, though, the French and British jointly promised the Arabs 'the setting up of national governments and administrations deriving their authority from the free exercise of the initiative and choice of the indigenous populations'. Two months later, on 3 January 1919, Weizmann and Feisal signed an agreement:

His Royal Highness the Emir FEISAL, representing and acting on behalf of the Arab Kingdom of Hedjaz, and Dr CHAIM WEIZMANN, representing and acting on behalf of the Zionist Organization. mindful of the racial kinship and ancient bonds existing between the Arabs and the Jewish people, and realising that the surest means of working out the consummation of their national aspirations is through the closest possible collaboration in the development of the Arab State and Palestine, and being desirous further of confirming the good understanding which exists between them, have agreed upon the following Articles;-

ARTICLE I The Arab State and Palestine in all their relations and undertakings shall be controlled by the most cordial goodwill and understanding and to this end Arab and Jewish duly accredited agents shall be established and maintained in the respective territories.

ARTICLE II Immediately following the completion of the deliberations of the Peace Conference, the definite boundaries between the Arab State and Palestine shall be determined by a Commission to be agreed upon by the parties hereto.

ARTICLE III In the establishment of the Constitution and Administration of Palestine all such measures shall be adopted as will afford the fullest guarantee for carrying into effect the British government's Declaration of the 2nd of November, 1917.

ARTICLE IV All necessary measures shall be taken to encourage and stimulate immigration of Jews into Palestine on a large scale, and as quickly as possible to settle Jewish immigrants upon the land through closer settlement and intensive cultivation of the soil. In taking such measures the Arab peasant and tenant farms shall be protected in their rights and shall be assisted in forwarding their economic development.

However, Feisal appended a note:

If the Arabs are established as I have asked in my manifesto of January 4th addressed to the British Secretary of State for Foreign Affairs, I will carry out what is written in this agreement. If changes are made, I cannot be answerable for failing to carry out this agreement.

Britain, bound by the Sykes-Picot Agreement, was unable to deliver the promises at the Paris Peace Conference and, granted a mandate to administer Palestine by the League of Nations, for the next thirty years found itself in the position of uneasy peacemaker, unable to offer satisfaction to either party.

ALSO ON THIS DAY

1570 A North Sea *tsunami* claims more than 1,000 lives between the Netherlands and Denmark.
1930 Emperor Haile Selassie is crowned in Ethiopia.
1975 The Italian film director Pier Paolo Pasolini is murdered near Rome.

3 NOVEMBER

NIXON APPEALS TO THE 'SILENT MAJORITY', 1969

And now I would like to address a word, if I may, to the young people of this nation who are particularly concerned, and I understand why they are concerned, about this war [in Vietnam]. I respect your idealism. I share your concern for peace. I want peace as much as you do... I have chosen a plan for peace. I believe it will succeed. If it does succeed, what the critics say now won't matter. If it does not succeed, anything I say then won't matter.

I know it may not be fashionable to speak of patriotism or national destiny these days. But I feel it is appropriate to do so on this occasion.

Two hundred years ago this nation was weak and poor. But even then, America was the hope of millions in the world. Today we have become the strongest and richest nation in the world. And the wheel of destiny has turned so that any hope the world has for the survival of peace and freedom will be determined by whether the American people have the moral stamina and the courage to meet the challenge of free world leadership. Let historians not record that when America was the most powerful nation in the world we passed on the other side of the road and allowed the last hopes for peace and freedom of millions of people to be suffocated by the forces of totalitarianism.

And so tonight – to you, the great silent majority of my fellow Americans – I ask for your support.

RICHARD NIXON, ADDRESS TO THE NATION, 3 NOVEMBER 1969.

∞

American military involvement in Vietnam, aimed at preventing US-aligned South Vietnam from falling to Communist North Vietnam, increased in intensity throughout the 1960s, scooping up thousands of young Americans as draftees. In 1969, faced with vociferous opposition among the young, President Nixon appealed to what he called the 'silent majority' to back his policy of 'Vietnamization' – the gradual withdrawal of US troops and the building-up of South Vietnamese forces. The further goal, as Nixon often asserted, was 'peace with honour', though the means involved coercive bombing campaigns and the extension of hostilities into Cambodia and Laos, before a deal was thrashed out in 1973. It failed to prevent the North's victory in 1975.

ALSO ON THIS DAY

1783 The last public hanging takes place at Tyburn gallows, London.
1918 WWI: an armistice signals the end of the Austro-Hungarian Empire.
1957 The Soviet satellite *Sputnik 2* is launched with Laika the dog on board.

4 NOVEMBER

THE DISCOVERY OF CHLOROFORM, 1847

Immediately, an unwarranted hilarity seized the party – they became very bright-eyed, very happy, and very loquacious. The conversation was of unusual intelligence, and quite charmed the listeners – some ladies of the family and a naval officer, brother-in-law of Dr Simpson. But suddenly there was a talk of sounds being heard like those of a cotton mill louder and louder; a moment more and then all was quiet – and then crash! On awakening Dr Simpson's first perception was mental – 'this is far stronger and better than ether,' he said to himself. The second was to note that he was prostrate on the floor, and that among his friends about him there was both confusion and alarm. Hearing a noise he turned round and saw Dr Duncan beneath a chair – his jaw dropped, his eyes staring, his head bent half under him, quite unconscious, and snoring in a most determined and alarming manner. Dr Keith was waving feet and legs in an attempt to overturn the supper table. The naval officer, Miss Petrie and Mrs Simpson were lying about on the floor in the strangest attitudes, and a chorus of snores filled the air. By and by the sitting was resumed. Each expressed himself delighted with his new agent, and its inhalation was repeated many times that night until the supply of chloroform was fairly exhausted.

H.L. GORDON, *SIR JAMES YOUNG SIMPSON AND CHLOROFORM*, 1897.

The Scottish obstetrician James Young Simpson (1811–70), experimenting regularly with chemicals in search of an effective anaesthetic, hit upon the newly discovered substance chloroform in November 1847, and shortly thereafter used it to ease the pain of childbirth for his patients. Initial opposition on religious grounds was dispelled when Queen Victoria agreed to use chloroform for the birth of her eighth child, Prince Leopold, in 1853.

Simpson's talent was recognized early – he was president of Edinburgh's Royal Medical Society by the age of 24 – and in 1840, aged only 29, he was appointed to the Chair of Midwifery (as the young discipline of obstetrics was then described) at Edinburgh University.

5 NOVEMBER

THE GUNPOWDER PLOT, 1605

This last night, the Upper House of Parliament was searched by Sir Thomas Knyvett, and one Johnson, servant to Mr Thomas Percy, was there apprehended, who had placed 36 barrels of gunpowder in the vault under the House with a purpose to blow it and the whole company when they should here assemble.

CLERK OF THE HOUSE RALPH EWENS, 5 NOVEMBER 1605.

It was the aim of the Gunpowder plotters to blow up the Houses of Parliament, and to kill James I as well as most of the royal family, the king's Council and most of the country's political leadership – and then put the young Prince Charles on the throne at the head of a Catholic faction. Their plans were foiled when the former soldier Guy Fawkes was captured red-handed with the gunpowder on 5 November 1605. Sir Edward Hoby, Gentleman of the Bedchamber, summarized the threat a few weeks later:

> On the 5th of November we began our Parliament, to which the king should have come in person, but refrained through a practice but that morning discovered. The plot was to have blown up the king at such time as he should have been set on his royal throne, accompanied with all his children, nobility and commoners and assisted with all bishops, judges and doctors; at one instant and blast to have ruin'd the whole State and Kingdom of England. And for the effecting of this, there was placed under the Parliament House, where the king should sit, some 30 barrels of powder, with good store of wood, faggots, pieces and bars of iron.

The existence of the plot had been revealed when Lord Monteagle, brother-in-law of one of the plotters, received an anonymous letter on 26 October, which advised him to 'retire yourself into your county whence you may expect the event in safety for... they shall receive a terrible blow this parliament'. Fawkes, who initially gave his name as John Johnson, was tortured and executed at the end of January 1606. Most of the other conspirators were captured or killed, including the leader Robert Catesby, besieged with his remaining supporters in Holbeche House, Staffordshire. While their plot had failed to harm anyone, several conspirators at the house were badly injured when their own stock of gunpowder caught fire.

ALSO ON THIS DAY

1831 The American slave revolt leader Nat Turner is tried and sentenced to death.
1854 Crimean War: the Russians fail to defeat the allies at Inkerman.
2006 Saddam Hussein is sentenced to death in Iraq.

6 NOVEMBER

THE DEATH OF GUSTAVUS ADOLPHUS, 1632

'Now, now is the time comrades, let us charge, let us charge in the name of God: Jesus, Jesus, Jesus, guide me in fighting this day and favour my right.'

He spurred his horse, and charged a battalion of 24 companies of cuirassiers, the flower of the Imperial army. Two Swedish regiments had orders to follow him. The king's artillery was brought up, and five cannon shot discharged upon the enemy, who answered with 200 of their own, which went off with a horrid noise and lightning, but with little loss to the Swedes, as Wallenstein's cannoniers had not aimed well.

However the first charge proved fatal to the king, and the whole army: for though the squadrons came on the enemy like thunder, a pistol shot pierced the king's arm, and broke the bone. When those next to the king saw him bleed, they cried out: 'The king is wounded.' The king heard this with much distaste, fearing it would abate the valour of his men. He replied: 'The hurt is slight, comrades, take courage, let us make use of our odds, and return to the charge.'

The assault was vigorously begun again, and the king again fought at the head of his troops, but the loss of blood weakened his spirits and voice, until he whispered to the Duke of Saxon of Lavenburg; 'Take me away, for I am dangerously wounded.' But a cuirassier saw him retreat, and galloped up from the battalion of the enemy, then discharged his carabine full in the shoulder of the king... When the king had received this wound, he fell from his horse, and gave up the ghost.

ANONYMOUS ACCOUNT, 1633.

∞

Gustavus II Adolphus, king of Sweden from 1611, entered the Thirty Years' War in 1630, aiding the Lutherans against the forces of the Catholic (and Habsburg) Holy Roman Emperor in 1630. Over the next two years he turned Sweden into a major European power with his disciplined cavalry, focused aggression and use of artillery on the battlefield. In 1632 his army won a decisive victory against Wallenstein, the imperial commander, at the Battle of Lützen, but the king – who had won himself the nickname of the 'Lion of the North' – was killed in the fighting. The Sweden he left behind was, though, just beginning its 'golden age' of empire.

ALSO ON THIS DAY

1860 Abraham Lincoln is elected as the 16th president of the United States.
1893 The death of the Russian composer Pyotr Ilyich Tchaikovsky.
1917 WWI: Passchendaele is captured by Canadian forces after a four-month battle.

7 NOVEMBER

THE STORMING OF THE WINTER PALACE, 1917

Like a black river, filling all the street, without song or cheer we poured through the Red Arch... In the open we began to run, stooping low and bunching together, and jammed up suddenly behind the pedestal of the Alexander Column.

...After a few minutes huddling there, some hundreds of men, the army seemed reassured and without any orders suddenly began again to flow forward... Over the barricade of firewood we clambered, and leaping down inside gave a triumphant shout as we stumbled on a heap of rifles thrown down by the yunkers [military cadets] who had stood there.

...Carried along by the eager wave of men we were swept into the right hand entrance, opening into a great bare vaulted room, the cellar of the East wing, from which issued a maze of corridors and stair-cases. A number of huge packing cases stood about, and upon these the Red Guards and soldiers fell furiously... pulling out carpets, curtains, linen, porcelain plates, glassware.

One man went strutting around with a bronze clock perched on his shoulder; another found a plume of ostrich feathers, which he stuck in his hat. The looting was just beginning when somebody cried, 'Comrades! Don't touch anything! Don't take anything! This is the property of the People!' Immediately twenty voices were crying, 'Stop! Put everything back! Don't take anything! Property of the People!' ...Roughly and hastily the things were crammed back in their cases, and self-appointed sentinels stood guard. It was all utterly spontaneous. Through corridors and up staircases the cry could be heard growing fainter and fainter in the distance, 'Revolutionary discipline! Property of the People.'

JOHN REED, *TEN DAYS THAT SHOOK THE WORLD*, 1919.

∞

The storming of the Winter Palace, the former residence of the tsars and the seat of the Russian government in St Petersburg, was the defining moment of 1917's October Revolution. Reed (1887–1920), an American socialist journalist, became close to many of the Bolshevik leaders, including Lenin and Trotsky, over the following six months. His early death, from typhus, preserved a reputation as a heroic idealist of a distinctly unusual American political hue. The Winter Palace now forms part of St Petersburg's vast collection of art, the Hermitage Museum.

ALSO ON THIS DAY

1913 The death of Alfred Russel Wallace, an early theorist of evolution.
1919 10,000 suspected US Communists and anarchists are arrested in the first Palmer Raid.
1929 The Museum of Modern Art opens in New York.

8 NOVEMBER

MONTEZUMA ENCOUNTERS
THE CONQUISTADORS, 1519

'I understand what you have said about the three gods and the cross... We have given you no answer since we have worshipped our own gods... and know them to be good. No doubt yours are good also but do not trouble to tell us any more about them at present, regarding the creation of the world, we have held the same belief for many ages and for this reason are certain that you are those who our ancestors predicted would come from the direction of the sunrise. As for your great king, I am in his debt and will give him of what I possess. Two years ago I had news of the captains who came in ships... and said they were servants of this great king of yours. I should like to know if you are all the same people.'

When Cortés answered that we were all brothers and servants of the Emperor... [Montezuma] said that ever since that time he had wanted to invite some of these men to visit his kingdom... and that now his gods had fulfilled his desire for we were in his house which we might call our own. Here we might rest and enjoy ourselves for we should receive good treatment. If on other occasions he had sent to forbid our entrance into his city, it was not of his own free will but because his vassals were afraid. For they told him we shot out flashes of lighting and killed many Indians with our horses... But now he had seen us he knew we were of flesh and blood and very intelligent. Therefore he... would share with us what he had.

BERNAL DÍAZ DEL CASTILLO, *THE TRUE HISTORY OF THE CONQUEST OF NEW SPAIN*, 1576.

Montezuma II, ruler (1502–20) of the Aztec Empire in what is now central Mexico, allowed the Spanish conquistador Hernán Cortés and his small army into his capital Tenochtitlan, on the site of modern-day Mexico City, thinking that they were the gods foretold by ancient prophecies. One of the 'gods' was the soldier Bernal Díaz del Castillo, who went on, years later, to create his retrospective narrative.

Nine months after the Spaniards arrived, as Aztec–Spanish relations deteriorated into violence, Montezuma was dead, possibly at Spanish hands and possibly at those of his people. The Aztec Empire fell shortly thereafter.

ALSO ON THIS DAY

1793 French Revolution: the former royal palace of the Louvre opens as a museum.
1889 Montana becomes the 41st US state.
1987 An IRA bombing kills 12 at a Remembrance Day ceremony in Enniskillen, Northern Ireland.

9 NOVEMBER

THE FALL OF THE BERLIN WALL, 1989

We have decided on a new regulation today that makes it possible for every citizen of the GDR [German Democratic Republic, i.e. East Germany] to exit via border crossing points of the GDR. Private trips abroad can be applied for without questions, and applications will be dealt with at high speed. The People's Police have been instructed to hand out long-term exit visas without delay, and the conditions which have applied up until now are redundant... As far as I know, immediately, without delay.

BERLIN COMMUNIST PARTY PRESS SECRETARY GÜNTER SCHABOWSKI,
6.53 P.M. ON 9 NOVEMBER 1989.

∞

[7.15pm] I wanted to know if it was right that GDR citizens were allowed to travel abroad, because it was clear that Schabowski could not just give such an order. There was a chain of command, measures that would have to be prepared and of course we would need extra personnel at the checkpoint to cope with such a measure: stamps, technical equipment, everything. There would have to be a regulation about which document they were allowed to travel abroad with. We didn't know which document we would have to ask citizens to present.

[7.30pm, 50–100 people assembled at the Bornholmer Strasse checkpoint.] They were asking if they could travel. I told them it was not possible because according to our regulations they needed a passport and visa. I told them to come back the following day, and some of them went away.

[11pm, a large crowd was demanding passage to the West.] Although I was their superior, the people I was working with that night were experiencing what I was. They kept demanding that I do something but I was not sure what to do. So I kept asking them: 'What shall I do? Order you to shoot?' We kept discussing what to do, discussing what to do, discussing what to do...

All I was thinking about now was how to avoid bloodshed. There were so many people and they didn't have space to move. If a panic developed, people would have been crushed. We had the pistols, there were instructions not to use them but what if any of the men had lost his nerve? Even if he had shot in the air I cannot imagine what reaction that might have provoked. [He called headquarters and] I said: 'We will have to let all of them out.' The boss replied: 'You know your instructions and you must do only what they say.' I replied: 'It cannot be held any longer. We have to open the checkpoint. I will discontinue the checks and let the people out.'

[He had opened the checkpoint shortly before midnight, and 20,000 people went through.] 'My knees began to tremble and I had a very bad feeling in my stomach. I went to the telephone and rang headquarters, and said, 'Comrade Oberst [his boss's rank], I opened the border. I just couldn't hold it any longer. I let them all out.' He said: 'It's OK, *junge*'.

HARALD JÄGER, PASSPORT CONTROL OFFICER, BORNHOLMER STRASSE CHECKPOINT, BERLIN, INTERVIEW.

∞

The wall dividing East and West Berlin, symbol of the Cold War since 1961 (*see* 13 August), was opened on the chaotic night of 9 November 1989, allowing East Germans to cross freely to the West for the first time in almost 30 years. The Communist East German government, abandoned militarily by the Soviet Union and facing massive demonstrations, suddenly decided to remove restrictions on leaving the country at noon, and at 6 p.m. Günter Schabowski, a Politburo member speaking for the government, announced that the borders would be opened.

As soon as the news was broadcast, crowds flooded to the crossing points, where the border guards had no instructions. By midnight the Stasi secret police had ordered the opening of all gates, and an hour later thousands had crossed and people were hacking at the wall with pickaxes.

The scenes – so vastly different to the Soviet and Warsaw Pact quashing of popular unrest in Hungary in 1956 and Czechoslovakia in 1968 – could not have been a more potent expression of the lifting of the Iron Curtain (*see* 5 March). Without Soviet economic backing and military muscle, the Communist elites across Eastern Europe were too weak to resist popular pressure, and they quickly caved in – peaceably, except for the immediate spasm of violence in Romania and the complex unravelling of Yugoslavia that would follow in the 1990s and early 2000s.

The political impetus to reunify Germany was realized relatively quickly, in 1991, with Berlin once again the capital. But the economic challenge of integrating the affluent West with the decayed economy of the East created a new challenge.

ALSO ON THIS DAY
———
1494 The Medici family are expelled from Florence.
1918 Kaiser Wilhelm II of Germany abdicates.
1923 An attempted Nazi coup in Munich – the Beer-Hall Putsch – fails.

10 NOVEMBER

THE PUBLICATION OF
LADY CHATTERLEY'S LOVER, 1960

For having published this book, Penguin Books were prosecuted under the Obscene Publications Act, 1959 at the Old Bailey in London from 20 October to 2 November 1960. This edition is therefore dedicated to the twelve jurors, three women and nine men, who returned a verdict of 'Not Guilty' and thus made D. H. Lawrence's last novel available for the first time to the public in the United Kingdom.

DEDICATION OF THE SECOND PENGUIN EDITION, *LADY CHATTERLEY'S LOVER*, 1961.

∞

D.H. Lawrence's novel *Lady Chatterley's Lover*, originally published privately in Italy in 1928, was first published in Britain by Penguin Books on 10 November 1960. Previously, it had been banned on the grounds of obscenity for its unembarrassed descriptions of sex and its unabashed sexual dialogue, explicit and colloquial. (The fact that the fictional context was an affair that crossed the class divide, between the upper-class Lady Constance Chatterley and her gamekeeper, only deepened the novel's perniciousness in the eyes of some.)

The prompt for publication was the passing in 1959 of the Obscene Publications Act, which allowed a defence of 'redeeming social merit'. Having printed 200,000 copies, Penguin challenged the Director of Public Prosecutions to prosecute, and the case was heard at the Old Bailey in October 1960. Penguin called many leading literary figures and scholars in its defence, while the prosecuting counsel Mervyn Griffith-Jones was ridiculed for asking the jury to consider: 'Is it a book you would wish your wife or servants to read?'

The high-profile trial proved powerful publicity for the publisher, and when the book was published a week later, with the advertising slogan 'Now YOU can read it', long queues formed outside bookshops all over the country, and the novel sold out within minutes. Within a few months more than 3 million copies had been sold.

The case proved a watershed not only in British publishing history, but in the changing mores of Britain; it is often cited as the moment at which the liberal 'Sixties' began.

ALSO ON THIS DAY

1674 The Treaty of Westminster cedes American 'New Netherland' to England.
1938 The death of Mustafa Kemal ('Atatürk'), founding father of modern Turkey.
2001 The first Apple iPod is sold.

11 NOVEMBER

RAGING AT THE ARMISTICE, 1918

I could stand it no longer. It became impossible for me to sit still one minute more. Again everything went black before my eyes; I tottered and groped my way back to the dormitory, threw myself on the bunk, and dug my burning head into my blanket and pillow. Since the day when I had stood at my mother's grave, I had not wept... When in the long war years death snatched so many a dear comrade and friend from out of the ranks, it would have seemed to me almost a sin to complain. And so it had all been in vain.

In vain all the sacrifices and privations; in vain the hunger and thirst of months which were often endless; in vain the hours in which, with mortal fear clutching at our hearts, we nevertheless did our duty; and in vain the deaths of the two million who died. Would not the graves of all the hundreds of thousands open, the graves of those who, with faith in the fatherland had marched forth never to return? Would they not open and send the silent mud- and blood-covered heroes back as spirits of vengeance to the homeland which had cheated them with such mockery of the highest sacrifice which a man can make to his people in this world? Had they died for this?... Was this the meaning of the sacrifice which the German mother made to the fatherland when, with sore heart, she let her best-loved boys march off, never to see them again?

...The shame of indignation and the disgrace of defeat burned my brow... In these nights, hatred grew in me, hatred for those responsible for this deed... I decided, for my part, to go into politics.

ADOLF HITLER, MEIN KAMPF, 1925.

∞

The armistice that ended the Great War came into effect at 11 a.m. on 11 November 1918, a relief for most. But the Germany that sued for peace was very different from the self-confident power of 1914; now Kaiser Wilhelm was in exile, and nationalists, such as the 29-year-old Hitler, saw the armistice as a betrayal of a German army un-defeated in the field. The belief grew that Germany had been 'stabbed in the back', and a search for scapegoats began. The reparations imposed on Germany at Versailles, in 1919, merely stoked the resentment, sowing the seeds of future conflict.

ALSO ON THIS DAY

1215 The Catholic doctrine of transubstantiation is defined at the Fourth Lateran Council.
1869 The Aboriginal Protection Act is passed in Australia.
1965 The white-minority government of Rhodesia makes a Unilateral Declaration of Independence.

12 NOVEMBER

JULES LÉOTARD FLIES TO FAME, 1859

He'd fly through the air with the greatest of ease
That daring young man on the flying trapeze.
His movements were graceful
All girls he could please
And my love he purloined away.

GEORGE LEYBOURNE, MUSIC-HALL SONG, 1867.

The original 'Daring young man on the flying trapeze', Frenchman Jules Léotard, gave his first performance for the Cirque de Napoléon in Paris on 12 November 1859, to huge acclaim: a commemorative medal was struck in his honour. The same year another circus performer, Blondin, achieved similar fame when he crossed the Niagara Falls on a tightrope.

Born in Toulouse in 1842, Léotard developed his novel aerial act over a swimming pool run by his father, though in public he used a pile of mattresses in case of accidents. Although he trained for the law, he found the flying trapeze, where he performed somersaults in mid-air while flying from trapeze to trapeze, more rewarding as a career.

His audience appeal was partly for his daring, and partly for his appearance, as he wore a one-piece body-hugging costume that left little to the imagination. It was not called a *leotard* until many years after his death, but the name stuck. Léotard earned a fortune performing across Europe – in London he performed above the heads of diners at the Alhambra Theatre – and the United States; but he died in 1870 in Spain, from smallpox or cholera, aged only 28. His achievements and allure were immortalized in George Leybourne's music-hall song.

ALSO ON THIS DAY

1912 The bodies of Robert Falcon Scott and his men are found in Antarctica.
1927 Leon Trotsky is expelled from Stalin's Soviet Union.
1969 Vietnam War: the first accounts of the My Lai massacre, by Seymour Hersh, appear.

13 NOVEMBER

CHARLES DICKENS ATTENDS A HANGING, 1849

I was a witness of the execution at Horsemonger Lane this morning... I believe that a sight so inconceivably awful as the wickedness and levity of the immense crowd collected at that execution this morning could be imagined by no man, and could be presented in no heathen land under the sun. The horrors of the gibbet and of the crime which brought the wretched murderers to it faded in my mind before the atrocious bearing, looks, and language of the assembled spectators. When I came upon the scene at midnight, the *shrillness* of the cries and howls that were raised from time to time... made my blood run cold. As the night went on, screeching, and laughing, and yelling in strong chorus of parodies on negro melodies... were added to these. When the day dawned, thieves, low prostitutes, ruffians, and vagabonds of every kind, flocked on to the ground, with every variety of offensive and foul behaviour. Fightings, faintings, whistlings, imitations of Punch, brutal jokes, tumultuous demonstrations of indecent delight when swooning women were dragged out of the crowd by the police, with their dresses disordered, gave a new zest to the general entertainment. When the sun rose brightly – as it did – it gilded thousands upon thousands of upturned faces, so inexpressibly odious in their brutal mirth or callousness, that a man had cause to feel ashamed of the shape he wore, and to shrink from himself, as fashioned in the image of the Devil. When the two miserable creatures who attracted all this ghastly sight about them were turned quivering into the air, there was no more emotion, no more pity, no more thought that two immortal souls had gone to judgement, no more restraint in any of the previous obscenities, than if the name of Christ had never been heard in this world, and there were no belief among men but that they perished like the beasts.

CHARLES DICKENS, LETTER TO *THE TIMES*, 13 NOVEMBER 1849.

∞

Thus Charles Dickens – forensic observer of London life – excoriated the baying multitudes that attended a public hanging. Eloquently, he characterized the 'spectacle' as one that degraded its onlookers. *The Times* opposed reform, but in May 1868 public executions were ended by the Capital Punishment Amendment Act.

ALSO ON THIS DAY

1002 The 'St Brice's Day' massacre of Danes in England.
1903 The death of the French Impressionist artist Camille Pissarro.
1979 *The Times* reappears after a year-long absence due to an industrial dispute.

14 NOVEMBER

THE DESTRUCTION OF COVENTRY CATHEDRAL, 1940

The famous Cathedral is little more than a skeleton, masses of rubble forming huge mounds within its bare walls... The Provost (the Very Rev. R. T. Howard) and a party of cathedral watchers attempted to deal with twelve incendiary bombs. They tackled them with sand and attempted to smother them, until a shower of other incendiaries, accompanied this time by high explosives, rendered impossible their efforts to save the cathedral, only the tower and steeple of which remain. 'The cathedral,' said the Provost, 'will rise again, will be rebuilt, and it will be as great a pride to future generations as it has been to generations in the past.'

Tonight the Cathedral was a reeking shell. Blackened arches and window faces of fretted stone, still stately for all their disfigurement, framed a picture of hideous destruction. Blocks of masonry, heavy pieces of church furniture, and plaques commemorating famous men were merged into a common dust. In addition to the two churches, a Methodist chapel was wrecked, as well as a library (with thousands of volumes and treasured manuscripts), a hall, a ward and operating theatre of one hospital, the outbuildings of an isolation hospital, two hotels, and a newspaper office.

Manchester Guardian, 16 November, 1940.

∞

On the night of 14–15 November 1940, German bombers dropped 500 tonnes of high explosives, including 36,000 incendiary bombs, on the industrial city of Coventry in the English Midlands. The raid destroyed the 14th-century St Michael's Cathedral, flattened 4,000 homes and killed more than 560 people in one of the most devastating raids of the Blitz. A new cathedral, designed by Basil Spence and built next to the remains of the old one, was reconsecrated on 25 May 1962. (*See also* 7 September.) Benjamin Britten's *War Requiem* was commissioned for the consecration of the new cathedral, and premiered there on 30 May 1962.

ALSO ON THIS DAY

1922 The BBC begins its radio service in the UK.
1969 The *Apollo 12* mission to the Moon is launched.
1990 A German–Polish treaty accepts their post-WWII border.

15 NOVEMBER

ATLANTA IN FLAMES, 1864

We rode out of Atlanta by the Decatur road, filled by the marching troops and wagons of the Fourteenth Corps; and reaching the hill, just outside of the old rebel works, we naturally paused to look back upon the scenes of our past battles. We stood upon the very ground whereon was fought the bloody battle [for Atlanta] of July 22nd [1864], and could see the copse of wood where McPherson fell. Behind us lay Atlanta, smouldering and in ruins, the black smoke rising high in air, and hanging like a pall over the ruined city. Away off in the distance, on the McDonough road, was the rear of Howard's column, the gun-barrels glistening in the sun, the white-topped wagons stretching away to the south; and right before us the Fourteenth Corps, marching steadily and rapidly, with a cheery look and swinging pace, that made light of the thousand miles that lay between us and Richmond. Some band, by accident, struck up the anthem of 'John Brown's soul goes marching on'; the men caught up the strain, and never before or since have I heard the chorus of 'Glory, glory, hallelujah!' done with more spirit, or in better harmony of time and place.

WILLIAM T. SHERMAN, *MEMOIRS OF GENERAL W.T. SHERMAN*, 1889.

∞

The Unionist general William Tecumseh Sherman, having driven back the Confederate Army of Tennessee during the summer of 1864, took the key city of Atlanta, Georgia, in September. On 15 November he left the city in flames, reflecting a new strategy that would not only fight enemy combatants but also destroy their material and economic infrastructure. On that day he and his men began what became known as their 'March to the Sea' through enemy territory, which ended in Savannah in December. *En route* they implemented a policy of scorched earth, to demoralize the enemy and undermine the South's will to fight on.

The exhausted Confederacy would finally surrender at Appomattox Court House, Virginia, the following spring (*see* 9 April), bringing America's Civil War to an end.

ALSO ON THIS DAY

1630 The death of the German astronomer-mathematician Johannes Kepler.
1917 The death of the French sociologist Émile Durkheim.
1942 WWII: US forces defeat the Japanese at Guadalcanal.

16 NOVEMBER

THE CAPTURE OF THE INCA EMPEROR, 1532

Few of us slept that night, and we kept watch in the square of Cajamarca, looking at the campfires of the Indian army... on a hillside and so close to each other that it looked like the sky brightly studded with stars...

Next morning a messenger arrived, and the governor said: 'Tell your lord to come when and how he pleases, and that I will receive him as a friend and brother. No harm or insult will befall him.' At noon Atahuallpa began to approach... Eighty lords carried him on their shoulders, all wearing a rich blue livery. Atahuallpa himself was richly dressed, with his crown on his head and a collar of large emeralds. The litter was lined with parrot feathers of many colours and decorated with plates of gold and silver.

...In the meantime all of us Spaniards were waiting, hidden in a courtyard, full of fear. Many of us urinated without noticing it, out of sheer terror. On reaching the centre of the plaza, Atahuallpa remained in his litter on high.

Governor Pizarro now sent Friar Vicente de Valverde to require Atahuallpa to subject himself to the law of our Lord Jesus Christ and to the service of His Majesty the King of Spain. Advancing with a cross in one hand and the Bible in the other, the friar addressed him: 'I am a priest of God, and I teach Christians the things of God, and in like manner I come to teach you. What I teach is that which God says to us in this book. Therefore, I beseech you to be their friend, for such is God's will, and it will be for your good.'

Atahuallpa asked for the book and the friar gave it to him closed. Atahuallpa did not know how to open the book, and the friar was extending his arm to do so, when Atahuallpa, in great anger, gave him a blow on the arm, not wishing that it should be opened. Then he opened it himself, and, without any astonishment at the letters and paper he threw it away from him five or six paces, his face a deep crimson.

...The governor gave the signal... to fire off the guns. The trumpets were sounded, and the Spanish troops sallied forth into the mass of unarmed Indians crowding the square. We had placed rattles on the horses to terrify the Indians. The booming of the guns, the blowing of the trumpets, and the rattles on the horses threw the Indians into confusion. The Spaniards fell upon them and began to cut them to pieces...

The governor himself... with great bravery reached Atahuallpa's litter. He grabbed Atahuallpa's left arm but he could not pull Atahuallpa out of his litter because it was held up high. Although we killed the Indians who held the litter, others took their places and held it aloft... Finally seven or eight Spaniards on horseback spurred on their horses, rushed upon the litter from one side, and heaved it over on its side. Atahuallpa was captured, and the governor took Atahuallpa to his lodging.

...If night had not come on, few out of the more than 40,000 Indian troops would have been left alive...

The governor ordered Atahuallpa to sit near him and soothed his rage at finding himself so quickly fallen from his high estate. The governor said: 'Do not take it as an insult that you have been defeated... I have conquered greater kingdoms than yours, and have defeated other more powerful lords than you, imposing upon them the dominion of the Emperor, whose vassal I am, and who is King of Spain and of the universal world... Our Lord permitted that your pride should be brought low and that no Indian should be able to offend a Christian.'

Francisco de Xeres, Narrative of the Conquest of Peru, 1530–34.

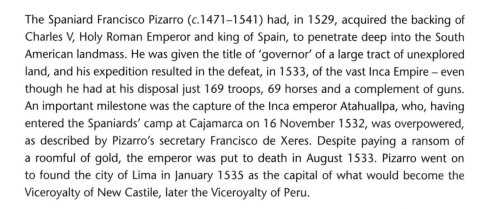

The Spaniard Francisco Pizarro (c.1471–1541) had, in 1529, acquired the backing of Charles V, Holy Roman Emperor and king of Spain, to penetrate deep into the South American landmass. He was given the title of 'governor' of a large tract of unexplored land, and his expedition resulted in the defeat, in 1533, of the vast Inca Empire – even though he had at his disposal just 169 troops, 69 horses and a complement of guns. An important milestone was the capture of the Inca emperor Atahuallpa, who, having entered the Spaniards' camp at Cajamarca on 16 November 1532, was overpowered, as described by Pizarro's secretary Francisco de Xeres. Despite paying a ransom of a roomful of gold, the emperor was put to death in August 1533. Pizarro went on to found the city of Lima in January 1535 as the capital of what would become the Viceroyalty of New Castile, later the Viceroyalty of Peru.

ALSO ON THIS DAY

1724 The English thief and serial prison escapee Jack Sheppard is hanged at Tyburn.
1938 The drug LSD is synthesized for the first time, by a Swiss chemist.
1979 Sir Anthony Blunt is revealed as the 'fourth man' in the Cambridge spy ring.

17 NOVEMBER

THE JOYOUSNESS OF STALINISM, 1935

Life has improved, comrades. Life has become more joyous. And when life is joyous, work goes well...

Our proletarian revolution is the only revolution in the world which had the opportunity of showing the people not only political results but also material results. Of all workers' revolutions, we know only one which managed to achieve power. That was the Paris Commune. But it did not last long. True, it endeavoured to smash the fetters of capitalism; but it did not have time enough to smash them, and still less to show the people the beneficial material results of revolution.

Our revolution is the only one which not only smashed the fetters of capitalism and brought the people freedom, but also succeeded in creating the material conditions of a prosperous life for the people. Therein lies the strength and invincibility of our revolution... But, unfortunately, freedom alone is not enough, by far.

If there is a shortage of bread, a shortage of butter and fats, a shortage of textiles, and if housing conditions are bad, freedom will not carry you very far. It is very difficult, comrades, to live on freedom alone. In order to live well and joyously, the benefits of political freedom must be supplemented by material benefits. It is a distinctive feature of our revolution that it brought the people not only freedom, but also material benefits and the possibility of a prosperous and cultured life. That is why life has become joyous in our country.

JOSEPH STALIN, SPEECH, CONFERENCE OF STAKHANOVITES, 17 NOVEMBER 1935.

∞

Despite the famine of 1932 caused by rapid collectivization of agriculture in the First Five-Year Plan for the Soviet Union (1928–33), Stalin launched a Second Five-Year Plan in 1933, this time focusing on a rapid expansion of industrial output. As part of this plan, he celebrated the indefatigable work of labourers such as the miner Aleksei Grigorievich Stakhanov, who was said to have extracted over 100 tons of coal in one five-hour period in August 1935.

Despite the sticks and carrots offered, not all the efforts of ordinary workers matched the feats of these Stakhanovite Heroes of Soviet Labour. And the lives of many Soviet citizens were rather less than 'joyous'.

ALSO ON THIS DAY

1558 The death of England's Queen Mary I ('Bloody Mary').
1869 The Suez Canal is opened to shipping.
1986 George Besse, the head of the Renault car company, is assassinated in Paris.

18 NOVEMBER

THE REVOLUTIONARY WILLIAM TELL, 1307

Gessler: Then, Tell, since at a hundred yards thou canst
Bring down the apple from the tree, thou shalt
Approve thy skill before me. Take thy bow –
Thou hast it there at hand – make ready, then,
To shoot an apple from the stripling's head!
But take this counsel, – look well to thine aim,
See, that thou hit'st the apple at the first,
For, shouldst thou miss, thy head shall pay the forfeit...

Walter: Grandfather, do not kneel to that bad man!
Say, where am I to stand? I do not fear;
My father strikes the bird upon the wing,
And will not miss now when 'twould harm his boy!

...Do you think I fear
An arrow from my father's hand? Not I!
I'll wait it firmly, nor so much as wink!
Quick, father, show them what thy bow can do.
He doubts thy skill – he thinks to ruin us.
Shoot then and hit, though but to spite the tyrant!

FRIEDRICH SCHILLER, *WILLIAM TELL*, SCENE III, 1804.

On 18 November 1307 William Tell, from the Swiss canton of Uri, refused to doff his hat to one placed on a post in the town square by the Austrian bailiff Gessler. As a punishment Gessler forced Tell to shoot an apple, placed on his son Walter's head, with his crossbow, from 100 paces. Although Tell succeeded, Gessler still held him in prison; but Tell escaped, ambushed and killed Gessler, and then led an uprising against Austrian rule.

Such, at any rate, is the legend of William Tell, as first recounted by Aegidius Tschudi in about 1570. There is, though, no evidence for Tell's existence or for the major uprising that he is supposed to have led. Nevertheless, the legend became a major theme in Swiss national identity after the German playwright Schiller adopted it.

ALSO ON THIS DAY

1922 The death of the French novelist Marcel Proust.
1962 The death of the Danish physicist Niels Bohr.
1978 918 cult members commit mass suicide at Jim Jones's People's Temple, Guyana.

19 NOVEMBER

THE GETTYSBURG ADDRESS, 1863

Four score and seven years ago our fathers brought forth on this continent a new nation, conceived in liberty, and dedicated to the proposition that all men are created equal.

Now we are engaged in a great civil war, testing whether that nation, or any nation, so conceived and so dedicated, can long endure. We are met on a great battle-field of that war. We have come to dedicate a portion of that field, as a final resting place for those who here gave their lives that that nation might live. It is altogether fitting and proper that we should do this.

But, in a larger sense, we can not dedicate, we can not consecrate, we can not hallow this ground. The brave men, living and dead, who struggled here, have consecrated it, far above our poor power to add or detract. The world will little note, nor long remember what we say here, but it can never forget what they did here. It is for us the living, rather, to be dedicated here to the unfinished work which they who fought here have thus far so nobly advanced. It is rather for us to be here dedicated to the great task remaining before us – that from these honoured dead we take increased devotion to that cause for which they gave the last full measure of devotion – that we here highly resolve that these dead shall not have died in vain – that this nation, under God, shall have a new birth of freedom – and that government of the people, by the people, for the people, shall not perish from the earth.

ABRAHAM LINCOLN, SPEECH, 19 NOVEMBER 1863.

US President Lincoln, facing growing opposition for the human cost of the American Civil War, gave this speech – just ten sentences long, taking two minutes to deliver – when dedicating the Soldiers' National Cemetery at Gettysburg, Pennsylvania, scene of what proved the war's decisive encounter four months previously (*see* 3 July). Despite a mixed initial reception – and Lincoln's own doubts about its memorability – the Gettysburg Address has become regarded as one of the great pieces of modern oratory, and its very concision seems to encapsulate the essence of American idealism.

ALSO ON THIS DAY

1942: WWII: Operation Uranus begins the Soviet counter-attack at Stalingrad.
1967 The British prime minister Harold Wilson defends the devaluation of sterling.
1977 Egypt's Anwar Sadat becomes the first Arab leader to visit Israel.

20 NOVEMBER

THE REAL MOBY-DICK, 1820

He was enveloped in the foam of the sea, that his continual and violent thrashing about in the water had created around him, and I could distinctly see him smite his jaws together, as if distracted with rage and fury. He remained a short time in this situation, then started off with great velocity across the bows of the ship to windward. By this time the ship had settled down a considerable distance in the water, and I gave her up as lost...

I turned around and saw him about a hundred rods directly ahead of us, coming down apparently with twice his ordinary speed, at to me at that moment it appeared with tenfold fury and vengeance in his aspect. The surf flew in all directions about him, and his course towards us was marked with a white foam of a rod in width, which he made with the continual violent thrashing of his tail; his head was about half out of the water, and in that way he came upon, and again struck the ship... He struck her to windward, directly under the cathead [a beam on the bow of a sailing-ship], and completely stove in her bows. He passed under the ship again, went off to leeward, and we saw no more of him.

OWEN CHASE, *NARRATIVE OF THE MOST EXTRAORDINARY AND DISTRESSING SHIPWRECK OF THE WHALE-SHIP ESSEX*, 1821.

The American whaler *Essex* was attacked and sunk in the Pacific by a huge sperm whale, apparently infuriated by hammering on the hull, on 20 November 1820. Of the crew, 21 men managed to reach an uninhabited island of the Pitcairns, where just eight survived to be rescued four months later, having had to survive through cannibalism.

The account of the tragedy by First Mate Owen Chase proved an inspiration to the young Herman Melville while he was himself serving on a whaler. He later adapted the story for his epic novel *Moby-Dick* (1851), which, with various digressions and a cornucopia of whaling lore, traces the vengeful hunt across the world's oceans by the one-legged Captain Ahab for the eponymous whale, which had, on an earlier occasion, relieved him of his other leg.

ALSO ON THIS DAY

AD 284 Diocletian becomes Roman emperor.
1945 The Nuremberg war crimes trials begin.
1975 The death of the Spanish dictator Francisco Franco.

21 NOVEMBER

THE FIRST MANNED BALLOON FLIGHT, 1783

Today... an experiment was made with the aerostatic machine of M. Montgolfier... The Marquis d'Arlandes and M. Pilâtre des Roziers were in the gallery. The first intention was to raise the machine and pull it back with ropes, to test it, to find out the exact weight which it could carry... But the machine, driven by the wind, far from rising vertically, was directed upon one of the walks of a garden, and the cords which held it shook with so much force that several rents were made in the balloon. The machine, being brought back to its place, was repaired in less than two hours. Being again inflated, it rose once more, bearing the same persons, and when it had risen to the height of 250 feet, the intrepid voyagers, bowing their heads, saluted the spectators. One could not resist a feeling of mingled fear and admiration. Soon the aeronauts were lost to view, but the balloon itself, displaying its very beautiful shape, mounted to the height of 3,000 feet, and still remained visible. The voyagers, satisfied with their experience, and not wishing to make a longer course, agreed to descend, but, perceiving that the wind was driving them upon the houses of the Rue de Sèvres, preserved their self-possession, renewed the hot air, rose anew and continued their course till they had passed Paris.

They then descended tranquilly in the country, beyond the new boulevard, without having experienced the slightest inconvenience, having still the greater part of their fuel untouched.

BENJAMIN FRANKLIN, QUOTED IN F. MARION, *WONDERFUL BALLOON ASCENTS*, 1870.

∞

Although a manned balloon flight had been made in June 1783, the first untethered flight took place in November of that year, setting off from the Bois de Boulogne in western Paris and crossing the city in 25 minutes. The finely decorated hot-air balloon, or *globe aerostatique*, was designed by the Montgolfier brothers Joseph-Michel (1740–1810) and Jacques-Étienne (1745–99), and it carried the Marquis d'Arlandes and Pilâtre des Roziers over the city's rooftops. The novelty of manned flight was a source of fascination for the American scientist Benjamin Franklin, then resident as a diplomat; and it caught the public imagination. However, hot air was soon superseded by hydrogen, and it was a hydrogen balloon that was the first to cross the English Channel in 1785.

ALSO ON THIS DAY

1811 The death of the German poet and dramatist Heinrich von Kleist.
1877 Thomas Edison unveils his 'phonograph'.
1974 The IRA's Birmingham pub bombings kill 21 people.

22 NOVEMBER

THE ASSASSINATION OF
PRESIDENT JOHN F. KENNEDY, 1963

Here is a bulletin from CBS News. Further details on an assassination attempt against President Kennedy in Dallas, Texas. President Kennedy was shot as he drove from Dallas Airport to downtown Dallas; Governor Connally of Texas, in the car with him, was also shot. It is reported that three bullets rang out. A Secret Service man has been... [sic] was heard to shout from the car, 'He's dead.' Whether he referred to President Kennedy or not is not yet known. The president, cradled in the arms of his wife Mrs. Kennedy, was carried to an ambulance and the car rushed to Parkland Hospital outside Dallas, the president was taken to an emergency room in the hospital. Other White House officials were in doubt in the corridors of the hospital as to the condition of President Kennedy. Repeating this bulletin: President Kennedy shot while driving in an open car from the airport in Dallas, Texas, to downtown Dallas.

WALTER CRONKITE, CBS BROADCAST, 22 NOVEMBER 1963.

∞

The assassination in Dallas of the US president John F. Kennedy was first reported on CBS Television by the anchorman Walter Cronkite, at 1.40 p.m. EST (Eastern Standard Time), just ten minutes after the shooting happened. A live broadcast of a soap opera was interrupted by audio bulletins from Cronkite several times as more information emerged; by 2.30 p.m. he had reported that the president was dead. It was the dramatic end to a presidency of which there had been much expectation, and which had grappled with crises such as the building of the Berlin Wall (*see* 13 August) and the Cuban Missile Crisis (*see* 22 October).

In the complex and chaotic events of the next 72 hours, during which Vice-President Lyndon Baines Johnson succeeded the murdered Kennedy as 36th US president, it was Cronkite (1916–2009) who became the lynchpin of the reporting, and many Americans associate his voice with one of the most traumatic and vividly remembered events of the 20th century. (*See also* 31 January.)

ALSO ON THIS DAY

1869 The last-surviving tea clipper the *Cutty Sark* is launched.
1916 The death of the US writer Jack London.
1928 Ravel's *Boléro* is first performed at the Paris Opera.

23 NOVEMBER

MILTON INVEIGHS AGAINST CENSORSHIP, 1644

Though all the winds of doctrine were let loose to play upon the earth, so Truth be in the field, we do injuriously, by licensing and prohibiting, to misdoubt her strength. Let her and falsehood grapple; who ever knew truth put to the worse, in a free and open encounter?

JOHN MILTON, *AREOPAGITICA*, 1644.

As a young man, the poet John Milton (1608–74) was a polemicist supporting the Parliamentarian cause in the English Civil War. Written at the height of the conflict, and in a period when governments and churchmen of all hues took for granted their right to vet material for publication, his tract *Areopagitica: A Speech for the Liberty of Unlicensed Printing* was published on 23 November 1644. It comprised a trenchant attack on censorship and has often been regarded since as one of the finest defences of free speech. In it, Milton argued that the interests of truth could never be advanced by restricting the right of others to speak.

Milton was writing in response to a Licensing Order issued the previous year, in which Parliament had attempted to reimpose controls over publication that had been removed when the traditional Court of the Star Chamber was abolished in 1641. Additionally, he had himself experienced, the previous year, an encounter with official censorship when he attempted to publish a pamphlet on the morality of divorce.

After the execution of Charles I in 1649 (*see* 30 January), Milton became a polemicist on behalf of republicanism, and he defended regicide in a tract published in October that year. Nevertheless, his greatest work, dictated after he had succumbed to blindness in the 1650s, appeared in print in the very different atmosphere of post-Restoration England: the epic poem *Paradise Lost*, published in 1667.

ALSO ON THIS DAY

1499 Perkin Warbeck, a pretender to the English throne, is hanged.
1940 WWII: Romania joins the Axis powers.
1963 The first episode of the science-fiction series *Dr Who* is broadcast on BBC TV.

24 NOVEMBER

ON THE ORIGIN OF SPECIES IS PUBLISHED, 1859

Owing to this struggle for life, any variation, however slight and from whatever cause proceeding, if it be in any degree profitable to an individual of any species, in its infinitely complex relationship to other organic beings and to external nature, will tend to the preservation of that individual, and will generally be inherited by its offspring. The offspring, also, will thus have a better chance of surviving, for, of the many individuals of any species which are periodically born, but a small number can survive. I have called this principle, by which each slight variation, if useful, is preserved, by the term Natural Selection, in order to mark its relation to man's power of selection.

CHARLES DARWIN, *ON THE ORIGIN OF SPECIES BY MEANS OF NATURAL SELECTION*, 1859.

∞

On the Origin of Species, published on 24 November 1859, was one of the most controversial books of the 19th century, being the means by which the naturalist Charles Darwin outlined, for a non-specialist readership, his theory of 'natural selection' – that species evolve and acquire distinctive characteristics not by adaptation but by a continual competition in which effective adaptations succeed while less effective ones tend to die out.

The book presented the evidence that Darwin had gathered during his expedition to South American waters and the Galápagos Islands in HMS *Beagle* in the 1830s (*see* 17 September), as well as findings from his long researches into barnacles and many other species. Darwin had in fact reached his conclusions by the late 1830s, but they worried him sufficiently for him to hold back from publication until he learned that another scientist, Alfred Russel Wallace, had come to similar conclusions. Darwin, a former student of divinity and well aware that the theory flew in the face of conventional Christian belief about Creation and Man's place within Nature, nevertheless asserted that 'There is grandeur in this view of life.'

The book sold out immediately and was reprinted several times. It was not until the fifth edition that the phrase 'survival of the fittest' was included.

ALSO ON THIS DAY

1642 The Dutchman Abel Tasman sights Van Diemen's Land (Tasmania).
1963 Lee Harvey Oswald, arrested for killing President Kennedy, is shot dead.
2005 New UK licensing laws allow some pubs to stay open round the clock.

25 NOVEMBER

THE GREAT STORM OVER ENGLAND, 1703

The author of this relation was in a well-built brick house in the skirts of the City [of London]; and a stack of chimneys falling in upon the next houses, gave the house such a shock, that they thought it was just coming down upon their heads: but opening the door to attempt an escape into a garden, the danger was so apparent, that they all thought fit to surrender to the disposal of Almighty Providence, and expect their graves in the ruins of the house, rather than to meet most certain destruction the open garden... the author of this has seen tiles blown from a house above thirty or forty yards, and stuck from five to eight inches into the solid earth.

...Indeed the City was a strange spectacle the morning after the storm, as soon as the people could put their heads out of doors... The streets lay so covered with tiles and slates, from the tops of the houses, especially in the out-parts, that the quantity is incredible: and the houses were so universally stripped, that all the tiles in fifty miles round would be able to repair but a small part of it. Something may be guessed at on this head, from the sudden rise of the price of tiles; which rise from 21s. per thousand to 6 l. [21 shillings to £6] for plain tiles; and from 50s. per thousand for pantiles, to 10 l. and bricklayers' labour to 5s. per day.

DANIEL DEFOE, *THE STORM*, 1704.

The young Daniel Defoe's first full-length book was a vivid survey, full of dramatic first-hand and eye-witness accounts, of a huge storm that ravaged southern and central England in November 1703. The storm killed an estimated 15,000 people, including the celebrated engineer Henry Winstanley who was working on his new Eddystone Lighthouse when it collapsed. The winds were said to have hit 120 mph, in what Defoe described as a 'perfect hurricane', and even the lead on Westminster Abbey's roof was 'rolled up like parchment and blown clear of the building'.

ALSO ON THIS DAY

1120 William, the heir of Henry I of England, drowns when the *White Ship* sinks.
1748 The death of the prolific English hymn writer Isaac Watts.
1938 Germany and Japan sign the Anti-Comintern Pact.

26 NOVEMBER

THE DISCOVERY OF TUTANKHAMUN'S TOMB, 1922

With trembling hands, I made a tiny breach in the upper left hand corner... widening the hole a little, I inserted the candle and peered in... at first I could see nothing, the hot air escaping from the chamber causing the candle to flicker. Presently, details of the room emerged slowly from the mist, strange animals, statues and gold – everywhere the glint of gold. For the moment – an eternity it must have seemed to the others standing by – I was struck dumb with amazement, and when Lord Carnarvon, unable to stand in suspense any longer, inquired anxiously: 'Can you see anything?', it was all I could do to get out the words: 'Yes, wonderful things'.

HOWARD CARTER, *THE TOMB OF TUTANKHAMUN*, 1923.

The most celebrated discovery in archaeology occurred in Egypt's Valley of the Kings in November 1923 when, after five years of fruitless searching, archaeologist Howard Carter, accompanied by his sponsor Lord Carnarvon, peered into the antechamber of the tomb of Tutankhamun. The steps leading down to it had been spotted three weeks earlier. Unlike all other important Egyptian tombs, it had somehow escaped the attentions of ancient grave robbers and still contained both the sarcophagus and the grave goods that had been buried with the teenaged pharaoh on his death in the 14th century BC. Carter and his team opened the door of the tomb itself a few months later.

Tutankhamun, a pharaoh during Egypt's New Kingdom (16th–11th centuries BC), reigned for only a few years (c. 1333–1323 BC), at a time of political uncertainty following the rule of his father Akhenaten, who had instituted the worship of a new god and built an entirely new capital at Amarna, both of which were immediately disowned by his young son. Although by Egyptian standards Tutankhamun's was probably not the most lavish of royal burials, the find proved sensational – not least in its dazzling and valuable artefacts – and continues to attract fascination all round the world.

ALSO ON THIS DAY

1504 The death of Queen Isabella I of Castile.
1855 The death of the Polish Romantic poet Adam Mickiewicz.
1983 Britain's largest robbery takes place, at the Brink's-MAT warehouse, Heathrow Airport.

27 NOVEMBER

POPE URBAN II EMBOLDENS THE CRUSADERS, 1095

All who die by the way, whether by land or by sea, or in battle against the pagans, shall have immediate remission of sins... O what a disgrace if such a despised and base race, which worships demons, should conquer a people which has the faith of omnipotent God and is made glorious with the name of Christ! With what reproaches will the Lord overwhelm us if you do not aid those who, with us, profess the Christian religion! Let those who have been accustomed unjustly to wage private warfare against the faithful now go against the infidels and end with victory this war which should have been begun long ago. Let those who, for a long time, have been robbers, now become knights. Let those who have been fighting against their brothers and relatives now fight in a proper way against the barbarians. Let those who have been serving as mercenaries for small pay now obtain the eternal reward. Let those who have been wearing themselves out in both body and soul now work for a double honour. Behold! On this side will be the sorrowful and poor, on that, the rich; on this side, the enemies of the Lord, on that, his friends. Let those who go not put off the journey, but rent their lands and collect money for their expenses; and as soon as winter is over and spring comes, let them eagerly set out on the way with God as their guide.

POPE URBAN II, QUOTED BY FULCHER OF CHARTRES,
A HISTORY OF THE EXPEDITION TO JERUSALEM, 1106.

∞

Pope Urban II initiated the first of the medieval crusades at the Church's Council of Clermont, in central France, in November 1095. There he urged Western Christians to stop fighting among themselves and to take up arms to assist the Byzantine emperor Alexis I Comnenus in his struggle against the Seljuk Turks in Anatolia, and to fight the Muslims occupying the sacred sites of the Holy Land. His speech was met by a general shout of *Deus vult*, 'God wills it'.

The crusading army, led mainly by French and Norman knights, left in August the following year, arriving at the Byzantine capital of Constantinople in the winter of 1096–7; they besieged and captured Antioch in 1098 (*see* 3 June) before taking Jerusalem in July 1099, slaughtering both Muslims and Jews in the aftermath.

ALSO ON THIS DAY

8 BC The death of the Roman lyric poet Horace.
1942 WWII: the French fleet scuttles its ships at Toulon to avoid German capture.
1967 French President de Gaulle vetoes UK membership of the EEC for a second time.

28 NOVEMBER

THE FIRST WOMEN VOTERS, 1893

I was first mistress at the Petone School. I was very interested in the women's franchise movement, organised by the Women's Christian Temperance Union.

Mrs Sheppard, who directed the franchise movement, would never have approved of violence. We put up with abusive criticism from our opponents, and some silly things were said about our ideas in Parliament. Many women wanted nothing to do with politics...

Before we could vote we had to enrol, and again we met many women who did not want the voting privilege. One of their strongest objections was that voting meant going to a public polling booth, among strange men. Women always had to have a male escort when they went out. The idea of asking them to enter a polling booth on election day, when things were rather lively, was so repellent to many people that an effort was made to introduce postal voting for women. That was not adopted.

But once the women had succeeded in getting the vote, all candidates were anxious to have their support. One candidate made a special appeal to the women. His baby son was paraded in a perambulator with a large placard – 'Vote for Daddy'.

MRS PERRYMAN, QUOTED IN NEW ZEALAND HISTORY ONLINE.

On 28 November 1893 New Zealand became the first country in the world where women voted in a general election, when universal suffrage was granted to women over the age of 21, including the indigenous Maori. Kate Sheppard, leader of the Temperance Union, had organized a petition in favour of the franchise, which was signed by a quarter of the potential female electorate. The *Christchurch Press* newspaper described the election as the 'best-conducted and most orderly' ever held, stating that 'the ladies and their smiling faces lighted up the polling booths most wonderfully'. (The Liberal Party won, and Richard Seddon became prime minister.) Kate Sheppard's image now appears on New Zealand's $10 note.

American women had wait until 1920 for similar rights, and British women until 1928.

ALSO ON THIS DAY

1859 The death of the US writer Washington Irving.
1905 Sinn Féin, an Irish nationalist party, is founded.
1990 The British prime minister Margaret Thatcher formally resigns.

29 NOVEMBER

ASIA'S FIRST PARLIAMENT, 1890

I have just seen the birth of a new Parliament, the first assembly of its kind known to the continent of Asia, modelled on European systems, traditions and precedents and meeting for its very first visible embodiment, with all constitutional forms and ceremonies under the imperial patronage and presence of the Mikado [the Japanese emperor], lately a sovereign so removed from mortal sight and spheres as to be almost regarded as a deity, but today viewed discharging the duties of a constitutional monarch…

…The government and the nation have been educating themselves up to this high point of progress ever since the opening of the Meiji era, a quarter of a century ago. Then, as you well know, the power of the Shogunate fell; authority was stripped from those proud and despotic lords who had kept the Mikado in seclusion like a gilded idol.

…They come! There is heard outside a fanfare of military music just as the clock strikes 11… The Emperor has reached the building and reposes awhile in the state apartment, while the peers and commons arrive and take their places. The peers of Dai Nippon [Great Japan] are led to their seats by Count Ito, all wearing coats of honour – deep blue, heavily embroidered with gold – and with the imperial kiku. It is an effect as of the plumage of pheasants, or a great jeweller's display of gold and diamonds on dark velvet… Then follow the faithful Commons, all to a man in evening costume of the strictest propriety, with high silk or opera hats…

The Lord High Chamberlain has informed His Imperial Majesty that all is ready and, conducted by that great official and the other court dignitaries, the Mikado enters through the right door of the elevated platform. At his side by a little behind walk the princes of the blood, and immediately before His Majesty paces a grandee carrying a copy of the constitution wrapped up in green silk powdered with gold chrysanthemums… As the emperor stands before the throne, all in the assembly bow profoundly. Every person present is reverentially attentive – it is the moment of the birth of the First Asiatic Parliament.

The emperor is dressed in the uniform of a generalissimo of the army, and wears the red *dai-gusho* ribbon of the Order of the Rising Sun as his principal decoration. Tall in comparison with most of his subjects, watchful dark eyes, a slight beard and moustache, and manners at once gracious yet imperturbably reserved, the Mikado looks as different from the pictures of his imperial ancestors as the spirit governing the proceedings of today differs from the ancient Japanese notions.

...A new Japan is definitely born – constitutional, progressive, energetic, resourceful, sure to become great and perhaps destined to become almost again as happy as of yore. Let the nations of the West receive and welcome as she deserves this immeasurably ancient empire, which thus renews her youth in the fountain of constitutional liberties and institutions. With one slight inclination of his august head, the Mikado saluted the vast assembly bending low before him and Japan had entered on the list of lands governed by an electoral regime as His Imperial Majesty passed through a guard of lancers to his equipage.

SIR EDWIN ARNOLD, *NEW YORK TIMES*, 26 JANUARY 1891.

With the Meiji Restoration of 1867, the emperor of Japan reasserted his authority after a long period of being eclipsed by his nominal subjects, the military *Shogun* and the feudal lords known collectively as *Daimyo*. The country had already begun to emerge from international isolation (*see* 8 July), and in 1889 Japan adopted a new constitution, which combined imperial authority with a Western-style democratic system. The two houses (Peers and Commons) of the new 'Parliament' – strongly influenced by the Prussian example, it was called the Diet – met for the first time in Tokyo in November 1890.

These constitutional developments reflected a wider desire to transform and modernize Japan based on Western models. And the country soon emerged as an Asian military power, defeating China in 1895 and Russia ten years later, and affirming Japanese dominance over Korea. The constitution endured until September 1945.

ALSO ON THIS DAY

1781 The crew of the British slave-ship *Zong* dumps 133 Africans in the sea.
1885 Burma is absorbed into the British Raj at the end of the Third Anglo-Burmese War.
1945 The Federal People's Republic of Yugoslavia is formally declared.

30 NOVEMBER

THE FIRST FOOTBALL INTERNATIONAL, 1872

A splendid display of football in the really scientific sense of the word, and a most determined effort on the part of the representatives of the two nationalities to overcome each other...

The only thing which saved the Scotch team from defeat, considering the powerful forward play of England, was the magnificent defensive play and tactics shown by their backs, which was also taken advantage of by the forwards.

BELL'S LIFE IN LONDON, AND SPORTING CHRONICLE, 1 DECEMBER 1872.

∞

The first ever international football match was played between teams representing England and Scotland at a cricket ground in Partick, Glasgow, on St Andrew's Day, 30 November 1872. Four thousand spectators watched the goal-less draw. Although there had been earlier matches in London between the two nations, the Scottish team had comprised only Scots resident in the capital.

To counter the criticism of this situation, the Football Association had issued a challenge to Scottish footballers, and this was accepted. The entire Scottish team comprised players from Queen's Park, the leading club (there was no Scottish Football Association, and few other footballers north of the Border played by the English Football Association's rules at this stage). In the first half the Scots had the upper hand, and had a goal controversially disallowed; in the second half the heavier English side was dominant. Shortly before the final whistle a Scottish shot fell on the tape that was used instead of a crossbar – the closest either side came to scoring a goal.

The annual fixture became the source of much rivalry over the succeeding 100 years, but in 1989 the tradition was abandoned.

ALSO ON THIS DAY

1900 The death of the Irish poet and playwright Oscar Wilde.
1936 The Crystal Palace, London, is destroyed by fire.
1939 Hostilities commence in the Soviet–Finnish Winter War.

DECEMBER

1 DECEMBER

THE BLUEPRINT FOR THE WELFARE STATE, 1942

Three guiding principles may be laid down at the outset.

1. The first principle is that any proposals for the future, while they should use to the full the experience gathered in the past, should not be restricted by consideration of sectional interests established in the obtaining of that experience. Now, when the war is abolishing landmarks of every kind, is the opportunity for using experience in a clear field. A revolutionary moment in the world's history is a time for revolutions, not for patching.

2. The second principle is that organization of social insurance should be treated as one part only of a comprehensive policy of social progress. Social insurance fully developed may provide income security; it is an attack upon want. But want is one only of live giants on the road of reconstruction and in some ways the easiest to attack. The others are disease, ignorance, squalor and idleness.

3. The third principle is that social security must be achieved by co-operation between the state and the individual. The state should offer security for service and contribution.

WILLIAM BEVERIDGE, THE 'BEVERIDGE REPORT', 1 DECEMBER 1942.

On 1 December 1942, less than a month after Winston Churchill had hailed the Eighth Army's victory at El Alamein as 'the end of the beginning' of the fight-back against Nazi Germany, Britain's coalition government marked a new start in the domestic sphere. It published economist William Beveridge's 'Report of the Inter-Departmental Committee on Social Insurance and Allied Services', which came to form the basis of Britain's postwar welfare state.

The Beveridge Report, as it became known, was hailed by many as a visionary document that would lay the foundations of a new society, ending the extreme poverty that had blighted Britain after the previous global war. All three political parties adopted its principles, which underlay many of the initiatives of Clement Attlee's Labour government, elected in 1945.

ALSO ON THIS DAY

1918 Icelandic sovereignty is recognized by Denmark.
1934 The murder of the Leningrad Communist Sergei Kirov gives a pretext for Stalin's Great Terror.
1955 The arrest of Rosa Parks in Montgomery, Alabama, escalates the civil rights movement.

2 DECEMBER

THE MONROE DOCTRINE, 1823

We owe it, therefore, to candour and to the amicable relations existing between the United States and those [European] powers to declare that we should consider any attempt on their part to extend their system to any portion of this hemisphere as dangerous to our peace and safety. With the existing colonies or dependencies of any European power we have not interfered and shall not interfere. But with the Governments who have declared their independence and maintain it, and whose independence we have... acknowledged, we could not view any interposition for the purpose of oppressing them, or controlling in any other manner their destiny, by any European power in any other light than as the manifestation of an unfriendly disposition toward the United States.

JAMES MONROE, STATE OF THE UNION ADDRESS, 2 DECEMBER 1823.

In his 1823 State of the Union Address, US President James Monroe asserted that the United States would consider any interference by others in the affairs of the western hemisphere as hostile to the nation. While he was mainly concerned with the newly independent, and soon-to-be independent, Latin American countries, his sentiments also applied to possible Russian expansion in the northwest.

The Monroe Doctrine, as it came to be known, was reasserted by President Theodore Roosevelt in the early 20th century, who remarked:

All that this country desires is to see the neighbouring countries stable, orderly, and prosperous... If a nation shows that it knows how to act with reasonable efficiency and decency in social and political matters, if it keeps order and pays its obligations, it need fear no interference from the United States. Chronic wrongdoing, or an impotence which results in a general loosening of the ties of civilized society, may in America, as elsewhere, ultimately require intervention by some civilized nation, and in the Western Hemisphere the adherence of the United States to the Monroe Doctrine may force the United States, however reluctantly... to the exercise of an international police power.

The doctrine became a major plank of anti-Communist policy, but it has also been interpreted as a statement of US imperialism in all but name.

ALSO ON THIS DAY

1805 Napoleon defeats a Russo-Austrian army at the Battle of Austerlitz.
1859 The militant abolitionist John Brown is hanged for treason in Virginia.
1917 WWI: Russian Bolsheviks and the Central Powers sign an armistice.

3 DECEMBER

HISTORY'S WORST INDUSTRIAL ACCIDENT, 1984

Everything is normal.

POLICE LOUDSPEAKER ANNOUNCEMENT, BHOPAL, INDIA, 3 DECEMBER 1984.

The release of a cloud of methyl isocyanate gas from the Union Carbide Bhopal pesticide plant in central India killed at least 2,000 people – and perhaps four times that number – during the night of 2/3 December 1984. People found themselves suddenly blinded, vomiting, and with burning lungs; a panicked stampede to escape the horror killed many others, before the police announcement at 6 a.m. wrongly claimed that matters were under control.

At least the same number of people died later, and some estimates have put the total death toll at 25,000. Many others suffered blindness. An investigation showed that the release was the result of negligence by the company, with inadequate staffing and lax safety procedures; there was possibly also some sabotage by employees. It was found that a leak of water into a tank of methyl isocyanate had created the conditions to cause the explosion.

Most of the victims were slum-dwellers or homeless people who slept on the streets, and more than 20,000 people needed hospital treatment. A prolonged legal battle resulted in a voluntary settlement by the company in 1989; but in 2002 India sought the extradition of the company's former chief executive, Warren Anderson, on charges of culpable homicide, and the Indian Supreme Court agreed compensation to be paid to more than half a million victims.

ALSO ON THIS DAY

1818 Illinois becomes the 21st US state.
1894 The death of the Scottish author Robert Louis Stevenson.
1971 Pakistani airstrikes on Indian airbases begin the short Indo-Pakistan War of 1971.

4 DECEMBER

BRITISH NEUTRALITY IN THE US CIVIL WAR, 1861

Our great advisers of the *Times* newspaper have been persuading people... [of] the determination of the Washington government to pick a quarrel with the people of England. Did you ever know anybody who was not very nearly dead drunk, who, having as much upon his hands as he could manage, would offer to fight everybody about him? Do you believe that the United States government, presided over by President Lincoln, so constitutional in all his acts, so moderate as he has been – representing at this moment that great party in the United States, happily now in the ascendency, which has always been especially in favour of peace, and especially friendly to England – do you believe that such a government, having now upon its hands an insurrection of the most formidable character in the South, would invite the armies and the fleets of England to combine with that insurrection, and, it might be, to render it impossible that the Union should ever again be restored? I say, that single statement, whether it came from a public writer or a public speaker, is enough to stamp him forever with the character of being an insidious enemy of both countries.

What can be more monstrous than that we, as we call ourselves, to some extent, an educated, a moral, and a Christian nation – at a moment when an accident of this kind occurs... should be all up in arms, every sword leaping from its scabbard, and every man looking about for his pistols and his blunderbusses? I think the conduct pursued – and I have no doubt just the same is pursued by a certain class in America – is much more the conduct of savages than of Christian and civilized men. No, let us be calm...

Now... let me ask you what is this people, about which so many men in England at this moment are writing, and speaking, and thinking, with harshness, I think with injustice, if not with great bitterness? Two centuries ago, multitudes of the people of this country found a refuge on the North American continent, escaping from the tyranny of the Stuarts and from the bigotry of [Archbishop] Laud. Many noble spirits from our country made great experiments in favour of human freedom on that continent...

At this very moment, then, there are millions in the United States who personally, or whose immediate parents have at one time been citizens of this country. They found a home in the Far West; they subdued the wilderness; they met with plenty there, which was not afforded them in their native country; and they have become a great people. There may be persons in England who are jealous of those States. There may be men who dislike democracy, and who hate a republic; there may be even those whose sympathies warm toward the slave oligarchy of the South. But of this I am certain, that only misrepresentation the most gross, or calumny the most wicked can sever the tie which unites the great mass of the people of this country with their friends and brethren beyond the Atlantic.

Now, whether the Union will be restored or not, or the South achieve an unhonoured independence or not, I know not, and I predict not. But this I think I know – that in a few years, a very few years, the twenty millions of freemen in the North will be thirty millions, or even fifty millions—a population equal to or exceeding that of this kingdom. When that time comes, I pray that it may not be said among them, that in the darkest hour of their country's trials, England, the land of their fathers, looked on with icy coldness and saw unmoved the perils and calamities of their children.

JOHN BRIGHT MP, ROCHDALE, 4 DECEMBER 1861.

In late 1861, with the American states sundered by civil conflict, a Unionist fleet seized a British ship, the *Trent*, carrying British diplomats to the Confederate Southern states. The seizure was seen by many in Britain as a *casus belli* with the North. The Quaker and Liberal reformer John Bright (1811–89) urged against military involvement, in a powerful speech delivered in Rochdale in December, and he denied that the confrontation had been intentionally engineered by Washington. He sought to remind his audience of the shared Anglo-American heritage and of the unattractiveness of the Southern 'slave oligarchy'. War was averted when President Lincoln released the diplomats in January 1862, though tensions between the North and Britain remained during the war.

ALSO ON THIS DAY

1745 The Jacobite army reaches Derby, its deepest penetration of England.
1791 The first edition of *The Observer* in London, the world's first Sunday newspaper.
1976 The death of the English composer Benjamin Britten.

5 DECEMBER

THE GREAT EUROPEAN WITCH-HUNT, 1484

Many persons of both sexes, unmindful of their own salvation and straying from the Catholic faith, have abandoned themselves to devils, incubi and succubi, and by their incantations, spells, conjurations, and other accursed charms and crafts, enormities and horrid offences, have slain infants yet in the mother's womb, as also the offspring of cattle, have blasted the produce of the earth, the grapes of the vine, the fruits of the trees, nay, men and women, beasts of burthen, herd-beasts, as well as animals of other kinds, vineyards, orchards, meadows, pasture-land, corn, wheat, and all other cereals; these wretches furthermore afflict and torment men and women, beasts of burthen, herd-beasts, as well as animals of other kinds, with terrible and piteous pains and sore diseases, both internal and external; they hinder men from performing the sexual act and women from conceiving, whence husbands cannot know their wives nor wives receive their husbands; over and above this, they blasphemously renounce that faith which is theirs by the Sacrament of Baptism, and at the instigation of the Enemy of Mankind they do not shrink from committing and perpetrating the foulest abominations and filthiest excesses to the deadly peril of their own souls, whereby they outrage the Divine Majesty and are a cause of scandal and danger to very many... the abominations and enormities in question remain unpunished not without open danger to the souls of many and peril of eternal damnation.

POPE INNOCENT VIII, *SUMMIS DESIDERANTES AFFECTIBUS*, 5 DECEMBER 1484.

∞

With his papal bull *Summis desiderantes affectibus* ('Desiring with extreme ardour'), the newly installed Pope Innocent VIII approved the suppression of witchcraft by the Inquisition. Some historians consider that he thereby launched an era of witch-hunting that would cause the deaths of an estimated 100,000 women across Europe during the early modern period. Two years later, in 1486, the Dominican inquisitor Heinrich Kramer – whose request for papal authority to prosecute witches in Germany had prompted Innocent to issue his bull – published *Malleus Malificarum* (literally, 'the hammer of witches'), an influential and misogynistic treatise that would be reprinted many times over the next 200 years.

ALSO ON THIS DAY

771 Charlemagne becomes king of the Franks.
1492 Christopher Columbus lands on Hispaniola.
1791 The death of the Austrian composer Wolfgang Amadeus Mozart.

6 DECEMBER

AN IRISH NATIONALIST FORESEES HIS DEATH, 1921

When you have sweated, toiled, had mad dreams, hopeless nightmares, you find yourself in London's streets, cold and dank in the night air. Think – what have I got for Ireland? Something which she has wanted these past seven hundred years. Will anyone be satisfied at the bargain? Will anyone? I tell you this; early this morning I signed my death warrant. I thought at the time how odd, how ridiculous – a bullet may just as well have done the job five years ago.

MICHAEL COLLINS, LETTER TO JOHN O'KANE, 6 DECEMBER 1921.

The Anglo-Irish Treaty, signed in London on 6 December 1921, ended the Anglo-Irish War of 1919–21, also called (by Irish republicans) the War of Independence or the Tan War, the latter after the Black and Tans, the nickname of a brutal armed force sent to reinforce the Royal Irish Constabulary. A vicious guerrilla conflict, it was triggered by the unilateral declaration of an Irish Republic by Sinn Féin MPs in January 1919, and was fought between republicans and British Crown forces. By the treaty's terms, 26 of Ireland's 32 counties became the Irish Free State, a self-governing dominion within the British Empire, while six northeastern counties stayed within the United Kingdom as Northern Ireland.

The treaty remained to be ratified in Westminster and Dublin, and the Irish negotiators included Michael Collins – veteran of the 1916 Easter Rising (*see* 24 April), Sinn Féin MP and Irish Republican Army (IRA) leader, who had masterminded the nationalist terror campaign. When the British lord chancellor Lord Birkenhead said to Collins: 'I may have signed my political death-warrant,' Collins replied: 'I may have signed my *actual* death-warrant.' He repeated the thought in a letter to an associate later that day.

Although the Irish Parliament, the *Dáil,* narrowly ratified the treaty, many republicans – notably the *Dáil* president Éamon de Valera – refused to accept it. Civil war ensued in Ireland and Collins – as he foresaw – was assassinated by anti-Treaty IRA men near Cork in August 1922.

7 DECEMBER

THE JAPANESE ATTACK PEARL HARBOR, 1941

Yesterday, December 7th, 1941 – a date which will live in infamy – the United States of America was suddenly and deliberately attacked by naval and air forces of the Empire of Japan.

The United States was at peace with that nation and, at the solicitation of Japan, was still in conversation with its government and its emperor looking toward the maintenance of peace in the Pacific.

Indeed, one hour after Japanese air squadrons had commenced bombing in the American island of Oahu, the Japanese ambassador to the United States and his colleague delivered to our Secretary of State a formal reply to a recent American message. And while this reply stated that it seemed useless to continue the existing diplomatic negotiations, it contained no threat or hint of war or of armed attack.

It will be recorded that the distance of Hawaii from Japan makes it obvious that the attack was deliberately planned many days or even weeks ago. During the intervening time, the Japanese government has deliberately sought to deceive the United States by false statements and expressions of hope for continued peace.

The attack yesterday on the Hawaiian islands has caused severe damage to American naval and military forces. I regret to tell you that very many American lives have been lost. In addition, American ships have been reported torpedoed on the high seas between San Francisco and Honolulu.

Yesterday, the Japanese government also launched an attack against Malaya.

Last night, Japanese forces attacked Hong Kong.

Last night, Japanese forces attacked Guam.

Last night, Japanese forces attacked the Philippine Islands.

Last night, the Japanese attacked Wake Island.

And this morning, the Japanese attacked Midway Island.

Japan has, therefore, undertaken a surprise offensive extending throughout the Pacific area. The facts of yesterday and today speak for themselves. The people of the United States have already formed their opinions and well understand the implications to the very life and safety of our nation.

As commander in chief of the Army and Navy, I have directed that all measures be taken for our defence. But always will our whole nation remember the character of the onslaught against us.

No matter how long it may take us to overcome this premeditated invasion, the American people in their righteous might will win through to absolute victory.

I believe that I interpret the will of the Congress and of the people when I assert that we will not only defend ourselves to the uttermost, but will make it very certain that this form of treachery shall never again endanger us.

Hostilities exist. There is no blinking at the fact that our people, our territory, and our interests are in grave danger.

With confidence in our armed forces, with the unbounding determination of our people, we will gain the inevitable triumph – so help us God.

US President Franklin D. Roosevelt, speech to Congress, 8 December 1941.

∞

In a brief speech to the US Congress on 8 December, President Franklin D. Roosevelt summed up the events of the preceding day – when the Japanese air force had struck the US naval base in Hawaii without warning, sinking or damaging 18 ships (including eight battleships), destroying 188 aircraft and killing over 2,400 people.

The Japanese intention had been to inform the US government that negotiations to preserve the tenuous peace were at an end some 30 minutes before the attack, but although the Japanese ambassador met the US secretary of state, the vital part of the message was not conveyed. In response to Roosevelt's speech, Congress immediately passed a formal declaration of war.

Later, the Japanese prime minister, Hideki Tojo, reflected: 'that the Pearl Harbor attack should have succeeded in achieving surprise seems a blessing from Heaven'. But on hearing the American declaration of war, Japan's Admiral Yamamoto's response was rather different, and prescient: 'I fear we have awakened a sleeping giant, and his reaction will be terrible.'

More than three and a half years of bitter warfare followed – fought on land, at sea and in the air. Carpet-bombing was used against the Japanese cities of Tokyo, Osaka, Kobe and Nagoya, killing hundreds of thousands in 1944–5, but the fighting only ceased after the United States dropped atom bombs on Hiroshima and Nagasaki (*see* 6 August).

ALSO ON THIS DAY

43 BC The Roman orator and statesman Marcus Tullius Cicero is assassinated.
1732 The Royal Opera House opens in London.
1917 WWI: the United States declares war on Austria-Hungary.

8 DECEMBER

THE ASSASSINATION OF JOHN LENNON, 1980

This morning I went to the bookstore and bought *The Catcher in the Rye*...

I'm sure the large part of me is Holden Caulfield, who is the main person in the book. The small part of me must be the Devil.

I went to the building. It's called the Dakota. I stayed there until he came out and asked him to sign my album [*Double Fantasy*]. At that point my big part won and I wanted to go back to my hotel, but I couldn't. I waited until he came back. He came in a car. Yoko walked past first and I said hello, I didn't want to hurt her.

Then John came and looked at me and printed me [sic]. I took the gun from my coat pocket and fired at him. I can't believe I could do that. I just stood there clutching the book. I didn't want to run away. I don't know what happened to the gun. I remember Jose [Perdomo], the doorman kicking it away. Jose was crying and telling me to please leave. I felt so sorry for Jose. Then the police came and told me to put my hands on the wall and cuffed me.

MARK CHAPMAN, STATEMENT TO NEW YORK POLICE, 9 DECEMBER 1980.

∽

The former Beatle John Lennon (1940–80) was murdered on entering the Dakota apartment block in New York by 25-year-old Mark Chapman, a man obsessed with J.D. Salinger's 1951 novel *Catcher in the Rye*, and identifying with its main character Holden Caulfield, a youth hyper-aware of the hypocrisies of the adult world. Chapman saw Lennon as a celebrity preaching peace while living in luxury, and claimed to have heard voices telling him to kill the rock star.

Chapman pleaded guilty, and was sentenced to life imprisonment: he currently resides in the Attica Correctional Facility, once called Attica State Prison – about which John Lennon recorded a protest song in 1972, over the killings of rioting prisoners.

One of the particular pleasures for Lennon of life in New York, as opposed to life in London, had been that he could freely walk the streets because people didn't 'bug' him.

ALSO ON THIS DAY

1941 WWII: the Japanese invade Hong Kong.
1974 The Greek monarchy is abolished by plebiscite.
1991 The Commonwealth of Independent States replaces the Soviet Union.

9 DECEMBER

THE VIRGIN OF GUADALUPE, 1531

A few days into December 1531, Juan Diego, a humble but respected Indian from Cuauhtitlán, drew near the little hill called Tepeyac. It was beginning to dawn. He heard singing, like the song of many precious birds; when the voices stopped, it was as if the hill were answering them; extremely soft and delightful, their songs exceeded the songs of the coyoltotl and the tzinitzcan and other precious birds.

...Juan Diego looked up the hill, toward where the heavenly song was coming from. And when the singing stopped, he heard someone calling him, from the top of the hill: 'Juan, dearest Juan Diego.'

And when he reached the top of the hill, a maiden who was standing there called him to her. Her clothing was shining like the sun, as if sending out waves of light, and the crag on which she stood seemed to be giving out rays; her radiance was like precious stones, like an exquisite bracelet, beautiful beyond all else; the earth shone with the brilliance of a rainbow in the mist.

She said: 'Know, my dear young son, that I am the perfect ever-virgin Holy Mary, mother of the one great God of truth who gives us life, the inventor and creator of people... I want very much that you build a sacred house here in which I will show Him; I will give Him to the people in all my love, in my compassionate gaze, in my help, in my salvation: because I am truly your compassionate mother, yours and of all the people who live together in this land.

MIGUEL SANCHEZ, *IMAGE OF THE VIRGIN MARY, MOTHER OF GUADALUPE*, 1648.

The miraculous appearance of the Virgin Mary to a Mexican peasant just ten years after the Spanish conquest of Mexico culminated in the appearance, three days later, of her image on a cloth that the peasant showed to the bishop of Mexico. The story was recorded in the native Nahuatl language and published by the Spanish priest Sanchez 100 years later. The image – sometimes called the 'Queen of Mexico' – became the symbol of the suffering of the Mexican and Creole people, and in 1810 Miguel Hidalgo led an independence movement with her image on his flag, and with the slogan, 'Death to the Spaniards and long live the Virgin of Guadalupe' (*see* 16 September).

ALSO ON THIS DAY

1917 WWI: General Allenby captures Jerusalem.
1960 The first episode of the TV soap opera *Coronation Street* is broadcast in Britain.
1979 The eradication of the smallpox virus is announced by scientists.

10 DECEMBER

THE 'BROWN DOG' VIVISECTION RIOTS, 1907

In Memory of the Brown Terrier Dog Done to Death in the Laboratories of University College in February 1903 after having endured Vivisections extending over more than two months and having been handed over from one Vivisector to another till Death came to his release. Also in memory of the 232 dogs vivisected in the same place during the year 1902. Men and Women of England – How long shall these things be?

INSCRIPTION ON A STATUE OF THE BROWN DOG,
LATCHMERE PARK, BATTERSEA, SOUTH LONDON, 1906.

∞

Britain's most violent demonstration over animal rights took place in London's Trafalgar Square in December 1907. Two Swedish women at the medical school of University College London had observed the dissection of a brown terrier with inadequate anaesthetic in December 1902 and again the following February, when the dog was deliberately killed in the lecture theatre. They later wrote:

> Its legs are fixed to the board, its head is firmly held in the usual manner, and it is tightly muzzled. There is a large incision on the side of the neck, exposing the gland. The animal exhibits all the signs of intense suffering; in his struggles, he again and again lifts his body from the board, and makes powerful attempts to get free. The lecturer, attired in the blood-stained surplice of the priest of vivisection... is now comfortably smoking a pipe... Now and then, he makes a funny remark, which is appreciated by those around him.

Physiologist William Bayliss, the discoverer of intestinal hormones, was accused of illegal dissection. The college sued successfully for libel, but the anti-vivisectionists raised a statue to the dog with a provocative inscription. 'Anti-dogger' medical students repeatedly attempted to destroy this statue, with their most determined effort – by 1,000 medical students after the Oxford–Cambridge rugby match on 10 December 1907 – resisted by local residents. They moved on to central London where prolonged clashes with police and anti-vivisectionists took place. In March 1910 Battersea Council removed the statue in the middle of the night and melted it down.

ALSO ON THIS DAY

1799 The metre is adopted as a unit of measurement in France.
1868 The world's first traffic lights are installed in London, powered by gas.
1948 The Universal Declaration of Human Rights is adopted by the UN General Assembly.

11 DECEMBER

THE ABDICATION OF KING EDWARD VIII, 1936

A few hours ago I discharged my last duty as king and emperor, and now that I have been succeeded by my brother, the Duke of York, my first words must be to declare my allegiance to him. This I do with all my heart.

You all know the reasons which have impelled me to renounce the throne. But I want you to understand that in making up my mind I did not forget the country or the empire, which, as Prince of Wales and lately as King, I have for twenty-five years tried to serve.

But you must believe me when I tell you that I have found it impossible to carry the heavy burden of responsibility and to discharge my duties as king as I would wish to do without the help and support of the woman I love.

And I want you to know that the decision I have made has been mine and mine alone. This was a thing I had to judge entirely for myself. The other person most nearly concerned has tried up to the last to persuade me to take a different course.

I have made this, the most serious decision of my life, only upon the single thought of what would, in the end, be best for all.

… I now quit altogether public affairs and I lay down my burden. It may be some time before I return to my native land, but I shall always follow the fortunes of the British race and empire with profound interest, and if at any time in the future I can be found of service to His Majesty in a private station, I shall not fail.

EDWARD VIII, BBC RADIO BROADCAST, 11 DECEMBER 1936.

On 10 December 1936, Edward VIII, 'King of the United Kingdom and Dominions and Emperor of India', agreed to lay down those burdens, abdicating the following day in favour of his brother who was now King George VI. He had been monarch for less than a year. On that same day he broadcast his decision to the nation from Windsor Castle, and, retitled as Duke of Windsor, he married the twice-divorced American Wallis Simpson, 'the woman I love', six months later. The rest of his life was spent in exile, mostly in Paris, with a wartime spell as Governor of the Bahamas.

ALSO ON THIS DAY

1282 The death of the last native Prince of Wales, Llewellyn.
1816 Indiana becomes the 19th US state.
1994 The First Chechen War: President Yeltsin orders Russian troops into Chechnya.

12 DECEMBER

THE FIRST TRANSATLANTIC RADIO SIGNAL, 1901

Shortly after midday I placed the single earphone to my ear and started listening. The receiver on the table was very crude – a few coils and condensers and a coherer – no valves, no amplifiers, not even a crystal. But I was at last on the point of putting the correctness of all my beliefs to test. The answer came at 12.30 when I heard, faintly but distinctly, pip-pip-pip. I handed the phone to Kemp. 'Can you hear anything?' I asked. 'Yes,' he said, 'the letter S' – he could just hear it. I knew then that all my anticipations had been justified. The electric waves sent out into space from Poldhu had traversed the Atlantic – the distance, enormous as it seemed then, of 1,700 miles – unimpeded by the curvature of the earth. The result meant much more to me than the mere successful realization of an experiment. As Sir Oliver Lodge has stated, it was an epoch in history. I now felt for the first time absolutely certain that the day would come when mankind would be able to send messages without wires not only across the Atlantic but between the farthermost ends of the earth.

GUGLIELMO MARCONI, QUOTED IN DEGNA MARCONI, *MY FATHER, MARCONI*, 2000.

∞

On 12 December 1901 the 25-year-old Italian inventor Guglielmo Marconi and his Canadian assistant, George Kemp, were sitting in a hut on a cliff in Newfoundland, having spent three days listening to atmospheric noise in their crude receivers – the aerial was a length of wire held up by kites. Suddenly, they thought they heard the Morse signal for the letter 's' which had been transmitted from the radio station Marconi had built at Poldhu in Cornwall. The original intention had been to receive the message at a site on Cape Cod, Massachusetts, but the aerial was destroyed in a gale.

The event was hailed as a historic moment in radio telegraphy, although there was no independent verification for the successful transmission of the signal. Many now consider it impossible for a medium-wave signal to have travelled so far during daylight hours. Nevertheless, it has gone down in modern history as a milestone in the rapid development of the new technology.

ALSO ON THIS DAY

1942 WWII: the start of the German Operation Winter Storm
to relieve encircled troops at Stalingrad.
1963 Kenya gains its independence from the UK.
1988 35 people die in the Clapham Junction rail crash, London.

13 DECEMBER

THE RAPE OF NANJING, 1937

Three of us drive out to military hospitals... whose doctors and nurses simply ran away when the shelling got too heavy... The dead and wounded lie side by side in the driveway leading up to the Foreign Ministry... At the entrance is a wheelbarrrow containing a formless mass, ostensibly a corpse, but the feet show signs of life.

We come across corpses every 100 to 200 yards. The bodies of civilians that I examined had bullet holes in their backs. These people had presumably been fleeing and were shot from behind.

The Japanese march through the city in groups of ten to twenty soldiers and loot the shops. If I had not seen it with my own eyes I would not have believed it. They smash open windows and doors and take whatever they like...

...We run across a group of 200 Chinese workers whom Japanese soldiers have picked up off the streets of the Safety Zone, and after having been tied up, are now being driven out of the city. All protests are in vain.

Of the perhaps one thousand disarmed soldiers that we had quartered at the Ministry of Justice, between 400 and 500 were driven from it with their hands tied. We assume they were shot since we later heard several salvos of machine-gun fire. These events have left us frozen with horror.

...Troops of Japanese soldiers enter my private residence as well, but when I arrive and hold my swastika armband under their noses, they leave. There's no love for the American flag.

JOHN RABE, DIARY, 13 DECEMBER 1937.

∞

In July 1937 Japan launched a full-scale invasion of China. Japanese troops occupied the city of Nanjing – at that time the Chinese capital – on 13 December. There, in six weeks of rape and pillage, at least 40,000 Chinese – and possibly as many as 200,000 – were massacred. The few Westerners remaining in the city attempted to create a 'safety zone' for some 200,000 Chinese civilians. Among them was the Nazi-sympathizing German businessman John Rabe, whose diary remains an important testimony to one of the worst atrocities of the 20th century.

ALSO ON THIS DAY

1577 Francis Drake begins his round-the-world voyage from Plymouth.
1867 A Fenian (Irish nationalist) bomb explosion in Clerkenwell, London, kills six.
1959 Archbishop Makarios becomes the first president of Cyprus.

14 DECEMBER

VICTORIA MOURNS PRINCE ALBERT, 1861

My Own Dearest, Kindest Father – For as such have I ever loved you!

The poor fatherless baby of eight months is now the utterly broken-hearted and crushed widow of forty-two!

My life as a happy one is ended!

The world is gone for me!

If I must live on, his spirit will guide and inspire me!

But oh! to be cut off in the prime of life when I had hoped with such instinctive certainty that God never would part us, and would let us grow old together is too awful, too cruel!...

I am also anxious to repeat one thing, and that one is my firm resolve, my irrevocable decision, namely that his wishes – his plans – about everything, his views about everything are to be my law!

And no human power will make me swerve from what he decided and wished...

And I live on with him, for him; in fact I am only outwardly separated from him, and only for a time.

God bless and preserve you, Ever your wretched but devoted Child,

Victoria R

QUEEN VICTORIA, LETTER TO KING LEOPOLD I OF THE BELGIANS, 20 DECEMBER 1861.

Prince Albert, the husband of Queen Victoria, died on 14 December 1861, apparently of typhoid fever, throwing the queen into a deep grief that overwhelmed her for decades; she wore black for the rest of her life. After pouring out her feelings to her uncle, Leopold I, who had advised and supported her ever since her accession, she largely withdrew from public life. She barely visited London for several years, which made her generally unpopular and fed a rising republican movement in the years around 1870. As time wore on she was coaxed gradually back into a more visible role in the nation's life, and Parliament bolstered her role as a global figurehead when it conferred on her the title 'Empress of India' in 1877.

ALSO ON THIS DAY

1287 Sea surges along the coast of the Netherlands kill at least 50,000 people.
1556 The death of the French 'prophet' Nostradamus.
1995 The Dayton Agreement signed in Paris ends the war in Bosnia-Herzegovina.

15 DECEMBER

THE TRIAL OF ADOLF EICHMANN, 1961

The trouble with Eichmann was precisely that so many were like him, and that the many were neither perverted nor sadistic, that they were, and still are, terribly and terrifyingly normal. From the viewpoint of our legal institutions and of our moral standards of judgment, this normality was much more terrifying than all the atrocities put together, for it implied – as had been said at Nuremberg over and over again by the defendants and their counsels – that this new type of criminal, who is in actual fact *hostis generis humani* ['the enemy of mankind'], commits his crimes under circumstances that make it well-nigh impossible for him to know or to feel that he is doing wrong.

HANNAH ARENDT, *EICHMANN IN JERUSALEM: A REPORT ON THE BANALITY OF EVIL*, 1963.

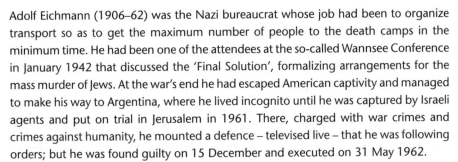

Adolf Eichmann (1906–62) was the Nazi bureaucrat whose job had been to organize transport so as to get the maximum number of people to the death camps in the minimum time. He had been one of the attendees at the so-called Wannsee Conference in January 1942 that discussed the 'Final Solution', formalizing arrangements for the mass murder of Jews. At the war's end he had escaped American captivity and managed to make his way to Argentina, where he lived incognito until he was captured by Israeli agents and put on trial in Jerusalem in 1961. There, charged with war crimes and crimes against humanity, he mounted a defence – televised live – that he was following orders; but he was found guilty on 15 December and executed on 31 May 1962.

The political philosopher Hannah Arendt reported on the trial for the *New York Times*. She noted his ordinariness and his hackneyed thinking. Ending her 1963 book with a description of his execution, she quoted his last words as: 'Long live Germany. Long live Argentina. Long live Austria. I shall not forget them,' and commented: 'In the face of death, he had found the cliché used in funeral oratory. Under the gallows, his memory played him the last trick; he was "elated" and forgot that this was his own funeral.'

ALSO ON THIS DAY

1675 The death of the Dutch painter Johannes Vermeer.
1911 Roald Amundsen's Norwegian team becomes the first to reach the South Pole.
1970 The *Venera 7* spacecraft lands on Venus.

16 DECEMBER

THE BOSTON TEA PARTY, 1773

It was now evening, and I immediately dressed myself in the costume of an Indian, equipped with a small hatchet, which I and my associates denominated the tomahawk, with which, and a club, after having painted my face and hands with coal dust in the shop of a blacksmith, I repaired to Griffin's wharf, where the ships lay that contained the tea. When I first appeared in the street after being thus disguised, I fell in with many who were dressed, equipped and painted as I was, and who fell in with me and marched in order to the place of our destination.

When we arrived at the wharf, there were three of our number who assumed an authority to direct our operations, to which we readily submitted. They divided us into three parties, for the purpose of boarding the three ships which contained the tea at the same time. The name of him who commanded the division to which I was assigned was Leonard Pitt. The names of the other commanders I never knew. We were immediately ordered by the respective commanders to board all the ships at the same time, which we promptly obeyed. The commander of the division to which I belonged, as soon as we were on board the ship, appointed me boatswain, and ordered me to go to the captain and demand of him the keys to the hatches and a dozen candles. I made the demand accordingly, and the captain promptly replied, and delivered the articles; but requested me at the same time to do no damage to the ship or rigging. We then were ordered by our commander to open the hatches and take out all the chests of tea and throw them overboard, and we immediately proceeded to execute his orders, first cutting and splitting the chests with our tomahawks, so as thoroughly to expose them to the effects of the water.

In about three hours from the time we went on board, we had thus broken and thrown overboard every tea chest to be found in the ship, while those in the other ships were disposing of the tea in the same way, at the same time. We were surrounded by British armed ships, but no attempt was made to resist us.

The next morning, after we had cleared the ships of the tea, it was discovered that very considerable quantities of it were floating upon the surface of the water; and to prevent the possibility of any of its being saved for use, a number of small boats were manned by sailors and citizens, who rowed them into those parts of the harbour wherever the tea was visible, and by beating it with oars and paddles so thoroughly drenched it as to render its entire destruction inevitable.

GEORGE HEWES, QUOTED IN JAMES HAWKES, *A RETROSPECT OF THE BOSTON TEA-PARTY*, 1833.

∞

On 16 December 1773 Samuel Adams, the Massachusetts Whig leader, held a mass meeting of the True Sons of Liberty, a group that had emerged in opposition to the Stamp Act of 1765, passed by the British Parliament. The Stamp Act, which imposed – without colonial assent – direct taxes on a wide range of printed papers, had been quickly repealed. But in 1773 the Tea Act aroused further ire. It gave near-monopolistic rights over the tea trade to the East India Company, and while this had an effect of lowering tea prices in the American colonies, it damaged the prospects of local merchants and local commerce, and fed an increasing sense of American disenfranchisement from the decision-making process concerning taxes and tariffs.

Adams's mass meeting was held in protest at the presence in Boston harbour of the *Dartmouth* and two other British vessels, the *Eleanor* and the *Beaver*, carrying cargoes of tea. When someone asked: 'Who knows how tea will mingle with salt water?', the meeting broke up, and a group of men disguised as Mohawk Indians and armed with tomahawks climbed aboard the ships and threw 342 chests into the harbour. The Boston shoemaker George Hewes was one of the group.

This act of defiance brought the American Revolutionary War (War of Independence) a step closer. Adams argued the justice of the deed, re-asserting the principle of 'no taxation without representation'. This slogan had first been used in 1750, but now it epitomized the American opposition to the Tea Act. And the Boston Tea Party turned those words into actions, giving the phrase a sense of actual, subversive consequences.

ALSO ON THIS DAY

1497 Vasco da Gama rounds the Cape of Good Hope.
1653 Oliver Cromwell becomes Lord Protector of England, Scotland and Ireland.
1944 WWII: a major German offensive in the Ardennes begins the Battle of the Bulge.

17 DECEMBER

THE FIRST SUCCESSFUL POWERED FLIGHT, 1903

Success four flights Thursday morning all against twenty one mile wind started from Level with engine power alone speed through air thirty one miles longest 57 second inform Press home Christmas.

ORVILLE WRIGHT, TELEGRAM TO HIS FATHER BISHOP MILTON WRIGHT, 1903.

∞

The cycle-repairing brothers Orville (1871–1948) and Wilbur Wright (1867–1912) from Dayton, Ohio, were both in their thirties when they made the world's first powered flight. It took place on a bitingly cold and windy December day, from the beach at Kitty Hawk, North Carolina. Having experimented with flying machines since the mid-1890s and devised a revolutionary system of control based on their observations of birds' flight, their machine proved capable of making four short flights – the longest being 852 feet – before a gust of wind picked up the embryonic biplane, smashing it irrevocably. Orville's telegram to his father conveyed his excitement about the achievement, but the press took little immediate interest.

Orville's handwritten notebook described the first flight in the precise language of the engineer:

> This flight lasted only 12 seconds, but it was nevertheless the first in the history of the world in which a machine carrying a man had raised itself by its own power into the air in full flight, had sailed forward without reduction of speed and had finally landed at a point as high as that from which it started.

Much later his older brother Wilbur adopted a loftier tone in describing their inspiration: 'The desire to fly is an idea handed down to us by our ancestors who looked enviously on the birds soaring freely through space on the infinite highway of the air.'

ALSO ON THIS DAY

1830 The death of the South American independence leader Simón Bolívar.
1939 WWII: the German battleship *Admiral Graf Spee* is scuttled after the Battle of the River Plate.
1983 An IRA car bomb kills six outside Harrods department store, London.

18 DECEMBER

THE BATTLE OF VERDUN, 1916

How depressing it was when they [the French troops] returned, whether singly as wounded or footsore stragglers, or in the ranks of companies impoverished by their losses! Their expressions, indescribably, seemed frozen by a vision of terror; their gait and their postures betrayed a total dejection; they sagged beneath the weight of horrifying memories; when I spoke to them, they could hardly reply, and even the jocular words of the old soldiers awoke no echo from their troubled minds.

PHILIPPE PÉTAIN, *LA BATAILLE DE VERDUN*, 1929.

∞

Marshal Pétain's description of French troops returning from the front line of the trenches sums up the horror of the ten-month Battle of Verdun, which finally ended on this day – leaving a toll of at least three-quarters of a million French and German casualties, a third of them killed or missing. The battle began in February 1916 when the Germans made a determined assault on the French fortified city of Verdun and its line of supporting fortresses on France's eastern border with Germany. It was launched with the intention of, in the later words of German commander Erich von Falkenhayn, 'bleeding France white'. The defence remained strong, mustered first by General Philippe Pétain, with the words *Courage! On l'aura* ('Courage! We shall get them!'), and then by Robert Nivelle, in June, who pronounced *Ils ne passeront pas* ('They shall not pass').

By this time the desperate defenders were being supplied by a constant stream of trucks, cars and even taxis from Paris. The disastrous Allied offensive on the Somme earlier in 1916 (*see* 1 July) was intended in part to relieve the pressure on Verdun, but the indescribably intense fighting went on in grotesque conditions, which led one French soldier to exclaim: 'Hell cannot be as terrible as this.' More than 23 million shells were fired before the Germans, who had lost much of the ground they had taken and had thousands taken prisoner, finally abandoned the attack on 18 December.

The Battle of Verdun remains as the ultimate monument to French suffering in the Great War.

ALSO ON THIS DAY

1642 The Dutch explorer Abel Tasman lands in New Zealand.
1737 The death of the Italian violin maker Antonio Stradivari.
1829 The death of the French naturalist Jean-Baptiste Lamarck.

19 DECEMBER

THE PUBLICATION OF DICKENS'S
A CHRISTMAS CAROL, 1843

'A merry Christmas, Bob!' said Scrooge, with an earnestness that could not be mistaken, as he clapped him on the back. 'A merrier Christmas, Bob, my good fellow, than I have given you for many a year! I'll raise your salary, and endeavour to assist your struggling family, and we will discuss your affairs this very afternoon, over a Christmas bowl of smoking bishop, Bob...'

Scrooge was better than his word. He did it all, and infinitely more; and to Tiny Tim, who did not die, he was a second father. He became as good a friend, as good a master, and as good a man, as the good old city knew...

Some people laughed to see the alteration in him, but he let them laugh, and little heeded them... His own heart laughed: and that was quite enough for him.

...and it was always said of him, that he knew how to keep Christmas well, if any man alive possessed the knowledge. May that be truly said of us, and all of us! And so, as Tiny Tim observed, God Bless Us, Every One!

CHARLES DICKENS, *A CHRISTMAS CAROL*, 1843.

∞

The 1840s were the pivotal decade in the invention of the modern Christmas with the publication on 19 December 1843 of Charles Dickens's tale *A Christmas Carol*. Henry Cole invented the commercial Christmas card the same year; and Prince Albert's enthusiasm for the decorated fir-tree was given huge publicity in 1848.

The notion of associating seasonal good cheer with Christian charity was already in the air: the very week that *A Christmas Carol*, with its memorable protagonist Ebenezer Scrooge, was published, *Punch* magazine asked: 'What have you done, this "merry Christmas", for the happiness of those about, below you? Nothing? Do you dare, with those sirloin cheeks and that port-wine nose, to answer – Nothing?'

A Christmas Carol was written in six weeks out of urgent financial need.

20 DECEMBER

THE BALLAD OF THE CAPTIVE LIONHEART, 1192

No prisoner can tell his honest thought
Unless he speaks as one who suffers wrong;
But for his comfort as he may make a song.
My friends are many, but their gifts are naught.
Shame will be theirs, if, for my ransom, here
   I lie another year.

They know this well, my barons and my men,
Normandy, England, Gascony, Poitou,
That I had never follower so low
Whom I would leave in prison to my gain.
I say it not for a reproach to them,
   But prisoner I am!

The ancient proverb now I know for sure;
Death and a prison know nor kind nor tie,
Since for mere lack of gold they let me lie.
Much for myself I grieve; for them still more.
After my death they will have grievous wrong
   If I am a prisoner long.

What marvel that my heart is sad and sore
When my own lord torments my helpless
   lands!
Well do I know that, if he held his hands,
Remembering the common oath we swore,
I should not here imprisoned with my song,
   Remain a prisoner long.

They know this well who now are rich and
   strong
Young gentlemen of Anjou and Touraine,
That far from them, on hostile bonds I strain.
They loved me much, but have not loved me
   long.
Their plans will see no more fair lists arrayed
   While I lie here betrayed.

RICHARD I, *c.*1192, TRANSLATED BY HENRY ADAMS.

When forced to travel back overland from the Third Crusade, Richard I of England donned a disguise, for he was passing through hostile territory. But in December 1192 he was captured by his erstwhile crusading ally Duke Leopold of Austria, with whom he had fallen out. Leopold held him captive for three months before handing him over to the Holy Roman Emperor, Henry VI. After payment of an enormous ransom, at a debilitating cost to his subjects, Richard was released in 1194.

While in prison he wrote this song to his half-sister Marie of Champagne, which told of his frustration at his incarceration, far from the comfort of home. It was composed in Occitan, the language then spoken across much of southwest France – including Gascony, a dukedom that Richard held – as well as some parts of Italy and Spain.

ALSO ON THIS DAY

1860 South Carolina becomes the first state to secede from the Union.
1917 The Cheka, the Soviet secret police, is created by V.I. Lenin.
1989 US forces invade Panama to remove its dictator Manuel Noriega.

21 DECEMBER

THE LOCKERBIE BOMBING, 1988

Flight PA103 took-off at 18.25 hrs. As it was approaching the Burnham VOR [VHF Omnidirectional radio range: a navigation aid for aircraft], it took up a radar heading of 350 and flew below the Bovingdon holding point at 6000 feet. It was then cleared to climb initially to flight level [FL] 120 and subsequently to FL 310. The aircraft levelled off at FL 310 north west of Pole Hill VOR at 18.56 hrs. Approximately 7 minutes later, Shanwick Oceanic Control transmitted the aircraft's oceanic clearance but this transmission was not acknowledged. The secondary radar return from Flight PA103 disappeared from the radar screen during this transmission. Multiple primary radar returns were then seen fanning out downwind for a considerable distance. Debris from the aircraft was strewn along two trails, one of which extended some 130 km to the east coast of England...

Two major portions of the wreckage of the aircraft fell on the town of Lockerbie; other large parts, including the flight deck and forward fuselage section, landed in the countryside to the east of the town. Residents of Lockerbie reported that, shortly after 19.00 hrs, there was a rumbling noise like thunder which rapidly increased to deafening proportions like the roar of a jet engine under power. The noise appeared to come from a meteor-like object which was trailing flame and came down in the north-eastern part of the town. A larger, dark, delta-shaped object, resembling an aircraft wing, landed at about the same time in the Sherwood area of the town. The delta-shaped object was not on fire while in the air, however, a very large fireball ensued which was of short duration and carried large amounts of debris into the air, the lighter particles being deposited several miles downwind. Other less well-defined objects were seen to land in the area.

BRITISH AIR ACCIDENTS INVESTIGATION BRANCH, REPORT, JULY 1990.

∞

Pan Am Flight 103, a Boeing 747 flying from London Heathrow to New York, was destroyed by a terrorist bomb that killed all 259 passengers and crew members (the majority of them US citizens) as well as 11 people in the town of Lockerbie, southern Scotland, on 21 December 1988. One of the Lockerbie residents described the disaster: 'At the time it went up there was a terrible explosion and the whole sky lit up. It was virtually raining fire – it was just liquid fire.'

Several different groups claimed responsibility for the bombing, but suspicions pointed to Libyan involvement. At that time the Libyan pariah regime of Colonel Muammar Muhammad al-Gaddafi (born 1942) was a known sponsor of terror groups; in 1986 US President Reagan had ordered airstrikes against Libya in retaliation for the

Libyan-inspired bombing of a West Berlin discotheque popular with American forces in that city.

As Libya began to reorientate its foreign policy, and following a decade of protracted negotiations between the British government and Libya, two Libyans accused of the Pan Am bombing were tried under Scottish law at a neutral venue, Camp Zeist, in the Netherlands, between May 2000 and January 2001. On 31 January 2001 Abdelbaset al-Megrahi was convicted on 270 counts of murder, having been found to have sent an explosive device from Malta, via Frankfurt, to London Heathrow where it was loaded on PA 103.

In 2001 al-Megrahi was sentenced to life imprisonment in Scotland; in 2002 Libya offered compensation to the families of the victims of the bombing, and in 2003 the regime finally admitted responsibility for the bombing. Al-Megrahi, suffering from prostate cancer, was released from prison on compassionate grounds, in circumstances of considerable transatlantic diplomatic controversy, in August 2009.

As Libya fractured into civil conflict in 2011, some leading defectors claimed to have evidence – unverified to date – that Gaddafi personally ordered the bombing of PA 103.

ALSO ON THIS DAY

1844 The 'Rochdale Pioneers' open their cooperative store, starting the Cooperative Movement.
1940 The death of the US novelist F. Scott Fitzgerald.
1979 The Lancaster House Agreement frames a future black-majority Zimbabwe.

22 DECEMBER

THE PREMIERE OF BEETHOVEN'S
FIFTH SYMPHONY, 1808

Can there be any work of Beethoven's that confirms all this to a higher degree than his indescribably profound, magnificent symphony in C minor? How this wonderful composition, in a climax that climbs on and on, leads the listener imperiously forward into the spirit world of the infinite!... No doubt the whole rushes like an ingenious rhapsody past many a man, but the soul of each thoughtful listener is assuredly stirred, deeply and intimately, by a feeling that is none other than that unutterable portentous longing, and until the final chord – indeed, even in the moments that follow it – he will be powerless to step out of that wondrous spirit realm where grief and joy embrace him in the form of sound. The internal structure of the movements, their execution, their instrumentation, the way in which they follow one another – everything among the themes that engenders that unity which alone has the power to hold the listener firmly in a single mood. This relationship is sometimes clear to the listener when he overhears it in the connecting of two movements or discovers it in the fundamental bass they have in common; a deeper relationship which does not reveal itself in this way speaks at other times only from mind to mind, and it is precisely this relationship that imperiously proclaims the self-possession of the master's genius.

E.T.A. HOFFMANN, *BEETHOVEN'S INSTRUMENTAL MUSIC*, 1813.

∞

Beethoven's Fifth Symphony in C minor, his Sixth Symphony, his Fourth Piano Concerto and six other works were all given their premieres in an single epic four-hour concert in Vienna in December 1808. The concert was not, though, a great success – the hall was cold and the orchestra poor, but subsequent performances of the Fifth Symphony made much more impact, not least with Romantic writer E.T.A. Hoffmann.

Five months after the concert, Napoleon's armies were bombarding Vienna and the increasingly deaf Beethoven desperately attempted to escape the noise of the barrage to preserve what was left of his hearing.

ALSO ON THIS DAY

1864 US Civil War: Sherman telegraphs Lincoln announcing the capture of Savannah, Georgia.
1880 The death of the English novelist George Eliot.
1972 Survivors of an Andean air crash are found after 10 weeks, surviving partly on human flesh.

23 DECEMBER

TOLSTOY AT SEVASTOPOL, 1854

There is so much simplicity and so little effort in what [the Russian soldiers] do that you are persuaded that they could, if it were necessary, do a hundred times more, that they could do everything. You judge that the sentiment that impels them is not the one you have experienced, mean and vain, but another and more powerful one, which has made men of them, living tranquilly in the mud, working and watching among the bullets, with a hundred chances to one of being killed, contrary to the common lot of their kind. It is not for a cross, for rank; it is not that they are threatened into submitting to such terrible conditions of existence. There must be another, higher motive power. This motive power is found in a sentiment which rarely shows itself, which is concealed with modesty, but which is deeply rooted in every Russian heart – patriotism... it is only now that the anecdote of Korniloff, who said to his troops: 'Children, we will die but we will not surrender Sevastopol', and the reply of our brave soldiers: 'We will die, hurrah!' – it is only now that these stories have ceased to be to you beautiful stories since they have become truth, facts.

Leo Tolstoy, Sevastopol Sketches, 1855.

∞

The siege of Sevastopol, the Russian fortress and capital of the Crimea, by the British and French between September 1854 and September 1855 was the central action of the Crimean War. The defence was initially organized by Admiral Kornilov until his death in October 1854; the eventual fall of the city was the signal for the end of the war.

The novelist Leo Tolstoy experienced the siege as a young army officer and mined the period for the three linked short stories of his *Sevastopol Sketches* – 'Sevastopol in December', 'Sevastopol in May' and 'Sevastopol in August'. Their strongly patriotic backbone and unprecedentedly vivid evocation of soldierly reality at the front proved a potent mix for the Russian reading public, and they were massively popular.

ALSO ON THIS DAY

1588 The Duke of Guise, founder of the Catholic League, is assassinated.
1688 After the Glorious Revolution, King James II flees to France.
1956 British and French troops withdraw from Suez.

24 DECEMBER

TRUCE ON THE WESTERN FRONT, 1914

A voice in the darkness shouted in English, with a strong German accent: 'Come over here!' A ripple of mirth swept along our trench, followed by a rude outburst of mouth organs and laughter. Presently, in a lull, one of our sergeants repeated the request: 'Come over here!'

'You come half-way, I come half-way,' floated out of the darkness.

'Come on, then!' shouted the sergeant. 'I'm coming along the hedge!'

After much suspicious shouting and jocular derision from both sides, our sergeant went along the hedge which ran at right-angles to the two lines of trenches.

Presently, the sergeant returned. He had with him a few German cigars and cigarettes which he had exchanged for a couple of Machonochie's [tins of meat stew] and a tin of Capstan, which he had taken with him.

On Christmas morning I awoke very early and emerged from my dug-out into the trench. It was a perfect day. A beautiful, cloudless blue sky. The ground hard and white, fading off towards the wood in a thin low-lying mist.

'Fancy all this hate, war, and discomfort on a day like this!' I thought to myself. The whole spirit of Christmas seemed to be there, so much so that I remember thinking, 'This indescribable something in the air, this Peace and Goodwill feeling, surely will have some effect on the situation here to-day!'

Walking about the trench a little later, discussing the curious affair of the night before, we suddenly became aware of the fact we were seeing a lot of evidences of Germans. Heads were bobbing about and showing over the parapet in a most reckless way, and, as we looked, this phenomenon became more and more pronounced.

A complete Boche [German] figure suddenly appeared on the parapet, and looked about itself. This complaint became infectious. It didn't take 'Our Bert' [the British sergeant who exchanged goods with the Germans the previous day] long to be up on the skyline. This was the signal for more Boche anatomy to be disclosed, and this was replied to by our men, until in less time than it takes to tell, half a dozen or so of each of the belligerents were outside their trenches and were advancing towards each other in no-man's land.

I clambered up and over our parapet, and moved out across the field to look. Clad in a muddy suit of khaki and wearing a sheepskin coat and Balaclava helmet, I joined the throng about half-way across to the German trenches.

This was my first real sight of them at close quarters. Here they were – the actual practical soldiers of the German army. There was not an atom of hate on either side that day; and yet, on our side, not for a moment was the will to beat them relaxed. It was just like the interval between the rounds in a friendly boxing match.

The difference in type between our men and theirs was very marked. There was no contrasting the spirit of the two parties. Our men, in their scratch costumes of dirty, muddy khaki, with their various assorted head-dresses of woollen helmets, mufflers and battered hats, were a light-hearted, open, humorous collection as opposed to the sombre demeanour and stolid appearance of the Huns in their grey-green faded uniforms, top boots, and pork-pie hats.

These devils, I could see, all wanted to be friendly; but none of them possessed the open, frank geniality of our men. However, everyone was talking and laughing, and souvenir hunting. Suddenly, one of the Boches ran back to the trench and presently reappeared with a large camera. I posed in a mixed group for several photographs, and I have ever since wished I had fixed up some arrangement for getting a copy.

BRUCE BAIRNSFATHER, *BULLETS AND BILLETS*, 1916.

∞

The Christmas truce that broke out along 500 miles of the Western Front in 1914 was a spontaneous fraternization of people who recognized they had more in common than divided them. It developed out of the Germans decorating their barbed wire on Christmas Eve and singing carols, and it culminated in groups meeting, exchanging gifts and playing football in no-man's-land. But it was too subversive to endure. Gustav Riebensahm of the 2nd Westphalian regiment commented: 'The English are extraordinarily grateful for the ceasefire, so they can play football again. But the whole thing has become ridiculous and must be stopped. I will tell the men that from this evening it's all over.' For his part, Sir John French, commander of the British Expeditionary Force, stamped firmly on peace on earth and goodwill to all men: 'I issued immediate orders to prevent any recurrence of such conduct, and called the local commanders to strict account, which resulted in a great deal of trouble.'

Bruce Bairnsfather fought in the Royal Warwickshire Regiment and became famous for his cartoons of trench life, based on a character known as 'Old Bill'.

ALSO ON THIS DAY

1524 The death of the Portuguese explorer Vasco da Gama.
1814 The Treaty of Ghent concludes the Anglo-US War of 1812.
1968 *Apollo 8* astronauts are the first to orbit the Moon.

25 DECEMBER

THE BIRTH OF JESUS, *c.*4 BC

And it came to pass in those days, that there went out a decree from Caesar Augustus, that all the world should be taxed.

(And this taxing was first made when Cyrenius was governor of Syria.)

And all went to be taxed, every one into his own city.

And Joseph also went up from Galilee, out of the city of Nazareth, into Judaea, unto the city of David, which is called Bethlehem; (because he was of the house and lineage of David.)

To be taxed with Mary his espoused wife, being great with child.

And so it was, that, while they were there, the days were accomplished that she should be delivered.

And she brought forth her firstborn son, and wrapped him in swaddling clothes, and laid him in a manger; because there was no room for them in the inn.

And there were in the same country shepherds abiding in the field, keeping watch over their flock by night.

And, lo, the angel of the Lord came upon them, and the glory of the Lord shone round about them: and they were sore afraid.

And the angel said unto them, Fear not: for, behold, I bring you good tidings of great joy, which shall be to all people.

For unto you is born this day in the city of David a Saviour, which is Christ the Lord.

And this shall be a sign unto you; Ye shall find the babe wrapped in swaddling clothes, lying in a manger.

And suddenly there was with the angel a multitude of the heavenly host praising God, and saying,

Glory to God in the highest, and on earth peace, good will toward men.

And it came to pass, as the angels were gone away from them into heaven, the shepherds said one to another, Let us now go even unto Bethlehem, and see this thing which is come to pass, which the Lord hath made known unto us.

And they came with haste, and found Mary, and Joseph, and the babe lying in a manger.

And when they had seen it, they made known abroad the saying which was told them concerning this child.

And all they that heard it wondered at those things which were told them by the shepherds.

But Mary kept all these things, and pondered them in her heart.

And the shepherds returned, glorifying and praising God for all the things that they had heard and seen, as it was told unto them.

And when eight days were accomplished for the circumcising of the child, his name was called JESUS, which was so named of the angel before he was conceived in the womb.

THE GOSPEL OF LUKE, CHAPTER 2.

∞

The most famous birth in Western history, that of Jesus the son of Mary, later called Christ, cannot be accurately dated, either to the year or to the month. Matthew's Gospel says it took place during the reign of King Herod of Judaea, who died in 4 BC; the Roman governor of Syria, Quirinus, ordered a general taxation in about AD 6, but there is no record that this involved a large movement of people to their ancestral homes. The date presently used for the start of the Christian era was calculated in the early sixth century by a Syrian monk known as Dionysius Exiguus.

Beyond the writings of the followers of Christ and those of the first-century AD Jewish historian Josephus, there is no independent record for the life of Jesus, but his influence on those followers was profound, and his life and teachings were recorded in oral form until being written down about 40 years after his death. The first Christians celebrated the birth of Jesus on 6 January; but from the fourth century it was more commonly celebrated on 25 December, coinciding with an ancient Roman festival of Saturnalia.

Worries that Christmas revelry was superseding the date's religious significance are nothing new. In England between 1647 and 1660, the Puritan-minded Cromwellian regime suspended the festival lest it encourage unseemly merrymaking. But it was the early Victorian era that brought much of the paraphernalia of the 'traditional' Christmas (*see* 19 December), and some 'traditions' – such as the giving of presents – came even later.

ALSO ON THIS DAY

1643 Christmas Island, in the Indian Ocean, is named by Captain William Mynors.
1977 The death of the English film comedian Charlie Chaplin.
1990 The Romanian dictator Nicolae Ceauşescu is executed.

26 DECEMBER

THE BOXING DAY *TSUNAMI*, 2004

It was 9.30am on Boxing Day. We were in our small hotel across the road from the beach and raised a few meters above sea level, maybe 4–5m. Unlike many, it was solid, brick and concrete and our rooms were on the second floor. The sky was clear blue. No wind. Hot. Preparing to go to the beach.

I was looking at the sea when suddenly it covered the short space from the beach to the road and was on the road. It was so fast. As it reached the road I saw a group of children watch petrified for a split second and then pick up the ball they were playing with and run. I find it hard to imagine they reached safety.

With 3–4 massive belches the sea rose and reached the base of the hotel. The force was incredible. It lifted cars and crashed through the corrugated iron roofs below us, planks of wood and other stuff swirling. People were screaming.

It was not a wave as such. It was more as if the sea simply overspilt its boundaries, overflowed, spewed out, only with tremendous force and power. It rose at such a rate that it seemed only seconds until we too would be engulfed by it. I felt completely trapped. I was terrified.

After what seemed ages but must have been a minute or two at most, the level of the sea had stopped rising – I could see from the house in front that it was stable at the level near the top of the windows. Then as suddenly as it came, the sea was sucked back in, again with tremendous force, as if to fill a vacuum…

At the end of the day the Sri Lankans living on the hillside took in the stranded tourists and we spent the night on the concrete floor of someone's house and were bought food parcels. For a brief window there was little them-and-us separation – until the third day, when we were bussed out in an air-conditioned coach and they stayed to bury the dead and rebuild their lives.

SARA BURNS, LETTER, JANUARY 2005

∞

On 26 December 2004 an earthquake off the western coast of Sumatra caused a *tsunami* that devastated coastal regions of Indonesia, Malaysia, Thailand, Sri Lanka and southern India. Holiday-makers, such as Sara Burns, and locals alike were caught by the wall of water; some 230,000 people lost their lives in fourteen countries.

ALSO ON THIS DAY

1776 American Revolutionary War: the British are defeated at Trenton, New Jersey.
1893 The birth of the Chinese Communist leader Mao Zedong.
1991 The USSR is formally dissolved by its Supreme Soviet.

27 DECEMBER

THE INAUGURATION OF HAGIA SOPHIA, 537

[The Church is]... distinguished by indescribable beauty, excelling both in its size and in the harmony of its measures, being more magnificent than ordinary buildings, and much more elegant than those which are not of so just a proportion. The church is singularly full of light and sunshine; you would declare that the place is not lighted by the sun from without, but that the rays are produced within itself... No one ever became weary of this spectacle, but those who are in the church delight in what they see, and, when they leave, magnify it in their talk. Moreover it is impossible accurately to describe the gold, and silver, and gems, presented by the Emperor Justinian, but by the description of one part, I leave the rest to be inferred. That part of the church which is especially sacred, and where the priests alone are allowed to enter, which is called the Sanctuary, contains forty thousand pounds' weight of silver.

PROCOPIUS, THE BUILDINGS OF JUSTINIAN, c.560.

The Hagia Sophia, or Church of the Holy Wisdom, in Constantinople (modern Istanbul), which was to be the world's largest church for 1,000 years, was completed in 537. The Byzantine emperor Justinian spared no expense to replace an earlier church, which had burned down in the city's violent eruption of factional fighting that was the 'Nika riots' of 532. His architects Isodorus and Anthemius devised a scheme that was massive – it included the world's largest dome – and innovative (in its 'pendentives', the concave arches springing from the huge pillars to support it) and exceptionally harmonious.

Justinian inaugurated the Hagia Sophia, which was often just called 'the great church', on 27 December 537, entering in a chariot and with words that expressed no false modesty: 'Solomon, I have outdone you.' Thus he proclaimed it finer even than the lost Temple of Jerusalem. Hagia Sophia's dome fell in an earthquake in 558, but it was immediately rebuilt, even lighter and higher than the original.

The building still stands as Istanbul's greatest monument: it was secularized in 1934, having served as a mosque from 1453, when Constantinople fell to the Ottoman Turks (*see* 29 May). It is now a museum and a much-visited tourist attraction.

ALSO ON THIS DAY

1945 A 28-nation agreement creates the World Bank.
1979 The Soviets invade Afghanistan.
2007 The former Pakistani premier Benazir Bhutto is assassinated.

28 DECEMBER

THE ADVENT OF THE MOVIES, 1895

The cinema is an invention without any future.

AUGUSTE AND LOUIS LUMIÈRE, 1895.

∞

The Lumière brothers Auguste (1862–1954) and Louis (1864–1948) unveiled their new invention – the cinematograph, a machine to take, develop and project moving images – to a paying public at the Grand Café of the Boulevard des Capucines, Paris, on 28 December 1895. The ten films they showed, each about 40 seconds long and some including gentle humour, portrayed such everyday subjects as parents feeding a baby, a gardener watering the roses and swimmers plunging into the sea. Perhaps the most well-known was *Workers Leaving the Lumière Factory*, which depicted exactly that.

The brothers, who had worked for their father's photographic studio in Besançon in eastern France, had given private demonstrations of the technology earlier in the year, but this was the first public viewing. They had described their invention a few weeks earlier:

> *The apparatus will be of considerable assistance to the photographic study of motion. Not only does it enable us to capture movement in its various stages, but we can recompose it at will, since the crank is hand-operated. Motions can be slow, very slow if we wish, so that no detail escapes our attention; and subsequently we can accelerate it, should we so desire, back to normal speed. We shall then possess perfect reproduction of real movement.*

The brothers went on to open theatres – which they called cinemas – across the world. Yet after making well over 1,000 shorts, they could see no way of furthering the invention, justifying their seemingly definitive statement of its limitations. The Lumière brothers sold the rights to the device and concentrated their own efforts instead on 'autochromes' – coloured still photographs. It would be other pioneers who would develop moving pictures and experiment with editing, to turn a novel means of recording actuality into a new medium for telling stories in images – and later in sound too (*see* 6 October).

29 DECEMBER

THE MURDER OF THOMAS BECKET, 1170

The murderers... tried to drag him out of the church to kill him or take him prisoner, as they claimed later... Becket pushed them off, saying: 'Don't touch me; you owe me fealty and subjection; you are behaving like madmen.'

The furious knight... shouted: 'I owe you no faith nor subjection above my fealty to the king'... The knight wounded him in the head, cutting the top of the crown; and with the same blow he wounded the arm of him who is writing this.

Becket received a second blow on the head. After a third he fell on his knees...

Then the third knight inflicted a terrible wound, breaking his sword against the pavement. Becket's crown was separated from the head so that the blood white with the brain, and the brain red from the blood, dyed the floor of the cathedral. The fourth knight stopped any from interfering, as a clerk who had come with the knights put his foot on the martyr's neck and scattered his brain and blood over the pavement, calling out, 'Let us go; he will rise no more.'

EDWARD GRIM, *LIFE OF THOMAS BECKET*, C.1180.

The murder of Archbishop of Canterbury Thomas Becket in his cathedral stemmed from an outburst by King Henry II on Christmas Day, 1170. 'Who will rid me of this turbulent priest?', the traditional version of his words, has a memorable ring but there is no contemporary evidence for them.

The row between the two former friends began when Henry appointed Becket – who was already his lord chancellor – archbishop in 1162. By appointing Becket to the archbishopric, Henry had hoped to have a compliant ally at the head of the Church; but instead Beckett went native. Amid deteriorating relations, in 1164 Becket fled England, and although an intervention by the pope meant he eventually returned in November 1170, the dispute escalated when Becket excommunicated several bishops who had proved amenable to the king.

While an official mission set off to confront Becket, four knights interpreted the king's angry words more aggressively, and rushed to Canterbury, where they gruesomely struck Becket down.

Edward Grim was a Cambridge clerk who happened to be visiting Canterbury on the day of the murder and who was himself wounded in the arm.

ALSO ON THIS DAY

1860 The Royal Navy's first 'ironclad', HMS *Warrior*, is launched.
1890 The Wounded Knee Massacre of the Lakota takes place in South Dakota.
1916 The Russian mystic and royal favourite Grigori Rasputin is murdered.

30 DECEMBER

A GRAND ALLIANCE FOR A GLOBAL WAR, 1941

The French Army collapsed, and the French nation was dashed into utter and, as it has so far proved, irretrievable confusion. The French government had at their own suggestion solemnly bound themselves with us not to make a separate peace. It was their duty and it was also their interest to go to North Africa, where they would have been at the head of the French Empire. In Africa, with our aid, they would have had overwhelming sea power... If they had done this Italy might have been driven out of the war before the end of 1940, and France would have held her place as a nation in the counsels of the Allies and at the conference table of the victors. But their generals misled them. When I warned them that Britain would fight on alone whatever they did, their generals told their prime minister and his divided Cabinet, 'In three weeks England will have her neck wrung like a chicken.' Some chicken; some neck.

What a contrast has been the behaviour of the valiant, stout-hearted Dutch! ... The Dutch nation are defending their empire with dogged courage and tenacity by land and sea and in the air... The British Empire and the United States are going to the aid of the Dutch. We are going to fight out this new war against Japan together. We have suffered together and we shall conquer together.

But the men of Bordeaux, the men of Vichy, they would do nothing like this. They lay prostrate at the foot of the conqueror. They fawned upon him. What have they got out of it?... Hitler plays from day to day a cat-and-mouse game with these tormented men.

WINSTON CHURCHILL, SPEAKING AT THE CANADIAN PARLIAMENT, 30 DECEMBER 1941.

∞

Churchill's famous words 'some chicken; some neck' were delivered to the Canadian Parliament during his visit to North America to meet President Roosevelt and the Canadian prime minister William Mackenzie King, a few weeks after Pearl Harbor (*see* 7 December) had made the war truly a global one. The speech brims with scorn for the Vichy collaborationist regime of France – a particular heartache for Churchill, a Francophile – but also with a bold confidence now that the prime minister's long-cherished goal of a grand 'Anglo-Saxon' alliance existed to challenge the Axis powers.

ALSO ON THIS DAY

1066 A Muslim mob massacres many of the Jews of Granada, Spain.
1460 Wars of the Roses: Lancastrian forces defeat the Yorkists at the Battle of Wakefield.
2006 The former Iraqi dictator Saddam Hussein is executed.

31 DECEMBER

THE HUMBLE END OF A WAR-TORN CENTURY, 1999

Today, on the last day of the outgoing century, I am retiring.

…Russia must enter the new millennium with new politicians, new faces, new intelligent, strong and energetic people. As for those of us who have been in power for many years, we must go.

…Today, on this incredibly important day for me, I want to say more personal words than I usually do. I want to ask you for forgiveness, because many of our hopes have not come true, because what we thought would be easy turned out to be painfully difficult.

I ask you to forgive me for not fulfilling some hopes of those people who believed that we would be able to jump from the grey, stagnating, totalitarian past into a bright, rich and civilized future in one go.

I myself believed in this. But it could not be done in one fell swoop. In some respects I was too naive. Some of the problems were too complex.

…A new generation is taking my place, the generation of those who can do more and do it better… I have signed a decree entrusting the duties of the president of Russia to Prime Minister Vladimir Vladimirovich Putin.

BORIS YELTSIN, RESIGNATION ADDRESS, 31 DECEMBER 1999.

The last significant political act of the 20th century revealed not just an unexpected humility in the actor, but hit a welcome tone at the end of a war-ravaged century in which humility had been rare amid the stridency of demagogues and ideologues.

At the beginning of the decade, as the last president of the Russian Soviet Socialist Republic, Boris Yeltsin had resisted the attempts of both the reformist Communist Mikhail Gorbachev and hardliners to preserve the Soviet Union. As president of the new Russian Federation from 1991, he had backed a rush to capitalism and multi-party democracy; but by the end of the decade he had overseen a chaotic selling-off of the state's assets and reverted to authoritarianism tempered by buffoonery and vodka, while the economy floundered.

Yeltsin had been expected to see out his time in office, but he surprised everyone by tearfully announcing his immediate retirement at noon on the last day of 1999.

ALSO ON THIS DAY

1909 Manhattan Bridge opens in New York.
1923 The chimes of Big Ben are broadcast on BBC radio for the first time.
1960 The British farthing coin ceases to be legal tender.

CHRONOLOGY OF EVENTS COVERED
IN HISTORY'S DAYBOOK

4004 BC According to the calculations of the 17th-century Irish archbishop James Ussher, the world is created on 23 October of this year (23 Oct.)

753 BC The traditional date of the founding of Rome by Romulus and Remus (21 April)

490 BC The citizens of Athens defeat the Persians at Marathon (12 Sept.)

323 BC Alexander the Great dies (10 June)

202 BC Publius Cornelius Scipio defeats the Carthaginian general Hannibal at Zama (19 Oct.)

52 BC Julius Caesar defeats the Gauls at Alesia (3 Oct.)

49 BC Julius Caesar crosses the Rubicon, making civil war inevitable (10 Jan.)

44 BC Julius Caesar is assassinated (15 March)

30 BC Cleopatra commits suicide (12 Aug.)

27 BC The Roman Senate confers the title 'Augustus' on Gaius Julius Caesar Octavian (16 Jan.)

c.4 BC Jesus Christ is born (25 Dec.)

4 BC Herod, king of Judaea, dies (31 March)

AD 14 Augustus, Rome's first emperor, dies (19 Aug.)

54 The Roman emperor Claudius dies by poisoning (13 Oct.)

68 The Roman emperor Nero commits suicide (9 June)

70 Roman soldiers destroy the Temple in Jerusalem (10 Aug.)

79 Vesuvius erupts, destroying the towns of Pompeii and Herculaneum (24 Aug.)

303 The Roman emperor Diocletian begins his 'great persecution' of Christians (24 Feb.)

312 The Roman emperor Constantine experiences a vision of a Christian cross before the Battle of Milvian Bridge (27 Oct.)

537 The church of Hagia Sophia is inaugurated in Constantinople (27 Dec.)

622 The Prophet Muhammad arrives in Medina (24 Sept.)

632 The Prophet Muhammad delivers his final sermon (23 Feb.)

642 Oswald, Christian king of Northumbria is killed at the Battle of Maserfield (5 Aug)

732 Charles Martel, king of the Franks, defeats an invading Arab army at Tours in central France (10 Oct.)

793 The Vikings raid the monastery of Lindisfarne in Northumbria (8 June)

871 Alfred of Wessex defeats the Danes at Ashdown (8 Jan.)

1066 Harold Godwinson defeats an invading Norse army at Stamford Bridge (25 Sept.)

1066 Duke William of Normandy defeats Harold Godwinson at Hastings (14 Oct.)

1087 William the Conqueror dies (9 Sept.)

1095 Pope Urban II preaches the First Crusade at Clermont (27 Nov.)

1098 The Crusaders capture Antioch (3 June)

1170 Thomas Becket, archbishop of Canterbury, is murdered in his cathedral (29 Dec.)

1179 The Third Lateran Council condemns the Cathars as heretics (19 March)

1187 Crusader-held Jerusalem surrenders to Saladin (2 Oct.)

1192 King Richard I ('the Lionheart') is captured in Austria (20 Dec.)

1204 Byzantine Constantinople falls to the Fourth Crusade (12 April)

1214 King Philip (II) Augustus of France defeats an imperial-Flemish-English alliance at Bouvines (27 July)

1227 The Mongol conqueror Genghis Khan dies (18 Aug.)

1268 The Mamluk sultan Baybars writes to Prince Bohemund VI of Antioch, describing his massacre of Christians in that city (18 May)

1282 The Sicilian Vespers: rebellion against the French rule of Charles of Anjou (30 March)

1307 The Austrian bailiff Gessler forces William Tell to shoot an apple placed on his son Walter's head (18 Nov.)

1314 The Scots under Robert Bruce defeat an English army at Bannockburn (24 June)

1327 King Edward II is murdered at Berkeley Castle (21 Sept.)

1346 An English army defeats the French at Crécy (26 Aug.)

1349 Flemish flagellants appear in London at the time of the Black Death (29 Sept.)

1381 Richard II faces down the Peasants' Revolt (15 June)

1429 Joan of Arc meets the Dauphin Charles at Chinon (6 March)

1453 Constantinople falls to the Ottoman Turks (29 May)

1478 The Duke of Clarence is murdered (18 Feb.)

1484 Pope Innocent VIII approves the suppression of witchcraft by the Inquisition (5 Dec.)

1485 Henry Tudor defeats Richard III, England's last Plantagenet king, at Bosworth Field (22 Aug.)

1492 The emirate of Granada falls to the forces of Ferdinand and Isabella of Spain (2 Jan.)

1492 Christopher Columbus reaches the Americas (12 Oct.)

1498 Savonarola is burnt at the stake in Florence (23 May)

1501 The Ballet of the Chestnuts – a papal orgy in Renaissance Rome (30 Oct.)

1504 Michelangelo's sculpture of David is unveiled (8 Sept.)

1515 The young Henry VIII impresses the Venetian ambassador (30 April)

1517 Luther posts his 95 theses on the door of the castle church in Wittenberg, beginning the Protestant Reformation (31 Oct.)

1519 The conquistador Hernán Cortés meets the Aztec ruler Montezuma in Tenochtitlan (8 Nov.)

1520 Henry VIII of England and Francis I of France meet at the Field of Cloth of Gold (7 June)

1521 Martin Luther insists on the authority of scripture at the Diet of Worms (18 April)

1521 The explorer Ferdinand Magellan dies in the Philippines (27 April)

1531 The Virgin of Guadalupe appears to a Mexican peasant (9 Dec.)

1532 The conquistador Francisco Pizarro captures the Inca emperor Atahuallpa (16 Nov.)

1535 Sir Thomas More, Henry's VIII's lord chancellor, is executed (6 July)

1536 Anne Boleyn, Henry VIII's second wife, is executed (19 May)

1537 Jane Seymour, Henry VIII's third wife, dies after giving birth to a son (24 Oct.)

1556 Thomas Cranmer is burnt at the stake for heresy, becoming a Protestant martyr (21 March)

1558 England loses Calais, its last French territorial possession (7 Jan.)

1559 Elizabeth I is crowned queen of England (15 Jan.)

1571 A Christian coalition defeats the Ottoman Turkish fleet at Lepanto (7 Oct.)

1572 Thousands of Huguenots die in the Massacre of St Bartholomew's Day (23 Aug.)

1579 Francis Drake lands in Nova Albion (California) (17 June)

1584 William the Silent, ruler of the United Provinces of the Netherlands, is assassinated by a Catholic fanatic (10 July)

1587 Mary, Queen of Scots, is executed (8 Feb.)

1588 Queen Elizabeth I addresses her troops at Tilbury during the attempted invasion of England by the Spanish Armada (9 Aug.)

1600 The Italian philosopher and astronomer Giordano Bruno is burnt at the stake for heresy (17 Feb.)

1603 Elizabeth I dies and is succeeded by the Stuart king James I (24 March)

1605 The Gunpowder Plot attempts to blow up James I and his Parliament (5 Nov.)

1607 The Jamestown Colony is established in Virginia (14 May)

1611 The King James Bible is published (2 May)

1613 Shakespeare's Globe Theatre burns down (29 June)

1632 Gustavus II Adolphus, Protestant king of Sweden, is killed at Lützen during the Thirty Years' War (6 Nov.)

1642 The speaker of the House of Commons defends its independence (4 Jan.)

1644 The English poet John Milton defends free speech in his tract *Areopagitica* (23 Nov.)

1645 King Charles I is defeated by a Parliamentary army at Naseby (14 June)

1649 Charles I is executed (30 Jan.)

1650 Oliver Cromwell urges the General Assembly of the Church of Scotland to reject an alliance with Charles II (3 Aug.)

1660 King Charles II of England issues a declaration of pardon and toleration (4 April)

1661 Samuel Pepys celebrates the coronation of Charles II (23 April)

1666 The Great Fire devastates the City of London (2 Sept.)

1670 The Treaty of Dover: Charles II secretly promises the French king Louis XIV that he will convert to Catholicism (26 May)

1671 Captain Blood attempts to steal the crown jewels (9 May)

1685 Louis XIV of France revokes the Edict of Nantes, ending toleration of Protestants (18 Oct.)

1687 Isaac Newton's *Principia* is published (5 July)

1690 William III's victory at the Boyne ensures the Protestant ascendancy in Ireland (12 July)

1692 Some 80 members of the Clan MacDonald are killed in the Massacre of Glencoe (13 Feb.)

1692 The Salem Witch Trials begin in Massachusetts (29 Feb.)

1703 A 'great storm' hits England (25 Nov.)

1709 Alexander Selkirk is rescued from the Pacific island of Juan Fernandez, where he has been marooned (2 Feb.)

1717 Mary Wortley Montagu, wife of the British ambassador, visits a Turkish bath in Sofia (1 April)

1738 John Wesley, founder of Methodism, experiences his religious conversion (24 May)

1746 Hanoverian forces defeat the Jacobites at Culloden Moor (16 April)

1755 The Portuguese capital Lisbon is destroyed by a massive earthquake (1 Nov.)

1756 More than 100 Britons and Anglo-Indians die in the 'Black Hole of Calcutta' (21 June)

1757 Admiral John Byng is executed (14 Feb.)

1759 Robert Burns, Scotland's national poet, is born (25 Jan.)

1759 British forces capture Quebec from the French (13 Sept.)

1763 France cedes Canada to Britain (10 Feb.)

1764 Edward Gibbon is inspired to write *The Decline and Fall of the Roman Empire* (15 Oct.)

1773 The Boston Tea Party (16 Dec.)

1775 The Virginian politician Patrick Henry calls for American resistance to British rule (23 March)

1775 The Battle of Lexington begins the American Revolution (19 April)

1776 The American Declaration of Independence (4 July)

1779 Samuel Johnson displays his talent for conversation (28 April)

1779 A Franco-American fleet raids a British convoy off Flamborough Head (23 Sept.)

1783 Benjamin Franklin observes the first untethered human flight in a hot-air balloon (21 Nov.)

1785 *The Times* newspaper is first published (1 Jan.)

1779 Captain James Cook is killed in Hawaii (14 Feb.)

1788 Captain Phillip disembarks at Sydney harbour (26 Jan.)

1789 The storming of the Bastille: start of the French Revolution (14 July)

1792 'La Marseillaise' is heard for the first time in Paris (30 July)

1793 King Louis XVI of France is guillotined (21 Jan.)

1794 Maximilien Robespierre justifies the 'terror' of revolutionary France (5 Feb.)

1800 Irish nationalist Robert Emmet speaks from the dock before his execution (19 Sept.)

1801 Vice-Admiral Horatio Nelson disobeys orders at the Battle of Copenhagen (2 April)

1803 The US Senate ratifies the Louisiana Purchase (20 Oct.)

1804 US Vice-President Aaron Burr kills his political rival Alexander Hamilton in a duel (11 July)

1805 The US explorers Meriwether Lewis and William Clark reach the Great Falls of the Missouri (13 June)

1805 Vice-Admiral Horatio Nelson defeats a Franco-Spanish fleet at Trafalgar (21 Oct.)

1807 The first commercial steamship service is launched in the USA (17 Aug.)

1808 Ludwig van Beethoven's Fifth Symphony premieres in Vienna (22 Dec.)

1810 The Mexican Revolution against Spanish rule begins (16 Sept.)

1812 The Russians burn Moscow during Napoleon's occupation of the city (14 Sept.)

1812 The British Prime Minister Spencer Perceval is assassinated (11 May)

1814 The British occupy Washington and burn the White House during the War of 1812 (25 Aug.)

1815 The British-Prussian victory over the French at Waterloo ends the Napoleonic Wars and results in the French emperor's abdication (18 June)

1815 Napoleon surrenders aboard HMS *Bellerophon* (15 July)

1819 Troops kill 11 demonstrators calling for parliamentary reform in the 'Peterloo Massacre' in Manchester (16 Aug.)

1820 Chilean patriots capture Valdiva from the Spanish (4 Feb.)

1820 The whale-ship *Essex* is rammed by a sperm whale in the South Pacific (20 Nov.)

1823 The English reformer William Cobbett defines the nature of good government (31 May)

1823 US President James Monroe outlines the 'Monroe Doctrine' (2 Dec.)

1827 The Baltimore & Ohio Railroad, America's first railway, is incorporated (28 Feb.)

1829 The Police Act establishes London's Metropolitan Police (19 June)

1830 The Liverpool and Manchester Railway opens in England (15 Sept.)

1832 The German polymath and poet Goethe dies (22 March)

1834 The Tolpuddle Martyrs are sentenced to transportation for swearing a secret oath as members of the Friendly Society of Agricultural Labourers (18 March)

1834 The Palace of Westminster is destroyed by fire (16 Oct.)

1835 Charles Darwin arrives in the Galápagos Islands (17 Sept.)

1837 Queen Victoria accedes to the British throne (20 June)

1840 Britain gains New Zealand by the Treaty of Waitangi (6 Feb.)

1843 Isambard Kingdom Brunel's iron-hulled steamship, SS *Great Britain*, is launched (19 July)

1843 Charles Dickens's *A Christmas Carol* is published (19 Dec.)

1845 William Cobden reveals the iniquities of the Corn Laws (13 March)

1847 The explorer Sir John Franklin dies in the Arctic (11 June)

1847 James Simpson discovers the anaesthetic effects of chloroform (4 Nov.)

1848 The Communist Manifesto is published (21 Feb.)

1848 The declaration of the Seneca Falls

Convention: birth of the US women's suffrage movement (20 July)

1849 Charles Dickens writes to the editor of *The Times* after witnessing a public hanging (13 Nov.)

1853 Admiral Perry's 'black ships' arrive in Japan (8 July)

1851 The Great Exhibition opens in London (1 May)

1852 Queen Victoria goes hunting in the Scottish Highlands (11 Oct.)

1853 The explorer Richard Burton visits Mecca (10 Sept.)

1854 Britain declares war on Russia and enters the Crimean War (28 March)

1854 The Charge of the Light Brigade (25 Oct.)

1854 Leo Tolstoy describes the Siege of Sevastopol (23 Dec.)

1857 The Indian Mutiny breaks out (10 May)

1857 The surrender of the Mughal emperor ends the Indian Mutiny (20 Sept.)

1858 Abraham Lincoln accepts the nomination as Republican senator for Illinois (16 June)

1859 Henry David Thoreau observes the first signs of spring near his cabin by Walden Pond (27 March)

1859 Jules Léotard, the aerial trapeze artist, gives his first performance in Paris (12 Nov.)

1859 Charles Darwin's *On the Origin of Species* is published (24 Nov.)

1860 Giuseppe Garibaldi recognizes Victor Emmanuel as ruler of an independent, unified Italy (26 Oct.)

1861 Tsar Alexander II emancipates Russia's serfs (3 March)

1861 John Bright argues against British involvement in the American Civil War (4 Dec.)

1861 Queen Victoria mourns the death of Prince Albert (14 Dec.)

1862 The Second Battle of Manassas (30 Aug.)

1862 US President Abraham Lincoln makes his first emancipation proclamation (22 Sept.)

1863 The final day of the Battle of Gettysburg (3 July)

1863 US President Abraham Lincoln makes the Gettysburg Address (19 Nov.)

1864 Unionist General William Tecumseh Sherman leaves the city of Atlanta in flames (15 Nov.)

1865 The French socialist Pierre-Joseph Proudhon dies (19 Jan.)

1865 Robert E. Lee surrenders at Appomattox Courthouse, ending the American Civil War (9 April)

1865 US President Abraham Lincoln is assassinated (14 April)

1865 William Booth is inspired to found the Salvation Army (2 July)

1870 Prussia defeats France at Sedan, in the decisive battle of the Franco-Prussian War (1 Sept.)

1871 The Paris Commune is crushed by French government forces (28 May)

1871 Henry Morton Stanley meets David Livingstone at Ujiji (17 Oct.)

1872 The Yellowstone National Park, in the northwestern USA, comes into being (1 March)

1872 Scotland and England play the first ever international football match (30 Nov.)

1876 Alexander Graham Bell makes the world's first telephone call (10 March)

1876 General George Custer is defeated and killed by the Sioux at Little Bighorn (25 June)

1879 152 British soldiers defy some 4,000 Zulus at Rorke's Drift in Natal (23 Jan.)

1882 The US outlaw Jesse James is killed (3 April)

1882 Australia's cricketers defeat England at the Kennington Oval, giving rise to the tradition of playing for 'the Ashes' (29 Aug.)

1883 The volcanic island of Krakatoa erupts in the Dutch East Indies (27 Aug.)

1884 W.T. Stead of the *Pall Mall Gazette* interviews General Gordon about the situation in the Sudan (9 January)

1885 The Congo becomes the property of Leopold II, king of the Belgians (26 Feb.)

1886 The Apache chief Geronimo surrenders (4 Sept.)

1887 Lord Acton explains his belief that power tends to corrupt (5 April)

1889 White settlers claim parcels of 'Unassigned Lands' in Indian Territory in Oklahoma (22 April)

1890 The artist Vincent van Gogh dies (29 July)

1890 The two houses of Japan's new 'parliament' meet for the first time in Tokyo (29 Nov.)

1893 In New Zealand, women vote for the first time in a national election (28 Nov.)

1894 Baron de Coubertin announces the creation of the modern Olympic movement (23 June)

1895 The National Trust is founded in Britain (12 Jan.)

1895 The Lumière brothers unveil the cinematograph (28 Dec.)

1896 The British journalist Augustus Wylde surveys the battlefield at Adowa, scene of an Ethiopian victory over the Italians (2 March)

1896 The *Daily Mail* is launched, introducing mass-market newspapers to Britain (4 May)

1898 The novelist Émile Zola identifies the guilty men in the Dreyfus case (13 Jan.)

1898 The Spanish–American War breaks out (15 Feb.)

1898 Joshua Slocum completes his solo circumnavigation of the world (27 June)

1899 French president Félix Faure dies in mysterious circumstances (16 Feb.)

1900 The British garrison of Mafeking is relieved after a lengthy siege during the Boer War (17 May)

1900 An international relief force reaches Beijing and ends the nationalist 'Boxer' rebellion (14 Aug.)

1901 US President McKinley is shot (6 Sept.)

1901 The Italian inventor Guglielmo Marconi receives the first radio signal sent across the Atlantic (13 Dec.)

1903 The Wright brothers make the first heavier-than-air flight (17 Dec.)

1906 San Francisco is devastated by an earthquake (17 April)

1907 A violent demonstration over animal vivisection takes place in London (10 Dec.)

1909 The Futurist Manifesto is published (20 Feb.)

1909 Louis Blériot becomes the first man to fly across the English Channel (25 July)

1910 The wife-murderer Dr Crippen is arrested on board the transatlantic liner SS *Montrose* (31 July)

1911 The 'Siege of Sidney Street', in London, follows the shooting of a policeman by a revolutionary group (3 Jan.)

1911 Hiram Bingham discovers Machu Picchu, lost city of the Inca (24 July)

1912 Captain Lawrence Oates dies in Antarctica (16 March)

1912 The RMS *Titanic* sinks on her maiden voyage (15 April)

1914 Archduke Franz Ferdinand is assassinated in Sarajevo (28 June)

1914 Britain declares war on Germany (4 Aug.)

1914 The German army enters Brussels (21 Aug.)

1914 The first day of the Battle of the Marne (5 Sept.)

1914 A Christmas truce breaks out on the Western Front (24 Dec.)

1915 ANZACS land at Gallipoli (25 April)

1915 John McCrae completes his poem 'In Flanders Fields' (3 May)

1916 The centre of Dublin is severely damaged in the nationalist Easter Rising (24 April)

1916 Henry Ford tells the *Chicago Tribune* his views on history (25 May)

1916 Some 19,500 British troops die on the first day of the Somme offensive (1 July)

1916 The Battle of Verdun ends after ten months of fighting and 300,000 battlefield deaths (18 Dec.)

1917 The Balfour declaration expresses British support for a Jewish national home in Palestine (2 Nov.)

1917 Bolsheviks storm the Winter Palace in St Petersburg (7 Nov.)

1918 The former Russian tsar Nicholas II and his family are executed (17 July)

1918 T.E. Lawrence leads an attack on a Turkish position during the Arab Revolt (27 Sept.)

1918 US corporal Alvin York single-handedly captures 35 German machine guns (8 Oct.)

1918 The Armistice ends the First World War (11 Nov.)

1919 The Paris Peace Conference opens (18 Jan.)

1919 The Greeks occupy Smyrna (15 May)

1919 British troops shoot dead at least 379 unarmed Indians in the Amritsar massacre (13 June)

1921 France's Marshal Foch honours Napoleon on the centenary of his death (5 May)

1921 101 die in the 'Great Train Wreck' in Nashville, Tennessee (9 July)

1921 The Anglo-Irish treaty is signed in London, ending the Anglo-Irish war of 1919–21 (6 Dec.)

1922 Howard Carter discovers the tomb of Tutankhamun (26 Nov.)

1923 V.I. Lenin's last testament denounces Joseph Stalin (9 March)

1924 Britain's first Labour government takes office (22 Jan.)

1925 The 'Scopes Monkey Trial' (13 July)

1926 Virginia Woolf's diary describes Britain's General Strike (7 May)

1927 Charles Lindbergh becomes the first man to fly the Atlantic solo (21 May)

1927 The premiere of *The Jazz Singer*, the world's first 'talkie' (6 Oct.)

1928 US presidential candidate Herbert Hoover predicts the imminent end of poverty in his acceptance speech at the US Republican Party convention (11 Aug.)

1928 Alexander Fleming discovers penicillin (28 Sept.)

1929 The Wall Street Crash (29 Oct.)

1930 Gandhi completes his Salt March (6 April)

1930 The last lynching in the Northern United States takes place in Marion, Indiana (7 Aug.)

1933 Former US president Calvin Coolidge dies (5 Jan.)

1933 The Reichstag, Berlin's Parliament building, is destroyed by fire (27 Feb.)

1934 Alexander I of Yugoslavia is assassinated (9 Oct.)

1935 Joseph Stalin celebrates the quality of life under Soviet Communism in a speech to the All-Union Conference of Stakhanovites (17 Nov.)

1936 The Jarrow marchers leave for London (5 Oct.)

1936 King Edward VIII of Great Britain abdicates (11 Dec.)

1937 The Basque town of Guernica is destroyed in a bombing raid by the German Condor Legion (26 April)

1937 The airship *Hindenburg* explodes on its maiden transatlantic journey (6 May)

1937 George Orwell is wounded by a sniper during the Spanish Civil War (20 May)

1937 Japanese troops occupy the Chinese city of Nanjing and massacre its inhabitants (13 Dec.)

1938 The Anschluss: Adolf Hitler annexes Austria (12 March)

1938 Neville Chamberlain signs the Munich Agreement (30 Sept.)

1939 Hitler and Mussolini agree the 'Pact of Steel' (22 May)

1939 Albert Einstein urges President Roosevelt to commence the building of a US atom bomb (2 Aug.)

1939 Britain declares war on Germany (3 Sept.)

1940 New British premier Winston Churchill promises 'blood, toil, tears and sweat' (13 May)

1940 The 'little ships' evacuate the British Expeditionary Force from Dunkirk (1 June)

1940 The French surrender to Nazi Germany at Compiègne (22 June)

1940 Churchill hails the heroes of the Battle of Britain (20 Aug.)

1940 The Luftwaffe begins its 'Blitz' on London (7 Sept.)

1940 German bombers devastate the town of Coventry in the English Midlands (14 Nov.)

1941 US President Franklin D. Roosevelt delivers his third inaugural presidential address

1941 The star, worn by Jews in Nazi Germany, is introduced (18 Sept.)

1941 The Japanese attack Pearl Harbor (7 Dec.)

1941 Churchill repeats his defiance of Nazi Germany (30 Dec.)

1942 US General Douglas MacArthur vows to retake the Philippines (20 March)

1942 The RAF's Bomber Command launches the first 'thousand-bomber raid' on Cologne (30 May)

1942 Anne Frank begins her diary (12 June)

1942 Stalin orders the Red Army to take 'not one step back' (28 July)

1942 The Beveridge Report, the basis of Britain's postwar welfare state, is published (1 Dec.)

1943 Hitler forbids the surrender of the German 6th Army at Stalingrad (24 Jan.)

1943 The Gestapo execute members of the White Rose Society (22 Feb.)

1943 Ireland's taoiseach Éamon de Valera celebrates St Patrick's Day (17 March)

1943 The Nazis destroy the Warsaw Ghetto (16 May)

1944 The D-Day landings (6 June)

1944 Anne Frank writes her last diary entry (1 Aug.)

1944 The Allies fail to take the bridge at Arnhem (26 Sept.)

1945 Auschwitz-Birkenau is liberated by the Red Army (27 Jan.)

1945 Hitler dictates his political testament (29 April)

1945 Victory in Europe day (8 May)

1945 The first atomic bomb is tested in the New Mexico desert (16 July)

1945 Clement Attlee's Labour Party defeats Churchill's Conservatives in the UK general election (26 July)

1945 The USA drops the atom bomb on Hiroshima (6 Aug.)

1946 Churchill sees the Iron Curtain fall across Europe (5 March)

1946 Zionist militants bomb the King David Hotel in Jerusalem (22 July)

1946 Eighteen leading Nazis are convicted of war crimes and crimes against humanity at Nuremberg (1 Oct.)

1947 India becomes an independent state (15 Aug.)

1950 US Senator Joseph McCarthy begins a witchhunt against suspected Communists (9 Feb.)

1952 The Free Officers movement seizes power in Egypt (23 July)

1953 Ethel and Julius Rosenberg are convicted of spying for the Soviet Union (29 March)

1953 The Kenyan nationalist Jomo Kenyatta is condemned to imprisonment by the British (8 April)

1954 US President Dwight Eisenhower argues for the domino theory of the spread of Communism (7 April)

1956 The Soviet leader Nikita Khrushchev denounces Stalin in his 'Secret Speech' (25 Feb.)

1957 *Sputnik*, the world's first artificial satellite, is launched (4 Oct.)

1960 In a speech in South Africa, British premier Harold Macmillan describes a 'wind of change' blowing through the African continent (3 Feb.)

1960 Penguin Books publish *Lady Chatterley's Lover* (10 Nov.)

1961 The Berlin Wall is built (13 Aug.)

1961 In Jerusalem, the Nazi bureaucrat Adolf Eichmann is found guilty of war crimes and crimes against humanity (15 Dec.)

1962 Douglas MacArthur addresses cadets at the US Army academy of West Point (12 may)

1962 US President John F. Kennedy broadcasts to the nation on the Cuban Missile Crisis (22 Oct.)

1962 Marilyn Monroe dies (5 Aug.)

1963 Betty Friedan's *The Feminine Mystique* is published (19 Feb.)

1963 The Beeching Report recommends drastic cuts in Britain's rail network (27 March)

1963 US President John F. Kennedy speaks in Cold War Berlin (26 June)

1963 Civil rights leader Martin Luther King makes his 'I Have a Dream' speech in Washington, DC (28 Aug.)

1963 US President John F. Kennedy is assassinated in Dallas (22 Nov.)

1964 Smoking and Health: report of the advisory committee to the Surgeon General of the United States (11 Jan.)

1964 Beatlemania hits New York (7 Feb.)

1964 Nelson Mandela defends himself in the Rivonia treason trial (20 April)

1965 Martin Luther King addresses civil rights marchers at Montgomery, Alabama (25 March)

1967 The Gathering of the Tribes for a Human Be-In, a radical counter-cultural event, takes place in San Francisco (14 Jan.)

1968 North Vietnam launches the Tet Offensive against South Vietnamese and US forces (31 Jan.)

1968 In Paris, the May protests reach their climax (27 May)

1968 Robert F. Kennedy, a Democratic candidate for the US presidency, is assassinated in Los Angeles (5 June)

1969 US Navy pilot Commander Neil Armstrong becomes the first man to land on the Moon (21 July)

1969 US President Richard M. Nixon appeals for the support of the 'silent majority' for America's military involvement in Vietnam (3 Nov.)

1971 Mujibur Rahman calls for Bangladeshi independence from Pakistan (7 March)

1974 US president Richard M. Nixon resigns in the wake of the Watergate scandal (8 Aug.)

1979 The Ayatollah Khomeini returns to Iran (1 Feb.)

1979 Pope John Paul II visits his native Poland (2 June)

1979 The Egyptian–Israeli Middle East peace treaty is signed on the White House lawn (26 March)

1979 Black-majority rule comes to Zimbabwe (4 March)

1980 The former Beatle John Lennon is murdered in New York (8 Dec.)

1983 Ronald Reagan argues against détente with the Soviet Union (8 March)

1984 A chemical leak at the Union Carbide pesticide plant at Bhopal in India kills more than 2,000 people (3 Dec.)

1985 Mikhail Gorbachev comes to power in the Soviet Union (11 March)

1986 The US space shuttle *Challenger* is destroyed in an explosion shortly after take-off (28 Jan.)

1988 Pan Am Flight 103 is destroyed by a terrorist bomb over Lockerbie, southern Scotland (21 Dec.)

1989 The Chinese authorities kill 2,000–3,000 demonstrators in the Tiananmen Square massacre in Beijing (4 June)

1989 The Berlin Wall is dismantled (9 Nov.)

1990 Nelson Mandela is released from prison (11 Feb.)

1991 A US-led coalition launches Operation Desert Storm, aiming to expel Saddam Hussein's Iraqi forces from Kuwait (17 Jan.)

1994 The Rwandan genocide gathers pace (11 April)

1995 The Srebrenica massacre of Bosnian Muslims enters its second week (18 July)

1997 Hong Kong returns to Chinese rule (30 June)

1997 Diana, Princess of Wales, dies in a car accident in Paris (31 Aug.)

1998 The Good Friday Agreement brings hopes of an end to Northern Ireland's 'Troubles' (10 April)

1998 The report of South Africa's post-*apartheid* Truth and Reconciliation Committee is published (28 Oct.)

1999 Boris Yeltsin resigns as Russian president (31 Dec.)

2001 Al-Qaeda attacks New York and Washington (11 Sept.)

2002 US President George W. Bush defines the 'axis of evil' (29 Jan.)

2002 US Secretary of Defence Donald Rumsfeld makes sense of the War on Terror (12 Feb.)

2004 An earthquake off the coast of Java causes a devastating *tsunami* (26 Dec.)

2005 Islamist suicide bombers attack London's transport network (7 July)

2009 The inauguration of US President Barack Obama (20 Jan.)

SOURCES AND CREDITS

JANUARY

1 January: John Walter, *Universal Register,* 1 January 1785.

2 January: Miguel Garrido Atienza, *Las capitulaciones para la entrega de Granada,* Granada: University of Granada, 1992.

3 January: Philip Gibbs, *Adventures in Journalism,* London: William Heinemann, 1923.

4 January: William Lenthall, in J. Rushworth (ed.), *Historical Collections of Private Passages of State,* 8 vols, London: James Astwood, 1721–2.

5 January: Dorothy Parker, quoted in Malcolm Cowley (ed.) *The Paris Review Interviews: Writers at Work,* New York: Viking, 1963

6 January: Franklin D. Roosevelt, quoted at Miller Center Presidential Speech Archive, www.millercenter.org/scripps/ archive/speeches. By permission of Nancy Roosevelt Ireland.

7 January: Raphael Holinshed, *Chronicles of England, Scotland and Ireland,* London: London Stationers, 1577.

8 January: Asser, *Life of Alfred* (9th century), in *Old English Chronicles,* London: Bell, 1906.

9 January: W.T. Stead, in *Pall Mall Gazette,* 9 January 1884.

10 January: Suetonius, *The Twelve Caesars,* trans. Alexander Thomson, London: Bell, 1893.

11 January: *Smoking and Health: Report of the Advisory Committee to the Surgeon General of the United States,* Washington, DC: US Government Printing Office, 1964.

12 January: Octavia Hill, quoted in G. Darley, *Octavia Hill: Social Reformer and Founder of the National Trust,* London: Francis Boutle, 2010.

13 January: Emile Zola, in *L'Aurore* newspaper, 13 January 1898.

14 January: *San Francisco Oracle* magazine, January 1967.

15 January: John Strype, *Annals of the Reformation ... During Queen Elizabeth's Happy Reign,* 4 vols, London: no publisher, 1709–31.

16 January: Senate decree quoted in Werner Eck, *The Age of Augustus,* Oxford: Blackwell, 2003.

17 January: Saddam Hussein, quoted in *Washington Post,* 17 January 1991.

18 January: T.E. Lawrence, in *The Letters of T E. Lawrence,* ed. David Garnett, London: Jonathan Cape, 1938.

19 January: Pierre-Joseph Proudhon, *General Idea of the Revolution in the Nineteenth Century,* 1845, trans. John Beverly Robinson, 1923: London: Freedom Press

20 January: Barack Obama, quoted at Miller Center Presidential Speech Archive, www. millercenter.org/scripps/archive/speeches.

21 January: Henry Essex Edgeworth, *Memoirs,* London: Rowland Hunter, 1815.

22 January: George V, quoted in Kenneth Rose, *King George the Fifth,* London: Weidenfeld & Nicolson, 1983.

23 January: Frederick Hitch, quoted in M. Boucher, 'Frederick Hitch and the Defence of Rorke's Drift', *Military History Journal,* Vol. 2, No. 6 (1973).

24 January: Adolf Hitler, quoted in Antony Beevor, *Stalingrad,* New York: Viking, 1998.

25 January: The Selkirk Grace, quoted in Mick Imlah (ed.), *Penguin Book of Scottish Verse,* Harmondsworth: Penguin, 2006.

26 January: Arthur Phillip, quoted in *Historical Records of New South Wales,* Vol. 1, Part 2 (1788–92).

27 January: Bart Stern, interview collected by the US Holocaust Museum, quoted at www.ushmm.org. Courtesy of US Holocaust Memorial Museum, Washington, DC.

28 January: Ronald Reagan, Miller Center Presidential Speech Archive, www.millercenter.org/scripps/archive/speeches.

29 January: George W. Bush, at Miller Center Presidential Speech Archive, www.millercenter.org/scripps/archive/speeches.

30 January: Philip Henry, in *Diaries and Letters of Philip Henry*, ed. Matthew Henry Lee, London: Kegan Paul, Trench, 1882.

31 January: Vo Nguyen Giap, reported message, 1968; Walter Cronkite, CBS Television News broadcast, 27 February 1968, as reproduced in *Reporting Vietnam, Part One: American Journalism, 1959–1969*, New York: Library of America, 1998

FEBRUARY

1 February: Ruhollah Khomeini, quoted in Amir Taheri, *The Spirit of Allah*, Castle Rock, CO: 1985.

2 February: Woodes Rogers, *A Cruising Voyage Round the World*, London: Bell and Lintot, 1712.

3 February: Harold Macmillan, *Pointing the Way 1959–1961*, London: Macmillan, 1972.

4 February: Thomas Cochrane, *Narrative of Services in the Liberation of Chili sic, Peru and Brazil, from Spanish and Portuguese Domination*, n.p.: James Ridgway, 1859.

5 February: Maximilien Robespierre, 'Report of the Principles of Public Morality', quoted in *Speeches of Maximilien Robespierre*, New York: International, 1927.

6 February: treaty text quoted in T. Lindsey Buick, *The Treaty of Waitangi; or, How New Zealand Became a British Colony*, Wellington: S & W. Mackay, 1916.

7 February: George Harrison, quoted in Bob Spitz, *The Beatles: The Biography*, New York: Little, Brown, 2005.

8 February: Robert Wynkefield, letter to Lord Burghley quoted in A. McLean (ed.), *The Execution of Mary Queen of Scots:*

An Eyewitness Account, Isle of Bute, Scotland: Mount Stuart Trust, 2007.

9 February: Joseph McCarthy, quoted in Robert Griffith, *The Politics of Fear: Joseph R. McCarthy and the Senate*, Lexington: University Press of Kentucky, 1970.

10 February: Text at Avalon Project, Yale Law School, www.avalon.law.yale.edu/18th century/paris763.asp.

11 February: Nelson Mandela, quoted at www.nelsonmandela.org.

12 February: Donald Rumsfeld, quoted at www.defense.gov/Transcripts/Transcript.aspx?TranscriptID 2636

13 February: John Dalrymple, orders to John Campbell quoted in John Prebble, *Glencoe: The Story of the Massacre*, London: Secker & Warburg, 1966.

14 February: John Rickman, 'Journal of Captain Cook's Last Voyage to the Pacific Ocean' (1781), The National Archives, Kew, Surrey.

15 February: 'A Few Spaniards Flee', *New York Times*, 21 April 1898.

16 February: Marguerite Steinheil, *My Memoirs*, London: Nash, 1912.

17 February: Giordano Bruno, quoted in Dorothea Waley Singer, *Giordano Bruno: His Life and Thought*, New York: Schuman, 1950.

18 February: William Shakespeare, *King Richard the Third*, London: Valentine Sims, 1597.

19 February: Betty Friedan, *The Feminist Mystique*, New York: Norton, 1963. Used by permission of WW Norton & Company Inc. and the Orion Publishing Group, London.

20 February: Filippo Marinetti, *Marinetti: Selected Writings*, ed. by R. W. Flint, trans. R. W. Flint and Arthur A. Coppottelli, New York: Farrar, Straus and Giroux, 1972. Translation copyright © 1972 by Farrar, Straus and Giroux, LLC. Reprinted by permission of Farrar, Straus and Giroux, LLC.

21 February: Karl Marx and Friedrich Engels, *The Communist Manifesto*, London: 1848 (edition in German).

22 February: Sophie Scholl, quoted in Jud Newborn and Annette Dumbach, *Sophie*

Scholl and the White Rose, Oxford: Oneworld, 2006.

23 February: Muhammad, Farewell Sermon, *Sahih al-Bukhari*, Cairo: Egyptian Press 1959.

24 February: Eusebius, *Historia Ecclesiae* (tr. Philip Schaff), Vol. 1 (Series II) of *A Select Library of the Nicene and Post-Nicene Fathers of the Christian Church*, Edinburgh: T. & T. Clark, 1890.

25 February: Nikita Khrushchev, *The Crimes of Stalin Era*, annotated by Boris Nikolaevsky, New York: The New Leader, 1956.

26 February: Leopold II, quoted in Arthur Conan Doyle, *The Crime of the Congo*, London: Hutchinson, 1909.

27 February: D. Sefton Delmer, *Daily Express*, 28 February 1933.

28 February: *Proceedings of Sundry Citizens of Baltimore, Concerned for the Purpose of Devising the Most Efficient Means of Improving Intercourse Between That City and the Western States*, Baltimore: William Woddy, 1827.

29 February: Sarah Good and John Hathorne, interrogation transcript in Paul Boyer and Stephen Nissenbaum (eds), *The Salem Witchcraft Papers*, Vol. 1, New York: DaCapo Press, 1977.

MARCH

1 March: Ulysses S. Grant, Act of Congress, quoted at www.yellowstone-online.com.

2 March: Augustus Wylde, *Modern Abyssinia*, London: Methuen 1901.

3 March: Tsar Alexander II, quoted in James Harvey Robinson and Charles Beard (eds), *Readings in Modern European History*, Vol. 2, Boston and New York: Ginn, 1908.

4 March: Robert Mugabe, in *SA Reporter*, March 2010.

5 March: Winston Churchill, quoted at www.winstonchurchill.org. Reproduced with permission of Curtis Brown, London, on behalf of the Estate of Sir Winston Churchill.

6 March: Lord Raoul de Gaucourt, transcript of the trial of Joan of Arc in Jules Quicherat (ed.) *Procès de condamnation et de réhabilitation de Jeanne d'Arc*

(1841–9), trans. Mathias Gabel, at www.stjoan-center.com/Trials/null05.html.

7 March: Mujibur Rahman, quoted in *Poet of Politics, Father of the Nation: Bangabandhu Sheikh Mujibur Rahman*, Dhaka: Sheikh Mujibur Rahman Memorial Trust, 1999

8 March: Ronald Reagan, quoted at Miller Center Presidential Speech Archive, www.millercenter.org/scripps/archive/speeches. Courtesy Ronald Reagan Library.

9 March: V.I. Lenin, *Collected Works*, Vol. 36, *1900–1923*, at www.marxists.org/archive/lenin/works/cw/volume36.htm

10 March: Alexander Graham Bell, journal entry, from the Alexander Graham Bell Family Papers: US Library of Congress, Washington, DC.

11 March: Margaret Thatcher, BBC interview transcript www.margaretthatcher.org/document/105592.

12 March: transcript of radio report (1938) for US Mutual Broadcasting System, at www.otr.com/austria.shtml.

13 March: Richard Cobden, *Hansard*, 13 March 1845.

14 March: Voltaire, *Candide*, Paris: Sirène, and London: Nourse, 1759.

15 March: Suetonius, *The Twelve Caesars* (AD 121), trans. Alexander Thomson, London: Bell, 1893.

16 March: Robin Falcon Scott, in Leonard Huxley (ed.) *Scott's Last Expedition: Being the Journals of Captain R.F. Scott*, London: Smith, Elder, 1913.

17 March: Eamon de Valera, Address on RTE radio; audio and transcript at www.rte.ie/laweb/ll/ll t09b.html.

18 March: George Loveless, *Victims of Whiggery*, London: no publisher, 1837.

19 March: From Canons of the Third Lateran Council, in Norman P. Tanner (ed.), *Decrees of the Ecumenical Councils*, 2 vols, London: Sheed and Ward, 1990

20 March: Douglas MacArthur, quoted in *The News* (Adelaide newspaper), 20 March 1942.

21 John Foxe, *Actes and Monuments*, London: John Day, 1563.

22 Johann Peter Eckermann, *Conversations of Goethe with Eckermann and Soret* (1832), trans. John Oxenford, London: Bell, 1906

23 March: Patrick Henry, quoted in William Wirt, *Sketches of the Life and Character of Patrick Henry*, Philadelphia: Webster, 1816.

24 March: Proclamation, quoted in James Larkin (ed.) *Royal Stuart Proclamations*, Oxford: Clarendon Press, 1973.

25 March: Martin Luther King, Jr., quoted at www.kinginstitute.info. Reprinted by arrangement with The Heirs to the estate of Martin Luther King Jr., c/o Writers House as agent for the proprietor New York NY. Copyright 1965 Dr. Martin Luther King Jr; copyright renewed 1993 Coretta Scott King.

26 March: Jimmy Carter, Anwar Sadat, Menachem Begin, transcript at www.jewishvirtuallibrary.org/jsource/US-Israel/Carter Peace9.html.

27 March: Henry David Thoreau, *The Journal of Henry David Thoreau*, Boston: Houghton Mifflin Co., 1906

28 March: Declaration of war quoted in Alexander Kinglake, *The Invasion of the Crimea*, Edinburgh and London: Blackwood, 1863–87.

29 March: Irving Kaufman, in trial transcript at www.law2.umkc.edu/faculty/projects/FTrials/Rosenberg/RosenbergTrial.pdf

30 March: Roger Mastrangelo, in the chronicle by Saba Malaspina (*c.*1285), quoted in Michele Amari, *History of the War of the Sicilian Vespers*, London: Richard Bentley, 1850.

31 March: Josephus, *The Antiquities of the Jews*, trans. William Whiston (1737), updated by Peter Furtado.

APRIL

1 April: Lady Mary Wortley Montagu, *The Complete Letters of Lady Mary Wortley Montagu*, ed. Robert Halsband, Oxford: Clarendon Press 1965

2 April: Robert Southey, *Life of Horatio Lord Nelson*, London: Dent, 1813.

3 April: Report in the *New York Times*, 4 April 1882.

4 April: Charles II, Declaration of Breda, quoted in *Journals of the House of Lords*, Vol. XI (1660).

5 April: Lord Acton (John Emerich Edward Dalberg-Acton), letter to Bishop Mandell Creighton (5 April 1887), quoted in his *Essays on Freedom and Power*, ed. Gertrude Himmelfarb, Boston: Beacon Press, 1949

6 April: Mohandas K. Gandhi, quoted in Stanley Wolpert, *Gandhi's Passion: The Life and Legacy of Mahatma Gandhi*, Oxford and New York: Oxford University Press, 2001.

7 April: Dwight D. Eisenhower, news conference transcribed in *The Pentagon Papers*, Vol. 1, Boston: Beacon Press, 1971.

8 April: Ransley Thacker, quoted in Rawson Macharia, *The Truth About the Trial of Jomo Kenyatta*, London: Longman, 1991.

9 April: Horace Porter, quoted in Robert Underwood Johnson and Clarence Clough Buel (eds), *Battles and Leaders of the Civil War*, New York: Century, 1887.

10 April: Northern Ireland Office, text of Good Friday Agreement at www.nio.gov.uk/agreement.pdf.

11 April: Roméo Dallaire, *Shake Hands with the Devil: The Failure of Humanity in Rwanda*, Toronto: Random House Canada. Copyright © 2003 Roméo A. Dallaire, LGen (ret) Inc. Reprinted by permission of Random House Canada and the Random House Group Ltd.

12 April: Niketas Choniates, in Harry J. Magoulias (ed.), *O City of Byzantium: Annals of Niketas Choniates*, Detroit: Wayne State University Press, 1984.

13 April: Girdhari Lal, Report of Commissioners, Vols I and II, Bombay: 1920; reprinted, New Delhi, 1976

14 April: Charles Sabin Taft ('The Assassination of Abraham Lincoln, 1865'), in *Century Magazine*, February 1893.

15 April: Harold Bride, *New York Times*, 18 April 1912.

16 April: Donald Mackay of Achmonie, account published at www.lochness1.hypermart.net/scottish-history-heritage/1745-bonnie-prince-charlie.html.

17 April: Enrico Caruso, *The Theatre* (magazine), 1906.

18 April: Martin Luther, quoted in Martin Brecht, *Martin Luther*, trans. James L. Schaaf, Minneapolis: Fortress Press, 1985–93.

19 April: John Robbins, *Providence Gazette*, 3 June 1775.

20 April: Nelson Mandela, quoted at www. nelsonmandela.org.

21 April: Livy, *History of Rome*, Book I, trans Rev. Canon Roberts, London: Dent, 1905.

22 April: Report in *Harper's Weekly*, 18 May 1889.

23 April: Samuel Pepys, *Diary*, at www. pepysdiary.com.

24 April: Padraig Pearse *et al.*, quoted in Arthur Mitchell and Padraig Ó Snodaigh (eds), *Irish Political Documents: 1916– 1949*, Dublin: Irish Academic Press, 1986.

25 April: Ellis Ashmead-Bartlett, *Sydney Morning Herald*, 8 May 1915.

26 April: George Steer, *The Times*, 28 April 1938. Courtesy of *The Times*/NI Syndication.

27 April: Antonio Pigafetta in Theodore J. Cachey (ed.), *The First Voyage Around the World, 1519–1522*, Toronto: University of Toronto Press, 2007.

28 April: James Boswell, *Life of Samuel Johnson, LL,D*, Volume III, London: Henry Baldwin for Charles Dilly, 1791.

29 April: Adolf Hitler, text from Office of United States Chief of Counsel for Prosecution of Axis Criminality, Nazi Conspiracy and Aggression, Washington, DC, 1946–48.

30 April: Piero Pasqualigo, letter (30 April 1515), trans. Rawdon Brown in *Four Years at the Court of Henry VIII*, London: Smith, Elder, 1854.

MAY

1 May: Charlotte Brontë, letter in Clement Shorter, *The Brontes' Life and Letters*, London: Hodder and Stoughton, 1908.

2 May: Preface, *The Holy Bible* (King James Bible), London: Robert Barker for the King, 1611.

3 May: John McCrae, *'In Flanders Fields' and Other Poems*, New York and London: Putnam, 1919.

4 May: *Daily Mail*, 4 May 1896.

5 May: Ferdinand Foch, in Lewis Copeland, Lawrence W. Lamm, Stephen J. McKenna (eds), *The World's Great Speeches*, New York: Dover, 1999.

6 May: Herb Morrison, in Michael Macdonald Mooney, *The Hindenburg*, New York: Dodd, Mead, 1972

7 May: Virginia Woolf, diary entry (6 May 1926) in *The Diary of Virginia Woolf*, ed. Anne Olivier Bell, London: The Hogarth Press. Reprinted by permission of The Random House Group and courtesy of The Society of Authors as the Literary Representative of the Estate of Virginia Woolf.

8 May: Mollie-Panter-Downes, *New Yorker*, 19 May 1945. Courtesy of the *New Yorker*.

9 May: Report in the *Newgate Calendar*, 1770.

10 May: Sita Ram, quoted in Joseph Coohill, 'Indian Voices from the 1857 Rebellion', *History Today*, Vol. 57, No. 5 (2007).

11 May: Report in *The Times*, 13 May 1812.

12 May: Douglas MacArthur, quoted in Department of Defense Pamphlet GEN-1A, Washington, DC: US Government Printing Office, 1964.

13 May: Winston Churchill, quoted at www. winstonchurchill.org. Reproduced with permission of Curtis Brown, London, on behalf of the Estate of Sir Winston Churchill.

14 May: John Smith, *The General Historie of Virginia, New England and the Summer Isles*, London: Printed for Michael Sparkes, 1624.

15 May: From the Introduction to *Greek Atrocities in the Vilayet of Smyrna (May To July 1919): Inedited Documents and Evidence of English and French Officers*, Permanent Bureau of the Turkish Congress at Lausanne, 1919.

16 May: Jürgen Stroop, report entitled *The Jewish Quarter of Warsaw is No More!*, 1943; Marek Edelman, *Resisting the Holocaust*, Melbourne: Ocean Press, 2004.

17 May: Robert Baden-Powell, *Lessons from the Varsity of Life*, London: Pearson, 1933. Reproduced by permission of The Scout Association. Registered Charity 306101 (England and Wales) and SC038437 (Scotland).

18 May: Baybars, letter quoted in Francesco Gabrieli, *Arab Historians of the Crusades*,

Berkeley: University of California Press, 1984.

19 May: Charles Wriothesley, *Chronicle of England During the Reign of the Tudors*, ed. W.D. Hamilton, London: Camden Society, 1875–7.

20 May: George Orwell, *Homage to Catalonia*, London: Secker & Warburg, 1938. Copyright © George Orwell, 1937. Reprinted by permission of Bill Hamilton as the Literary Executor of the Estate of the Late Sonia Brownell Orwell and Secker & Warburg Ltd.

21 May: Charles Lindbergh, *We*, New York: Putnam, 1927.

22 May: Text of Italo-German Alliance, Translation Office of United States Chief of Counsel for Prosecution of Axis Criminality, Nazi Conspiracy and Aggression, Vol. 453, Doc. No. 2818-PS, Washington, DC: US Government Printing Office, 1946–8.

23 May: Luca Landucci, quoted in U. Baldassarri and A. Saiber (eds) *Images of Quattrocento Florence*, New Haven, CT: Yale University Press, 2000.

24 May: John Wesley, *The Journal of the Rev. John Wesley*, ed. Nehemiah Curnock, 8 vols, London: Epworth, 1909.

25 May: Henry Ford, *Chicago Tribune*, 25 May 1916.

26 May: Treaty text in J.P. Kenyon, *The Stuart Constitution, 1603–1688: Documents and Commentary*, Cambridge and New York: Cambridge University Press, 1966.

27 May: Slogans quoted in Marc Rohan, *Paris '68: Graffiti, Posters, Newspapers and Poems of the May 1968 Events*, London: Impact Books, 1988.

28 May: Edmond de Goncourt, *Pages from the Goncourt Journals*, trans. and paraphrased by Richard Milbank.

29 May: Niccolo Barbero, *Diary of the Siege of Constantinople, 1453*, trans. John Melville-Jones, New York: Exposition Press, 1969.

30 May: Arthur Harris, recorded statement; George Orwell, BBC Radio Broadcast (June 1942). Copyright © George Orwell, 1942. Reprinted by permission of Bill Hamilton as the Literary Executor of the Estate of the Late Sonia Brownell Orwell

and Secker & Warburg Ltd.

31 May: William Cobbett, *Political Register*, 31 May 1823.

JUNE

1 June: John Masefield, *The Nine Days Wonder: The Operation Dynamo*, London: Heinemann, 1941. Reproduced courtesy of The Society of Authors as the Literary Representative of the Estate of John Masefield.

2 June: Pope John Paul II, text of address at www.vatican.va.

3 June: Raymond d'Aguiliers, *Historia Francorum*, as reproduced in Paul Halsall (ed.) Internet Medieval Sourcebook (Fordham University, New York), www.fordham.edu/halsall/source/raymond-cde.asp

4 June: telegram from the American Embassy, Beijing, to the US State Department, Washington, DC: National Archives.

5 June: Pete Hamill, *The Village Voice*, Vol. XIII, No. 35, 1968. Courtesy of Pete Hamill and Village Voice.

6 June: Dwight D. Eisenhower, text of broadcast from Dwight D. Eisenhower Memorial Commission, Washington, DC.

7 June: Ambassador Soardino, in Rawdon Brown (ed.) *Calendar of State Papers Relating to the Reign of Henry VIII in the Archives of Venice*, Vol. 3, 1869.

8 June: Alcuin and *Anglo-Saxon Chronicle*, in Dorothy Whitlock (ed.) *English Historical Documents 500–1042*, London: Eyre & Spottiswoode, 1955.

9 June: Suetonius, *The Twelve Caesars* (AD 121), trans. Alexander Thomson, London: Bell, 1893.

10 June: Arrian of Nicomedia, *The Life of Alexander the Great*, trans. Aubrey de Sélincourt, Harmondsworth: Penguin, 1958.

11 June: Francis Crozier and James Fitzjames, quoted in Ann Savours, *The Search for the North West Passage*, New York: St Martin's Press, 1999.

12 June: Anne Frank, *Diary of a Young Girl: The Definitive Edition*, ed. Otto H. Frank and Mirjam Pressler, trans. Susan

Massotty, New York: Doubleday, 1995 and Harmondsworth: Penguin, 1997. English translation copyright © 1995 by Doubleday, a division of Random House, Inc., 1995, 2001. Used by permission of Doubleday, a division of Random House Inc. Reproduced by permission of Penguin Books Ltd. Copyright © The Anne Frank Fonds, Basel, 1982, 1991, 2001.

13 June: Meriwether Lewis, in M.M. Quaife (ed.), *The Journals of Captain Meriwether Lewis and Sargeant John Ordway, Kept on the Expedition of Western Exploration, 1803–1806*, Madison: State Historical Society of Wisconsin, 1916.

14 June: Eliot Warburton (ed.) *Memoirs of Prince Rupert and the Cavaliers*, Vol. III, London: Richard Bentley, 1899.

15 June: *Anonimalle Chronicle*, as reproduced in Paul Halsall (ed.) Internet Medieval Sourcebook (Fordham University, New York), www.fordham.edu/halsall/source/anon1381.asp

16 June: Abraham Lincoln, *Writings of Abraham Lincoln*, Vol. III, ed. Arthur Brooks Lapsley, New York: Putnam, 1923.

17 June: Francis Pretty, *Sir Francis Drake's Famous Voyage Round the World* (1580).

18 June: Captain J.H. Gronow, *The Reminiscences and Recollections of Captain Gronow*, ed. R.H. Gronow, London: Smith, Elder, 1862–66.

19 June: Sir Richard Mayne, *General Instruction Book*, London: 1829

20 June: Queen Victoria, *The Letters of Queen Victoria 1837–1861*, ed. Arthur Christopher Benson and Viscount Eshers, London: John Murray, 1907.

21 June: John Zephaniah Holwell, *A Genuine Narrative of the Deplorable Deaths of the English Gentlemen and Others who were suffocated in the Black Hole*, London: Millar, 1758.

22 June: William Shirer, *Berlin Diary: The Journal of a Foreign Correspondent, 1934–1941*, 1941; reprinted Baltimore: Johns Hopkins University Press, 2002. Reprinted here by permission of Don Congdon Associates, Inc. © 1941, renewed 1968 by William L. Shirer.

23 June: Pierre de Coubertin, quoted (reprinted) in *LA84* newsletter, July 1969.

24 June: Sir Thomas Gray, *Scalacronica*, ed. and trans. Andy King, Woodbridge, Suffolk: Boydell Press, 2005.

25 June: Chief Red Horse, recorded in pictographs and text at the Cheyenne River Reservation (1881), in Garrick Mallery, *Picture Writing of the American Indians, 10th Annual Report of the Bureau of American Ethnology*, Washington, DC: US Government Printing Office, 1893.

26 June: John F. Kennedy, speech at www.millercenter.org.

27 June: Joshua Slocum, *Sailing Alone Around the World*, New York: Century, 1900.

28 June: Borijove Jevtic, quoted in Tamara Orr (ed.), *Critical Perspectives on World War I*, New York: Rosen Publishing, 2005.

29 June: Henry Wotton, *The Life and Letters of Sir Henry Wotton*, ed. Logan Pearsall Smith, Oxford: Clarendon Press, 1907.

30 June: Chris Patten, quoted at bbc.co.uk/news.

JULY

1 July: Lieutenant Alfred Bundy, quoted in Malcolm Brown (ed.), *The Imperial War Museum Book of the Somme*, London: Imperial War Museum, 1996. Courtesy of the Estate of Lieutenant Alfred Bundy and Gloria Siggins.

2 July: William Booth, *In Darkest England, and the Way Out*, London: International Headquarters, 1890.

3 July: Tillie Pierce Alleman, *At Gettysburg; or, What a Girl Saw and Heard of the Battle: A True Narrative*, New York: W. Lake Borland, 1889.

4 July: Text of Declaration at www.ushistory.org.

5 July: Isaac Newton, *Philosophiae naturalis principia mathematica*, London: Pepys Press, 1687

6 July: Edward Hall, *Chronicle; or, The Union of the Two Noble and Illustrioous Families of Lancaster and York* (1548), reprinted London: Johnson *et al.*, 1809.

7 July: Alice O'Keeffe, *The Observer*, 10 July 2005. Copyright ©Alice O'Keeffe, 2005.

8 July: William Heine, *With Perry to Japan: A Memoir* (1876), translated by Frederic Trautmann, Honolulu: University of Hawaii Press, 1990.

9 July: Report in *Nashville Tennessean*, 10 July 1918.

10 July: John Lothrop Motley, *The Rise of the Dutch Republic*, New York: Harper, 1856.

11 July: Nathaniel Pendleton, in Harold C. Syrett (ed.), *The Papers of Alexander Hamilton*, Vol. 26, New York: Columbia University Press, 1961.

12 July: Robert Aleway, as reproduced in *Notes and Queries*, March 1923.

13 July: Clarence Darrow, trial transcript at www.law2.umkc.edu/faculty/projects/ftrials/scopes/scopes2.htm

14 July: Thomas Jefferson, letter to Secretary of State John Jay (16 July 1789),Washington, DC: National Archives.

15 July: Ephraim Graebke, quoted in Frederick Lewis Maitland, *The Surrender of Napoleon, Being the Narrative of the Surrender of Buonaparte, and of His Residence on Board H.M.S. Bellerophon* ..., Edinburgh and London: Blackwood, 1904.

16 July: General Thomas Farrell, US War Department Release on New Mexico Test, quoted in Henry de Wolf Smyth (ed.), *Atomic Energy for Military Purposes: The Official Report on the Development of the Atomic Bomb Under the Auspices of the United States Government* (August 1945), Princeton, New Jersey: Princeton University Press, 1945.

17 July: Pavel Medvedev, quoted in Edvard Radzinsky, *The Last Tsar: The Life and Death of Nicholas II*, trans. Marian Schwartz, New York: Doubleday, 1992.

18 July: Text from the *Report of the Secretary-General Persuant to General Assembly Resolution 53/35: The Fall of Srebrenica*, New York: United Nations, 1999. Reproduced courtesy of the United Nations.

19 July: Report in the *Bristol Mercury*, 22 July 1843.

20 July: Seneca Falls Convention Declaration of Sentiments, quoted at www.nps.gov/wori/historyculture/declaration-of-sentiments.htm.

21 July: Neil Armstrong, quoted by NASA at www.hq.nasa.gov/alsj/a11/a11.step.html.

22 July: Report in *Palestine Post*, 23 July 1946.

23 July: General Muhammad Naguib, quoted at www.news.egypt.com/en/egyptian-revolution-of-1952.html.

24 July: Hiram Bingham, *Inca Land*, New York: Houghton Mifflin, 1922.

25 July: Louis Blériot, *New York Times*, 26 July 1909.

26 July: Winston Churchill, *War Memoirs*, Volume 6, *Triumph and Tragedy*, New York: Houghton Mifflin Harcourt, 1953. Reproduced with permission of Curtis Brown, London, on behalf of the Estate of Sir Winston Churchill.

27 July: William the Breton, in George Duby, *The Legend of Bouvines: War, Religion and Culture in the Middle Ages*, trans. Catherine Tihanyi, Berkeley: University of California Press, 1990.

28 July: Joseph Stalin, Order No. 227, 28 July 1942

29 July: Émile Bernard, letter quoted in Vincent Van Gogh, *Letters Unabridged and Annotated*, trans. Robert Harrison, at www.webexhibits.org/vangogh/letter/21/etc-Bernard-Aurier.htm.

30 Claude Joseph Rouget de Lisle, 'La Marseillaise' (anthem), 1792.

31 July: Captain H.G. Kendall, quoted in Leslie Bailey, *Scrapbook 1900–1914*, London: Frederick Muller, 1974.

AUGUST

1 August: Anne Frank, *Diary of a Young Girl*, New York: Doubleday, 1952.

2 August: Albert Einstein, quoted by Manhattan Project Heritage Preservation Association, www.mphpa.org.

3 August: Oliver Cromwell, letter to the Scottish Kirk, 1650, from Thomas Carlyle, *Oliver Cromwell's Letters and Speeches: with elucidations*, Vol. 3, letter 136, 1871.

4 August: Herbert Asquith and Edward Goschen, quoted at www.firstworldwar.com.

5 August: Bede, *History of the English Church and People* (731), accessible at

www.questia.com, from *History of the English Church and People*, Book iii, ch 9; trans. Leo Shirley-Price, Penguin, 1955.

6 August: Tokyo Radio, quoted by United Press, Guam, 8 August 1945; Harry S. Truman Press release, from Harry S. Truman Library, 'Army press notes', Box 4, Papers of Eben A. Ayers.

7 August: James Cameron, *A Time of Terror: A Survivor's Story*, self-published, 1982; reprinted Baltimore: Black Classics Press, 1994; Abel Meeropol, 'Strange Fruit', quoted in David Margolick, *Strange Fruit: Billie Holiday, Café Society, and an Early Cry for Civil Rights*, Philadelphia: Running Press, 2000.

8 August: Richard M. Nixon, quoted at Miller Center Presidential Speech Archive, www.millercenter.org/scripps/archive/speeches.

9 August: Queen Elizabeth I, cited in letter from Leonel Sharp to the Duke of Buckingham (1623), quoted in J.E. Neale *Queen Elizabeth I*, London: Jonathan Cape, 1934.

10 August: Flavius Josephus, *The Jewish War Book VI*, trans. William Whiston (1737), updated by Peter Furtado.

11 August: Herbert Hoover, quoted at Miller Center Presidential Speech Archive, www.millercenter.org/scripps/archive/speeches.

12 August: Plutarch, *Life of Antony*, London: Heinemann (Loeb Classical Library) 1920, updated by Peter Furtado.

13 August: Erdmute Gries-Behrendt, quoted in Christopher Hilton, *The Wall: The People's Story*, Stroud, Gloucestershire: Sutton Publishing, 2001. Reprinted courtesy of The History Press.

14 August: Miner Luella ('The End of the Boxer Rebellion, 1900'), quoted in Hart Albert Bushnell, *American History Told by Contemporaries* v. 5, Macmillan, New York, 1929

15 August: Jawaharlal Nehru, quoted in *The Guardian*, 1 May 2007.

16 August: Samuel Bamford, *Passages in the Life of a Radical*, London: Simpkin Marshall, 1840–44.

17 August: James Dabney McCabe, in *Great Fortunes, and How They Were Made*, Philadelphia: George Maclean, 1871.

18 August: Genghis Khan, quoted in John Man, *Genghis Khan: Life, Death and Resurrection*, London: Transworld, 2005.

19 August: Suetonius, *Life of Augustus*, London: Heinemann (Loeb Classical Library), 1920.

20 August: Winston Churchill, quoted at www.winstonchurchill.org. Reproduced with permission of Curtis Brown, London, on behalf of the Estate of Sir Winston Churchill.

21 August: Richard Harding Davis, *News Chronicle*, 23 August 1914.

22 August: Text quoted in J.W. Hales and F.J. Furnivall (eds), *Bishop Percy's Folio Manuscript: Ballads and Romances*, 3 vols, London: Trübner, 1867–8.

23 August: Marguerite de Valois, *Memoirs*, Boston: L.C. Page, 1899.

24 August: Pliny the Younger, *The Letters of Pliny the Younger*, trans. William Melmoth, rev. F.C.T. Bosanquet, London: Heinemann, 1915 (Loeb Classical Library).

25 August: Paul Jennings, *A Coloured Man's Reminiscences of James Madison*, Brooklyn: George Beadle, 1865.

26 August: Jean Froissart, *Chronicles*, trans Lord Berners (1523–5), text accessible at www.fordham.edu/halsall/basis/froissart-full.asp.

27 August: Johanna Beijerinck, diary reproduced at www.dsc.discovery.com/convergence/krakatoa/diaries/johanna 02.html.

28 August: Martin Luther King, Jr, quoted by the Martin Luther King Jr. Research and Education Institute, www.mlk-kpp01.stanford.edu. Reprinted by arrangement with The Heirs to the estate of Martin Luther King Jr., c/o Writers House as agent for the proprietor New York NY. Copyright 1963 Dr. Martin Luther King Jr; copyright renewed 1991 Coretta Scott King.

29 August: Reginald Brooks 'Bloobs', *Sporting Times*, 2 September 1882.

30 August: 'P.W.A.', *Savannah Republican*, August 1862, quoted at www.civilwarwiki.net/wiki/Eyewitness Account - 2nd Battle of Manassas.

31 August: Tony Blair, quoted at www.bbc.co.uk/news/special/politics97/diana/blairreact.html.

SEPTEMBER

1 September: Helmut von Moltke and Auguste Alexandre Ducrot, quoted in Michael Howard, *The Franco-Prussian War*, London: Routledge, 1961.

2 September: Samuel Pepys, *Diary*, at www.pepysdiary.com.

3 September: Neville Chamberlain, reproduced in facsimile at www.bbc.co.uk/archive/ww2outbreak/7957.shtml.

4 September: Geronimo, *Story of His Life*, ed. S.M. Barrett, New York: Duffield, 1906.

5 September: Barbara Tuchman, *The Guns of August*, New York: Random House, 1962. Reproduced courtesy of Russell & Volkening, Inc.

6 September: Leon Frank Czolgosz, *New York Times*, 8 September 1901.

7 September: Desmond Flower, *The War 1939–1945*, London, Cassell, 1960.

8 September: Giorgio Vasari, *Lives of the Artists* (1550), trans. Gaston du C. de Vere as *Most Eminent Painters, Sculptors and Architects*, 10 vols, London: Macmillan/Medici Society, 1912–15.

9 September: Orderic Vitalis, *Gesta Regum Anglorum*, ed. and trans. Marjorie Chibnall as *The Ecclesiastical History of Orderic Vitalis*, 6 vols, Oxford: Clarendon Press, 1968–80.

10 September: Richard Burton, *A Personal Narrative of a Pilgrimage to El-Medinah and Meccah*, London: Longman, 1855.

11 September: George W. Bush, quoted at www.americanrhetoric.com/speeches/gwbush11addresstothenation.htm.

12 September: Herodotus, *Histories*, translated by G.C. Macaulay, London: Macmillan, 1890.

13 September: James Wolfe, quoted in Christopher Hibbert, *Wolfe at Quebec: The Man Who Won the French and Indian War*, London: Longman, 1959.

14 September: Claude François de Méneval, *Memoirs*, 1827; trans. Robert H. Sherard, London: Hutchinson, 1894.

15 September: Frances Kemble, *Record of a Girlhood*, 3 vols, London: Richard Bentley, 1878.

16 September: Miguel Hidalgo ('The Stirrings of Mexican Revolution, 1810'), quoted in

Hugh M. Hammill, *The Hidalgo Revolt: Prelude to Mexican Independence*, ABC-Clio, 1981.

17 September: Charles Darwin, *Diary of the Voyage of H.M.S. 'Beagle'*, ed. Nora Barlow, Cambridge: Cambridge University Press, 1933.

18 September: Victor Klemperer, *I Will Bear Witness: A Diary of the Nazi Years*, New York: Random House, 1998.

19 September: Robert Emmet, quoted in Marianne Elliott, *Robert Emmet: The Making of a Legend*, London: Profile Books, 2003.

20 September: Report in *Illustrated London News*, March 1858.

21 September: Brut Chronicle, quoted in Ian Mortimer, *The Greatest Traitor: The Life of Sir Roger Mortimer, 1st Earl of March, Ruler of England 1327–1330*, London: Jonathan Cape, 2003.

22 September: Abraham Lincoln, text of proclamation at Library of Congress, Washington, DC.

23 September: Richard Dale, quoted in John Henry Sherburne, *The Life and Character of John Paul Jones*, Washington, NY: Wilder & Campbell, 1825.

24 September: Ibn Ishaq, *Life of God's Messenger*, ed. Ibn Hisham, trans. Edward Rehatsek, published by Royal Asiatic Society, London, 1898

25 September: Snorri Sturelson, quoted at Online Medieval and Classical Library, www.omacl.org/Heimskringla/hardrade1.html.

26 September: Bernard Montgomery, *The Memoirs of Field-Marshal the Viscount Montgomery of Alamein*, London: Collins, 1958. Reproduced courtesy of Pen and Sword Books.

27 September: T.E. Lawrence, *Seven Pillars of Wisdom*, privately published, 1926.

28 September: Alexander Fleming, *British Medical Bulletin*, Vol. 23, No. 1 (1944).

29 September: Robert of Avesbury, quoted in Norman Cohn, *The Pursuit of the Millennium: Revolutionary Millenarians and Mystical Anarchists of the Middle Ages*, Oxford: Oxford University Press, 1970.

30 September: Neville Chamberlain, quoted in the Modern History Sourcebook, www.fordham.edu/halsall/mod/1938PEACE.html.

OCTOBER

1 October: G.M. Gilbert, *Nuremberg Diary*, New York: Farrar, Straus 1947.

2 October: *De expugnatione terrae sanctae per Saladinum*, ed. Joseph Stevenson, London, Oxford and Cambridge: Longman, Trübner, Row, Parker and Macmillan, 1875.

3 October: Julius Caesar, *On the Gallic War*, trans. H. Edwards, London: Heinemann, 1919 (Loeb Classical Library).

4 October: Edward Teller, quoted in Walter B. Wriston, 'Technology and Sovereignty', *Foreign Affairs*, Vol. 67, No. 2 (Winter 1988–9)

5 October: Ellen Wilkinson, *The Town That Was Murdered*, London: Gollancz for Left Book Club, 1939.

6 October: Al Jolson, quoted in Robert L. Carringer, *The Jazz Singer*, Madison: University of Wisconsin Press, 1979.

7 October: Pope Pius V, quoted in Roger Crowley, *Empires of the Sea: The Siege of Malta, the Battle of Lepanto and the Contest for the Center of the World*, New York: Random House, 2008

8 October: Alvin York, *Sergeant York: His Own Life Story and War Diary*, ed. in Tom Skeyhill, New York: Doubleday, 1928.

9 October: Graham McNamee, transcript from *Alexander Murdered* newsreel, produced by Universal Studios, October 1934.

10 October: *Mozarabic Chronicle*, quoted in Edward Creasy, *Fifteen Decisive Battles of the World*, New York: Dutton, 1851.

11 October: Queen Victoria, *Journal of Our Life in the Highlands*, London: Smith, Elder,1868.

12 October: Christopher Columbus (ed. Bartolomé de las Casas), *The Journal of Christopher Columbus (During His First Voyage)*, ed. Clements R. Markham, Cambridge: Cambridge University Press, 1893.

13 October: Cassius Dio, *Roman History*, London: Heinemann, 1924 (Loeb Classical Library).

14 October: William of Malmesbury, *Gesta Regum Anglorum*, in James Harvey Robinson (ed.), *Readings in European History*, Boston: Ginn, 1904–6.

15 October: Edward Gibbon, *Miscellaneous Works ... with Memoirs*, ed. Lord Sheffield, 2 vols, London, and 3 vols, Dublin: no publisher, 1796.

16 October: Report in *Manchester Guardian*, 17 October 1834.

17 October: Henry M. Stanley, *How I Found Livingstone*, New York: Scribner, Armstrong, 1872.

18 October: Edict quoted in J.H. Robinson (ed.), *Readings in European History*, Boston: Ginn, 1906.

19 October: Polybius, *Histories*, London: Heinemann, 1922 (Loeb Classical Library).

20 October: Napoleon Bonaparte, quoted in John P. Foley (ed.), *Jeffersonian Cyclopedia*, New York and London: Funk & Wagnells, 1900

21 October: John Pasco, quoted in RoyAdkins, *Trafalgar: The Biography of a Battle*, Boston and London: Little, Brown, 2004.

22 October: John F. Kennedy, quoted at Miller Center Presidential Speech Archive, www.millercenter.org/scripps/archive/speeches.

23 October: James Ussher, *The Annals of the World Deduced from the Origin of Time ...*, London: Tyler for J. Crook, 1658.

24 October: Ballad in Francis James Child, *The English and Scottish Popular Ballads*, 5 vols, Boston: Houghton Mifflin, 1882–98.

25 October: William Howard Russell, *The Times*, 14 November 1854

26 October: Giuseppe Garibaldi, *Autobiography*, London: Smith & Innes, 1889.

27 October: Eusebius, *Church History*, in Philip Schaff and Henry Wace (eds), *Nicene and Post-Nicene Fathers*, Second Series, Vol. 1, New York: Christian Literature Publishing, 1890.

28 October: Desmond Tutu, *Truth and Reconciliation Commission Report*, Cape Town: Truth and Reconciliation Commission, 1998.

29 October: Jonathan Norton Leonard, *Three Years Down*, New York: Carrick & Evans, 1944.

30 October: Johannes Burchard, *At the Court of the Borgia: Being an Account of the Reign of Pope Alexander VI Written by His Master of Ceremonies*, London: Folio Society, 2002

31 October: Martin Luther, *Works of Martin Luther*, trans. Adolph Spaeth, L.D. Reed, Henry Eyster Jacobs *et al.*, Philadelphia: Holman, 1915.

NOVEMBER

1 November: William Stephens, quoted in Jenefer Roberts, *Glass: The Strange History of the Lyne Stephens Fortune*, no place: Templeton Press, 2003.

2 November: Text in the British Library, London.

3 November: Richard Nixon, quoted at Miller Center Presidential Speech Archive, www. millercenter.org/scripps/archive/speeches.

4 November: H.L. Gordon, *Sir James Young Simpson and Chloroform*, London: Unwin, 1897.

5 November: Ralph Ewens, *The Gunpowder Plot*, House of Commons Factsheet, 2010.

6 November: Jacob Baum (ed.), *The Great and Famous Battel sic of Lützen … Faithfully translated out of the French Coppie*, London: no publisher, 1633.

7 November: John Reed, *Ten Days That Shook the World*, New York: Boni & Liveright, 1919.

8 November: Bernal Díaz del Castillo, *The True History of the Conquest of New Spain*, 1576, trans. A.P. Maudsley, 5 vols, London: Hakluyt Society, 1908–16.

9 November: Günter Schabowski and Harald Jäger, quoted in Christopher Hilton, *The Wall: The People's Story*, Stroud, Gloucestershire: Sutton, 2001. Reprinted courtesy of The History Press.

10 November: Dedication in D.H. Lawrence, *Lady Chatterley's Lover*, second edition, London: Penguin Books, 1961.

11 November: Adolf Hitler, *Mein Kampf* (1925), trans. James Murphy, London: Hurst and Blackett, 1939.

12 November: George Leybourne, broadside ballad (1874), National Library of Scotland, Edinburgh.

13 November: Charles Dickens, letter to *The Times*, 13 November 1849.

14 November: *Manchester Guardian*, 16 November 1940.

15 November: William T. Sherman, *Memoirs of General W.T. Sherman*, New York: Appleton, 1889.

16 November: Francisco de Xeres, *Narrative of the Conquest of Peru*, 1530–34, translated and edited, with Notes and an Introduction, by Clements R. Markham, London: Hakluyt Society, 1872.

17 November: Joseph Stalin, *Works*, Moscow: Foreign Languages Publishing, 1953–5.

18 November: Friedrich Schiller, *William Tell* (1804), trans. Theodore Martin, Philadelphia: David McKay, 1898.

19 November: Abraham Lincoln, quoted at Miller Center Presidential Speech Archive, www.millercenter.org/scripps/archive/speeches.

20 November: Owen Chase, *Narrative of the Most Extraordinary and Distressing Shipwreck of the Whale-Ship Essex*, New York: W.B. Gilley, 1821.

21 November: Benjamin Franklin, quoted in Fulgence Marion, *Wonderful Balloon Ascents; or, The Conquest of the Skies*, New York: Charles Scribner, 1870.

22 November: Walter Cronkite, CBS, November 1963.

23 November: John Milton, *Areopagitica: A Speech of Mr Milton*, London (?): no publisher, 1644.

24 November: Charles Darwin, *On the Origin of Species By Means of Natural Selection*, London: John Murray, 1859.

25 November: Daniel Defoe, *The Storm*, London: Sawbridge, 1704

26 November: Howard Carter, *The Tomb of Tutankhamun*, New York: George Doran, 1923.

27 November: Pope Urban II, quoted in Fulcher of Chartres, *A History of the Expedition to Jerusalem, 1095–1127*, trans. Francis Rita Ryan, ed. Harold S. Fink, New York: Norton, 1969.

28 November: Mrs Perryman, quoted at www.elections.org.nz/study/

education-centre/history/history-sound.
html#transcripts.

29 November: Sir Edwin Arnold, *New York Times*, 26 January 1891.

30 November: *Bell's Life in London, and Sporting Chronicle*, 1 December 1872.

DECEMBER

1 December: William Beveridge, *Report of the Inter-Departmental Committee on Social Insurance and Allied Services*, London: HMSO, 1942

2 December: James Monroe, quoted at Miller Center Presidential Speech Archive, www.millercenter.org/scripps/archive/speeches.

3 December: Report in *The Hindu* newspaper, 7 June 2010.

4 December: John Bright, *Speeches of John Bright, M.P., on the American Question*, Boston: Little, Brown, 1865.

5 December: Innocent VIII, quoted in George Lincoln Burr (ed.) *The Witch-Persecutions*, Philadelphia: University of Pennsylvania, 1907.

6 December: Michael Collins, quoted in Tim Pat Coogan, *Michael Collins: The Man Who Made Ireland*, Basingstoke: Palgrave Macmillan, 2002.

7 December: Franklin D. Roosevelt, quoted at Miller Center Presidential Speech Archive, www.millercenter.org/scripps/archive/speeches. By permission of Nancy Roosevelt Ireland.

8 December: Mark Chapman, quoted in Jack Jones, *Let Me Take You Down: Inside the Mind of Mark David Chapman, the Man Who Killed John Lennon*, New York: Villard, 1992.

9 December: Miguel Sanchez, *Image of the Virgin Mary, Mother of Guadalupe* (1648), quoted at http://web.archive.org/web/20071022042328/www.interlupe.com.mx/nican-e.html.

10 December: Hilda Kean, 'The "Smooth Cool Men of Science": The Feminist and Socialist Response to Vivisection', *History Workshop Journal*, Vol. 40, No. 1 (1995).

11 December: Edward VIII, BBC Archive, London.

12 December: Guglielmo Marconi, quoted in Degna Marconi, *My Father, Marconi*, Toronto: Guernica Editions, 2001. Reproduced courtesy of Guernica Editions.

13 December: John Rabe, in Erwin Wickert (ed.), *The Good German of Nanjing: The Diaries of John Rabe*, trans. John E. Woods, New York: Knopf, 1998. Copyright © 1998 by Alfred A. Knopf, Inc. Used by permission of Alfred A. Knopf, a division of Random House, Inc and reproduced courtesy of Little, Brown Book Group Ltd.

14 December: Queen Victoria, *Letters of Queen Victoria*, ed. Arthur Christopher Benson and Viscount Esher, Vol. 3, London: John Murray, 1907.

15 December: Hannah Arendt, *Eichmann in Jerusalem: A Report on the Banality of Evil*, New York: Viking Press, 1963. Reproduced by permission of Penguin Books Ltd.

16 December: George Hewes, quoted in James Hawkes, *A Retrospect of the Boston Tea-Party*, New York: Bliss, 1834.

17 December: Orville Wright, text at Library of Congress, Washington, DC.

18 December: Marshal Philippe Pétain, *La Bataille de Verdun*, Paris: Payot, 1929.

19 December: Charles Dickens, *A Christmas Carol*, London: Chapman & Hall, 1843.

20 December: Richard I, trans. Henry Adams, in Samuel N. Rosenberg (ed.), *Songs of the Troubadours*, New York: Garland, 1998.

21 December: British Air Accidents Investigation Branch, *Report No: 2/1990 – Report on the Accident to Boeing 747-121, N739PA, at Lockerbie, Dumfriesshire, Scotland on 21 December 1988*, accessible at www.aaib.gov.uk/publications/formal reports/21990n739pa.cfm.

22 December: E.T.A. Hoffmann, 'Beethoven's Instrumental Music', in *Zeitung für die elegante Welt* (1813).

23 December: Leo Tolstoy, *Sevastopol Sketches* (1855), trans. W.D. Howells, New York: Harper, 1887.

24 December: Bruce Bairnsfather, *Bullets and Billets*, London: Grant Richards, 1916. Courtesy of the Bairnsfather Estate and Great Northern Publishing.

25 December: Luke's Gospel, Chapter 2, *The Holy Bible* (Authorized or King James Version)

26 December: Sara Burns, private correspondence (January 2005). Courtesy of Sara Burns.

27 December: Procopius, *The Buildings of Justinian*, translated by William Richard Lethaby and Harold Swainson in *The Church of Sancta Sophia Constantinople*, New York: Macmillan, 1894.

28 December: Auguste and Louis Lumière, quoted in David Cook, *A History of Narrative Film*, fourth edition, New York: Norton, 2004.

29 December: Edward Grim, in James Craig Robertson (ed.), *Materials for the Life of Thomas Becket*, 7 vols, London: Longman, 1875–85.

30 December: Winston Churchill, quoted at www.winstonchurchill.org. Reproduced with permission of Curtis Brown, London, on behalf of the Estate of Sir Winston Churchill.

31 December: Boris Yeltsin, quoted at www.news.bbc.co.uk/1/hi/world/ monitoring/584845.stm.

INDEX

484